D1582337

ENGLISH PLACE-NAME SOCIETY. VOLUME LXXXVIII
FOR 2010

GENERAL EDITOR

RICHARD COATES

PRODUCTION EDITOR

PAUL CAVILL

THE PLACE-NAMES OF
LEICESTERSHIRE

PART V

THE SURVEY OF ENGLISH PLACE-NAMES
UNDERTAKEN WITH THE APPROVAL AND SUPPORT OF
THE ARTS AND HUMANITIES RESEARCH COUNCIL
AND
THE BRITISH ACADEMY

THE PLACE-NAMES OF

LEICESTERSHIRE

BY

BARRIE COX

PART FIVE

GUTHLAXTON HUNDRED

NOTTINGHAM
ENGLISH PLACE-NAME SOCIETY
2011

Published by the English Place-Name Society,
School of English Studies, University of Nottingham,
Nottingham NG7 2RD.

Registered Charity No. 257891

ISBN-10: 0 904889 87 4
ISBN-13: 978 0 904889 87 1

Typeset by Paul Cavill & Printed in Great Britain
by 4Word, Bristol.

Published as part of the project
Perceptions of Place
funded by the
Arts and Humanities Research Council

CONTENTS

PREFACE

My fifth volume of *The Place-Names of Leicestershire* retains the format which I adopted for my four previous volumes, in that each as far as possible is self-contained and, I believe, user-friendly. Materials for a wide range of disciplines are here readily available for those who wish to focus only on this particular area of the county.

Again I extend my grateful thanks to the staffs of the Record Office for Leicestershire, Leicester and Rutland at Wigston Magna and of the Lincolnshire Archives Office, Lincoln, for their splendid assistance in locating and presenting such documents as I requested to study in researching the place-names of the Guthlaxton Hundred.

I am indebted to Dr Anne Tarver for her work on the parish map of the Hundred. She gives gladly of her time and expertise. And as always, my very best thanks are due to Dr Paul Cavill of the English Place-Name Society for his meticulous care in the typesetting of this volume. His presentation is unfailingly elegant.

Barrie Cox
January 2011

INTRODUCTION
TO THE PLACE-NAMES
OF GUTHLAXTON HUNDRED

Guthlaxton Hundred consists of a wedge of land which opens out southwards from Leicester to the river Avon and to Roman Watling Street. To its east lies Gartree Hundred and to its west Sparkenhoe Hundred. The earlier Guthlaxton Wapentake comprised a much larger area, from Gartree Wapentake to its east as far as the old Goscote Wapentake and Derbyshire's Repton Wapentake in the north-west. Its moot-site was at Guthlac's Stone, a possible Roman milestone on the Fosse Way on the bounds of Cosby parish. At what date Sparkenhoe Hundred was carved from Guthlaxton Wapentake is uncertain. The Guthlaxton administrative unit is styled as a wapentake as late as 1203 and as a hundred from 1184, while the Sparkenhoe Hundred first appears in the Leicestershire Survey of c.1130.

The north-western limit of the redefined Guthlaxton Hundred is the Roman Fosse Way. It constitutes the north-western parish bounds of Claybrooke, Frolesworth, Broughton Astley and Cosby. Just beyond Fosse Way and bordering Watling Street lies the isolated little parish of Wigston Parva, now surrounded by Sparkenhoe territory, with fields of Sharnford to its east and Smockington to its west. South-east from Fosse Way, Watling Street forms parish boundaries of Claybrooke, Ullesthorpe, Bittesby, Lutterworth, Cotesbach, Shawell and Catthorpe.

The territory of Guthlaxton thus defined comprises roughly two different regions. In the north is the upper Soar Valley, of alluvium studded with gravel patches and drained by the river Soar and its tributaries, especially the river Sence, an area rich in arable and meadow. In the south is the Lutterworth Upland, a region with ground almost all over 400ft above sea-level, with much Boulder Clay, drained by the river Swift which runs into the Warwickshire Avon in its south and by various tributaries of the upper Soar in its north.

At High Cross, the crossing point of the two great Roman roads Watling Street and Fosse Way, developed the Romano-British settlement of *Venonis*. The name may be interpreted as 'the place of the tribe', and if so, would have referred to the Corieltauvi whose principal settlement was *Ratae* (Leicester). The *territorium* of this township may well be traced in present-day parish bounds both north and south of Watling Street. From the point at which the eastern boundary of Bittesby meets Watling Street close to the Cross in Hand, the line of the parish bounds of Bittesby, Ullesthorpe and Claybrooke is continuous to Fosse Way from where it skirts the northern portion of Sharnford and runs along the northern and western limits of Wigston Parva to meet Watling Street. Crossing Watling Street into Warwickshire, this significant boundary continues along the stream which marks the western bounds of Copston Magna parish to meet the ancient Mere Lane (Old English (*ge*)*mǣre*) 'a boundary') which then runs south-east, encompassing Wibtoft and Willey parishes, and so back to the Cross in Hand at Watling Street. The south-eastern stretch of the old Mere Lane eventually became known as Coal Pit Lane, the route bringing pit coal from the Bedworth area into south-eastern Leicestershire from at least the early seventeenth century. That the detached Wigston Parva parish remained as part of Guthlaxton Hundred may reasonably be accounted for in its having once been a part of this probable former *territorium* of *Venonis*, although the particular processes of such a continuity via a possible large Anglo-Saxon estate here are all but lost to us.

South-west on Watling Street at Cave's Inn in Shawell parish lay the Romano-British settlement of *Tripontium* ('(the place of) three bridges'). Since there is no river at the site of the township to have warranted a major bridge, it is possible that the 'bridges' of the name referred to causeways crossing wet land here. Alternatively, *Tripontium* may have been so called since, being fairly equidistant between what became Bransford Bridge carrying Watling Street over the river Swift in Cotesbach parish to its north-west and Dow Bridge carrying the road over the river Avon in Catthorpe parish to its south-east, a causeway or culvert over the stream at Cave's Inn could have been construed as the third 'bridge' of three. The names *Venonis* and *Tripontium* survive only in the Antonone Itinerary, the various parts of which may be dated only generally between the reigns of Trajan and Diocletian (i.e. c.100 × c.300).

Pre-English names which do survive in Guthlaxton Hundred are Leire and Glen (Parva). Both are probably river-names which became attached to riverine settlements, Glen the earlier name of the river Sence and Leire that of a tributary of the river Soar. To these may perhaps be added two minor pre-English stream-names, the *Dove* in Oadby and the *Lugge* in Lutterworth. However, any evidence for Romano-British survival in the place-names of the Hundred is sparse. Both Walton and Walcote have as their specifics OE *walh* 'a Briton, a serf', while in Cosby, *Walschemore* and in Leire *welchmore* ('moorland of the *wælisc* (British, unfree)') are all that survive, apart from *Bretterhul* 'hill of the Britons' in Wigston Magna and perhaps Barom Hill in Gilmorton, with the British root *barro-* 'a summit, a hill'. Both Churchill in Shearsby and Church Hill in Frolesworth may record a Proto-Welsh *crūg* 'hill', but the forms are too late to be anything but matters of speculation.

In the southern half of Guthlaxton Hundred, OE place-names predominate. Apart from names derived from features of topography, such as Bitteswell, Claybrooke, Cotesbach, Shawell and Swinford which cannot be dated but which may well be early, there are two names which record early Anglo-Saxon folk-groups. They are the continguous Peatling Magna and Peatling Parva (with a possible outlier at *Peatling* in Claybrooke Parva) and the lost *Lilinge*, to be located either in Ullesthorpe or in Westrill and Starmore. They record the people of *Pēotla* and *Lilla* respectively. Another early OE place-name type is *wīchām*, typifying an Anglo-Saxon settlement adjacent to a surviving Romano-British small township. Whether the lost *dunninc wicon*, which can be reasonably located in the later Ullesthorpe parish, contains such a name is open to question. Its relationship to *Venonis* conforms to the pattern of such sites, adjacent to Romano-British townships and Roman roads, but whether *wicon* here is the dative plural *wīcum* of *wīc* or a reduced *wīchām* is difficult to tell, except it should be noted that *wīchām* in all other recognized instances stands alone (*v.* Margaret Gelling, 'English place-names derived from the compound *wīchām*', *Medieval Archaeology* XI (1967), 87–104.

Other important OE settlement names are Misterton, the site of an Anglo-Saxon minster which was a large church served by a priest and monastic or secular assistants and responsible for the cure of souls of a wide range of nearby townships, and the group comprising Frolesworth, Kilworth, *Stormsworth* (Starmore) and Lutterworth. This southern quarter of Leicestershire is particularly *worð* country. The first three of these names in *worð* have OE masculine personal names as their specifics, while Lutterworth has *Hlūtre*, the ancient English name of the river Swift. Such place-names relate to waterways, here the rivers Avon, Swift and a tributary of the river Soar. They appear to belong to the eighth century (*v.* Barrie Cox, 'Aspects of place-name evidence for early medieval settlement in England', *Viator* 11 (1980), 35–50), although little work has been done on them to make this dating safe.

Place-names with Scandinavian elements lie for the most part in the upper Soar Valley in the north of the Hundred. Only two may relate to the earliest settlement of Danes after the break-up of their great army in 877. These are Wigston (Magna) and perhaps a lost *Nafferton* in Foston (Kilby parish). In Wigston, the compounded personal name may be an English *Wicing, Wīcing* rather than a Scandinavian *Víkingr*, while the late-recorded *Nafferton* in Foston could (but at its date probably not) contain a surn. taken from Nafferton in Yorkshire rather than the Scandinavian personal name *Náttfari*. Three names near Leicester with the later *bȳ* generic have Scandinavian personal names as their specifics: Arnesby, Blaby and Oadby. The personal names in Cosby and Shearsby could be either OE or Scandinavian. Other than these, Ashby Magna, Ashby Parva and Willoughby Waterleys (~ Waterless) which lie further south have OE tree-names as their specifics, while their generics may once have been OE *tūn* Scandinavianized to *bȳ*.

The names with *þorp* appear to be even later. Catthorpe in the far south, Countesthorpe, Littlethorpe and Primethorpe are all initially recorded as the simplex *þorp*. Catthorpe eventually takes on a feudal affix, as perhaps does Primethorpe, while Countesthorpe and Littlethorpe have Middle English prefixes. Only Bruntingthorpe (with an OE personal name) and Ullesthorpe (with a Scandinavian personal name) have unadapted forms from the time of the Domesday Survey.

The few place-names with Scandinavian elements on Watling Street in the south of the Hundred are worthy of note. The tiny Catthorpe, squeezed between the Anglo-Saxon Swinford and Shawell, is obviously a late-comer and not indicative of early Scandinavian settlement. Towards High Cross at the junction of Watling Street with Fosse Way, the land unit that eventually became Bittesby and Ullesthorpe parishes is of particular interest. It was most probably simply once called

Bittesby. The name has an OE specific and a Scandinavian generic. The *byttel* 'stumpy hill' which gave its name to the township is on the later boundary with Ullesthorpe. Bittesby is now a deserted medieval village, but Ullesthorpe which thrived at its expense was obviously carved out of Bittesby territory. The whole land unit of Bittesby with Ullesthorpe may well have been previously that of the lost *dunninc wicon* recorded in the Anglo-Saxon charter of 962 for the Claybrooke estate. Although the specific of Ullesthorpe is the Scandinavian personal name *Ulf*, Scandinavian settlement in the southern half of the Hundred appears minimal. Indeed, such a common Scandinavian word as *bekkr* 'a stream' survives only in two field-names in the Hundred as compared with the ubiquitous OE *brōc* with the same meaning.

A few other survivals from the medieval past of the Hundred may be noted. Perhaps the Bridewell of Kilworth and the Ladywell of Whetstone record sites sacred to fertility, while Shawell and Wigston Magna each had its Holy Well. Ashby Parva, Catthorpe and Lutterworth possessed their local giant or demon (OE *þyrs*), Broughton Astley, Frolesworth and Leire had their spectres or wraiths (OE *scinn*), while a hobgoblin is recorded for Whetstone. Tom Thumb, the little fellow of the nursery tale, perhaps had as a precursor a *þūma* (OE, '?dwarf, hobgoblin') in Tomley.

What is modern has also left an impact on the names of the Hundred. For each parish, the inns and taverns have been listed and such names are often valuable evidence of local trades, tradesmen and families. So too is the canal system of the county, although only the Grand Union Canal has left its legacy of names in the north of Guthlaxton Hundred, in those of the bridges and locks created during its eastward progress through Glen Parva and Wigston Magna. As for the railways that were built through the region during the nineteenth century, the line of the Hitchin Branch of the old Midland Railway survives and has left a few field-names in Wigston Magna parish, while the line of the former Midland Counties Railway through Countesthorpe, Broughton Astley, Leire and Ullesthorpe, although dismantled, has given several field-names by which remember it, and so has the line south from Leicester through Whetstone, Dunton Bassett, Lutterworth and Shawell. The former Rugby and Stamford Branch Railway clipped the Hundred in its south-east at North Kilworth, but that line too is long gone apart from its surviving earthworks and an occasional name.

NOTES ON ARRANGEMENT

1.   The Guthlaxton Hundred name is discussed first. After this, the place-names are treated within the civil parishes. Within each civil parish, the townships are dealt with in alphabetical order. For each township, the township name is followed by names of primary historical or etymological interest, also arranged in alphabetical order. At the end of these sections, all the remaining names related to the township appearing on the 1956–67 O.S. 6" maps, on the 1951–66 O.S. 2½" maps and on the 1967–8 O.S. 1" maps (and any names recorded only locally) are listed with such early forms and etymological comment as can be provided. These names, however, are sometimes of obvious origin or are ones about whose history it is unwise to speculate. The forms of all names in the above sections are presented in the order: spelling, date, source. The final section for each township lists field-names, divided into modern (i.e. post-1750) and earlier. The pre-1750 field-names are printed in italic.

2.   Place-names believed to be no longer current are marked '(lost)', e.g. 'STORMSWORTH (lost)'. This does not necessarily mean that the site to which the name was once applied is unknown. We are dealing primarily with names and it is the names which are lost. Such names are printed in italic in the index. Place-names marked '(local)' are believed to be current or recently current locally.

3.   In explaining the various toponyms, summary reference is always made, by printing the elements in bold type, to the analysis of elements at the end of this volume and to the more extended treatment of these in *English Place-Name Elements* (EPNS 25 and 26), in the *Addenda and Corrigenda* to these volumes and in *The Vocabulary of English Place-Names*, in progress: e.g. '*Caldewellegrindel* 1467 × 84 (*v.* **cald**, **wella**, **grendel**)'.

4.   Manuscript sources of early spellings of the names are indicated by printing the abbreviations for the sources in italic. The abbreviations for published sources are printed in roman type.

5.   Where two dates are given for a spelling, e.g. '1189 (1332)' or '1477 (e.16)', the first date is the date at which the document purports to have been composed, the second the date of the copy that has come down to us. Sources whose dates cannot be fixed to a particular year are dated by century, e.g. '12', '13', '14' etc. (often more specifically 'e.13', 'm.13', 'l.13' etc., i.e. early, mid and late thirteenth century respectively); by regnal date, e.g. 'Hy 2', 'Edw 1', 'Stephen' etc.; or by a range of years, e.g. '1467 × 84', such a date meaning that the form belongs to a particular year within those limits but cannot be more precisely fixed.

6.   The sign '(p)' after a source indicates that the particular spelling given appears in that source as a person's surname, not primarily as a reference to a place; thus '*Butlesby* 1327 SR (p)' refers to one *Johannes de Butlesby*, bearing *Butlesby* as his surname.

7.   When a letter or letters (sometimes words or phrases) in an early place-name form are enclosed in parentheses, it means that spellings with and without the enclosed letter(s) occur; e.g. '*As(s)cheby*' means that the forms *Ascheby* and *Asscheby* are found. When only one part of a place-name spelling is given as a variant, preceded or followed by a tilde, it means that the particular spelling only differs in respect of the cited part from the preceding or following spelling, e.g. '*Ulesthorpe* ~, *Ullesthorpe Meer*'.

8.   When an entry reads, e.g. 'THE GREEN, 1788 *EnclA*', the name appears in its modern spelling in the source quoted.

9.   Names presented in capital letters are those which appear on the Ordnance Survey maps used in preparing the Leicestershire survey.

10.   Cross references to other names are sometimes given with *supra* or *infra*, the former referring to a name already dealt with, the latter to a name dealt with later in the text.

11.   When a place-name is compared with an example from another county, that county is indicated; e.g. 'Ailsworth, Nth 228' which refers to Ailsworth in Northamptonshire and to a specific page in the EPNS survey *The Place-Names of Northamptonshire*.

12.   In order to save space in presenting early spellings of a name, *et passim* and *et freq* are sometimes used to indicate that the preceding form occurs from time to time or frequently from the date of the last quoted source to that of the following one.

13. Hypothetical forms of place-name elements which appear asterisked in the analysis of elements at the end of this volume are not asterisked in the text, although the discussion will often make it clear which are on independent record and which are inferred.

ABBREVIATIONS AND BIBLIOGRAPHY

Abbreviations printed in roman type refer to printed sources and those in italic to manuscript sources.

a.   *ante.*
AAS   Reports and Papers of the Associated Architectural Societies.
Abbr   *Placitorum Abbrevatio* (RC), 1811.
AD   *Catalogue of Ancient Deeds* (PRO), in progress.
adj.   adjective, adjectivally.
AFr   Anglo-French.
AILR   Auditors' Inrolements – Land Revenues, in various publications.
AllS   Manuscripts in the Muniments Room of All Souls' College, Oxford.
AN   Anglo-Norman.
Angl   Anglian dialect of Old English.
Anglo-Scand   Anglo-Scandinavian.
Ass   Assize Rolls in the Public Record Office.
Ass   Assize Rolls in various publications.
ASWills   *Anglo-Saxon Wills*, ed. D. Whitelock, 1930.
Ave   Avenue (in street names).
Bahlow   H. Bahlow, *Deutschlands geographische Namenwelt*, Frankfurt am Main 1985.
Banco   *Index of Placita de Banco 1327–28* (PRO Lists and Indexes 32), 1909; De Banco Rolls in Farnham.
BCS   *Cartularium Saxonicum*, ed. W. de G. Birch, 3 vols., 1885–93.
Bei   H. B. Beighton, *A Map of Warwickshire*, 1725.
Berkeley   *Catalogue of the Charters at Berkeley Castle*, ed. I. H. Jeayes, 1892.
Bk   *The Place-Names of Buckinghamshire* (EPNS 2), 1925.
BL   British Library, London.
BM   *Index to the Charters and Rolls in the Department of Manuscripts, British Museum*, 1900–12.
BodlCh   *Calendar of Charters and Rolls preserved in the Bodleian Library*, ed. W. H. Turner and H. O. Coxe, 1878.
Braye   Braye MSS, The Record Office for Leicestershire, Leicester and Rutland, Wigston Magna.
Brit   British.
Brk   *The Place-Names of Berkshire* (EPNS 49–51), 1973–6.

Bu	*The Burton Chartulary*, ed. G. Wrottesley (Salt 5), 1884.
Burton	W. Burton, *The Description of Leicestershire*, 1622.
c.	*circa.*
Ca	*The Place-Names of Cambridgeshire and the Isle of Ely* (EPNS 19), 1943.
Camden	W. Camden, *Britannia*, 1586.
CDEPN	Victor Watts, *The Cambridge Dictionary of English Place-Names*, 2004.
Census	Censuses variously published.
cent.	century.
cf.	compare.
Ch	*Calendar of Charter Rolls* (PRO), 6 vols., 1903–27.
Ch	*The Place-Names of Cheshire* (EPNS 44–7), 1970–2, (EPNS 48, 54), 1981, (EPNS 74), 1997.
ChAccts	Chamberlains' Accounts in RBL.
ChancP	*Calendar of Proceedings in Chancery in the Reign of Queen Elizabeth*, 3 vols., 1827–32; *Index of Chancery Proceedings* (series ii) (PRO Lists and Indexes 7, 24, 30).
ChancR	Chancellor's Rolls (as footnotes to *Pipe Rolls* (PRS), in progress).
Chap	*Chapter Acts, Lincoln Cathedral* (LRS 12, 13, 15).
Charyte	Charyte's Novum Rentale of Leicester Abbey, incorporating Geryn's Rental (Bodleian Laud Misc. 625), Bodleian Library, Oxford.
ChR	*Rotuli Chartarum* (RC), 1837.
Cl	*Calendar of Close Rolls* (PRO), in progress.
Cl(s)	Close(s) (in field-names).
ClR	*Rotuli Litterarum Clausarum* (RC), 1833–44.
Combe	Cartulary of Combe Abbey (BL Cotton Vitellius A i).
Comp	Compotus Rolls, Duke of Rutland's Muniments Room, Belvoir Castle, Leics.; The Record Office for Leicestershire, Leicester and Rutland, Wigston Magna; in the Middleton MSS, Nottingham University Archives, Nottingham.
comp.	comparative.
ConstR	Constables' Records for Shearsby in The Record Office for Leicestershire, Leicester and Rutland, Wigston Magna.
ContGerm	Continental Germanic.
CoPleas	Common Pleas in various publications.
Cor	Coroners' Rolls in various publications.
Coram	Coram Rege Rolls in various publications.
Cox[1]	Barrie Cox, *English Inn and Tavern Names*, 1994.
Cox[2]	Barrie Cox, *A Dictionary of Leicestershire and Rutland Place-Names*, 2005.
CPT	*Clerical Poll-Taxes of the Diocese of Lincoln, 1377–1381*, ed. A. K. McHardy (LRS 81).

CRCart	Roll Cartulary of Croxton Abbey (II 29 iii), Duke of Rutland's Muniments Room, Belvoir Castle, Leics.
CroxR	Croxton Abbey Register (Add. MS 71), Duke of Rutland's Muniments Room, Belvoir Castle, Leics.
Ct	Miscellaneous Court Rolls in various publications.
Ct	Court Rolls in the Ferrers MSS, the Hazlerigg MSS, the Rothley Temple Deeds and the Winstanley MSS, The Record Office for Leicestershire, Leicester and Rutland, Wigston Magna; in the Middleton MSS, University of Nottingham Archives.
Cur	*Curia Regis Rolls* (PRO), in progress.
Curtis	J. Curtis, *A Topographical History of the County of Leicester*, 1831.
D	*The Place-Names of Devon* (EPNS 8–9), 1931–2.
Dan	Danish.
Dane	F. M. Stenton, *Documents illustrative of the Social and Economic History of the Danelaw*, 1920.
dat.pl.	dative plural.
DB	Domesday Book; *Domesday Book: Leicestershire*, ed. P. Morgan, 1979.
Db	*The Place-Names of Derbyshire* (EPNS 27–9), 1959.
DBPN	A. D. Mills, *A Dictionary of British Place-Names*, 2003.
Deed	Miscellaneous published deeds.
Deed	Miscellaneous deeds in The Record Office for Leicestershire, Leicester and Rutland, Wigston Magna; in Lincolnshire Archives Office, Lincoln; in private collections.
Dep	Exchequer Special Depositions in the Public Record Office.
DEPN	E. Ekwall, *The Concise Oxford Dictionary of English Place-Names*, 4th edn, 1960.
Derby	*Descriptive Catalogue of Derbyshire Charters*, ed. I. H. Jeayes, 1906.
dial.	dialect(al).
Dixie	Dixie or Market Bosworth Grammar School MSS, The Record Office for Leicestershire, Leicester and Rutland, Wigston Magna.
DKR	*Reports of the Deputy Keeper of the Public Records* (PRO).
DLPN	K. Cameron (with J. Insley), *A Dictionary of Lincolnshire Place-Names*, 1998.
Do	*The Place-Names of Dorset* (EPNS 52, 53, 59, 60, 86, 87), 1977–2010, in progress.
Du	V. Watts, *A Dictionary of County Durham Place-Names*, 2002.
Dugd	W. Dugdale, *Monasticon Anglicanum*, 6 vols. in 8, 1817–30.
e.	early.
ECP	*Early Chancery Proceedings* (PRO Lists and Indexes 1–12).
ed.	edited by.
EDD	J. Wright, *The English Dialect Dictionary*, 6 vols., 1898–1905.
edn	edition.
Edw 1, Edw 2	Regnal date, t. Edward I, t. Edward II etc.

el.	place-name element.
Elements	A. H. Smith, *English Place-Name Elements*, (EPNS 25–6), 1956.
ELiW	*Early Lincoln Wills*, ed. A. Gibbons, 1888.
eModE	early Modern English.
EnclA	Enclosure Awards in various publications.
EnclA	Unpublished Enclosure Awards, The Record Office for Leicestershire, Leicester and Rutland, Wigston Magna.
EpCB	*An Episcopal Court Book for the Diocese of Lincoln 1514–20* (LRS 61), 1967.
EPNS	Publications of the English Place-Name Society.
esp.	especially.
Ess	*The Place-Names of Essex* (EPNS 12), 1935.
et freq	*et frequenter* (and frequently (thereafter)).
et passim	and occasionally (thereafter).
ExchSpC	Exchequer Special Commissions in PRO.
FA	*Feudal Aids* (PRO), 6 vols., 1899–1920.
Farnham	G. F. Farnham, *Leicestershire Medieval Village Notes*, 6 vols., 1929–33.
Fd(s)	Field(s) (in field-names).
Fees	*The Book of Fees* (PRO), 3 vols., 1921–31.
Feilitzen	O. von Feilitzen, *The Pre-Conquest Personal Names of Domesday Book*, Uppsala 1937.
fem.	feminine.
Ferrers	Ferrers MSS, The Record Office for Leicestershire, Leicester and Rutland, Wigston Magna.
FF	Feet of Fines in various publications.
Field	J. Field, *A History of English Field-Names*, 1993.
Fine	*Calendar of Fine Rolls* (PRO), in progress.
FineR	*Excerpta e rotulis finium* (RC), 2 vols., 1835–6.
Fm	Farm.
f.n(s).	field-name(s).
Forssner	T. Forssner, *Continental-Germanic Personal Names in England in Old and Middle English Times*, Uppsala 1916.
France	*Calendar of Documents preserved in France* (RS), 1899.
freq.	frequently.
GarCart	Cartulary of Garendon Abbey (BL Lansdowne 415), British Library, London.
gen.pl.	genitive plural.
gen.sg.	genitive singular.
GildR	Merchant Gild Rolls in RFL and RBL.
Gl	*The Place-Names of Gloucestershire* (EPNS 38–41), 1964–5.
Goodacre	Goodacre MSS, The Record Office for Leicestershire, Leicester and Rutland, Wigston Magna.
Ha	R. Coates, *The Place-Names of Hampshire*, 1989.

Harl	Harley MSS, British Library, London.
Hastings	*The Manuscripts of the late Reginald Rawdon Hastings of the Manor House, Ashby de la Zouch*, vol. 1 (HMC), 1928.
Hazlerigg	Hazlerigg MSS, The Record Office for Leicestershire, Leicester and Rutland, Wigston Magna.
HB	Hall Books in RBL and RFL.
HMC	Historical Manuscripts Commission.
Ho.	House.
Hosp.	*The Hospitallers in England* (Camden Society 65), 1855.
Hy 1, Hy 2	Regnal date, t. Henry I, t. Henry II etc.
ib, *ib*	*ibidem*.
IE	Indo-European.
infra	below.
Inqaqd	*Inquisitiones ad quod Damnum* (RC), 1803.
Ipm	*Calendar of Inquisitions post mortem* (PRO), in progress.
IpmR	*Inquisitiones post mortem* (RC), 4 vols., 1802–28.
ISLR	F. A. Greenhill, *The Incised Slabs of Leicestershire and Rutland*, 1958.
JEPNS	Journal of the English Place-Name Society.
John	Regnal date, t. John.
Kelly	*Kelly's Directory of the Counties of Leicester and Rutland*, 1925.
l.	late.
La	David Mills, *The Place-Names of Lancashire*, 1976.
LAS	Transactions of the Leicestershire Archaeological Society, later Leicestershire Archaeological and Historical Society.
Lat	Latin.
Laz	Cartulary of Burton Lazars (BL Cotton Nero C XII), British Library, London.
LCDeeds	Leicester Corporation Deeds, The Record Office for Leicestershire, Leicester and Rutland, Wigston Magna.
LCh	Leicestershire Charters, The Record Office for Leicestershire, Leicester and Rutland, Wigston Magna.
Lei	*The Place-Names of Leicestershire* (EPNS 75, 78, 81, 84), 1998–2009, in progress.
LeicSurv	*The Leicestershire Survey*, ed. C. F. Slade, 1956.
LeicW	*Leicester Wills*, ed. H. Hartopp, 2 vols., 1902–20.
LEpis	*Lincoln Episcopal Records* (LRS 2), 1912.
Letter	Miscellaneous letters in various publications.
LibCl	Liber Cleri in *The State of the Church*, vol. 1 (LRS 23), 1926.
Lind	E. H. Lind, *Norsk-Isländska Personbinamn från Medeltiden*, Uppsala, 1920–1.
LML	*Leicestershire Marriage Licences 1570–1729*, ed. H. Hartopp, 1910.
LN	*Liber Niger Scaccarii*, 1774.
LRS	Publications of the Lincoln Record Society.

LTD	Liber de terris Dominicalibus of Leicester Abbey (BL Cotton Galba B III), British Library, London.
LWills	*Lincoln Wills* (LRS 5, 10, 24), 1914–30.
m.	mid.
Map	Various printed maps.
Map	Unpublished maps in local and private collections.
masc.	masculine.
MB	Minutes Books in local collections.
Mdw	Meadow (in field-names).
ME	Middle English.
MemR	*Memoranda Rolls* (PRS NS 11, 21, 31).
MHW	The Matriculus of Hugh of Wells in *Rotuli Hugonis de Welles* (LRS 3), 1912.
MI	Monumental inscription.
MiD	Middleton MSS, University of Nottingham Archives, Nottingham.
MinAccts	*Ministers' Accounts: List of the Lands of Dissolved Religious Houses* (PRO Lists and Indexes, Supplementary Series III, vols. 1–4).
MinAccts	Unpublished Ministers' Accounts, The Record Office for Leicestershire, Leicester and Rutland, Wigston Magna.
Misc	*Calendar of Inquisitions Miscellaneous* (PRO), in progress.
MiscAccts	Miscellaneous accounts in local and private collections.
MktHPR	Market Harborough Parish Records, The Record Office for Leicestershire, Leicester and Rutland, Wigston Magna.
MLat	Medieval Latin.
ModE	Modern English.
Morden	R. Morden, *Map of Warwickshire*, 1695.
Morgan	*Domesday Book: Leicestershire*, ed. P. Morgan, 1979.
Mx	*The Place-Names of Middlesex* (EPNS 18), 1942.
n.d.	not dated.
neut.	neuter.
num.	numeral.
Nf	*The Place-Names of Norfolk* (EPNS 61, 72, 79), 1989–2002, in progress.
Nichols	J. Nichols, *The History and Antiquities of the County of Leicester*, 4 vols. in 8, 1795–1811.
nom.pl.	nominative plural.
NS	New series in a run of publications.
Nt	*The Place-Names of Nottinghamshire* (EPNS 17), 1940.
Nth	*The Place-Names of Northamptonshire* (EPNS 10), 1933.
O	First edition O.S. 1" maps.
OblR	*Rotulis de Oblatis* (RC), 1835.
obl.sg.	oblique singular.
OBret	Old Breton.
ODan	Old Danish.

OE   Old English.
OED   *A New English Dictionary*, ed. J. A. H. Murray *et al.*, 1884–1928; re-
                issued with a supplement in 1933 as *The Oxford English Dictionary*.
OFr   Old French.
OGer   Old German.
OHGer   Old High German.
OIr   Old Irish.
ON   Old Norse.
ONFr   Old Norman French.
Ord   Ordericus Vitalis, *Ecclesiasticae Historiae*, vols. 2–3, Paris 1840–5.
O.S.   The Ordnance Survey.
OScand   Old Scandinavian.
OSut   *The Rolls and Registers of Bishop Oliver Sutton* (LRS 39, 43, 48, 52,
                60), 1948–65.
OSw   Old Swedish.
Ox   *The Place-Names of Oxfordshire*, (EPNS 23, 24), 1953–4.
P   *Pipe Rolls* (PRS), in progress.
p.   *post.*
(p)   place-name used as a personal name or surname.
Paget   Paget MSS, The Record Office for Leicestershire, Leicester and
                Rutland, Wigston Magna.
Palmer   The Palmer MSS, The Record Office for Leicestershire, Leicester and
                Rutland, Wigston Magna.
Pap   *Calendar of Entries in the Papal Registers* (PRO), in progress.
pa.part.   past participle.
Pat   *Calendar of Patent Rolls* (PRO), in progress.
Pat   Patent Rolls in the Public Record Office.
Peake   Peake MSS (Nevill of Holt), The Record Office for Leicestershire,
                Leicester and Rutland, Wigston Magna.
perh.   perhaps.
pers.n(s).   personal name(s).
P.H.   Public House.
Pipewell   Cartulary of Pipewell Abbey (BL Cotton Julius A I), British Library,
                London.
PK   Powys-Keck Estate Documents, The Record Office for Leicester-
                shire, Leicester and Rutland, Wigston Magna.
Plan   Unpublished plans in The Record Office for Leicestershire, Leicester
                and Rutland, Wigston Magna.
p.n.   place-name.
PNLeiR   Barrie Cox, *The Place-Names of Leicestershire and Rutland*,
                unpublished Ph.D. thesis for the University of Nottingham, 1971.
PN -ing   E. Ekwall, *English Place-Names in -ing*, 2nd edn, Lund 1962.
poss.   possible, possibly.
ppl.adj.   participial adjective.

PR	Parish Registers in various publications.
PRep	*The Register of Bishop Philip Repingdon* (LRS 57–8), 1963.
prep.	preposition.
pres.part.	present participle.
presum.	presumably.
PRO	Records preserved in or published by the Public Record Office.
prob.	probable, probably.
PRS	Publications of the Pipe Roll Society.
PrW	Proto-Welsh.
QH	Quorn House MSS, The Record Office for Leicestershire, Leicester and Rutland, Wigston Magna.
q.v.	*quod vide.*
RB	Romano-British.
RBE	*Red Book of the Exchequer* (RS 99), 1896.
RBL	*Records of the Borough of Leicester*, vols. 1–3, ed. M. Bateson 1899–1905; vol. 4, ed. H. Stocks 1923; vols. 5–6, ed. G. A. Chinnery 1965–7.
RC	Publications of the Record Commission.
Rd	Road (in street-names).
Reaney	P. H. Reaney, *A Dictionary of English Surnames*, revised by R. M. Wilson, 3rd edn with appendix by D. Hey, 1995.
Redin	M. Redin, *Uncompounded Personal Names in Old English*, Uppsala 1915.
Reg	*Regesta Regum Anglo-Normannorum*, 1913–68.
RegAnt	*Registrum Antiquissimum of the Cathedral Church of Lincoln* (LRS 27–9, 51), 1931–58.
Rental	Various published rentals.
Rental	Various unpublished rentals in local and private collections.
Rey	Reynolds and Blackwell Deeds, The Record Office for Leicestershire, Leicester and Rutland, Wigston Magna.
RFL	*Register of the Freemen of Leicester*, ed. H. Hartopp, 2 vols., 1927–33.
RGrav	*Rotuli Ricardi Gravesend Episcopi Lincolniensis* (LRS 20), 1925.
RGros	*Rotuli Roberti Grosseteste Episcopi Lincolniensis* (LRS 11), 1914.
RH	*Rotulis Hundredorum* (RC), 1812–18.
RHug	*Rotuli Hugonis de Welles Episcopi Lincolniensis* (LRS 3, 6), 1912–13.
RN	E. Ekwall, *English River-Names*, 1928.
RotNorm	*Rotuli Normanniae in Turri Londiniensi* (RC), 1835.
RS	Rolls Series.
RTAL	*Rotuli Taxationis Archidiaconatus Leicestrie* (LRS 3), 1912.
RTemple	Rothley Temple Deeds, The Record Office for Leicestershire, Leicester and Rutland, Wigston Magna.
Ru	*The Place-Names of Rutland* (EPNS 67–9), 1994.
Rut	Duke of Rutland's MSS, Muniments Room, Belvoir Castle, Leics.

S	P. H. Sawyer, *Anglo-Saxon Charters*, 1968.
s.a.	*sub anno.*
Sale	Particulars of sales in local and private collections.
Salt	Publications of the William Salt Society.
Saxton	Christopher Saxton, *Atlas of England and Wales*, 1576.
sb.	substantive.
Scand	Scandinavian.
Searle	W. G. Searle, *Onomasticon Anglo-Saxonicum*, 1897.
Segrave	The Segrave Cartulary (BL Harl MS 4748).
Selby	*The Selby Abbey Cartulary* (YAA 10, 13), 1891–3.
Seld	Publications of the Selden Society.
ShR	Shangton Records, The Record Office for Leicestershire, Leicester and Rutland, Wigston Magna.
Sloane	Sloane MSS, The British Library, London.
s.n(n).	*sub nomine, sub nominibus.*
Speed	J. Speed, *The Theatre of the Empire of Great Britain*, 1610.
SPNLY	G. Fellows Jensen, *Scandinavian Personal Names in Lincolnshire and Yorkshire*, Copenhagen 1968.
SR	Subsidy Rolls in various publications.
Sr	*The Place-Names of Surrey*, (EPNS 11), 1934.
SSNEM	G. Fellows Jensen, *Scandinavian Settlement Names in the East Midlands*, Copenhagen 1978.
St	*The Place-Names of Staffordshire* (EPNS 55), 1984, in progress.
St	Street (in street-names).
StH	D. Horovitz, *The Place-Names of Staffordshire*, Brewood 2005.
superl.adj.	superlative adjective.
supra	above.
surn(s).	surname(s).
Surv	Surveys in various publications.
Surv	Surveys in local and private collections.
s.v.	*sub voce.*
Swed	Swedish.
t.	*tempore.*
TA	Tithe Awards, The Record Office for Leicestershire, Leicester and Rutland, Wigston Magna.
Tax	*Taxatio Ecclesiastica* (RC), 1802.
Terrier	Various published terriers.
Terrier	Terriers in local and private collections.
TRE	*tempore Regis Edwardi*, the DB term for 'on the day that King Edward the Confessor was alive and dead'.
v.	*vide.*
Val	*The Valuation of Norwich*, ed. W. E. Lunt, 1926.
Valuation	Valuations in local and private collections.
vbl.sb.	verbal substantive.

VCHL	*Victoria County History of Leicestershire*, in progress.
VE	*Valor Ecclesiasticus* (RC), 1810–34.
VEPN	*The Vocabulary of English Place-Names*, in progress.
Visit	*Visitations of Religious Houses in the Diocese of Lincoln* (LRS 14, 21, 33, 35, 37), 1918–47.
W	*The Place-Names of Wiltshire* (EPNS 16), 1939.
Wa	*The Place-Names of Warwickshire* (EPNS 13), 1936.
We	*The Place-Names of Westmorland* (EPNS 42–3), 1967.
White	*History, Gazetteer and Directory of Leicestershire and Rutland*, ed. W. White, 1846, 1863, 1877.
Will	Wills in various publications.
Will	Unpublished wills in local and private collections.
Win	Winstanley MSS, The Record Office for Leicestershire, Leicester and Rutland, Wigston Magna.
wk.obl.	weak oblique.
Wo	*The Place-Names of Worcestershire* (EPNS 4), 1927.
WoCart	John de Wodeford's Cartulary (BL Claudius A XIII), British Library, London.
Wyg	Wyggeston Hospital MSS, The Record Office for Leicestershire, Leicester and Rutland, Wigston Magna.
YAA	Publications of the Yorkshire Archaeological Association; Record Series.
YN	*The Place-Names of the North Riding of Yorkshire* (EPNS 5), 1928.
YW	*The Place-Names of the West Riding of Yorkshire* (EPNS 30–7), 1961–3.
*	a postulated form.
1"	O.S. 1" maps, editions of 1967–8.
2½"	O.S. 2½" maps, editions of 1951–66.
6"	O.S. 6" maps, editions of 1956–67.

GUTHLAXTON HUNDRED

Guthlaxton Hundred

Gvtlakiston 1086 DB (freq.), *Gutlakestan* 1202 ChancR
Guðlachestan 1167 P, *Guthlakestan* 1247 Fees
Gudlachestan 1176 P, *Gudlakestan* 1170, 1171 ib, 1175 ChancR,
   1177, 1178 P *et freq* to 1210 ib, *Gudlakistan* 1175 ib,
   Gudelakestan 1183 ib, *Gudlacstan* 1180 ib
Guðlakeston 1166 P, *Guthlakeston* 1195 ib, 1272 Cur, *Guthlacston*
   l.13 GarCart, *Guthlaxton* 1254 Val, 1301 Ass, 1332 SR,
   Guthlaxton 1316 FA, 1327 SR, 1402, 1428 FA *et passim*
Gutlacston 1265 Misc, 1274 Ipm, *Gutlaxston* 1314 GarCart,
   Gutlaxton 1375 IpmR
Gudlaceston 1167 P, *Gudlakeston(e)* 1197, 1198, 1203 ib,
   Gudlakston c.1291 Tax (freq.), 1342 Pat, 1428 FA, *Gudlaxton*
   1443 Pat, 1449 Fine, 1518 Visit
Goudlokston 1392, 1397 Pat *et passim* to 1441 Cl
Godlaxton 1413 Fine, 1457 Ct, 1465, 1550 Pat, *Godlokston* 1441 ib,
   Godloxton 1432 ib
Goodlaxton 1510 Visit, 1535 VE *et passim* to 1610 Speed

The division is styled: *wapent(ac)* 1086 DB, 1166 P *et freq* to 1203
ib, *hundred* 1184, 1185 ib *et freq*, *v.* **vápnatak, hundred**.

'Guthlac's stone', *v.* **stān**. The masc. pers.n. *Gūðlāc* is Old English.
Both the identity of Guthlac and the nature of the stone from which the
wapentake took its name are uncertain.

At the time of the Domesday Survey, an extensive Guthlaxton
Wapentake stretched from the bounds of the Gartree Wapentake in the
east to those of the old Goscote Wapentake and Derbyshire's Repton
Wapentake to the north and north-west. By the date of the Leicestershire
Survey of c.1130, roughly two-thirds of the former Guthlaxton's territory
north-west of the Roman Fosse Way had been separated from it to form
the Sparkenhoe Hundred. The moot-site of the original wapentake lay
beside Fosse Way at Guthlaxton Gap near *Guthlaxton Bridge* (SP 527961)

which carried the road across a tributary of the river Soar at the north-western bounds of Cosby parish. Cosby's north-western great open-field is recorded in the *Liber de terris Dominicalibus* of Leicester Abbey of 1467 × 84 as *Gutlakestonfelde*. Writing c.1807, Nichols noted, 'A piece of land in this (i.e. Cosby) lordship is called *Guthlaxton Meadow*; and near it still remains a tumulus upon which, it is said, the Hundred Court was formerly held' (Nichols **4** 1 140). The 'tumulus' may be the small narrow ridge shown as crossing Fosse Way at this point on the 1st edn O.S. map of 1835. Otherwise, no tumulus is marked here on any later map and none is evident on the ground.

The presumed location of the erstwhile stone on the Fosse Way is six Roman miles from the western entrance to Roman Leicester (*Ratae Corieltavorum*) which suggests that, rather than this being a glacial erratic such as is Hunbeorht's Stone in Humberstone (Lei **3** 133), it was a surviving Roman milestone on the Fosse Way, but what function it had in the Anglo-Saxon period is obscure. The fact that it marked the moot-site of Guthlaxton Wapentake may imply that it was more than simply a boundary-marker of an estate belonging to a local landowner called Guthlac. Did it rather in some sort relate to St Guthlac of Crowland?

St Guthlac (c.674–714), son of Penwald (or Penwalh), a minor prince of the royal Mercian house of the Icelingas, after a period as a warrior fighting on the western boundaries of Mercia, entered the monastery of Repton. After several years there, he moved to become a hermit in the Fens at Crowland in Lincolnshire. There is a tradition, probably spurious, that Æthelbald of Mercia founded a monastery in Guthlac's memory at Crowland on the site of his cell in 716, but his cult certainly became extensive later in eastern Mercia and his tomb was popular with pilgrims as early as the ninth century. St Guthlac's Abbey of Crowland was raised subsequently on the site of his hermitage, possibly having been laid down before the Norman Conquest, but it is recorded that the building of a great church commenced here for certain in 1114. There is a boundary marker three miles north-east of Crowland Abbey which is inscribed *Hanc petram Guthlacus habet sive metam*, literally 'This stone Guthlac has as his limit': another Guthlac's Stone, but this relating directly to the saint.

In the Domesday Survey, Crowland Abbey is shown to hold in Leicestershire two carucates of land in Sutton Cheney, two carucates more in Stapleton, both townships in the original Guthlaxton Wapentake, ten and a half carucates in Beeby in the former Goscote Wapentake, as well as three messuages in Leicester itself. Brian Rich (personal communication) has noted that the abbey also held two virgates of land in Barkby ante 1275, a township also in the old Goscote Wapentake (*v. Rotuli Hundredorum* **1** 238).

There are twelve church dedications to St Guthlac in the East Midlands and East Anglia, of which five are in Lincolnshire, three are in Northamptonshire and two are in Leicestershire. The Leicestershire instances are of the churches of the adjoining former parishes of Stathern and Branston in the north-east of the county in Framland Hundred. That the churches of these two contiguous parishes relate to St Guthlac may indicate a pre-Conquest estate here also belonging to Crowland Abbey. However, nothing else of a Guthlac, other than the name of the stone, survives in Guthlaxton Hundred.

The personal-name *Gūðlāc* is not common in Anglo-Saxon records, apart from its recurrence in various Latin and Old English accounts of the saint's life and in two Old English poems concerning him. Only four other instances are listed in Searle's personal-name collection (*v.* Searle 273) and the name is not recorded in sources after 824. It is the importance of the moot-site that suggests the Guthlac of this Guthlac's Stone may have been more than a local landowner. Otherwise, its position conforms to the pattern of moot-sites in the county in relation to its Roman road system and principal township (*v.* Barrie Cox, 'Leicestershire moot-sites: the place-name evidence', *Transactions of the Leicestershire Archaeological and Historical Society*, Vol. 47 (1971–2), 14–21).

Arnesby

ARNESBY

> *Erendesbi* 1086 DB, 1169, 1170 P, *Erendesby* 1227, 1229 Ch, 1231
>   Fine, *Herendesby* 1265 Misc, *Herendisby* c.1280 *Wyg*
> *Erendesberie* 1086 DB
> *Erndesby* 1227 ClR, 1230 Fin *et passim* to 1285 FA, *Herndesbi* 1199
>   Cur (p)
> *Ernesbi* 1202 FF, 1205 Pap *et passim* to c.1251 *RTemple, Ernesby*
>   1212 RBE, 1225 ClR *et freq* to 1493 *Rey*, 1522 *RTemple,*
>   *Hernesb'* 1236 Fees, *Hernisby* 1272 Ipm
> *Ernebi* 1177, 1178 P *et freq* to 1215 ib, *Erneby* 1224 Cur, 1266 Pat
>   (p), *Hernebi* 1176 P, *Herneby* 1335 (p), 1344 *Peake* (p) *et freq* to
>   1356 *ib* (p)
> *Yerenesby* 1518 Visit
> *Earnsby* 1576, 1601 LibCl, *Earnesbie* 1603 LibCl, *Earnesby* 1606,
>   1630 LML
> *Armesby(e)* 1548 Fine, 1576 Saxton
> *Arnesby(e)* 1610 Speed, 1695 LML *et freq*

Either 'the farmstead or village of a man called Erendi' or 'the
farmstead or village of a man called Iarund', *v.* **bȳ**. The recorded ODan
masc. pers.n. *Iarund* (ON *Iǫrundr*) may have given a ME gen.sg.
*Erendes, but Fellows-Jensen (SSNEM 31) argues that the specific is
more likely to be an appellative, perhaps Scand *erendi* 'errand, message'
used as an unrecorded by-name, since Scand initial *ja*- survives almost
without exception in Scand names in England. Only the form *Yerenesby*
1518 contains any indication of an initial diphthong, but is very late. The
isolated -*berie* form in DB is erratic and no doubt should be ascribed to
the compiler of the Leicestershire returns. Seven other instances of such
DB -*berie* forms occur in the county: those for Appleby (Sparkenhoe
Hundred, PNLeiR 559), Asfordby (Lei **3** 9), Barkby (Lei **3** 21), Old
Ingarsby (Lei **3** 152), Quenby (Lei **3** 154), Shoby (Lei **3** 111) and
Somerby (Lei **2** 225). For comment on this feature, *v.* PNLeiR 74–7, Lei
3 10 and SSNEM 13–15.

ARNESBY LODGE, ~ ~ COTTAGES, *Arnesby Lodge* 1835 O, *v.* **loge**.
BAPTIST CHAPEL, built 1795, extended 1839 and 1857; cf. *First* ~ ~,
Second ~ ~, *Third Chapel Field* 1968 *Surv*, *v.* **chapel(e)**. BAULK LANE,
v. **balca**. BLUE BELL (P.H.) (lost), *Blue Bell* 1846, 1863, 1877 White,
Bell Inn 1925 Kelly. CHURCH LANE, *v.* St Peter's Church *infra*. FACTORY
LANE. FLAXHILL BUNGALOW, cf. *Big* ~, *Little Flaxhill* 1968 *Surv*, *v.*
fleax, **hyll**. FLECKNEY RD, Fleckney lying 2 miles to the north-east.
GRANGE FM, *v.* **grange**. LUTTERWORTH RD, Lutterworth lying 8 miles to
the south-west. MANOR FM (×2), *v.* **maner**. MILL HILL RD, MILL HO.,
v. The Windmill *infra*. OLD COCK (P.H.), *Old Cock* 1846, 1863, 1877
White, *Old Cock Inn* 1925 Kelly. ST PETER'S CHURCH, *Church (St Peter)*
1846, 1863, 1877 White, 1925 Kelly; it is earlier recorded as *ecclesie de
Ernesby* 1220 MHW, 1489 *Pat, ecclesiam de Ernesb'* 1249 RGros,
ecclesie de Ernysby 1376 *Pat, ecclesiam de Ernesby* 1377 *ib, ecclesiam
Sancti Petri Ernesby* 1389 *ib, ecclesie de Ernesbye* 1550 *ib*. ST PETER'S
RD, *v.* St Peter's Church *supra*. SHOULDER OF MUTTON (P.H.) (lost),
Shoulder of Mutton 1846, 1863, 1877 White, 1925 Kelly. THE
VICARAGE, 1925 Kelly; earlier is recorded *The Vicarage House* 1700,
1708 *Terrier*, *v.* **vikerage**. WELFORD RD, Welford lying 8 miles to the
south in Northants. WESTFIELD COTTAGE. WESTFIELD HO., *Westfield
House* 1877 White, 1925 Kelly. THE WHITE HO. THE WINDMILL, built
1815, *v.* **wind-mylne**.

FIELD-NAMES

In (a), forms presented without dates are 1968 *Surv*; those dated 1795 are
EnclA; 1837 are *Deed*; 1843, 1907, 1910 and 1928 are Sale; 1882 are
Plan. Forms throughout dated a.1250 are *RTemple*; 1332 are SR; c.1550
and e.17 are *Rental*; 1554 and 1609 are Nichols; 1601, 1625, 1673, 1679,
1694, 1700 and 1708 are *Terrier*.

(a) Four Acre, Six ~, Seven ~, Eight ~, Top Eight ~, Nine ~, Ten ~, Twelve Acre
(*v.* **æcer**); Ant Bank (*v.* **æmette, banke**); Arkwright's Mdw 1882 (with the surn.
Arkwright (from OE *arc* + *wyrhta* 'a maker of chests')); Great ~, Little Asgates 1907,
Big Asgate (or Big Barn) 1968 (*Ashgates* 1673, 1679, 1694, 1700, 1708, *v.* **æsc,
gata**); Back Allotment (*v.* **back, allotment**); Barn Cl 1928, 1968, Barn Fd 1968 (*v.*
bern); Bell Paddock (*v.* **paddock**; rather than *Bell* as a surn., this may refer to an
endowment for the upkeep of bells in the parish church, or even to the shape of the
enclosure); Bennett's Cl (with the surn. *Bennett*, from OFr *Beneit* (Lat *benedictus*
'blessed'), a common Christian name from the 12th cent.); Big ~, Little Barn (*v.*
bern and Big Asgate *supra*); Big Cl 1907, 1968; Big Fd; Binger's Hill (*binggers hill*
1601, *Binger Hill* 1673, 1679, 1694, *Bingershill* 1708; earlier forms are needed, but

poss. with shortening is a name meaning 'wooded slope growing with berries', *v.* **begen, hangra, (hyll)**); Blackthorn Bottom (*v.* **blakthorn, botm**); Bottle Neck (referring to the shape of the enclosure); Brant Hill 1843, 1968, Little ~, Brantles 1907, Little Brant Hill 1968, Brant Hill Mdw 1843 (*v.* **brant, hyll**); Bridle Road Fd, ~ ~ Mdw, Top Bridle Road (*v.* **brigdels**); Brook Fd 1795 (*Brookfield* c.1550, (*the*) *Brook(e) feild* e.17, 1673, 1679, 1694, 1700, *the Brook field* 1708, *v.* **brōc, feld**; one of the great open-fields of the township, also called *the bridge feild* 1601 (*v.* **brycg**)); Brown's (the surn. *Brown* in the possessive case); Chapman's Mdws (with the surn. *Chapman*, cf. *Matthew Chapman* 1839 Census, *Thomas Chapman* 1841 ib and *Samuel Chapman* 1851 ib of Arnesby); Church Cls (*v.* St Peter's Church *supra*); The Cock Cl, Second Cock Cl (*v.* Old Cock (P.H.) *supra*); Cottage Fd (*v.* **cotage**); First ~ ~, Second Cow Cl (*v.* **cū**); Cowdale Mdw 1837, Caldwell ~ 1910, Caudle Mdw 1968 (*Caudwell* 1601, *Caudhil* 1673, 1679, 1694, *Cowdwell* 1708, *v.* **cald, wella**); Crab Tree (*v.* **crabtre**); Crooked Tree Cl 1795, Crooked Tree Allotment 1968 (*v.* **allotment**) (*Crooktree* 1601, *Crooke Tree* 1673, 1679, 1694, 1700, *Crook-tree* 1708, *v.* **trēow**; the earlier forms suggest **krókr** 'a crook, a bend; land in the bend of a stream' as the first word but it may simply be a shortened **croked** 'crooked, twisted'); Draw Rails (*v.* **raile**; the specific is problematical); (The) Englands 1794, 1882, 1968 (*v.* **eng, land**); Far Fd, ~ Mdw (*v.* **feor**); Finger Post Fd 1882, Fingerpost 1968 (*v.* **finger-post**); First Fd; Fleckney Brook 1795, Fleckney Hill Fd 1795, 1968 (*Fleckney Hill feild* 1673, 1679, 1694, *Fleckley Hill feild* (sic) 1700, *Fleckley Hill Field* (sic) 1708 (*v.* **feld**; one of the great open-fields of the township, earlier called *Eastfeld* c.1550, *the East feild* e.17 (*v.* **ēast**)), First ~ ~ ~, Second Fleckney Lane Cl 1968 (Fleckney parish in Gartree Hundred adjoins to the north-east); Foston Hill Fd 1795 (*Foston hill* 1601, *Foston Hill Feild* 1673, 1679, *Fauston Hill Feild* 1694, 1700, *Foston Hill Field* 1708, *v.* **feld**; one of the great open-fields of the township, earlier called *Northfeld* c.1550, *the North feild* e.17 (*v.* **norð**); Foston parish adjoins to the north); Garden Fd (*v.* **gardin**; land used for horticulture); First ~, Long ~, Twin Glebe (*v.* **twinn**) (*v.* **glebe**); Glover's Mdw (with the surn. *Glover*, cf. *Ann Glover* 1806 Census, *Richard Glover* 1815 ib and *Daniel Glover* 1823 ib of Arnesby); Gravel Cl 1907, Gravel Hill, Gravel Hole, Gravel Pit 1968 (*v.* **gravel**); the Green 1795 (*the Greene* 1601, 1673, 1679, 1694, 1700, *v.* **grēne**²); Green Cl 1928, 1968; Middle ~, Old Greenleys 1928 (*v.* **leys**; prob. with **grēne**¹); The Grove 1928, 1968 (*v.* **grāf**); Hagglespit 1882, 1910, Agglespit 1968 (*v.* **pytt**; earlier forms are needed, but if the name is ancient, then the ON masc. pers.n. *Hagleikr* (Lind 130), with shortening, is poss. as the specific, although apart from the township's name, Scand influence appears minimal in the parish; otherwise, perh. with *haggle* 'to dispute'); Hall's First ~ ~, Hall's Second Cow Fd (*v.* **cū**; with the surn. *Hall*); Bottom ~ ~, Top Hardy's Fd (with the surn. *Hardy*, cf. *John Hardy* 1827 Census of Arnesby); Headlands (*v.* **hēafod-land**); Home Cl 1843, 1928, 1968, Home Fd 1968 (*v.* **home**); Horse Cl (*v.* **hors**); Horton's Mdw 1882, Orton's Mdw 1968 (with the surn. *Horton*, cf. *Mary Horton* 1832 Census of Arnesby); Hut Cl (*v.* **hut**); Isle of Wight (a 'remoteness' name for parish ground distant from the township); Kilby Cl (at the boundary with Kilby parish which adjoins to the north); Langham's Big Fd (with the surn. *Langham*, (cf. *Willielmus de Langham* 1327 SR of Leics.), presum. that of a family originally from Langham in Rutland); Little Mdw; Long Leas (*v.* **leys**); Lowe's Big ~, Lowe's Little Fd, Lowe's Mdw (with the surn. *Lowe*, cf. *Helen Lowe* 1859 Census and *Annie Lowe* 1860 ib, both of adjacent Peatling Magna); Man's Fd (although *Mann* is a common surn. in Leics., this f.n. may remember the *Mansfield* family in Arnesby, as *Maunsfeild Hedg* 1700, *Mansfields Hedge* 1708 (v. **hecg**)); Mawby's Fds (with the surn. *Mawby*, cf. *George Mawby* 1831 Census and *Josiah Mawby* 1850 ib of Arnesby); The Meadow 1928, 1968; Middle Fd 1928, 1968; Middle Mdw; Mill Cl 1928, Mill Fds 1968 (cf. *the Mill Furlong* 1673, 1679, 1694, 1700, 1708 (v. **furlang**), (*the*) *Mill Hedge* 1673, 1679, 1694, 1700, 1708 (v. **hecg**), v. **myln**); Mount Pleasant (usually a complimentary name, but occasionally bestowed ironically); New Mdw 1907; Oxhall (*Oxhole* 1673, 1679, 1694, 1700, 1708, v. **oxa**; with **hol**¹ or **halh**); The Paddock (v. **paddock**); Old Ploughed Fd; Pollard's (the surn. *Pollard* in the possessive case, cf. *Thomas Pollard* 1824 Census, *Harriet Pollard* 1837 ib and *Fred Pollard* 1861 ib, all of Arnesby); Primrose Hill (v. **primerole**; land on which primroses grew); Ram's Cl (v. **ramm**); Red Barn Fd (v. **bern**); Rickyard Fd (v. **reke-yard**); Saddington Lane Cl (cf. *Sadington way* 1601, *Saddington waye* 1625, ~ *Way* 1673, 1679, 1694, 1700, 1708 (v. **weg**); Saddington lies 3 miles to the east); The Sandhill, Second ~, Third Sandhill (*Sand hill* 1601, *Sandhil* 1673, 1679, 1694, *Sand-hill* 1708, v. **sand**, **hyll**); Second Fd; Bottom ~ ~, Top Seed Cl 1882, Bottom ~, Top Seeds 1968 (v. **sǣd**; in modern f.ns., used of grasses sown for one year's mowing or grazing as distinguished from permanent pasture); Shallow Thistles 1928, 1968 (1673, 1679, 1694, 1700, 1708, v. **þistel**), Second Shallow 1928 (v. **sceldu**; used of a 'a shallow dip, a shallow valley'); Sharman's (the surn. *Sharman* in the possessive case, cf. *Rogerus sereman* 1207 RFL of Leicester; common in adjacent Fleckney, as *Nicholas Sharman* 1816 Census, *Randal Sharman* 1821 ib and *John Sharman* 1857 ib; an occupational surn., 'one who removes the nap of cloth by shearing'); The Slades (v. **slæd**); (The) Slang 1907, 1968 (v. **slang**); Snipes ~ 1928, Snipe's Corner 1968 (v. **corner**; with the surn. *Snipe*, either from the OE masc. pers.n. *Snīp* or from the ON masc. pers.n. *Snípr*); Square Fd (v. **squar(e)**); Stackyard (v. **stackyard**); Stonebridge Flat 1968 (v. **flat**), Stone Bridge Mdw 1795 (v. **stān**, **brycg**); Stonehill (v. **stān**, **hyll**); Bottom ~ ~, Little ~ ~, Middle Swans Nest 1907 (v. **swan**¹, **nest**); The Ten acres Mdw 1882 (v. **æcer**); Three Corner Fd (v. **three-corner**); First ~, Middle ~, Top Tithe (v. **tēoða**); Top Bridge (cf. *the bridge* 1601, v. **brycg**); Top Mdw; Turnpike Mdw (v. **turnepike**); Washbrook Fd, ~ Mdw (v. **brōc**; prob. with **wæsce**, but **wæsse** is poss.); Washpit Cl 1882, Washpit 1968 (v. **wæsce**, **pytt**); Waterlees Mdw 1882, Warterley Meer 1837, Waterly Mere 1910, Waterfly Mere (sic) 1968 (v. **mere**¹) (v. **wæter**, **leys**); Wiggins Hole (*wigins hole* 1601, *Wiggin(s) hole* 1625, 1673, 1679, 1694, 1700, 1708 (v. **hol**¹; with the surn. *Wiggins*, cf. *Radulfus filius Wigein* 1163 P of Leics.; *Wigein* was an OFr pers.n. of Breton origin (OBret *Wicon*, *Guegon*), introduced at the Norman Conquest).

(b) Armitage 1673, 1679, 1694, 1708, *Armitadge* 1700 (v. **ermitage**); *Ashby slade* 1601, 1700, 1708 (v. **slæd**; prob. with the surn. *Ashby*); *burdich* (or *burdith*) *hedge* 1601 (v. **hecg**; if the first word is a surn., then *Burdet* is poss., cf. *Radulfus Burdet* 1160 Dane of Leics., otherwise perh. **burh**, with **dīc**); *Breddles* 1601 (unexplained; poss. from **brigdels**); *Bridgers Hill* 1700 (with the surn. *Bridger*); *Broad(e) Ashpitt* 1679, 1694, *Broad Ashpit* 1700, 1708 (v. **brād**, **æsc**, **pytt**); *Broad Wells* 1673, 1679, 1694, 1700, 1708 (v. **brād**, **wella**); (*the*) *Brook(e) Slade* 1673, 1679, 1697, 1700, 1708 (v. **brōc**, **slæd**); *Cludhils* 1673, 1679, 1694, *Cloude Hills* 1700, *Cludhills* 1708 (v. **clūd**, **hyll**); *Colepitt Road* 1708 (v. **col-pytt**; poss. a route for the transportation of pit coal from the Bedworth area of Warwks.); *Dopscroft* 1673, 1679, 1694, *Dobscroft* 1708 (v. **croft**; with the surn. *Dobb(s)*, from a pet-form of Robert); *dawnes hadland* 1625 (*v.* **hēafod-land**; with the surn. *Dawn, v.* Reaney *s.nn.* Daw and Geffen); (*at*) *the Farm gate* 1673, 1679, 1694, 1700, *the Farme Gate* 1708 (*v.* **ferme, gata**); *Fleckly Meere* (sic) 1700, *Fleckley Meer* (sic) 1708 (*v.* **(ge)mǣre**; the boundary with Fleckney parish which adjoins to the north-east); *ad fontem* 1332 SR (p) ('at the spring or well'; MLat *ad* 'at' with *fons* (*fontem* acc.sg.) 'a spring, a well'); *Foston Gate* 1673, 1679, 1694, 1708 (*v.* **gata**; Foston parish adjoins to the north); *the hall mere* 1625 (*v.* **hall, (ge)mǣre**); *Hangarshull'* a.1250 (*v.* **hangra, hyll**); *Hayes Croft* 1700 (*v.* **croft**; with the surn. *Haye*(*s*), *v.* Reaney *s.n.*); *the Hill Farme* 1708 (*v.* **hyll, ferme**); *Kerbidge* 1601, *Kirbrik* 1679, *Kirbridge* 1694, *Kirbidge* 1708 (*v.* **kjarr**; with either **brycg** or **bece**[1]); *Kill Well Hedg* 1700, *Kilwell Hedge* 1708 (poss. with a Scandinavianized **cildawella* (*v.* **cild, wella**, cf. Chilwell, Nt 142) and either **hecg** or **edisc**); *Kirbie grownde* 1700 (*v.* **grund**; *Kirbie* may be either a surn. here or a misconstrued *Kilbie* (with long *l* for *r*), Kilby parish adjoining to the north); *Langedich* a.1250, *Languish Way* (sic) 1673, 1679, 1694, 1700, 1708 (*v.* **lang**[1], **dīc**); *London way* 1601, *London waye side* 1625 (*v.* **sīde**), *London Road* 1700, 1708 (*v.* **weg**; the route to London, now the A 5199 road to Northampton and then via Watling Street); *Many Banks* 1673, 1679, 1694 (*v.* **manig, banke**); *Mickle Med*(*d*)*ow* 1673, 1679, 1694, 1700, 1708 (*v.* **micel, mikill, mēd** (**mēdwe** obl.sg.)); *Mid*(*d*)*dle Hills* 1673, 1679, 1694, 1700, 1708 (*v.* **middel, hyll**); *Money Balk* 1700, *~ Baulk* 1708 (*v.* **moneye, balca**; presum. the site of the discovery of a coin hoard); *Mussel Bush* 1673, 1679, 1694, *Moossels Bush* 1700, *Muzzles Bush* 1708 (*v.* **busc**), *Mosshels Hedg* 1673, 1679, 1694 (*v.* **hecg**) (*v.* **mos, wella**; the surn. *Mussell* (from OE *muscelle* 'a mussel, a shell fish' and metonymic for a gatherer of these) is unlikely, since found only belonging to four incomers from the south to Leicester and Melton Mowbray in the 1881 Census); *peasseland way* 1625, *Peeseland ~* 1673, 1679, 1694, *Peasland way* 1700, 1708 (*v.* **pise, land, weg**); *Peatlinge waye* 1601, *Peatlin ~* 1673, 1679, *Peatling Way* 1700, 1708 (*v.* **weg**; the road to Peatling Magna which lies 1½ miles to the west); *pippines well* 1625, *Pipins Well* 1673, *Pippings Well* 1679, *Pipineswell* 1694, *Pippins Well* 1700, *Pippinwell Farme* 1708 (*v.* **ferme**) (*v.* **wella**; it is uncertain whether *Pip*(*p*)*in* here represents the ContGerm masc. pers.n. *Pipin* or a surn. derived from it (as for *Radulphus Pipin* 1086 DB who held 6 carucates of land in Goadby Marwood (Lei **2** 125) and *Willielmus Pipin* 1199 Cur, a canon of Leicester); in compound with *wella*, the pers.n., which occurs early as in *pippenespenne* 949 (12) BCS 882 (S 550), is perh. to be preferred, *v.* Forssner 204); *Ravens Well* 1673, 1679, 1694, 1700, 1708 (*v.* **wella**; either with the OE masc. pers.n. *Hræfn* or the ON masc. pers.n. *Hrafn* or the surn. *Raven* derived from them, the raven (bird) (OE *hræfn*, ON *hrafn*) being less likely); *Seusbys croft close* 1554 (*v.* **croft, clos**(**e**)), *Shearsby slade* 1601 (*v.* **slæd**), *Shersby meere* 1700, *Shearsby Meer* 1708 (*v.* **(ge)mǣre**; Shearsby parish adjoins to the south-east; cf. the 1554 spelling with earlier forms for Shearsby, as *Seusbi* 1197); *the Thornes* 1673, 1679, 1694, 1700, 1708 (*v.* **þorn**); *Toote Hill* 1673, 1679, 1694, 1700, 1708 (*v.* **tōt-hyll**; *the Vicars peice* 1700 (*v.* **pece**), *Vicars willows* 1625, 1673, 1679, 1694, 1700, 1708 (*v.* **wilig**) (*v.* **vikere**); *white hill* 1601, *Whitehill Hollow* 1673, 1679, 1694, 1708 (*v.* **holh**) (*v.* **hwīt, hyll**; as well as referring to appearance, in eModE, *white* may indicate 'infertile' (in contrast to *black* 'fertile'), while dial. *white* may refer to 'dry open pasture').

Ashby Magna

Essebi 1086 DB (×2), l.12 Dane, 1210 Cur (p), 1210 (p), 1211 P (p), 1221 RHug, *Essebiam* c.1175 *MiD*

Esseby 1221 RHug, 1226 Fine (p), 1254 Val *et passim* to c.1291 Tax, l.13 *CRCart*

Eissebi 1203 (p), 1207 (p), 1212 P (p)

Aissebi 1189 × 95 AD, l.12 Dane (p)

Assheby 1316, 1320 Cl, 1330 Ipm *et freq* to 1428 FA, 1460 *Wyg et passim* to 1569 Fine, 1579 CoPleas

Asscheby 1316 Misc, *Ascheby* 1330 FA

Ashby 1518 Visit, 1535 VE, 1610 Speed *et freq*

Affixes are variously added as:

Magna ~ l.12 Dane, 1209 × 35 RHug, 1266 Pat (p) *et passim* to 1330 FA

~ *Magna* 1254 Val, 1316 Misc, 1320 Cl *et freq*

Mekyll ~ 1492 RBL

Miche ~ 1518 RBL, *Myche* ~ 1558 AAS, *Much(e)* ~ 1576 LibCl, 1638 ChancP, *Mutche* ~ 1595, 1603 RBL

Great ~ 1610 Speed

'The farmstead or village where ash-trees grow', *v.* **æsc, bȳ**. Spellings with *Esse-* may be due to the influence of ON **eski** 'a place growing with ash-trees' or even OE **esce** 'a stand of ash-trees'. The affixes MLat *magna*, ON **mikill** and ME **muche**, all meaning 'great', distinguish the township from Ashby Parva *infra*, which lies some three miles to the south-west. Ashby is a common place-name, but it is uncertain whether in individual cases the name is an Old English creation modified by Scandinavian (say with *bȳ* for *tūn*) or whether it is wholly Scandinavian in origin, with OE *æsc* (ME *ash*) replacing ON *askr*.

ASHBY MAGNA STATION, on the former LNER (Sheffield to London) line, closed in the 1960s. BRICKYARD FM, *v.* **brike-yard**. BRICKYARD

LANE (now HOLT LANE, *v*. Holt Fm *infra*), *v*. **brike-yard**. BRIDGE FM.
BROXTOWE FM. CHEQUERS (P.H.), *Chequers* 1846, 1863, 1877 White,
1925 Kelly. CHURCH FM, *Church farm* 1925 Kelly, *v*. St Mary's Church
infra. THE COPPICE, *v*. **copis**. FLAT HOUSE FM (FLAT HO. 2½"), *Flat
House* 1835 O, 1846 White, *Flat Farm* 1862 ib, *v*. **flat**. GILMORTON
LODGE FM (GILMORTON LODGE 2½"). GILMORTON RD, Gilmorton lying
two miles to the south-east. GRANGE FM, *v*. **grange**. GWENS GORSE, *v*.
gorst. THE HALL FM, *the Hall farme* 1697 Terrier, *the Hall* 1606 ib,
1925 Kelly, *v*. **hall**, **ferme**. HOLT FM. HOLT LANE, *v*. **wald** and the
adjacent Holt Ho. in neighbouring Dunton Bassett. HUBBARDS FM, cf.
Wm. Hubbard 1846 White, *John Hubbard* and *Thomas Hubbard* 1877
ib, farmers and graziers; earlier are *Humfridus Hubbard* and *Mattheus
Hubbard* 1685 Deed. LOW SPINNEY, *v*. **spinney**. MAIN ST is *the towne
street* 1606 Terrier, *v*. **tūn**, **strēt**. MANOR FM, cf. *Manor House* 1877
White, 1925 Kelly, *v*. **maner**. OAK FM. OAK SPINNEY, *Oak Spinny* 1835
O, *v*. **āc**, **spinney**. THE RETREAT. ST MARY'S CHURCH, *Church (St Mary)*
1846, 1863, 1877 White, 1925 Kelly; it is earlier recorded as *ecclesie de
Magne Esseby* 1220 MHW. Note also *the Churchyard* 1601, 1606
Terrier et passim to 1745 ib, *v*. **churchyerd**. SPRING HILL FM (local), *v*.
spring[1]. STATION FM, *v*. Ashby Magna Station *supra*. THE VICARAGE,
1877 White, 1925 Kelly; earlier is recorded *the Vicarage House* 1606,
1700, 1724, 1745 Terrier, *the Vicaridge House* 1674, *The Vicaradge
House* 1697 ib, *v*. **vikerage**. WILLOUGHBY RD, Willoughby Waterleys
lying 2 miles to the west. WILLOW FM.

FIELD-NAMES

In (a), forms dated 1821 are *Terrier*; those dated 1825 are *Plan*; 1835 are
O. Forms throughout dated l.12 are Dane; p.1242 are AD; 1330 are Ipm;
1579 are CoPleas; 1601, 1625, 1674, 1679, 1697, 1700, 1724 and 1745
are *Terrier*; 1630 and 1685 are Deed; 1638 are ChancP; 1747 are
Nichols.

(a) Churchyard Croft 1821 (*v*. **churchyerd**, **croft**); Bottom Piece 1825 (*v*.
bottom, **pece**); Conduit Spinny 1835 (*v*. **cundite**, **spinney**); The Croft 1825 (*v*.
croft); Home Mdw 1825 (*the Home Meddow* 1674, *v*. **mēd** (**mēdwe** obl.sg.); most
prob. with **holmr** rather than **home**, *v. the holme, infra*); North ~ ~, South Little Fd;
Middle Cl 1825; Top Cl 1825; The Walks 1825 (*the Walk*(e) 1601, 1625, 1638; cf.
Brooksbyes Walke 1697, *Brooksbys Walk* 1745, *v*. **walk**; note *Master Broxesbye* 1601
of Ashby Magna, with the surn. of a family originally from Brooksby, 18 miles to the
north-east in East Goscote Hundred and note also *Brooksbyes farme* 1697 *infra*).

(b) *Aylthmesty* p.1242 (*v.* **stig**; prob. with a poor form of the OE masc. pers.n. *Æðelmǣr*); *Bates Cottage* 1694 (*v.* **cotage**; with the surn. *Bates*, cf. *Johannes Bates* 1685); *Blacwellam* l.12, *Blackwell leyes* 1638 (*v.* **leys**) (*v.* **blæc**, **wella**); *Bradewelle* p.1242 (*v.* **brād**, **wella**); *Mr Bradgate his heath* 1601, *Mr Broadgates heath* 1625 (*v.* **hǣð**), *Mr Bradgates lands* 1697 (*v.* **land**) (the *Bradgate* family prob. came originally from Bradgate, 12 miles to the north-east); *Cowakars* 1601, *cow agares* 1625 (*v.* **cū**, **æcer**); *Dayrie close* 1638 (*v.* **deierie**); *Erewerde Wongge* 1330 (*v.* **vangr**; with the OE masc. pers.n. *Hereweard*); *Eychuls* p.1242 (*v.* **ēcels**); *the Flatt* 1674 (*v.* **flat**); *the ford* 1601 (*v.* **ford**); *the holme* 1601, *the Home close* 1638 (*v.* **clos(e)**), *the holmes leese* 1601, *the home lease* 1625 (*v.* **leys**) (*v.* **holmr**); *the homestall* 1606 (*v.* **hāmstall**); *Inggesickefeld* 1638 (*v.* **sík**, **feld**; with the ON masc. pers.n. *Ingi*; one of the great open-fields of the township); *Judds Cottage* 1697 (*v.* **cotage**; with the surn. *Judd*, cf. *Thomas Judd* 1685); *Kilne close* 1638 (*v.* **cyln**); *the long leys* 1579 (*v.* **lang**[1], **leys**); *the Lower close* 1697; *the mid(d)le ground* 1674, 1697 (*v.* **middel**, **grund**); *Moreton Meere* 1579 (*v.* **(ge)mǣre**; Gilmorton parish adjoins to the south-east); *Neddrewong* p.1242 (*v.* **neoðera**, **vangr**); *Osberneswelle* p.1242 (*v.* **wella**; with the OE masc. pers.n. *Ōsbern* (from ON *Ásbjǫrn*)); *Rams close* 1638 (*v.* **ramm**); *Sallowe pitte* 1638 (*v.* **salh**, **pytt**); *Shardelowe* p.1242 (*v.* **sc(e)ard**, **hlāw**; cf. Shardlow, Db 501); *Shepehusflatte* p.1242 (*v.* **scēp-hūs**, **flat**; cf. *the sheephosse* in Beeby, Lei **3** 45); *Shilborne meddow* 1674, *Shilbing Medow* (sic) 1679, *the Shelbourne meadow* 1697 (*v.* **sc(e)alu**, **burna**, **mēd** (**mēdwe** obl.sg.)); *Swinsties* 1638 (*v.* **swīn**, **stig**); *le Thernefeld* 1579 (*v.* **þyrne**, **þynir**, **feld**; one of the great open-fields of the township); (*the*) *Upper close* 1638, 1674, 1697; *the wagonested* 1625 (*v.* **wagan**, **stede**; as a compound, this is unrecorded in OED); *Warhthou* p.1242 (*v.* **varði**, **haugr**; perh. a Scandinavianization of an earlier OE **weard-hōh, v.* **weard**, **hōh**); *Westbrookfeild* 1638 (*v.* **west**, **brōc**, **feld**; another of the great open-fields of the township); *willowbye meare or brok* 1601, *willoweby brok* 1606, *Willoweby Meare, Willowby mere* 1625, *Willowby meere* 1674, *Willowby brooke* 1697 (*v.* **(ge)mǣre**, **brōc**; the boundary with Willoughby Waterleys parish was defined by the stream).

In the parish's Glebe Terrier for 1697, the following farms are listed by tenant or owner:
Brooksbyes farme, Byards ~, *Clowes* ~, *Cookes* ~, *Coopers farme* (cf. *John Cooper* 1630), *Froanes farme* (cf. *Christopher Frone* 1630, *Thomas Froane* 1685), *Gambles farme* (cf. *Davenport Gamble* 1747), *Gilberts farme, Harris his farme, Heafords* ~, *Hunts* ~, *Iliffes farme* (cf. *Edmond Iliffe* 1685), *Mussons farme* (cf. *Hugh Musson* 1630), *Orams* ~, *Prats* ~, *Wards farme, v.* **ferme**. Of these local surnames, the following are of interest because of their Scand origins: *Gamble* (from the ON masc. pers.n. *Gamall*, ODan *Gamal*, an original by-name 'old'); *Iliffe* (from the ON masc. pers.n. *Eilífr*); *Oram* (from the ON masc. pers.n. *Ormr*, ODan *Orm*, an original by-name 'snake, serpent').

Ashby Parva

> *Essebi* 1086 DB, 1176 BM, *Essebia* c.1130 LeicSurv, *Esseby* 1212
> FF, 1209 × 35 RHug, 1243 Fees *et freq* to 1278, 1280 *Goodacre*
> *et passim* to 1301 *ib*, 1316 FA
> *Asseby* 1287, 1295 Cl
> *Assheby* 1251 Cur, 1274 Coram, 1285 Banco *et freq* to 1384
> *Goodacre*, 1397 Cl *et passim* to 1502 *MiscAccts*, 1506 Ipm, 1541
> MinAccts, *Asshebi* 1383 *Goodacre*
> *As(s)cheby* 1352 *Goodacre*
> *Asshby* 1518, 1528 *Comp*, *Ashby* 1515 *Deed*, 1535 VE, 1610 Speed
> *et freq*, *Ashbie* 1572 LEpis, 1576 LibCl, 1583 DKR

Affixes are variously added as:
> *Parua* ~ 1086 DB, *Parva* ~ c.1130 LeicSurv, 1212 FF *et passim* to
> 1278, c.1280 *Goodacre et freq* to 1384 *ib*, 1444 *Peake* 1502
> *MiscAccts*
> ~ *Parva* 1176 BM, 1251 Cur, c.1300 *Goodacre et passim* to 1510
> Visit *et freq*
> *Luytel* ~ 1347 Ipm, *Litle* ~ 1441 (e.16) *Will*, *Lytell* ~ 1515 *Deed*, 1583
> DKR

'The farmstead or village where ash-trees grow', *v.* **æsc, bȳ**. As for
Ashby Magna *supra*, note the possible influence of ON **eski** 'a place
growing with ash-trees' or OE **esce** 'a stand of ash-trees'. The township
was distinguished by the MLat affixes *parva* 'small' and ME **litel** 'little'
to avoid confusion with Ashby Magna *supra*.

ASHBY LODGE is *Boggy Brays* 1835 O, 1846, 1863 White, *Boggy Brae*
farm 1925 Kelly, *v.* **boggy, brēg**; to what extent *Brays* is early here is
uncertain, but likely is the late borrowing of a northern form. CANAAN
FM, a transferred biblical name for land remote from the village; cf.
Canaan Fm, Rempstone (*v.* Nt 255). DUNTON LANE, Dunton Bassett
lying 2 miles to the north-east. FROLESWORTH RD is *Frolesworth Way*

1847 *TA*, Frolesworth lying 2 miles to the north-west. HOME FM (2½"),
v. **home**. IVY HOUSE FM, *v.* **īfig**. LEIRE LANE, 1847 *TA*, Leire lying one
mile to the north-west. MAIN ST is *the streete* 1625 *Terrier*, *the Town-
Street* 1709 *ib*, *v.* **tūn**, **strēt**. MANOR FM, *Manor farm* 1925 Kelly, *v.*
maner. MERE BARN, cf. *Ulsthrope meere* 1625 *Terrier*, *Ulesthorpe* ~
1709 *ib*, *Ullesthorpe Meer* 1745 *ib*, *v.* **(ge)mǣre**; the barn lies at the
parish boundary with Ullesthorpe. PINK'S PARK, *Pinks Park* 1762, 1781
Terrier, 1847 *TA*; with the surn. *Pink* (from OE **pinca* 'a finch') and
referring to **park** as a small enclosure. THE RECTORY, 1877 White, 1925
Kelly, *v.* **rectory**; earlier is recorded *the Parsonage House* 1625, 1709,
1762, 1781 *Terrier*, *v.* **personage**. ST PETER'S CHURCH, *Church (St
Peter)* 1846, 1863, 1877 White, 1925 Kelly; it is earlier recorded as
ecclesie Parve Esseby 1220 MHW. Note also *the Church Yard* 1709,
1781 *Terrier*, *v.* **churchyerd**. SHOULDER OF MUTTON (P.H.) (lost),
Shoulder of Mutton 1846, 1863, 1877 White, 1925 Kelly. *Benjamin
Steven*, mine host in 1846 White, was also a butcher and this may have
been instrumental in the naming of the tavern. SLIP INN FM, outlying on
Lutterworth Rd and presumably a former wayside hostelry.
ULLESTHORPE RD, Ullesthorpe lying one mile to the south-west.

FIELD-NAMES

In (a), forms presented without dates are 1847 *TA*; those dated 1762 and
1781 are *Terrier*; 1831 are *Goodacre*. Forms throughout dated c.1220,
c.1230, Hy 3, 1301, 1589, 1618, 1639, 1648, 1669, 1670, 1671, 1673,
1678, 1680, 1686, 1695, 1697 and 1716 are *Goodacre*; those dated 1601,
1625, 1638, 1674, 1709 and 1745 are *Terrier*.

(a) Two Acre, Four Acre 1831, 1847, Fore Acre Mdw (sic) 1831, Five Acre
1847, ~ ~ Cl, ~ ~ Mdw 1831, Six Acre 1831, 1847, ~ ~ Cl 1831, Seven Acres Cl
1831, Eight Acre, Eight Acres Mdw, Nine Acre, ~ ~ Mdw 1847, Nine Acres Cl 1831,
Ten Acre 1847, ~ ~ Mdw 1831 (*v.* **æcer**); Ant Hills (*v.* **ǣmett-hyll**); Ashall, ~ Mdw
(*Ashe hill*, *Ashhill* 1601, *Ashill* 1625, 1638, 1639, cf. *Ashehill Crosse* 1601 (*v.* **cros**),
Ashhill Way 1625 (*v.* **weg**), *v.* **æsc**, **hyll**); Far ~, Great Ashwell 1831 (*Ashwell* 1670,
1673; this may belong with the previous f.n., otherwise *v.* **æsc**, **wella**); Ayres Mdw
(with the surn. *Ayres*, cf. *Mary Ayres* 1836 Census of Ashby Parva); Barn Cl, ~ Mdw
(*v.* **bern**); Beales Cl (with the surn. *Beale*, cf. *Thomas Beale* 1625, *Eliza Beale* 1825
Census and *Sarah Beale* 1828 ib of Ashby Parva); Blacksitch 1831 (1697, *blacke
sytche* 1601, *Blakesick* 1625, *v.* **blæc**, **sīc**; the 1625 form has **sík**); Bog Mdw (*v.* **bog**);
Bogmore (1716, *v.* **bog**, **mōr**¹); Boss Mdw (prob. with the Leics. surn. *Bosse* (*v.*
Reaney *s.n.*), since the survival of OE *bōs* 'a cowstall' is unlikely); Bottom Mdw,
Bottom Orchard (*v.* **orceard**), Bottom piece (*v.* **pece**) (*v.* **bottom**); Bounds Cl, ~

Mdw (with the surn. *Bounds*); Bowks 1831 (*v.* **balca**); Bowbrook 1847, Bow Brook
Hill 1831 (*Bubbrooke* 1601, 1625, *Bowbrooke* 1670, *v.* **boga, brōc**); Broadmore
1847, Far ~, Second Broadmore 1831 (*Broodmoore* 1601, cf. *Broodmore Feilde*
1601, *Broadmore Feild*(*e*) 1625, 1638, *Broademoore feild* 1625 (*v.* **feld**; one of the
great open-fields of the township), *Broadmore Well* 1625 (*v.* **wella**), *v.* **brād, mōr**[1]);
Great ~, Little Buckleys 1847, Top Buckleys, Buckleys Barn Cl, Buckleys Mdw
1831 (with the surn. *Buckley*); Burrows Cl (with the surn. *Burrows*); Bush Cl, ~ Mdw
(*v.* **busc**); Buswells Cl (with the surn. *Buswell*); Butts Hill 1831, ~ Mdw 1847 (*Buttes*
1601, *v.* **butte** and *Bookes leyes* in f.ns. (b)); Church Cl (*v.* St Peter's Church *supra*);
Church Hadland (*the Church Hadland* 1709, *v.* **hēafod-land**); Clarkes Cl, Clarks
Orchard (*v.* **orceard**) (with the surn. *Clark*(*e*)); Constables Cl (*v.* **conestable**);
Cordwell Hole 1831, Caudle Hole 1847 (*Cawdwell Hole* 1697, *v.* **cald, wella**; with
hol[1] or **halh**, *v. Springale hill* in f.ns. (b)); Coventry Orchard 1831, 1847 (*v.* **orceard**;
presum. the property of one of the almshouses called Bablake Hospital and Ford's
Hospital in Coventry, cf. *Coventry land* in Bittesswell f.ns. (b)); Cow Cl 1831 (*v.* **cū**);
Crabtree Cl (*v.* **crabtre**); Crow Trees (*v.* **crāwe, trēow**); Bottom ~ ~, Dairy Cl (*v.*
deierie); Dastals, ~ Mdw 1831, Dystalls, Great Dyestalls 1847 (*Dytche doles* 1601,
Ditchdoles 1625, *Diestall Close*, ~ *Meadow* 1695, *v.* **dīc, dāl**); Debsdale 1847, First
~ ~, Second Depdale Mdw 1831 (*Debsdale* 1671, cf. *Depdale Hill* 1601, *Depdill hill*
1625 (*v.* **hyll**), *v.* **dēop, dalr**); Deepslade, Deep Slade Mdw 1831 (*Depslade* 1601,
1625, 1638, *Debslade* 1670, *v.* **dēop, slæd**); Great ~, Little Duddle, Duddle Mdw
(*Dudwell* 1625, cf. *Dudwell Goore* 1601, ~ *gore* 1625 (*v.* **gāra**), *v.* **wella**; with the
OE masc. pers.n. *Dudda*); Far Cl 1831, 1847, Far Mdw 1847 (*v.* **feor**); Filley Cl
1831, Fillow ~ 1831, Filley Mdw 1847 (*Philomedowe* 1601, *Fillaw* ~ 1625, *Fillow
Meadow* 1745 (*v.* **mēd** (**mēdwe** obl.sg.)), *Phillowmedowe Feilde* 1601, *Fillaw
meadow feilde* 1625, *Fillow Meadow Field* 1709 (*v.* **feld**; one of the great open-fields
of the township), *v.* **fille, hlāw**); Fishers piece (*v.* **pece**; with the surn. *Fisher*); Freers
Cl (with the surn. *Freer*); Front Orchard (*v.* **front, orceard**); Frowlesworth Lanes
End 1762, 1781 (*Frolesworth Lane End* 1745, *v.* **lane-ende** and Frolesworth Rd
supra); Grange Mdw (*v.* **grange**); Gravel Pit(s) 1831, 1847, Gravel Pitt Mdw 1831
(*Gravill pitts* 1625, cf. *Gravill pitt furlong* 1638 (*v.* **furlang**), *v.* **gravel, pytt**); the
Great Cl 1762, 1781 (*Great Close* 1697), Great Mdw (*v.* **grēat**); Green Kettle 1831,
1847 (*Greene Kettle* 1601, 1625, ~ ~ *furlong*(*e*) 1601, 1625, 1638 (*v.* **furlang**), *Green
Kettle Close* 1670, *v.* **grēne**[1], **cetel**); Lower ~ ~, Upper Green Lane (*v.* **grēne**[1]);
Bottom ~ ~, Top Hacketts Cl (with the surn. *Hackett*, from an AN diminutive of the
ON masc. pers.n. *Haki* (ODan *Hake*), prob. an original by-name 'chin'); Hall Cl
1831, 1847 (*the Hall Close* 1709, *v.* **hall**); Great ~, Little Harestile(s) 1831, 1847
(earlier forms are needed, but poss. is either 'boundary slope', *v.* **hār**[2], **stigel**, or 'hare
slope', *v.* **hara**); Harrolds Barn Cl, ~ Bottom Cl 1831 (with the surn. *Harrold*, from
the ON masc. pers.n. *Haraldr* (ODan *Harald*)); Hazlewood (*v.* **hæsel, wudu**);
Highleys 1831, High Leys 1847 (*Heighe Lees* 1601, *hie leyes* 1625, *v.* **hēah**[1], **leys**);
Home Cl 1831 (1673; prob. with **holmr**); Home piece (*v.* **home, pece**); Homestead
1831 (*v.* **hām-stede**); Holt Cl (*Oult Close* 1669), Holts Mdw (*the owlte* 1601, *the
Wolt* 1625, cf. *the owlte feilde* 1601, *the Wolte feild* 1625, *the Oult Field* 1709 (*v.*
feld; one of the great open-fields of the township), *Wolt*(*e*) *Furlonge* 1601, 1625 (*v.*
furlang), *v.* **wald**); House Cl; Hut Cl, ~ Mdw (*v.* **hut**); Kings Cl (with the surn.
King); Lambs Cl (*v.* **lamb**); Lammas Cl (1618, *Lamas Close*, 1678, *v.* **lammas**);
Langham, ~ Mdw (*Langham* 1601, 1625, 1697, *v.* **lang**[1], **hamm**); Leir Hill 1831, Leir

Lane Cl, ~~ Fd 1847 (Leire lies one mile to the north-east); Lincroft Gap 1762, 1781 (*Lincrofte* 1625, *Lingcroft gap* 1674, *Lincroft Gap* 1709, *v.* **līn, croft, gap**); Little Cl 1831, 1847, Lower Little Cl 1831, Bottom ~ ~, Top Little Cl 1847; Far ~ ~, Little More 1831, Great ~, Little Littlemore 1847, Little More Mdw 1831, Littlemore Mdw 1847 (*Littlemore* 1601, *Littlemoor* 1697, cf. *Little More Bank* 1670 (*v.* **banke),** *Littlemoore heade* 1625 (*v.* **hēafod),** *v.* **lȳtel, mōr**[1]); Little Orchard 1831 (*v.* **orceard**); Long Roods, ~ ~ Mdw (*Longe roodes* 1601, 1625, *v.* **lang**[1]**, rōd**[3]); Lower Orchard; Meach Cl (with the surn. *Meach, Meech*); Middle Cl; Mill Croft, ~ ~ Mdw (*Mylne crofte* 1601, *Milcroft* 1625, *Millcroft* 1716, *v.* **myln, croft**); Second ~ ~, Mill Hill 1831 (*v.* **myln**; a windmill site); Near Mdw; New piece (*v.* **pece**); Oak Cl (*v.* **āc**); Oat Fd (*v.* **āte**); Old Barn Cl (*v.* **bern**); Overplus 1831, 1847 (*v.* **plysc**. prob. with **ofer**[3]); Palmers Cl, ~ Mdw 1831 (with the surn. *Palmer*); Path Cl (*v.* **pæð**); Pen Cl (*v.* **penn**); Pikes Cl 1831, 1847, ~ Mdw 1847 (with the surn. *Pike*); Plough Cl (*v.* **plōg**); Porters Cl (with the surn. *Porter*, cf. *Thomas Porter* 1776 MI); Railway 1847 (land near to the old Midland Counties Railway line, the Leicester to Rugby section of which opened in 1840); Bottom ~, Top Redham (*v.* **hrēod, hamm**); Rights Cl (sic) 1831, Wrights Cl, ~ Mdw 1847 (with the surn. *Wright*); Rye Cl (*Gaules or Rye Close* 1697, *v.* **ryge** and *gaales* in f.ns. (b)); Bottom Sallands, Second ~ ~, Top Sallands Cl (*Salents* 1601, *Sallands* 1625, *Sallars, Nether Sallows* 1625; the base of these forms is **salh** 'a willow, a sallow', but it is uncertain whether a second el. **land** pertains in the 1601 and the first of the 1625 forms); Sandpit Cl (*v.* **sand-pytt**); Long ~ ~, Sheep Cl (*v.* **scēp**); Showell (1601, cf. *Showell ste*[…] 1601, *Shouel steale* 1625 (*v.* **stell**), *v.* **wella**; these late forms poss. disguise a specific **seofon**, hence 'seven springs', a common name, cf. Showell, Ox 249, 291 and *v.* K. Briggs, 'Seven wells', JEPNS 39 (2007), 7–44; otherwise with **sc(e)eald** or **sc(e)ealu**); Slip in Fd, ~ ~ Mdw (*v.* Slip Inn Fm *supra*); Spinney Cl (*v.* **spinney**); Square Mdw 1831 (*v.* **squar(e)**); Starlands 1831, Starnels (sic) 1847 (*Starlandes* 1601, *Starlands* 1625, 1638, 1671, *Starelands* 1670, *v.* **storr**[2]**, land**); Stoxwell 1831, Stockswell 1847 (*Stokkes Hill* 1601, *Stockshill* 1625, *Stocksall* 1670 (*v.* **stocc, hyll**); Stone Pit (*v.* **stān-pytt**); Street Cl, Street Seed Cl (*v.* **sǣd**) (*v.* **strēt**); Strip (*v.* **strīp**); Thrush Slade Cl, ~ ~ Mdw 1831, Thrashlaid, ~ Mdw (sic) 1847 (*Thurse slade* 1601 (×2), *Thrush slade* 1625, *v.* **þyrs, slǣd**); Three Corner Cl (*v.* **three-corner**); Tibbles Great Cl, Tibbles Mdw (with the surn. *Tibble*, *v.* Reaney *s.n.*); Top Cl; Top Mdw; Top Orchard (*v.* **orceard**); Town Cl 1831 (*v.* **tūn**); Turnip Cl, ~ Fd (*v.* **turnepe**); Varnhams Cl, ~ Mdw (with the surn. *Varnham*, a late form of the common surn. *Farnham*); Wheat Cl, ~ Fd (*v.* **hwǣte**).

(b) *Baggemulnedam* Hy 3 (*v.* **myln, damme**; prob. with the common ME surn. *Bagge*, *v.* Reaney *s.n.* and Bag Mdw in adjoining Leire f.ns. (a) *infra*); *Banlondis* 1301 (*v.* **bēan, land**); *Bitswell meere* 1625, *Bitteswell Meer* 1709, 1745 (*v.* **(ge)mǣre**; the parish boundary of Bitteswell which adjoins to the south); *Nether Blacke landes* 1601, *Nether Blakelands* 1625 (*v.* **neoðera**), *Over blacklandes* 1601 (*v.* **uferra**), *Blakelands Close* 1680, 1697 (*v.* **blæc, land**); *Bowthe* 1601 (*v.* **būð**); *Broodcrofte* 1601, *Broadcrofte, Broade Croft* 1625, *Broadcraft* 1638 (*v.* **brād, croft**); *the brooke* 1625 (*v.* **brōc**); *Richard Burroughes's Homestall* 1709 (*v.* **hām-stall**); *Byte* 1601, *Bite* 1625 (*v.* **bit**); *Church-Land Plot* 1709 (*v.* **plot**), *Church leyes* 1625 (*v.* **leys**) (*v.* St Peter's Church *supra*); *Coates Close* 1648, *Coates hedge* 1625 (*v.* **hecg**) (with the surn. *Coates*); *Cole Corner* 1589 (*v.* **corner**; poss. with **col**[1], with reference to a charcoal-making site); *the Comon* 1601, *the Common* 1625 (*v.* **commun**); *the Common Balke* 1601, ~ ~ *baulke* 1625 (*v.* **commun, balca**);

Crothorne 1625, *Crow Thorne* 1697 (*v.* **crāwe, þorn**); *Dawthames* 1601, *Dowtham* 1670, 1671 (the OE generic is either **hamm** or **hām** in its sense 'homestead'. The original specific was prob. OE **dēad**, but has been replaced either by ON **dauðr** 'dead, disused' or by ON **dauði** 'death'. OE *dēad* in its sense 'infertile' was often used of poor moorland (*v.* Lei 4 319 *s.v.* **dēad**) and no doubt could also have been applied to a boggy *hamm*. If the generic is *hām*, perh. the site was thought to be that of a ruined and haunted dwelling (or dwellings, given the earlier plural form)); *Ducketts Close* 1648 (with the surn. *Duckett*, cf. *Francis Duckett* 1741 MI); *Flaxen Knowles* 1601, 1625 (*v.* **flaxen, cnoll**); *Fullpittes* 1601, *Fulpits* 1625, *Full pitt Furlonge* 1601, *Fulpit furlonge* 1625 (*v.* **furlang**) (*v.* **fūl, pytt**); *the furres of Thomas Beale* 1625 (*v.* **fyrs**); *gaales* 1601, *Galls* 1625, *Gaules* 1697, *Nether* ~, *Upper Galls* 1625 (*v.* **galla** and Rye Cl *supra*); *the glebe hadlande* 1625 (*v.* **glebe, hēafod-land**); *Grafton Hill* 1601, 1625, 1697 (with the surn. *Grafton*, cf. *Willelmus de Graftona* 1130 P of Leics.); *the hadland of William Pabody* 1625 (*v.* **hēafod-land**); *Hardwyke* 1601, *Hardwicke* 1625 (*v.* **heorde-wīc**); *Hempbrookes* 1625 (*v.* **hænep, brōc**); *Homes* 1601, 1625, ~ *leyes* 1625 (*v.* **leys**) (*v.* **holmr**); *Horsein Hylles* 1601 (*v.* **hors, eng, hyll**); *the Kings Hie way* 1625 (*v.* **hēah-weg**; with reference to James I); *Lairesty* 1625 (*v.* **stīg**; the footpath to Leire which lies one mile to the north-west); *Langefurlong* c.1230, Hy 3, *Langfurlonges* 1601, *Langfurlong* 1625 (*v.* **lang**[1], **furlang**); *Leare meare* 1601, ~ *meere* 1625 (*v.* **(ge)mǣre**; the boundary with Leire parish which adjoins to the north); *Learemoore* 1625 (*v.* **mōr**[1]; moorland towards the Leire boundary); *the Leyes of Thomas Beale, the Leyes of John Pabody, the Leyes of Phillip Wale* 1625 (*v.* **leys**); *Limbers House* 1673 (with the surn. *Limber*, cf. *John Limber* 1850 Census of adjacent Leire); (*in*) *Longe* 1625 (*v.* **lang**[2]); *Lysslade* 1601, *Lisslade* 1625 (*v.* **lisc, slæd**); *Merridews Close* 1697 (with the surn. *Merridew*); *Mill leyes* 1625 (*v.* **myln, leys**); *Moore furlonge* 1601, 1625 (*v.* **mōr**[1], **furlang**); *Pease close* 1697 (*v.* **pise**); *Peshull'* Hy 3, *Pessell Forlonge* 1601 (*v.* **furlang**), *Nether* ~, *Over Pessell* 1601 (*v.* **neoðera, uferra**), *Nether* ~, *Upper Pessill* 1625, 1638 (*v.* **pise, hyll**); *Queenes high way called common street* 1589, *the Queenes heigh way* 1601 (*v.* **hēah-weg, commun, strēt**; with reference to Elizabeth I); *Rayneswombe* 1601, *Raynesonge* 1625 (*v.* **vangr**; prob. with the surn. *Raynes* (*v.* Reaney *s.n.*), although a shortening of the ON masc. pers.n. *Ragnhildr* may also be thought of); *Redding Close* 1625 (*v.* **clos(e)**), *Reddinge End* 1625 (*v.* **ende**) (*v.* **hrēod, eng**); *Reddwombe* 1601 (*v.* **hrēod, vangr**); *Sachdole* Hy 3 (*v.* **sacu, dāl**); *Shorte Crofte* 1601, *Short Croft* 1625 (*v.* **sc(e)ort, croft**); *Shorte Roodes* 1601, *short roodes* 1625 (*v.* **sc(e)ort, rōd**[3]); *Six Leys Close* 1680 (*v.* **six, leys**; an enclosure comprising six grassed-over selions of a former great open-field); *Smale thorne* 1601, *Small thorne* 1625 (*v.* **smæl, þorn**); *Smeythe Meddowe* 1601, *Smith meadow* 1625, *Smiths Meadow* 1669 (*v.* **smēðe**[1], **mēd** (*mēdwe* obl.sg.)); *Springale hill* 1601, *Springhole Hill* 1625 (*v.* **spring**[1], **halh, hyll**); *Nether* ~ ~, *Over Throwlesworthe waye* 1601, *Nether* ~ ~, *Over Froulesworth way* 1625 (*v.* **neoðera, uferra, weg** and Frolesworth Rd *supra*); *Throwlesworthe Meare* 1601, *Frolesworth Meer* 1745 (*v.* **(ge)mǣre**; the boundary with Frolesworth parish which adjoins to the north-west); *Thwertdole* Hy 3 (*v.* **þverr** (**þvert** neut.), **dāl**); *the tith peece* 1625 (*v.* **tēoða, pece**); *tounge* 1601, *tonge* 1625 (*v.* **tunge**); *the Townes ende* 1601 (*v.* **tūn, ende**); *Wakeley* 1625 (this is most prob. Waklin listed in adjoining Leire f.ns. (a) *infra*, *v.* **wacu, hlāw**); *Watergall Closes* 1686 (*v.* **wæter, galla**); *Water furrowes* 1601, *Waterthurrows* 1625 (*v.* **wæter, furh**; prob. 'furrows where water tends to lie'; Field 50 argues that these were deeper furrows so ploughed in order to carry off surface water, but such furrows appear to be called alternatively *Wet furrowes* in Coston (Lei **2** 155–6) and *Watriforowis* in Eaton (Lei **2** 121)); *Weste Well* 1601, *Westwell Close* 1680 (*v.* **west, wella**); *Woefull Lees* 1601, *Woolfale Leyes* 1695 (*v.* **waful, leys**; presum. a disparaging name for pastures of poor quality); *Wollandes gutter* 1601, *Woollands gutter* 1625 (*v.* **wald, land, goter**).

Aylestone

Aylestone is now part of the Borough of Leicester.

AYLESTONE

> *Ailestone* 1086 DB (×3), a.1238, 1283 Hastings, *Aileston* 1086 DB,
> e.13 *Rut*, e.hy 3 Hastings *et passim* to Hy 3, 1334 *Rut*, *Ailestona*
> 1209 × 19 RHug, *Ailiston* 1199 GildR
>
> *Ayleston* e.13 *Rut*, 1237 RGros *et passim* to c.1250 *RTemple*, 1272
> *Rut et freq* to 1480 *ib et passim* to 1518 Visit, *Aylestone* 1272,
> 1313, 1356 *Rut et passim* to 1630 LML *et freq*, *Aylleston* 1283
> Banco, 1315 GildR (p) *et passim* to 1361, 1363 *Rut et freq* to 1381
> *ib et passim* to 1494 *Comp*, 1501, 1508 *Rut*
>
> *Ailston* 1285 × 93 Hastings, 1305 *AllS*, 1611 LML, *Aylston* 1337 *Rut*,
> 1451, 1452 *LCDeeds*, 1617 *Rut*, 1630 LML
>
> *Egilston* 1307 Pap
>
> *Eyleston* 1234 Cl, 1253 × 58 RHug *et passim* to 1379 Pat (p), 1447
> *Rut*, *Eyliston* 1209 × 35 RHug, *Eylistona* c.1250 *Rut*
>
> *Eylston* 1420 *Wyg*, 1485 *Rut et passim* to 1522 *ib*, 1558 *Wyg*
>
> *Elston* 1549 Pat, 1571 SR *et passim* to 1617, 1641 LML, *Elson* 1725
> *ib*

Most probably 'the farmstead or village of a man called Ægel', *v.* **tūn**.
The OE masc. pers.n. *Ægel* is not recorded independently, but appears
also in such p.ns. as Ailsworth (Nth 228), Aylesbury (Bk 145) and
Aylworth (Gl 1 199). The Scand masc. pers.n. *Egill* is formally possible
but less likely as the specific since there is no certain evidence of its use
in England. (However, note what may be a unique archaic form surviving
in the Papal Registers of 1307.) In either case, medial *g* would have been
vocalized after a front vowel to *i* to form a diphthong with the preceding
vowel.

AYLESTONE HALL, 1877 White; earlier are *Hallehouse* 1424 *Rut* (*v.* **hūs**)
and *The Hall* 1708, 1745 *Terrier*, *v.* **hall**. AYLESTONE MILL LOCK (2½"),
Aileston mill 1795 Nichols, *v.* **myln**, **lock**; an early mill is recorded as

molendinum de Ayleston 1367 *Rut* (with MLat *molendinum* 'a mill'). AYLESTONE PARK, 1877 White, *v.* **park**. BLACK HORSE (P.H.), *Black Horse* 1846, 1877 White. CANAL ST, named from the Union Canal. CHURCH RD, *v.* St Andrew's Church *infra*. COTTAGERS CLOSE, *v.* **cotager** and *Cottiers Close* in f.ns. (b) *infra*. CRABTREE CORNER, *v.* **crabtre**, **corner**. DIAMOND JUBILEE COVERT, commemorating the Diamond Jubilee of the reign of Queen Victoria in 1897, *v.* **cover(t)**. DISRAELI ST, named from Benjamin Disraeli, Prime Minister in 1868 and 1874–80. GOLDHILL, 1756 *EnclA*, *v.* **hyll**; either with **gold** (poss. used of 'gold treasure', perh. that discovered in an early burial since the site is at the old parish boundary (but also used in the sense 'golden-hued')), or with **golde** 'a golden flower', such as the marigold. HALL LANE, *v.* Aylestone Hall *supra*. HAWKES HILL, prob. with the surn. *Hawkes*, cf. *Diana Hawkes* 1851 Census of adjoining Wigston Magna. HOLYWELL RD, *v.* Holowell Fd in f.ns. (a) *infra*. THE HOLT, *v.* **holt**. KING'S LOCK, on Union Canal; with the surn. *King*, *v.* **lock**. KNIGHTON LANE, early Knighton lying 2 miles to the north-east. LUTTERWORTH RD, Lutterworth lying 10 miles to the south. MANOR HO., 1846, 1863 White, *v.* **maner**. MARSDEN LANE, with the surn. *Marsden*. MARQUIS OF GRANBY (P.H.) (lost), *Marquis of Granby* 1846 White. NARROW LANE. OLD CHURCH ST, *v.* St Andrew's Church *infra*. PEN CLOSE, *v.* **penn**. THE RECTORY, 1877 White, *The Rectory House* 1821 *Terrier*, *v.* **rectory**; earlier is recorded *The Parsonage* 1601, 1674 *ib*, *the parsonage house* 1605 *ib*, *v.* **personage**. SAFFRON HILL, 1638, 1708, 1745 *Terrier*, SAFFRON LANE, *v.* Saffron Brook, Lei **1** 226. ST ANDREW'S CHURCH, *Church (St Andrew's)* 1846, 1863, 1877 White, 1925 Kelly; it is earlier recorded as *ecclesiam de Ailestona* a.1219 RHug, *ecclesie de Eyliston* 1220 MHW, *ecclesiam ~ ~, ecclesie de Ayleston* 1237 RGros, 1293, 1307 *Pat et passim* to 1406, 1458 *ib*, *la eglise de Aileston* 1328 BM (with OFr *eglise* 'a church'). Note also *the Churchyard* 1605, 1674, 1708, 1745, 1821 *Terrier*, *v.* **churchyerd**. SANVEY LANE provides no early forms, but poss. as for Sanvey Gate (Lei **1** 61), *v.* **sand**, **weg**. SHARPLAND, *Sharplandes* 1605 *Terrier*, *Sharpe Lands* 1638, 1708, 1745 *ib*, *Sharplands* 1674 *ib*, *v.* **sc(e)arp**, **land**. STOCKLAND RD, *v.* *Stock Lands* in f.ns. (b) *infra*. TWO ACRE SPINNEY, *v.* **tū**, **æcer**, **spinney**. UNION (P.H.), *Union* 1846, 1877 White; beside Union Canal. WHEAT SHEAF (P.H.) (lost), *Wheat Sheaf* 1846 White. WIGSTON LANE is *Wigston Way* 1745 *Terrier*; early Wigston Magna lying 2½ miles to the south-east.

Street-names in areas of recent urban development for which no early forms have been found:

ALLENWOOD RD. ALTON RD. ARNESBY CRESC. ASPLIN RD. AWFORD RD.
AYLESTONE DRIVE. BABINGDON ROW. BANKS RD. BARFOOT RD.
BATTEN ST. BELTON CL. BELVOIR DRIVE. BENTINGHOUSE RD.
BERKSHIRE RD. BLOOMFIELD RD. BOULDER DRIVE. BOUNDARY RD.
BRETBY RD. BRETTELL RD. BRIDEVALE RD. BROOKFIELD RISE.
BROUGHTON RD. BURGESS RD. BURNASTON RD. BURNSIDE RD.
CAMFIELD RISE. CAVENDISH RD. CHESHIRE GARDENS. CHESHIRE RD.
CLIFTON RD. CONAGLEN RD. COPINGER RD. CRANFIELD RD. THE
CROSSWAY. CYPRUS RD. DARTFORD RD. DUNCAN RD. EASTWOOD RD.
ELSTON FIELDS. ERITH RD. FAIRHURST RD. FERRERS ST. FRANKLYN RD.
GLENBOURNE RD. GLENHILL BOULEVARD. GRACE RD. GRANBY RD.
GREENHITHE RD. GREENSIDE PLACE. HALLATON ST. HAMPSHIRE RD.
HANDLEY ST. HEATHCOTE RD. HEREFORD RD. HIGHGATE. HOWDEN RD.
HUGHENDEN DRIVE. KEMPSON RD. KEPSTON CL. KNIGHTON FIELDS RD.
LANSDOWNE RD. LEESON ST. LINWOOD LANE. LITTLEGARTH.
LITTLEJOHN RD. LORRAINE RD. LOTHAIR RD. LYDALL RD. MARKLAND.
MEADOW GARDENS. MIDDLESEX RD. MIDDLETON ST. MONSELL DRIVE.
MONTROSE RD. MORBAN RD. PAGET ST. PAIGLE RD. PARK HILL DRIVE.
PASLEY RD. PAVIAN RD. PAWLEY GARDENS. PERCY RD. PLANTATION
AVE. REPPINGTON ROW. RICHMOND RD. RYE CL. ST ANDREWS RD. ST
ANNES DRIVE. SCHOOLGATE. SEAFORD RD. SHAKESPEARE ST. SHERIDAN
ST. SHROPSHIRE RD. SIMMINS CRESC. SPENDLOW GARDENS. SPONNE
RISE. SPRING CL. STANTON ROW. STONESBY AVE. STURDEE CL.
STURDEE RD. TAMERTON RD. THE FAIRWAY. THE NEWRY. THE SLADE
GREEN. TOVEY CRESC. TRENANT RD. UPLANDS RD. VAUGHAN RD.
VERNON RD. WHITTENEY DRIVE. WHITTIER RD. WHITWELL ROW.
WINDLEY RD. WORCESTER RD.

FIELD-NAMES

In (a), forms presented without dates are 1768 *EnclA*; those dated 1806
are Map; 1821 are *Terrier*; 1835 are O; 1877 are White. Forms
throughout dated c.1220 × 37, c.1250, l.Hy 3, 1285 × 93 and Edw 1 are
Hastings; those dated c.1312, 1313, 1332, 1352, 1365, 1371, 1372, 1394,
1424, 1426, 1469, 1470, 1494, 1617, 1626, 1628, 1632, 1633 and 1637
are *Rut*; 1590 are *Win*; 1601, 1605, 1638, 1674, 1708 and 1745 are
Terrier; 1688 are LML.

(a) Aylestone Gorse 1806 (*v.* **gorst**); Aylestone Spinny 1835 (*v.* **spinney**);
Aylestone Wharf 1877 (*v.* **wharf**); Benting Holme Cl (*Bentingholme* 1688, 1708,
Benting home furlong 1605, 1674 (*v.* **furlang**), *v.* **beonet, -ing**^{2}, **holmr**); the Hay

Croft 1821 (*v.* **hēg, croft**); Holowell Fd (*Halywell feild* 1605, *Hollowel Field or the Middle Field* 1674 (*v.* **feld** and Middle Fd *infra*; one of the great open-fields of the township), *Haliwell furlong* 1605, *Hollowel Furlong* 1674 (*v.* **furlang**), *Neather ~*, *Hollywell* 1638, *Neither ~*, *Hollywell* 1708, *Nether ~*, *Hollywell* 1745 (*v.* **neoðera**)), Hollywell farm 1877 (*v.* **ferme**) (*v.* **hālig, wella**); Middle Fd (*the midle feeld* 1601, (*the*) *Middle Feild* 1638, 1708, 1745, *Hollowel Field or the Middle Field* 1674 (*v.* **middel, feld** and Holowell Fd *supra*; one of the great open-fields); Mill Fd (*the Milne feild* 1605, (*the*) *Mill Feild* 1638, 1708, 1745, *Milne field or the North field* 1674, *v.* **myln, feld**; one of the great open-fields, named from a windmill); Mill Holme (*Mulneholme* 1371, *Nethirmylnholm* 1469 (*v.* **neoðera**), *le ouermylneholme* 1424, *Ouermilneholme* 1469 (*v.* **uferra**), *v.* **myln, holmr**; at the site of a watermill); Nether Mdw (1745, *Neither meadow* 1605, *Neather meadow* 1638, 1708, *the Nether great Meadow* 1674, *v.* **neoðera, mēd** (**mēdwe** obl.sg.)); Parsons Piece 1821 (*v.* **persone, pece**); the Pasture (*v.* **pasture**); Saffron Farm 1877 (*v.* **ferme**; named from Saffron Brook, a pre-English stream-name *Severne, v.* Saffron Lane *supra*); South Fd (1674, *Southfeild* 1605, *v.* **sūð, feld**; one of the great open-fields of the township, also called *Arnest feld* and *Little Feild* (both listed in f.ns. (b) *infra*)); the Wall Cl (*v.* **wall**).

(b) *Akeryerd* c.1312, *Acreyard* 1469 (*v.* **æcer, geard**); *Applebystub furlong* 1605 (*v.* **stubb**), *Applebee-stump Furlong* 1674 (*v.* **furlang**), *Appleby Stumpe* 1638, 1708, 1745 (*v.* **stump**) (originally with **æppel-trēow**); *Archers crofte* 1601 (*v.* **croft**; with the surn. *Archer*); *Arnest brooke* 1601 (*v.* **brōc**), *Arnest feld*, *Arnest feeld way* 1601 (*v.* **feld**; one of the great open-fields, later called *Little Field* (*v. infra*) and South Fd (*v.* f.ns. (a)) (*v.* **earn, nest**; named from the nest of a fish-eagle or sea-eagle, *v.* M. Gelling, 'Anglo-Saxon Eagles', *Leeds Studies in English* XVIII (1987), 177–81); *Blaby Way* 1605, *Long ~ ~*, *Short Blaby Way* 1605, 1638, 1674, 1708, 1745 (*v.* **weg**; land beside the road to Blaby which lies 2 miles to the south); *Black Hill* 1638, 1708, 1745 (*v.* **blæc**; may describe the former aspect, but in eModE, *black* also had the sense 'fertile' in contrast to *white* 'infertile'); *Robert Bonner's Close* 1745; *Bowling layes* 1674, *Neather ~ ~*, *Over Bowling Leyes* 1638, *Neither ~ ~*, *Over Bowling Leys* 1708, *Nether ~ ~*, *Over Bowling Leys* 1745 (*v.* **neoðera, uferra**) (*v.* **bowling, leys**); *Bradefordehurst* 1285 × 93 (*v.* **brād, ford, hyrst**); *branston hill* 1601, *Branston ~* 1708, *Braunston Meadow* 1745 (land towards Braunstone which lies 1½ miles to the north-west); *Breake acre* 1605, *Break Acre* 1674 (*v.* **bracu, æcer**); *Brokeswode* 1365 (*v.* **brōc, wudu**); *the Brook(e)* 1708, 1745, *Brook(e)furlong* 1605, 1638, 1708, 1745 (*v.* **furlang**) (*v.* **brōc**); *John Burneys Hadland* 1708 (*v.* **hēafod-land**); *Byholme* 1469, 1494, 1638, 1708, 1745, *Byhome* 1605, 1674 (*v.* **byge**[1], **holmr**); *Canunesholm* c.1250 (*v.* **canon, holmr**); *Mr Carters Close* 1708, 1745; *Cartwrightes close* 1605 (*v.* **clos(e)**; the land of *Thomas Cartwright* 1605); *Catshouse* 1605 (*v.* **hūs**), *Cattes crosse* 1605 (*v.* **cros**) (with the surn. *Catt*, as in Catthorpe *infra*); *Church Hadland* 1605, 1638, 1708, 1745 (*v.* **hēafod-land**), *the church hedg* 1601 (*v.* **hecg**) (*v.* St Andrew's Church *supra*); *the fare cley, the hither cley* 1601 (*v.* **feor, hider, clǣg**); *Clover Grass Close* 1708 (*v.* **clǣfre, græs**; grown as a fodder crop); *the constables peece* 1605 (*v.* **conestable, pece**); *Cookes Close* 1617 (with the surn. *Cook*); *copmores slade* 1601 (*v.* **copp, mōr**[1], **slæd**); *Cottiers Close* 1638, 1674, 1708, 1745 (*v.* **cottere** and cf. Cottagers Close *supra*); *le Crowne* 1469 (the name of an early inn or tavern, *v.* Cox[1] 83); *the Deane* 1601 (*v.* **denu**); *Donkkesteles* 1285 × 93, *the Donxtills* 1638 (*v.* **donke, stell**); *the Drove* 1601 (*v.* **drāf**); *Ellevyn rodes* 1469 (*v.*

elevyn, rōd³); *Elleridges* ~ 1605, *Eldriges Furlong* 1674 (*v.* **furlang**), *Ellridges* 1638, 1708, 1745 (with the surn. *Eldridge,* cf. *Annie Eldridge* 1858 Census of nearby Oadby; furlongs are occasionally defined by family names in 17th-cent. Glebe Terriers, cf. *Catts furlong* (Lei **4** 123) and *Stannion furlong* (Lei **3** 17)); *Short Fawston Way* 1638, 1708 (land beside the road to Foston which lies 4 miles to the south-west); *Flaxdale* 1674 (*v.* **fleax, dalr**); *Flaxstaves* 1605, 1638, 1708, 1745 (*v.* **stæf** (ME **staves** pl.); either referring to a place where suitable wood for staves for barrel-making could be obtained (with OE **flaxe** 'a wooden vessel for liquids') or to a marshy place where a series of poles were used for markers of some kind (with ODan **flask** 'swampy grassland' metathesized)); *Foale close* 1674 (*v.* **fola**); *Folehouse* 1605, 1745 (*v.* **fola, hūs**); *atte Forth'* 1332, 1372 (*v.* **atte, ford**); *Fowlewells* 1638, 1745, *Fowlwells* 1708, *Fowlewell* ~ 1605, *Fowlwels furlong* 1674 (*v.* **furlang**) (*v.* **fūl, wella**); *Furr leyes* 1638, 1708, 1745 (*v.* **feor, leys**); *Fyssherscroft* 1424 (*v.* **croft**; with the surn. *Fisher*); *Gibbet Close* 1590, *Jebett Close* 1626 (*v.* **gibet, clos(e)**); *Gilford Low* 1638, ~ *Lowe* 1708, *Gilford low furlong* 1605 (*v.* **furlang**) (*v.* **gylde, ford, hlāw**); *Glen haggs* 1605 (*v.* **hogg**), *Little Glen hedg(e)* 1605, 1674 (*v.* **hecg**, the parish boundary hedge with Glen Parva), *Glenmedo* 1424, *Glene medowe* 1469, *Glenn* ~ 1708, *Glen Meadow* 1745 (*v.* **mēd** (**mēdwe** obl.sg.)), *Glen Meeare* 1605, ~ ~ *furlong* 1605 (*v.* **furlang**) (*v.* **(ge)mǣre**; boundary land at Glen Parva parish limits), *Glen piece* 1745 (*v.* **pece**), *Glen Stile* 1638, *Glenn* ~ 1708, *Glen Style* 1745 (*v.* **stīg**; the path to Glen Parva); *Gosmore* 1638, 1708, 1745 (*v.* **mōr**¹; poss. with dial. **goss(e)** (for **gorst**) rather than with **gōs** 'goose'); *Great Close* 1590 (*v.* **grēat, clos(e)**); *Greate bridge* 1617 (*v.* **grēat, brycg**); *Green(e)well Haggs* 1638, 1708, 1745 (*v.* **grēne**¹, **wella, hogg**); *First* ~ ~, *Second* ~ ~, *Third greenhill furlong* 1605, *Green Hill Furlong* 1674 (*v.* **grēne**¹, **hyll, furlang**); *Green(e) Yard* 1638, 1708, 1745 (*v.* **grēne**¹, **geard**); *Green's close* 1674, *Greens Closes* 1708, 1745 (with the surn. *Green*); *gregories hedland* 1601 (*v.* **hēafod-land**; with the surn. *Gregory*); *le Halle cloos* 1424, *Hall Close* 1638, 1708, 1745 (*v.* **hall, clos(e)** and *Aylestone Hall supra*); *Hanginhill* 1605 (*v.* **hangende, hyll**); *hardwicke way* 1601 (*v.* **heorde-wīc, weg**); (*at*) *harpston, harpston way* 1601 (*v.* **weg**) (earlier forms are needed since the generic may be either **stān** or **tūn**; if **stān**, then poss. with **here-pæð**, referring to the Fosse Way and perh. to a Roman milestone 2 miles from Leicester (*Ratae*); if a lost **tūn**, then **hearpere** may be thought of as the specific); *Hat* 1674, *Hatt* 1745, *Hatthill* 1628, *Hat hills* 1674, *Hatt Hills* 1708, 1745 (*v.* **hæt(t), hyll**); *Hautestrete* 1352, *the streat* 1601 (*v.* **strēt**; with OFr *haut* 'high', poss. alluding to the Fosse Way); *Neyther Hawthornebush furlong* 1605 (*v.* **neoðera, hagu-þorn, busc**); *Hawthorne hill furlong* 1605 (*v.* **hagu-þorn, hyll, furlang**); *Hawysemylle* 1424 (*v.* **myln**; with the surn. *Haw(y)es*, from the OFr fem. pers.n. *Haueis*); *Hodale* 1605, *Hodell* 1638, 1708, 1745 (*v.* **hōh, dæl**¹, **dalr**; cf. *houdale*, Lei **4** 77); (*at*) *hogges wateringe* 1601 (*v.* **hogg, wateryng**); *the Holme* 1626 (*v.* **holmr**); *Hortons close* 1605 (with the surn. *Horton*); *Husland slade* 1605 (*v.* **hūs, land, slæd**); *le Inmedewe* c.1250 (*v.* **in, mēd** (**mēdwe** obl.sg.)); *Innecrofte* 1469 (*v.* **in, croft**); *Langdale moore* 1601 (*v.* **lang**¹, **dalr, mōr**¹); *the kinges highway* 1605, *the King's highway* 1674 (*v.* **hēah-weg**; with reference to James I and Charles II respectively); *Knighton balke* 1605 (*v.* **balca**), *Knighton Meeare* 1605 (*v.* **(ge)mǣre**), *Knighton Way,* ~ ~ *bank* (*v.* **banke**) 1674 (Knighton parish adjoins to the north-east); *Lecester high way* 1605 (*v.* **hēah-weg**; early Leicester once lay 2 miles to the north-east); *Lechpittes* c.1220 × 37 (*v.* **lǣce**², **pytt**); *Linches* 1605, 1638, 1674, 1708, 1745,

Lynches 1745 (*v.* **hlinc**); *Littell brooke* 1601 (*v.* **lȳtel**, **brōc**); *Littelwell style* 1601 (*v.* **lȳtel**, **wella**, **stig**); *Little Home* 1590 (*v.* **lȳtel**, **holmr**); (*the*) *Little Feild* 1638, 1708, 1745 (*v.* **feld**; one of the open-fields, also called *Arnest feld* and *Southfeild, supra*); *Lubsthorp grounds* 1674 (*v.* **grund**; Lubbesthorpe lies 1½ miles to the west); *Lubstock* 1688 (*v.* **stoc**; with the OE masc. pers.n. *Lubb*, as in adjacent Lubbesthorpe); *le lytelend* 1394, *Littlin* 1708 (*v.* **lȳtel**; the generic may well be **eng** rather than **ende**); *Marle pitt* 1605 (*v.* **marle-pytt**); *Martins Meadow* 1632 (with the surn. *Martin*); *the meadow hedg(e)* 1605, 1674 (*v.* **hecg**); *le Milnedam* 1426, (*le*) *milnedame* 1469, 1470 (*v.* **myln**, **damme**; alluding to a watermill); *Milne peece* 1674 (*v.* **myln**, **pece**); *Mugecroft* 1424 (*v.* **croft**; prob. with the ME surn. *Mugge*, from an OE masc. pers.n. *Mugga*); *Mylne Hill Close* 1590 (*v.* **clos(e)**), *Milne hill* 1605, 1674, *Mill Hill* 1638, 1708, 1745, *Ouermylnehill* 1494 (*v.* **uferra**) (*v.* **myln**, **hyll**; a windmill site); *Nayles* ~ 1605, *Neales Hill* 1638, 1674, 1708, 1745 (with the surn. *Nail*, metonymic for ME *nailere* 'a maker of nails'); *New closse* 1470, *New Close* 1708, 1745, *the new close hedge* 1674 (*v.* **hecg**) (*v.* **nīwe**, **clos(e)**); *Newetoft* 1426, *Newtoftes* 1469 (*v.* **nīwe**, **toft**); (*at*) *newton stone* 1601 (*v.* **stān**), *newton way* 1601 (*v.* **weg**) (it is uncertain what the stone could have been, but it was poss. some sort of way-marker on the road to Newton Harcourt which lies 4½ miles to the southeast); *le Nortmedewe* c.1250 (*v.* **norð**, **mēd** (**mēdwe** obl.sg.)); *Northentowne* 1424, (*le*) *Northyn Towne* 1469, 1470, (*a close called*) *Norton towne* 1605 (('the place or land lying) north of the village', *v.* **norðan**, **tūn**); *Over meadow* 1605, *Ailston over Meadow, far* ~ ~, *hither over Meadow* 1708, 1745 (*v.* **uferra**); *Pawmers lane end* 1605 (*v.* **lane-ende**; with the surn. *Palmer*); *Paynes hadland* 1605 (*v.* **hēafod-land**; with the surn. *Payne* (cf. *Rotrotus Pagani* 1195 P of Leics.), from OFr *Paien* (from MLat *paganus* 'heathen'); in the 12th and 13th cents., *Payn* was a very common Christian name); *peaseland busshe* 1601 (*v.* **pise**, **land**, **busc**); *le Pollelane* 1313 (*v.* **pōl**[1], **lane**); *pooles headland* 1601 (*v.* **hēafod-land**; prob. with the surn. *Pool*, but **pōl**[1] may pertain here); *Pooleyard* 1605, *the Pool(e) Yard* 1638, 1674, 1708, 1745, *the pooll yard* 1708 (*v.* **pōl**[1], **geard**); *the Queens highway* 1708 (*v.* **hēah-weg**; with reference to Queen Anne); *Ranglands* 1638, 1708, 1745, *Wronglands* 1674 (*v.* **wrang**, **land**); *Red Bank(e)* 1638, 1708, 1745, *Redbanke Furlong* 1605, 1674 (*v.* **furlang**) (*v.* **banke**; with **hrēod** or **rēad**); *Redholme* 1637 (*v.* **hrēod**, **holmr**); *le Redy* 1424 (perh. 'the reedy (one)', **hrēodig** rather than **hrēod** with **ēg**, cf. *Reedye* in Sutton in the Elms f.ns. (b)); *Reede forlong* 1601 (*v.* **hrēod**, **furlang**); *the ricke place* 1605 (*v.* **hrēac**, **place**); *the Round Close* 1590, 1626 (*v.* **round**, **clos(e)**); *the Rud Closse* 1637 (*v.* **ryde**, **clos(e)**); *Ruelowe* c.1250, l.Hy 3, *Rouwelowe*, *Rowelawe*, *Ruwelowe* Edw 1 (*v.* **rūh**, **hlāw**); *Russcheheye* 1371, *le Russhey* 1424 (*v.* **risc**, (**ge**)**hæg**); *Rydesholme* 1424, *Riddeshom* 1469 (*v.* **ryde**, **holmr**); *Ryelandesiche* 1424 (*v.* **sīc**), *Ryland* 1605 (*v.* **ryge**, **land**); *Ryemede* 1424, *Ruyemedowe* 1469, *Rye Meadow* 1638, 1674, 1708, 1745 (*v.* **ryge**, **mēd** (**mēdwe** obl.sg.)); *Saffron Furlong* 1674 (*v.* **furlang**), *Saffron Slade* 1674 (*v.* **slæd**) (*v.* Saffron Farm in f.ns. (a)); *St Andrews peece* 1674, ~ ~ *peice* 1745 (*v.* **pece**; a perquisite of St Andrew's Church *supra*); *St Johns* 1674 (if not the property of St John Baptist's Church in adjacent Enderby, then either once that of the Hospitallers of St John or else the site of Midsummer bonfires on St John's Day (24 June)); *Sand Landes* 1601 (*v.* **sand**, **land**); *Sealom* 1601 (with **hamm** or **holmr**), *Seales close* 1674 (with the surn. *Seal*, *v.* Reaney *s.n.*); *Severne bridge* 1605 (*v.* **brycg**; crossing Saffron Brook (Lei **1** 226), *v.* Saffron Farm *supra*); *Shackadale furlong* 1605 (*v.* **furlang**), *Shackadale slade* 1605 (*v.* **slæd**) (*v.* **scēacere, dæl**[1], **dalr**; cf. Shackerdale, Nt 223); *the Shoulder peice* 1745 (*v.* **pece**; poss. with **sceldu** 'a shallow place', since *shoulder* transferred to a hill feature is not recorded until 1817 OED); *six roode peece* 1605 (*v.* **pece**), *the 6 Roode* 1674 (*v.* **six, rōd**[3]); *Skatescroft* 1605 (*v.* **croft**; prob. with the surn. *Skate*, otherwise with **skeið**); *the Slade* 1605, 1638, 1674, 1708, 1745 (*v.* **slæd**); *Slaters close* 1605 (the property of *William Slater* 1605); *Slawston Way* 1605, *Short Slauston Way* 1745 (the road to Slawston, 1¼ miles to the south-east); *Slithers* 1605, 1674, 1708, *Slethers* 1638 (*v.* **slidor**); *Smetholme* 1494 (*v.* **smēðe**[1], **holmr**); *le Smythesacre* 1424, *Smytheacre* 1469 (*v.* **smið, æcer**); *Stamford Way* 1601 (*v.* **weg**; presum. the road to the important Stamford in Lincs., 30 miles to the north-east, rather than to little Stanford on Avon, 14 miles to the south); *the farr Stanehill* 1601 (*v.* **feor**), *Ston(e)hill furlong* 1605, 1674 (*v.* **furlang**), *Neather ~, Over Stonehill* 1638, *Neither ~, Over Stonehill* 1708, *Nether ~, Over Stonehill* 1745 (*v.* **neoðera, uferra**) (*v.* **stān, hyll**); *Stock Lands* 1638, *Stocky Lands* 1674, 1708, 1745, *Stokey landes furlong* 1605, *Stockyland Furlong* 1674 (*v.* **furlang**) (*v.* **stocc, -ig**[3], **land**); *Stonie crose* 1601 (*v.* **stānig, cros**); *le thisteliholm* 1313, *Thystelyholme* 1424 (*v.* **thist(e)ly, holmr**); *Thorney Close* 1605, 1638, 1674, 1708, 1745 (*v.* **þornig**); *Threthen rodes* 1469 (*v.* **threten, rōd**[3]); *the toftes* 1601 (*v.* **toft**); *Toot(e)hill* 1605, 1638, 1674, 1708, 1745 (*v.* **tōt-hill**); *the Town Closes* 1674, *Town(e) Furlong* 1638, 1708, 1745 (*v.* **furlang**), *Townhill* 1605, 1674 (*v.* **hyll**), *the Townsend, ~ ~ Close* 1674 (*v.* **ende**), *Townsend furlong* 1674, *the Parsons Townsend close* 1674 (*v.* **persone**) (*v.* **tūn**); *Trawlyng* 1469, 1494, *Thrallyn* 1637 (*v.* **þræll, eng**); *Turners headland* 1601 (*v.* **hēafod-land**; with the surn. *Turner*); *the Tyth peece* 1674, *the Tyth(e) piece* 1708, 1745 (*v.* **tēoða, pece**); *Further ~ ~, Hither upper meadow* 1708, *Far ~ ~, Hither upper Meadow* 1745; *Walteresheye* 1285 × 93 (*v.* **(ge)hæg**; either with the ContGerm masc. pers.n. *Walter* or with the surn. derived from it); *the Water close* 1601 (*v.* **wæter, clos(e)**); *Waterfurrowes* 1605, *Water Thurrowes* 1638, 1708, 1745 (*v.* **wæter, furh** and *Water furrowes* in Ashby Parva f.ns. (b)); *the watring pitt* 1605 (*v.* **wateryng, pytt**); *le Waynford* 1494, *Wainsford, ~ meare* 1601 (*v.* **mere**[1]) (*v.* **wægn, ford**); *the Well* 1674, *Well Slade* 1601 (*v.* **slæd**) (*v.* **wella**); *Wethington'* 1494 (prob. a lost 'farmstead at the willows', *v.* **wīðign, tūn**); *Whetstone way* 1708, 1745 (the road to Whetstone which lies 2½ miles to the south-west); *Wigston Way* 1605, 1638, 1674, 1708, 1745, *Wigston Way side* 1605 (*v.* **sīde**) (the road to Wigston Magna which lies 2½ miles to the south-east); *Willowes ~* 1638, 1708, *Willows Close* 1745 (*v.* **wilig**); *the Windmill* 1605 (*v.* **wind-mylne**; from which *the Milne field* was named); *Witcham corner* 1605 (*v.* **wice, hamm, corner**); *Woollats close* 1674 (with the surn. *Woollatt*, derived from the OE masc. pers.n. *Wulfweard*).

Bittesby

Bichesbie (sic) 1086 DB
Bittlesby 1258 Ch, 1327 SR, *Bitlesby* 1315 Cl, 1329, 1335 Ipm, 1344
  Cl, *Bittelesby* 1428 FA
Buttelesby 1274 IpmR, *Buttlesby* 1275 Cl, *Butlesby* 1285 FA, 1327
  SR (p), *Butlisby* 1271, 1274 Ipm, 1277 Hastings, *Bytlesby* 1328
  Banco
Bettelesby 1383 Ipm, *Bettesby* 1383 Cl
Bittesby 1507 Ipm, 1515 AD, 1540 MinAccts *et passim*

'The farmstead or village at the stumpy hill', *v.* **byttel**, **bȳ**. The
stump-like hill at SP 503864 rises some 500 yards north of the deserted
settlement of Bittesby, at the parish boundary with Ullesthorpe. The hill-
name survives in two adjacent f.ns., *Bittell* and *Short Bittell* in the
Ullesthorpe Tithe Apportionments of 1843. From the *TA* map, these can
be precisely located. The unrecorded OE sb. **byttel** is a diminutive of an
(unrecorded) OE *butt* 'a (tree-) stump, a mound', related to ON *bútr* 'a
log', Swed *but* 'a stump' and to the ON adj. *buttr*, Dan *but* 'short, stocky,
stumpy' and is here transferred topographically as a hill-name.
Presumably because of the genitival composition-joint, Ekwall
incorrectly in DEPN takes the specific to be an unrecorded OE masc.
pers.n. *Byttel*, similar to the recorded *Byttic* (Redin 151).
   The earthworks at the centre of deserted medieval village of Bittesby
lie at SP 500859, stretching north and south for 500 yards on both sides
of a stream, but in part, the house platforms were destroyed by an
embankment of the former Midland Counties Railway line. The village
was depopulated in 1494 to make way for sheep pasture.

BITTESBY COTTAGES. BITTESBY HO. is *Bittesby Lodge* 1835 O, *v.* **loge**.
BITTESBY SPINNEY, *Bittesby Spinny* 1835 O, *v.* **spinney**. WILLEY
CROSSING (WILLEY GATES 2½"), Willey parish in Warwks. adjoining to
the south-west. The gates were those of an early crossing of the
dismantled Midland Counties Railway.

FIELD-NAMES

In (a), forms presented without dates are 1842 *TA*. In (b), 1600 is DKR.

(a) Far ~ ~, Near ~ ~ North Barn Cl, Barn Mdw (*v.* **bern**); Big ~ ~, Little Barley Mdw (*v.* **bærlic**); Boggy Mdw (*v.* **boggy**); Clover Cl (*v.* **clāfre**; grown as a fodder crop); Corner Cl (*v.* **corner**); Near ~ ~, Cow Cl, Cow Close Mdw (*v.* **cū**); Eight Acres (*v.* **æcer**); Far Piece (*v.* **pece**); Fourteen Acre Spinny 1835 O (*v.* **æcer, spinney**); Hill Ground (*v.* **grund**); Home Cl (*v.* **home**); Horse Close Mdw (*v.* **hors**); James Lower Mdw (with the surn. *James*); Little Mdw; Long Mdw; Middle Ground (*v.* **grund**); New Mdw; North Hill, ~ ~ Mdw; Oat Mdw (*v.* **āte**); Pigeon Cl (*v.* **pigeon**; the site of a pigeon-house); Ploughed Cl; Poole's Cl, ~ Hill Cl, ~ Mdw, ~ Spinney Cl (*v.* **spinney**) (with the surn. *Poole*, cf. *Ann Poole* 1816 Census and *Joseph Poole* 1817 ib of nearby Claybrooke Parva); Ram Mdw (*v.* **ramm**); Spinney Piece (*v.* **spinney, pece**); Stevens Cl (with the surn. *Stevens*); Township (*v.* **tūnscipe**; the site of the deserted medieval village, now pasture); Wale's Cl, ~ Mdw (with the surn. *Wale*, cf. *George Wale* 1818 Census, *Joseph Wale* 1820 ib and *John Wale* 1831 ib of adjacent Lutterworth); Ward's Upper Mdw (with the surn. *Ward*; perh. cf. *Willielmus de la Warda* 1176 P of Leics., from OE *weard* 'watching, ward'); Willey Fd 1863, 1877 White (a close bordering Willey parish, adjacent to the south-west in Warwks.).

(b) *the Little Feild* 1600 (*v.* **feld**).

Bitteswell

BITTESWELL

Betmeswel, Betmeswelle 1086 DB, *Behtmeswelle* l.12 Dane,
   Betmeswell e.Hy 3 BM
Buthmeswell(e) l.12 Dane, e. Hy 3, 1245 × 50 BM, *Buthmeswella* 12
   Dane
Butimeswell(e) l.12 Dane, 1254 Val, *Butemuswell* 1342 Pap
Butmeswell 1220 MHW, 1238 RGros, *Buttmeswelle* 13 *Goodacre,*
   Butmuswell(e) 1299 Ipm, 13, a.1300 *Goodacre,* 1301 IpmR
Bythemeswell 1287 OSut, *Bytemeswell, Bittemeswell* c.1291 Tax
Bitmeswell(e) 1199 FF, 1221 Fine *et passim* to 1355 Hastings, 1361
   Inqaqd, *Bytmeswell* 1327, 1328 Banco *et passim* to 1352
   Goodacre, 1361 Pat
Byttuswelle 1407 *Wyg, Bytteswell* 1416 Fine, 1428 FA *et passim* to
   1539, 1542 MinAccts, *Byttyswell* 1434, 1437 *Wyg et passim* to
   1497 *Braye,* 1524 Fine, *Bytyswell* 1535 VE, 1553 Pat
Bitteswell 1437 *RTemple,* 1447 Pat, 1524 Ipm, 1576 LibCl *et freq*
Bichwell 1674 *Terrier, Bitchwell* 1720 LML, c.1720 *Terrier*

'The stream in the broad valley', *v.* **bytme (bytmes** gen.sg.), **byðme,**
wella and A. Cole, 'The distribution and usage of the place-name
elements *botm, bytme* and *botn*', JEPNS 20, 38–46.

ASHBY HO. ASHBY LANE is *Asscebywey* 1467 × 84 *LTD, Ashby way* 1670
Terrier, v. **weg**; Ashby Parva lies 2 miles to the north-west. ASH TREE
HO. BITTESWELL AERODROME. BITTESWELL GRANGE, *Bittsewell
Graunge* 1361 Ipm, *v.* **grange**. BITTESWELL HALL, ~ ~ PARK, *Bitteswell
Hall* 1831 Curtis, 1846, 1863 White, 1925 Kelly, *The Hall* 1877 White,
v. **hall, park**. BITTESWELL HO., *Bitteswell House* 1925 Kelly.
BITTESWELL LODGE, 1925 Kelly, *v.* **loge**. BLAKENHALL FM, *Blakinhil*
1467 × 84 *LTD, Blakenhall* 1835 O, 1925 Kelly, *Blacken Hall* 1846,
1863 White, *v.* **blæc (blacan** wk.obl.), **hyll**. CAULDWELL FM,
CAULDWELL LANE, *Cauldwell* 1835 O, 1846, 1863 White, 1925 Kelly,
cf. *Caldewellefelde* 1467 × 84 *LTD, Caudell feild* 1670 *Terrier (v.* **feld**;

one of the early great open-fields), *Caldewellegrindel* 1467 × 84 *ib* (*v.* **grendel**), *v.* **cald, wella**. THE CHAIN, 1925 Kelly, *v.* **chain**; unexplained, unless this was an early toll site at the junction of Hall Lane and Lutterworth Rd, *v.* OED chain, sb. II 6. There is Toll Gate Fm some 1000 yards further north. COTTAGE FM. THE ELMS. FIELD FM (BITTESWELL FIELDS 2½"), *Bitteswell Field* 1847, 1863 White, *v.* **feld**. FIR TREE LODGE, *v.* **loge**. FOX COVERT, *v.* **cover(t)**. GLEBE FM, *Glebe farm* 1925 Kelly, *v.* **glebe**. THE GREEN, 1788 *EnclA*, cf. *a la grene* 1327 SR (p), *super le Grene* 1467 × 84 *LTD* (p), *v.* **grēne**². HALL FM, *Hall farm* 1925 Kelly, HALL LANE, *v.* Bitteswell Hall *supra*. KIBBLED OAKS, *v.* **āc**; the specific appears to be a ppl.adj. from the verb *to kibble* in a sense 'to cut severely, to pollard', *v.* EDD 430–1. THE LODGE (×3), *The Lodge* 1877 White, 1925 Kelly, *v.* **loge**. LUTTERWORTH RD, Lutterworth lying a half mile to the south-east. MANOR HO., *v.* **maner**. THE NOOK, *v.* **nōk**. OLD ROYAL OAK (P.H.) (lost), *Old Royal Oak* 1846, 1863 White, *Old Royal Oak Inn* 1925 Kelly. PLOUGH (P.H.) (lost), *Plough* 1846 White. ROYAL OAK (P.H.) (lost), *Royal Oak* 1846, 1863 White, *New Royal Oak* 1877 ib, 1925 Kelly. ST MARY'S CHURCH, *Church (St Mary)* 1846, 1863, 1877 White, 1925 Kelly; it is earlier recorded as *ecclesie de Butmeswell* 1220 MHW, *ecclesia de Bithmiswell* 1253 × 58 RTAL. Note also *the churche yarde* 1606 *Terrier*, *the Church Yard* 1700, 1724, 1762 *ib*, *v.* **churchyerd**. THRONE'S BARN, with the surn. *Throne*, *v.* **bern**. ULLESTHORPE RD is *Olesthorpwey* 1467 × 84 *LTD*, *v.* **weg**; Ullesthorpe lies 2 miles to the north-west. VALLEY FM, VALLEY LANE, cf *Bitteswell valley* 1877 White, *The Valley* 1925 Kelly, *v.* **valeie**. THE VICARAGE, 1877 White, 1925 Kelly; recorded earlier is *the vicaredge house* 1606 *Terrier*, *the Vickridge house* 1674 *ib*, *The Vicorage House* 1690 *ib*, *the Vicarage House* 1762 *ib*, 1846 White, *v.* **vikerage**. WEST END FM (local), *v.* **ende**. WOODBY LANE, prob. to be identified with *Wood way road* 1788 *EnclA*, cf. *Wodewayfurlong* 1467 × 84 *LTD* (*v.* **furlang**), *v.* **wudu, weg**. WOOD END FM, *v.* **wudu, ende**.

FIELD-NAMES

In (a), forms presented without dates are 1968 *Surv*; those dated 1788 are *EnclA*; e.19 are *Plan*; 1835 are O. Forms throughout dated Hy 3 are LAS; 13 are *Goodacre*; 1327 and 1332 are SR; 1467 × 84 are *LTD*; 1477 (e.16) are *Charyte*; 1606, 1670, 1674 and 1690 are *Terrier*.

(a) 4 Acre, 5 ~, 6 ~, 7 ~, 8 ~, Ten ~, Twelve Acre, 19 Acres (*v.* **æcer**); The Allotments (*v.* **allotment**); Bottom Ashby Way (*v.* Ashby Lane *supra*); Ashton's, ~

Fd (with the surn. *Ashton*, cf. *John Ashton* 1864 Census of adjacent Ullesthorpe);
Back Cl, ~ Fd, ~ Mdw (*v*. **back**); Baldwin's Cl (with the surn. *Baldwin*); First ~ ~,
Second ~ ~, Barn Cl, Big ~ ~, Little ~ ~, Bottom Barn Fd (*v*. **bern**); Bean Fd (*v*.
bēan); Bear Lane 1788 (prob. the site of an inn or tavern called The Bear, cf.
Berelane 1472 in Bristol (Gl **3** 86), *the Bear* 1528 in Gloucester (Gl **2** 135) and *v*.
Cox[1] 85); Bee Fd (*v*. **bēo**; land on which bees were hived or where bees abounded);
Belcher's Cl (with the surn. *Belcher*); Belt Cl (*v*. **belt**); Big Fd, ~ Mdw; the Bite (*v*.
bit); Bitteswell House Paddock (*v*. **paddock** and Bitteswell Ho. *supra*); Bogg Fd (*v*.
bog); Boundary Fd (*v*. **boundary**); Bowling Alley (*v*. **bowling-alley**); Brick Kiln,
Brickhill Mdw (*v*. **brike-kiln**); Old Brickyard (*v*. **brike-yard**); Brooder Fd (*v*.
brooder 'a device or structure for the rearing of young chickens or other birds'; note
Chicken Fd *infra*); Brook Fd, ~ Mdw (*le Brok'* 1467 × 84, *the brooke* 1670, *v*. **brōc**);
Cattern (*Catthorn* 1467 × 84, *v*. **cat(t)**, **þorn**); Caudale Hill, Cauldwell Hole (with
hol[1] or **halh**, *v*. Caldwell Lane *supra* and Cordwell Hole in Ashby Parva f.ns. (a));
Cemetery Fd (abutting a graveyard); Little Chain Cl (*v*. The Chain *supra*); First
Charity Cl (land endowed for charitable purposes); Chicken Fd (*v*. **cīcen** and Brooder
Fd *supra*); Clover Fd (*v*. **clāfre**; grown as a fodder crop); Cow Cl (*v*. **cū**); First ~,
Second Cowage (*v*. **cū**, **edisc**); Cowhead (*Couhaueden* 1467 × 84, *Cowhaden* 1670,
v. **cū**, **hēafod**; note the survival of the archaic -*en* plural, freq. in the south of the
Hundred); The Cricket Fd, The Old Cricket Fd (for the game of cricket); Dam Cl, ~
Mdw (*the Dam* 1670, *Dam furlong* 1467 × 84 (*v*. **furlang**), *v*. **damme**); First ~ ~,
Second Drive Fd (fields beside a driveway); Dunton Lane Cl (beside the road to
Dunton Bassett which lies 3 miles to the north); Faggot Fd (*v*. **faggott**); Far Fd, ~
Mdw (*v*. **feor**); First Mdw; Fish Pond (*v*. **fisshe-ponde**); The Football Fd; Front Fd
(*v*. **front**); Glover's Fd (with the surn. *Glover*, a common family name in Bitteswell,
cf. *William Glover* 1809 Census, *Francis Glover* 1818 ib, *Frederick Glover* 1823 ib
and *John Glover* 1841 ib); Gravel Hole (*v*. **gravel**, **hol**[1]); Hand Fd 1788 (of uncertain
meaning; poss. sited near a hand-post (*v*. Field 222)); Hankin's Fd (sic) (presum.
with the surn. *Hankins*, the Leics. form, rather than *Hankin*); Harris's Fd (with the
surn. *Harris*); Haybox (*v*. **hēg**, **box**; a small enclosure, esp. retained for mowing
grass); Hill Fd; Home Cl, ~ Fd (*v*. **home**); Horse Cl (*v*. **hors**); Houndsacre (*v*. **æcer**;
either with the OE masc. pers.n. *Hund* or with the sb. **hund** or with the surn. *Hound*
derived from these, cf. Hounds Acre, Lei **2** 292); House Fd; Hovel Cl e.19 (*v*. **hovel**);
Hubbard's Fd, ~ Mdw (with the surn. *Hubbard*, from the ContGerm masc. pers.n.
Hubert; cf. *Elizabeth Hubbard* 1836 Census, *John Hubbard* and *Sarah Hubbard*
1842 ib of Bitteswell); Hut Mdw (*v*. **hut**); Jackson's Lane 1788 (with the surn.
Jackson); Lamb Fd (*v*. **lamb**); Lane Cl (*v*. **lane**); Leicester Road Cl (Leicester lying
12 miles to the north); Little Fd, ~ Mdw; Little Hill 1788 (1670, *Littelhille* 1467 ×
84, *v*. **lȳtel**, **hyll**); Lodge Fd (*v*. The Lodge *supra*); Little ~, Longlands e.19 (*v*. **lang**[1],
land); Long Fd, ~ Mdw; L-Shaped Fd; Manor Fd (*v*. Manor Ho. *supra*); The
Meadow; Mick's Fd (with the familiar form *Mick* of the masc. pers.n. Michael); The
Middle Fd 1788, 1968 (*the Midle Feild* 1670, *v*. **middel**, **feld** and *Woldfelde* in f.ns.
(b); one of the great open-fields of the township); Middle Six (presum. a close of six
acres); Milestone Fd (*v*. **mīl-stān**); Mill Fd 1788, 1968 (*v*. **myln**); The Moors (*v*.
mōr[1]); Morebarns (*v*. **mōr**[1], **bern**); Murnhill well (sic) 1835 (*Mirnewelhill*,
Mirnewellehil 1467 × 84, *v*. **wella**, **hyll**; the prototheme is difficult, but poss. is a
reduced OE masc. pers.n. *Merewine*); New Fd; Oak Tree Ground (*v*. **āc**, **grund**); the
Old Ark (sic) (*v*. **āc**); Old Ted's (with the familiar form *Ted* of the masc. pers.n.

Edward); the Paddock (*v*. **paddock**); The Parlour (*v*. **parlur**); The Piece (*v*. **pece**); First ~ ~, Second Pond Cl (*v*. **ponde**); Bottom ~ ~, Top Pump Fd (with reference to a wind-pump); Rickyard Cl (*v*. **reke-yard**); Road Cl e.19, Roadside 1968 (these are prob. the same field); Scotton's Mdw (with the surn. *Scotton*, that of a family originally from Scotton in Lincs., cf. *Charles Scotton* 1806 Census, *Thomas Scotton* 1824 ib and *John Scotton* 1853 ib, all of Bitteswell); Second Fd; Side Cl, ~ Mdw (*v*. **sīde**); Cold ~, Sizeham e.19 (*Sysom feild* 1670 (*v*. **feld**; one of the great open-fields), *v*. **hamm**; poss. with a shortened OE masc. pers.n. *Sigehǣð* or *Sigefrið*, *v*. *Sitheswong* in f.ns. (b) and Syston, Lei **3** 227); The Slang (*v*. **slang**); Second ~ ~, Small Fd; Smid's Mdw (*Smethemedewe, Smethemedow* 1467 × 84, *Smethemedo furlang* 1477 (e.16) (*v*. **furlang**), *Smidmeadow* 1670, *v*. **smēðe**[1], **mēd** (**mēdwe** obl.sg.)); Spinney Cl, ~ Mdw 1968, Spinney Fd e.19 (*v*. **spinney**); Spring Fd, Sharpe's Spring Mdw, Smith's Spring Mdw (*v*. **spring**[1]; with the surns. *Sharpe* and *Smith*); Square Fd (*v*. **squar(e)**); Stable Fd (*v*. **stable**); Stanhope's (the surn. *Stanhope* in the possessive case, cf. *Mary Stanhope* 1846 Census of nearby Claybrooke Parva); Stevenson's Cl, ~ Park (*v*. **park**) (with the surn. *Stevenson*, cf. *Charles Stevenson* 1843 Census, *Anna Stevenson* 1851 ib and *Bertrum Stevenson* 1877 ib, all of Bitteswell); Straw Rick Cl (*v*. **strēaw**, **hrēac**); Temple Cottage Paddock (*v*. **paddock**; there is no immediate evidence to explain *temple* here); Thistle Fd (*v*. **þistel**); Thorn Bush Cl (*v*. **þorn**, **busc**); Tollgate Cl (*v*. **toll-gate**); Top Fd; Trench Cl (*v*. **trenche**); Turnpike Cl (*v*. **turnepike**); Twelve Acre Wood e.19 (*Twelueacris* 1467 × 84, *v*. **twelf**, **æcer**); Twining's (the surn. *Twining* in the possessive case); Ullesthorpe Gap 1788 (*v*. **gap**; at the boundary with Ullesthorpe, such names referring to gaps in parish boundary fences or hedges); Uncle Tom's (with the familiar form *Tom* of the masc. pers.n. *Thomas*); Village Mdw (*v*. **village**); West Croft 1788 (*v*. **west**, **croft**); White Gate Fd; Windmill Fd (*v*. **wind-mylne**); Woodyard (*v*. **wodyard**); Wormleighton's Fd (with the surn. *Wormleighton* of a family originally from the township of this name, 21 miles to the south-west in Warwks., cf. *Mary Wormleighton* 1804 Census of Bitteswell); Woulands (*Woulonds* 1467 × 84, *v*. **wōh**, **land**); The Yerricks, Great Yerrick (cf. *Hericke furlong* 1670 (*v*. **furlang**); prob. with the surn. *Herrick*, from the ON masc. pers.n. *Eiríkr* (ODan *Erik*), cf. *Johannes Eirich* 1211 RFL of Leicester, but ME **heyrek** 'a haystack' is poss.).

(b) *Apiltrefurlong* 1467 × 84, *Apletree furlong* 1670 (*v*. **æppel-trēow**, **furlang**); *Aylwordwaye* 1467 × 84 (*v*. **weg**; with the surn. *Aylward*, from the OE masc. pers.n. *Æðelweard*); atte Barr 1327 (p), 1332 (p), *atte barre* (p), *at the barre* (p) 1467 × 84 (*v*. **atte**, **barre**); *Banebut* 1467 × 84 (*v*. **bēan**, **butte**); *Banlondhill, Littilbanlondhill* 1467 × 84 (*v*. **lȳtel**), *Great Ballan Hill* 1670 (*v*. **bēan**, **land**, **hyll**); *Bitlysbymere* 1467 × 84 (*v*. **(ge)mǣre**; land at the boundary with Bittesby parish which adjoins to the south-west); *le Longbreche, le Schortbreche* 1467 × 84 (*v*. **lang**[1], **sc(e)ort**, **brēc**); (*upon*) *Catherine* 1670 (a furlong name with the surn. *Catherine, Catlin* (from OFr forms of the fem. pers.n. Catherine), cf. (*upon*) *Normans, infra*); *Cecesslade* 1467 × 84 (*v*. **slæd**; the specific may be **chike** 'a chicken'; otherwise, *v*. **cheker**); *Littelclarouhull, Mikelclarouhil* 1467 × 84, *Little Clarauhill* 1670 (*v*. **clāfre**, **hōh**, **hyll**, **lȳtel**, **micel**); *Coppedhill* 1467 × 84 (*v*. **copped**[1], **hyll**); *Corland* 1467 × 84 (*v*. **land**; perh. with **corn**[1], but additional forms are necessary since this single spelling is from an abbey register of property); *Coventry land* 1670 (*v*. **land**; charity land belonging either to Bablake Hospital or to Ford's Hospital, both almshouses in Coventry, cf. Coventry Orchard in Ashby Parva f.ns. (b)); *Crosfurlong* 1467 × 84 (*v*.

cross, furlang); *Crowethorne* 1467 × 84 (*v.* **crāwe, þorn**); *Edrichewey* 1467 × 84
(*v.* **weg**; with the surn. *Edrich*, from the OE masc. pers.n. *Ēadrīc*); *Elrynstub* 1467
× 84 (*v.* **ellern, stubb**); *Erewygfurlong* 1467 × 84 (*v.* **erewygge, furlang**);
Flaggefurlong 1467 × 84 (*v.* **furlang**), *flagspitt* 1670 (*v.* **pytt**) (*v.* **flagge**); *le Gore*
1467 × 84 (*v.* **gāra**); *Grasfeelde* 1467 × 84 (*v.* **græs, feld**); *the Heath* 1670 (*v.* **hǣð**);
the Hedge furlong 1670 (*v.* **hecg, furlang**); *le Hert* 1467 × 84 (presum. an inn or
tavern name, *v.* Cox[1] 82); *Hornlowe* 1467 × 84 (*v.* **horn, hlāw**); *Houeres in the
medue* 13 (*v.* **ofer**[2], **in, mēd** (**mēdwe** obl.sg.); perh. 'ridges in the meadow', with
reference to former arable selions grassed over); *Kembirweye* 1467 × 84 (*v.* **weg**;
with the surn. *Kember*, an occupational surn. from ME *kembere* 'a comber of wool
or flax'); *the kinges high streete* 1606 (*v.* **hēah**[1], **strēt**; with reference to James I); *le
knolles* 1467 × 84 (*v.* **cnoll**); *Lambhill* 1467 × 84, *Lamwell* 1670 (*v.* **lamb, hyll**; the
later form is no doubt a garbled version of the earlier, since sheep are kept away from
waterside fields because of liver fluke); *Littulfurlong* 1467 × 84 (*v.* **lȳtel, furlang**);
John Lords hedge 1670 (*v.* **hecg**); *long foreland* 1670 (this may belong with *little
long furlong, infra*, otherwise *v.* **fore, land**); *little long furlong* 1670 (*v.* **lang**[1],
furlang); *le Merefurlong* 1467 × 84 (*v.* **(ge)mǣre, furlang**); (*upon*) *Normans* 1670
(a furlong name with the surn. *Norman*, cf. (*upon*) *Catherine, supra*); *Nortmest* (sic)
1467 × 84 (*v.* **norðmest**; a furlong name); *Pasfurlong* 1467 × 84 (*v.* **furlang**; perh.
with OE **pæsc(e)** '?a muddy place', the source of ModEdial. *pash* 'a soft mass, a
puddle'); *le Portwey* 1467 × 84 (*v.* **port-wey**; the road to Leicester); *little Quicks
hills* 1670 (*v.* **quyk**); *Aboueriggewey, Binetheriggewey* 1467 × 84 (*v.* **above,
benethe, hrycgweg**); *Robynetisknolle* 1467 × 84 (*v.* **cnoll**; with the masc. pers.n.
Robinet, an *-ette* diminutive of *Robin*, in turn a diminutive of *Robert*); *Sand furlong*
1467 × 84 (*v.* **sand, furlang**); *Schortgathyll* (*v.* **hyll**), *Schortgatetunge* (*v.* **tunge**)
1467 × 84 (*v.* **sc(e)ort, gata**); *Shackits furs* (*v.* **fyrs**), *Sharcutt hill* (*v.* **hyll**) 1670
(perh. 'the boundary cottage', *v.* **sc(e)aru, cot**); *Shortleyes* 1670 (*v.* **leys**); *Sitheswong*
1467 × 84 (*v.* **vangr**; with a shortened OE masc. pers.n. *Sigehǣð* or *Sigefrið*, *v.*
Sizeham in f.ns. (a)); *le Sladole* 1467 × 84 (*v.* **slæd, dāl**); *Smalerodes* 1467 × 84,
Small roodes 1670 (*v.* **smæl, rōd**[3]); *the Small orchard* 1690 (*v.* **orceard**); *le
Smalthorn* Hy 3, 1467 × 84 (*v.* **smæl, þorn**); *Stansladefurlong* 1467 × 84 (*v.*
furlang), *Stoneslaide, Stoun Slaide* 1670 (*v.* **stān, slæd**); *Stanywelfurlong* 1467 × 84
(*v.* **stānig, wella, furlang**); *Stony furlong* 1670 (*v.* **stānig, furlang**); *Stotfoldlow* 1467
× 84 (*v.* **stōd-fald, hlāw**); *Stounemore pitt* 1670 (*v.* **stān, mōr**[1], **pytt**); *the Towne
Streete* 1674 (*v.* **tūn, strēt**); *Usom* 1670 (*v.* **hūs, hamm**); *Wolfoushull* Hy 3,
Wlfousul, Lutlewolfoushul 13 (*v.* **lȳtel**), *Woulfoxhill, Mikilwoulfoxhill* 1467 × 84 (*v.*
micel) (*v.* **wulf, hūs, hyll**; the reference appears to be to the dens of wolves (which
could be freshly dug in the earth or in re-used old fox holes or in old badger holes),
the wolf becoming extinct in England during the reign of Henry VII (1486–1509);
this Leics. instance, now in addition to Woolfox (Ru 24), suggests that the latter may
well have been wrongly interpreted as with an OE masc. pers.n. *Wulfa*); *le
Netherwold* 1467 × 84 (*v.* **neoðera**), *le Ouerwold* 1467 × 84, *over Olt* 1670 (*v.*
uferra) (*v.* **wald**); *Woldfelde* 1467 × 84 (*v.* **wald, feld**; prob. an earlier name for
Middle Fd in f.ns. (a), the location of *over Olt, supra*); *Wolleswong* 1467 × 84 (*v.*
vangr; with the OE masc. pers.n. *Wulf*, cf. *Wolueswong* in Catthorpe f.ns (b)); *Wyses
layes* 1670 (*v.* **leys**; with the surn. *Wyse, Wise*).

Blaby

BLABY

Bladi (sic) 1086 DB

Blabi 1175 P (p), 1196 GildR (p), 1204 Cur, e.13 (1404) *Laz* (p),
a.1250 *LCDeeds* (p)

Blaby 1220 MHW, 1222, 1235 RHug *et freq*, *Blabye* 1557 Pat, 1576
Saxton

Blayby 1518 Visit, *Blaybie* 1576 LibCl

Probably 'the farmstead or village of a man called Blar', *v.* **bȳ**. A
Scand masc. pers.n. *Blár* is unrecorded, but appears to be a by-name
from the ON adj. *blár* 'dark'. Note *Randulfus Bla* 1202 Ass of
Lincolnshire and the later *Iusse bla* (Lind 29).

ALL SAINTS' CHURCH, *Church (All Saints)* 1846, 1863, 1877 White,
1925 Kelly; it is earlier recorded as *ecclesia(m)* ~ ~, *ecclesie de Blaby*
a.1219 RHug, 1220 MHW, 1235 RGros *et passim* to 1411, 1446 *Pat*.
Note also *The Churchyard* 1821 Terrier, *v.* **churchyerd**. ASH SPINNEY,
v. **æsc, spinney**. BAKER'S ARMS, 1846 White, 1925 Kelly, *Bakers Arms*
1863, 1877 White. BLABY BRIDGE. BLABY HALL, 1863, 1877 White,
1925 Kelly, *The Hall* 1846 White, *v.* **hall**. BLABY HILL, 1835 O, 1846,
1863, 1877 White, 1925 Kelly, *v.* **hyll**. BLABY HOSPITAL. BLABY MILL,
1740 LeicW, 1835 O, 1846, 1863 White; a watermill, *v.* **myln**. BLABY
STATION. BLACK HORSE (P.H.), *Black Horse* 1846, 1863, 1877 White,
1925 Kelly. BLACK SPINNEY, *v.* **spinney**. BULL'S HEAD (P.H.), *Bull's
Head* 1832 Deed, 1846, 1863, 1877 White, 1925 Kelly. CHAPEL ST.
CHURCH ST, *v.* All Saints' Church *supra*. THE COTTAGE. DOG AND GUN
INN (lost), *Dog and Gun* 1925 Kelly. THE ELMS. GEORGE (P.H.), 1846,
1877 White. GLEBE FM, *v.* **glebe**. GOLDEN BALL (P.H.) (lost), *Golden
Ball* 1846, 1863, 1877 White. HIGHFIELDS FM. HILL LANE. HOSPITAL
LANE, *v.* Blaby Hospital *supra*. KEEPERS FM, in origin a gamekeeper's
house. THE LEYSLANDS, *Leysland'* 1467 × 84 *LTD*, *Leaslands* 1835 O,
Leaselands 1849 Surv, *v.* **læs, land**. THE LIMES. LODGE FM, *v.* **loge**.
LONG WALK, *v.* **lang**[1], **walk**. LUTTERWORTH RD, Lutterworth lying 9

miles to the south. MILL LANE is *Milnwey, Mylnwey* 1467 × 84 *LTD*, (*the*) *Milne way* 1625, 1638 *Terrier, the mylne way* 1638 *ib, the Mill Way* c.1740, m.18 *ib, v.* **weg**; leading to Blaby Mill *supra*. MILL LANE FM. NORTHFIELD HO., *Northfield house* 1925 Kelly. NORTHFIELD RD, 1925 Kelly. OAK FM. PORT HILL, 1638, c.1740, m.18 *Terrier*, 1766 *EnclA*, 1925 Kelly, *v.* **port**[2]; probably named from a **port-wey** and referring to the road from Countesthorpe to Leicester since this is unlikely to be an early market site so close to the principal town, *v.* Cox[2] 81 *s.n.* THE RECTORY, 1925 Kelly, *the Rectory House* 1821 *Terrier, v.* **rectory**; earlier recorded is *the parsonage howse* 1638 *ib, The Parsonage House* c.1740, m.18 *ib, v.* **personage**. STULT BRIDGE, crosses Whetstone Brook at the parish boundary; the early bridge must have been carried on piles, *v.* **stylt, brycg**. THREE OWLS (P.H.) (lost), *the Three Owles* 1726 *Deed*. UNION WORKHOUSE (lost), *Union Workhouse* 1846, 1863, 1877 White, *v.* **workhouse**; a Poor Law institution. WELFORD RD, Welford in Northants. lying 12 miles to the south-east. WIGSTON RD, Wigston Magna lying 2 miles to the north-east. WILLOW FM. WINCHESTER RD is *Winchester way* c.1740, m.18 *Terrier*; a major route south to Winchester in Hampshire.

Street-names in recent urban development:

AUBURN RD. DARLEY RD. DOVEDALE RD. GROVE RD. JAMES ST. KESWICK RD. NEW ST. PARK RD. QUEEN'S RD. SYCAMORE ST. THE CRESCENT. THE FAIRWAY. WESTERN DRIVE. WEST ST.

FIELD-NAMES

In (a), forms presented without dates are 1849 *Surv*; those dated 1776 are *EnclA*; 1846, 1863 and 1877 are White; 1925 are Kelly; 1935 are *Deed*; 1969 are *Surv*. Forms throughout dated Edw 1 are *Rut*; those dated 1467 × 84 are *LTD*; 1535 are Ipm; 1625, 1638, 1674, c.1740 and m.18 are *Terrier*; 1627 are Surv; 1726 are *Deed*.

(a) 5 Acre 1935, The Six ~, The Eight ~, 9 Acres 1849 (*v.* **æcer**); Little ~ ~, Barn Cl (*v.* **bern**); Big Birches or Binks (the surn. *Binks* in the possessive case), Little Birches (*v.* **birce**); Bosses Cl 1776 (with the surn. *Boss, v.* Reaney *s.n.*); Brickhill Cl 1776, Brittle Pits 1935 (*v.* **pytt**) (*v.* **brike-kiln**); Bridle Road Cl (*v.* **brigdels**); Broad Hurst (*v.* **brād, hyrst**); Bruin's Cl 1776 (with the surn. *Bruin*, cf. *Richard Bruin* 1776); Chester Cl (with the surn. *Chester*, cf. *Charles Chester* 1638); Church Headland Fd 1776 (*Longhadland alias Church hadland Feild* c.1740, *Long-hadland* *alias Church-hadland Feilde* m.18, *The Hadlandfelde* 1467 × 84, *Long Headland feild* 1625, *Long Hadland Feild* 1638, 1674, *v.* **hēafod-land**, **feld** and All Saints' Church *supra*; one of the great open-fields of the township); Clarkes Cl 1935 (with the surn. *Clarke*, cf. *Clement Clarke* 1674, *John Clarke* c.1740, both of Blaby); Far ~ ~, Clay Acres (*Cleyacres* 1467 × 84, *Longe* ~, *Short Cleyacres* 1638, *Long* ~ ~, *Short Clay Acres* c.1740, m.18, *v.* **clǣg**, **æcer**); Clear Cl, ~ ~ Part 1935 (*v.* **part**) (prob. cleared of stones or other obstructions to efficient management); Corthouse Cl (sic) (poss. with **court-hous** in the sense 'a manorial dwelling'); Crosspit (*Cros(e)pitt'* 1467 × 84, *the Crosse pitts* c.1740, m.18, *Crosspits furlonge* 1638, *Crospitts furlong* 1674 (*v.* **furlang**), *v.* **pytt**; most prob. with **cross**, but *v. Crosfelde, infra*); Crow Spinney 1969 (*v.* **crāwe**, **spinney**); Cuckoo Cl (*v.* **cuccu**); Dale Cl (*le Dale* Edw 1, *þe Dale, þe Dall'* 1467 × 84, *Dale furlonge* 1467 × 84, ~ *furlong* 1625, 1638, 1674, c.1740, m.18 (*v.* **furlang**), *v.* **þe**, **dalr**); Bottom ~ ~, Top ~ ~, Far Cl (*v.* **feor**); Foston Way, Bottom Foston Way Cl (*Foston wey, Longfostonwey, Schortfostonwey* 1467 × 84 (*v.* **lang**[1], **sc(e)ort**), *Foston way side* 1638, c.1740, m.18 (*v.* **sīde**), *v.* **weg**; the road to Foston which lies 3 miles to the south-east); Glen Hill 1925 (Glen Parva parish adjoins to the north); Bottom ~, Top Gorse 1849, Gorse Farm 1877, Gorse Pit 1849 (*v.* **pytt**) (*v.* **gorst**); Gravel Hill (*v.* **gravel**); Great Mdw; Haggs Fd, Top Haggs 1935 (*the haggs* 1625, m.18, *the Hags* c.1740, *v.* **hogg**); the Hall Cl 1776, Hall Piece 1849 (*v.* **pece**) (*v.* Blaby Hall *supra*); High Leys 1776 (c.1740, m.18, *High leyes* 1625, *v.* **hēah**[1], **leys**); Hog's Gore 1935 (*Hoggerds gore* 1625, *Hoggheards goar* 1638, *Hoggheards-goare* c.1740, *Hog-heard-goare* m.18, *v.* **hogghirde**, **gāra**); Home Cl 1849, 1935 (*v.* **home**); Homestead (*v.* **hām-stede**); Honey Bags (sic) (this may be a miscopied or misheard Money Bags; but if accurate, then *v.* **hunig**, either alluding to the location of beehives or to very good land ('flowing with milk and honey') or even to ground with sticky soil); Horse Cl (*v.* **hors**); House Cl; Hovel Fd 1969 (*v.* **hovel**); Jimmy Laws Mdw 1969; The Lunns, Bruins ~, Fludes Lunns 1776 (*the Lons* 1627, *v.* **land**, in its sense 'selion, strip'; with the surns. *Bruin* and *Flude*, cf. *Richard Bruin* 1776 and *James Flude* 1759 MI); Kinton's Cl 1846, 1863, 1877 (with the surn. *Kinton*, cf. *Robert Kinton* 1836 Census, *Henrietta Kinton* 1839 ib and *Mark Kinton* 1843 ib, all of adjacent Wigston Magna); Knight's Cl 1846, 1863, 1877 (with the surn. *Knight*, cf. *George Knight* 1833 Census, *Sharrett Knight* 1846 ib and *Annie Knight* 1852 ib, all of adjacent Wigston Magna); The Five Lands, Ten Lands (*v.* **land**; enclosures comprising five and ten selions of a former great open-field, cf. The Lunns *supra*); Little Cl; Little Jonathan (prob. with the masc. pers.n. *Jonathan*; as a surn., it is rare and not evidenced in Leics. in the 19th cent.); First ~, Second Lodge (*v.* Lodge Fm *supra*); Meadow Pastures 1776 (*v.* **pasture**); Middle Cl; Middle Fd 1776 (c.1740, *the Middle feild* 1625, 1674, *the Midle-Feilde* m.18, *v.* **middel**, **feld**; one of the great open-fields, earlier called *Crosfelde, infra*); Mill Dam 1776, ~ ~ Cl 1849 (*the Dam* 1625, c.1740, m.18, *v.* **damme** and Blaby Mill *supra*); Mill Fd 1776 (c.1740, *Mylnefelde* 1467 × 84, *the Milne feilde* 1625, *the Mill Field(e)* 1674, m.18, *v.* **myln**, **feld**; one of the great open-fields); 1st ~ ~, 2nd ~ ~, Mill Hill, Great Mill Hill (*Milnhyll* 1467 × 84, *Milnehill* 1638, *Mill Hill* 1674, c.1740, m.18, *v.* **myln**, **hyll**); Mill Holme 1776 (*Mylnholm* 1467 × 84, *v.* **myln**, **holmr**); Mill Mdw; Nether Mdw 1776 (*the neather meadow commonly called Hammer meadow* 1625, *Homer mead'* 1638, *the homer meadow* c.1740, m.18, *v.* **hamer**); North Croft 1776, 1849, the Great ~ ~, Little North Croft 1776 (*North Croft* 1627, *v.* **croft**); Far ~ ~, Near Old Fd (*Old feild* 1625,

1674, ~ *feild* 1638, c.1740, m.18, *v*. **feld**; most likely with **wald** (as for the names of great open-fields in Ashby Parva, Bruntingthorpe, Dunton Bassett etc.); the third common field of this township); the Old Orchard 1776 (*v*. **orceard**); Next Ortons (with the surn. *Orton* in the possessive case, cf. *Thomas Orton* 1826 Census, *Henry Orton* 1834 ib and *John Orton* 1841 ib, all of Blaby); Osier Bed Cl (*v*. **oyser**, **bedd**); Paddock ((*on*) *Paddock* 1638, *v*. **paddock**); Paddy's Nest (*Padognest* 1467 × 84, *paddock nest* 1625, *Poddocks-neast* c.1740, *Poddock's nest* m.18, *v*. **padduc**, **nest**); Park Seeds 1969 (*v*. **park**, **sǣd**; in modern f.ns. *seed*(*s*) is used for grasses grown for one year's mowing or grazing as distinguished from permanent pasture); the Peice 1776, The Piece 1969 (*v*. **pece**); Pen Cl (*v*. **penn**); Pettites Cl 1969 (with the surn. *Pettit*, cf. *Mary Pettitt* 1853 Census of adjacent Glen Parva); Place's Cl or Slang Fd 1935 (with the surn. *Place*, *v*. Reaney *s.n.* and Slang Fd *infra*); Short Port 1849, Long Port 1935 (*Longe* ~, *Short Portfurlonge* 1638, *Long-Port-furlong*, *Short-Port-furlong* c.1740 (*v*. **furlang**); beside Port Hill *supra*); Pye ~ 1849, Pie Dyke 1969 (*Pydyk* 1467 × 84, *v*. **dík**; prob. with **pīe**² rather than **pīe**¹); Short Bit 1935 (*v*. **bit**); Far ~, Middle ~, Near ~, Slade, Slade Cl, Great Slade Mdw (*v*. **slæd**); Slang Fd 1935 (*v*. **slang** and Place's Cl *supra*); Small Cl; Stable Cl (*v*. **stable**); Straw Cl (*v*. **strēaw**); Big Stub Stile (*v*. **stubb**, **stigel**); Swing Gates 1969 (with reference to enclosure gates); Ten Cl (a field either of ten acres in area or comprising ten selions enclosed from a great open-field); Thistly Mdw (*v*. **thist(e)ly**); Top Cl 1849, 1935, Far ~ ~, Near Top Cl 1849; Three Corner Bit 1935 (*v*. **three-corner**, **bit**); Three Cornered Piece (*v*. **three-cornered**, **pece**); Turnpike Cl (*v*. **turnepike**); Upper Mdw 1776 (*the upper meadowe* 1625, *the Over Meadowe* 1638, *the overmeadow* c.1740, *v*. **upper**, **uferra**); Upper Row (with **rāw** or **rǣw**); Water Furrows (c.1740, m.18, *Waterfurrowes* 1638, 1674, *Water Furrowes furlonge* 1625 (*v*. **furlang**), *v*. **wæter**, **furh** and *Waterfurrowes* in Aylestone f.ns. (b)); Western Holmes (*v*. **holmr**; prob. with an altered *Whetstone* rather than *Western*); Wheat Cl (*v*. **hwǣte**); Whetstone Leys 1776 (*Whetston Leyes* 1625, 1638, ~ *Leys* c.1740, *v*. **leys**; Whetstone parish adjoins to the west); 1st ~ ~, 2nd ~ ~, 3rd ~ ~, 4th Willow Pits (cf. *willowe pit furlonge* 1625, *Willopit furlonge* 1638, *Willopitt furlong* 1674, *Willo-pitt-furlong* c.1740 (*v*. **furlang**), *willowpit way* 1625, *Willopit way* 1638 (*v*. **weg**), *v*. **wilig**, **pytt**); Far ~ ~, Near Winchester Way (cf. *Winchester way furlong*(*e*) 1625, 1638, 1674, c.1740, *v*. **furlang** and Winchester Rd *supra*).

(b) *Alblasters land* 1535 (*v*. **land**; with the surn. *Alblaster*, *Arblaster*, from AFr *alblaster*, *arblaster* 'crossbowman, a maker of crossbows', cf. *Ricardus le Arbelaster* 1198 P of Rutland); *Mr Ashbys Close*, ~ ~ *hades*, ~ ~ *hadland* c.1740, m.18 (*v*. **hēafod**, **hēafod-land**); *the bark milne holme* 1625, *the Barke mill holme* 1638, m.18, *the Barkmill-holme* c.1740 (*v*. **bark-milne**, **holmr**; a mill for grinding bark, normally used for tanning; the earliest citation in OED for such a structure is dated 1885); *Barton poole* 1638, c.1740, m.18 (*v*. **bere-tūn**, **pōl**¹); *Blabye Mylne fludgate* 1638, *Blaby mill Flood-gate* c.1740, m.18 (*v*. **flodegate** and Blaby Mill *supra*); *Blakmyle* 1467 × 84 (*v*. **blæc**, **mylde**); *Brachou* 1467 × 84 (*v*. **bracu**; with **hōh** or **haugr**); *Brathethe hill* 1625, 1638, 1674, *Bradthern-hill* c.1740, m.18 (*v*. **brād**, **breiðr**, **þyrne**, **þyrnir**); *Broadarse* 1638, 1674, *broad-arse furlong* c.1740, m.18 (*v*. **furlang**) (*v*. **brād**, **ears**; a common f.n., presum. with reference to the shape of a rounded hill, but some such names may disguise an earlier *herse* 'hill-top'); *Brodeacre* 1625 (*v*. **brād**, **æcer**); *Brodegrenys* 1467 × 84 (*v*. **brād**; with **grēne**² or **grein**); *Broke* 1467 × 84, *Brook*(*e*) *furlong* 1625, 1638, c.1740, m.18 (*v*. **furlang**) (*v*. **brōc**); *Brookes*

Hadland c.1740, m.18 (*v.* **hēafod-land**; with the surn. *Brookes*, cf. *Charlotte Brookes* 1811 Census and *Joseph Brookes* 1820 ib of Blaby); *Brier Hill furlonge* 1625, *Bryere furlonge* 1638, *Bryerfurlong* 1674, c.1740, m.18 (*v.* **brēr, furlang**); *Bulhadland* 1467 × 84 (*v.* **bula, hēafod-land**; land on which a bull was kept); *the Bulhooke* 1625, *the Bullhook*(*e*) 1638, *the Bull-hooke* c.1740, m.18 (*v.* **bula, hōc**; land on which a bull was kept); *the Bull peice* c.1740, m.18 (*v.* **bula, pece**; as for the two previous f.ns.); *Butchers acre* 1625, c.1740 (*v.* **æcer**; with the surn. *Butcher*); *Catishill, Cattyshyll* 1467 × 84 (*v.* **hyll**; either with **cat(t)** or with the surn. *Catt, v.* Catthorpe *infra*); *Clement Clarkes ditch* 1674, *John Clarkes Ditch* c.1740, m.18 (*v.* **dīc**), *John Clarkes hadland* c.1740, m.18 (*v.* **hēafod-land**); *the Colledge Land* 1625, c.1740, m.18, *the College land* 1638 (*v.* **land**), *the Colledge meadow* c.1740, m.18 (*v.* **college**; *the land of Trinitie College in Caymbridge* 1638); *the comon* 1625, *the Common ground* 1638 (*v.* **commun, grund**); *John Coopers ground* 1625 (*v.* **grund**); *Crosfelde* 1467 × 84 (*v.* **feld**; most prob. with **cross**, but **cros** is poss.; an early name for the great Middle Fd, the location of *Cros*(*e*)*pitt'*, *supra*); *Cunningre close* 1627 (*v.* **coningre**); *the Deyne* 1467 × 84 (*v.* **denu**); *Estmedow, Estmedohaddis* 1467 × 84 (*v.* **hēafod**) (*v.* **ēast, mēd** (**mēdwe** obl.sg.)); *Flaxlandis* 1467 × 84, *the Flaxlands* 1625, *Flax-lands* c.1740, m.18 (*v.* **fleax, land**); *Flax leyes* 1625, 1638, *Flax-leys* c.1740, m.18 (*v.* **fleax, leys**); *Fordols, the Fordolys* 1467 × 84, *the foredoles* 1625, c.1740, *the Fordoles* m.18 (*v.* **fore, dāl**); *Fosters hadland* 1625, c.1740, *Fosters headl'* 1638, *Forster's hadland* m.18 (*v.* **hēafod-land**; with the surn. *Foster*); *Foston Thorne* c.1740, ~ ~ *furlong*(*e*) 1638, c.1740, m.18, *Fawston thorne furlonge* 1625 (*v.* **furlang**) (*v.* **þorn**; thorn-scrub towards Foston which lies 2½ miles to the south-east); *Wm. Foxons ground* 1625 (*v.* **grund**; Foxon's family originally came from Foxton, 9 miles to the south-east, the surn. showing typical Leics. 17th-cent. loss of *t* from the final group -*ston*); *Willm. Freers hadland* 1674 (*v.* **hēafod-land**); *Glencaluerley fen* 1467 × 84 (*v.* **calf** (**calfra** gen.pl.), **lēah, fenn**), *Glendame* 1467 × 84, *Glen Dam* 1638, m.18, *Glenn-Dam* c.1740 (*v.* **damme**), *Glen hedge* 1638, m.18, *Glenn hedge* c.1740 (*v.* **hecg**; a parish boundary hedge) (all alluding to Glen Parva which adjoins to the north); *Gorsehurst* 1467 × 84 (*v.* **gorst, hyrst**); *Grensty* 1467 × 84, *Greenstie way* 1638 (*v.* **grēne¹, stīg, weg, sty-way**); *Mr Halfords hadl'* 1638 (*v.* **hēafod-land**); *Heycroft* 1467 × 84 (*v.* **hēg, croft**); *Heythingwong* (×2) 1467 × 84 (*v.* **vangr**; prob. with the surn. *Heathen*, from a by-name formed from OE *hæðen* 'heathen', there being no surviving evidence hereabouts for *hæð* or *heiðr* 'heath'); *Horslandis* 1467 × 84, *Horse lands* 1638, c.1740, m.18 (*v.* **hors, land**); *Huddunsty, Hudwynsty* 1467 × 84 (*v.* **stīg, stig**; with an unrecorded OE masc. pers.n. *Hudwine* (or *Hūdwine*)); *Julianwong* 1467 × 84 (*v.* **vangr**; with the surn. *Julian, v.* Reaney *s.n.*); *the kinges highe way* 1625, *the Kings hieway* 1638, ~ ~ *highway* c.1740 (*v.* **hēah-weg**; with reference to Charles I and George II respectively); *Kyrkehadland, Kyrk*(*e*)*hadlond* (*v.* **hēafod-land**), *Kyrkland* (*v.* **land**) 1467 × 84 (*v.* **kirkja** and All Saints' Church *supra*); *Lancoldale* 1467 × 84 (*v.* **lang¹, dalr**; perh. with **kollr** 'hill'); *Langdal*(*e*), ~ *heyde* (*v.* **hēafod**) 1467 × 84 (*v.* **lang¹, dalr**); *Lese hadland* 1467 × 84 (*v.* **lǣs, hēafod-land**); *Lituldykes, Lytuldykys* 1467 × 84 (*v.* **lȳtel, dīk**); *Longams* 1625, *Longhams* ~ 1638, *Langham*(*s*) *close* c.1740, m.18 (*v.* **clos**(**e**)), *Longhams furlong*(*e*) 1638, 1674, *Langhams furlong* c.1740, m.18 (*v.* **furlang**) (*v.* **lang¹, hamm**); *Long hadland* 1638, 1674, c.1740, m.18 (*v.* **lang¹, hēafod-land**); *Lotherworth Way* 1467 × 84 (*v.* **weg**; the road to Lutterworth which lies 8½ miles to the south); *Medodyke*, (*the*) *Midodyke, Mydodyke* 1467 × 84 (*v.* **dīk**), *the mead' ditch* 1638, *the Meadow*

Ditch c.1740, m.18 (*v.* **dīc**) (*v.* **mēd** (**mēdwe** obl.sg.)); *Midulwong* 1467 × 84 (*v.* **middel, vangr**); *Middulwey, Mydulwey* 1467 × 84 (*v.* **middel, weg**); *milfurlonge* 1625, *Mill furlong* 1638, c.1740, m.18 (*v.* **myln, furlang**); *Mydohad*(*d*)*ys* 1467 × 84, *Meadow heads* 1625, *Mead' hades* 1638 (*v.* **mēd** (**mēdwe** obl.sg.), **hēafod**); *Newfurlong* 1467 × 84 (*v.* **nīwe, furlang**); *Nygunholmes* 1467 × 84 (literally 'nine water-meadows' (*v.* **nigon, holmr**) seems unlikely; this may well be a Scandinavianized **atten innome*, *v.* **atte, atten, innām**, cf. Ninehams, Sr 312); *the over furlong* c.1740, m.18 (*v.* **uferra, furlang**); *Henry Palmers ground* 1625 (*v.* **grund**); *the Parsonage Yard* 1638, c.1740 (*v.* **personage, geard**); *the Parsons hook*(*e*) 1625, 1638, c.1740, m.18 (*v.* **persone, hōc**); *the Pingle* 1627 (*v.* **pingel**); *Poole yard* 1627 (*v.* **geard**; either with the surn. *Poole* or with **pōl**[1]); *Port fyrsse* 1467 × 84, *Port-furze* c.1740, *Port-furzes* m.18 (*v.* **fyrs** and Port Hill *supra*); *Reydgreys* 1467 × 84 (*v.* **hrēod, græs, gres**); *Reynolds howse* 1625 (*v.* **hūs**; with the surn. *Reynold*(*s*) (from a masc. pers.n., OFr *Reinald*, ContGerm *Raginald*); *Rush-leys* c.1740, m.18, *Rush leyes furlong*(*e*) 1625, 1638, 1674 (*v.* **furlang**) (*v.* **risc, leys**); (*in*) *þe Ryme*, (*in*) *the Ryne*, *þe Ryn* 1467 × 84 (*v.* **þe, rūm**[1], **rúm**); *Thomas Saviles ground* 1625 (*v.* **grund**); *Scalbaro, Scalboro, ~ furlong* 1467 × 84 (*v.* **furlang**) (*v.* **skalli, berg**); *Schakulwade, Shakulwade* 1467 × 84 (*v.* **scacol, shackle, (ge)wæd** and cf. Shackleford, Sr 199; the allusion may be to a ford with a loose or shaking bottom or to an area of quaking-grass at its location); *Schortforrou* 1467 × 84 (*v.* **sc(e)ort, furh**); *the Sheep Pen* 1627 (*v.* **scēp, penn**); *þe Slade* 1467 × 84 (*v.* **þe, slæd**); *Smythlanesende* 1467 × 84 (*v.* **lane, ende, lane-ende**; prob. with the surn. *Smith*, otherwise, *v.* **smið**); *Steanes hadland* 1625, *Steynes hadland* 1625, 1638, c.1740, m.18 (*v.* **hēafod-land**; with the surn. *Steyne*, from the ON masc. pers.n. *Steinn*); *Styway* 1467 × 84 (*v.* **sty-way**); *Swannes nest* 1625, *the Swans-neast* c.1740, *the Swans nest* m.18 (*v.* **swan**[1], **nest**); *Syndrus, Syndurs* 1467 × 84 (*v.* **sinder**; in allusion to a place where cinders and slag were dumped); *Thefdayle* 1467 × 84 (*v.* **dalr**; either with **þefa** 'brushwood, bramble' or with **þeof** 'thief', and if in the latter case, cf. Thievesdale, Nt 109); *Henry Thorntons ground* 1625, *William Thorntons ground* c.1740 (*v.* **grund**); *Thorpdal*(*e*), *Thorpdall*(*e*), *Thorpdalys* 1467 × 84 (*v.* **dalr, deill**; land near the Countesthorpe parish boundary to the south); *Thorpway, Thorpwey* 1467 × 84 (*v.* **weg**; the road to Countesthorpe which lies 2 miles to the south-east); *Threos* (sic, ×2) 1467 × 84 (*v.* **þrēo**; presum. a particular group of three selions); *Henry Tilleys ground, Robert Tilleyes ground* 1625 (*v.* **grund**); *Toft'* 1467 × 84 (*v.* **toft**); *Wastrow* 1467 × 84 (*v.* **west**; with **rāw** or **rǣw**); *Welgate* 1467 × 84 (*v.* **wella, gata**); *Westonbroke* 1467 × 84 (*v.* **brōc**; flowing into Whetstone parish which adjoins to the west); *Whetston hedge* 1638, 1674 (*v.* **hecg**; the boundary hedge with Whetstone); *Wheston mere* 1467 × 84, *Whetston meare* 1638 (*v.* **(ge)mǣre**; Whetstone boundary land); *Wiggeston ditch* 1625, *Wigston Ditch* c.1740, m.18 (*v.* **dīc**; a boundary ditch with Wigston Magna parish which adjoins to the east); *Wodewey, Wodgate* 1467 × 84 (*v.* **wudu, weg, gata**; two styles for the same road).

Broughton Astley

1. BROUGHTON ASTLEY

Broctone 1086 DB, *Brocton* 1195 P (p), 1196 ChancR, 1220 MHW
  et passim to 1299 Ipm, 1303 Pat
Brohtone 1086 DB
Brotone 1086 DB, *Brotton* c.1291 Tax, 1301 Ipm
Broxtona 1190 × 1204 France
Bruchton 1205 Pap
Brochton 1322 Pat, 1428 FA, (~ *Astele* 1322 Pat)
Brouton 1240 × 46 BM, 1266 Pat, 1301 Ipm, *Broutton* 1316 FA,
  Brouhton 1308 Misc
Broghton 1286 Pat, 1296 OSut *et passim* to 1385, 1423 AD, (~
  Asteley(e) 1322 Pat *et passim* to 1385 ib, ~ *Astley* 1423 AD)
Broughton 1327 SR, 1330 FA, 1376 Cl *et freq*, (~ *Asteley(e)* 1376 ib,
  1377 ELiW *et passim* to 1492 Cl, ~ *Astley* 1535 VE, 1576 Saxton
  et freq, ~ *Ashley* 1518 Visit, 1608, 1624 LML)
Browhton 1417 *MiD*, (~ *Asteley* 1417 *ib*), *Browthton* 1459 Pap

'The farmstead or village by the brook', *v.* **brōc, tūn**. The affix ~
Astley is the family name of *Walterus de Estley* who held the manor
c.1210 RHug, followed by *Thomas de Estlee* 1220 Cur to 1266 Pat,
Andreas de Estleye 1285 FA, 1286 Pat, *Egidius de Estleye* 1316 FA to
1322 Pat, another *Thomas de Asteleye* 1327 SR to 1361 Cl and *Joanna
de Asteley* 1445 ib.

ARKWRIGHT COTTAGES, named from *Arthur William Arkwright* 1881
Census of The Hall *infra*. CLUMP HILL, 1967 *Surv*, cf. *Best ~, Far Clump*
1844 *TA*, *v.* **clump**. COLES BARN, cf. *Coles Barn Close* 1844 *TA*, with
the surn. *Cole*. COSBY RD is *Cosby Lane* 1844 *TA*, Cosby lying 2 miles
to the north-east. COTTAGE LANE, cf. *Cottage Close* 1844 *TA*, *v.* **cotage**.
FROLESWORTH RD, Frolesworth lying 2 miles to the south-west. GLEBE
FM. GLEBE RD, *v.* **glebe**. GRANGE FM, *v.* **grange**. THE HALL (2½"), *The
Hall* 1925 Kelly, *v.* **hall**. HALL FM. JUBILEE RD, named from one of the
Jubilees of Queen Victoria (Golden 1887, Diamond 1897). LEIRE LANE,

Leire lying 1½ miles to the south. LINDEN LODGE, *v.* **linden**, **loge**.
LODGE FM (BROUGHTON ASTLEY LODGE 2½"), *Broughton Lodge* 1863,
1877 White, *v.* **loge**. MANOR FM (local), *Manor farm* 1925 Kelly, *v.*
maner. THE MILL, a watermill. MILL FM, 1925 Kelly. NEW INN (lost),
New Inn 1846, 1863 White. OLD MILL RD, *v.* The Mill *supra*. OLD
RECTORY CLOSE. OLD WINDMILL (2½"), *Broughton Mill* 1835 O, 1863
White, *v.* **myln**. THE RECTORY, 1877 White, 1925 Kelly, *v.* **rectory**;
earlier recorded is *the Parsonage House* 1605, 1700 *Terrier*, *v.*
personage. SIX ACRES, *The Six Acres* 1700 *Terrier*, 1844 *TA*, *v.* **æcer**.
ST MARY'S CHURCH, *Church (St Mary)* 1846, 1863, 1877 White, 1925
Kelly; it is earlier recorded as *ecclesie de Brocton* 1220 MHW, ~ *de
Broghton Asteleye* 1322, 1324 *Pat*, *ecclesie parochialis de Broughton
Asteley* 1462 *ib* (with MLat *parochialis* 'parochial'), *The Church* 1605
Terrier; also *the Church yard* 1700 *ib*, *v.* **churchyerd**. Both Sutton in the
Elms and Primethorpe once had their own chapels, presumably
dependant on St Mary's Church, as *capellam de Sutton* 1220 MHW and
capellam de Torp 1220 ib. Note *atte Chapell* 1332 SR (p) (*v.* **atte**,
chapel(e)), but to which chapel the name refers is uncertain. STATION
FM. STATION HOTEL (lost), *Station Hotel* 1925 Kelly. STATION RD, cf.
Broughton Station 1854 O; on the former Midland Counties Railway.
STONEY BRIDGE, 1811 Nichols, *v.* **stānig**. SUTTON LODGE, 1835 O, *v.*
loge. WHITE HORSE (P.H.) 1846, 1863, 1877 White, 1925 Kelly.
WILLOWBANK.

2. SUTTON IN THE ELMS

Sutone, Svton(e) 1086 DB
Sutton 1220 MHW, 1241 Abbr *et freq*, (~ *iuxta Brocton* 1303 Pat, ~
iuxta Brouhton 1308 Misc, ~ *iuxta Broughton Asteley* 1430 *Peake*,
1445 Cl), (~ *in the Elms* 1835 O, 1932 Kelly).

'The south farmstead or village', *v.* **sūð, tūn**. The affix ~ *in the Elms*
is recent.

BAPTIST CHAPEL, the original small brick chapel being prob. that
licensed in 1700, with the added chapel building of 1815 adjacent. FOSSE
COTTAGE, FOSSE HO., both beside the Roman Fosse Way. GRANGE FM
is *The Grange* 1925 Kelly, *v.* **grange**. HIGHLAND FM. IRELAND HO.,
Ireland House 1717 LeicW, 1835 O, poss. named from William of
Orange's defeat of Jacobite forces at the Battle of the Boyne in 1690 in
Ireland and his becoming King of Ireland in 1691. But note *Irelandes*

close 1626 in neighbouring Frolesworth parish, with the surn. *Ireland*, which may pertain here. LEICESTER RD is *Leaster* ~ 1601 *Terrier*, *Lecester Way* 1605, 1625 *ib*; now the principal road through the village and leading to Fosse Way, with Leicester lying 8 miles to the north-east. LODGE FM is *Sutton Lodge* 1846, 1863, 1877 White, 1925 Kelly, *v*. **loge**. MESSENGER'S BARN, with the surn. *Messenger*, cf. *Joanne Messenger* 1846 White, a tenant farmer. QUAKER COTTAGE (local), the location of a 17th-cent. Quaker meeting-house. ROYAL HOTEL (lost), *Royal Hotel* 1925 Kelly. SOAR MILL, 1718 LML, 1807 Map, 1835 O, 1863 White, *v*. **myln**; a watermill on the river Soar. SUTTON FM. SUTTON FIELDS FM (×2). SUTTON HILL BRIDGE, ~ ~ FM. THREE BOUNDARY FM, at the junction of the parish boundaries of Broughton Astley, Cosby and Croft (Sparkenhoe Hundred). WALTON LODGE FM, *v*. **loge**; with the surn. *Walton*, cf. *Mary Walton* 1806 Census of adjacent Cosby parish and *Emily Walton* 1868 ib, *Clara Walton* 1870 ib and *Ellen Walton* 1880 ib, all of adjacent Dunton Bassett parish.

3. PRIMETHORPE

> *Torp* 1203 Cur, 1220 MHW
> *Thorp* 1260, 1272 Cur, 1285, 1330 FA, (~ *iuxta Brocton* 1285 ib),
> > *Thorpe* 1346 Pat, (~ *iuxta Browgton* 1539 MinAccts)
> *Prymesthorp* 1316 FA
> *Primethorpe* 1575, 1622 LeicW, *Prymethorp(e)* 1601, 1614 Ipm,
> > 1637 Fine

'The outlying farmstead', later associated with Prim, *v*. **þorp**. The *Torp* 1086 DB of folio 234b is usually identified with Primethorpe (as Stenton VCHL **1** 326, Morgan DB Leics. 19.3 and Ekwall DEPN 374), but Elmesthorpe may well be its preferred identification. This *Torp* was held TRE by one *Aelmer* who may be the *Æðelmǣr* (> *Æilmer*, *v*. Feilitzen 184) whose name appears compounded in Elmesthorpe in that part of the Guthlaxton Wapentake which was later incorporated in Sparkenhoe Hundred. Whether the *Prim* of the later Primethorpe is an OE masc. pers.n. (the name recorded as that of a moneyer in the reign of Eadmund (939–46) and of Edgar (959–75)) or is a ContGerm masc. pers.n. as suggested by Smart, is uncertain, *v*. Veronica Smart, 'Economic migrants? Continental moneyers' names on the tenth-century English coinage', *Nomina* 32 (2009), 121 and 150. Less likely is a feudal surn. affix *Prime* (from OFr *prim(e)* 'excellent, fine') in the style of Herringthorpe, YW **1** 185, and Perlethorpe, Nt 91.

BULL'S HEAD (P.H.) (lost), *Bull's Head* 1846, 1863, 1877 White, 1925 Kelly. GEORGE AND DRAGON (P.H.), *George and Dragon* 1846, 1863, 1877 White, 1925 Kelly. GREEN RD. MAIN ST. PLATT HO. is *Platt House farm* 1925 Kelly, *v.* **plat**^{2}. SPION KOP, a transferred name commemorating the Battle of Spion Kop in Natal in 1900 during the Boer War. WITHAM VILLA.

FIELD-NAMES

In (a), forms presented without dates are 1844 *TA*; those dated 1803 are *Deed*; 1967 are *Surv*. Forms throughout dated 13 are Misc; 1601, 1605, 1625, 1674 and 1700 are *Terrier*; 1627 and 1634 are Ipm. The Glebe Terriers for Broughton Astley of 1601, 1605 and 1625 show the ecclesiastical holdings itemized in six great open-fields which appear to relate only to Broughton and to Sutton, these two townships each having three great open-fields, as was usual in the county pre-Enclosure. There is no record of Primethorpe's having had open-fields of its own. Field-names in (b) are separately listed as far as is possible for Broughton and for Sutton, although such earlier names for these townships as relate to any closes recorded post-1750 in (a) are included and treated there. On occasion, the names of the same landholders relate to furlongs and headlands in the great fields of both townships.

(a) The Two ~, The Three Acres, Little Three Acres 1844, Four Acres 1844, 1967, Far Four Acres 1844, Five Acres 1844, 1967, Five Acre Cl 1844, Wapples Six Acres 1844 (with the surn. *Waple*, *Walpole*, cf. *Galfridus Waupol* 1271 RBL of Leicester and later, *Ann Walpole* 1821 Census of adjacent Frolesworth), Six Acres Platt 1967 (*v.* **plat**^{2}), Nine Acre, ~ ~ Mdw 1967, The Ten Acres 1844, Ten Acre 1967, (The) Twelve Acres 1844, 1967, Thirteen ~, Fifteen Acre 1967 (*v.* **æcer**); Allotment Fd 1967 (*v.* **allotment**); The Banks 1967 (*v.* **banke**); Far ~ ~, Barn Cl 1844, Barn Fd 1967, Close behind the Barn 1844 (*v.* **bern**); Big Cl; First ~ ~, Big Mdw; Big Platt 1844, 1967 (*v.* **plat**^{2}); Biggs Cl (with the surn. *Biggs*); Bilstons Cottage Cl (*v.* **cotage**; with the surn. *Bilston* of a family originally from Bilstone, 12 miles to the north-west); Blacksmith's Cl (*v.* **blacksmith**); Top ~, Blackwells (*Blackwell* 1601, cf. *Blackwell haggs* 1605, ~ *hagges* 1625 (*v.* **hogg**) (*v.* **blæc**, **wella**; in *Hongrye Fielde* of Sutton in the Elms); Boggy Mdw (*v.* **boggy**); Bottom Cl, ~ Mdw; Bottom Platt (*v.* **plat**^{2}); Brick Kiln Cl, Brickkiln Spinney (*v.* **spinney**) (*v.* **brike-kiln**); Brickyard Cl (*v.* **brike-yard**); Brobsons Cl (with the surn. *Brobson*, a form of *Brabazon*, from AFr *Brabançon* 'a native of Brabant'); Far ~ ~, Brook Cl 1844 (*the brooke* 1601, 1605, *the bruck* 1625, *the common brooke* 1625 (*v.* **commun**) (*v.* **brōc**); Brookfield Cl; Big Broughton Mdw; Browns Cl (with the surn. *Brown*); First ~ ~, Second Bull Banks 1844, Bull Banks 1967 (*v.* **bula**, **banke**; grazing for a bull); Near ~ ~ ~, Burbages Barn Cl (*v.* **bern**; with the surn. *Burbage*, cf. *John*

Burbage 1834 Census and *William Burbage* 1843 ib of adjacent Cosby, *Emma Burbage*1874 ib and *William Burbage* 1878 ib of Broughton Astley, the family originally from Burbage, 5 miles to the west); Burdetts Far Cottage Cl (*v.* **cotage**; with the surn. *Burdett*, cf. *Hugo Burdet* 1086 DB who held land in Lowesby, Rearsby and Welby in East Goscote Hundred, and *Radulfus Burdet* c.1160 Dane of Leics.; later are *William Burdett* 1800 Census of Broughton, *William Burdett* 1828 ib of Primethorpe and *Hardy Burdett* 1861 ib, also of Broughton); Buxtons Cl, ~ Mdw (with the surn. *Buxton*, cf. *John Buxton* 1816 Census and *Mary Buxton* 1864 ib, both of Broughton); Cabbage Croft (*v.* **cabache, croft**); Calves Cl (*v.* **calf**); Chandlers Mdw 1967 (with the surn. *Chandler*, cf. *William Chandler* 1831 Census, *Edward Chandler* 1834 ib of Broughton and *Lizzie Chandler* 1878 ib of Sutton); Chapel Fd 1967 (*v.* Baptist Chapel in Sutton in the Elms *supra*); Cheney Cl (with the surn. *Cheney* as in Sutton Cheney, 8 miles to the north-west, of families which may have come variously from Quesnay (Calvados, La Manche) or Quesnay-Guesnon (Calvados) or Le Quesnay (Seine-Inferieure)); Far ~ ~, Church Hadland (*v.* **hēafod-land** and St Mary's Church *supra*); Clarkes Cl (with the surn. *Clarke*, cf. *Eliza Clarke* 1863 Census of Broughton); Clover Cl (*v.* **clāfre**; grown as a fodder crop); Coles Big Cl, ~ Five Acre Cl, ~ Halfords Cl (earlier owners, cf. *William Halford* 1811 Census and *Mary Halford* 1815 ib of Broughton), Coles Long Cl (with the surn. *Cole*); Little ~, Nether Conery 1844, Conery 1967 (*the Connygray* 1601, 1605, *Connygray Fielde* 1601, ~ *Feeld* 1605, 1625 (*v.* **feld**; one of the three great open-fields of Broughton township) (*v.* **coningre**); Corner Cl (*v.* **corner**); Cosby Lane Cl (Cosby lies 2 miles to the north-east); First ~ ~, Second ~ ~, Little ~ ~, Cow Cl, Bottom ~ ~, Middle ~ ~, Top Cow Pasture (*the kow pasture* 1605, *the cow pasture* 1625, *v.* **pasture**; in Broughton); Cow Plat (*v.* **plat**²), Cows Croft (*v.* **croft**) (*v.* **cū**); Top ~ ~, Dam Mdw 1844, Dam Fds 1967 (*v.* **damme**); Double Gate Cl (*v.* **duble, geat**); Ducketts Cl, ~ Hill, ~ Hovel Cl (*v.* **hovel**), Ducketts Long Cl, ~ Mdw (with the surn. *Duckett*, cf. *Francis Duckett* 1625 of Broughton); Dysons Yard (*v.* **geard**; with the surn. *Dyson*); Bottom ~ ~, Far Cl, Far Mdw (*v.* **feor**); Feeding Cl (*v.* **feeding**); Flat Cl 1844, 1967 (*v.* **flat, flatr**); Floodgate Mdw (*v.* **flode-gate**); Bottom ~ ~ ~, Foot Road Cl (*v.* **foot-road**); Bottom ~ ~, Top ~ ~, Fosse Cl (beside the Roman Fosse Way); Garden Allotments, ~ ~ Cl (*v.* **gardin, allotment**); Gees Cl, ~ Mdw (with the surn. *Gee*, cf. *James Gee* 1830 Census of Broughton); Gravel Pit Cl (*v.* **gravel, pytt**); Hacketts Cl 1967, ~ Mdw 1844, 1967 (with the surn. *Hackett*, an AN diminutive of the ON masc. pers.n. *Haki* (ODan *Hake*)); The Hades (*v.* **hēafod**); Hall Hay Mdw (*the Haul Hey* 1601, *the hall hay* 1605, 1625 (*v.* **halh, (ge)hæg**; in Broughton); Hammonds Little Cl, ~ Top Cl (with the surn. *Hammond*, from the OFr masc. pers.n. *Hamond* (ContGerm *Hamon*)); Top ~ ~ ~, Harris Cottage Cl (*v.* **cotage**), Far ~ ~ ~, Harris Gorse Cl (*v.* **gorst**) (with the surn. *Harris*); Harrow Cl (perh. cf. *Arrow furlong* 1601, 1605, 1625 (*v.* **furlang**), *the Arrow hades* 1605, 1625 (*v.* **hēafod**) (in *Soare Fielde* of Sutton); the name *Harrow* recurs in the Leics. Hundreds so far researched, as *Harrowe* 1601, *the furlonge called harro* 1625 (Lei **2** 214), *Harrowefeld* 1412 (Lei **3** 278), *Harrow hole* 1689 (Lei **4** 115), *Harrow akers* 1638 in Bruntingthorpe f.ns. (b) *infra* and *harrow slade* 1601 in Peatling Parva f.ns. (b) *infra*; formally OE *hærg* 'a heathen temple' is a poss. source, but the many instances argue against such a presence in most cases; ME *harwe* 'a harrow' (from an OE *hearge* or *hearwe*) is recorded from a.1300, but while a modern f.n. such as Harrow Close may contain this word, in earlier compounds with *æcer, feld, furlong,*

hēafod, *hol* and *slæd*, as well as the simplex *Harrow*, it is most unlikely; it may be
that we have, rather, **hǫrgr** 'a heap of stones, a cairn' (the ON cognate of OE *hærg*)
as the base of these names); Hickleys Cl (with the surn. *Hickley*, cf. *Abraham Hickley*
1813 Census, *Samuel Hickley* 1817 ib, *Benjamin Hickley* 1825 ib and *William
Hickley* 1836 ib, all of Broughton); Higginsons Mdw (with the surn. *Higginson*, cf.
John Higginson 1842 Census of Broughton); Hill Cl; Great ~ ~, Little ~ ~, Home Cl
(cf. *the Home Close of Thomas Everard* 1674, *the Home Close* 1700), Home Close
Mdw 1844, Home Fd 1967 (*v.* **home**); Homestead Cl (*v.* **hām-stede**); Bottom ~,
Middle ~, Top Hondsway (*v.* **weg**) (cf. *Hounsplack, Hounsplak* 1605, *hounesplacke,
hounsplack* 1625, *Little Hounsplack* 1605, 1625, *Hunsplack end* 1605, *hounsplack
end* 1625 (*v.* **ende**) (*v.* **plek**) (with the surn. *Hound*; in *Soare Fielde* of Sutton); Horse
Cl 1844, 1967 (*v.* **hors**); Little ~ ~, House Cl; Hovel Cl, ~ Mdw (*v.* **hovel**); Hulses
Barn Yard and Cl (*v.* **barn-yard**; with the surn. *Hulse*); Far ~, Near Husks (*v.*
hassuc); Hussocky Cl (*v.* **hassuc**, **-ig**³); Island Pit Cl 1844, 1967 (*v.* **island**, **pytt**);
Jordans Cl, ~ Mdw (with the surn. *Jordan*, from the name of the river Jordan in
Israel; it was used as a Christian name by returning Crusaders who brought back with
them Jordan water for the baptism of their children); the L-Cl (referring to an L-
shaped enclosure); Land Hill (*v.* **land**); Big ~ ~, Little Larra Hill, Brook Larra Hill
(*v.* **brōc**) (*Larow hill* 1605, 1625 (it is uncertain whether **hōh** is appended to Leire
in these forms rather than *Larow, Larra* simply being local developments of that
township-name), Brook Larra Mdw 1844, Larra Mdw 1844, 1967, *Larow way* 1605,
1625 (*v.* **weg**), *Leire meire* 1601, *Leare meere* 1605, *Lare meere* 1625 (*v.* (**ge**)**mǣre**);
all in *Bradstone Fielde* of Broughton, Leire parish adjoining to the south); Leir Cl
(towards the Leire parish boundary); The Ley 1844, The Lea 1967 (*v.* **ley**²); The Leys
(*v.* **leys**); Lileys Cl 1844, Lyleys Fd 1967, Lileys Hill 1844, Lyleys Hill 1967 (with
the surn. *Lil(l)ey*); Bottom ~ ~, Top ~ ~, Little Cl 1844; Little Fd 1967; Near ~ ~, Top
~ ~, Little Mdw 1844; Little Platt 1967 (*v.* **plat**²); Bottom ~ ~, Top ~ ~, Long Cl
1844; The Long Fd 1967; Long Lands 1967 (*v.* **land**); Lucas Cl (with the surn.
Lucas, cf. *Daniel Lucas* 1805 Census of Broughton); Maltkiln Orchard (*v.* **malt-
kylne**, **orceard**; the compound *malt-kiln* is not recorded in OED); The Manor (*v.*
Manor Fm in Broughton *supra*); Marlpit Cl (*v.* **marle-pytt**); Marvins Cottage Cl (*v.*
cotage), Marvins Soar Mill Mdw (alluding to a watermill on the river Soar) (with the
surn. *Marvin*); First ~, Second Mdw 1844, The Meadow 1844, 1967 (*the Meadow
1605, the me(a)dowe* 1625, *v.* **mēd** (**mēdwe** obl.sg.)); Meeting House Cl, Far ~ ~ ~,
Near Meeting House Mdw (alluding to the early Quaker meeting-house in Sutton, *v.*
Quaker Cottage *supra*); Mere Cl (*le Mayre close* 1627, *v.* (**ge**)**mǣre**); Far ~ ~, First
Messengers Cl (*v.* Messenger's Barn in Sutton *supra*); Middle Cl (*The Middle Close*
1700); Middle Mdw; Moor Cl (*the Moore* 1601, 1605, 1625, cf. *the Moore dykes*
1601, 1605, *the moor dikes* 1625 (*v.* **dík**), *the moore hades* 1605, 1625 (*v.* **hēafod**)
(*v.* **mōr**¹; in *the Nether Fielde* of Sutton); Moores Cl (with the surn. *Moore*, cf.
Thomas Moore 1834 Census and *Edwin Moore* 1856 ib of adjacent Dunton Bassett);
Mowing Mdw 1967 (*v.* **mowing**); New Inn Cl, ~ ~ Mdw (*v.* New Inn in Broughton
supra); Nichols Mdw (with the surn. *Nicholl(s)*); The Nook (*v.* **nōk**); Oak Tree Cl (*v.*
āc); Odd House Cl (*v.* **odde**; a house standing alone, cf. Odd House, Ru 117); Close
below Old Barn; Far ~ ~, Little ~ ~, Middle Old Fd (*Oalde Fielde* 1601, *Oulde
Feelde, the Ould Feelde* 1625, *v.* **wald**, **feld**; one of the great open-fields of
Broughton); Old Home Cl (*v.* **ald**, **home**); Orton's Mdw 1967 (with the surn. *Orton*);
Palmers Cl (with the surn. *Palmer*, cf. *Thomas Palmer* 1817 Census and *John Palmer*

1856 ib of adjacent Dunton Bassett); Paradise 1967 (*v.* **paradis**); the Park Fd 1967 (cf. *the Parke corner* 1605, 1625, *v.* **park**, **corner**; in the *Oalde Fielde* of Broughton); Parlour (*v.* **parlur**); Paynes Fd 1967 (with the surn. *Payne*); Phillips Cottage Cl (*v.* **cotage**), Phillips Mdw (with the surn. *Phi(l)lips*, cf. *Sarah Philips* 1862 Census of Broughton); Pit Cl (*v.* **pytt**); Pleck (*v.* **plek**); The Pound 1967 (*v.* **pund**); Bottom ~ ~, Top Porters Cl (with the surn. *Porter*, cf. *Rebecca Porter* 1804 Census of nearby Claybrooke Parva); Porteys Piece (*v.* **pece**; cf. *Porty knoale* 1601, *Porty Knowle* 1605, *porty knole* 1625, *portlie knowle* (sic) 1625, *v.* **cnoll**; poss. with a reduced **port-wey**; in *Oalde Fielde* of Broughton); Poughers Cl (with the surn. *Pougher*, cf. *Abraham Pougher* 1825 Census and *Ambrose Pougher* 1862 ib of adjacent Cosby); Far ~ ~, Near Pratts Cl (with the surn. *Pratt*, common in Broughton and Primethorpe, cf. *Joseph Pratt* 1834 Census, *George Pratt* 1847 ib of Broughton and *Edward Pratt* 1843 ib, *Joseph Pratt* 1865 ib of Primethorpe); Ralphs Barn Cl (*v.* **bern**), Ralphs Cl, ~ Mdw (with the surn. *Ralph*, cf. *Mary Ralph* 1833 Census, *Sarah Ralph* 1836 ib and *John Ralph* 1862 ib of adjacent Dunton Bassett; from the ContGerm masc. pers.n. *Radulf* (AN *Radulf*, *Raulf*)); Ratley (*Ratlye* 1601, *Ratley* 1605, 1625, cf. *ratlye* ~ 1605, *ratley furlong* 1625 (*v.* **furlang**), *Ratlye haggs* 1605, *Ratley hagges* 1625 (*v.* **hǫgg**) (perh. 'red clearing', *v.* **rēad**, **lēah**, cf. Radley, Brk **2** 316, 445, but earlier forms are needed and **hrēod** might be thought more likely in such a compound; in *Hongrye Fielde* of Sutton); Reads Cl (with the surn. *Read*, cf. *Reades hadland* 1625, *v.* **hēafod-land**); Richardsons Brick Kiln Cl (*v.* **brike-kiln**; with the surn. *Richardson*); Rickyard (*v.* **reke-yard**); Round Cl (*v.* **round**); Rushy Piece (*v.* **riscig**, **pece**); Sandhill 1967 (1601, cf. *Sandhill hades* 1605, 1625 (*v.* **hēafod**), *v.* **sand**, **hyll**; in *Connygray Fielde* of Broughton); Bottom ~ ~, Top ~ ~, Far ~ ~, Near Saunts Cl (with the surn. *Saunt*, common in the 19th cent. in Burbage, 5 miles to the west, as *Jane Saunt* 1858 Census, *Martha Saunt* 1868 ib and *John Saunt* 1867 ib); Sawpit Cl (*v.* **saw-pytt**); Seed Cl (*v.* **sǣd**; used of grasses sown for one year's mowing or grazing as distinguished from permanent pasture); Sheen Mdw (prob. with the surn. *Sheen*, cf. *Albert Sheen* 1827 Census, *Elizabeth Sheen* 1837 ib and *Benjamin Sheen* 1870 ib, all of adjacent Cosby; a complimentary name with *sheen* in the sense 'clean, beautiful' (from OE **scēne**) is less likely); Shingles Mdw (with the surn. *Shingles*, from ME *shingle* 'a wooden tile'; metonymic for the occupational *shinglere* 'a roofer'; cf. *Mary Shingles* 1811 Census and *William Shingles* 1812 ib, both of Claybrooke Magna, 3 miles to the south-west); First ~ ~, Second Short Cl, Short Leys (*v.* **leys**) (*v.* **sc(e)ort**); The Sitch 1844, 1967, Sitch Cl, ~ Mdw 1844 (*the Syche* 1601, 1605, *Sich* 1625, cf. *Syche furlong* 1605 (*v.* **furlang**), *v.* **sīc**; in *Connygray Fielde* of Broughton); Skinsmore Cls 1803 (*Skinsmeare*, *Skynsmeare* 1601, *Skinsmore* 1605, 1625, *Skinmor* 1625, cf. *Skinsmore House* 1718 LeicW; 'the demon-haunted moor', *v.* **scinn**, **mere**[1], **mōr**[1]; the specific has been Scandinavianized with *sk-* for *sc-*, while the generic varies between 'wetland' (*mere*) and 'wet moorland' (*mōr*); the name occurs also as *Skinsmeere* 1605 in adjoining Frolesworth parish, the moorland in part bordering *Bradstone Fielde* of Broughton and Skinsmoor in adjoining Leire); Slade (*the Slade* 1605, 1625, *v.* **slæd**; in *the Nether Fielde* of Sutton); Slang 1967 (*v.* **slang**); Sleaths Cl, ~ Mdw (with the surn. *Sleath*, cf. *John Sleath* 1853 Census of adjacent Leire); Smiths Cl (with the surn. *Smith*, cf. *Richard Smith* 1625 of Sutton and *Will' Smith* 1625 of Broughton); Big ~ ~ ~, Far ~ ~ ~, Far Bottom ~ ~ ~, Little ~ ~ ~, Near ~ ~ ~, Soar Mill Mdw, Soar Mill Dam Mdw (*v.* **damme**) (closes at the watermill on the river Soar); Somervilles Mdw (it is uncertain whether this is with the surn. *Somerville* or whether there was confusion with Summerfield, *infra*); Sough Cl (*v.* **sōg**); Spoil Bank (from workings for the former Midland Counties Railway); Station Fd 1967 (*v.* Station Fm in Broughton *supra*); Steers Cl, ~ Mdw (either referring to land on which young bullocks were kept (*v.* **stēor**) or with the surn. *Steer(s)*); Stubble Cl (*v.* **stubbil**; land on which stubble was allowed to remain for long periods for sheep-grazing and stubble-mulching); Far ~, Top Summerfield, Big ~ ~, Little Summerfields Cl (prob. with the surn. *Summerfield*, cf. *John Summerfield* 1819 Census of Claybrooke, 3 miles to the south-west; but note Somervilles Mdw *supra*); Sutton Cl (at Sutton in the Elms); Sutton's Orchard (*v.* **orceard**; with the surn. *Sutton*, cf. *Charles Sutton* 1840 Census of adjoining Dunton Bassett and *Henry Sutton* 1838 ib of adjoining Leire); Swathes Mdw (*the Swathes* 1601, 1605, *v.* **swæð**; in Sutton); Tebbs Brobsons Cl (*v.* Brobsons Cl *supra*), Tebbs Hall Hay Mdw (*v.* Hall Hay Mdw *supra*), Far ~ ~, Near Tebbs Cl, Tebbs Homestead (*v.* **hām-stede**) (with the surn. *Tebb(s)*, cf. *Johannes Tebbe* 1316 FA of Leics.); Thorny Fd (*v.* **þornig**); The Little ~ ~, Thorpe Cl, Westons Thorpe Cl (with the surn. *Weston*) (all closes at Primethorpe); Top ~ ~, Tobins Plat (*v.* **plat**²; with the surn. *Tobin*); Far ~ ~, Middle ~ ~, Top Cl 1844, Top Fd 1967, Top Mdw, Top Plat 1844 (*v.* **plat**²) (*v.* **top**); Big ~ ~, Little ~ ~, Top Hill (*v.* **topp**); Town Hay (*the towne hay* 1601, 1605, 1625, *v.* **tūn**, **(ge)hæg**); Big Bottom ~ ~, Little Bottom ~ ~, Far ~ ~, Little ~ ~, Middle Townsend Cl 1844, Top Townsend 1967 (*v.* **tūn**, **ende**); Triangle Bit (*v.* **triangle**, **bit**); Turnip Cl, Big ~ ~, Little Turnip Hill (*v.* **turnepe**); Twiggs Barn Cl, ~ Middle Cl, ~ Top Cl (with the surn. *Twiggs*, cf. *John Twiggs* 1840 Census and *Sarah Twiggs* 1862 ib of Broughton); Walnut Cl 1967 (*v.* **walh-hnutu** (literally 'the foreign nut'); walnut-trees which were originally from the Mediterranean were grown for nuts and for timber); Westons Willows (*Weston Willows* 1605, *weston willows* 1625, *v.* **wilig**; poss. with the surn. *Weston* (cf. *Jane Weston* 1841 Census of adjacent Dunton Bassett and note Westons Thorpe Cl *supra*), but the early forms without genitival composition may indicate rather a lost 'west farmstead' (*v.* **west**, **tūn** and cf. *Sutton Willowes* in f.ns. (b) *infra*), although there is no other evidence for such; an earlier disguised **westerne** 'western' may also be thought of; in *Hongrye Fielde* of Sutton); Far ~ ~, Windmill Cl, Windmill Piece (*v.* **pece**) (cf. *Windemill hill* 1601, *the Windmill hill* 1605, 1625, *v.* **wind-mylne** and Old Windmill in Broughton *supra*); Wrights Mdw (with the surn. *Wright*, cf. *Robert Whright* 1625 of Broughton).

(b) **Broughton Astley**: *Bosse his hadland* 1605 (*v.* **hēafod-land**), *Bosse his lea* 1601 (*v.* **ley**²) (with the surn. *Bosse*, cf. *Richard Boss* 1700 MI and *William Boss* 1775 ib of Broughton); *the bradston* 1605, *Highe* ~, *the middle Bradstone*, *the Neather Bradstone* (*v.* **neoðera**) 1601, *high* ~, *the middle Bradston* 1605, *high* ~, *the middle Bradstone* 1625, *high Broadstone* 1625, *Bradstone Fielde* 1601, *the feeld called* ~ 1605, *the field called Bradstone* 1625 (*v.* **feld**; one of the great open-fields of Broughton) (*v.* **brād**, **stān**); *the brooke side* 1601, *the brook syde* 1605 (*v.* **brōc**, **sīde**); *la Brouce* 13 (*v.* **bryce**); *Broughton greene* 1605, 1625 (*v.* **grēne**²), *Broughton townes end* 1601 (*v.* **tūn**, **ende**); *Burges* ~ ~ 1605, *Burgis townes end* 1625 (*v.* **tūn**, **ende**; with the surn. *Burges*, *Burgis*, cf. *Philippus Burgis* 1199 RFL); *Butlers hadland* 1605 (*v.* **hēafod-land**; with the surn. *Butler*); *Cookes ground* 1625 (*v.* **grund**), *Cookes hadland* 1605 (*v.* **hēafod-land**), *Cookes half yardland* 1627 (*v.* **yerdland**) (with the surn. *Cooke*); *Copthorne furlong* 1605, 1625 (*v.* **copped**², **þorn**, **furlang**); *the Deacon cloase* 1605 (*v.* **deakne**, **clos(e)**); *Debdale* 1601, 1605,

Depdale 1625 (*v.* **dēop, dalr**); *Duckettes hadland* 1601, *Francis Ducketts hadland* 1605, 1625 (*v.* **hēafod-land**), *Duckettes hedge* 1601 (*v.* **hecg**)); *Dunton Meare* 1605, ~ *meere* 1625 (*v.* **(ge)mǣre**), *Dunton Way*, ~ ~ *furlong* 1601, 1605, 1625 (*v.* **furlang**) (Dunton Bassett lies 2 miles to the south-east); *Foxall way* 1605, 1625 (*v.* **fox, halh**); *the Fosse high way* 1605 (*v.* **hēah-weg**; the Roman Fosse Way); *the furrs* 1605, *the furres* 1625 (*v.* **fyrs**); *Groocock(e)s hadland* 1605, 1625 (*v.* **hēafod-land**; with the surn. *Groocock*); *Hasty(e)* 1601, *Hastie* 1605, 1625, *v.* **stīg**; the specific may be **hǣs** 'brushwood'); *the Haul* 1601, *the Haules* 1605, 1625, *the Halles* 1605, 1625 (*v.* **halh**); *the horsegrasse* 1605, *the horsgras* 1625 (*v.* **hors, græs**); *the kings highway* 1605 (*v.* **hēah-weg**; with reference to James I); *Knightly's Nether* ~, *Knightly's Upper Close* (with the surn. *Knightly*); *(the) Lammas close* 1605, 1625, *lamas cloose* 1625, *the Lammas cloase gate* 1601 (*v.* **geat**) (*v.* **lammas, clos(e)**); *Laughton Way* 1605, 1625 (Laughton lies 9 miles to the east); *Leare medowe* 1625 (Leire parish adjoins to the south); *litle hill* 1601, *Little* ~ 1605, *Littell hill* 1625, *Little hill slade* 1605, 1625 (*v.* **slæd**) (*v.* **lȳtel, hyll**); *Little Meadow* 1601, 1605, ~ *medowe* 1625; *the litle Stock, Little Stock* 1601, (*in the*) *little stock(e)* 1625 (*v.* **lȳtel, stoc**); *Lordes* ~ 1601, 1625, *Lords hadland* 1605 (*v.* **hēafod-land**; with the surn. *Lord*, which lived on in Broughton, as *John Lord* 1830 Census, *Mary Lord* 1831 ib and *Thomas Lord* 1856 ib); *Mallens hooke* 1601, 1605, *Mallows hooke* 1625 (*v.* **hōc**; with the surn. *Mallen*, from *Mal-in*, a diminutive of *Malle*, a pet-name for Mary); *Matts Close* 1700 (with the surn. *Matt*, from the diminutive *Mat(t)* of Matthew); *le Mayre half yardland* 1627 (*v.* **(ge)mǣre, yerdland**); *The Middle Close* 1700; *the Myres* 1601 (*v.* **mýrr**); *the myry gutter* 1605, *my(e)rie gutter* 1625 (*v.* **myry, goter**); *neeles hadland* 1625 (*v.* **hēafod-land**; with the surn. *Neal, Neel*, from the ON masc. pers.n. *Njáll* (from OIr *Niall*)); *The Nether Close* 1700; *Orams* ~ 1601, *Thomas Orams hadland* 1605, 1625 (*v.* **hēafod-land**; with the surn. *Oram*, from the ON masc. pers.n. *Ormr* (ODan *Orm*), an original by-name 'serpent'); *the Parsonage cloase* 1605 (*v.* **clos(e)**), *the Parsonage Pykes* 1601, *personage pykes* 1605 (*v.* **pīc**) (*v.* **personage**), *the parsons pykes* 1625 (*v.* **persone**) (*v.* **pīc**); *The Pen Close or Wards Close* 1700 (*v.* **penn** and *Wards Close, infra*); *Proctors* ~ 1605, *procters hadland* 1625 (*v.* **hēafod-land**; with the surn. *Proctor*, from ME *prok(e)tour*, a contraction of Lat *procurator* 'a manager, an agent'); *the Rushes* 1601, 1605, 1625 (*v.* **risc**); *Will' Smiths hadland* 1625 (*v.* **hēafod-land**); *the Stock* 1601, 1605, *stocke* 1625, *Stock Slade* 1605, 1625 (*v.* **slæd**) (*v.* **stoc**); *Tallys his hadland* 1605, *tallis his hadland* 1625 (*v.* **hēafod-land**; with the surn. *Tallis*); *Thion* ~ 1601, *Thyon hedge* 1605, 1625 (*v.* **þyrne, hecg**); *Thorny slade* 1601, 1605, 1625 (*v.* **þornig, slæd**); *Thurnborow* 1625, *Thurnborough bush* 1601 (*v.* **busc**) (*v.* **þyrne, berg**); *Towborrowe* 1601, *Towborough* 1605, 1625, *towborowe* 1625 (*v.* **tōh, berg**); *The Upper Close* 1700; *Wales half yardland* 1634 (*v.* **yerdland**; with the surn. *Wale*, cf. *William Wale* 1832 Census and *John Wale* 1828 ib of adjacent Cosby); *Wards Close* 1700 (with the surn. *Ward*, cf. *William Ward* 1812 Census of Broughton, *v. The Pen Close, supra*); *le Well yard* 1627 (*v.* **wella, geard**); *Mr Whright his cloase* 1601, *Mr Whrites close* 1605, *Whrites clo(o)se* 1625 (*v.* **clos(e)**), *Mr Whrites close end* 1605 (*v.* **ende**), *Mr Whrites hadland* 1605, *Whrightes hadland* 1625 (*v.* **hēafod-land**), *Mr Whrightes hedge* 1601 (*v.* **hecg**) (cf. *Robert Whrite* 1625 of Broughton); *Wightmans hadland* 1625 (*v.* **hēafod-land**), *Wightmans Middle* ~, *Wightmans Nether* ~, *Wightmans Upper Close* 1700 (with the surn. *Wightman*, cf. *Edward Wightman* 1844 Census and *Charles Wightman* 1849 ib, both of Burbage, 5 miles to the west); *Willoughby Way* 1601, 1605, 1625 (Willoughby

Waterleys lies 3 miles to the east); *Woolmans meire* 1601, ~ *meare* 1605, ~ *meere* 1625 (*v.* **(ge)mǣre**; with the surn. *Woolman*, a ME occupational surn. meaning 'a dealer in wool'); *Wythy beddes* 1601 (*v.* **wīðig, bedd**).

(b) **Sutton in the Elms**: *Armesons hadland* 1605, 1625 (with the surn. *Arm*(*i*)*son*, from the ME masc. pers.n. *Ermin*, a hypocoristic form of ContGerm pers.ns. such as *Ermenwald, Ermingard*, cf. *Thomas Armson* 1819 Census and *Fanny Armson* 1821 ib of nearby Claybrooke); *Bosses hadland* 1625 (*v. Bosse his hadland* in Broughton f.ns. (b) *supra*); *Bradfoarde, Bradforde, Broadford* 1605, *Bradfo*(*o*)*rd* 1625 (*v.* **brād, ford**); *Brisway* 1601, 1605, 1625, *Brysway* 1625 (*v.* **weg**; the specific may be the surn. *Brice, Bryce*, common in nearby Narborough in the 19th cent. (as *Amy Brice* 1817 Census and *Christopher Brice* 1820 ib); otherwise **brīosa** 'gadfly' may be thought of); *Bull meadow*(*e*) 1601, 1605, ~ *medowe* 1625, *Bull Meadow hagges* 1605, *bull medowe hagges* 1625 (*v.* **hǫgg**), *the Bull peece* 1605, 1625 (*v.* **pece**) (*v.* **bula**); *Cookes hadland* 1605 (*v.* **hēafod-land**; cf. *Cookes hadland* in Broughton f.ns. (b)); *Cosby Meare*, ~ *Meire* 1601, *Cosbie meare, Cosbye meare*, ~ *meere* 1605, *Cosbie meere* 1625 (*v.* **(ge)mǣre**; Cosby parish adjoins to the north-east); *the dale* 1601 (*v.* **dalr**); *deadhurst* 1605, 1625 (*v.* **dēad, hyrst**); *Fen hades* 1601, 1605, 1625, (*the*) *Fenne hades* 1605, 1625 (*v.* **fenn, hēafod**); *the mor fernes* (*v.* **mōr**[1]), *the nether* ~, *the upper fernes* 1605, 1625 (*v.* **fearn**); *the fosse* 1625 (the Roman Fosse Way); *Garbrod* 1605, 1625 (*v.* **garebrode, gorebrode**); *the haggs* 1605, *the hagges* 1625 (*v.* **hǫgg**); *the halles* 1605, 1625 (*v.* **halh**); *Hincly Way* 1601 (*v.* **weg**; the road to Hinckley which lies 6 miles to the west); *Hongrye Fielde* 1601, *Hungrye Feeld* 1605, (*the*) *Hungri*(*e*) *Feeld* 1625 (*v.* **hungrig, feld**; one of the three great open-fields of Sutton); *the horsegrasse* 1605, *the horse grase, Sutton horsegras*(*s*) 1605, 1625 (*v.* **hors, grǣs**); *Hulstye* 1605, 1625, *hillstie, hulste* 1625 (*v.* **hyll, stīg**); *Jefcocks hadland* 1605 (*v.* **hēafod-land**; with the surn. *Jefcock*, a *cock*-diminutive of *Jeff*, a pet-form of Geoffrey, *cock* being used of a pert boy who strutted like a cock-bird, hence used of a cocky young lad, cf. OED cock II 7); *the Kylne yard* 1627 (*v.* **cyln, geard**); *lit*(*t*)*le* ~ 1605, 1625, *littell dale* 1625 (*v.* **lȳtel, dalr**); *Long hill*; *Lord*(*e*)*s hadland* 1605, 1625 (*v. Lordes hadland* in Broughton f.ns. (b)); *the Mare, meare hades* 1605 (*v.* **hēafod**) (*v.* **(ge)mǣre**); *Myles his hadland* 1605, *miles* (*his*) *hadland* 1605, 1625 (*v.* **hēafod-land**; with the surn. *Miles*); *Myrye foarde* 1605, *myrie ford* 1625 (*v.* **myry, ford**); *myrye gutter* 1605 (*v.* **myry, goter**); *the Nether Fielde* 1601, *Nether Feeld* 1605, *the Nether feelde* 1625 (*v.* **neoðera, feld**; one of the great open-fields of Sutton); *Nether holmes* 1601, ~ *homes* 1605, 1625 (*v.* **holmr**); *Nether Way* 1601, 1605, 1625; *the New cloase* 1601, *New close* 1605, 1625, *the new close furlong* 1605, 1625 (*v.* **furlang**) (*v.* **nīwe, clos**(*e*)); *Nutons hadland* 1605 (*v.* **hēafod-land**; with the surn. *Newton*); *Orams hadland* 1605, 1625 (*v. Orams hadland* in Broughton f.ns. (b)); *the Paches* 1601, 1605, 1625, *the Patches* 1601, 1605 (*v.* **patche**); *Pedlers* ~ 1601, *Pedlars goare* 1605, *Pedlers goore* 1625 (*v.* **pedlere, gāra**); *Perkins close* 1605, *perkines cloase* 1625 (*v.* **clos**(*e*); with the surn. *Perkins*); *Rank*(*e*) *slade* 1605, 1625 (*v.* **ranke, slæd**); *Redhill* 1605, 1625, *Reedhill* 1625 (*v.* **hyll**; **rēad** or **hrēod** is poss. as the specific); *Reedye* 1601, 1605, *Reedie* 1625 (perh. 'the reedy (one)', **hrēodig** rather than **hrēod** with **ēg**, cf. *le Redy* in Aylestone f.ns. (b)); *Ridg*(*e*)*way Greene* 1605, 1625 (*v.* **grēne**[2]), *Ridgway haggs* 1605, *Ridg*(*e*)*way hagges* 1625 (*v.* **hǫgg**) (*v.* **hrycgweg**); *Rye Furlonge* 1601 (*v.* **ryge, furlang**); *Short meadow* 1605, ~ *medowe* 1625 (*v.* **sc**(*e*)**ort**); *Richard Smithes hadland* 1625 (*v.* **hēafod-land**); *Soare Fielde* 1601, ~ *feeld* 1605, 1625 (*v.* **feld**; one of the great open-fields of Sutton, beside the river Soar); *the Soare furlonge* 1601, *the Middle* ~ ~, *the Nether Soare furlong(e)* 1605, 1625 (*v.* **furlang**; all butting on the river Soar); *the Soare meadow* 1601, 1605, (*the*) *Soare medowe* 1605, 1625 (a meadow beside the river); *Sutton Ballans* 1601 (*v.* **bēan, land**), *Sutton Pasture* 1601, 1605, 1625 (*v.* **pasture**), *Sutton townes end* 1601, 1605, ~ *towne end* 1625 (*v.* **tūn, ende**); *Sutton Willowes* 1601 (*v.* **wilig**) (all with reference to Sutton township); *Thurnboro(u)gh* 1605, 1625 (*v.* **þyrne, berg**); (*in*) *Thyon* 1601, 1605, 1625 (*v.* **þyrne**); *Tookes hadland* 1625 (*v.* **hēafodland**; with the surn. *Tooke*, from the ON masc. pers.n. *Tóki* (ODan *Tōke*)); *the towne hadland* 1601, 1605, 1625 (*v.* **tūn, hēafod-land**); *Wales house* 1601 (*v.* **hūs** and *Wales half yardland* in Broughton f.ns. (b)); *Rob. Whrites* ~ 1601, 1605, *Robert Whrightes hadland* 1625 (*v.* *Mr Whrites hadland* in Broughton f.ns. (b)); *Wightman(e)s hadland* 1605, 1625 (*v.* *Wightmans hadland* in Broughton f.ns. (b)); (*in*) *Whytston* 1605, (*in*) *Whitstone* 1625 (*v.* **hwīt, stān**); *Wigston(e) hill* 1601, 1605, 1625 (with the common Leics. surn. *Wigston*, formed principally on the p.n. Wigston Magna *infra*).

Bruntingthorpe

Brandinestor (sic) 1086 DB

Brentingestorp 1199 FF, 1200 Fine, 1220 MHW *et passim* to 1243
Fees, 1247 Abbr, *Brentingstorp* e.13 *RTemple, Brentingesthorp*
1232 Fine, 1236 RGros

Brentyngthorp(e) 1299 Ipm, 1441 (e.16) *Will*, 1507 *Wyg*, 1528 *Comp*,
1559 Ipm, *Brentingthorp(e)* 1370 *MiD*, 1441 (e.16) *Will et passim*
to 1607, 1626 LML

Brantingestorp 1228 *Rut*, 1247 Abbr, 1254 Val, *Brantingestorph*
1339 *Wyg, Brantingesthorp* 1232 Fine, 1236 RGros *et passim* to
1311 Coram, 1348 *Wyg, Brantyngesthorp* 1261 Cur, 1280 Banco
et passim to 1424, 1435 *Wyg*

Brantingthorp(e) 1236, 1243 Fine *et passim* to 1318, 1335 *Wyg*, 1505
Banco, 1549 Pat *et freq* to 1601 LibCl, 1610 Speed,
Brantyngthorp(e) 1291 Tax, 1296 Banco *et freq* to 1571 LeicW,
1573 Ipm

Bruntingthorp(e) 1496 *Wyg*, 1523 AAS *et passim* to 1627 LML, 1641
Fine *et freq, Bruntyngthorp* 1502 Pat, 1535 VE, 1570 Fine,
Brountyngthorp 1519 *Wyg*

'The outlying farmstead of a man called Branting or Brenting', *v.*
þorp and cf. Brentingby, Lei **2** 132. OE masc. pers.ns. *Branting* and
Brenting are both recorded (Searle 113, 114). Forms for Bruntingthorpe
with *Brenting* tend to be earlier than those with *Branting*, with the
exception of the poor DB spelling, but the evidence here is inconclusive.

BATH LANE, leading to Bath Hotel in neighbouring Shearsby, a relic of
spa days. BRUNTINGTHORPE AIRFIELD. BRUNTINGTHORPE HALL (lost),
Brantingthorpe Hall 1613 *Deed, v.* **hall**. BRUNTINGTHORPE HOLT (2½"),
v. **wald**; the development of *wald* locally was **wald > *wold > olde >
oult > olt > holt, v. the Olt field* in f.ns. (b) and cf. Walton Holt in
Kimcote and Walton. BRUNTINGTHORPE HO., *Bruntingthorpe House*
1877 White. CHURCH WALK, *v.* **walk** and St Mary's Church *infra*.

COTTAGE FM. GRANGE FM is *The Grange* 1877 White, 1925 Kelly, *v.*
grange. HOLT FM, ~~ COTTAGE, *v.* Bruntingthorpe Holt *supra*. JOINERS'
ARMS (P.H.), *Joiners' Arms* 1846, 1863, 1877 White, 1925 Kelly. LITTLE
END, ostensibly with **ende**, but a disguised earlier **eng** is possible.
MANOR HO., *Manor House* 1925 Kelly, *v.* **maner**. MAIN ST. PLOUGH
(P.H.), *Plough* 1863 White, *Plough Inn* 1877 ib, 1925 Kelly. THE
RECTORY, 1925 Kelly, *v.* **rectory**; earlier is *the mansion house* 1601
Terrier (i.e. the principal residence of the Parsonage, *v.* **mansion-house**),
the Parsonage House e.18, c.1708 *ib*, *the parsonidge house* 1724 *ib*, *v.*
personage. ST MARY'S CHURCH, *Church (St Mary)* 1925 Kelly; earlier
is recorded *ecclesie de Brentingestorp* 1220 MHW, *ecclesiam de
Brantingesthorp* 1236 RGros, *ecclesia parochiali de Brantingthorpe*
1549 *Pat* (with MLat *parochialis* 'parochial'); note also *the Church-yard*
c.1708 *Terrier*, 1776 *EnclA*, *v.* **churchyerd**. WHITE HOUSE FM.

FIELD-NAMES

In (a), forms presented without dates are 1843 *Paget*; those dated 1776
are *EnclA*; 1807 are *Nichols*; 1895 are *MiscAccts*. Forms throughout
dated 1601, 1606, 1625, 1638, 1679, l.17, 1701, 1702, e.18, 1708,
c.1708, 1724, 1742, 1745 and 1748 are *Terrier*; those dated 1613 are
Fine; 1691 are *Deed*; 1713 are *Nichols*.

(a) Ash Dikes 1843, Ashdykes 1895 (*Ashdickes* l.17, *v.* **æsc**, **dík**); Bottom ~ ~,
Top Barn Cl (*v.* **bern**); Braceford (*v.* **ford**; the specific may be **bræsc** 'brushwood',
alluding to a causeway; cf. Bracebridge, DLPN 18; otherwise perh. with **breiðr**);
Broadway (1702, e.18, 1708, c.1708, *Brodeway* 1625, *broodeway* 1638), Broadway
Hollow (*broad way hallow* 1679, *v.* **holh**) (*v.* **brād**, **weg**); The Bundards, East ~,
West Bundards, Bundards Cl, ~ Mdw, The Bundards Mdw (*Bundards* l.17; earlier
forms are needed, but perh. 'the peasant landowner's enclosure' may be thought of,
with ON **bóndi** (ODan **bunde**) and **geard** (cf. Dan *bundegaard* 'farmyard')); Church
Headland 1807 (*Church hadeland* l.17, *v.* **hēafod-land** and St Mary's Church *supra*);
Clip Yard (*v.* **geard**; an enclosure where sheep were sheared or clipped); The Cottage
Mdw (*v.* Cottage Fm *supra*); Bottom ~ ~, Cow Cl, Cow Leys (*Cowleyes* 1638,
Cowlayes 1702, *Cowlays* e.18, 1708, c.1708, 1724, *Cowleys furlong* 1745, 1748 (*v.*
furlang), *v.* **leys**) (*v.* **cū**); Crabtree Cl (*v.* **crabtre**); Cragdale, ~ Mdw (*v.* **cragge**,
dalr; a 1625 form is recorded in adjoining Peatling Parva f.ns. (b)); Dead Lane 1776
(*v.* **dēad**; usually used in reference to a violent death or to the discovery of human
bones, but this lane may have lead to the churchyard or to a dead-end); Dick's Cl
(with the surn. *Dicks*, from *Dick*, a pet-form of Richard, cf. *Mary Dicks* 1837 Census
of adjoining Peatling Magna); Dikes Cl, ~ Mdw, Dikes Bottom ~, Dikes Top Mdw
(the surn. *Dicks* as in the previous f.n. is often found as *Dikes*, which may pertain
here; otherwise *v.* **dík**); Dole Mdw (*v.* **dāl**); Bottom ~ ~, Top ~ ~, Frankley Mdw

(perh. with the surn. *Frankley*, but there is no 19th-cent. evidence for this in Leics.; otherwise *v.* **lēah**, with the OE masc. pers.n. *Franca*, cf. Frankley, Wo 346); Gorsy Fd 1835 (*v.* **gorstig**); Great Hill Banks (*v.* **banke**); Hobill's Mdw (with the common Bruntingthorpe surn. *Hobill*, as *William Hobill* 1723 MI, *Thomas Hobill* 1763 ib, *William Hobill* 1811 Census and *Sarah Hobill* 1817 ib); Holme Cl (*v.* **holmr**); Lammas Mdw (*v.* **lammas**); Bottom ~ ~, Top ~ ~, Little Cl; The Long Sides (*v.* **sīde**); The Meadow; Bottom ~ ~, Top ~ ~, Midgley Mdw (poss. with the surn. *Midgley* (but rare in 19th-cent. Leics.); otherwise, *v.* **mycg**, **lēah** and cf. Midgley, Ch **1** 167 and YW **3** 132); Far ~ ~, Moor Fd ((*the*) *Moore Field* 1601, 1606, 1679, *Morefeild* 1724, *Moor*(*e*)*feild* 1742, *the Moor Feild* 1745, ~ ~ *Field* 1748, *the Midle Feild called Strete and More Feild* 1625 (*v.* **middel**), *the Moore Feild and Streete Feild* 1638, *Morefield and Street field* 1702, *Moore field and Street field* e.18, *the Moorfild and Street fild* 1708, *Moorfield and Streetfield* c.1708, *Streetfield* 1713, *v.* **mōr**[1], **strēt**, **feld**; one of the three great open-fields of the township, its alternative name with 'street' alluding to the ancient trackway running south-west here via Kibworth Harcourt, Saddington and Shearsby (and not with its main route via Mowsley as postulated in Lei **4** xi), known to the Anglo-Saxons as *le Ferdgate* 'the army road'); The Oak Yard (*v.* **āc**, **geard**; described as pasture); The Orchard (*v.* **orceard**); Parsons Piece (*the Parsons piece* 1702, e.18, ~ ~ *peece* 1745, ~ ~ *peice* 1748 (*v.* **persone**); also called *the Parsonage peece* 1601, 1606, 1625, 1638, ~ ~ *piece* 1702, e.18, 1708, c.1708 (*v.* **personage**), *v.* **pece**); Second ~ ~, Peas Land (*Pease landes* 1679, *Peaselands* l.17, *Peaslands* 1745, 1748, *v.* **pise**, **land**); Pedlar's Well Cl (*v.* **pedlere**, **wella**); the Quitall 1776 (*Kitehill* 1601, 1625, e.18, 1708, c.1708, *Kytehill* 1606, 1638, *Kitehil* 1702, *Kitehill or Tything piece* 1708, *Kiteall or Titheall peice* 1724, *Keytall or Tythall peice* 1745, 1748 (*v.* **tēoðung**, **pece**), cf. *Kitehil*(*l*) *doles* 1702, e.18, 1708, c.1708 (*v.* **dāl**), *Kitehill guttor* 1702, ~ *gutor* 1708, ~ *gutter* e.18 (*v.* **goter**), *v.* **cȳta**, **hyll**); Bottom ~, Top Riggs (cf. *Short Riggs* l.17, *v.* **hryggr**); Rye Hill (l.17, *v.* **ryge**, **hyll**); The Smee (sic) (prob. with **smēðe**[1]); Spinney Cl (*v.* **spinney**); Springwell Cl (*Springwell* 1606, *Springswelles* (sic) 1638, *Springwells* l.17, 1701, 1702, 1708, c.1708, cf. *Springwell Lees* 1625 (*v.* **leys**), *v.* **spring**[1], **wella**); Stone Hill (*Stanhill* l.17, cf. *Stonhill* ~ 1638, *Stonehill slade* 1679, 1702, e.18, 1708, c.1708 (*v.* **slæd**), *v.* **stān**, **hyll**); Three-Corner Cl (*v.* **three-corner**); Top Cl, ~ Fd, Top Field Mdw; Ward's Cl, ~ Top Cl, ~ Bottom Mdw (with the surn. *Ward*, cf. *Elizabeth Ward* 1810 Census of adjoining Peatling Parva and *Joseph Ward* 1820 ib, *William Ward* 1831 ib of neighbouring Kimcote).

(b) *Armesby way* 1702, e.18, *Armsby way* 1708, c.1708 (the road to Arnesby which lies 2 miles to the north-east); *Bastard Lees* 1606 (*v.* **bastard**, **leys**); *Brantingtyhorpe Hall place* 1613 (*v.* **place** and Bruntingthorpe Hall *supra*); *Great* ~, *Little Brograss* l.17 ('the slope grass', *v.* **bro**, **græs**); *Carbrook* l.17 (*v.* **kjarr**, **brōc**); *Carre field* 1601, 1606, *the Carfielde* 1638, *Carr Field* 1679, l.17, *Carfield* e.18, 1702, 1708, *Carefield* c.1708 (*v.* **kjarr**, **feld**; one of the great open-fields, also called *Carbrookfield* 1713 (*v.* Carbrook, *supra*), *the Neather feild* 1625, 1724 (*v.* **neoðera**) and *the Lower field* 1742, 1745, 1748); *Cawdwell Close* 1691 (*v.* **cald**, **wella**); *the Common* 1742, 1745, 1748 (*v.* **commun**); *Constable baulk* 1679, ~ *balk* 1702, *Constables balk* e.18, c.1708, *cunstables balke* 1708 (*v.* **conestable**, **balca**); *dead mans piece* 1748 (*v.* **dede-man**, **pece**); *Dryland* 1606, 1625, 1702, *Drylands* 1625, 1638, e.18, 1745, 1748, *drilonds* 1724, *Drylands forelands* 1708, ~ *fourlands* c.1708 (prob. with **furlang** rather than **fore** + **land**), *v.* **drȳge**, **land**); *Fellings* l.17

(either **felging** or **felling**); *Freewells* l.17 (*v.* **frēo**, **wella**); *the Glebe* 1745, 1748 (*v.* **glebe**); *the green swerd* 1745 (*v.* **greeneswarth**); *Hall baulk* l.17 (*v.* **balca** and Bruntingthorpe Hall *supra*); *Harrow akers* 1638, 1708, *Harrow acres* e.18, c.1708 (*v.* **æcer** and Harrow Cl in Broughton Astley f.ns. (a)); *the Homestall* 1702, e.18 (*v.* **hām-stall**); *Hole dale* l.17 (*v.* **hol**[2], **deill**); *Little Cliffe* 1638, c.1708, *Litle Cliffe* 1702, e.18, *littel cleft* (sic) 1708 (*v.* **lȳtel**, **clif**); (*on*) *Longdale* l.17 (*v.* **lang**[1], **deill**); *Marlepitt* l.17 (*v.* **marle-pytt**); *Milne hill* l.17 (*v.* **myln**; a windmill site); (*the*) *Moore furlong*(*e*) 1601, 1625, 1638, 1679, e.18, *More furlonge* 1606, 1702, *Moreforlong* 1724, *Moor furlong* 1708, c.1708, 1745, 1748 (*v.* **furlang**), *Morehaden* 1702, *Moor*(*e*) *haden* e.18, 1708, c.1708 (*v.* **hēafod**; note the survival of the -*en* plural), *moorehaden common* 1708 (*v.* **commun**) (*v.* **mōr**[1]); *the Neatheards Baulk* 1742, 1745, *the neatherds balk* 1748 (*v.* **neetherd**, **balca**); *the Olt field* 1601, 1702, e.18, 1708, c.1708, *the Upper Feild called the Olte Feild* 1625, *the Olde Feilde* 1638, (*the*) *Oult Field* 1679, l.17, 1713, *the Olt field alias the upper field* 1742, *the holt feild* 1745, 1748 (*v.* **wald**, **feld**; one of the great open-fields, also called *Este Field* 1606 (*v.* **ēast**) and *the Overfeild* 1724 (*v.* **uferra**)); *Parsonage lays* c.1708 (*v.* **personage**, **leys**); *the Parsons hadland* l.17 (*v.* **persone**, **hēafod-land**); *Peatling meer* e.18, ~ *mear* 1708, *Great Peatling meer* c.1708 (*v.* (**ge**)**mǣre**; Peatling Magna parish adjoins to the north); *Pillit land* 1601, 1606, 1625, 1679, l.17, *Pyllitland* 1638, *Pillet land* e.18, *pilot land* 1708, *Pillett land furlong* 1742, 1745, 1748 (*v.* **furlang**) (*v.* **pil-āte**, **land**); *Shaltwells* l.17 (*v.* **wella**; perh. with **sc**(**e**)**ald** 'shallow', but an intrusive *h* may conceal **salt**[2] 'salty, brackish'); *Shearesby way* 1702, e.18, *Chearesby way* (sic) 1708 (the road to Shearsby which lies one mile to the north-east); *Short buttes* 1638 (*v.* **sc**(**e**)**ort**, **butte**); *Sprinkley* l.17 (perh. an altered form of *Stinkley* which is recorded more frequently in adjoining Peatling Parva parish; if not, then *v.* **spring**[1], **ley**[2]); *Stamford way*(*e*) 1601, 1606, 1702, 1708, c.1708, *Stamford Road* 1742, 1745, 1748 (the road to the important town of Stamford in Lincs., 29 miles to the north-east); *Tailors way* e.18, 1708, c.1708, *Taylers way furlong* 1679, *Taylor's way furlong* 1745, 1748 (*v.* **furlang**), *Taylors way meer* c.1708 (*v.* (**ge**)**mǣre**) (with the surn. *Taylor*, cf. *Edith Taylor* 1870 Census of Bruntingthorpe); *the Thick* l.17 (*v.* **þicce**[1]); *Tongue doles* 1702, e.18, c.1708, *tong doles* 1708 (*v.* **tunge**, **dāl**); *the Town Side* l.17 (*v.* **tūn**, **sīde**); *the Wash Pit* l.17 (*v.* **wæsce**, **pytt**).

Catthorpe

Torp 1086 DB, 1209 × 35 RHug, 1243 Cur, 1243 Fees
Thorp(e) 1243 Cur, 1269, 1279 RGrav *et passim* to 1343 *LCh*, 1352
   AD, (~ *iuxta Lilleburne(e)* 1269 RGrav, 1284 Cl *et passim* to 1360
   Ipm)
Kattorpt 12 AD
Torpkat 1276 RH
Thorp le Cat 1232 Fine, n.d. (1477) *Charyte*
Thorpcat 1285 FA, *Thorpe Cat* 1410 Pat
Catthorp(e) 1218 ClR, 1232 Cl, 1242 Cur *et freq* to 1343 *LCh et*
   passim to 1497 *Braye*, 1517 EpCB, 1576 Saxton *et freq*, (~ *iuxta*
   Lilleburn 1343 *LCh*)
Cattesthorp(e) 1289, 1311, 1328, 1397 Banco, (~ *iuxta Lilleburn*
   1311 ib), *Catesthorp* 1311, 1330 ib
Cathorp 1381, 1391 Pat, 1417 AD, 1477 Pap, 1627 LML
Catethorpe alias Thorp Thomas 1574 LEpis, *Cathorpe alias Thorpe*
   Thomas 1635 LeicW
Thorpthomas 1344 Tax, 1377 CPT, *Thorpthomes* 1510 Visit
Thorp(e) Thomas 1518 Visit, 1535 VE *et passim* to 1601, 1603
   LibCl, 1637 LeicW

'The outlying farmstead', *v.* **þorp**. The vill is later distinguished by
the manorial affix (*le*) *Cat*. In Charyte's Rental, it is recorded that
Leicester Abbey held a virgate of land in Catthorpe *ex dono Simonis*
Mallore de Thorp le Cat et assensu Ysabelle uxoris sue. In the same
register, the lady is called *Ysabelle Chat de Thorp* and *Ysabelle le Chat*.
The township is recorded with the affix ~ *Thomas* in 1344 and 1377.
Apart from these 14th-cent. instances, other spellings with *Thomas* are
found only in late ecclesiastical sources which suggests clerical copying
from earlier Church records. The affix presumably refers to that Thomas,
son of Edmund, Earl of Lancaster, who held Catthorpe from 1295 to
1321. The dedication of Catthorpe's medieval parish church of St
Thomas may have reinforced the late ecclesiastical usage. Catthorpe lies

one mile north-west of Lilbourne in Northants., hence ~ *iuxta Lilleburn(e)* in several forms.

DOW BRIDGE

Duuebrigge c.1150 *Pipewell, Douuebrugge* 1293 *Ass, pons de Douuebrigge in Watlingstrete* 1330 *ib* (with MLat *pons* 'a bridge'), *Doebrege* 1477 (e.16) *Charyte, Dowbridge* 1590 Camden, 1656 Dugd, *Dove Bridge* 1656 ib, 1831 Curtis, c.1840 *TA, Dowbridge or Dovebridge* 1846, 1863, 1877 White; a bridge carrying Watling Street across the river Avon. Either 'bridge frequented by doves', *v.* **dūfe, brycg**; or, more likely, with a 12th-cent. pers.n. *Duva* as the specific (from an OE fem. pers.n. **Dūfe*), as *Duua* Hy 2 Dane (cf. *Robertus filius Duue* 1166 P (Yorks.)), *Doue* 1195 ib (Notts.) or as a surn., cf. *Radulfus Duue* 1197 ib (Norfolk). The precursor of Dow Bridge was the most southerly of three closely consecutive bridges which may have given the important Romano-British settlement of *Tripontium* ('(the place of) three bridges') on Watling Street its name, *v.* Bransford Bridge in Cotesbach *infra*. For *Tripontium, v.* A. L. F. Rivet and Colin Smith, *The Place-Names of Roman Britain* (1979), 476.

BLUE BELL (P.H.) (lost), *Blue Bell* 1846, 1863 White. CATTHORPE HALL, 1846, 1863 White, *The Hall* 1925 Kelly, *v.* **hall**. CATTHORPE TOWERS, 1863 White, 1925 Kelly. CHERRY TREE (P.H.), *Cherry Tree* 1846, 1863 White, 1925 Kelly, *Cherry Tree Inn* 1877 White. MODEL FM, a 'Model Farm' being a 19th-cent. experimental farm, organized according to certain principles, rather than a traditional farm. THE RECTORY, 1877 White, 1925 Kelly, *v.* **rectory**; earlier is *the Parsonage House* 1606, 1625, 1700, 1703, 1708, 1724 *Terrier, v.* **personage**. ST THOMAS'S CHURCH, *Church (St Thomas)* 1846, 1863, 1877 White, 1925 Kelly; earlier it is recorded as *ecclesie de Torp* 1220 MHW, ~ *de Catthorp* 1300 *Pat*. Note also *the Church Yard* 1690, 1700, 1703, 1708 *Terrier, v.* **churchyerd**. TOMLEY HALL, 1877 White, *Thomley Hall* 1846, 1863 ib (*v.* **hall**), *tomlowe* 1343 *LCh, Tomley* 1606, 1625 *Terrier*; the generic was originally **hlāw** 'a hill, a burial mound', while the specific may be **þūma** 'a thumb' used in a transferred sense such as 'a dwarf, a hobgoblin' (cf. Tom Thumb), hence 'the dwarf's or hobgoblin's mound', perh. a p.n. recording an early local superstition. Prof. R. Coates suggests as an alternative specific the OE adj. **tōm** 'empty, void of contents'.

FIELD-NAMES

In (a), forms presented without dates are 1846 *TA*; those dated 1821 are *Terrier*. Forms throughout dated 1218 are ClR; those dated 1343 are *LCh*; 1477 (e.16) are *Charyte*; 1606, 1625, 1674, 1679, 1690, 1700, 1703, 1708 and 1724 are *Terrier*; 1694 and 1695 are Deed.

(a) Back Cl, ~ ~ and Spinny (*v.* **back, spinney**); The Bank 1821, 1846 (*v.* **banke**); Barn Cl, ~ Ground (*v.* **bern, grund**); Bottom Cl; Brook Mdw (*v.* **brōc**); Browns Cl (*Brownes Close* 1695), Browns Mdw (with the surn. *Brown*); Copthorn (*v.* **copped**[2], **þorn**); Crabtree Mdw (*v.* **crabtre**); Dairy Ground (*v.* **deierie, grund**); Dove Bridge Ground (*v.* **grund** and Dow Bridge *supra*); Dowses Cl (with the surn. *Dowse*, from ME *dowce* 'sweet, pleasant', used freq. as a fem. pers.n.); First ~ ~, Second Five Acres (*v.* **æcer**); Flavells Cl (with the surn. *Flavell*); Garden Cl (*v.* **gardin**); First ~ ~, Second Gents Slade (*v.* **slæd**; with the surn. *Gent*, from ME *gente* 'well-born, courteous'); Great Cl, Great Mdw (*the Great Meadow* 1694) (*v.* **grēat**); Hall Cl (*v.* Catthorpe Hall *supra*); Hill Ground (*v.* **hyll, grund**); Honey Pot (*v.* **hunig, pot(t)**; a common f.n. style, alluding to places where honey was found or produced, or to 'sweet land', but sometimes also used of sites with sticky soil); House Cl; Hutchins Cl (with the surn. *Hutchin(s)*; from the OFr masc. pers.n. *Huchon*, a diminutive of *Hue* (Hugh)); Kimbles Homestead (*v.* **hām-stede**; with the surn. *Kimble*); Lammas Cl 1821, 1846 ((*the*) *Lammas Close* 1700, 1703, *Josephe Smithes lammas closse* 1606, *v.* **lammas**); Langhams Ground (*v.* **grund**) (*Lanckham* 1606, 1625, *v.* **lang**[1], **hamm**); The Leys (*v.* **leys**); Lilburne ~ 1821, Lilbourn Mdw 1846 (land adjoining Lilbourne parish which lies to the south-east in Northants.); Little Mdw; Long Mdw; Bottom ~ ~, Top Love Park (cf. *Luffemilne* 1477 (e.16) (*v.* **myln**), *loofepath* 1606, *aboue Louepathe, under louepath* 1625 (*v.* **pæð**); originally either with the OE masc. pers.n. *Luffa* (as in Luffenham, Ru 256) or with its surn. issue *Luff*, here later confused with *Love* and with *path* replaced late by *park*); First ~ ~, Second Middle Cl; Middle Ground 1821 ((*the*) *Middle Ground* 1690, 1703, *v.* **middel, grund**); Far ~ ~, Near Mill Fd (*the Myll fielde* 1606, *the Myllfield* 1625, *Mill Field* 1694, *v.* **myln, feld**; one of the great open-fields of the township); Moor Pit Cl (*v.* **mōr**[1], **pytt**); The Pastures (*v.* **pasture**); Pen Cl (*v.* **penn**[2]); Penfold Cl (*v.* **pynd-fald**); Rackley, ~ Mdw (*Rackley* 1606, 1625, *v.* **racu, lēah**; alluding to land beside a long reach of the river Avon); Round Mdw (*v.* **round**); Rye Cl (*v.* **ryge**); The Slade 1821, 1846 (1690, *Slade* 1703, *v.* **slæd**); Small Spinny 1821 (*v.* **spinney**); Smiths Mdw (*Smith meadowe* 1606, *Smythmeaddoe* 1625; poss. with **smēðe**[1], but the surn. *Smith* is poss., note *Joseph Smith* 1606 of Catthorpe); Betty Smith's Mdw; Spring Cl (*v.* **spring**[1]); Little Tomley (cf. *Longetomlowe* 1343, *Long Tomley* 1606, 1625 (*v.* **lang**[1]), *hie Tomley* 1606 (*v.* **hēah**[1]), *Over Tomley* 1625 (*v.* **uferra**), *nether Tomley* 1606, *Tomley Field(e)* 1606, 1625 (*v.* **feld**; one of the great open-fields), *v.* Tomley Hall *supra*); Top Cl 1821, 1846; Vanns Cl 1821, 1846 (with the surn. *Vann*, from a form of OE *fenn* 'a marsh'); Walls Homestead (*v.* **hām-stede**; prob. with the surn. *Wall*, but *v. Wallslade* in f.ns. (b)); Winter Gutter (*v.* **winter**[1], **goter**; a watercourse which flowed only in the winter months).

(b) *the Acre* 1703 (*v.* **æcer**); *Barlyhull* 1343 (*v.* **bærlic, hyll**); *Biggin Field* 1625 (*v.* **bigging, feld**; one of the great open-fields, earlier called *the Streete Fielde, infra*, with reference to Watling Street, the parish adjoining to the west being Newton and

Biggin in Warwks., *v.* Wa 117); (*the*) *Brooke furlong* 1606, 1625 (*v.* **brōc, furlang**); *the bull close* 1606 (*v.* **bula**); *but leyes* 1606, *Butleyes* 1625 (*v.* **leys**; with either **butte** or **butt**²); *castro de Catthorp* 1218 (with MLat *castrum* 'a castle'; it is uncertain whether this refers to the motte and bailey castle at SP 561775 just across the river Avon in Lilbourne parish, since no defensive earthworks are evident in Catthorpe); *the Church Headland* 1690, *the upper and neather Church Headland* 1703 (*v.* **hēafod-land** and St Thomas's Church *supra*); *the Cottagers close* 1674 (*v.* **cotager**); *the Cowe pasture* 1606, 1625 (*v.* **cū, pasture**); *the Crofts* 1625 (*v.* **croft**); *Derneslade* 1343, *dearneslade* 1606, 1625 (*v.* **derne, slæd**); *fullwell* 1606, *Fulwell* 1625 (*v.* **fūl, wella**); *gilden furlong* 1625 (*v.* **gylden, furlang**); *gilden roodes* 1606 (*v.* **gylden, rōd**³); *Gostill* 1606, 1625 (*v.* **gorst, hyll**); *the Harpe* 1606 (*v.* **hearpe**; a piece of land resembling a harp in shape); *the Haywardes peece* 1606 (*v.* **heiward, pece**); *hollme waye* 1606 (the road to Holme in Newton and Biggin parish, Warwks., *v.* Wa 18); *le Hurst* 1343 (*v.* **hyrst**); *Thomas Killpackes headland* 1606 (*v.* **hēafod-land**); *the kinges highe way* 1606 (*v.* **hēah-weg**; with reference to James I); *the Laming close* 1690 (*v.* **lambing**); *Langlond* 1343, 1606, *Langland* 1625 (*v.* **lang**¹, **land**); *Lilborne Waye* 1625, *Lilbourne Road* 1695 (the road to Lilbourne, one mile to the south-east); *the meadowe* 1606, *le medewefurlong* 1343, (*the*) *meadowe furlong* 1606, 1625, *le smalemedewefurlong* 1343, *Smallmeadowe furlong* 1606 (*v.* **smæl**) (*v.* **mēd** (**mēdwe** obl.sg.), **furlang**); *Long ~ ~, Short ~ ~* 1606, *Meere furlong* 1606, 1625 (*v.* **(ge)mǣre**); *the mill* 1606, *le milnefurlong* 1343 (*v.* **furlang**), *the Mill holmes* 1606 (*v.* **holmr**) (*v.* **myln** and Mill Fd *supra*); *le morfurlong* 1343, *the More ~* 1606, *Moore furlong* 1625 (*v.* **mōr**¹, **furlang**); *the parsonage hedge furlong* 1625 (*v.* **hecg**), *the parsonage homestall* 1606 (*v.* **hām-stall**), *the parsonage yards end* 1625 (*v.* **geard, ende**) (*v.* **personage** and The Rectory *supra*); *Parsons Meadow* 1694, 1695 (*v.* **persone**); *Pesefurlong* 1343 (*v.* **pise, furlang**); *Pikefurres* 1625 (*v.* **pīc, fyrs**); *long ~, Riehill* 1606, *Long Ryhill* 1625, *under Rie hill* 1625 (*v.* **under**) (*v.* **ryge, hyll**); *the River Side* 1679 (*v.* **sīde**; with reference to the river Avon); *the Streete Fielde* 1606 (*v.* **strēt, feld**; one of the great open-fields, adjoining Watling Street and later called *Biggin Field*, *supra*); *Swinford Meere* 1625 (*v.* **(ge)mǣre**; (land at) the parish boundary with Swinford which lies to the north-east); *Thorowe acres* 1606, 1625 (*v.* **furh, æcer**); *Thorp medow* 1625 (*v.* **þorp**; with reference to Catthorpe); *Thurspitt dike* 1625 (*v.* **dík**), *Thurspitt slade* 1606 (*v.* **slæd**), *Thursputwelle* 1343 (*v.* **wella**) (*v.* **þyrs, pytt**; a name indicative of early popular superstition, cf. Tomley *supra*); *the tithe peece* 1606 (*v.* **tēoða, pece**); *the Towne furlong* 1625 (*v.* **furlang**), *the towne headland* 1606 (*v.* **hēafod-land**) (*v.* **tūn**); *Underthorpe* 1708, 1724 (*v.* **under, þorp**; a meadow so called, with reference to Catthorpe); *Wallslade* 1606, 1625, 1700, *Walslade* 1625 (*v.* **slæd** and cf. Walls Homestead in f.ns. (a); it is just poss. that rather than the surn. *Wall* for which there is no surviving evidence in the parish, the specific of these names is **wall**, perh. alluding to foundations of outlying buildings related to the former the Roman settlement of *Tripontium* nearby on Watling Street); *Waterie ~* 1606, *Watery furlong* 1625 (*v.* **wæterig, furlang**); *le Wold'* 1343 (*v.* **wald**); *Wolueswong* 1343 (*v.* **vangr**; with the OE masc. pers.n. *Wulf*, cf. *Wolleswong* in Bitteswell f.ns. (b)).

Claybrooke Magna

clæg broc, (*to*) *clæg broce* 962 (13) BCS 1096 (S 833)
Claibroc 1086 DB, a.1186, l.Hy 2 Dane *et freq* to 1205, 1210 P,
  Claibrok(*e*) 1220 MHW, 1316 FA
Claebroc c.1200 Dane
Cleibroc e.Hy 2 Dane, 1199 FF (p), 1200 Cur, 1224 RHug, *Cleibroke*
  1335 Ipm
Cleybroc 1212 RBE (p), 1224 RHug, *Cleybrok*(*e*) 1265 Abbr, 1267
  Cur *et passim* to 1515 *Deed*, 1548 Pat, 1571 LEpis
Claybroc 1259 GildR, 1261 RGrav, 1274 Ipm, 1282 *LCDeeds* (p),
  Claybrock 1261 RGrav, 1307 *Wyg*, 1414 *LCDeeeds*, *Claybroke*(*e*)
  1267, 1268 Cur *et freq* to 1494 Banco, 1495 Ipm *et passim* to
  1541 ib, 1576 Saxton, 1725 LML, *Claybrouk* 1384 *Wyg*,
  Claybrook(*e*) 1396, 1397 Cl, 1428 *Peake et passim* to 1535 VE *et*
  freq
Clebrooke 1528 LWills, 1549 Pat, *Clebrowke* 1528 LWills,
  Clebrocke 1576 LibCl

Affixes are added as:
Magna ~ 1261 RGrav, 1285, 1316 FA
~ *Magna* 1428 FA
Nether ~ 1397 Ipm, 1399 Cl, 1414 *LCDeeds*, 1515 AD, 1701, 1725
  LML, *Neither* ~ 1702 ib
Lower ~ 1784 *Terrier*, 1807 Nichols

'The stream with the clayey bed', *v.* **clæg**, **brōc**. The settlement was later afforded the affixes MLat *magna* 'great', and *nether* and *lower* to distinguish it from adjoining Claybrooke Parva which stands on higher ground.

For Claybrooke (both ~ Magna and ~ Parva) within a Romano-British *territorium* and early Anglo-Saxon estate context, *v.* C. Phythian-Adams, *Continuity, Fields and Fission: the Making of a Midland Parish*, Leicester University Department of English Local History, Occasional Papers (Third Series 4), 1978.

BELL ST, the site of the former Blue Bell hostelry. BLUE BELL (P.H.) (lost), *Blue Bell* 1846, 1863, 1877 White, *Blue Bell Inn* 1925 Kelly. BULL'S HEAD (P.H.), *Bull's Head* 1846, 1863, 1877 White, 1925 Kelly. CLAYBROOKE LODGE FM, *Claybrook Lodge* 1877 White, 1925 Kelly, *v.* **loge**. CLAYBROOKE MAGNA MILL, *Claybrook Mill* 1835 O, *v.* **myln**. THE COTTAGE. FROLESWORTH LANE, Frolesworth lying 1½ miles to the north-east. GABLES FM. THE GRANGE is *High Cross Grange* 1877 White, 1925 Kelly, *v.* **grange**; beside High Cross *infra.* THE HALL, *Claybrook Hall* 1807 Nichols, *v.* **hall**. HIGH CROSS, 1656 Dugd, 1846, 1863, 1877 White, *Hie Crosse* 1561 *Rental*, 1625 *Terrier*, *High Crosse* 1638, 1674 *ib*, *v.* **hēah**[1], **cros**; presum. once the location of a medieval wayside cross raised at the junction of the great Roman roads Watling Street and Fosse Way at the site of the small Romano-British settlement of *Venonis*, where in 1712 a fine monument (since lost) was erected by Samuel Dunckley, *v.* Nichols **4** 1 126a. MANOR COTTAGE. MANOR FM, 1925 Kelly, *v.* **maner**. MOUNT PLEASANT, usually a complimentary name for a location, but occasionally bestowed ironically. ROYAL OAK (P.H.) (lost), *Royal Oak* 1877 White. VICTORIA FM, named from Queen Victoria (1837–1901).

FIELD-NAMES

In (a), forms presented without dates are 1839 *Map*; those dated 1762 and 1821 are *Terrier*; 1786 are *Surv*; 1807 are Nichols; 1832 and 1840 are *Deed*. Forms throughout dated 1577 are Cl; those dated 1625, 1638, 1674 and 1708 are *Terrier*.

(a) The Bank (*v.* **banke**); Barn Cl 1786, First ~ ~, Second ~ ~, Barn Cl 1839 (*v.* **bern**); Bassets Cl, ~ Mdw (with the surn. *Bassett*, cf. *Richard Bassett* 1694 Deed, *Thomas Bassett* 1814 Census, *Joseph Bassett* 1815 ib, *Mary Bassett* 1820 ib, all of Claybrooke Magna); Beamishes Cl, ~ Mdw (with the surn. *Beamish*, introduced by Normans originally from Beaumais-sur-Dive in Calvados); Big Mdw; Black Roods (*v.* **blæc**, **rōd**[3]; alluding to the colour of the soil); Blockley's Bogg (*v.* **bog**), ~ Farm, ~ Second Cl (cf. *Jonathan Blockley* 1681 *Deed*, *John Blockley* 1754 MI and *William Blockley* 1839 *Map*); Boarded Cl (a close provided in some sort with boards or planks, presum. as a form of fencing); Boggy Mdw (*v.* **boggy**); Bottom Garden (*v.* **gardin**); Bottom Hill (*v.* **botm**); Bottom Mdw (*v.* **bottom**); Brick-Kiln Cl (*v.* **brike-kiln**); Bridleway Cl (*v.* **brigdels**); Far ~, Near Brinks, Corner Brinks (*v.* **corner**) (*v.* **brink**); Bryan's Cl (with the surn. *Bryan*, a Breton name introduced by the Normans and found in ON as *Brján*); Budmore, ~ Mdw 1786, Buddmore, East and West Budmore Mdws 1839 (*v.* **mōr**[1]; prob. with the OE masc. pers.n. *Budda*; otherwise, with **budda** 'a beetle'); Burrows Farm (with the surn. *Burrows*, cf. *Hannah Burrows* 1839 *Map*); Carters Farm (with the surn. *Carter*); Church Lea (*v.* **ley**[2] and St Peter's

Church in Claybrooke Parva); Close Hedge (*v.* **clos(e)**, **hecg**); Far ~ ~, Middle ~ ~, Top ~ ~, Clover Cl (*v.* **clāfre**); Cow Cl; Great ~ ~, Large ~ ~, Small Cow Pasture (*v.* **cū**, **pasture**); Dairy Cl (*v.* **deierie**); Great ~ ~, Little Dole Mdw (*v.* **dāl**); Ell Hole (sic) (a disparaging name for infertile or otherwise unattractive land, a form of 'Hell Hole', altered by Victorian squeamishness about 'strong' language); Fawkes Mill (*v.* **myln**; with the surn. *Fawkes*, from OFr *Fauques* ('falcon'), cf. *Marmaduke Fawkes* 1839 *Map*); Far ~ ~, First Fenny (*v.* **fennig**); Ford Mdw (*v.* **ford**); Bottom ~ ~, Far ~ ~, First ~ ~, Second ~ ~, Little ~ ~, Fosse Cl (bordering Fosse Way); Great ~, Little Foxhall 1786, Great ~ ~, Little Fosse Hill (sic) 1839 (attracted to Fosse Way) (*Foxholes* 1577, *v.* **fox-hol**); Great Cl; Great Mdw; Great North Fallow (*v.* **falh**); Great Old Mdw; Green Cl 1786; Green Furlong 1786, 1839 (*v.* **grēne**[2], **furlang**); Far ~ ~, First Haines Cl (with the surn. *Haines*, from the ODan masc. pers.n. *Haghni*, prob. a Scand form of ContGerm *Hagano*); Nether ~ ~, Upper Hanging Hill 1786, Nether ~, Upper Hanging (sic) 1839 (*v.* **hangende**); Big ~ ~, Little Harrolds Cl, Harralds Mdw (with the surn. *Harrold*, from the ON masc. pers.n. *Haraldr* (ODan *Harald*), cf. *William Harrold* 1800 MI and *Mary Harrold* 1803 ib of Claybrooke Magna); Hide Mdw (*v.* **hīd**; may remember a former hide of land, since the surn. is consistently spelled *Hyde*, cf. *Hede medow* in Oadby f.ns. (b)); High Headland 1786, 1839 (*v.* **hēah**[1], **hēafod-land**); Hill Cl; Hill Mdw; Hill Path Croft 1786, 1839 (*v.* **hyll**, **pǣð**, **croft**); Home Cl, Great ~ ~, Little Home Mdw (*v.* **home**); Hull Pits 1786, 1839 (*v.* **hyll**, **pytt**); Hut Cl (*v.* **hut**); Island Mdw (*v.* **island**; used of a field completely surrounded by others and thus without independent access by road); Far ~ ~, Near ~ ~, Upper ~ ~, Far Upper Lane Piece (*v.* **lane, pece**); The Lea (*v.* **ley**[2]); Legates Cl, ~ Mdw (with the surn. *Legate*, cf. *Rev. Lionel Legat* 1694 Deed, vicar of Claybrooke); Little Cl; Little Mdw; Little North Cl; Long Cl 1821, 1839; Long Mdw 1786, 1839; Middle Cl; Bottom ~ ~, Nether ~ ~, Upper ~ ~, Little ~ ~, Mill Cl, Mill Mdw (*v.* **myln**); Mill Dam, ~ ~ House (*the mill dame* 1638, *v.* **myln**, **damme** and Fawkes Mill *supra*; Claybrooke's water-mill); Moat Furlong (*v.* **mote**, **furlang**; alluding to a small rectangular earthwork which appears on an 1839 map of Claybrooke but which is absent from modern large scale O.S. maps of the parish); Occupation Road (a common name, often dating from the Enclosures and signifying a private road for the use of the occupiers of the land, an access road, usually a green lane); Old House Cl; Ozier Bed (*v.* **oyser**, **bedd**); Parish Yard (*v.* **geard**; official land owned by the parish); Pen Cl 1786, 1839 (*v.* **penn**); Pike Cl, Pike Hill (*v.* **pīc**); Pit Mdw (*v.* **pytt**); (The) Plash 1786, 1839 (*v.* **plæsc**); Plough Cl (*v.* **plōg**); The Poor's Plott 1807, First ~ ~, Second Poors Plot 1839 (*v.* **pouer(e)**, **plot**); land dedicated to poor-law relief or charity); Ravens Hill (later names of hills in Leics. are often compounded with surns., but while the surn. *Raven* is common in the north of the county, it is not recorded in its south; poss. with the bird **hræfn**, cf. *Raven Willow Leyes* in Claybrooke Parva f.ns. (b)); Rodmore Mdw (*Radmore* 1625, 1638, *Redmoor* 1674, *v.* **mōr**[1]; prob. with **rēad** 'red' since this is on clay, but **hrēod** 'reed' is common in compound with *mōr* in Leics. and preferable as a name relating to early agricultural economy); Sandhill 1786, 1839, Sand Hill Cl 1839 (*v.* **sand**, **hyll**); Sand Pit Cl (*v.* **sand-pytt**); Seed Cl (*v.* **sǣd**; in f.ns., used of grasses sown for one year's mowing or grazing as distinguished from permanent pasture); Six Acre Cl (*v.* **æcer**); Slang above Mill Dam (*v.* **slang** and Mill Dam *supra*); Small Mdw 1786, 1839; Spencers Farm (cf. *Francis Spencer* 1839 *Map*); Spiney ~ 1786, Spinney Mdw 1839, The Spinney Cl 1832, Far Spinney Cl 1839 (*v.* **spinney**); Spring Cl 1839, First ~ ~,

Second Spring Cl 1840 (*v.* **spring**[1]); Bottom ~ ~, Square Mdw (*v.* **squar(e)**); First ~, North ~, South Stanymere (*Stoniemere* 1625, *Stouny Meere* 1638, *Stony meere* 1674, *v.* **stānig**, **(ge)mǣre**); Street Cl (*v.* **strēt**; alluding to Watling Street and in a once detached portion of the parish bordering it, as for Wibtoft Mdw *infra*); First Sweetham, Sweetham Mdw (*v.* **swēte**, **hamm**); Three Corner Cl (*v.* **three-corner**); Three Corner'd Cl (*v.* **three-cornered**); Tithe Mdw 1762, 1786, the Tythe Mdw 1821 (*v.* **tēoða**); Great ~, Little Toft (*v.* **toft**); First ~ ~, Second ~ ~, Third ~ ~, Fourth ~ ~, Top Cl; Town Hill, ~ ~ Cl, ~ ~ Mdw (*v.* **tūn**, **hyll**); Turnpike Road (*v.* **turnepike**); Wakefields Farm (cf. *William Wakefield* 1638 *Terrier*, *Anne Wakefield* 1780 MI, *Joseph Wakefield* 1794 ib, all of Claybrooke); Wardens Mdw (with the surn. *Warden*, from AFr *wardein* 'a warden, a guardian'); Wibtoft Mdw (in a once detached portion of Claybrooke Magna bordering Watling Street, with Wibtoft parish in Warwks. beyond it, cf. with Street Cl *supra*).

(b) *the mill home* 1638, 1674 (*v.* **holmr**), *the Mill way* 1708 (*v.* **weg**) (*v.* **myln** and Fawkes Mill *supra*).

Claybrooke Parva

For Claybrooke forms and interpretation, *v.* Claybrooke Magna *supra.*

Affixes are added as:
Parva ~ 1261 RGrav, 1285, 1316 FA *et passim*
Over ~ 1596 Fine, 1721 LML
Church ~ 1784 *Terrier*

The village stands higher than adjoining Claybrooke Magna, hence the affix *Over* ~ (*v.* **uferra**). From the mid 13th cent., forms for it appear with the MLat affix *parva* 'small, little', but at what date it became a separate parish remains uncertain. The bounds detailed in the Anglo-Saxon charter of 962, analysed below, are of former woodland which once lay entirely within the limits of the present parish. The village contains the old church dedicated to St Peter which served the entire land unit called Claybrooke. There is, and has been, no parish church in adjacent Claybrooke Magna. The surviving Glebe Terriers of St Peter's Church, which are entitled simply *Claybrooke*, relate only to land in the later three great fields of Claybrooke Parva.

ALMA HO., named from the Battle of the Alma (1854) in the Crimean War. AVENUE VILLAS. CLAYBROOKE HALL, *Claybrook Hall* 1807 Nichols, 1839 *Map*, 1846, 1863 White, 1925 Kelly, *v.* **hall**. GLEBE FM, 1925 Kelly, *v.* **glebe**. LAUREL BANK, *v.* **banke**. ST PETER'S CHURCH, *Church (St Peter)* 1846, 1863, 1877 White, 1925 Kelly; it is earlier recorded as *ecclesie de Claibroke* 1220 MHW, ~ *de Claybrok(e)* 1371, 1454 *Pat, ecclesie parochialis de Cleybrooke* 1555 *ib* (with MLat *parochialis* 'parochial'), *the Church* 1708 *Terrier*. Note also *the Churchyard* 1708 *ib*, *v.* **churchyerd**. THE VICARAGE, 1925 Kelly; earlier is *the Vicarage House* 1638, 1708, 1724, 1742, 1762, 1768, 1784 *Terrier*, 1839 *Map*, *v.* **vikerage**. WOODWAY COTTAGE. WOODWAY LANE, 1835 O; it is *the Woodway* 1708, e.18 *Terrier*, *v.* **wudu**, **weg**.

FIELD-NAMES

In (a), forms presented without dates are 1839 *Map*; those dated 1762, 1768, 1784, l.18 and 1821 are *Terrier*; 1832 and 1840 are *Deed*; 1846, 1863 and 1877 are White. Forms throughout dated 962 (13) are BCS 1096 (S 833); those dated 1577 are Cl; 1625, 1638, 1674, 1708, e.18, 1724 and 1742 are *Terrier*.

(a) Six ~, Nine Acres (*v.* **æcer**); Back Garden Cl (*v.* **back, gardin**); Balls Spinney (*v.* **spinney**; with the surn. *Ball*); Baldwin's Green 1724, 1846, 1863, 1877 (*v.* **grēne**[2]; with the surn. *Baldwin*, from the ContGerm masc. pers.n. *Baldwin*; note Baldwin's Spinney in adjacent Ullesthorpe parish); Bottom ~, Middle Banky (*v.* **banke, -ig**[3]); Far ~ ~, First ~ ~, Second ~ ~, Barn Cl (*v.* **bern**); Bath Mdw 1821, 1839 (*v.* **bæð**; alluding to land containing a pond); the Big Cl; Bittesby Mdw (land overlooking nearby Bittesby); Bottom Cl 1832, 1839; Brick Kiln Cl (*v.* **brike-kiln**); Browns Cl, ~ Mdw (with the surn. *Brown*); Bull Gore (1625, 1638, 1674, *v.* **bula, gāra**); Chidmans Mores 1762, ~ Mires 1768, 1784, l.18, Chitmans ~ 1821, Chidmores Mires 1839 (*Chidmore furlong* 1638, *chidmearfurlong* 1674 (*v.* **furlang**), *Chitman Mires* 1708, *Chidmans Mores close* 1724, 1742 (*v.* **mōr**[1]; prob. originally with the OE masc. pers.n. *Cidda*, the generic later influenced by Scand **mýrr**, perh. through settlement at neighbouring Bittesby and Ullesthorpe); Church Land (*v.* St Peter's Church *supra*); Clarkes Bottom ~, Clarkes Top Cl, Clarkes Mdw (with the surn. Clarke; cf. *John Clarke* 1815 Census, *Stephen Clarke* 1836 ib and *William Clarke* 1845 ib, all of Claybrooke Parva); Great ~ ~, Little Clover Cl (*v.* **clāfre**; a fodder crop); Coopers Cl (with the surn. *Cooper*; cf. *William Cooper* 1822 Census, *Thomas Cooper* 1826 ib and *Edward Cooper* 1832 ib of Claybrooke Parva); Copwell Mdw (*Copwell* 1577, *Copwel(l) furlong* 1625, 1638 (*v.* **furlang**), *Copwell medowe* 1625, ~ *meddow* 1674, ~ *Meadow* 1708, e.18, *Copwell Slade* 1638 (*v.* **slæd**), *v.* **copp, wella**); Dairy Leys 1762, 1768, 1784, l.18, ~ Leayes 1821, Far ~ ~, First Dairy Lea (*v.* **deierie, leys, ley**); Darleys Cl 1762, 1768, 1784, l.18 (1724, 1742; prob. with the surn. *Darley* of a family originally from one of the two villages of this name in Derbyshire (*v.* Db 81 and 443); otherwise, as this was once a woodland area, then 'woodland clearing frequented by deer', *v.* **dēor, lēah**); Doctors Cl 1821, 1839 (*v.* **doctour**); Dovecote Cl (*v.* **dove-cot(e)**); Dumbletons Cl, ~ Spinney (*v.* **spinney**) (with the surn. *Dumbleton*, from the village of this name (*v.* Gl 2 9); common in 19th-cent. Warwks., but rare in Leics., cf *Hannah Dumbleton* 1832 Census of Leicester); the East Cl 1821; Far Cl 1832; Goldpit (*v.* **pytt**; prob. with **golde** rather than with **gold**); The Great Cl 1762, 1768, 1784, l.18 (1708, 1724, 1742, *v.* **grēat**); The Green (1708, *v.* **grēne**[2]); Hall Cl (*v.* **hall** and Claybrooke Hall *supra*); Bottom ~ ~ ~, Middle ~ ~ ~, Top High Cross Cl 1821, High Cross Cl 1839 (*Hie Crosse Closse* 1625, *High Cross(e) Close* 1638, 1674, cf. *Hie Crosse feilde* 1625, *High Cross(e) Feild* 1638, 1674 (*v.* **feld**; one of the great open-fields of Claybrooke Parva), *v.* High Cross in Claybrooke Magna *supra*); Hill Cl; Hipwell Mdw 1762 (1724, 1742; with the surn. *Hipwell*, cf. *Caroline Hipwell* 1829 Census of adjoining Ullesthorpe parish); Hollyoaks Cl (with the surn. *Holyoak*, common in Leics., cf. *Hannah Holyoak* 1804 Census of nearby Frolesworth, *George Holyoake* 1817 ib and *Henry Holyoak* 1823 ib of nearby Lutterworth; the Leics. instances are prob. of a family originally from Holyoaks on the Rutland border, *v.* Lei **4** 250); Home Cl 1832, 1839 (*v.* **home**); Home Mdw (poss. with **holmr** (as in *Coulmanns Holme* in f.ns. (b)); otherwise with **home**); Hop Yard (*v.* **hop-yard**); Hughes Pasture (*v.* **pasture**; with the surn. *Hughes*); Hut Cls 1821, Bottom ~ ~, Top Hut Cl 1839 (*v.* **hut**); (The) Lammas Cl 1762, 1768, 1784, 1839, Lamas Cl 1821 (*The Lammas Close* 1638, 1708, e.18, 1724, 1742, *v.* **lammas**); Long Cl 1821, 1839; Long Mdw 1786; Lower ~ ~, Upper Magpie Cl (land frequented by the common magpie (*Pica caudeta*)); The Meadow 1768, l.18; Middle Cl; Mill Hill Cl 1840; Mott Cl 1821, Moat Cl 1839 (*v.* **mote**; at the site of the early manor house); Pasture Cl (*v.* **pasture**); the Pingle (*v.* **pingel**); Portway Cl 1762, 1768, 1784, l.18 (1724, 1742, *Portway* 1638, 1708, *v.* **port-wey**; presum. the road to Lutterworth); Potatoe Ground (*v.* **potato**, **grund**); Pridmores Mdw 1821, 1839 (with the surn. *Pridmore*; cf. *William Pridmore* 1830 Census of nearby Sapcote); Rookery (*v.* **rookery**); Small Mdw 1786, 1839 (1708, *v.* **smæl**); South Cl 1821; Spencers Pasture (*v.* **pasture**; note *Francis Spencer* 1839 *Map* of Claybrooke Parva); The Spinney (*v.* **spinney**); Stony Lea (*v.* **stānig**, **ley**[2]); Streetway Cl (*the Streete way* 1638, *v.* **strēt**, **weg**; beside Watling Street); Taylors Cl, ~ Mdw (with the surn. *Taylor*); Tews Cl (with the surn. *Tew*; cf. *Edward Tew* 1824 Census, *Stephen Tew* 1828 ib and *Ann Tew* 1833 ib, all of nearby Lutterworth); Top Cl; Wells Cl, ~ Mdw (with the surn. *Wells*; cf. *Emma Wells* 1805 Census, *William Wells* 1822 ib and *Hannah Wells* 1823 ib, all of Claybrooke Parva); Great Wheatly (poss. with the common Leics. surn. *Wheatley*; otherwise, *v.* **hwǣte**, **lēah**); Wibtoft Cl (adjacent to Wibtoft parish which lies beyond Watling Street in Warwks.); Woodway Cl 1762, 1768, 1784, l.18, Far ~ ~, Near Woodway Cl 1839 (*Woodway Close* 1724, 1742, *v.* Woodway Lane *supra*).

(b) *Apelnodes gemære* 962 (13) (*v.* **(ge)mǣre**; with the OE masc. pers.n. *Æðelnōð*); *barearsse* ~ 1625, *Barearss* ~ 1638, *Barearse furlong* 1674 (a common derogatory name for unproductive land, *v.* **bær**[1], **ears**, **furlang**); *Basil* ~ 1638, *Basill furlong* 1674 (poss. with the surn. *Basil*, from the OFr masc. pers.n. *Basile*, but likelier is an allusion to Basil, Earl of Denbigh, who held land in the great open-fields of Claybrooke in the 17th cent., *v.* Nichols **4** 1 104); *Blackhill* 1577 (*v.* **blæc**, **hyll**); *blake yearth furlonge* 1625, *Nether* ~ ~, *Upper Black Yearth* 1638, *Blackearth* 1674 (*v.* **blæc**, **eorðe**); *Nether* ~ ~, *Upper Breer*(*e*) *furlong* 1638 (*v.* **brēr**); *the bridge* 1625, *the church brigg* 1638 (*v.* **brycg** and St Peter's Church *supra*); *the Brooke* 1638, (*the*) *Brooke close* 1625, 1638, *the Brooke furlong* 1638 (*v.* **furlang**) (*v.* **brōc**); *the Butte Close* 1638 (*v.* **butte**); *the Coal Pit Way* 1638 (*v.* **col-pytt**; a route for carrying pit coal from the mines in the Bedworth area to the south and east of the county); *the Common waie* 1625 (*v.* **commun**, **weg**); *the Constables Peice* 1638 (*v.* **conestable**, **pece**); *Coulmanns Holme* 1577 (*v.* **holmr**; with the surn. *Coulman*, *v.* Reaney *s.n.*); *The Cow Close* 1708 (*v.* **cū**); *Cowdale* ~ 1638, *Caudel slade* 1674 (*v.* **slæd**; prob. with a reduced **Caldwell* (*v.* **cald**, **wella**), cf. *Cawdel well* 1807 in adjacent Ullesthorpe parish; but note *George Cowdell* 1681 *Deed* and *William Cowdell* 1756 MI of Claybrooke Parva, so a surn. is poss. here); *þa ealdan stræt* 962 (13) (*v.* **ald**, **strēt**; alluding to Watling Street); *le Hall land, Hall lands* 1625 (*v.* **land** and Claybrooke Hall *supra*); *the hie waie* 1625 (*v.* **hēah-weg**); *Hinckl*(*e*)*y balke* 1638, 1674 (*v.* **balca**; Hinckley lies 5½ miles to the north-west and since there is no record of any territorial relationship between these townships, this f.n. appears to contain the surn. *Hinckley* of a family originally from there; the surn. is more frequent in Warwks.); *the Homestall* 1708 (*v.* **hām-stall**); *the Homesteede* 1625 (*v.* **hām-stede**);

the Horse close 1708 (*v.* **hors**); *Mr Legats Close* 1708 (*Rev. Lionel Legat* 1694 Deed, 1708 *Terrier*, was vicar of Claybrooke 1685–1715); *Little* ~, *Mansemore* 1638, *little mansmore* 1674 (*v.* **(ge)mǣnnes, mōr**¹); (*the*) *Middle Feild* 1625, 1638, 1674 (*v.* **middel, feld**; one of the great open-fields of the township); *the Neither feild* 1625, (*the*) *Nether Feild* 1638, 1674 (*v.* **neoðera, feld**; another of the great open-fields); *the New close* 1625, 1638, 1674; *path lands* 1625, *Great Path lands* 1638, *great pathlands* 1674 (*v.* **pæð, land**; this no doubt alludes to the ancient track or pathway described in Note 9 concerning the Claybrooke Anglo-Saxon charter *infra*); (*on*) *Peatling* 1638, *Peatlin thorne* 1674 (*v.* **þorn**) (it is uncertain whether *Peatling* here is the surn. of a family originally from either Peatling Magna or Peatling Parva, respectively 7 miles and 6 miles to the north-east; the simplex form of 1638 hints at another possible survival in this area of the folk-name **Pēotlingas* (*v.* **-ingas**)); *Pitts* 1638, 1674 (*v.* **pytt**); *The Priors Peeces* 1708 (*v.* **pece**; the def.art. suggests the sb. **prior** rather than the surn. *Prior*, but there appears to be no record of any association of the township with an abbey or priory, although the Prioress and Convent of Nuneaton were patrons of St Peter's Church from 1220 to 1524, *v.* Nichols **4** 1 114; the nearest poss. prior would have been that of the small, lost, Holywell Priory in Shawell, 7 miles to the south-east); *Raven Willow Leyes* 1638, 1674 (*v.* **wilig, leys**; either with **hræfn** or with the surn. *Raven*, cf. Ravens Hill in Claybrooke Magna f.ns. (a)); *Ridgeway* 1577 (*v.* **hrycgweg**); (*andlang*) *riþiges* 962 (13) (*v.* **rīðig**); *þone rodweg* 962 (13) (this may rather be *wodweg* (*v.* Note 10 in the discussion of the Claybrooke Anglo-Saxon charter *infra*); otherwise, *v.* **rād-weg**); *Short Leys* 1674 (*v.* **sc(e)ort, leys**); *Stounie hill* 1625, *Stouny Hill* 1638, *Stonyhill* 1674 (*v.* **stānig**); *streete leas* 1625, *Nether* ~ ~, *Upper Street(e) Leyes, Street Leyes Close* 1638 (*v.* **strēt, leys**; alluding to Watling Street); *Swallowgore bauke* 1625, *Swallow Gore Balk* 1638 (*v.* **balca**), *Swallowgore* 1674 (*v.* **swalg, gāra**); *Sydlings* 1577 (*v.* **sīdling**); *Thornborrow* 1577 (*v.* **þorn, berg**); *the Tofts* e.18 (*v.* **toft**); *the townes end* 1625, *the Townsend* 1674 (*v.* **tūn, ende**); *towne hill, the towne hill furlong* 1625, *Town Hill furlong* 1638 (*v.* **furlang**) (*v.* **tūn, hyll**); *the Tyth Piece* 1638, ~ ~ *Peice* 1674 (*v.* **tēoða, pece**); *the Vicars Cowe Close,* ~ ~ *Great Close,* ~ ~ *Horse Close* 1708 (*v.* **vikere**); *Wakefields Close* 1638 (*v.* Wakefields Farm in Claybrooke Magna f.ns. (a)); *waterfurrowes* 1674 (*v.* **wæter, furh** and *Water furrowes* in Ashby Parva f.ns. (b)); *wileardes hyrste* 962 (13) (*v.* **hyrst**; with the OE masc. pers.n. *Wilheard*); *Woodway side* 1638 (*v.* **sīde** and Woodway Lane *supra*).

AN ANGLO-SAXON WOODLAND ESTATE AT CLAYBROOKE
962 (13) BCS 1096 (S 833)¹

Þis his þæs wudes land gemære þe Aþelred² cyning bocað Leofrice his þegene on ece yrfe: ærest of clæg broce³ on þa ealdan stræt⁴ be westan dunninc wicon⁵ andlang stræt on norþewerde wileardes hyrste⁶ on þone feld⁷ þanon on þe riþi⁸ andlang riþiges on Aþelnodes gemære⁹ þanon on þone rodweg¹⁰ andlang weges þe eft on clæg broc.

'This is the boundary of the woodland which King Athelred grants in perpetuity to Leofric his thane: first from the clayey brook to the ancient street to the west of *dunninc wicon*, along the street to the north of Wilheard's wooded hill to the open country, thence to the little stream, along this stream to Athelnoth's boundary, thence to the bridle-way (or to the Woodway) and along the track back again to the clayey brook.'

1. This is the sole surviving Anglo-Saxon charter with Old English bounds for a location in Leicestershire. It is extant as a 13th-cent. copy in BL Cotton Claudius B vi, folio 93. It is clearly evident that scribal errors have occurred in transmission. Where significant, these are specified below.

2. Athelred reigned from 979 to 1013. The charter is dated 962, which places it as originally granted in the reign of Edgar (959–75) and presumably later confirmed by Athelred.

3. The major watercourse *clæg broc* 'the clayey brook' which gave the Claybrooke parishes its name rises near Wood Farm (at SP 472861) in Willey parish, beyond Watling Street in Warwks., flows hard by the deserted medieval village site of Bittesby, is crossed by the road running between Claybrooke Parva and Ullesthorpe, then runs north between Claybrooke Magna village and Claybrooke Grange in Frolesworth parish to join the river Soar east of Sharnford. The charter bounds begin at SP 500878 where the clayey brook is crossed by the road between Claybrooke Parva and Ullesthorpe.

4. From SP 500878, the perambulation in general followed what is now the south-eastern parish boundary of Claybrooke Parva to meet *þa ealdan stræt* (Watling Street) at about SP 486869. This point is to the west of the lost *dunninc wicon*. The zigzag line of the existing parish boundary from the *clæg broc* to the *ealdan stræt* may well have been governed by the shapes of the later medieval furlongs of *the Neither Feild* after the clearing of the woodland. Otherwise, its present tortuous route must follow later close boundaries.

5. The site of *dunninc wicon* appears to have been in the south-western corner of what is now Ullesthorpe parish, which with the present Bittesby parish, strongly suggests that this was a subdivided early land unit. The generic *wicon* of the place-name appears to be a poor rendering of the dat.pl. *wīcum* of OE *wīc*, perhaps indicating a group of farm buildings (the OE prep. *be westan* required a following dative case). An alternative original for *wicon* could be *wīchām* 'an Anglo-Saxon settlement adjacent to a former Romano-British small town', which with *Venonis* (at High Cross) only a little over one mile away on Watling Street, would fit perfectly the pattern of such sites in relation to Roman roads and to small Romano-British settlements first recognized by Margaret Gelling (*v.* M. Gelling, 'English place-names derived from the compound *wīchām*', *Medieval Archaeology* 9 (1967), 87–104, a study extended in her *Signposts to the Past*, 3rd edn (1997), 67–74). It should be noted, however, that *wīchām* invariably survives as a simplex. The specific *dunninc* may be the OE masc. pers.n. *Dunning*, with copying loss of the genitival composition-joint *-es-*, or an OE masc. pers.n. *Dunn* or *Dunna* with the added connective particle *-ing-*[4] linking the pers.n. to the generic *wīc(um)* (or *wīchām*), signifying an association of the site with *Dunn(a)*. A further possibility is that *dunninc* is a reduced **Dunninga* (from **Dunningas* 'the family or people of

Dunn(a)') with the folk-name-forming suffix *-ingas*. Since the place-name appears in the manuscript as two words, in this case there may have been a copying loss of medial *a*.

6. The perambulation turned north-west along Watling Street, the hill called *wileardes hyrste* (*Wilheardes hyrst*) rising to the south-west of the ancient road, the bounds following Watling Street over the hill's north-eastern slopes.

7. The woodland of the charter ceased as the boundary reached *þone feld* 'the open country' at about SP 481875.

8. The boundary continued downhill along Watling Street to *þe riþi*, which is the stream crossed by Watling Street at SP 481876. Judging by the following gen.sg. *riþiges* of the neuter noun *rīðig* 'a small stream', the original word here presum. was *riþige* (*rīðige*), with copying loss of *-ge*, rather than the dat.sg. *riþe* (*rīðe*) of the feminine noun *rīð*, also 'a small stream'.

9. The bounds then turned away from Watling Street and followed the stream north-east until they met *Apelnodes gemære* 'Athelnoth's boundary'. This boundary may be represented nowadays by the path which runs from High Cross to the old school site in Claybrooke Parva and so straight on via a sunken, overgrown lane to Ullesthorpe. This track has every appearance of being an ancient one whose destination was once *Venonis* (*v. path lands* in f.ns. (b) *supra*). If so, the little stream met Athelnoth's boundary at SP 484881; but if this boundary is that now represented by Claybrooke Parva's northern parish boundary, then the stream met it at SP 485882.

10. The perambulation then followed Athelnoth's boundary eastwards to meet *þone rodweg*. This is presumably now the road from Claybrooke Magna to Claybrooke Parva. The *rodweg* may be from an OE *rād-weg* 'riding way, bridle-way' or the form which survives may be a misscript from an original *wudu weg > wodweg* 'the Woodway, the track to the wood', with a misreading of an Anglo-Saxon initial character 'win' (*w*) as the very similarly-shaped *r*. Indeed, this road now continues south-west to Watling Street as modern Woodway Lane. It should be noted, however, that in the OE preamble to the bounds, *wudes land* retains the early *u*, which may argue against *u* having here given *o*, and thus for *rodweg* as the authentic form. If Athelnoth's boundary is represented nowadays by the northern parish boundary of Claybrooke Parva, it met this bridle-way (or 'wood way') at SP 493882. The bounds would then have turned south along the track to meet the beginning of what is now the overgrown sunken lane at SP 494878 and next have turned east along this lane, continuing eastwards to the crossing of the *clæg broc* at SP 500878 where the perambulation began. If Athelnoth's boundary was the old pathway or track to *Venonis* described in Note 9, then it met the bridle-way (or 'wood way') at about SP 494878. Next, the bounds would have proceeded directly east along the sunken lane (which continues as the modern road to Ullesthorpe) to the *clæg broc* at SP 500878.

Cosby

1. COSBY

Cossebi 1086 DB (×2), Hy 2 Dugd, 1207 GildR, *Cosseby* c.1130
   LeicSurv, c.1200 *LCDeeds et freq* to 1406 *Ferrers*, 1504 Banco
Cosbi 1086 DB, *Cosby* 1502 *MiscAccts*, 1505 Ipm *et freq*
Coseby 1212, 1261 Cur

Either 'the farmstead or village of a man called *Kofsi* or *Kopsi*', with
a Scand masc. pers.n., or 'the farmstead or village of a man called Cosa
or Cossa', with an unrecorded OE masc. pers.n. *Cos(s)a* which appears
in such place-names as Cosham (Ha 59), Corsham (W 95) and
Cossington (Lei **3** 59), *v.* **bȳ**. It should be noted, however, that in the case
of a Scand masc. pers.n. *Kofsi* or *Kopsi*, *fs* or *ps* would have been
expected to leave some trace in early forms, although their assimilation
to *ss* would be regular.

ASHPOLE SPINNEY, *v.* **æsc**, **pāl**, **spinney**; cf. Ashpole Spinney, Lei **4** 205.
BAPTIST CHAPEL. BLACKSMITHS' ARMS (P.H.), *Blacksmiths' Arms* 1846,
1863, 1877 White, 1925 Kelly. BROUGHTON RD, Broughton Astley lying
2 miles to the south-west. BULL'S HEAD (P.H.), *Bull's Head* 1846, 1863,
1877 White, 1925 Kelly. CAMBRIDGE RD. CLARKE'S SPINNEY, *v.*
spinney; cf. Clarke's Lodge *infra* and *Wm. Clarke, farmer* 1846 White.
COSBY HILL, ~ ~ FM, *Cosby Hill* 1835 O, 1925 Kelly, *v.* **hyll**. COSBY
HO., *Cosby House* 1877 White, 1925 Kelly. COSBY LODGE, ~ ~ FM, *v.*
loge. COSBY SPINNEYS, *Cosby Spinnies* 1877 White; the site is called
Bosworth Spinny 1835 O, presum. with the surn. *Bosworth*, *v.* **spinney**.
CROFT RD, Croft in Sparkenhoe Hundred lying 2½ miles to the north-
west. CROSS KEYS (P.H.) (lost), *Cross Keys* 1863, 1877 White.
GUTHLAXTON GAP, 1807 Nichols, *v.* **gap**, cf. *Guthlaxton Bridge* 1835 O
at this site; *v.* Guthlaxton Hundred *supra* and *Gutlakestonfelde* in Cosby
f.ns. (b) *infra*. THE HALL, *v.* **hall**. THE HILL FM. HILL FIELD FM. THE
HIVE. KINGSFIELD RD. LADY LEYS, *v.* **ladi**, **leys**. LANGHAM BRIDGE FM,
named from Langham Bridge in Narborough parish, Sparkenhoe
Hundred. LEICESTER ROAD FM. LOWLANDS FM. MANOR FM, 1925 Kelly.

67

MANOR HO., *Manor House* 1846, 1877 White, *v.* **maner**. MAIN ST.
METHODIST CHAPEL. MOUNT RD. NARBOROUGH RD, Narborough lying
1½ miles to the north-west. NEW INN (lost), *New Inn* 1863, 1877 White,
1925 Kelly. THE NOOK, cf. *The Nook Farm* 1925 Kelly, *v.* **nōk**. PARK
RD. PORTLAND ST. ROAD BARN FM (OLD ROAD BARN 2½"). ROSE
MOUNT (2½"), *Rose Mount* 1877 White. ST MICHAEL'S CHURCH, *Church
(St Michael)* 1846, 1863 White, *Church (St Michael and All Angels)*
1877 ib, 1925 Kelly; it is earlier recorded as *ecclesie de Cosseb'* 1220
MHW and in the group *ecclesiarum de Buckmynster Disworth Cosby
Wyggeston et Sancta Maria Leicestre* 1558 Pat. Note *the vicaridge house*
e.18 *Terrier, v.* **vikerage**. SHUTTLEWORTH LANE, presum. with a garbled
version of the surn. of *Joseph Shuttlewood, farmer* 1846 White. SPINNEY
LODGE (CLARKE'S LODGE 2½"), *Clarke's Lodge* 1846 White, *v.* **loge**.
VICTORY PARK. THE VINERIES, 1925 Kelly, 1936 Sale; the home of
Thomas Scarborough, fruit grower 1925 ib. WALNUT FM, 1925 Kelly.
WHITE BARN DRIVE. WHITE BARN FM (~ ~ COTTAGE 2½"). WILLIAM IV
(P.H.) (lost), *William IV* 1863 White.

FIELD-NAMES

In (a), forms presented without dates are 1972 *Surv*; those dated 1764,
1771, 1772, 1775, 1777, 1786, 1789, 1840, 1844, 1847, 1851 and 1857
are *Deed*; 1819 are Sale; 1850 are *Plan*. Forms throughout dated 1221
are Fine; those dated 1397 are Banco; 1467 × 84 are *LTD*; 1477 (e.16)
are *Charyte*; 1539 are MinAccts; 1555 and 1584 are Ipm; 1590 × 1631
are Terrier; 1674, 1702, 1709, 1720, 1726, 1734, 1739, 1741 and 1747
are *Deed*; e.18 are *Terrier*.

(a) 5 Acre(s), 6 ~, 7 ~, 8 ~, 9 ~, 10 Acre(s), Long ~ ~, 11 Acre(s), 13 ~, 14 ~, 17
~, Middle ~ ~, 20 Acre(s), Bottom ~, Top Acres (*v.* **æcer**); Allotment Fd (*v.*
allotment); Armston's Mdws (with the surn. *Armston* of a family originally from the
village of this name, 33 miles to the east in Northants.; cf *William Armston* 1815
Census, *Elizabeth Armston* 1848 ib and *John Armston* 1879 ib, all of Cosby); Ash
Tree Cl (*v.* **æsc, trēow**); Back Fd, Back Lane (*v.* **back**); The Banks, Banks Cl (*v.*
banke); First ~, Second Banlands (*v.* **bēan, land**); Little ~ ~, Barn Cl, Barn Fd (*v.*
bern); Big Mdw; Blakeland ~ 1775, Blackland Cl 1840, 1844 (*Blakelond'*,
Blakelondes ouerende 1467 × 84, *v.* **blæc, land**); Bog Fd (*v.* **bog**);
Bottom Hill 1772, ~ ~ Cl 1850 (*v.* **botm**); Bottom of the Orchard (*v.* **botm, orceard**);
Brook Fd 1777, 1789 (*Brokefelde* 1467 × 84, *Brookfeild* e.18, *v.* **brōc, feld**; one of
the great open-fields); Broughton Fd (Broughton Astley parish adjoins to the south-
west); Bull Furlong (*v.* **bula, furlang**); The Burning Up Fd (poss. alluding to land
once prepared by paring and burning, with the ash produced by slow combustion of

heaps of turf and weeds then ploughed in; otherwise, a site for the burning of unwanted agricultural waste); The Captain (if not indicating ownership by a retired army or naval officer or recording a field with the common name of a farm horse, then unexplained); Clankers Cl (named from the harsh metallic noises of railway traffic on a now defunct railway line); Clarke's Paddock (*v.* **paddock**; with the surn. *Clarke*, cf. *Wm. Clarke, farmer* 1846 White; note Clarke's Spinney *supra*); Clover Cl (*v.* **clāfre**; a fodder crop); Cock Hill Cl (*le Cochull, Hy Cokyll* (*v.* **hēah**[1]), *Litell kokell* (*v.* **lȳtel**) 1467 × 84, *Cokhullfeld* 1397, *Cokelfelde* 1467 × 84 (*v.* **feld**; one of the early great open-fields, poss. shared with Littlethorpe), *Cokkelemedew* 1477 (e.16) (*v.* **mēd** (**mēdwe** obl.sg.), *v.* **hyll**; prob. with **cocc**[1] 'a hillock', but **cocc**[2] 'a cock bird' is also poss.); Cocksfoot (pasture where Cocksfoot (*Dactylis glomerata*) abounded; Cocksfoot is a type of grass which is an important ingredient of hay meadows and natural pastures, the way its lowest flowering branch sticks out on its own, reminiscent of a chicken's foot, giving the plant its name); Colelane Fd formerly New Cl or Saunts Cl 1771 (*v.* Saunts Cl *infra*), Coal Lane Fd 1777, 1786 (*Cole lane* 1590 × 1631, *Colelanefelde* 1467 × 84, *Colelanefeild* e.18 (*v.* **feld**; a great open-field, poss. shared with Littlethorpe), *v.* **col**[1], **lane**); Cosby Road Great ~, Cosby Road Little Cl; Cottage Fd (*v.* **cotage**); First Cow Cl 1847, 1851, 1857, Cow Cl 1972; Cow Lane (*v.* **cū**); Cox's Little Meer (*v.* (**ge**)**mǣre**; a boundary plot, with the surn. *Cox*); Crabbies (either with the surn. *Crabbe* in the possessive case or a close containing crab-apple-trees, *v.* **crabbe**); Crick's First ~, Crick's Middle ~, Crick's Top Fd, Crick's Mdw (with the surn. *Crick*, perh. of a family originally from Crick, 14 miles away to the south-east in Northants.; cf. *Thomas Crick* 1873 Census of Cosby); Cricket Fd (for the game of cricket); Dew Pond Fds (*v.* **dew-pond**; an artificially-created pond used for watering livestock; despite its name, the primary source of water in a dew-pond is believed to be rainfall rather than dew); Far Cl; Fen Cl (*v.* **fenn**); First Fd; The Flashes (*v.* **flasshe**); Flaxnorrs (poss. is a metathesized **flask** 'swampy grassland', with **knorre** 'rough, gnarled ground', perh. with reference to projecting stone or stumps of trees; otherwise with **fleax**); Flaxlands (*Flaxlandes, Flaxlandis, Flaxlandeswong* (*v.* **vangr**) 1467 × 84, *v.* **fleax**, **land**); Flint's Fd (with the surn. *Flint*, from an unrecorded OE masc. by-name *Flint* 'rock; hard as rock'; cf. *Arthur Flint* 1854 Census and *Amy Flint* 1879 ib, both of adjacent Broughton Astley parish); The Football Fd; First ~ ~, Second Foot Road Fd (*v.* **fōt**; cf. ModEdial *fotewaye* 'a footpath'); Front Fd; Fullmore Mdw (*Fulmeere* 1467 × 84, *v.* **fūl**, **mere**[1]); Gipsy Lane Cl (a camping place for itinerants); Golf Links Fd (part of, or bordering a golf course); Goodspeed Cl 1775 (maybe with the surn. *Goodspeed* (from ME *god speid* 'success', in turn from the phrase *God spede you* 'God prosper you'); otherwise perh. a fond name for fertile ground); Gorse Cl, ~ Fd (*v.* **gorst**); Grass Cl (*v.* **græs**; pasture or meadow land); Great Cl 1764; Hagg (*v.* **hogg**); Hall Nook Cl 1847, 1851, 1857 (1709, 1720, 1726, 1739, 1747, *v.* **hall**, **nōk** and The Hall *supra*); Hennams Cl 1775, First ~, Second Hennams 1847, 1851, 1857, Heynams Cls 1972 (*Heynames, Mydul heynams* (*v.* **middel**), *Heyman buskys* (sic) (*v.* **buskr**) 1467 × 84, *v.* **hēah**[1] (**hēan** wk.obl.); with **hām** or **hamm** or even **nām**); Hill Cl 1772, Big ~~, Little Hill Fd (*le Hull* 1467 × 84 (*v.* **hyll**); Hill or Rye Grass Fd (*v.* Rye Grass Fd *infra*); Hills Orchard 1850 (*v.* **orceard**; with the surn. *Hill*); Hollows (*atte holu* (*v.* **atte**), *le Holu* 1467 × 84, *v.* **holh**); Home Cl, ~ Fd (*v.* **home**); Horse Cl (*v.* **hors**); House Cl 1850, House Fd 1972, Bottom House Cl 1850; Kendal's Mdw (with the surn. *Kendal*; cf. *John Kendal* 1813 Census of Cosby); Kings Fd (with the surn. *King*, common in

Cosby from *William King* 1836 Census to *William John King* 1871 ib); Lady Cl
(*Lady clos* 1555, *v.* **ladi, clos(e)**); Lambing Mdw (*v.* **lambing**); Langmore Cl
(*Langemore, Langemoor* 1467 × 84, *v.* **lang**[1], **mōr**[1]); Over the Line, Side of the Line
(fields adjoining a now defunct railway, cf. Big Railway *infra*); Little Fd; Little
Mdw; Little Hill 1772; Little Spinney Fd (*v.* **spinney**); Long Fd; Long Mdw; Manor
Hill (*v.* Manor Ho. *supra*); Marl Hill Cl (prob. related to *Marlhowey* 1467 × 84, *v.*
marle, hōh, weg); Middle Cl; Far ~ ~, Middle Fd; Middle Hill 1772; Mushroom Fd
(land on which mushrooms abound); Mussons Fd (with the surn. *Musson* of a family
originally from Muston, 32 miles to the north-east, with typical Leics. loss of *t* from
the group -*ston* in p.ns., *v.* Muston, Lei **2** 35); Narborough Mdw (Narborough parish
adjoins to the north); Near Cl; Nettle Mdw (*v.* **netel(e)**; usually indicative of high
phosphate content in the soil, signalling former habitation sites); New Cl 1771; The
Park (*v.* **park**); Petrol Fd (beside a former petrol station on Fosse Way); Piggins Fd
(prob. with the surn. *Piggin* which occurs fairly freq. (perh. a garbled form of ME
pilegrim 'pilgrim'); much less likely is a toponymic compound of **pigga** with **eng**);
Pit Cl 1850 (*le Pit* 1467 × 84, *v.* **pytt**); First ~ ~, Second Ploughed Fd; Pump Fd (*v.*
pumpe; a close with a water-pump); Rabbit Warren (*v.* **rabet, wareine**); Big
Railway (beside a now disused railway line, cf. Over the Line *supra*); Bottom ~, Top
Riggs (cf. *Schort Ryggus* (*v.* **sc(e)ort** 1467 × 84, *v.* **hryggr**); The Road Fd, Over the
Road; Round Cl (*v.* **round**; the field is now rectangular); Rye Grass Fd (Common
Ryegrass (*Lolium perenne*) is a valuable pasture grass and early was deliberately
cultivated on sown meadows); Saunts Cl, 1771, 1819, 1847, 1851, 1857, New ~, Old
Saunts 1840, 1844, 1850 (with the surn. *Saunt*, a nickname from ME *saint, seint*
'saint'; cf. *Mary Saunt* and *Thomas Saunt* 1702 *Deed* of Cosby); Search Light Fd (the
location of a searchlight battery in the Second World War); Second Fd; Seeds (*v.*
sǣd; used of grasses sown for one year's mowing or grazing as distinguished from
permanent pasture); Seeres half yardland 1764 (cf. *Seares quarterne of yardland*
1674, *v.* **quarterne, yerdland**; with the surn. *Sear*, cf. *Will'us Seer* 1467 × 84 *LTD*);
Seven Furlongs (*v.* **seofon, furlang**; an enclosure comprising seven furlongs of a
former great open-field); Slade Cl 1847, 1851, 1857 (*v.* **slæd**); The Slang (*v.* **slang**);
the Spinnies (*v.* **spinney**); the Splash (*v.* **splash**; land at a shallow ford); Stanlins
(prob. a late form of *Stainlands* in f.ns. (b)); Steven's Fd (with the surn. *Steven*);
Sutton Garbage (*v.* **garebrode, gorebrode**; towards Sutton in the Elms in adjacent
Broughton Astley parish); Thistle Hill (*Thistelhull, Thistilhull* 1467 × 84, *v.* **þistel,
hyll**); Three Sisters (unexplained; poss. a close with a group of three large trees);
Lower ~ ~, Upper Tilbram Cls (earlier forms are needed; poss. is a name with the OE
fem. pers.n. *Tilburh* and **hām**, perh. the settlement preceding Cosby); Tin Hut Cl (*v.*
hut); Top Cl; Top Hill Cl 1850; Top Mdws; The Turn Fd (poss. with **trun**; but the
close lies at a sharp angle of road); Turnpike Cl 1772 (*v.* **turnepike**); Two Acre
Paddock (*v.* **æcer, paddock**); Tythe Land (*v.* **tēoða, land**); Upper Furlong (*v.*
furlang); Varnhams Fd (with the surn. *Varnham*, a variant of the surn. *Farnham*; cf.
Sarah Varnham 1855 Census of adjacent Narborough parish); First ~, Second
Wadders (*Wadhow, Wadow* 1467 × 84, *v.* **wād, hōh**); Watson's Fd (with the surn.
Watson; cf. *John Watson* 1827 Census and *Henry Watson* 1866 ib of Cosby); Well
Fd (*le Well* 1467 × 84, cf. *Wellefurlong* 1467 × 84, 1477 (e.16) (*v.* **furlang**), *v.*
wella); White Barn; Willow Cl 1850 (*v.* **wilig**); Witherbed (*v.* **wīðig, bedd**).

(b) *les Acres* 1467 × 84 (*v.* **æcer**); *Assheby land* 1555, 1584 (*v.* **land**; adjoining
Ashby Magna parish which borders to the south-east); *le Blakedole* 1467 × 84 (*v.*

dāl; with **blāc** or **blæc**); *Boycroftes* 1467 × 84 (*v.* **boi(a)**, **croft**); *Bradmere*, *Brademeereheuedes* (*v.* **hēafod**) 1467 × 84 (*v.* **brād**, **(ge)mǣre**); *Brakenholm* 1467 × 84 (*v.* **braken**, **holmr**); *Bretlong* 1467 × 84 (*v.* **breiðr**, **lang**[2]); *Branhowstyes* 1467 × 84 (*v.* **brant**, **hōh**, **stig**); *the Breches* 1467 × 84 (*v.* **brēc**); (*in to*) *Brokes*, *le Brokesende* (*v.* **ende**) 1467 × 84 (*v.* **brōc**); *Broughton land* 1555, 1584 (*v.* **land**; ground adjoining Broughton Astley parish which marches to the south-west); *Broutonmere* 1467 × 84 (*v.* **(ge)mǣre**; the parish boundary of Broughton Astley); *Chestreway* 1397, *Chasterwey*(*e*), *Chasturwey* 1467 × 84 (*v.* **weg**; the long-distance route to Chester via Leicester); *le Cleypittis* 1467 × 84, *Cleypyttes* 1477 (e.16) (*v.* **cley-pytt**); *le Communpitt'* 1467 × 84 (*v.* **commun**, **pytt**); *Cosby Mill* 1539 (*v.* **myln**); *le Cros* 1467 × 84 (*v.* **cros**); *Docepittewey*, *Docepitwey* 1467 × 84 (*v.* **docce**, **pytt**, **weg**); *le Dokestile* 1467 × 84 (*v.* **docce**, **stig**); *Dunting'*, *Duntyng'* 1467 × 84 (the first element appears to be ME **dunt** (from OE *dynt* 'a blow', cf. ON *dyntr*) in a topographical sense such as 'a small narrow hollow', transferred descriptively from the notion of 'a dent, a dint, a dunt' (the result of a blow); either with **-ing**[2] or **eng**); *Estfurlonges* 1467 × 84 (*v.* **ēast**, **furlang**); *Falstedes* 1467 × 84 (*v.* **(ge)fall**, **stede**); *Fermforlang'* 1467 × 84 (*v.* **ferme**, **furlang**); *Finland* 1477 (e.16) (*v.* **finn**, **land**); *Flaxyard* 1555 (*v.* **fleax**, **geard**); *le Flodgates* 1467 × 84 (*v.* **flodegate**); *Flotegres* 1467 × 84 (*v.* **fljót**, **græs**); *le Formedewe* 1467 × 84 (*v.* **fore**, **mēd** (**mēdwe** obl.sg.)); *Godescroft* 1467 × 84 (*v.* **croft**; with the surn. *Good*, either from OE *gōd* 'good' or from the OE masc. pers.n. *Goda* (or the fem. pers.n. *Gode*); note *godscroft hollow* in nearby Frolesworth f.ns. (b)); *Brodegrendale* (*v.* **brād**), *Smalegrendale* (*v.* **smæl**) 1467 × 84 (*v.* **grēne**[1], **dāl**); *Grenegate* 1467 × 84 (*v.* **grēne**[1], **gata**); *Grenestokysmere* 1467 × 84 (*v.* **stoc**, **(ge)mǣre**; poss. with **grein**); *Gudlokeston*, *Gutlakestonfelde* 1467 × 84 (*v.* **feld**; one of the early great open-fields of Cosby, abutting Fosse Way, *v.* Guthlaxton Gap *supra*; poss. an alternative name for *Cokhullfeld*, *v.* Cock Hill Cl *supra*); *Halyday clos* 1555, *Holidaye close* 1584 (*v.* **clos(e)**), *Haliday land or Broughton land* 1555, *Holydayes land or Broughton land* 1584 (*v.* **land**) (with the surn. *Haliday*, from OE *hālidæg* 'a holy day, a religious festival', a name often given to a person born on such a day; *v. Broughton land*, *supra*); *Hareland* 1555, 1584 (*v.* **land**; either with **hær** or **hār**[2]); *Hilliforlang* 1467 × 84 (*v.* **hyllig**, **furlang**); *Holdingsik*, *Holdyngesyke* 1467 × 84 (*v.* **sík**; poss. suffixed to a toponym meaning 'the place of shelter', *v.* **hald**[1], **-ing**[2]; otherwise the surn. *Holdin* may be thought of, *v.* Reaney *s.n.*); *le Holm* 1467 × 84 (*v.* **holmr**); *Holoughtherne* 1397, *Holetherne*, *Holtherne*, *Holthirne* 1467 × 84 (*v.* **holh**, **þyrne**); *Hungurhull* 1467 × 84 (*v.* **hungor**, **hyll**); *Kynseman clos* 1555 (*v.* **clos(e)**), *Kynseman land* 1555, 1584 (*v.* **land**) (with the surn. *Kinsman*); *Langedike*, *Langedicsti* (*v.* **stīg**) 1467 × 84 (*v.* **lang**[1], **dík**); *Langedole*, *Longedole* 1467 × 84 (*v.* **lang**[1], **dāl**); *Lodyngtonweye* 1467 × 84 (*v.* **weg**; the road to Loddington which lies 16 miles to the north-east); *Longfurlong'* 1467 × 84 (*v.* **lang**[1], **furlang**); *Lortewell* 1467 × 84 (*v.* **lort(e)**, **wella**); *Maidethorne* 1221 (*v.* **þorn**; the specific is prob. **mægð**[2], indicating that this thorn-scrub was the common property of the township, but if **mægð**[1], then it either belonged to an unmarried woman or was a place frequented by the village girls); *Mariots risich*, ~ *rysich* 1467 × 84 (*v.* **ryge**, **sīc**; with the surn. *Marriott*, from *Mari-ot*, a diminutive of Mary; the surn. is very common nowadays in Framland Hundred); *le Medudykys* (*v.* **dík**), *le Meduplott'* (*v.* **plot**) 1467 × 84 (*v.* **mēd** (**mēdwe** obl.sg.)); *Middelforlong'*, *le Middel furlong'*, *Middelfurlonges* 1467 × 84 (*v.* **middel**, **furlang**); *Milnfeild* e.18, *Milnhyll* 1467 × 84 (*v.* **hyll**) (*v.* *Cosby Mill*, *supra*); *Mongereswell*(*e*), *Mongerwell* 1467 × 84

(v. **wella**; it is uncertain whether the specific is the surn. *Monger* or its source **mangere** 'a monger, a dealer'); *New Close* 1702, 1734, 1741; *le Oldgore* 1467 × 84 (v. **ald, gāra**); *Osbernwong'* 1467 × 84 (v. **vangr**; with the late OE masc. pers.n. *Ōsbern*, from ON *Ásbjǫrn* (ODan *Asbiorn*)); *le Patthes* 1467 × 84 (v. **pæð**); *Peselond* 1467 × 84 (v. **pise, land**); *Polwelthirne* 1467 × 84 (v. **wella, þyrne**; the prototheme may be either **pōl**[1] or the OE masc. pers.n. *Pol*); *Rasson* ~ 1555, *Rason land* 1584 (v. **land**; prob. with the surn. *Rason* (from the Lincs. place-name (Market) Rasen etc.), but **ræsn**, alluding to a plank bridge, is poss.); *Ryelond*(*e*) 1467 × 84 (v. **ryge, land**); *le Scheld ad le Cros* 1467 × 84 (v. **sceld**; some kind of shelter at the village cross is indicated); *Schortacres* 1467 × 84 (v. **sc(e)ort, æcer**); *Schortmorsikes* 1467 × 84 (v. **sc(e)ort, mōr**[1], **sík**); *Sereland* 1555, 1584 (v. **land**; with the surn. *Sear*, cf. *Will'us Seer* 1467 × 84 *LTD*, v. Seeres half yardland in f.ns (a)); *le Sikes, le Sikefurlonges* (v. **furlang**) 1467 × 84 (v. **sík**); *Sourdole* 1467 × 84, 1477 (e.16), *Sowerdoles* 1477 (e.16) (v. **sūr, dāl**); *le Spitelwong'* (v. **vangr**), *le Spitelyerd* (v. **geard**) 1467 × 84 (v. **spitel**; properties of the Hospital of St John the Evangelist in Leicester, v. Lei **1** 93); *Stainlandes, Stainlondfelde* (v. **feld**; one of the great open-fields) 1467 × 84 (v. **steinn, land**); *le Stok', le Stokis* 1467 × 84 (with **stoc** or **stocc**); *le Swetegres* 1467 × 84 (v. **swēte, græs**); *Toftes* 1467 × 84 (v. **toft**); *Twerforlonghauedlandes* 1467 × 84 (v. **þverr, furlang, hēafod-land**); *Tweyston', Twostones* 1467 × 84 (v. **twēgen, stān**; presum. boundary markers); *Wadgorslade* 1467 × 84 (v. **wād, gāra, slæd**); *Wakelow* 1467 × 84 (**wacu, hlāw**); *Waldeforlong'* 1467 × 84 (v. **wald, furlang**); *Walschemor*(*e*) 1467 × 84 (v. **wælisc, mōr**[1]); *Waterforowes* 1467 × 84 (v. **wæter, furh** and *Water furrowes* in Ashby Parva f.ns. (b)); *Wartres* 1467 × 84 (v. **weargtrēow**; the site of a gallows); (*le*) *Westing', Westyng, the Westynges, Westingesnetherende* (v. **neoðera, ende**), *Westyng' furlong* (v. **furlang**), *Westyngmeer* (v. **(ge)mǣre**), *Westingtherne* (v. **þyrne**), all 1467 × 84 (v. **west, eng**); *Whetstonmere* 1467 × 84 (v. **(ge)mǣre**; Whetstone parish adjoins to the east); *Wilkynescroft*(*e*) 1467 × 84 (v. **croft**; with the surn. *Wilkin*, a -*kin* diminutive of *Will* (a pet-form of William)); *Willugby meere* 1467 × 84 (v. **(ge)mǣre**; Willoughby Waterleys to the south-east has a small mutual boundary with Cosby); *le Wokehauedeland* 1467 × 84 (v. **wōh, hēafod-land**); *Wolewell* 1467 × 84 (v. **wella**; prob. with the OE masc. pers.n. *Wulfa*); *Wranglandes, Wranglandys* 1467 × 84 (v. **wrang, land**); *Wrensloes* 1467 × 84 (v. **wrenna, slōh**; the habitat of the wren (*Troglodytes troglodytes*) is often marsh edges and reed beds); *le Wrongweye* 1467 × 84, *Wronge way* e.18 (v. **wrang, weg**); *le Wroo* 1467 × 84 (v. **vrá**).

2. LITTLETHORPE

Torp 1086 DB, c.1130 LeicSurv, 1209 × 35 RHug, (~ *iuxta Cosseby* c.1130 LeicSurv)

Thorp 1254 Val, 1257 Fine *et passim* to 1398 Banco, (*Parva* ~ 1254 Val, c.1291 Tax), (~ *iuxta Northbur'* l.13 (1449) *WoCart*)

Thorpe 1269 Ch, 1285 FA, (*Parva* ~ 1285 FA, 1324 Abbr), (~ *iuxta Northburgh* 1314 Banco, 1330, 1331 Ch, 1352 Pat), (~*iuxta Cosseby* 1397 Banco)

Litilthorp iuxta Northburgh 1416 Cl, *Litelthorpe iuxta Northburgh*
1424 Pat, 1500 Ipm
Litylthorp 1449 Fine, 1500 Ipm, *Litelthorp(p)* 1502 *MiscAccts*, 1535
VE, *Lyttelthorp* 1544 Fine, *Lyttlethorpe* 1550 Pat, 1551 Fine,
Littlethorp(e) 1610 Speed, 1627 LML *et freq*

'The little farmstead', *v.* **lȳtel**, **lítill**, **þorp**. In 1807, it is noted by
Nichols that 'Littlethorpe ... is a member of Cosby'. Eventually it was
annexed to Narborough parish in Sparkenhoe Hundred, but lies away
from it to the south of the river Soar, a major boundary, so it is preferable
to include the township here.

LODGE FM (LITTLETHORPE LODGE 2½"), *Littlethorpe Lodge* 1877 White,
1925 Kelly, *v.* **loge**. PLOUGH (P.H.), *Plough* 1925 Kelly, *Old Plough*
1877 White. THE SQUARE. STATION RD, leading to the railway station at
Narborough.

FIELD-NAMES

In (a), forms presented without dates are 1972 *Surv.* Forms throughout
dated 1467 × 84 are *LTD*; those dated 1477 (e.16) are *Charyte*; 1604 are
Nichols; 1641 are Ipm; e.18 are *Terrier*.

(a) Biddles Mdw (with the surn. *Biddle*; cf. *Ann Biddle* 1818 Census of Cosby
and *Mary Biddle* 1846 ib of Littlethorpe); The Bogs (*v.* **bog**); The Charltons (with the
surn. *Charlton*, cf. *John Charlton* 1584 Nichols of Littlethorpe and *Mary Charlton*
1856 Census of Cosby); Big ~, Cuckoo (perh. alluding to the cuckoo (*Cuculus
canorus*), but note Echo Mdw *infra*, of which this may be a garbled form); Dog Leg
(referring to the angled shape of the field); Echo Mdw (*Hechow* 1467 × 84, *Hekho*
1477 (e.16); cf. *Longhekko* (*v.* **lang**[1]), *Schort hekkoo*, *Schortehechowe* (*v.* **sc(e)ort**),
Hechowfelde, *Hekkofelde* (*v.* **feld**; this is the only great open-field that can safely be
attributed solely to Littlethorpe; it is poss. that Littlethorpe once shared *Cokhullfeld*,
Colelanefelde and *Gutlakestonfelde* with Cosby), *Hechowsty* (*v.* **stīg**), all 1467 × 84,
v. **hæc(c)** (here showing Scand influence); with **hōh** or **haugr**); the Flewitts (with the
surn. *Flewitt*, cf. *Hubertus Flohardus* 1130 P of Leics.; from the ContGerm masc.
pers.n. *Hlodhard* (OFr *Floutard*)); The Hatcham (*v.* **hæc(c)**, **hamm**); Holmes or
Biddles Mdw (*v.* **holmr** and Biddles Mdw *supra*); Lammas Piece (*v.* **lammas**, **pece**);
Littlethorpe Cow Cl (*v.* **cū**); The Leys (*v.* **leys**); Osier Beds (*v.* **oyser**, **bedd**); Reins
Mdw (perh. with **rein** 'a boundary strip'); The Ridgeway (*le Rigeweye*, *le Riggeway*,
le Riggeweye, *Rigweye*, *Rydchewey*, *le Riggeweyende* (*v.* **ende**), all 1467 × 84 (*v.*
hrycgweg); South Hams (*v.* **hamm**); Tom Toon's Mdw (cf. *Rachael Toon* 1823
Census, *Henry Toon* 1825 ib and *Mary Toon* 1872 ib, all of Cosby).

(b) *Alforthwey*, *Alforteway* 1467 × 84 (*v.* **ald**, **ford**, **weg**; cf. Alford, DLPN 2; *forth* for *ford* is thought to be due to Scand influence); *Banlondis* 1467 × 84 (*v.* **bēan**, **land**); *Bewcroft* 1467 × 84 (*v.* **croft**; the first el. may be either OE **bēag** or ON **bjúgr**, both meaning 'a river bend', or OE **bū** or ON **bú**, both meaning 'a dwelling, a homestead'); *Blaklond* 1467 × 84 (*v.* **blæc**, **land**, alluding to the colour of the soil); *Bradmere* 1467 × 84 (*v.* **brād**, **(ge)mǣre**); *Brokefurlong* 1467 × 84 (*v.* **brōc**, **furlang**); *le Bull piece* 1641 (*v.* **bula**, **pece**); *Calver pastur* 1467 × 84 (*v.* **calf** (**calfra** gen.pl.), **pasture**); *Cleylond* 1467 × 84, 1477 (e.16) (*v.* **clǣg**, **land**); *Cleypittes* 1467 × 84 (*v.* **cley-pytt**); *Cornerwylow* 1467 × 84 (*v.* **corner**, **wilig**); *Fulwell*, *Fulwellfurlong* (*v.* **furlang**) 1467 × 84 (*v.* **fūl**, **wella**); *Fyssher mydo* 1467 × 84 (*v.* **mēd** (**mēdwe** obl.sg.); with either the surn. *Fisher* or its source **fiscere** 'a fisherman'); *above the gaytes* (*v.* **above**), *inter the gaytes* (with MLat *inter* 'between') 1467 × 84 (*v.* **gata**); *abbutant in Gudloxton* 1467 × 84 (with MLat *abbutto* 'to border upon, to adjoin'); alluding either to 'Guthlac's stone' or to *Gutlakestonfelde*, *v.* Guthlaxton Hundred *supra* and the great open-field of this name in Cosby f.ns. (b) *supra*); *Langfurlong* 1467 × 84 (*v.* **lang**[1], **furlang**); *Langmore* 1467 × 84 (*v.* **lang**[1], **mōr**[1]); *Leeke bedys* 1467 × 84 (*v.* **lēac**, **bedd**); *Longlandis* 1467 × 84 (*v.* **lang**[1], **land**); *Mowshow* 1467 × 84 (*v.* **mūs**; with **hōh** or **haugr**); *Ouergreyndall'* 1467 × 84 (*v.* **uferra**; this may be the *grendale* of Cosby f.ns. (b), but otherwise, *v.* **grein**, **deill**); *Pittholm(e)* 1467 × 84 (*v.* **pytt**, **holmr**); *Rigdole*, *Rygdole* 1467 × 84 (*v.* **hryggr**, **dāl**); *Seares Close* 1604 (with the surn. *Sear*, cf. *Will'us Seer* 1467 × 84 *LTD* of Cosby); *Segbrygfurlong'* 1467 × 84 (*v.* **secg**[1], **brycg**, **furlang**); *le Sixpenny piece* 1641 (*v.* **pece**; land valued at sixpence, presum. at this date its annual rental); *Stanydolis*, *Stanydolys* 1467 × 84 (*v.* **stānig**, **dāl**); *Stokfurlong'* 1467 × 84 (*v.* **stoc**, **furlang**); *Stonys* 1467 × 84 (*v.* **stān**); *Thacheholme* 1467 × 84 (*v.* **þæc**, **holmr**).

Cotesbach

Cotesbece 1086 DB, *Cotesbech*(*e*) 1274 Ipm, 1280 Misc *et freq* to
    1406 Prep, 1507 Pat, *Cotisbech* l.13 *CRCart*, Edw 1 *CroxR*
Codesbech(*e*) 1205 FF, 1253 × 58 RHug, 1268 RGrav *et passim* to
    1327 Pat, *Codesb'* 1220 MHW
Godesbech(*e*) 1222, 1224 RHug, *Godebeche* 1224 ib
Cottesbec 1254 Val, *Cottesbech*(*e*) 1274 IpmR, 1295 OSut, 1336
    IpmR
Cotesbac 1236 Fees, *Cotisbache* 1274 Cl, *Cotesbach*(*e*) 1307, 1308
    Fine *et passim* to 1576 Saxton *et freq*
Cottysbych 1524 SR, *Cottesbiche* 1541 Ipm, *Cottisbich*(*e*) 1576
    LibCl, 1581 LEpis, 1608 LML, *Cottesbitch* 1612, 1621 ib

Probably 'Cott's broad valley with a stream', *v.* **bece**, **bæce**. The
stream in the valley here is the river Swift. The specific of the settlement-
name appears to be an OE masc. pers.n. *Cott*, as in Cottesmore (Ru 16)
and in *Cottes hyrst* 962 (10^2) BCS 1085 (S 703). An alternative OE masc.
pers.n. *Codd* may also be thought of, as in The Cotswolds (Wo 1),
Cutsdean (Wo 120) and perhaps in Cottesbrooke (Nth 67). Early
published forms for Cotesbach with initial *g* are no doubt misreadings of
upper case *c* rather than evidence for a voiced consonant.
    Note that Dodgson prefers to interpret the lost *Cotesbache* (Ch **3** 206),
with forms from 1278 to 1559, as 'stream and valley at a cot', with OE
cot (*cotes* gen.sg.) 'a cottage' as the specific.

pons de Brunesford 1284 *Ass* (with MLat *pons* 'a bridge'), *Bensford
Bridge* 1610 Speed, *a Bridge called now Benesford bridge but antiently
Brunesford bridge* 1656 Dugd, *Bensford Bridge* 1695 Morden, *v.* **brycg**;
Brinsford 1606, 1625 *Terrier*, *Brynesford* 1612 LAS, *Brinesford* 1629
Nichols, *v.* **ford**; the specific is a masc. pers.n. as in the township-name
of Brownsover, adjacent to the south in Warwks., which was held by a
man called *Bruno* in 1086 DB (from either OE *Brūn* or ON *Brúnn*). This
bridge over the river Swift is at the site of the most northerly of three

closely consecutive bridges which may have given the important
Romano-British settlement of *Tripontium* on Watling Street its name, *v.*
Dow Bridge in Catthorpe *supra.*

BURROW SPINNEY (*v.* **spinney**), *Burrow* 1720 *Map*, *v.* **berg**. BUTTON'S
HILL SPINNEY (*v.* **spinney**), *Button Hill* 1720, e.19 *Map*, 1850 *TA*; with
the surn. *Button*, cf. *Isaac Button* 1854 Census of nearby Ashby Parva.
COTESBACH FIELDS FM. COTESBACH HALL, 1925 Kelly, *The Hall* 1877
White, *v.* **hall**. COTESBACH HO. HALL FM. HILL FM. HOLLY WALK
SPINNEY, *v.* **holegn**, **walk**, **spinney**. HOME FM (is COTESBACH LODGE FM
2½"), *The Lodge* 1877 White, *v.* **loge**. HOME FARM LODGE, *v.* **home**,
loge. HOMELEIGH FM. HOME SPINNEY, *v.* **spinney**. JEREMY'S GROUND
SPINNEY (*v.* **spinney**), *Jeremy's Ground* e.19 *Map*, 1850 *TA*, *v.* **grund**,
with the surn. *Jeremy*, *v.* Reaney *s.n.* LODGE PLANTATIONS, *v.*
plantation. LONG SPINNEY, *v.* **spinney**. MAIN RD. MANOR HO. (~ ~ FM
2½"), *Manor House* 1846, 1877 White, *Cotesbach Manor* 1925 Kelly,
v. **maner**. NEW COVERT, *v.* **cover(t)**. ORCHARD FM, *v.* **orceard**. THE
PARK, *v.* **park**. THE RECTORY, 1877 White, 1925 Kelly, *v.* **rectory**;
earlier recorded is *the Parsonage House* 1625, 1674, 1679, 1690, 1697,
1700 *Terrier*, *v.* **personage**. ROAD BARN. RUGBY RD is *Rigbee way* 1606
Terrier, Rugby in Warwks. lying 5 miles to the south-west. ST MARY'S
CHURCH, *Church (St Mary)* 1846, 1863, 1877 White, 1925 Kelly; it is
earlier recorded as *ecclesie de Codesb'* 1220 MHW, ~ *de Codesbeche*
1319 *Pat*, ~ *de Cotesbech(e)* 1318, 1336, 1337, 1340, 1344, 1507 *ib*, ~
de Cotebech 1375 *ib*, *ecclesiam de Cotesbecche* 1383 *ib*. Note also *the
Church Yard* 1745 *Terrier*, *v.* **churchyerd**. SHAWELL RD, Shawell lying
one mile to the south-east. SOUTH LODGE, *v.* **loge**. TOWN END FM, *v.* **tūn**,
ende. WEST COTTAGES.

FIELD-NAMES

Forms in (a) presented without dates are 1850 *TA*; those dated e.19 are
Map. Forms throughout dated 1332 are SR; those dated 1589 are
ExchSpC; 1606, 1625, 1700, 1709 and 1745 are *Terrier*; 1612 are LAS;
1615 are DKR; 1720 are *Map*.

(a) Back Croft (*v.* **back**, **croft**); Bank(e)y Mdw e.19, 1850 (*Banke Meddow* 1720,
v. **banke**, **-ig**[3]); Upper ~ ~, Barn Cl, Barn Mdw e.19, 1850 (*v.* **bern**); Bath Cl (*v.*
bæð; at a pool); Big Cl e.19, Far ~ ~, Near Big Cl 1850; Boggy Mdw e.19, 1850
(1720, *v.* **boggy**); Branseed ~ (sic) e.19, Bransted Mdw (sic) 1850 (*Bransford
Meddow* 1720, *v.* Bransford Bridge *supra*); Brick Kiln Road Cl (*v.* **brike-kiln**);

Broadwell Cl, Little Bush(e)y Broadwell (*v.* **busshi**), Long Broadwell, Pen Broadwell (*v.* **penn**) e.19, 1850, Second ~, Third Broadwell 1850 (cf. *Upper Broadwell* 1720, *v.* **brād, wella**); Button Hill Mdw e.19, 1850 (*v.* Button's Hill Spinney *supra*); Clover Cl e.19, 1850 (*v.* **clāfre**; a fodder crop); Lower ~ ~, Upper Cold Slade e.19, 1850 (*Coslade* 1625, cf. *Coslade hill* 1606, 1625, *Nether* ~ ~, *Ouer Coslade Hill* 1606 (*v.* **uferra**), *Coslade medowe* 1625, *v.* **cald, slæd**; appears as *Colslade* (1606) in adjoining Shawell); Corn Cl e.19, 1850 ((*the*) *Corn*(*e*) *Close* 1709, 1720, 1745, *v.* **corn**[1]); Great Forest e.19, Far ~ ~, Near Great Forest 1850, Little Forest e.19, Far ~ ~, Near Little Forest 1850 (*v.* **forest**; it is uncertain whether these f.ns. remember the former Forest of Arden, *v.* Church of St Mary in Arden, 13 miles to the east (Lei **4** 177–8)); Further Cl e.19, 1850 (*v.* **furðra**); Gibbet Cl e.19, Far ~ ~, Near Gibbet Cl 1850 (*v.* **gibet**; the gibbet was positioned on the main road (Watling Street) for major impact on travelling malefactors); Further Ground (*v.* **furðra**), Great Ground e.19, Further ~ ~, Great Ground, Further Oat Ground 1850, Lower Oat Ground e.19, Top ~ ~, Top Road Oat Ground 1850 (*the Oat ground* 1709, 1745, *v.* **āte**), Short Furlong Ground 1850 (*v.* **furlang**), Upper Ground e.19, Upper Ground First Part, ~ ~ Second Part 1850, Upper Ground Mdw e.19, 1850 (*Upper ground* 1720) (*v.* **grund**); Hall Fd e.19 (1720), First ~ ~, Second Hall Fd 1850 (*the Hall field*(*e*) 1606, 1612, *Hallefeild* 1625, *v.* **feld**; one of the great open-fields of the township), Hall Field Mdw 1850 (*Hall field meddow* 1720) (*v.* **hall** and Cotesbach Hall *supra*); Hard Mdw e.19, 1850 (*Hard meddow* 1720, *v.* **heard**; land with a hard surface); Holmes (1720, *le holme* 1606, *v.* **holmr**); Home Cl, Home Mdw e.19, 1850 (*v.* **home**); Horse Cl e.19, First ~ ~, Second Horse Cl 1850, Great ~ ~, Little Horse Cl e.19, 1850 (*v.* **hors**); House Cl e.19, 1850, ~ Mdw 1850; Upper Kiln Cl e.19, 1850 (*v.* **cyln**); Little Hill e.19, 1850 (1720, *litle hill, the little hill* 1625), Little Hill Mdw e.19 (*Little hill meddow* 1720); Little Mdw (1709, 1745); Lole's Cl, ~ Mdw e.19, 1850 (with the surn. *Lolle*, cf. *Johannes Lolle* 1327 SR of Leics.; either from the OE masc. pers.n. *Lulla* or a nickname from ME *lollen* 'to droop'); Long Cl e.19, Bottom ~ ~, Top ~ ~, Long Cl 1850; Lower ~ ~, Upper Long Mdw e.19, 1850 (*Long meaddow* 1720); Mill Cl, Far Mill Fd 1850, Great Mill Fd e.19, Little ~ ~, Lower ~ ~, Near Mill Fd 1850 (*Nether* ~, *Upper Millfield* 1720, *v.* **myln**); Great ~, Nether ~, Wood Misterton (*v.* **wudu**) e.19, 1850, Road Misterton 1850 (abutting a roadway) (*Great* ~, *Little Mesterton* 1720; Misterton parish adjoins to the north-east); Nether Fd e.19, 1850 (1720); New Cl e.19, 1850 (1720); New Mdw e.19, 1850 (*the newe medowe* 1625, *New Meaddow* 1720); New Piece e.19, 1850 (*v.* **pece**); Old Orchard e.19, 1850 (*v.* **orceard**); Lower ~ ~, Upper Pen Cl e.19, 1850 (*v.* **penn**); Pit Cl 1850 (*v.* **pytt**); Plot Cl e.19 (*v.* **plot**); First ~ ~, Further ~ ~, Middle ~ ~, Upper Poor Cl e.19, 1850 (*v.* **pouer**(**e**); land endowed for charity, for the relief of the poor); Rickyard Cl (*v.* **reke-yard**); Road Cl e.19, 1850 (abutting a roadway); Seed Mdw e.19, 1850 (*v.* **sǣd**; in modern f.ns., used of grasses sown for one year's mowing or grazing as distinguished from permanent pasture); Slipes e.19, Big ~, Little Slipes 1850 (*v.* **slipe**); Lower ~ ~, Upper Smart Mdw e.19, 1850 (with the surn. *Smart*, common in adjoining Lutterworth parish from *William Smart* 1810 Census to *Thomas Smart* 1874 ib); Smith's ~ e.19, Smiths Mdw 1850 (with the surn. *Smith*); Three Corner Cl e.19 (*v.* **three-corner**); Three Cornered Cl 1850 (*v.* **three-cornered**); Top Cl e.19, 1850; Town end Cl e.19, Townsend Cl 1850, Town end Mdw e.19, Townsend Mdw 1850 (*v.* Town End Fm *supra*); Well Cl (*v.* **wella**); Wheat Cl e.19, Little ~ ~, Wheat Cl 1850 ((*the*) *Wheat close* 1709, 1720, 1745, *v.*

hwǣte); Wood Cl (v. **wudu**); Winneymeg (sic) 1850 (this may either be a misscript or a misheard Winnipeg (the site of a Scottish colony founded in 1811 and of a trading post established by the Hudson's Bay Company in 1821 and thus a 'remoteness' name for land well away from the village); but if the first six letters represent *whinny* 'growing with whins and gorse bushes', then *meg* could be ModEdial. *meg*, used of a halfpenny and thus denoting land of inferior worth, or even be an affectionate *Meg*, the pet-form of Margaret).

(b) *Ashbies corner* 1606 (v. **corner**; with the surn. *Ashby*); *Brinsford(e) fielde* 1606, *Brynesford Feild* 1612 (v. **feld**; one of the great open-fields), *Short Brinsford furlonge* 1606 (v. **furlang**), *Great Bransford* 1720 (v. Bransford Bridge *supra*); *Broad medowe leyes* 1606 (v. **leys**); *Short Brodelandes* 1606, *long broadelandes* 1625 (v. **brād**, **land**); *Brode old fielde* 1606, *the Broadolde Feild* 1612, *Broadeold feilde* 1625, *the Middle alias Broadold feild* 1625, *Broad Old Feilds* 1709, ~ ~ *Fields* 1745 (v. **brād**, **wald**, **feld**; one of the great open-fields); *Cornelandes* 1606 (v. **corn**[1], **land**); *Nether ~*, *Upper Croslands* 1720 (v. **land**; prob. with **cross**, but note *Crosse hill*); *Crosse hill* 1606, 1625 (v. **cros**); *Ditch furlonge* 1606 (v. **dīc**, **furlang**); *Gilbert Buttes* 1606, *~ Butts* 1625 (v. **butte**; with the surn. *Gilbert*, from the ContGerm masc. pers.n. *Gisilbert* (OFr *Gilebert*)); *Goddards Farm*; with the surn. *Goddard*, from the ContGerm masc. pers.n. *Godhard* (OFr *Godard*), cf. *Fras. Goddard* 1615 DKR of Cotesbach); *Gorebroad(e)* 1605, 1625 (v. **garebrode**, **gorebrode**); *grindle* 1606 (v. **grendel**); *the Hall clos* 1589 (v. **hall**, **clos(e)** and Cotesbach Hall *supra*); *(where) hallesgate* (*standeth*) 1625 (v. **hall**, **geat**); *Henme(e)re* 1606, 1625 (v. **henn**, **mere**[1]); *Highhill* 1606, 1625 (v. **hēah**[1]), *othe Hill* 1332 (p) (v. **hyll**); *the Hollow* 1709, 1745 (v. **holh**); *the Kinges high way* 1606, 1625 (v. **hēah-weg**; with reference to James I and to Watling Street); *Lang(e)landes* 1606, 1625 (v. **lang**[1], **land**); *Over Locke* 1606 (v. **uferra**), *the Locks* 1709, 1745 (v. **loca**); *Longeslade* 1625, *Long(e)slade furlonge* 1605, 1625 (v. **furlang**) (v. **lang**[1], **slæd**); *the meere hedge* 1625 (v. **(ge)mǣre**, **hecg**; a parish boundary); *the Middle alias Broadold feild* 1625 (v. *Brode old fielde*, *supra*); *Middle hill* 1605, 1625; *Middle Meeres* 1606 (v. **(ge)mǣre**); *the mires* 1606 (v. **mýrr**); *Misterton leyes* 1625 (v. **leys**), *Misterton Warren* 1625 (v. **wareine**), *Mesterton Meddow* 1720 (land abutting Misterton parish which adjoins to the north-east); *Mug pitt* 1720 (v. **pytt**; poss. with the ME surn. *Mugge*, from the OE masc. pers.n. *Mugga*, otherwise with **mug**; perh. cf. *firkinhole* in Wigston Magna f.ns. (b) or *Mugecroft* in Aylestone f.ns. (b)); *Newton way(e)* 1606, 1625 (the road to Newton which lies 2 miles to the south in Warwks.); *the old ditch* 1625 (v. **dīc**; with **wald** or **ald**); *the parsons piece* 1606 (v. **persone**, **pece**); *Rootes hedge* 1625 (v. **hecg**; with the surn. *Root*, from OE *rōt* 'cheerful'); *Rye more* 1606 (v. **ryge**, **mōr**[1]; poss. with reference to rye-grass); *Shawell hedge* (v. **hecg**), *Shawell mere* (v. **(ge)mǣre**) 1625 (a boundary with hedge to Shawell parish which adjoins to the south-east); *Sidemedowe* 1606 (v. **sīde**, **mēd** (**mēdwe** obl.sg.)); *Slithers* 1606, 1625 (v. **slidor**); *Smale old* 1625, *Smallard* 1720, *Smalleold fielde* 1606, *the Smallold or Misterton Feild* 1612 (v. **feld**; one of the great open fields, Misterton parish adjoining to the north-east), *Small Old Meadow* 1709, 1745, *Smalard Meaddow* 1720 (v. **smæl**, **wald**); *Stones* 1606, 1625 (v. **stān**); *the street* 1625, *Streete furlonge* 1606, 1625 (v. **furlang**) (v. **strēt**; alluding to Watling Street); *Thakeslade* 1606, 1625 (v. **þak**, **slæd**); *Thisle close* 1720 (v. **þistel**); *thorough acres* 1606, 1625 (v. **furh**, **æcer**); *twelue acres* 1625 (a close so called, v. **twelf**, **æcer**); *Upper meddow* 1720.

Countesthorpe

Torp 1156 (1318) Ch, 1220 MHW

Thorp Cuntasse 1276 RH, *Thorp Contasse* 1284 Fine, *Thorpe Countasse* 1284 Ass

Cuntassethorp 1242 GildR (p), 1261 Cur *et passim* to 1283 Fine, *Cuntasthorp*(*e*) 1284 Fine, 1299 Ipm *et passim* to 1397, 1399 *Rut*, *Cuntesthorp*(*e*) 1350 Pat, 1425 *Wyg et passim* to 1488 Ipm

Contassethorp 1272 GildR (p), 1344 Cl *et passim* to 1369, 1397 *Rut*

Countassethorp 1314 Ass, 1343 Cl, *Countasthorp*(*e*) 1314 Ass, 1316 Cl, 1330 FA, 1345 Banco

Countesthorp(*e*) 1395 Fine, 1400 Pat, 1427 *Wyg et passim* to 1626 LML *et freq*

Cuntysthorp(*e*) 1510 Visit, 1526 AAS, *Countysthorpe* 1562 CoPleas, 1627 LML, *Countisthorp*(*e*) 1576 Saxton, 1610 Speed, 1626 LML

'The outlying farmstead', *v.* **þorp**; later affixed with ME **cuntesse** 'a countess'. Nichols notes that this manor 'was antiently assigned in dower to the Countesses of Leicester', while in 1265, Simon de Montfort, Earl of Leicester, died seised of lands in Countesthorpe, *v.* Nichols **4** 1 56.

AXE AND SQUARE (P.H.), *Axe and Square* 1846, 1863, 1877 White, 1925 Kelly; a craft-related tavern name of a type which developed in the first half of the 19th cent., here poss. an indication of its landlord's subsidiary occupation, *v.* Cox[1] *passim*. BULL'S HEAD (P.H.), *Bull's Head* 1846, 1863, 1877 White, 1925 Kelly. CHURCH ST, *v.* St Andrew's Church *infra*. COTTAGE HOMES (local), built in 1884 for the Leicester Board of Guardians to house pauper children. FOSTON RD, Foston lying one mile to the east. GLEBE FM, *v.* **glebe**. HILL FM is *Blaby Lodge* 1835 O, *v.* **loge**; named from Blaby which lies 1½ miles to the north. LEICESTER RD is *Lester way* 1625, 1703 *Terrier*, *Leicester way* 1638, c.1674, 1639 *ib*, *v.* **weg**; early Leicester lay 4 miles to the north. LINDEN HO., *Linden House* 1877 White, 1925 Kelly, *v.* **linden**. PEATLING RD, Peatling lying 2 miles to the south-east. THE POPLARS. RAILWAY (P.H.), *Railway Hotel* 1925

Kelly. ROEBUCK (P.H.) (lost), *Roebuck* 1846, 1863, 1877 White. ROSE
FM. ST ANDREW'S CHURCH, *Church (St Andrew's)* 1846, 1863, 1877
White, 1925 Kelly; it is earlier recorded as *capellam Torp* 1220 MHW
(with MLat *capella* 'a chapel'). STATION RD, leading to the former
Countesthorpe Station 1854 O on the now defunct Midland Counties
Railway. THE VICARAGE, 1925 Kelly, *v.* **vikerage**. WILLIAM IV (P.H.),
William IV 1846 White, *William the Fourth* 1877 ib.

Street-names in recent urban developments:

BASSETT AVE. CENTRAL ST. HALLCROFT AVE. LINDEN AVE. MAIN ST.
NEW ST. REGENT RD. THE DRIVE. WATERLOO CRESC. WESTFIELD AVE.
WIGSTON ST.

FIELD-NAMES

In (a), names presented without dates are 1968 *Surv*. Names throughout
dated 1467 × 84 are *LTD*; those dated 1625, 1638, c.1674, 1679, l.17 and
1703 are *Terrier*; 1729 are MiscAccts.

(a) Four Acre, Five ~, Seven ~, Nine ~, Ten Acre (*v.* **æcer**); Lower ~ ~, Ballast
Hole (a former source of ballast for the dismantled railway which the close abuts);
Banky Cl (*v.* **banke, -ig³**); Big Fd; Blaby Cl, ~ End (*v.* **ende**) (Blaby parish adjoins
to the north); Brick Cl (the site of former brick-kilns); Lower ~ ~, Old Bridge Cl
(*ould bruge* 1703, *v.* **ald, brycg**); The Buildings; Bulls Piece (*v.* **pece**; prob. with
bula as in the common f.n. Bull Piece, but because of the apparent possessive case,
a surn. *Bull* is poss.; note *Mary Bull* 1825 Census of Countesthorpe); Burleys Cl
(with the surn. *Burley*, cf. *Abraham Burley* 1808 Census, *James Burley* 1815 ib, the
surn. found in this township through to *Ernest Burley* 1880 ib); Butts Cl (*v.* **butte**);
Chapmans Big Fd, Chapmans Fds (with the surn. *Chapman*, cf. *William Chapman*
1630 Nichols, *Thomas Chapman* 1815 Census, the surn. common in Countesthorpe
through to *Alfred Chapman* 1863 ib); Cheese Cake Mdw (*v.* **chese-cake**; used
topographically of a wedge-shaped field, alluding to a slice of the tart so called);
Clarks Cl (with the surn. *Clark*, cf. *Job Clark* 1821 Census, *Joseph Clark* 1848 ib,
a surn. common in the village through to *Prudence Clark* 1879 ib); Clover Cl (*v.*
cläfre; a fodder crop); Cosbys Fd (with the surn. *Cosby* of a family originally from
the township of this name, 2 miles to the west; cf. *William Cosby* 1802 Census and
Joseph Cosby 1834 ib of adjoining Blaby parish); Cross Roads Fd; First ~ ~, Second
Dairy Cl (*v.* **deierie**); Dale Acre (*v.* **æcer**) (*the dale* 1703, *v.* **dalr**); Dunmores Mdw
(this may be with a surn. *Dunmore* in the possessive case, but note *Dunspitt* 1638,
c.1674, 1703 (*v.* **pytt**), with the OE masc. pers.n. *Dunn*, so that a 'Dunn's moor' is
prob., *v.* **mōr¹**); First Cl; Gallaway (sic) (the surn. *Galloway* (perh. deriving from the
district of this name in Scotland) occurs occasionally in Leics. from 1829 to 1880
Census, but here this uncompounded f.n. may be rather a topographical 'road to the

gallows', *v.* **galga, weg**); Gibbins Mdw (with the surn. *Gibbin*(*s*)); Gilliams Butts (*v.* **butte**; with the surn. *Gillam*, cf. *Francis Gillam* 1630 Nichols, *John Gillam* 1630 ib, *Thomas Gillam* 1772 MI, *Sarah Gillam* 1808 Census, the surn. common in Countesthorpe through to *Thomas Gillam* 1848 ib); Gravel Hole (*v.* **gravel, hol**[1]); The Hagg (*v.* **họgg**); Top Hallcroft (*v.* **hall, croft**; remembered in the modern Hallcroft Ave *supra*); Left ~ ~, Right Hand Mdw; Bottom ~, Top Harton (*v.* **tūn**; a lost settlement, either with **hār**[2] in its sense 'a boundary' or with **hær**; *v.* also *Harton field* in neighbouring Whetstone f.ns. (b) and Top 'Arton in Willoughby Waterleys f.ns. (a)); Hollow Fd (*v.* **holh**); Home Cl, ~ Fd (*v.* **home**); Hubbards Cl, ~ Orchard (*v.* **orceard**) (with the surn. *Hubbard*, cf. *John Hubbard* 1802 Census, *Thomas Hubbard* 1813 ib, a surn. common in Countesthorpe through to *William Hubbard* 1880 ib); Kelhams Cl (with the surn. *Kelham* of a family originally from Kelham, 40 miles to the north-east in Notts., cf. *Willielmus Kelom* 1327 SR of Leics. and *William Kelham* 1821 Census of Countesthorpe); Leicester Road Fd (*v.* Leicester Rd *supra*); Masons Fd (with the surn. *Mason*); Moores Cl, ~ Mdw (with the surn. *Moore*, cf. *William Moore* 1827 Census of Countesthorpe); The Nook (*v.* **nōk**); The Orchard, Orchard Cl (*v.* **orceard**); Packman (sic) (this may be the surn. *Packman*, from the medieval occupation of *packeman* 'a hawker, a pedlar', cf. *Simon Pakeman* 1221 Cur of Leics.; otherwise denoting a place frequented by pedlars, as in *Packman way*, Lei **3** 270, *v.* **packeman**); The Paddock (*v.* **paddock**); Penns Cl (with the surn. *Penn*); Pit Fd (*v.* **pytt** and *Dunspitt* considered with Dunmores Mdw *supra*); Pump Cl (*v.* **pumpe**); Railway Cl (beside the dismantled Midland Counties Railway line); Reed Pool Cl (*v.* **hrēod, pōl**[1]); Bottom ~, Top ~, Scalborough (*Scalbaro, Scalboro* 1467 × 84, *Scalborow* 1703, *v.* **skalli, berg**; a hill at the Blaby boundary); Second Cl; Spanglands (1625, 1638, c.1674, 1679, l.17, *v.* **spang, land**); Spinney Fd, Top Spinney (*v.* **spinney**); Spoil Bank (excavated material from the building of the line of the now dismantled Midland Counties Railway); Sweets End (*v.* **ende**; prob. with the surn. *Sweet*); Tebbs Cl (with the surn. *Tebb*(*s*), cf. *Johannes Tebbe* 1316 FA and *Adam Tebbe* 1316 ib of Leics., *Richard Tebbs* 1841 Census, *Thomas Tebbs* 1847 ib and *Robert Tebbs* 1854 ib, all of adjacent Kilby); Thick Mdw (*v.* **þicce**[1]); Second ~ ~, Tipster Hill (meaning uncertain; modern hill-names are often compounded with surns., here poss. with the rare surn. *Tipster*, the 1881 Census recording only one instance of this name nationwide, that of *George Tipster* of London's Spitalfields; *Tipster* may well be a reduced form of the more common *Tipstaff*); Top Fd; Wards Fd, Wards Pit Fd (*v.* **pytt**) (with the surn. *Ward*, cf. *Austin Ward* 1801 Census, *Joseph Ward* 1817 ib, a surn. frequent in the township through to *William Ward* 1879 ib); West Mdw.

(b) *Claver leyes* c.1674, 1679 (*v.* **clǣfre, leys**); *the Common streete* 1638 (*v.* **commun, strēte**); *Countisthorpe Mill* 1729 (*v.* **myln** and *the Milfilde, infra*); *Farmoor Leases* 1679 (*v.* **feor, mōr**[1], **leys**); *at the footbrig*(*g*) 1679, 1703 (*v.* **fote-brydge**); *Mrs Gees close* 1703 (cf. *Mary Gee* 1816 Census and *John Gee* 1819 ib, both of neighbouring Cosby); *gildenebutes* 1625, *Gilden buttes* 1638, *Gildenbutts* c.1674, *giltonbuts* 1679, *gilton buts* 1703 (*v.* **gylden, butte**); *Goddins Hedge* 1679 (*v.* **hecg**; with the surn. *Goodwin*, cf. *Mary Goodwin* 1842 Census, *Jannett Goodwin* 1875 ib and *William Goodwin* 1879 ib, all of Countesthorpe); *grinste waye* 1625, *Greenstie way* 1638, *Greenstee way* c.1674, *Greensty way* 1679, *grinsty way* 1703 (*v.* **grēne**[1], **stīg, weg**; **sty-way**); *Richard Gumlis hadland* 1625 (*v.* **hēafod-land**; with the surn. *Gumley* of a family originally from the township of this name 8 miles to the south-east, cf. *Lydia Gumley* 1854 Census of adjacent Blaby); *hell hole* l.17, *Hell hole leases* 1679 (*v*. **leys**) (*v*. **hell-hole**; used of infertile or otherwise unattractive land); *Hoden Haggs* 1679, *hourding hags* 1703 (*v*. **họgg**; the first word may mean 'dirty valley', *v*. **horh**, **denu**); *hylese* 1625, *High leyes* 1638, c.1674, *highleases* 1679 (*v*. **hēah**[1], **leys**); *Longdoles* 1638 (*v*. **lang**[1], **dāl**); *Thomas Lords Cloose* 1625 (*v*. **clos(e)**; the surn. *Lord* was still common in Countesthorpe from *Thomas Lord* 1808 Census, *Samuel Lord* 1811 ib to *Martha Lord* 1835 ib); *Luterworth way* 1703 (Lutterworth lies 7 miles to the south); *Marlepitt* 1638, c.1674 (*v*. **marle-pytt**); *Maryroodes* 1625, *Marry Roodes* 1679 (*v*. **rōd**[3]; perh. with **myry** 'muddy' rather than alluding to land endowed for a chapel to the Virgin Mary in the parish church); *Meadwellgate* 1679, *medwell gate* 1703 (*v*. **mēd**, **wella**, **gata**); *the Midelfilde* 1625, *the Middle Fielde* 1638, ~ ~ *Feild* c.1674, 1679, l.17, *the Meadell field* 1703 (*v*. **middel**, **feld**; one of the great open-fields of the township; the 1703 form approximates to *Meadwell*, *supra*, which was in *the Midelfilde*); *the Milfilde* 1625, *the Milne fielde* 1638, ~ ~ *feild* c.1674, *the Mill field* 1679, 1703 (*v*. **feld**; one of the great open-fields), *milforland* 1625 (*v*. **furlang**), *Milne way* 1638, c.1674, 1679, *the Mill way* 1703 (*v*. **weg**) (*v*. **myln**; note *Countisthorpe Mill*, *supra*); *(the) Moore* 1625, c.1674, 1679, *the more* l.17, *more forland* 1625 (*v*. **furlang**) (*v*. **mōr**[1]); *Ould Mill Hill* 1679 (*v*. **ald**, **myln**); *padackkesden* 1625, *Paddocksden* 1638, 1674, 1679, 1703 (*v*. **padduc**; perh. with **denn** rather than with **denu**, the generic appearing to be in the sense 'a pit, a den', cf. Paddy's Nest (*Padognest* 1467 × 84, *paddock nest* 1625) in adjoining Blaby and Podocks Nest in Countesthorpe *supra*); *Long Rathes* 1679, ~ *Raths* 1703 (of uncertain meaning; perh. with **wraðu** 'a prop, a support', used of timbers or piles on which a building was erected as protection against floods, or timbers used as a flood barrier, cf. Rath Hades in Willoughby Waterleys f.ns. (a)); *Sharwood* 1638, c.1674, *Showward furlong* 1679, *Showard fourlong* 1703 (*v*. **furlang**) (*v*. **sc(e)aru**, **wudu**); *the South feelde* 1625, ~ ~ *Feild* 1679, l.17, ~ ~ *field* 1703 (*v*. **sūð**, **feld**; one of the great open-fields); *stanlands* 1703 (*v*. **stān**, **land**); *Stavens* ~ 1638, *Steevens hedge* c.1674, 1679 (*v*. **hecg**; note *Wm. Steevens* 1638 *Terrier* of Countesthorpe); *Synderlands* 1638 (*v*. **sundor-land**); *Thorpp Woldfeld*, *Thorpwoldefelde* 1467 × 84 (*v*. **wald**, **feld**; an early great open-field of Countesthorpe, perh. the precursor of *the South feelde*, *supra*); *Whetstone brooke* c.1674 (*v*. **brōc**; Whetstone parish adjoins to the south-west); *Woodway* 1679 (*v*. **wudu**, **weg**).

Dunton Bassett

Donitone 1086 DB, *Donton* 1254 Val, 1308 *Deed et passim* to 1518
   Visit, 1539 *Ferrers*, (~ *Bassett* 1539 *ib*)
Dunetunam 12 Nichols
Dunton(e) c.1130 LeicSurv, 1166 LN, e.13 *Dixie et freq*, (~ *Basset(t)*
   1526 Fine, 1535 VE, 1591 *Terrier*), *Duntona* 1148 Nichols,
   Duntun 1241 RGros
Dounton 1403, 1424 AD, 1431, 1447 *Ferrers*, 1489 Pat, 15 *Ferrers*,
   1537 MinAccts, (~ *Bassett* 1537 ib)

'The farmstead or village on the hill', *v.* **dūn**, **tūn**. *Radulfus Basset*
held the manor in 1166 LN and his family retained possession as late as
Ricardus Basset 1411 Pat.

ALL SAINTS' CHURCH, *Church (All Saints)* 1846, 1863, 1877 White,
1925 Kelly; it is earlier recorded as *ecclesie de Dunton* 1220 MHW, ~ *de
Duntun* 1241 RGros, *ecclesiam de Dunton* 1411 *Pat*, *the churche* 1601,
1606 *Terrier*, *the Church* 1709, 1724, 1745, 1762 *ib*. Note also *the
Churche yarde* 1606 *ib*, *the Church Yard* 1709, 1724, 1767 *ib*, *v.*
churchyerd. BLOOMHILLS FM, *Bloomhill* 1697, 1700, 1703, 1709
Terrier, *Bloonhill* (sic) 1724 *ib*, *Blomhill* 1745, 1762 *ib*, *Bloom Hills*
1925 Kelly; no early forms, but poss. with **blōma** 'a lump or ingot of
metal', denoting a place used for smelting, the surn. *Bloom*, metonymic
for *blōmere* 'a smelter, an iron-worker' also being possible. CHURCH
LANE, *v.* All Saints' Church *supra*. COOPER'S LANE, with the surn.
Cooper, cf. *John Cooper* 1823 Census of Dunton Bassett. CROOKED
BILLET (P.H.) (lost), *Crooked Billet* 1846, 1863, 1877 White, 1925 Kelly.
CROWN AND THISTLE (P.H.), *Crown and Thistle* 1846, 1863, 1877 White,
1925 Kelly. DUNTON MILL, 1835 O, *the Mill* 1700, 1703 *Terrier et
passim* to 1762 *ib*, *v.* **myln**. ELWELLS FM, *hillwells* 1591 *Terrier*, *v.* **hyll**,
wella. HOLMFIELD, *v.* **holmr**. HOLT HO., *Holt House* 1925 Kelly, *the olt*
1601, 1674, 1690 *Terrier*, *the olte* 1606 *ib*, *the oult* 1697, 1700 *ib et
passim* to 1762 *ib*, *v.* **wald**. LEIRE LANE, Leire lying one mile to the west.

LITTLE LUNNON, the local form of 'Little London'. Field 151 notes that sometimes fields so called were set aside for cattle drovers en route to London. LODGE FM (DUNTON LODGE 2½"), *Dunton Lodge* 1877 White, 1925 Kelly, *v.* **loge**. LOVES LANE, with the surn. *Love*, cf. *Jane Love* 1828 Census of nearby Kilworth. LUTTERWORTH RD, Lutterworth lying 4 miles to the south. MAIN ST. MANOR HO., *Manor House* 1925 Kelly, *v.* **maner**. RAILWAY HOTEL (lost), *Railway Hotel* 1925 Kelly. THE RISE, 1925 Kelly, *v.* **rise**. SHOULDER OF MUTTON (P.H.) (lost), *Shoulder of Mutton* 1846, 1863, 1877 White, 1925 Kelly. STATION RD, leading to the former Ashby Magna railway station; this is the direct route to Ashby Magna and must represent the former *asbygate* 1690 *Terrier*, *ashbyway* 1690 *ib*, *Ashby lane* 1698 *ib*, *v.* **gata**, **weg**, **lane**. STOKES CROFT, *Crafte* 1601, 1606 *Terrier*, *Croft* 1674 *ib*, *Crofts* 1697, 1700 *ib et passim* to 1762 *ib*, *v.* **croft**; presum. the eventual property of Thomas Stokes, a wealthy hosier of Leicester who was lord of the manor and founded the local school in 1849. THE VICARAGE, 1877 White, 1925 Kelly; earlier is recorded *the vicaridge house* 1601, 1606 *Terrier*, *the Vicarage House* 1700, 1703 *et passim* to 1762 *ib*, *v.* **vikerage**. WEST COTE (local), *West-Cote* 1925 Kelly, *v.* **cot**. WHITE LODGE, *v.* **loge**.

FIELD-NAMES

In (a), forms presented without dates are 1967 *Surv*; those dated 1762 are *Terrier*; 1796 are Nichols; 1797 are *EnclA*; 1835 are O; 1846, 1863 and 1877 are White. Forms throughout dated 1327 are SR; those dated 1336 are AD; 1489 are Pat; 1591, 1601, 1606, 1674, 1690, 1697, 1700, 1703, 1709, 1724 and 1745 are *Terrier*.

(a) Five Acre, the 12-Acre (*v.* **æcer**); Aikmans Cls, ~ Mdws (with the surn. *Aikman*, from OE *æcermann* 'a farmer, husbandman, ploughman'); The Allotment, Allotment Gardens, First Allotments or Shepherd's Bush (*v. infra*), Second Allotments (*v.* **allotment**); Ashby Lane End 1762 (1700, 1703, 1709, 1724, 1745, *v.* **lane-ende** and Station Rd *supra*; Ashby Magna parish adjoins to the east); Ashby Path Noles 1762, Far ~ ~, Near Path Knowle 1967 (*Ashby Path Noles* 1700, 1703, 1709, 1724, 1745, *v.* **pæð**, **cnoll**; with reference to Ashby Parva); Back Cl or Elwell Cl (*v.* **back** and Elwells Fm *supra*); Baker's Cl (with the surn. *Baker*); The Barn Cl, Barn Mdw (*v.* **bern**); Beaman's ~, Beaumont's Cl (with the surn. *Beaumont* (variant *Beaman*); from one of several places in Normandy named Beaumont 'beautiful hill'); Berridge's Mdw (with the surn. *Berridge*, prob. from the OE masc. pers.n. *Beornrīc*; cf. *William Berridge* 1800 MI, *Catherine Berridge* 1821 Census, *Annie Berridge* 1855 ib and *Ethel Berridge* 1880 ib, all of Dunton Bassett); Black Holme (*v.* **blæc**, **holmr**); Far ~, Near Bloomhills, Far Bloomhills Mdw, Bloomhills Haggs (*v.* **hogg**) (*v.* Bloomhills Fm *supra*); The Bog (*v.* **bog**); Bottom Fd (with **bottom** or **botm**); Bottoms 1762 (1697, 1700, 1703, 1709, 1724, 1745, *hitherbottomes* (*v.* **hider**), *netherbottomes furlong* (*v.* **furlang**) 1591, *the ne*(*i*)*ther* ~, *the ouer bottomes* 1601, 1606, *nether* ~, *over bottoms* 1674, 1690 (*v.* **neoðera, uferra**), *v.* **botm**); Botts Cl (prob. with the surn. *Bott,* from the OE masc. pers.n. *Botta,* cf. *Sarah Bott* 1838 Census of adjoining Leire parish; but **butte** is poss.); The Breach, Middle ~, Upper Breach (*v.* **brēc**); Brethren Cl (*v.* **bretheren**; the word was freq. applied to the 'brothers' or members of a religious or guild community but there appears to be no evidence for such in Dunton, apart from the recently demolished Methodist chapel, and no Quaker meeting house is recorded; the Prior and Convent of Canwell in Staffs. held the advowson of All Saints' Church from 1220 to 1565 and the Prior possessed several yardlands in the parish (*v.* Nichols **4** 1 153, 155) but it is doubtful whether this late f.n. is a memory of these); Briar Furlong 1797 (*v.* **brēr, furlang**); Broadway (*v.* **brād, weg**); the Bull Peice 1762 (*v.* **bula, pece**); Broughton Mdw (Broughton Astley parish adjoins to the north-west); Bungalow Fd; Butway Hedge 1762 (1591, *buttwaie* ~ 1601, *Buttway*(*e*) *hedge* 1606, 1674, *Butway heg* 1690, ~ *hedg* 1697, 1700, 1709, ~ *Hedge* 1724, 1745 (*v.* **hecg**), *butwaie hedge ende* 1601 (*v.* **ende**), cf. *butway furlonge* 1591 (*v.* **furlang**), *v.* **weg**; with **butt**[2] or **butte**); Chambers Cl, ~ Mdws (with the surn. *Chambers,* cf. *John Chambers* 1821 Census, *Mary Chambers* 1825 ib, *Hariet Chambers* 1863 ib and *Kate Chambers* 1865 ib, all of Dunton); The Church Cl 1797, Church Fd 1762, 1797 (1724, 1745), Church Piece or Church Furlong 1797 (*v.* **pece**) (*Churche furlonge* 1591, 1606, *Church furelonge* 1601, *Church Furlong* 1674, 1690 (*v.* **furlang**), cf. *Church Crofte or Lamas Close* 1606 (*v.* **croft, lammas**), *the Church Side* 1697, 1700, 1703, 1709 (*v.* **sīde**), *v.* All Saints' Church *supra*); Clover Cl, The Clover Fd (*v.* **clāfre**; a fodder crop); Cooper's Cl (with the surn. *Cooper,* from ME *couper* 'a maker of wooden casks, tubs etc.'); Cotes Long Mdw, Cotes Lower ~, Cotes Upper Piece (*v.* **pece**), Far ~ ~, Middle Great Cotes (*cottes* 1601, *Cotes* 1606, cf. *the cootes feild, the cootesfielde* 1606 (*v.* **feld**), *cottes syde* 1601, *Cotes side* 1606 (*v.* **sīde**), *v.* **cot**); Paul Crane's Cl (cf. *Edmund Crane* 1827 Census, with a surn. common in Dunton to *William Crane* 1867 ib; from OE *cran* 'a crane (bird)', hence it is a nickname signifying 'long-legged, like a crane'); Cricket Fd (for the game of cricket); Far ~, Near Croft, Middle Croft Mdw (*v.* Stokes Croft *supra* and cf. *craftslaid* 1591, *crafte slaide* 1601, *Craft slaid* 1606, *Croft slade* 1674, 1690, *v.* **slæd**); Dairy Cl (*v.* **deierie**); Deadmer or Deadman's Furlong (*deadmore,* ~ *furlonge* (*v.* **furlang**) 1591, cf. *Deadmore yate* 1606, 1674, 1690 (*v.* **gata**), *v.* **dēad, mōr**[1]; a common Leics. toponym for infertile moorland, but whether the later discovery of an ancient burial site at such an outlying location occurred (hence **dede-man**) is unrecorded; Dunton Gorse 1835, The Gorse 1967 (*v.* **gorst**); Dunton Mdw; Dutton's Orchards 1762 (*Duttons Orchards* 1703, 1709, 1724, 1745, *v.* **orceard**; with the surn. *Dutton* (there is no evidence for the place-name *Dunton* > *Dutton* by assimilation)); Elwell Cl (*v.* Elwells Fm *supra*); Lower ~, Upper Exchange or Parson's Piece (the nature of an exchange is unrecorded; *v.* Parson's Piece *infra*); Far Exton's Hill or Top Hill (*v.* **topp**), Near Exton's Hill or Little Hill (with the surn. *Exton* of a family originally from Exton, 27 miles to the north-east in Rutland; cf. *Robertus de Exton* 1327 SR of Leics.); Fielding's Cls (with the surn. *Fielding,* from OE *felding* 'a dweller in open country'); Finger Post Cl (*v.* **finger-post**); Flude's Cl (with the surn. *Flude,* either from OE *flōd* 'a stream' or OE *flōde* 'a channel, a gutter'; cf. *fluthes yate* 1601, *Fluttes yatt* 1606 (*William Flutt* is cited

1606 *Terrier*), *Fludes gate* 1674, 1690, *Thomas Fludes gate* 1697, (*at*) *Benjamin Fludes gate* 1700, 1703, 1709, 1724, (*at*) *John Fludes Gate* 1745 (replaced in the Glebe Terrier sequence by (*at*) *Mr Grundy's Gate* 1762), *v.* **geat**); Little Fordborough (*v.* **ford, berg**); Football Fd (for the game of football); Footpath Fds (*v.* **fote-path**); Front Fd (*v.* **front**); Gorse Cl or Paintbrooke Fd (*v.* **gorst** and Paintbrooke Fd *infra*); Gravel Hole Fd (*v.* **gravel, hol**[1]); Greensitch 1762 (*greensich, greensige* 1591, *gre(e)nsedge* 1601, 1606, *Greensich* 1674, 1690 *et passim* to 1724, 1745, cf. *greensiche way* 1591 (*v.* **weg**), *v.* **grēne**[1], **sīc**); Greenwells Cl (with the surn. *Greenwell*, cf. *Ambrose Greenwell* 1801 Census and *Lancelott Greenwell* 1846 ib of Dunton); Greeping 1762 (1674, 1690 *et passim* to 1745, *grypinge* 1591, *grippinge* 1601, 1606, *gripping* 1606, *v.* **grȳpe, gryppe**; with either **-ing**[2] or **eng**); Hall Cl 1797, 1846, 1863, 1877 (*v.* **hall**); Harbour Cl (*v.* **erber**); Hay Barn Cl (*v.* **hēg, bern**); Home Cl 1762 (1697, 1700, 1703, 1709, *the home closse* 1601, cf. *the vicaridge home close* 1606 (*v.* **vikerage**), *v.* **home**); Home Fd; The Horse Fd (*v.* **hors**); Horston Hill, ~ ~ Mdw (*whorestone* 1690, *horstenhilles* 1591; at the parish boundary and thus 'boundary-stone (hill)', *v.* **hār**[2], **stān, hyll**); South or Nether House Cl, Upper or North House Cl, The House Fd; Hungerlands 1762 (1745, *hangerlandes* 1591, *hanggerlandes* 1601, 1606, *Hangerlands* 1674, 1690, 1697, 1745 *Hanggerlands* 1700, 1703, 1709, 1724, *v.* **hangra, land**); Lower ~ ~, Upper ~ ~, Top James Cl (with the surn. *James*); Far ~ ~, Middle ~ ~, Near Joiner's Hook (*v.* **hōc**; with the surn. *Joiner*, from the occupational AFr *joignour* 'a joiner'); Kenny Cl (with the surn. *Kenny*, common in adjoining Cosby parish from *John Kenny* 1811 Census, *Thomas Kenny* 1821 ib to *Arthur Kenny* 1873 ib, *Joseph Kenny* 1879 ib); Far ~ ~, Knights Cl (with the surn. *Knight*); Lambcote 1762, 1967 (*lamscote* 1591, *v.* **lamb, cot**); Langslade Fd 1762 (*lanckslaid* 1601, *langslaide feilde* 1591, *lanckslaide feild* 1601, 1606, *Langslade Feild* 1674, 1690 *et passim* to 1724, ~ *Field* 1745 (*v.* **feld**; one of the great open-fields of the township), cf. *langesladegutter, langslaidgutter* 1591 (*v.* **goter**), *langeslaideleyes* 1591 (*v.* **leys**), *v.* **lang**[1], **slæd**); Leicester Mdw (beside *leicester waie* 1601, *v.* **weg**; the road to Leicester); Lever's Fd (with the surn. *Lever*, cf. *Radulphus le Levere* 1276 RH of Leics.; either a nickname from OFr *levre* 'a hare', alluding either to its speed or timidity, or metonymic for ME *leverer* 'a hare-hunter, a harrier'); Little ~, Long ~, Near Leyborough (*Leareborow, Learborowe* 1591, *v.* **berg**; prefixed by Leire, the name of the parish which adjoins to the west); Ley Cl (*v.* **ley**[1]); Lilbourne Corner (*v.* **corner**; perh. with the surn. *Lilbourne*, of a family originally from the village of this name 8 miles to the south in Northants., since there is no evidence of a connection between Lilbourne and Dunton or of a named road to Lilbourne); Little Barrow 1762, Littleborough Leys 1967 (*v.* **leys**) (*littelborowe* 1591, *little barrowe* 1601, *litlebarowe* 1606, *Littlebarrow* 1674, 1690 *et passim* to 1745, *v.* **lȳtel, berg**); Little Cl; Little Fd; Little Hill (*v.* Exton's Hill *supra*); Long Cl; Longdoles 1762 (1674, 1697 *et passim* to 1745, *langdales* 1601, *longdooles* 1606, *Longdoles End* 1700, 1703, 1709, 1724, 1745 (*v.* **ende**), *v.* **lang**[1], **dāl**); Long Slade Cl, ~ ~ Mdw or Oulton Cl (*v.* **slæd** and Oulton Cl *infra*); Lutterworth Mdw (beside the road to Lutterworth which lies 4 miles to the south); Mickling Fd 1762, The Micklin Fd 1797, Far ~, Near Micklin 1967 (*michilhill* 1591, *myckylhillfylde* 1591, *micklelefeild* (sic) 1601, *mycklingfeild* 1606, *Mickle Hill Feild* 1674, 1690, *Mickling Field* 1697, 1700 *et passim* to 1745 (*v.* **feld**; one of the great open-fields), cf. *michilhil knowles* 1591 (*v.* **cnoll**)), Mickling Ford 1762 (1724, *mickleford* 1606, *Micklehill foord* 1674, 1690, *Mickling Foard* 1697, 1700 *et passim* to 1745 (*v.* **ford**) (*v.* **micel, mikill, hyll**); Middle Furlong (*midell furlonge* 1591, *v.* **middel, furlang**); Mill Cl, Millcrofts (*v.* **croft**), Upper Mill or Road Mdw (*v.* **myln** and Road Mdw *infra*); Moor's Cl, Moore's Mdw (with the surn. *Moore*; cf. *Katherine Moor* 1724 *Terrier, Margaret Moore* 1821 Census, *Thomas Moore* 1834 ib and *Edwin Moore* 1856 ib, all of Dunton); the Nether Cl 1762 (*the Neather Close* 1697, 1700 *et passim* to 1745, *v.* **neoðera**); the Nurseries (*v.* **nursery**); Oak Tree Cl (*v.* **āc, trēow**); Orchard Cl (*v.* **orceard**); Oult Fd 1762, 1797 (1703, 1709, 1724, 1745, *Olte feilde* 1591, *the olt ~, the old feild* 1601, *the Olte Fielde* 1674, 1690, *Oult feild* 1697, 1700, *v.* **wald, feld**; one of the great open-fields); Oulton Cl (with the surn. *Oulton, v.* Long Slade Mdw *supra*); the Oult Highway 1762, Far ~ ~, Middle ~ ~, Oultway Mdw 1967 (*the oldway* 1591, 1690, *the olt highway* 1697, *the Oult Highway* 1700, 1703 *et passim* to 1745, cf. *old waie side, ~ ~ syde* 1601, *old way(e) sid* 1606, *Old way side* 1674 (*v.* **sīde**), *v.* **wald, weg, hēah-weg**); the Paddock (*v.* **paddock**); Paintbrooke Fd (*v.* **brōc** (and Gorse Cl *supra*); an intriguing late form and earlier spellings are needed; partly unexplained, unless the first element is an OE stream-name **Pante*, from PrW *pant*, Brit **panto*- 'a valley', as is the river Pant (Ess 9)); Parson's Piece (*v.* **persone, pece** and Exchange *supra*); Nether Pasture 1797, Lower ~, Middle ~, Upper Pasture 1967 (*v.* **pasture**); the Pit Fd (*v.* **pytt**); The Plash 1762, 1796, 1967 (1697, 1700 *et passim* to 1745, *plashe* 1591, 1601, *playshe* 1606, *plash* 1690), Plash Furlong 1797, 1967 (*v.* **furlang**), Plash Mdw 1967 (*v.* **plæsc**); Little Plough Cl (*v.* **plōg**); Ploughed Fd; Pylon Cl (on the route of a row of electricty pylons); Rabbit Burrow Cl (*v.* **rabet, borow**); The Railway Cl (alluding to the now dismantled railway line to the south-east of the township); First ~ ~, Second Ralph's Cl (sic) (with the surn. *Ralphs*, cf. *Joseph Ralphs* 1811 Census, *Sarah Ralphs* 1836 ib and *John Ralphs* 1862 ib of Dunton); Rangmore Slade 1762 (1700, 1724, *rannsmore* 1591, 1601, *Rangmore* 1674, *Rangmor slad* 1690, *Rangemore Slade* 1697, 1703, 1709, 1745, *v.* **mōr**[1], **slæd**; the prototheme may be either **hræfn** or the OE masc. pers.n. *Hræfn*, **wrang** 'crooked, twisted in shape' being less likely; for a similar phonetic development, cf. Rangemore, StH 452); The Road Fd, Road Mdw (*v.* Upper Mill Mdw *supra*; roadside closes); Thomas Roe's Cl 1797; The Rushes, Rushes Mdw (*v.* **risc**); Seeds Cl or Moor's Cl or the 12-Acre (*v.* **sǣd**, used of grasses sown for one year's mowing or grazing; note Moor's Cl *supra*); Seddon's Mdw or Cotes Upper Piece (with the surn. *Seddon; v.* Cotes Long Mdw *supra*); Shepherd's Bush (cf. *Shepherds Bush* (1841) in Dorking (Sr 394) and *Sheppards Bush* (1635) in London (Mx 109); evidently referring to some kind of shelter or grazing ground for shepherds and their flocks, *v.* **scēp-hirde, busc** and The Allotment *supra*); Short Kennell 1762 (*kennill* 1606, *Short(e) Kennell* 1697, 1700 *et passim* to 1745, *v.* **kennell**); Slowes 1762, Far ~ ~, Near Slough Cl 1967 (*slowes* 1591, 1697, 1700 *et passim* to 1745, *slowse* 1601, 1606, *slous(e)* 1674, 1690, *v.* **slōh**); Spinney Cl (*v.* **spinney**); Stockshill 1762 (1697, 1700 *et passim* to 1745, *stokeshill* 1591, *v.* **hyll**; with **stoc** or **stocc**); Thone (sic) 1762 (1700, 1703 *et passim* to 1745, *thornes* 1601, *Thorne* 1674, 1690, 1697, cf. *long smalthornes, shortsmallthornes* 1591, *small thorn* 1601 (*v.* **smæl**), *v.* **þorn**); Three Cornered Cl (*v.* **three-cornered**); the Three Rood Land 1762 (1724, *v.* **þrēo, rōd**[3], **land**); Tinkers Hill (*v.* **tinkere**); First ~ ~, Second Top Cl (*v.* **top**); Top Hill (i.e. '(land at the) top of the hill', *v.* **topp**); the Town Fd 1762 (1724, 1745), the Towns End 1762 (1697, 1700 *et passim* to 1745, *v.* **ende**), Townsend Leys 1797 (*v.* **leys**) (*v.* **tūn**); Tunnel Top (*v.* **topp**; above the local railway tunnel, now disused); the Upper Cl 1762 (1697, 1700 *et passim* to 1745); The

Wakelins or Wakelins Cl (*wackley* 1591, *v.* **wacu, hlāw**; the name occurs as *Wakeley* in adjoining Ashby Parva parish and Waklin in adjoining Leire); Old ~ ~, Wey Cl (*v.* **wald, weg**); Mr Wigley's Grounds 1762 (*Mr Edmund Wigley Grounds* 1724, *v.* **grund**); Windmill Cl 1967, (the) Windmill Hill 1762, 1967 (1697, 1700 *et passim* to 1745, cf. *winmille furlonge* 1591 (*v.* **furlang**), *v.* **wind-mylne**).

(b) *Ashby* ~ ~1601, *Ashbie magna hedge* 1606 (*v.* **hecg**; a parish boundary hedge, Ashby Magna adjoining to the east); *Ashby* ~ ~ 1601, *Ashby parva hedge* 1606 (*v.* **hecg**; another parish boundary hedge, Ashby Parva adjoining to the south-west); *austenhuke, austenshooke* 1591 (*v.* **hōc**; with the surn. *Austen*, from OFr *Aoustin*, the vernacular form of Augustine); *brackney* 1601, *brakney* 1606 (the name appears as Bracknell Cl in adjoining Leire f.ns. (a) (*braknell* 1601, *Bracknill* 1625), *v.* **braken, hyll**); *brimsiche* 1591, *brimsedge* 1601, *Brimsige* 1674, 1690, *brimsiche slaid* 1591 (*v.* **slæd**) (*v.* **brimme, sīc**); *the brockes* 1591, 1601, *the brokes* 1606 (*v.* **brōc**); *brodholme* 1591, *broade home* 1601, *broadhome* 1606 (*v.* **brād, holmr**); *broughton meir* 1591, *browghton* ~ 1601, 1606, *broughton meare* 1606, *Brouton Meare*, ~ *meir* 1674 (*v.* **(ge)mǣre**), *broughton slade* 1591 (*v.* **slæd**) (Broughton Astley parish adjoins to the north-west); *brownes haidland* 1601 (*v.* **hēafod-land**; with the surn. *Brown*); *Buristede* 1336 (*v.* **burh-stede**); *cocesleyes, cocsleyes, cocseleyes* 1591 (*v.* **leys**; prob. with **cocc**[1] rather than with the surn. *Cox*); *the comon cowe pasture* 1606 (*v.* **commun, cū, pasture**); *conningrye, corningras*, ~ *furlonge* 1591 (*v.* **coningre**); *cosbee meire* 1591 (*v.* **(ge)mǣre**; Cosby parish adjoins to the north); *the dames* 1601 (*v.* **damme**); *est medow* 1591 (*v.* **ēast, mēd** (**mēdwe** obl.sg.)); *fishedame* 1606 (*v.* **fisc, damme**; an artificial pool created for fishing); *flaxbrokeleyes* 1591 (*v.* **fleax, brōc, leys**; a brook where flax was retted); *ad fonte'* 1327 ('at the spring', with MLat *ad* 'at' and MLat *fons* (*fontem* acc.sg.) 'a spring, a well'); *gonnelesbrige, gunnelsebrige* 1591, *gonnelle bridge* 1601, 1606 (*v.* **gonele, brycg**); *greate more feylde* 1591, *greatemore field* 1601, *great more feild* 1606, *Greatmore Field* 1674, 1690 (*v.* **grēat, mōr**[1], **feld**; one of the open-fields); *the homestall* 1606 (*v.* **hām-stall**; belonging to the early vicarage); *inkereshill* 1591, *inkershill* 1591, 1601, *Inkareshill* 1606 (either with the surn. *Inker*, from ON masc. pers.n. *Yngvarr* (ODan *Ingvar*) or with the pers.n. itself); *littell haden* 1591 (*v.* **lȳtel, hēafod**; note the archaic -*en* plural); *littlemor* 1606, *littellmore feilde* 1591, *littlemore feild* 1601, *Littlemore Field* 1674 (*v.* **feld**; one of the open-fields), *littelmorehill, littlemoorhill* 1591 (*v.* **hyll**), *littelmor(e) pitt* 1601, 1606 (*v.* **pytt**), *littelmoreslad* 1591 (*v.* **slæd**) (*v.* **lȳtel, mōr**[1]); *Longhades* 1690 (*v.* **lang**[1], **hēafod**); *longhomes* 1591 (*v.* **lang**[1], **holmr**); *Longslade* 1674, 1690 (*v.* **lang**[1], **slæd**); *michillhaden, mikelhaden, mikilhaden, michilhaden slade* (*v.* **slæd**) 1591 (*v.* **micel, mikill, hēafod**; f.ns. with the archaic -*en* plural); *the mildam* 1591, *mylldame* 1601, *milldame* 1606 (*v.* **myln, damme**); *Katherine Moors Grounds* 1724 (*v.* **grund**); *more yate* 1601 (*v.* **mōr**[1], **gata**); *Morton way* 1690 (the road to Gilmorton which lies 2 miles to the south-east); *olt furlonge* 1591 (*v.* **wald, furlang**); *olteslade, oltslaid, oltslaide furlonge* (*v.* **furlang**) 1591 (*v.* **wald, slæd**); *Pallmers yearde* 1591 (*v.* **geard**; with the surn. *Palmer*, still to be found in Dunton much later, as *Thomas Palmer* 1817 Census and *John Palmer* 1856 ib); *ranglandes* 1591 (*v.* **wrang, land**); *rihill(e)* 1591, *Rihill, Ryhill* 1601, *Riehill* 1606 (*v.* **ryge, hyll**); *rowhill* 1601 (*v.* **rūh, hyll**); *Ryvellys landis* 1489 (*v.* **land**; with the surn. *Rivell*, a variant of *Revell*, from the OFr masc. pers.n. *Revel* (OFr *revel* 'pride, rebellion'); the surn. was also metonymic for *Reveler* (from *reveler* 'to rebel')); *smale thorowes* 1606 (*v.* **smæl, furh**); *Smiths hadland* 1674, 1690 (*v.* **hēafod-land**; with the surn.

Smith); *snayth* 1601 (*v.* **sneið**); *steane* 1591, (*under*) *steine* 1601, *Steane furlong* 1591 (*v.* **furlang**) (*v.* **steinn**); *stockwell* 1601, 1606, *stockswell* 1674, 1690 (*v.* **stocc**, **well**); *stodyhill* 1591 (*v.* **stōd**, (**ge**)**hæg**, **hyll**; cf. Stody, Nf); *stone meadowe* 1601 (*v.* **stān**; either 'the stony meadow' or 'the stoned meadow', i.e. one having been cleared of stones, cf. *the stone middow* (1601), Lei **2** 19 and *the stone meadow* (1625), Lei **4** 57); *stringlandes* 1591 (*v.* **strengr**, **land**); *torningsway* 1591, *turnyng waye* 1606 (*v.* **þorn**, **-ing**², **þyrning**, **weg**); *neather ~ ~, ouer tyth peece* 1606 (*v.* **neoðera**, **uferra**, **tēoða**, **pece**); *wagonewaye* 1591 (*v.* **wagan**, **weg**); *waie gore syde* 1601, *wayegoresyd* 1606 (*v.* **weg**, **gāra**, **sīde**); *waie hill* 1606 (*v.* **weg**, **hyll**); *watrie* 1591, 1606, *watrye* 1591, (*in*) *waiterie* 1601, *wateryhades* 1591 (*v.* **hēafod**) (*v.* **wæterig**); *wellandes* 1591 (*v.* **wella**, **land**; perh. cf. *ad fonte'*, *supra*); *wide dickes* 1601, *widedikes*, *wydedikes* 1606 (*v.* **wīd**, **dík**).

Frolesworth

Frelesworde 1086 DB (×2), *Frelesworth* Hy 1 Nichols, 1294 *MiD*
Frellesworde 1086 DB (×2), 1209 × 19 RHug, *Frelleswortha* 1209 ×
    19 ib, *Frellesworth*1220 MHW, e.14 Peake, *Frelleswrth* 1230 ×
    60 Goodacre, *Frellusworth* a.1300 *ib*
Fredleswurð 1175 ChancR (p), *Fredlesuuða* 1175 P (p),
    Fredleswurða 1176 ib (p)
Frolliswrthe c.1130 LeicSurv, *Frollisworthe* 1276 Goodacre, 1313
    Pat, *Frolleswrth* 1208 FF, 1254 Val *et passim* to c.1280, 1275 ×
    96 Goodacre, *Frollesworth*(*e*) 1235 Cl, 1261 RGrav *et passim* to
    1305 GildR (p), 1312 Peake *et freq* to 1547, 1549 Pat
Frolesworth 1518 Visit, 1535 VE, 1576 Saxton *et freq*
Frowlesworth 1611, 1614 LML, *Froulesworth* 1627 ib

'The enclosure belonging to a man called Freothuwulf or Freothulf',
v. **worð**. The OE masc. pers.n. *Freoðuwulf* gave the recorded shortened
form *Freoðulf*.

THE ALMSHOUSES, 1846, 1863, 1877 White, *v.* **almes-hous**; also called
Frolesworth Hospital 1807 Nichols, *v.* **hospital**. Founded in 1725 for 22
poor women by John Smith, Lord Chief Baron of the Exchequer for
Scotland, who was born in Frolesworth in 1656. THE BRINDLES, with no
early forms, but if a surviving ancient name, then a poss. meaning is
'place cleared by burning'; the base of the name may be OE **brend**
'burnt, cleared by burning', but whether with the OE noun suffix -**el**[3] or
a reduced generic **hyll** is uncertain. BROUGHTON RD is *Broughton Lane*
1781 *Terrier*, Broughton Astley lying 2 miles to the north-east. CHURCH
HILL FM, *Church hill* 1605 *Terrier*, *v.* **hyll**; the farm lies beside St
Nicholas's Church *infra*, but whether the name conceals PrW **crŭg** 'a
hill' is uncertain. CLAYBROOKE GRANGE, ~ ~ FM, *Claybrooke Grange*
1925 Kelly, *v.* **grange**. FOSSE FM, lies beside Fosse Way, early local
forms for which are *Fosse Lane*1674 *Terrier*, (*the*) *Fosse* 1605, 1700 *ib*,
the Fosse way 1708 *ib*, *the Fosse Road* 1781 *ib*, *v.* **foss**[1]; also called *le*

Porteweye e.14 *Peake, port way* 1605 *Terrier, v.* **port-wey**.
FROLESWORTH HILL, 1835 O, 1846 White, *Frowlesworth Hill* 1877 ib,
1925 Kelly, *the Hill* 1700, 1703 *Terrier et passim* to 1821 *ib, v.* **hyll**.
FROLESWORTH HO. FROLESWORTH LODGE, *v.* **loge**. GABLES FM. HALL
FM, cf. *Hall close* 1626 LAS, *v.* **hall, clos(e)**. THE HOLLIES. HOME FM,
v. **home**. THE HOMESTEAD, cf. *Far ~, First Homestead* 1838 *TA, v.* **hām-
stede**. LEIRE RD is *lare way* 1605 *Terrier, v.* **weg**; Leire lying one mile
to the south-east. LODGE FM (FROLESWORTH LODGE 2½"), *Frowlesworth
Lodge* 1835 O, *The Lodge* 1925 Kelly, *v.* **loge**. LODGE FARM COTTAGES.
MAIN ST. MANOR FM, *v.* **maner**. PLOUGH AND HARROW (P.H.), *Plough
and Harrow* 1863, 1877 White, 1925 Kelly. THE RECTORY, 1877 White,
1925 Kelly, *v.* **rectory**; earlier is *the parsonage house* 1605, 1708
Terrier, v. **personage**. ROYAL OAK (P.H.) (lost), *Royal Oak* 1846, 1863,
1877 White, 1925 Kelly. ST NICHOLAS'S CHURCH, *Church (St Nicholas)*
1846, 1863, 1877 White, 1925 Kelly; it is earlier recorded as *ecclesiam
de Frelleswortha* a.1219 RHug, *ecclesie de Frellesworth* 1220 MHW,
the Church 1605 *Terrier*. Note also *the Church-yard* 1708 *ib, v.*
churchyerd.

FIELD-NAMES

In (a), forms presented without dates are 1838 *TA*; those dated 1751,
1772, 1793 and 1814 are MiscAccts; 1781 and 1821 are *Terrier*; 1805
and 1807 are Nichols. Forms throughout dated 1275, 1657, 1660 and
1701 are Nichols; those dated l.13, e.14 and 1378 are *Peake*; 1546 are
AAS; 1549 are Pat; 1605, 1625, 1674, 1679, 1690, 1700, 1703, 1708 and
1724 are *Terrier*; 1626 are LAS.

(a) The Acre, Three Acres, Five ~, Six ~, Watts Seven ~ (with the surn. *Watts*),
Eight Acres (*v.* **æcer**); Ashby Nook (*v.* **nōk**; Ashby Parva parish adjoins to the south-
east); The Barks (*v.* **berc**; with unassibilated final consonant); Far ~ ~, Lower ~ ~,
Top ~ ~, Barn Cl (*v.* **bern**); Battle Flat (*v.* **bataille, flat**; presum. land subjected to
some sort of juridical battle, since no military conflict is recorded here); Big Cl, ~
Mdw; Boggy Mdw (*v.* **boggy**); Bottom Mdw, ~ Piece (*v.* **pece**); Brays Cl, ~ Barn Cl,
~ Mdw (with the surn. *Bray*, cf. *Thomas Bray* 1811 Census, *William Bray* 1816 ib
and *John Bray* 1853 ib of adjoining Ullesthorpe parish); Great ~, Little Breaknel (*v.*
braken, hyll); Far ~ ~, First Broad Cl (*v.* **brād**); Browns Cl, ~ Mdw (with the surn.
Brown); Second ~ ~, Broughton Cl (Broughton Astley parish adjoins to the north-
east); Cabbage Piece (*v.* **cabache, pece**); Calves Cl (*v.* **calf**); Cheesecake Cl (*v.*
chese-cake); Cottage Far Pasture, ~ Middle Pasture (cf. *Cottyers pasture* 1660, *v.*
cotage, cottere, pasture); Cow Cl (1660), Cow Mdw (*v.* **cū**); Craddocks Cl (with the
surn. *Craddock*); Daglock Cl (*v.* **dag-lock**; alluding to sheep husbandry and the

dampness of the ground in the close); Daniels Mdw (with the surn. *Daniel(s)*);
Dawkins Hill, ~ Mdw (with the surn. *Dawkins*; cf. *Mary Dawkins* 1807 Census of
adjoining Ullesthorpe parish); Double Fence (*v.* **duble, fense**); Earls Mdw (with the
surn. *Earl*; cf. *Selena Earl* 1850 Census of adjoining Claybrooke Magna parish); Top
Emmertons (with the surn. *Emmerton* in the possessive case); Far Pasture (*v.*
pasture); Feeding Mdw (*v.* **feeding**); Finger Post Cl (*v.* **finger-post**); First Mdw;
Bottom ~ ~ ~, Top Fish Pond Cl (*v.* **fisshe-ponde**); the Fosse Cl 1751, 1772, 1793,
1814, Bottom ~ ~, Lower ~ ~, Middle ~ ~, Top ~ ~, Upper Foss Cl 1838 (*Fosseclose*
1626, *the Fosse Close* 1730), Foss Lane Cl, ~ ~ Mdw, Middle Foss Lane Cl 1838, the
Fosse Mdw 1751, 1772, 1793, 1814 (1730) (closes bordering the Roman Fosse
Way); Gravel Hole Cl, Gravel Pit Cl (*v.* **gravel, hol**[1], **pytt**); Great Mdw (*the Great
Meddow* 1679); Greenway Cl, Top Greenway (*le greneweye* e.14, *greene way* 1605,
v. **grēne**[1], **weg**); Near ~, Top Far Hacketts (with the surn. *Hackett*, an AN diminutive
of the ON masc. pers.n. *Haki* (ODan *Hake*); cf. *Ann Hackett* 1806 Census of adjacent
Ullesthorpe parish); Hall Mdw (*v.* Hall Fm *supra*); Hill Cl, Far ~ ~, Near Hill Cl
((*the*) *Hill close* 1679, 1700, 1703, 1708); The Hole Cl (*v.* **hol**[1]); Home Cl (*the Home
close* 1625), Home Fd (*the Homefeild* 1626), Home Fd East, Lower Home Fd (*v.*
home); First ~ ~, Second ~ ~, Horse Cl (*Horse Close* 1660), Horse Mdw (*v.* **hors**);
Bottom ~ ~, Top ~ ~, House Cl, Second ~ ~, Old House Cl, Big ~ ~, Little House
Ground (*v.* **grund**); Hovel Cl (*Hovell close* 1626), Hovel Close End (*v.* **ende**) (*v.*
hovel); Hubbards Cl (with the surn. *Hubbard*, cf. *Elizabeth Hubbard* 1820 Census
and *Samuel Hubbard* 1857 ib of adjoining Broughton Astley parish); Jones First ~,
Jones Second Cl (with the surn. *Jones*); Kiln Cl (*v.* **cyln**); Lower ~ ~, Lane Cl (*v.*
lane); Lingham's (sic) (*nether linghams* 1605, cf. *Lyngholmsyke ouerhende* e.14 (*v.*
sík, uferra, ende), *v.* **lyng, holmr; hamm** replaced *holmr*); Far ~ ~, Near ~ ~, Top
~ ~, Little Cl (*Little Close* 1657); Little Mdw; Top ~ ~, Bottom ~ ~, Long Cl (*Long
Close* 1657, 1660); Lower ~ ~, Upper Long Ground (*v.* **grund**); Long Mdw; Far
Lower Cl; The Meadows 1821 (*the Meadow* 1724, cf. *meadow ditch side* 1605 (*v.*
dīc, sīde), *v.* **mēd** (**mēdwe** obl.sg.)); Far ~ ~, Middle Cl; Middle Mdw; Moors (*the
moores* 1605, *v.* **mōr**[1]); Morris Cl (with the surn. *Morris*); Neals Cl (with the surn.
Neal); Near Cl; Nine Lands (*v.* **land**; a close formed by nine selions of an earlier
great open-field); Big ~, Little Nursery (*v.* **nursery**); Big ~, Top Orchard (*v.*
orceard); Lower ~ ~, Over Cl (*v.* **uferra**); Ox House (*v.* **oxa, hūs**); Park Cl, ~ Mdw
(*v.* **park**); The Pasture 1805, Pasture Cl, The Pastures 1838 (*v.* **pasture**); Bottom ~
~, Lower ~ ~, Top Pen Cl (*v.* **penn**); Plants Cl (with the surn. *Plant* in the possessive
case; there is no evidence for f.ns. compounded with *plant*, i.e. 'something which can
be planted'); Randles Mdw, Stock Randles (perh. with **stock** 'livestock') (with the
surn. *Randle*, cf. *Thomas Randle* 1822 Census, *Ann Randle* 1827 ib and another
Thomas Randle 1855 ib, all of adjoining Claybrooke Magna parish); Rickyard Cl (*v.*
reke-yard); Road Mdw (a roadside enclosure); Robins Cl, ~ Lower Cl (with the
surn. *Robins*); Rotten Mdw (a derogatory name applied to soft, boggy ground);
Rough Cl (*v.* **rūh**); Top ~ ~, Round Cl (*Round Close* 1657, *v.* **round**); Bottom ~ ~,
Top Rushy Cl (*v.* **riscig**); Rye Cl (*v.* **ryge**); Second Mdw; Seed Cl (*v.* **sǣd**; in modern
f.ns., used of grasses sown for one year's mowing or grazing as distinguished from
permanent pasture); Shorts Mdw (with the surn. *Short*); Side Cl (*v.* **sīde**); Siden Cl,
~ Mdw (presum. with a survival of OE **sīd** (**sīdan** wk.obl.) 'large, extensive'); Small
Brook Mdw, Bottom Small Brook (*Smalbrooke* 1605, ~ *meadow* 1626, *v.* **smæl,
brōc**); Smiths Mdw (with the surn. *Smith*); Smock Cl (referring to *smoke-silver*, a tax

paid in lieu of tithewood to the incumbent of a parish); Spiers Cl (with the surn. *Spiers*); Spinney Cl (*v.* **spinney**); Springes, ~ Mdw, Little Springes (*le Sprung* l.13, *the Springes* 1660, cf. *Springe slade* 1605 (*v.* **slæd**), *v.* **spring**[1], **spryng**); Ten Foot Mdw (alluding to the breadth of a piece of grassland as opposed to its length); Top Hill (i.e. '(land at the) top of the hill', *v.* **topp**); Top Mdw (*v.* **top**); Far ~ ~, Townsend Cl (*v.* **tūn**, **ende**); East ~ ~, West ~ ~, Lower ~ ~, Upper Ward's Cl (with the surn. *Ward*, cf. *Willielmus de la Warda* 1176 P of Leics., *Elizabeth Ward* 1812 Census and *William Ward* 1812 ib of adjacent Broughton Astley parish); Great ~, Little ~, Middle ~, Near Warden, Lower Wardens Cl (*Waddon* e.14, *Whoddon* 1605, cf. *Waddonesykeplot* e.14 (*v.* **sík**, **plot**), *v.* **wād**, **dūn**); Wash Pit Mdw (*v.* **wæsce**, **pytt**); the Watery Cl 1781, Far ~ ~, Near Watery Cl 1838 ((*the*) *Watry close* 1625, 1690, 1700, 1703, (*the*) *Watery close* 1674, 1708, *the Watrey close* 1679, *v.* **wæterig**); Far ~ ~, Top Watts Cl (with the surn. *Watts*).

(a) *Anstye way* 1605 (*v.* **weg**; in the great *East feilde* and thus prob. with **anstig** 'a steep path' rather than *ānstīg* 'a (?narrow) footpath', as better suiting the topography); *Archingnolds* 1674, (*The*) *Archinolds* 1690, 1700, 1703 (a close so called; with the surn. *Archinold* in the possessive case, from the ContGerm masc. pers.n. *Archenbald*, *Erchenbald* via OFr *Archambaut*, *Erchembaut*); *Arlingward close* 1605, *the great ~, the little Arlingwade* 1625 (unexplained; earlier forms are needed); *Arsward meadowe* 1605 (also unexplained since again earlier forms are needed; but both *Arlingward* and *Arsward* may contain *ward* in its sense 'a district, a division'); *Astewell* e.14 (*v.* **ēast**, **wella**); *Ashby meere* 1605 (*v.* **(ge)mǣre**; the boundary with Ashby Parva which adjoins to the south-east); *Barbereyslond* 1378 (*v.* **land**; with the surn. *Barbery*, cf. *Ricardus de Barbary* 1327 SR of Leics. Reaney *s.n.* Barbary, Barbery assumes this surn. to be from 'the usual vernacular form of Barbara'. Nichols **4** 1 180, in discussing the history of the parish of Frolesworth, reproduces a charter concerning a grant of two virgates of land here to Thomas, son of Walter de Frolesworth. Among the witnesses of this undated charter (the copy of which Nichols considers to be prob. of the early 17th cent.) are *Willielmo de Barberi*, *Ancketillo de Craft* and *Rogero de Craft*, all local landowners. Anketill and Roger of nearby Croft date this Frolesworth charter firmly to the late 12th cent., since they also are present in other charters of this period (*v.* Dane 290 and 312). William de Barberi is otherwise unrecorded. It is most unlikely that *Barberi* in the late 12th cent. was a surn. derived from the fem. pers.n. Barbara. Both l.12 cent. and 1327 Leics. forms appear as personal names based on a toponym. Was William distinguished by his having been to the Barbary Coast as a Crusader to North Africa, Egypt and the Holy Land, on either the Second Crusade (1147–9) or the Third (1189–92)? Did his family retain this name as an escutcheon of honour? An alternative, more mudane, source of the name is that of the tiny village of Barberry, in Calvados (recorded from 1050), *v.* A. Dauzat and C. Rostaing, *Dictionnaire étymologique des noms de lieux en France*, 2nd edn, Paris 1968); *barefote* 1605 (*v.* **berg**, **fōt**; cf. *Barefoot Slade*, Lei **4** 60, *Barfoote*, Lei **4** 199 and Barfoot Lodge, Lei **4** 224); *blindemans wong* 1605, *Blindwing Close* (sic) 1657 (*v.* **blindman**, **vangr**; these forms presum. belong together, the 1657 form being prob. a poor reading and/or printing by Nichols); *Bodingtons Close* 1657 (with the surn. *Boddington* of a family originally from the village of this name, 24 miles to the south in Northants.; cf. *Sophia Boddington* 1815 Census and *Samuel Boddington* 1850 ib of nearby Dunton Bassett); *broade wong* 1605, *Broadwongfeild*, ~ *meadow* 1626 (*v.* **brād**, **vangr**); *Broughton meere* 1605 (*v.*

(ge)mǣre; Broughton Astley parish adjoins to the north-east); *the Common*, ~ ~ *ground* 1605 (*v.* **commun, grund**); *Conston* e.14 (evidently a lost settlement, with **tūn**; partly uncertain of interpretation, but an original **cyningestūn* (Scandinavianized as **konungstún*, *v.* **konungr**), although formally poss., seems unlikely); *Coopers Long Close, Coopers Meadow* 1657 (with the surn. *Cooper*); *Coops hadland* 1605 (*v.* **hēafod-land**; with the surn. *Coop*, metonymic for ME *couper* 'a maker of wooden casks, tubs etc.'; cf. *Hugo le Coupe* 1327 SR of Leics.); *Cowsleyes* 1605 (*v.* **cū, leys**); *Crum dike* 1605 (*v.* **crumb, dík**); *East feilde* 1605 (*v.* **ēast, feld**; one of the great open-fields of the township); *fenn hades* 1605 (*v.* **fenn, hēafod**); *le fordoles* e.14 (*v.* **fore, dāl**); *the Furry close* 1708 (*v.* **fyrsig**); *Godewynwong* e.14 (*v.* **vangr**; with the OE masc. pers.n. *Godwine*); *godscroft hollow* 1605 (*v.* **holh** and *Godescroft* in nearby Cosby f.ns (b) *supra* to which this name appears to relate); *the hall(e) hadland* (*v.* **hēafod-land**), *the hall peece* (*v.* **pece**) 1605 (*v.* Hall Fm *supra*); *heath furlong* 1605 (*v.* **hǣð, furlang**); *(the) Hill close* 1679, 1700, 1703, 1708, *Hills end* 1605, ~ ~ *meadow* 1626 (*v.* **hyll, ende**); *the Hull acres* 1625, 1674, 1690, *the Hulacres Close* 1679, *Hull Acres Close* 1701 (*v.* **æcer**; with the surn. *Hull*, from the ME masc. pers.n. *Hulle*, a pet-form of Hugh or of its diminutives *Hulin, Hulot*; cf. *Andrew Hull* 1691, 1701 Deed and *Francis Hull* 1701 ib of Frolesworth, Andrew Hull owning *Hull Acres Close* in 1701); *Irelandes close* 1626 (with the surn. *Ireland*); *lambcoates* 1605 (*v.* **lamb, cot**); *Langhams sich* 1605 (*v.* **sīc**; prob. with the surn. *Langham* rather than with a toponym **lang-hamm*); *Langhull* e.14, *Lanckhill, Langhill* 1605, *Longhill feild* 1626 (*v.* **lang¹, hyll**); *Lecester way, Leicester way side* (*v.* **sīde**) 1605 (*v.* **weg**; early Leicester lay 10 miles to the north-east); *Martines Croft* 1605 (*v.* **croft**; with the surn. *Martin*; cf. *William Martin* 1817 Census and *Harriett Martin* 1866 ib of adjacent Broughton Astley parish); *Mill Hill, Mill Way, (at) mill stile* (*v.* **stigel**) 1605 (with reference to a windmill); *North feilde* 1605 (*v.* **norð, feld**; one of the great open-fields); *Northling* 1275 (*v.* **norð, lyng**); *oxemeere* 1605 (*v.* **oxa, (ge)mǣre**; a boundary grazing strip (or turning strip?) for oxen); *parsonage hadland* (*v.* **hēafod-land**), *the parsonage willowes* (*v.* **wilig**) 1605 (*v.* **personage**); *Pesehull* e.14 (*v.* **pise, hyll**); *pitt furlonge* 1605 (*v.* **pytt, furlang**); *Pycrofts yard* 1606 (*v.* **geard**; with the surn. *Pycroft*); *the red way* 1605 (*v.* **rād-weg**); *long Roes* 1605 (*v.* **vrá**); *Ryhill* 1605, *Rye Hill* 1674, 1690, ~ ~ *close* 1625, ~ ~ *ditch* 1605 (*v.* **dīc**), *Ryhill meadowe* 1605, *Rye hill medow(e)* 1605, 1625 (*v.* **ryge, hyll**); *Sandhill way*, ~ ~ *hades* (*v.* **hēafod**) 1605 (*v.* **sand, hyll, weg**); *Simonds Landis* 1546, *Symondes Landes* 1549 (*v.* **land**; with the surn. *Simond(s)*, from the ON masc. pers.n. *Sigmundr* (ODan *Sigmund*)); *Skinsmeere* 1605 (occurs also in adjoining Broughton Astley and in adjacent Leire as *Skins(e)more* 1625, 1673 etc., 'the haunted marshland', *v.* **scinn, mere¹ (mōr¹)**; the OE specific *scinn* 'a spectre, an evil spirit' perh. alluded to 'phantoms' formed by marsh gas; the name has been Scandinavianized (sc > sk)); *Sort fures* (sic) 1605 (*v.* **sc(e)ort, furh**); *water leas* 1605 (*v.* **wæter, leys**); *West feilde* 1605 (*v.* **west, feld**; one of the three great open-fields of the township).

Gilmorton

1. GILMORTON

Moretone 1086 DB, 1209 × 19 RHug, *Moreton* 1173 ChancR, 1243
Fees, 1373, 1379 *LCDeeds*
Mortona c.1130 LeicSurv, 1209 × 19 RHug, c.1225 GildR (p), c.1230
RTemple (p), *Mortun* 1166 P (p), *Morton* 1170 ib (p) *et freq* to
1352 *LCDeeds*, 1357 Pat *et passim* to 1428 FA, 1510 Visit, 1576
Saxton
Aurea Morton 1248 RGros (×2)
Gildenemorton 1303 IpmR, 1328 Banco, 1341 Pat, *Guldenemorton*
1293 Ipm, *Gyldenemorton* 1322 Cl, 1328 Banco
Gildenmorton 1327 SR, 1344 *Deed*, 1438 Banco, *Gyldenmorton* 1406
LCh, 1420 Cl, 1509 Fine, *Gildynmorton* 1343 *MiD*, 1389 *Deed*,
Gyldynmorton 1397 Cl
Gildenmoreton 1402 *Hazlerigg*, *Gyldenmoreton* 1417 *ib et freq* to
1424 *ib*, *Gyldon Moreton* 1471 *ib*, 1547 Pat
Gildemorton 1540 *Hazlerigg*, *Gyldemorton* 1561, 1564 LeicW,
Gyldmorton 1551 Fine, 1556 ECP
Gylemorton 1515 ECP, *Gilmoreton* 1535 VE, *Gilmorton* 1573 LEpis,
1576 LibCl, 1610 Speed *et freq*

'The farmstead or village at the wet moorland', *v.* **mōr**[1], **tūn**. The
later affixes MLat *aurea* and ME **gilden** 'golden' could simply indicate
a prosperous settlement. It is noteworthy, however, that nearby Moreton
Pinkney, which was *Geldenemoretone* in 1221, *Guldenemorton* in 1226
(Nth 41) and Guilden Morden (Ca 61) also combine 'wetland, marsh'
with 'golden', so that the reference in each case could be rather to the
striking presence of gold-coloured wetland flowers such as the marsh-
marigold.

2. COTES DE VAL

Toniscote 1086 DB

Cotes 1194 Abbr, 1220 MHW *et passim* to 1814 *MiscAccts*, (~ *Deyvill* 1285 FA, ~ *Devile* 1301 Ass, ~ *Dayville* 1330 Ipm, ~ *Devyle* 1507 ib, ~ *Devyll* 1550 Pat, ~ *Deval* 1814 *MiscAccts*)
Cotes iuxta Morton al' Cotyn 1330 Ipm
Coates 1606 *Terrier*, 1709, 1730 *MiscAccts*

Originally 'the cottage(s) of a man called Tone', *v.* **cot** (**cotu** nom.pl.), with the OE masc. pers.n. *Tone* (Redin 137). Later, simply 'the cottages', as a ME secondary plural **cotes**. The single surviving form *Cotyn* of 1330 preserves the early dat.pl. **cotum**. Eventually, the feudal affix *Deyvill* was added, the name of a family possibly in origin from Deville in Normandy. Also styled *D'Eyvill*, they held land in Warwickshire in the 13th cent., but the affix here is the only evidence to indicate that they held land in Leicestershire also. Modern misdivision (metanalysis) of the feudal surname has created a pseudo-French form, ~ *de Val* 'of the Vale'.

ALL SAINTS' CHURCH, *Church (All Saints)* 1846, 1863, 1877 White, 1925 Kelly; it is earlier recorded as *ecclesiam de Mortona* a.1219 RHug, *ecclesie de Morton* 1220 MHW, *ecclesiam de Aurea Morton* 1248 RGros. Note also *the Church Yard* 1606, 1703 *Terrier et passim* to 1821 *ib*, *v.* **churchyerd**. ASHBY RD, Ashby Magna lying 2 miles to the north-west. BONEHAM'S LANE, with the surn. *Boneham*, common in adjacent Lutterworth 1841–79 Census. BOSTON LODGE, *Boston* 1835 O; whether this is the surviving name of an early farmstead or a transferred name is uncertain, *v.* **loge**. CHURCH DRIVE. CHURCH LANE, 1821 *Terrier*; it is *Allhollen Lane* 1606, *Church lane called Allhollen lane* 1709, 1745 *ib*, leading to All Saints' (i.e. All Hallows') Church *supra*, *v.* **hālga**. COOKE'S FM, cf. *Wm. Cooke* 1846 White of Gilmorton. CROWN (P.H.), *Crown* 1846, 1863, 1877 White, *Crown Inn* 1925 Kelly. GAWNEY LANE is *Mere Road* 1835 O (*v.* (**ge)mǣre**); *galney* 1601 *Terrier*, *gawne* 1606 *ib*, *Gawney* 1674, 1690, 1724, 1762 *ib*, *Gawnee* 1690, 1709, 1724, 1745 *ib*, *Gauni* 1694 *ib*, *Gaunee* 1700 *ib*, *Gawne* 1703, 1709 *ib*, cf. *nether gawne* 1606, 1703 *ib*, *neather gawnee* 1674, 1690, 1745 *ib*, *Neither Gaunee* 1700 *ib*, *the neither Gawnee* 1724 *ib*, *Nether Gawney* 1762 *ib* (*v.* **neoðera**), *Upper gawne* 1606, 1703, 1709, ~ *Gaunee* 1700 *ib*, ~ *Gaunee* 1700 *ib*, ~ *Gawnee* 1674, 1690, 1724, 1745, 1762, *Gawne feild* 1606, 1700, 1709 *ib*, *Gawnee* ~ 1674, 1690, 1709 *ib*, *Gaunee Feild* 1700, *Gawney* ~ 1724, 1762 *ib*, *Gawnee Field* 1724, 1745 *ib* (*v.* **feld**; one of the great open-fields of the township), *v.* **galla** (**gallan** gen.sg., dat.sg.), **ēg**; presum. meaning 'dry raised ground within wetland'; note also Gurney Lane in adjoining Kimcote and Walton parish, the same lane. GILMORTON HOLT (local), *the Oult* 1606, 1724 *Terrier*, *the Holt* 1821 *ib*,

Gilmorton Holt 1925 Kelly, *v.* **wald** and cf. Bruntingthorpe Holt *supra*);
GILMORTON HO. GILMORTON LODGE is *Gilmorton Field* 1835 O, *v.* **loge**.
GILMORTON SPINNEY, *Gilmorton Spinny* 1835 O, *v.* **spinney**.
GOODMAN'S FM, cf. *Wm. Goodman* 1846 White and *Ann Goodman,
cowkeeper* 1877 ib. HOLT FM, *v.* Gilmorton Holt *supra*. INKERSALL FM
(~ LODGE 2½"), either a transferred name from Inkersall in Derbys. (Db
302) or with a surn. taken from that township, *v.* **loge**. THE LODGE
(GILMORTON LODGE 2½"), *Gilmorton Lodge* 1877 White, *v.* **loge**.
LUTTERWORTH RD, Lutterworth lying 3 miles to the south-west. MAIN
ST is *the Town Street* 1821 *Terrier*, *v.* **tūn**. MILL HO. MILL LANE, cf.
Gilmorton Mill 1863 White, *v.* **myln**. OAK FM. OLD RED LION (P.H.),
Old Red Lion 1846, 1863 White, *Red Lion* 1877 ib, *Old Red Lion Inn*
1925 Kelly. PARSONS BARN, with the surn. *Parsons*, cf. *George Parsons*
1829 Census and *Arthur Parsons* 1865 ib of adjacent Misterton. THE
RECTORY, 1821 *Terrier*, 1925 Kelly, *v.* **rectory**; earlier is recorded *the
Parsonage House* 1606, 1709, 1745 *Terrier*, *Gilmorton parsonage* 1703
ib, *v.* **personage**. STOCKWELL HO. (local), *Stockwell House* 1925 Kelly;
Stockwell 1606, 1674 *Terrier et passim* to 1745 *ib*, cf. *Nether Stockwell*
1606, 1674 *ib et passim* to 1762 *ib*, *Neither Stockwell* 1745 *ib* (*v.*
neoðera), *Upper Stockwell* 1700, 1709 *ib et passim* to 1762 *ib*, *v.* **stocc**,
wella. TALBOT (P.H.), *Talbot* 1846, 1863 White, 1925 Kelly, *Talbot Inn*
1877 White. TEALBY'S FM (local), *Tealby farm* 1925 Kelly, cf. *George
Tailby, farmer* 1846 White; the surn. is taken from Tealby in Lincs. (*v.*
L **3** 131). TOLL GATE FM, a former toll-house, *v.* **toll-gate**. ULLESTHORPE
RD, Ullesthorpe lying 4 miles to the west. USHER FM, *Ursaw* 1606, 1674
Terrier et passim to 1745 *ib*, *Urser* 1762 *ib*, *Usser* 1821 *ib*, cf. *Long(e)
Ursaw* 1606, 1674, 1690, 1703 *ib* (*v.* **lang**[1]), *Ursaw feild* 1606, 1674 *ib
et passim* to 1709 *ib*, *Oursor Field* 1694 *ib*, *Ursaw* ~ 1724, 1745 *ib*,
Urser ~ 1762 *ib*, *Usser Field* 1821 *ib* (*v.* **feld**; the name of one of the
great open-fields of Gilmorton), *Ursaw furlong* 1700, 1709 *ib* (*v.*
furlang), *Ursaw Leys* 1700, 1709, 1745, 1762 *ib* (*v.* **leys**). The meaning
is uncertain and earlier forms are needed, but possible is 'the ploughed
enclosure', *v.* **ersc**, **haga**[1]. OE *ūr* 'a bison' (cf. ON *úrr* 'a kind of ox') is
unlikely as the specific in the East Midlands, even though the animal is
recorded in the north in Urpeth (Du 128) and in Urswick (La 144) where
the sense 'wild cattle' was probably intended, but this is a specific which
would sit unhappily with *haga* 'an enclosure' or *scaga* 'a small wood, a
copse'. The masc. pers.n. *Urri* (a Norman form of OE *Wulfrīc*) in the
possessive case would be formally acceptable as the specific, but one
would expect with it a generic in (*ge*)*hæg* rather than the earlier *haga* (cf.
Urishay, DEPN *s.n.*).

FIELD-NAMES

In (a), forms presented without dates are 1762 *Terrier*; those dated 1821 are also *Terrier*; 1843 are Sale; 1846, 1863 and 1877 are White. Forms throughout dated 1417, 1418 and 1421 are *Wyg*; those dated 1606, 1674, 1690, 1694, 1700, 1703, 1709, 1724 and 1745 are *Terrier*; 1648 and 1720 are *Deed*; 1713 are AAS.

(a) Ansdoles (1606, 1700, 1703, 1709, 1724, 1745, *v.* **dāl**; with the OE masc. pers.n. *Ān(n)*, cf. Annesley, Nt 112); Short Arbour (*Arbor* 1694, cf. *Arbor forlonge* 1606, ~*furlong* 1674, 1690, 1700, 1709, 1745, ~*forlang* 1703, *Arbour furlong* 1724 (*v.* **furlang**), prob. with **erber**; but in such names, a reduced early **eorð-burh** is always poss.); Assmore Pitt (*Astmore* 1724, ~ *Pitt* 1700, 1745 (*v.* **pytt**), *v.* **ēast**, **mōr**¹); Barom Hill (1745, *borromhill* 1606, *Barrom* ~ 1674, 1690, *Barrham* ~ 1700, *Barram* ~ 1709, *Baram Hill* 1724, *v.* **hyll**), Hanging Barom (1745, *Hanging Barrom* 1606, 1674, 1690, ~ *Barrham* 1700, ~ *Baram* 1709, 1724, *v.* **hangende**) (*v.* **barro-**, **hamm** (perh. influenced later by **holmr**)); Baxsters Cl (1694, 1700, 1724, *Baxstars* ~ 1709, *Baxter's Close* 1745; with the surn. *Baxter*); Bennetts Leys (*Benits Leyes* 1694, *Bennets Leys* 1745 (*v.* **leys**), cf. *Bennits hadland* 1606 (*v.* **hēafod-land**), *Bennits townsend* 1606, *Benitstownesend* 1674, 1690, (*at*) *Bennet Townsend* 1703 (*v.* **tūn, ende**); *Thom. Bennet* is cited in Gilmorton 1703 *Terrier*, the surn. *Bennet* from the OFr masc. pers.n. *Beneit* (Lat *benedictus* 'blessed')); Short ~, Blackhill (1700, 1709, 1724, 1745, *blachill* 1606, *Blackhill* 1674, 1690, 1694, *Blackill* 1703, *v.* **blæc**, **hyll**); Boyam (*boyom* 1606, *Boyhome* 1674, 1690, *Boyem* 1700, 1724, 1745, cf. *Boyom hole* 1709 (*v.* **hol**¹), *v.* **hamm** (prob. influenced later by **holmr**); with either the OE masc. pers.n. *Boia* or with **boi(a)**); Brickiln Cl 1843 (*v.* **brike-kiln**); the Broad Ley (*v.* **brād, ley**); Broadwell (1674, 1690, 1700, 1709, 1724, 1745, *Brodwell* 1606, cf. *Broadwell furlong* 1709, 1724, 1745 (*v.* **furlang**)), Broadwell Hole 1762, Broadle-hole 1846, Broadle-hole Spring 1863, Broadwell-hole Spring 1877 (*v.* **spring**¹) (*Brodwell hole* 1606, *Broadwellhole* 1674, *Broadwell Hole* 1690, 1694 *et passim* to 1745 (*v.* **hol**¹)), Broadwell Leys (*v.* **leys**) (*v.* **brād, wella**); Broxwell (1606, 1674 *et passim* to 1745, cf. *Broxwell Feild* 1648 (*v.* **feld**)), Broxwell End (1709, 1724, 1745, *Broxswell end* 1700, *v.* **ende**) (*v.* **wella**; either with the OE masc. pers.n. *Brocc* or with **brocc**); Bull Furlong (1674, 1690, 1700, 1709, 1724, 1745, *Bulforlong* 1606, 1703, *v.* **bula, furlang**); Cawsam (1690, 1709, 1745, *Cawsome* 1606, *Carsam* 1674, *Cawsom* 1700, 1724; earlier forms are needed, but poss. is a generic **holmr** with as specific the ON masc. pers.n. *Kálfr* (*Kálfs* gen.sg.), showing early loss of *l* due to Norman influence); Mrs Chandler's Land (cf. *Simon Chandler* 1782 MI, *Anne Chandler* 1789 ib and *Susannah Chandler* 1792 ib, all of Gilmorton); Clarks Land (*Clarke's Land* 1745, cf. *Clarkes hadland* 1674, 1690 (*v.* **hēafod, hēafod-land**); with the surn. *Clarke*, cf. *William Clarke* 1713 MI); Clay Furlong (1700, 1709, 1745, *Clay forlonge* 1606, *Cley furlong* 1724, *v.* **clǣg, furlang**); Clifts (1674, 1690 *et passim* to 1745, *Clift* 1606, *Cliffs* 1700, 1724, *Cliffts* 1745, *v.* **clif**); Coates Gate (*v.* **gata**), Coats Side (1709, 1745, *Cotes Side* 1694, 1700, 1709, 1745, *Coates Side* 1724, *v.* **sīde** and Cotes de Val *supra*); Colemans Home (1674, 1690 *et passim* to 1745, *Colmans home* 1606, *v.* **holmr**; with the surn. *Coleman*, in this region prob. from the ContGerm masc. pers.n. *Col(e)man* (*v.* Reaney *s.n.*), cf. *John Coleman* 1811 Census, *Charlotte*

Coleman 1813 ib and *Joseph Coleman* 1817 ib, all of Gilmorton); (a lane called) Common Baulk 1831 (*v.* **commun, balca**); Coppidmoore (1694, *Coppydmore* 1674, 1690, *Coppidmore* 1700, 1703, 1709, 1724, 1745, *Coppidmoor* 1745, *v.* **copped**[1], **mōr**[1]; cf. *Copedmore* (1467 × 84), Lei **4** 199); the Cow Cl 1843 (*v.* **cū**); Crate (1674, 1690 *et passim* to 1745), Nether Crate (1724, *Neither* ~ 1700, 1709, *Neather Crate* 1745, *v.* **neoðera**) (*v.* **croft**); Crickway Hedge (1694, 1700, 1724, 1745, *Grigway hedge* 1606, *Crickway hedg* 1709 (*v.* **hecg**), *gricway, grickway* 1606, *Crickway* 1674, 1690, 1703, *v.* **weg**; the road to Crick, which lies 10 miles to the south in Northants.); Croftlands (1674, 1690 *et passim* to 1745, *croftlandes* 1606, *Crafts Lands* 1694, *Craftlands* 1709, *v.* **croft, land**); Dry House (1674, 1690, 1694, *driars* 1606, *Dryas* 1700, *Drias* 1703, *Dryass* 1709, 1745, *Dryers* 1724, *v.* **drȳge, ears**); Dust Furlong 1762, 1843, Upper Dust Furlong 1843 (*Dus forlong* 1606, *Dust Furlong* 1700, 1724, 1745, *v.* **furlang**; prob. with **dūst** rather than with an unrecorded OE **dus** 'a heap' (deemed cognate with ON *dys*, ODan *dus* 'a heap, a grave mound')); (on) Ferey (*Ferry* 1606, *Fearey* 1674, 1690, *Fery* 1700, 1724, 1745), Ferey Furlong (*fery furlong* 1700, 1709, 1724, 1745, *v.* **furlang**) (*v.* **feor, ēg**); Flat Side (1674, 1690, 1703, 1709, 1724, *flatsyde* 1606, *Flattside* 1700, 1745, *Flat syde* 1703, *v.* **flat, sīde**); Fleet Slade (1700, 1709, 1724, 1745, *v.* **flēot, slæd**); Flitters pit (*v.* **pytt**; either with the (principally) southern surn. *Flitter* in the possessive case (from OE *flītere* 'a disputer') or with the plural of ME **flite** (OE (*ge*)*flit*) 'dispute' with an intrusive *r*); Fostons Lane 1821 (prob. with the surn. *Foston* of a family originally from the village of this name 6 miles to the north-east, but otherwise naming a lane leading to Foston itself); Foxholes (1700, 1703, 1709, 1724, 1745, cf. *neather foxholes* 1674, 1690 (*v.* **neoðera**), *v.* **fox-hol**); Hall Croft (1674, 1690 *et passim* to 1745, *Halcraft* 1709, *v.* **hall, croft**); Harris's Hill (1745, *Harrisis Hill* 1700, 1724, *Harriseshill* 1709; with the surn. *Harris*); Heath furlong 1762 (1674, 1690 *et passim* to 1745, ~ *forlong* 1606, *v.* **furlang** and Kimcote Heath *infra*); Hobrook (1745, *Holbrook(e)* 1694, 1700, 1709, 1724, *holebrock* ~ 1606, *Holebrooke medow* 1703 (*v.* **mēd** (**mēdwe** obl.sg.)), *v.* **hol**[2], **brōc**); the Holt, ~ ~ furlong (*the oult forlong* 1606, ~ ~ *furlong* 1674, 1690 *et passim* to 1745 (*v.* **furlang**), *v.* **wald** and Gilmorton Holt *supra*); Homemeadow (*homedow* 1606, *Homeadow* 1700, 1745, *Home Meadow* 1724; no early forms, so that the specific could be either **hōh**, **holmr** or **home**); Kelmidge (1700, 1724, 1745, *Celmidge* 1674, 1690, *Kelmige* 1709; again earlier forms are needed, but prob. with **edisc** as the generic and poss. with the OE masc. pers.n. *Cēnhelm* as the specific); Kimcote Heath 1821, The Heath 1843 (*v.* **hǣð**; bordering Kimcote which adjoins to the south-east); Nether ~, Upper Langlands, Longlands (*Longlands* 1606, 1674, 1690, 1700, 1703, 1709, *Nether* ~ 1606, *Neather* ~ 1674, 1690, *Neither Langlands* 1700, 1724, 1745, *Neither* ~ 1700, 1709, 1724, *Neather Longlands* 1745 (*v.* **neoðera**), *Upper* ~ 1606, 1700, 1703, 1724, 1745, *Uppar Langlands* 1674, 1690, *Uper Longlands* 1694, 1709 (*v.* **upper**), *v.* **lang**[1], **land**); Little Cl 1843; Littlewells (1606, 1674 *et passim* to 1745, *v.* **lȳtel, wella**); Marslin Tofts (*Maslin Tafts* 1745, *v.* **toft**; with the surn. *Maslin*, from the OFr masc. pers.n. *Masselin* (ContGerm *Mazelin*, a diminutive of *Mazo*)); the Meadow (1700, 1709, 1724, 1745); Measures Cl 1843 (with the surn. *Measure*); Micklidge (1745, *Miclidge, Miklidge* 1606, *Micheledge* 1674, 1690, *Mickledge* 1694, *Mickelidge* 1700, *Mickeledg* 1709), New Micklidge Hedge (*New Micledge hedge* 1700, 1724, *New Miclidge hedg* 1709, *New Micklidge Hedge* 1745, *v.* **hecg**), Old Micklidge Hedge (*Old Micledge hedge* 1700, 1724, *Old Mickle hedg* 1709, *Old Micklehedge* 1724, *Old*

Micklidge Hedge 1745, *v.* **hecg**) (*v.* **micel, mikill, edisc**); Millbrook (1700, 1709, *Mill brocke* 1606, ~ *brooke* 1674, 1690, 1703, *Milbrook* 1724, 1745, *v.* **myln, brōc**); Mill Furlong (1700, 1709, 1745, *Mill forlong*(*e*) 1606, *Milfurlonge* 1674, 1690, *Milforlonge* 1703, *v.* **myln, furlang**); Mill Heath 1762, Far ~ ~, Near Mill Heath 1843 (*Mill heath* 1606, 1703, 1709, 1745, *Milheath* 1674, 1690, 1724, *v.* **myln, hǣð**); Moult Thorne Leys (1709 (*v.* **leys**), *Mouldthorn*(*e*) 1606, 1674, 1690, *Moulthorn*(*e*) 1674, 1690, 1700, *Moult thorne* 1724, 1745, *v.* **molda, þorn**); the Parsons Piece (1724, *v.* **persone, pece**); Peasom (1694, *Pessam* 1606, *Pesam* 1674, 1690, *Peasam* 1700, 1724, cf. *Peasom* ~ 1709, 1724, *Peasum furlong* 1745 (*v.* **furlang**)), Peasom Slade (1700, 1724, *v.* **slæd**), Peasom Well (1700, 1709, *Pessam well* 1606, *Pesam* ~ 1674, 1690, *Peasam* ~ 1700, 1724, *Peasum Well* 1745, *v.* **wella**) (*v.* **pise, hamm** (perh. later influenced by **holmr**)); Podocks Nest (1674, 1690 *et passim* to 1745, *poddoxnest* 1606, *v.* **padduc, nest**; the name also appears as Paddy's Nest (*Padognest* 1467 × 84) in Blaby *supra*; note also *Paddocksden* (1638) in Countesthorpe f.ns. (b)); Poor Cross (1709, 1745, *portcross* 1606, *poowers cross* 1674, 1690, *porecross* 1700, *Pore Cross or Port Cross* 1703, *Port Cross* 1724, *v.* **port**[2], **cros**; *port* later confused with **pouer**(**e**)); Pultney Leys (*Poultney Leyes* 1674, 1690, 1724, *Poulteny layes* 1700, *Poltney* ~ 1709, *Poultney Leys* 1745, *v.* **leys**), Pultney Stones (1745, *Poulteney* ~ 1700, *Poultney stones* 1709, *v.* **stān**; prob. township boundary markers) (Poultney adjoins to the south); Ridgeway (1724, 1745, *Ridgway* 1606, 1674, 1690, 1700, 1703), Ridgeway Fd 1763, 1821 (1720, 1724, 1745, *Ridgway Feild* 1690, 1709, *Ridgway Field* 1694, *v.* **feld**; a later name for *Old Milfeild, infra*) (*v.* **hrycgweg**); Rooks Church (1703, 1709, 1724, 1745, *Rookes Church* 1606, 1674, 1690, 1700, *v.* **hrōc**; *church* is presum. in the sense 'a congregation', hence 'a rookery'); Rye Crofts (1745, *Ricroftes* 1606, *Rycrofts* 1674, 1679, *Rye croft* 1700, *Rye craft* 1709, *Riecroft* 1724, *v.* **ryge, croft**); Rye Hill (1700, 1724, 1745, *v.* **ryge**); Rye Tofts (*Rye Tafts* 1745, *v.* **ryge, toft**); Sand Pits (*Sandpit* 1606, *sandepits* 1674, 1690, *Sandpitts* 1700, 1709, 1724, 1745, *v.* **sand-pytt**); Seven Ridges 1762, 1843 (1700, 1724, 1745, *Seaven Ridges* 1606, *seuven ridgis* 1674, 1690, *Saven Ridges* 1709, *v.* **seofon, hrycg**); Rye Sharlings (1745, *Sharlinges* 1606, *Charleings* 1674, 1690, *Sharlings* 1694, 1703, *the Rie Sharlings* 1694, *v.* **ryge**), Short Sharlings (1700, 1709, 1724, 1745), Upper Sharlings (1700, 1709, 1724, 1745, cf. *Nether Sharlinges* 1606, *neather charlings* 1674, 1690, *Neither* ~ 1700, 1703, 1709, *Nether Sharlings* 1724, *v.* **neoðera** ('little shares (of common land)', *v.* **sc**(**e**)**aru, -ing**[1], **-ling**); Sidlings (1674, 1690 *et passim* to 1745, *sidlinges* 1606, *Sedlinges* 1703, *v.* **sīdling**); Sowledge (*Soulidge* 1606, *Sowlidge* 1690, 1700, 1709, 1724, 1745, *Sowledg* 1709), Upper Sowledge (*Upper Sowlidge* 1700, 1709, 1724, 1745, cf. *Nether* ~ 1606, *Neither Soulidge* 1674, 1690 (*v.* **neoðera**)) (*v.* **sulh, edisc**); Snelson's Homestead 1846, 1863 (*v.* **hām-stede**; with the surn. *Snelson* of a family originally from Snelston, 44 miles to the north-west in Derbys., with typical local 17th-cent. loss of *t* from the group *-ston*); Spillmans Home (*Spillmanshom* 1606, *Spilmans home* 1674, 1690, 1724, 1745, *Spellmanshome* 1694), Spillmans Home Hades (*Spilmans home hades* 1724, 1745, *v.* **hēafod**) (*v.* **holmr**; with the surn. *Spillman*, from OE *spilemann* 'a juggler'); Stonetree (1745, *Stontree* 1700, 1709, 1724; this is unlikely to be a Scand 'tree from which poles are cut' (*v.* **stong, tré**) in this area of low Scand topographical influence; better is 'stone trough' (*v.* **stān, trog**), since OE **trēow** 'a tree' remained sometimes as *trow*, which could be confused with the *trow* which developed from **trog**; whether this alluded literally to a stone trough for watering animals or was a topographically transferred name for a hollow resembling a trough is uncertain); Stullidge (1700, 1703, 1709, 1724, 1745, *Stallidge* 1606, 1674, 1690, *Stulledge* 1694, *Stullidg* 1709, *v.* **stall, edisc**); Throwsmoore (*frawsmore* 1606, *Frowsmoor* 1674, 1690, *Frowesmore* 1700, *Frowsmore* 1703, 1709, 1724, *Throwsmoor* 1745, *v.* **mōr**[1]; prob. with the OE masc. pers.n. *Freoðulf*, as in the name Frolesworth, 4½ miles to the north-west); Thurnborow (*Thurnborough* 1674, 1690, *Thurnbrow* 1703, cf. *Thurnborow Stile* 1745 (*v.* **stigel**), *v.* **þyrne, berg**); the Town Land (*v.* **tūn**); (at) Views (1700, 1745, *vewes* 1606, *Veiwes* 1674, 1690, 1709, *Viewes* 1724; of uncertain meaning, but perh. simply the sb. **vewe**, alluding to a view-point affording a range of prospects of the landscape or else an expectation of good produce; Prof. R. Coates notes an earlier meaning of *vewe* which may apply here, that alluding to a formal survey of land for valuation, *v.* OED view sb. I 1 a); Walton Meer (1700, 1724, 1745, *Walton meere* 1606, 1703, 1709, ~ *Meare* 1674, 1690, *v.* **(ge)mǣre**; the parish boundary with Walton which adjoins to the south-west); Warden Hill (1606, 1674 *et passim* to 1745; with the surn. *Warden*, cf. *Andrew Warden* 1700 *Terrier*, *Jo. Warden* and *Wm. Warden* 1703 *ib* and *Henry Warden* 1724 *ib*, all of Gilmorton); Willowbeds (1674, 1690, 1700, 1709, 1745, *Willoues beeds* 1694, *the Willobed* 1703, *Willowbed* 1724, *v.* **wilig, bedd**); Wormleightons Cl 1821 (with the surn. *Wormleighton* of a family originally from the village of this name, 23 miles to the south-west in Warwks.; cf. *Mary Wormleighton* 1804 Census of adjoining Bitteswell parish and *Robert Wormleighton* 1810 ib of adjoining Walton).

(b) *the beere balke* 1606 (*v.* **bere, balca**; in this Glebe Terrier, it is associated with the parish churchyard, hence *bere* 'a bier' (with *balke* as a pathway) is to be preferred to *bǣr* 'pasture'); *Bloxam's Land* 1745 (with the surn. *Bloxam* of a family originally from Bloxholm, 50 miles to the north-east in Lincs.; cf. *Ann Bloxam* 1796 MI); *Chapman's Land* 1745 (cf. *John Chapman* 1630 Nichols, a resident of Gilmorton); *the Common Ground* 1700, 1703, 1724, 1745 (*v.* **commun, grund**); *Cotes Forlong* 1606, 1674, 1690 (*v.* **furlang**), *Cotes ~* 1606, *Coates Slade* 1674, 1690 (*v.* **slæd**) (*v.* Cotes de Val *supra*); *the Dam* 1700, ~ ~ *on Rye hill* 1724 (*v.* Rye Hill *supra*), *the Dam Hill* 1724 (*v.* **damme**); *Fee Furlong* 1674, 1690, *fee forlonge* 1703 (*v.* **feoh, furlang**; alluding here to the payment of money (a fee)); *Field Close or Lammas Close* 1720 (a close adjoining one of the great open-fields, *v. Lammas Close, infra*); *Grass plots* 1694 (*v.* **græs, plot**); *Grinway* 1606 (*v.* **grēne**[1], **weg**); *atte Halle* 1416 (p), 1417 (p), 1421 (p) (*v.* **atte, hall** and note Hall Croft *supra*); *the homeward forlonge* 1606 (*v.* **hāmweard, furlang**); *hookesickmiddo* 1674, 1690 (*v.* **hōc, sík, mēd** (**mēdwe** obl.sg.)); *Kelingway* 1606, *Kilingway* 1703 (*v.* **weg**; the road to North Kilworth which lies 4 miles to the south-east; these forms contain abbreviations of *Kelingworth* and *Kilingworth*, in turn shortenings of the early spellings *Kevelingworth*, *Kivelingworth* of North ~, South Kilworth *infra*); *the kinges hie way* 1606, *the kings highway* 1703 (*v.* **hēah-weg**; with reference to James I in 1606, while the 1703 instance of ~ *kings* ~ from the reign of Queen Anne is the result of a lazy copying of the 1606 Glebe Terrier); *knockstone* 1694 (*v.* **cnocc**[2], **stān**); *Lammas Close* 1720 (*v.* **lammas** and *Field Close, supra*); *The Leyes* 1674, 1694 (*v.* **leys**); *Oddcrofts* 1700, *Odd Craftes* 1709, ~ *Crofts* 1724 (*v.* **ald, croft**); *Old Milfeild* 1606, *Old Mill Feild now called Ridgeway Feild* 1690, 1709, *The Old Milfeild now called Ridgway* 1700, *Old Mill Field now called Ridgeway Field* 1724, 1745, *v.* **ald, myln, feld**; one of the great open-fields of Gilmorton); *New-found-pool close* 1713 (*v.* **pōl**[1]; cf. New Found Pool, Lei **1** 222); *the Parsons Closses* 1724 (*v.* **persone**,

clos(e)); *peateling* ~ 1606, *Peatling hedge* 1674, 1690, 1703 (*v.* **hecg**; the boundary hedge with Peatling Parva parish which adjoins to the north-east); *poltny yate* 1606, *Poltny gate* 1703 (*v.* **gata**; the road to the original Poultney township which lay 7 miles to the south-east); *the Queens highway* 1709 (*v.* **hēah-weg**; alluding to Queen Anne); *Safforn or Kelmidge furlong* 1690, *Saffron or Kelmidge furlong* 1700, *Safforn furlong or Kelmidge* 1709, *Saffron Furlong or Kelmidge* 1724 (*v.* **furlang** and Kelmidge *supra*; the reference here may be to **safron** 'saffron', the cultivation of which was introduced into England c.1350 rather than to a third Leics. pre-English stream-name *Severne* (as Saffron Brook (*Severne* 1558, *Safforn* 1756)), Lei 1 226 and *Seuene* (13), Lei 3 212, later styled *Severn*, Lei 3 270); *sotham* 1606 (*v.* **sūð, hamm**); *Stanforlong(e)* 1606, *Stanfurlong* 1674, 1690 (*v.* **stān, furlang**); *the Streme lane* 1606, *the Stream Lane* 1709, 1745 (*v.* **strēam**); *Toftes* 1606, *Taftes* 1674, 1690, *Tofts* 1700, *Tafts* 1709, 1724 (*v.* **toft**); *Walton broocke* 1606, ~ *brook* 1674, 1690, 1703 (*v.* **brōc**; Walton lies 1½ miles to the south-east); *Waschpitt* ~ 1700, *Washpitt footway* 1709 (*v.* **wæsce, pytt, fote-waye**); *Whorelidge* 1606, 1674, 1690, 1703 (*v.* **hwerfel, edisc**); *Woodcock's Land* 1745 (cf. *Mrs Woodcock jun.* 1745 *Terrier* of Gilmorton).

GLEN PARVA

Glen e.13 *Rut*, 1220 MHW, 1227 Cur *et passim* to 1260 *Wyg et freq*
Gleen 1323 Misc, 1352 Ipm, 1389 *Rut*

Affixes are added as:
Parua ~, Parva ~ e.13 *Rut*, 1243 Fees *et passim* to 1491 *Rut*
~ Parua, ~Parva 1389 *Rut*, 1494 *Comp*, 1576 Saxton *et passim*
Little ~ 1605 *Terrier*, 1610 Speed

With MLat *parva* 'little, small' in contrast to Great Glen in Gartree
Hundred.

This place-name is identical in origin with that of Great Glen which
lies five miles to the east (*v.* Lei **4** 79). Early forms which are presumed
to relate to Great Glen are (*in loco qui nominatur*) *æt glenne* 849 (11)
BCS 455 (S 1272), *Glen* 1086 DB, 1140 Reg and *Glenne* 1199 FF. Glen
is probably a place-name formed from an earlier name for the river
Sence, a Brit **Glaṇi̯ā* from **glano-*'clean, beautiful', hence 'the clean
one' alluding to a clear stream, giving an early OE settlement-name '(the
place called) At the Glen', cf. R. Glen, DLPN 50. Alternatively, because
of early spellings with *-nn-* for Great Glen, a Brit **glennos* (Brythonic
*glïn, Gaelic *gleann*) 'a valley' may also be considered. However,
although Great Glen lies in a pronounced valley of the river Sence at its
particular location, Glen Parva, which is situated further west on the
same stream, was established where a valley is much less noticeable.
Hence, a British river-name seems likelier for the origin of both Glen
Parva and Great Glen. The notion of the river as having a British name
meaning 'the clean one' is supported by its Anglo-Saxon name Sence
(OE *senc* 'a draught, a drink'), implying a copious supply of good
drinking water.

If the origin of the names Glen Parva and Great Glen is indeed Brit
*glennos 'a valley', it is possible that the name of the valley at Great
Glen was extended to become a British district-name, eventually applied

to two settlements within its compass which were only coincidentally beside the river.

AYLESTONE GRANGE (2½") is *Aylestone Lodge* 1835 O, *v.* **loge, grange**. AYLESTONE HOLT, *v.* **holt**. BLUE BANK LOCK, *v.* **lock**; on the Grand Union Canal. CATHERINE SPINNEY, *v.* **spinney**; note Kitty's Big Mdw *infra*. CORK LANE, no early forms survive, but perh. with **calc**. DUNN'S LOCK, *v.* **lock**; with the surn. *Dunn*. GEE'S LOCK, *v.* **lock**; with the surn. *Gee*, cf. *George Gee* 1824 Census, *John Gee* 1833 ib of neighbouring Blaby and *Elizabeth Gee* 1828 ib of neighbouring Aylestone. GLEN FORD, *v.* **ford**. GLEN HILL LODGE, *v.* **loge**. GLEN HILLS NURSERY, *Glen Hills* 1795 Nichols, *v.* **nursery**. GLEN PARVA LODGE, *v.* **loge**. GRANGE SPINNEY, cf. *The Grange* 1877 White, *Glen Parva grange* 1925 Kelly, *v.* **grange, spinney**. JUBILEE COVERT (2½") (lost), *v.* **cover(t)**; named from one of Queen Victoria's national jubilees (Golden 1887, Diamond 1897). KNIGHT'S BRIDGE, cf. *Joseph Knight, lord of the manor* 1846 White. LATTICE COPPICE, *v.* **latis, copis**; perhaps referring to its original geometrical lattice-work pattern of planting. LITTLE GREEN BRIDGE. THE MANOR is *Manor House* 1863, 1877 White, *Glen Parva manor* 1925 Kelly, *v.* **maner**. ST THOMAS'S CHURCH, *Church (St Thomas)* 1925 Kelly; built 1892–3, but a chapel of ease is recorded here in *capellas Lubstorp et Glen* 1220 MHW (with MLat *capella* 'a chapel', also referring to nearby Lubbesthorpe in Sparkenhoe Hundred). SIMPKIN'S BRIDGE (2½"), with the surn. *Simpkin(s)*, cf. *Thomas Simpkin* 1630 Nichols, *John Simpkins* 1828 Census and *Samuel Simpkins* 1852 ib, all of Glen Parva. SIR JOHN'S WOOD, named from Sir John Manners (c.1534–1611) of Haddon Hall, Derbys., once a landowner in Glen Parva. UNION (P.H.) (lost), *Union Inn* 1835 O, *Union* 1846, 1863, 1877 White; a bargemen's tavern on the former Union Canal (now the Grand Union Canal).

Street-names in recent urban developments:

ALDERLEIGH RD. AMBLESIDE DRIVE. DOROTHY AVE. EBCHESTER RD. EDEN WAY. FEATHERSTONE DRIVE. GARNETT CRESC. GLEN RISE. GLENVILLE AVE. GREENDALE RD. HENRAY AVE. HILLSBOROUGH RD. HOWARD RD. IRIS AVE. KELSO GREEN. LEICESTER RD. LITTLE GLEN RD. MONMOUTH DRIVE. NEEDHAM AVE. NEW BRIDGE RD. OAKLEIGH AVE. QUEEN'S PARK WAY. RED HOUSE RD. RICHMOND DRIVE. RUNCORN RD. SAXON DALE. SCOTSWOOD CRESC. SHIELD CRESC. STRENSALL RD. SWINFORD AVE. TADCASTER AVE. THE BRIDLE. TWICKENHAM RD.

WESTDALE AVE. WESTLEIGH RD. WESTVIEW AVE. WINDSOR AVE.
WOKINGHAM AVE.

FIELD-NAMES

In (a), forms presented without dates are 1839 *TA*; those dated 1795 are
Nichols. Forms throughout dated c.1247 and 1260 are *Wyg*; those dated
1324 and Ric 2 are *Rut*; 1327 are SR; 1727 are *Deed*.

(a) Abbots Cl, ~ Land (with the surn. *Abbot*, cf. *James Abbott* 1824 Census of
Glen Parva); The Four ~, The Six ~, The Seven Acres, The Twelve Acre, Five Acre
Cl, Two and a half acre Mdw (*v.* **æcer**); Barn Cl (*the Barn Close* 1727, *v.* **bern**);
Bents Mdw (with the surn. *Bent*; cf. *James Bent* 1842 Census of Glen Parva); Biggin
Mdw (*v.* **bigging**); Breeches Mdw (cf. *le Breche* 1324, *v.* **brēc**); Bridge Cl, Bridge
Foot Cl (*v.* **fōt**) (*v.* **brycg**); Bush Cl (*v.* **busc**); Canal Cl (beside *Union Canal* 1846
White, later the Grand Union Canal); Caters Mdw (with the surn. *Cater*; from ME
catour 'a buyer of provisions for a large household' (from AFr *acatour*, OFr
achatour 'a buyer')); Clover Cl (*v.* **clāfre**; a fodder crop); Collum Mdw, Brewins
Collum (with the surn. *Brewin*; of Glen Parva, 'the principal inhabitant is Mr Bruin,
a reputable and wealthy grazier' 1807 Nichols; cf. also *Benjamin Brewin* 1812
Census and *John Brewin* 1837 ib of adjacent Wigston Magna) (*the Collums* 1727;
earlier spellings are needed but **hamm**, with as the specific an OE masc. pers.n. *Cola*,
is formally poss.); Coltmans First Cl, Coltmans Five Acres (with the surn. *Coltman*,
cf. *Thomas Coltman* 1806 Census and *William Coltman* 1844 ib of neighbouring
Wigston Magna); First ~ ~ 1839, Flax Leys 1795, 1839 (*v.* **fleax**, **leys**); Foot Road
Cl (*v.* **foot-road**); Front Cl (*v.* **front**); George's Cl (with the surn. *George*); First ~
~, Middle Glen Hills (*v.* Glen Hills Nursery *supra*); Great Brick Kiln (*v.* **brike-kiln**);
Great Denshire (with *denshire*, a syncopated form of *devonshire*, used as a verb
meaning 'to clear or improve land by paring off stubble, turf, weeds etc., burning
them and spreading the ashes'; the method was originally practised in Devon and was
the equivalent of the more usual Midlands style 'to burn-bake, to burn-beak', *v.* Field
88–90); The Hand Post (a close beside a guide-post or finger-post; the earliest
citation in OED for **hand-post** is dated 1791); Hewitts Cl, Far ~, Farthest ~, Top
Hewitts (with the surn. *Hewitt*); Hill Cl (*the Hill Close* 1727); Far ~ ~, Home Cl
(because of implied distance, the first form may suggest **holmr** rather than **home**);
House Cl, ~ Orchard (*v.* **orceard**); Kirkdale 1795, 1839 (cf. *Shortekirkedale* 1324 (*v.*
sc(e)ort), *v.* **kirkja**, **dalr**); Kitty's Big Mdw (with the fem. pers.n. *Kitty*, a pet-form
of Catherine; it is uncertain whether Catherine Spinney *supra* is related); Lewis's
Piece (*v.* **pece**; with the surn. *Lewis*, cf. *Joseph Lewis* 1857 Census of Glen Parva);
Little Cl, ~ Mdw; Lock Cl (*v.* **lock**; the close has a canal lock at its south-west
corner); Long Bit (*v.* **bit**); Long Mdw 1795, 1839; Mill Mdw (*v.* **myln**; note the local
ad molendinum c.1247 (p), 1260 (p) 'at the mill', with MLat *molendinum* 'a mill');
Nether Top (*v.* **topp**); Occupation Lane (a common post-Enclosure name alluding to
an access road through what was formerly a great open-field); Parsons Piece (*v.*
persone, **pece**); Pawleys Mdw (with the surn. *Pawley*; cf. *Sarah Pawley* 1837 Census
of adjoining Blaby, *Elizabeth Pawley* 1800 ib, *Thomas Pawley* 1805 *ib* and *George*

Pawley 1817 ib, all of adjacent Wigston Magna parish); Peakes Cl (with the surn.
Peake); Pitt Cl (*v.* **pytt**); Road Cl, Next Road (roadside closes); Round Cl 1795, 1839
(*v.* **round**); Rye Hill (*v.* **ryge**); Sickle Hill (earlier forms are needed; poss. is a name
with **sikel**, signifying a hill with a curving, sickle shape, or a **sík** + **hyll**, with later
reduplicated *hill*); Simpkins Mdw (*v.* Simpkin's Bridge *supra*); Great ~, Little Slade
(*v.* **slæd**); South Barn Cl (*v.* **bern**); the Turnpike Road (*v.* **turnepike**; the road to
Lutterworth, now the A426); Whattons Mdw (with the surn. *Whatton* of a family
prob. originally from Long Whatton, 16 miles to the north-west); Bottom Whetstone,
Whetstone Brook (*v.* **brōc**), Whetstone Holmes (*v.* **holmr**), Whetstone Lane,
Whetstone Mdw (Whetstone parish adjoins to the south).

(b) *Askecroft* 1324 (*v.* **askr, croft**); *Brookes's Main Plott* 1727 (*v.* **plot**; with the
surn. *Brookes*; cf. *William Brookes* 1630 Nichols, *Mary Brookes* 1727 *Deed* and
Alice Brookes 1727 *ib*, all of Glen Parva); *ad fonte'* 1326 (p) ('at the spring or well',
with MLat *fons* (*fontem* acc.sg.) 'a well'); *Glen Dam* 1727 (*v.* **damme**); *la Gore* Ric
2 (*v.* **gāra**); *Gorzey Close* 1727 (*v.* **gorstig**); *le Hallecroft(e)* 1324, Ric 2 (*v.* **hall,
croft**); *le Holmes* 1324 (*v.* **holmr**); *the Homestead* 1727 (*v.* **hām-stede**); *le Hull* 1324
(*v.* **hyll**); *Long Close*; *Nicketts Holme* 1727 (*v.* **holmr**; with the surn. *Nickett*, a
diminutive of *Nick*, the pet-form of Nicholas); *Osemondeshoc* 1324 (*v.* **hōc**; the surn.
Osmond developed from the OE masc. pers.n. *Ōsmund* and from Norman *Osmund*
(in turn from the ON masc. pers.n. *Ásmundr* (ODan *Asmund*); either a pers.n. or a
surn. is poss. here); *Pipendeput* 1324 (*v.* **pīpe, ende, pytt**); *Redehull* 1324 (*v.* **hyll**;
with **rēad** or **hrēod**); *Ridgeway* 1727 (*v.* **hrycgweg**); *le Roudik, Smale Roudik* (*v.*
smæl) 1324 (*v.* **rūh, dík**; cf. Raw Dykes, Lei **1** 5); *Stockwell sik Field* 1727 (*v.* **stocc,
wella, sík**); *the Stone Meadow* 1727 (*v.* **stān**; either 'the stony meadow' or 'the
stoned meadow', i.e. one having been cleared of stones, *v. the stone middow* (1601),
Lei **2** 19, *the stone meadow* (1625), Lei **4** 57 and *stone meadowe* (1601) in Dunton
Bassett f.ns. (b) *supra*); *le Styes* 1324 (*v.* **stig**); *Twotherenhul* 1324 (*v.* **tū, þyrne,
hyll**); *in Venell'* 1327 (p) ('in the lane', with MLat *venella* (*venellam* acc.sg.) 'a
lane'); *Wester Holme* 1727 (*v.* **vestr, holmr**); *Wrangelondes* 1324 (*v.* **wrang, land**);
Wrongedole 1324 (*v.* **wrang, dāl**).

Kilby

1. KILBY

Cilebi 1086 DB
Chilebi e.13 *RTemple* (p)
Kildebi 1195 P (p), 1196 ChancR (p), 1197 (p), 1199 P (p), *Kildeby*
 1209 × 19 RHug
Kilebi 1165 P, e.13 *RTemple* (p), e.13 *Wyg* (p), 1202 Ass (p) *et*
 passim to c.1220 *Hazlerigg* (p), *Kileby* 1209 GildR, 1210 Cur (p)
 et passim to 1269 *Wyg*, 1316 FA, *Kyleby* 1236 (p), 1242 Fees (p)
 et passim to 1350, 1353 Ipm
Kelebi 1156 (1318) Ch, *Keleby* 1258 Pat (p), 1265 Hastings (p) *et*
 passim to 1431 *Wyg*, *Kelleby* 1262 Fine (p), 1344 Coram (p),
 Kelby 1363 *Wyg* (p)
Kylby 1305 Banco, 1327 SR *et passim* to 1395, 1417 *Wyg et freq* to
 1559 Ipm, *Kilby* 1328 Banco, 1332 Ipm *et passim* to 1610 Speed
 et freq

Probably in origin an OE **cildatūn* 'the estate of young men of noble
birth', *v.* **cild** (**cilda** gen.pl.), **tūn**, but Scandinavianized with the generic
replaced with **bȳ** and with the use of initial ON [k]. The e.13th-cent.
spelling with *Ch-* is an AN style for the voiceless stop. Forms with *Ke-*
are due to AN substitution of *e* for *i*.

AMBERDALE SPINNEY appears to represent the *Foryste of Annurdale*
1467 × 84 *LTD*. If this cartulary copy of the place-name is accurate, then
probably 'Einarr's valley', *v.* **dalr**; with the common ON masc. pers.n.
Einarr, which would be acceptable in this township with a Scandinavianized name. But the *nn* of the copy may be an original *m* as in the modern
form, hence poss. rather 'valley frequented by buntings', with **amer** as
the specific, *v.* **forest**, **spinney**. BLACK SWAN (P.H.) (lost), *Black Swan*
1828 *Deed*, 1846, 1863, 1877 White. CONGREGATIONAL CHURCH. DOG
AND GUN (P.H.), *Old Dog and Gun* 1846, 1863 White, *Dog and Gun*
1877 ib, 1925 Kelly. FLECKNEY RD, Fleckney lying 2 miles to the south-
east. KILBY BRIDGE, 1846, 1863, 1877 White. KILBY GRANGE, 1835 O,

1877 White, *v*. **grange**. KILBY LODGE, 1835 O, 1877 White, *The Lodge* 1925 Kelly, *v*. **loge**. MAIN ST. ST MARY MAGDALENE'S CHURCH, *Church (St Mary)* 1846 White, *Church (St Mary Magdalene)* 1863, 1877 ib, 1925 Kelly; it is earlier recorded as *ecclesiam de Kildeby* a.1219 RHug. THE VICARAGE, 1925 Kelly; earlier is recorded *the Vicaridge house* 1674, 1700 *Terrier*, *v*. **vikerage**. WELFORD RD, Welford lying 10 miles to the south in Northants. WISTOW RD is *Wistow lane* 1725 *Terrier*, Wistow situated 1½ miles to the north-east.

FIELD-NAMES

Forms dated 1455 are Hastings; those dated 1477 (e.16) are *Charyte*; e.16 are *LTD*; 1725 are *Terrier*.

(b) *Abbethirne* 1477 (e.16) (*v*. **abbey, þyrne**; the thorn-land was the property of the Abbey of St Mary de Pratis, Leicester); *Barlykhul* 1477 (e.16), *Barly hill* e.16, *barley hill furlong* 1725 (*v*. **furlang**) (*v*. **bærlic, hyll**); *þe Beke* 1477 (e.16) (*v*. **bekkr**); *Brode water* e.16, *broadwater furlong* 1725 (*v*. **furlang**) (*v*. **brād, wæter**); *John Chamberlins hadland* 1725 (*v*. **hēafod-land**; cf. *John Chamberlin* 1806 Census of adjacent Arnesby parish); *Chanel seke,* ~ *syke* e.16, *chaniel sick* 1725 (*v*. **chanel, sík**); *þe clincis, Clyng* e.16, *clink bank* 1725 (*v*. **banke**) (*v*. **clinc**); *colt slade* 1725 (*v*. **colt, slæd**); *crofte acer* e.16 (*v*. **croft, æcer**); *the Cross feild* 1725 (*v*. **feld**; one of the great open-fields of the township), *crossway* 1725 (*v*. **weg**) (*v*. **cros**); *crucked tree* 1725 (*v*. **trēow**; perh. with **croked**, but note the comment on Crooked Tree Cl in adjoining Arnesby f.ns. (b) which relates to this feature); *Mr farmers hadland* 1725 (*v*. **hēafod-land**); *Fernedale* 1477 (e.16) (*v*. **fearn, dalr**); *Foston* ~ e.16, *fawson dale* 1725 (*v*. **dalr**; towards Foston *infra*); *goose acres* 1725 (*v*. **gōs, æcer**); *the Great Meddow,* ~ ~ *Middow* 1725 (*v*. **mēd** (**mēdwe** obl.sg.)); *Guttulmesholm* 1477 (e.16) (*v*. **holmr**; with the OE masc. pers.n. *Gūðhelm*); *Halebergh* 1477 (e.16) (*v*. **halh, berg**); *honey rushes* 1725 (*v*. **hunig, risc**; a rush-bed with sticky, boggy soil); *Leicester way* 1725 (the road to Leicester which once lay 6 miles to the north-west); *the Little Meddow* 1725 (*v*. **mēd** (**mēdwe** obl.sg.)); *Long furlong* e.16 (*v*. **lang**[1], **furlang**); *the Long hadland* 1725 (*v*. **hēafod-land**); *Long hedge end* 1725 (*v*. **hecg, ende**); *Marymawdelyn hadeland* e.16 (*v*. **hēafod-land**; lying next to the parish church of St Mary Magdalene *supra*); *Magsley* 1725 (*v*. **lēah**; an early name, poss. with the OE masc. pers.n. *Mæg* as the specific, with the final consonant Scandinavianized); *Mill hill, the Mill hill close, the Milln hill feild* 1725 (*v*. **feld**; one of the great open-fields) (*v*. **myln, hyll**); *Muklyng'* 1477 (e.16) (*v*. **micel, mikill, eng**); *the Mydull Feild* e.16, *the Middle feild* 1725 (*v*. **middel, feld**; one of the great open-fields); *Nedurfurlong* e.16 (*v*. **neoðera, furlang**); *Nedertoftes* e.16 (*v*. **neoðera, toft**); *Noke medow* e.16 (*v*. **nōk, mēd** (**mēdwe** obl.sg.)); *Ouer furlong* e.16 (*v*. **uferra, furlang**); *the Pasture* e.16, *the pastor, pastor furlong* 1725 (*v*. **furlang**) (*v*. **pasture**); *peatling way* 1725 (*v*. **weg**; the road to Peatling Magna which lies 2 miles to the south-west); *persons leas* 1725 (*v*. **persone, leys**); *Phillipes hadley* 1725 (*v*. **headley**; with the surn. *Phillips*); *Ry* ~ e.16, *rie hill* 1725 (*v*. **ryge, hyll**); *Sandelands* e.16 (*v*.

sand, **land**); *Schepecotes* 1455 (*v.* **scēp-cot**); *Shreeves furlong* 1725 (*v.* **furlang**; with the surn. *Shreeve*, from OE *scīrgerēfa*; cf. *Hugo le Sirreve* 1212 Cur of Leics.); *Skynner* ~ e.16, *Skinner hill* 1725 (*v.* **hyll**), *Neder Skynner* e.16 (*v.* **neoðera**) (with the surn. *Skinner*); *Thurnedale* 1477 (e.16) (*v.* **þyrne, dalr**); *the town furlong* 1725 (*v.* **tūn, furlang**); *Tythe medo(w)* e.16, *the tithe meddow* 1725 (*v.* **tēoða, mēd** (**mēdwe** obl.sg.)); *Tytman hyll* e.16 (*v.* **hyll**; with the surn. *Titman*, from OE *tēoðingmann* 'the chief man of a tithing' (a tithing originally consisted of ten householders)); *Vicar leyis* e.16 (*v.* **vikere, leys** and The Vicarage *supra*); *Waterforos* e.16 (*v.* **wæter, furh** and *Water furrowes* in Ashby Parva f.ns. (b)); *the Weste felde* e.16 (*v.* **west, feld**; one of the early great open-fields of Kilby, prob. an earlier name for *the Milln hill feild*, *supra*); *Whyte gresse* e.16, *whitt grass* 1725 (*v.* **hwīt, græs**; in eModE, *white* was sometimes used of dry, open pasture); *Wistow mere* e.16 (*v.* (**ge)mǣre**; the parish boundary with Wistow which lies 1½ miles to the north-east); *Wranglondes* e.16 (*v.* **wrang, land**).

2. FOSTON

> *Fostone* 1086 DB, *Foston* 1207 GildR (p), e.13 *Wyg*, 1220 MHW *et passim* to 1233 Cl *et freq*, (~ *iuxta Kyl(e)by* 1305, 1306 Banco, 1308, 1309 Cl), *Fostona* e.Hy 3 Berkeley, e.13 *Wyg*, *Fostun* 1205 Pap, *Fozton* 1194, 1199 P *et freq* to 1207 ib
>
> *Foteston* 1169, 1170, 1171 P *et freq* to 1208 ib, *Fotestona* a.1108 (1317) Dugd, 1155 (1316) Ch, *Fotiston* 1199 MemR, *Fotistona* 1109 × 22 (1356) Ch
>
> *Foscinton* 1197, 1198, 1199 P, *Fozinton* 1193 ib (p), 1196 ChancR
>
> *Fosceton* 1203, 1230 P
>
> *Fotstun* 1202 FF (p), *Fotston* 1233 Cl
>
> *Forston* 1493 Pat, 1539 MinAccts, *Fawston* 1693 LML, *Fawson* 1725 *Terrier*

'The farmstead or village belonging to a man called Fot', *v.* **tūn** The ON masc. pers.n. *Fótr* is an original by-name 'foot'. The Scand gen.sg. *Fóts* survives in the forms dated 1202 and 1233.

FOSTON COTTAGES. FOSTON HALL FM (HALL FM 2½"), *The Hall* 1846, 1863, 1877 White, *Foston Hall farm* 1925 Kelly, *v.* **hall**. FOSTON HO. FOSTON LODGE, 1835 O, 1846, 1863 White, *v.* **loge**. MOAT SPINNEY, at the site of the deserted medieval village of Foston, *v.* **mote**; it is *Foston Spinney* 1806 Map, *v.* **spinney**. NEW COTTAGES. THE RECTORY, 1877 White, 1925 Kelly, *v.* **rectory**; earlier is recorded *The Parsonage house* 1708 *Terrier*, *v.* **personage**. REED POOL (2½") is *the great poole* 1641 Ipm, *v.* **hrēod, grēat, pōl**[1]. REED POOL SPINNEY, *Reed-pool Spinny* 1835

O, *v.* **spinney**. ST BARTHOLOMEW'S CHURCH, *Church (St Bartholomew)* 1846, 1863, 1877 White, 1925 Kelly; earlier is recorded *ecclesie de Foston* 1220 MHW, 1340, 1341 *Pat et passim* to 1373, 1379 *ib*, *ecclesiam de Foston* 1237 RGros, 1242 RGrav, *ecclesie de Fostone* 1337 *Pat*, the Church 1700, 1703, 1708 *Terrier*. Note also *the Church Yard* 1742 *ib, v.* **churchyerd**. SOARS LODGE FM, with the surn. *Soars* (from OFr *sor* 'reddish brown' and not to be confused with the county's river Soar); cf. *John Soars* 1838 Census and *Rebecca Soars* 1838 ib, both of adjacent Countesthorpe, *v.* **loge**.

FIELD-NAMES

In (a), forms presented without dates are 1850 *TA*; those dated 1835 are O. Forms throughout dated e.13 are *Wyg*; those dated 1285 are Banco; n.d. are Nichols; 1548 are Pat; c.1575 and 1637 are *Deed*; 1619 are ChancP; 1641 are Ipm; 1690, 1700 and 1703 are *Terrier*.

(a) The four acres, The 4 acres east of Barn, the Barn 4 acres (*v.* **bern**), The six ~, The eight ~, The ten ~, The 12 ~, The 18 Acres (*v.* **æcer**); Allotment Ground (*v.* **allotment**, **grund**); Bann Cl (prob. with the surn. *Bann*, from an OE masc. pers.n. *Ban(n)a*; cf. *Willielmus Bann* 1327 SR of Leics.); Bog Cl (*v.* **bog**); Clover Cl (*v.* **clāfre**; a fodder crop); Cow Mdw (*v.* **cū**); Bottom ~, Top Croft (*v.* **croft**); Cunnery Mdw (*v.* **coningre**); East Cl; Gorse Cl, Great ~ ~, Little Gorse Holme (*v.* **holmr**) (*v.* **gorst**); Hall Cl (*v.* Foston Hall Fm *supra*); Hawcott Mdw (1619, *v.* **haga**[1], **cot**); Highway Cl (1690, 1703, *v.* **hēah-weg**); Horse Cl (1641, *v.* **hors**); Nether ~ ~, House Cl; Kilby Cl (*Kilbye close* 1703; bordering Kilby *supra*); Top Lady Mdw (*v.* **ladi**); East ~ ~, West Long Cl (*Long close* 1619, 1641, ~ *Closse* 1637); Bottom ~ ~, Top Long Mdw (*Long(e) meadow* 1619, 1641); Lowsy Mdw (1619, 1641; the reference may be to Lousy Grass, otherwise called Stinking Hellebore (*Helleborus fœtidus*), but note *Lousie Bush*, Lei **2** 49, Lousy Bush, Lei **2** 92 and *lowsy bushe*, Lei **3** 124, all of which appear to allude to infestation by insects of some sort); Middle Cl; Millers Mdw (no 19th-cent. surns. in *Miller* are recorded for the region in the 1881 Census, so prob. with **millere** 'a miller'); Millfield Mdw (*Mill feild* 1619, ~ *fyeld* 1637, *v.* **myln**, **feld**; one of the great open-fields of the township); Moor Fd (*Moore feild* 1619, 1641, *More fyeld* 1637, *v.* **mōr**[1], **feld**; one of the great open-fields); Far ~ ~, Middle ~ ~, Nether Cl; New Piece (*v.* **pece**); Northern Cl (*v.* **northerne**); Old Cl (*v.* **ald**); Little ~, Middle Packmans (with the surn. *Packman*, from ME *packeman* 'a pedlar, a hawker'; cf. *Simon Pakeman* 1221 Cur of Leics.); Paled Park (land enclosed by palings), Walled Park (land surrounded by walls), Pegs Park (with the surn. *Pegg*, from ME *pegg* 'a peg', metonymic for a maker or seller of pegs) (*v.* **park**); Bottom ~ ~, Middle ~ ~, Top Parsons Mdw (*v.* **persone**; note *The Parsonage house, supra*); Pool Cl (*poole close* 1641, *v.* **pōl**[1] and Reed Pool *supra*); The Ram Pen (*v.* **ramm**, **penn**); Bottom ~ ~, Range Mdw (of uncertain meaning; poss. with **hrynge** 'a pole, a stake' and alluding to land enclosed by palings or poles (cf. Paled Park *supra*) or to poles set rung-wise to form a track across marshy ground); Reedfield (*Reed Feild* 1690, *the Reed field* 1703, *v.* **hrēod**); Simpkins Cl (with the surn. *Simpkin*; cf. *Elizabeth Simpkin* 1876 Census of adjacent Wigston Magna); South Bridge Mdw (cf. *Brygg* ~ 1619, *Brigg meadow* 1641, *v.* **brycg, bryggja**); The Far ~, The Near Spinney (*v.* **spinney**); Spring Cl, ~ Mdw (*v.* **spring**[1]); Stephens Mdw (with the surn. *Stephens, Stevens*, cf. *Henry Stevens* 1818 Census and *Jane Stevens* 1832 ib of adjoining Arnesby parish); Stones Cl (with the surn. *Stones*, cf. *Hannah Stones* 1804 Census and *Maria Stones* 1841 ib, both of adjoining Wigston Magna parish); Far ~, Little Sunderlands (*Synderland* 1619, *Sinderland meadow* 1641, *v.* **sundor-land**); Ten Pound Piece (*v.* **pece**; alluding to rental); Three Cornered Piece (*v.* **three-cornered, pece**); Tollgate Mdw (*v.* **toll-gate**; cf. *Foston gate* 1835, which was a toll-gate); Upper Cl; Bottom ~ ~, Middle ~ ~, Top Walles Cl (with the surn. *Wall*, cf. *John Wall* 1845 Census of adjacent Wigston Magna); Washpit Cl, ~ Mdw (*v.* **wæsce, pytt**); Upper ~ ~, West Mdw; Bottom ~ ~, Top Wethers Cl (*v.* **weðer**).

(b) *Arnesby(e) close* 1700, 1703 (Arnesby parish adjoins to the south); *Bowling closes* 1690, 1700, *the Bouling Closes* 1703, *v.* **bowling**); *Buueton* 1285 ('(land) above the village', *v.* **bufan, tūn**). *Foston Grounds* 1703 (*v.* **grund**); *Goose holmes* 1641 (*v.* **gōs, holmr**); *Haigescroft* n.d. (*v.* **croft**; with the surn. *Haig*, from OE *haga*, ON *hagi* or the ON masc. pers.n. *Hagi*); *the Hall Land* c.1575 (*v.* **hall, land** and Foston Hall Fm *supra*); *Holegatemede* n.d. (*v.* **hol**[1], **gata, mēd**); *Kilby feild close* 1641 (a close adjoining the great *Weste felde* of Kilby; perh. to be identified with Kilby Cl *supra*); *Milne holme* 1641 (*v.* **myln, holmr**); *Nafferton close* 1619, ~ *closse* 1637 (perh. recording a lost early farmstead, *v.* **tūn**; with the ON masc. pers.n. *Náttfari* (ODan *Natfari*), cf. Nafferton, YE 94; the transferred name of the Yorks. Nafferton (some 110 miles to the north-east) this early is unlikely, as is a surn. here formed from it); *Northeng* c.13 (*v.* **norð, eng**); *le North Feld* 1548 (*v.* **norð, feld**; one of the great open-fields of Foston); *the park close* 1641 (*v.* **park**); *Peatling Grounds* 1703 (*v.* **grund**; adjoining Peatling Magna parish which marches to the south-west).

Kimcote and Walton

1. KIMCOTE

Chenemvndescote 1086 DB

Kinemundescot' 1167 ChancR (p), 1199 FF, *Kynemundescote* 1220 RHug

Kynemundeskote 1243 Cur, *Kynemoundescote* 1382 *Wyg*

Kinemundecot(e) 1195 P, 1196 ChancR (p) *et passim* to 1335 *Wyg*, 1340 Banco, *Kynemundecot(e)* 1160 × 1200 *Rey*, e.13 *Wyg* (freq.), 1232 RHug *et passim* to 1315 *Wyg*, 1317 *Rey et freq* to 1376, 1379 *Wyg et passim* to 1431 *ib*, *Kynemondecote* l.13 *Wyg*, 1344 *Rey*, 1368 AD, *Kynemundecotes* l.13, 1318, 1325, 1326 *Wyg*

Kilemundecot(e) 1220 MHW, 1243 Cur, 1277 Coram, *Kylemundecote* 1239, 1243 Cur, c.1295 Ipm

Kilmundecote l.13 *Wyg*, 1322 *Deed*, 1432 *Wyg*, *Kylmundecote* 1297 Banco, 1303 Ass *et passim* to 1465, 1469 *Wyg*, *Kylmondecote* 1473 *ib*, 1480 Cl, 1493 *Rey*

Kylmondcote 1327 SR, 1392 Cl, 1473 *Wyg*, *Kylmundkote* 1375 *ib*, *Kylmoundcote* 1384 *ib*, *Kilmondcote* 1492 *ib*

Kinmundecote 1325 *Wyg*

Kynemoundecote 1344 *Rey*, 1359 *Wyg*, *Kynemoundekote* 1367 *Rey*, *Kynemoundkote* 1380 *Wyg*, *Kynemoundcote* 1383 *ib*, *Kynemuncote* 1384 Goodacre

Kylmyncote 1424, 1427 *Wyg et passim* to 1469, 1481 *ib*

Kylmecote 1453, 1454 Pat, *Kilmecoat(e)* 1610, 1614 LML, *Kilmecote* 1612, 1626 *ib*

Kymcote 1507 Ipm, 1518 Visit, 1521 *Wyg et passim* to 1538 Fine, *Kimcot(e)* 1610 Speed, 1720 LML *et freq*

'The cottage(s) belonging to a man called Cynemund', *v.* **cot** (**cotu** nom.pl.). The masc. pers.n. *Cynemund* is Old English.

ALL SAINTS' CHURCH, *Church (All Saints)* 1846, 1863, 1877 White, 1925 Kelly; it is earlier recorded as *ecclesie de Kilemundecot* 1220 MHW, *ecclesie parochialis de Kymcote* 1422 *Pat* (with MLat *parochialis* 'parochial'). CROFT, *v.* **croft**. GURNEY LANE, *Gawney* 1579, 1601, 1606, 1656 *Terrier*, *Gawnye* 1606 *ib*, *Gawnie* 1625 *ib*, *v.* **galla** (**gallan** gen.sg.), ēg; this area of dry raised ground in surrounding wetland stretched into Gilmorton parish, *v.* Gawney Lane in Gilmorton *supra*. HIGHFIELDS FM. LUTTERWORTH RD, Lutterworth lying 3 miles to the south-west. MAIN ST is *the Towne Streett* 1709 *Terrier*, *v.* **tūn**, **strēt**. MANOR FM, 1925 Kelly; it is *Manor House* 1846, 1863, 1877 White, *v.* **maner**. MODEL FM, *v.* Model Fm in Catthorpe *supra*. THE PADDOCKS, *v.* **paddock**. POPLAR FM. POULTNEY LANE, Poultney lying one mile to the south. THE RECTORY, 1877 White, 1925 Kelly, *v.* **rectory**; earlier is *the parsonage howse* 1601 *Terrier*, *the Parsonage House* 1606, 1674 (18), 1709, 1745, 1751 *ib*, *v.* **personage**. RUSHBROOKE FM, *v.* **risc**, **brōc**.

2. WALTON

> *Waltone* 1086 DB, *Walton* 1160 × 1200 *Rey*, 1202 Cur, e.13 *Wyg et freq*, (~ *iuxta Kynemundecot'* c.1290 *Rey*, ~ *iuxta Kynemundecotes* 1.13 *Wyg* and with various spellings of Kimcote to 1524 Ipm, ~ *negh' Kymcoyte* 1538 *Ferrers*), *Waltona* e.13 *Wyg*, *Waltun* 1367 *Rey*, 1380 *Wyg*
> *Waleton* 1199 ChR, 1209 × 35 RHug
> *Wauton* 12341 Fine (p), 1243 Fees, 1268 Misc
> *Wollton* 1679 *Terrier*

'The farmstead or village of the Britons or (British) serfs', *v.* **walh** (**wala** gen.pl.), **tūn**. Affixes with MLat *iuxta* 'next to' and ME **nighe** 'near'.

BACK SIDE, *v.* **bak-side**. BAPTIST CHAPEL. BOSWORTH RD is *Bosswo(o)rth Waye* 1606, 1625 *Terrier*, *Bos(s)worth way* 1674 (18), 1703 *ib*, *v.* **weg**; Husbands Bosworth lies 3½ miles to the south-east. BREACH FM (BREACH BARN 2½"), *Breche* 1467 × 84 *LTD*, (*the*) *Breach* 1579, 1601, 1606 *Terrier*, *Breache* 1709 *ib*, *v.* **brēc**. BRIDGEMERE FM (BUDGEMERE FM 2½"), *Bridgemere farm* 1925 Kelly; *Bodlismere* m.13, 1.13 *Wyg*, *Bodlesmere* 1333 *Rey*, *Buddesmere* 1467 × 84 *LTD*, 1579, 1625 *Terrier*, *Buddysmere*, *Buggymere* (sic) 1579 *ib*, *Buddesmeere*, *Budsmeere* 1601 *ib*, *Budgemere* 1656 *ib*, *Buddsmeer(e)* 1674 (18), 1679, 1745, 1751 *ib*, *Nether Buddesmeere*, ~ *Budssemeere* 1606 *ib*, ~ *Buddesmere* 1625 *ib*, ~ *Budsmeer* 1709 *ib* (*v.* **neoðera**), *Buddesmeere heade* 1606 *ib*, *Buddesmere* ~ 1625 *ib*, *Budsmeer Head* 1709 *ib* (*v.*

hēafod), *Budds Meer Leays* 1674 (18) *ib*, *Buddesmeer Leys* 1703 *ib*, *Buddsmeer(e) Leyes* 1745, 1751 *ib* (*v.* **leys**), *v.* **bōðl, mere**[1]; a large pool survives close to the farmstead. CAMP BARN: a group of disused military camps relating to Bruntingthorpe Airfield appears located north-east of Walton on the O.S. 6″ map (1967), but the barn (a farm site) is one mile distant from the nearest of these, to the south-east of the village, with no evidence of military camps at or near. One hesitates to propose the survival here of **camp** 'open land' beside this 'farmstead or village of the Britons' since no early spellings are present in the many records for the parish. But note the late evidence for OE *camp* in Belgrave (Lei **3** 49) and Lat *campus* may have survived among the Romano-British inhabitants of Walton. CHAPEL LANE, the site of the Baptist Chapel *supra*. DOG AND GUN (P.H.), *Dog and Gun* 1846, 1863, 1877 White, 1925 Kelly. THE HALL, *The Old Hall* 1925 Kelly, *v.* **hall**. HALL LANE. HILL TOP FM, *Hill top* 1925 Kelly, *v.* **topp**. HILL TOP LODGE, *v.* **loge**. HOLLYTREE FM. HOLTON FM, either with the surn. *Holton*, most infrequent in the county, or with a modern portmanteau fabrication combining Holt with Walton, since very close to Walton Holt *infra*. KILWORTH RD, North Kilworth lying 2½ miles to the south-east. KIMCOTE RD is *Kimcote Lane* 1703 *Terrier*. MAIN ST. MISSION HALL (lost), a small corrugated iron chapel built in 1886, now demolished. MOWSLEY LANE, Mowsley lying 3½ miles to the north-east. RED LION (P.H.) (lost), *Red Lion* 1846, 1863 White. TABBERMEAR'S FM, *Tebberdemeyre* m.13, l.13 *Wyg*, *Teberdesmeyre* 1328, 1344 *Rey*, *Teyburmeyre* 1467 × 84 *LTD*, *Tebbermeres* 1579 *Terrier*, *Tebbermess(e)* 1601, 1625, 1703 *ib*, *Tebbermes* 1606 *ib*, *Tabermeeres* 1656 *ib*, *Tebbermeers* 1674 (18), 1709, 1751 *ib*, *Tebbermess* 1745 *ib*, 'Theodberht's boundary', *v.* **(ge)mǣre**; with the OE masc. pers.n. *Þēodberht*, *v.* Tibbits Haden and Tibblecotes in f.ns. (b) *infra*. TALBOT (P.H.) (lost), *Talbot* 1846, 1863, 1877 White. WALTON GRANGE, 1877 White, *The Grange* 1863 *ib*, *v.* **grange**. WALTON HOLT, 1806 Map, 1835 O, 1863 White, *The Holt* 1781 *Plan*, 1846, 1877 White; earlier it is *le Wold* 1339 *Wyg*, *the Olde* 1601, 1606 *Terrier*, *the Oulde* 1606 *ib*, *the Old* 1625, 1709 *ib*, *the Oult* 1656, 1679, 1692 *ib*, *the Owld* 1674 (18), 1745 *ib*, *the Ould* 1703, *v.* **wald**. WALTON HOLT GORSE, 1835 O, *v.* **gorst**. WALTON LODGE, 1877 White, *v.* **loge**. WILLOW BROOK FM, *v.* **wilig, brōc**. WINDMILL (P.H.) (lost), *Windmill* 1846, 1863 White, *Windmill Inn* 1877 *ib*, 1925 Kelly. WINDMILL FM.

FIELD-NAMES

Kimcote and Walton shared three great open-fields. In (a), forms
presented without dates are 1751 *Terrier*; those dated 1781 are *Plan*;
1807 are Nichols; 1843 are Sale. Forms throughout dated e.13, m.13,
l.13, 13, 1315, 1318, 1321, 1326, 1335, 1339, 1343, 1359, 1379, 1423,
1428 and 1469 are *Wyg*; those dated c.1290, 1328, 1333, 1334 and 1344
are *Rey*; 1392 are Banco; 1467 × 84 are *LTD*; 1579, 1601, 1606, 1625,
1656, 1674 (18), 1679, 1697, 1703, 1709, 1720 and 1745 are *Terrier*;
1612 are PR; 1639 are Ipm.

(a) Balney way, Balnyway (*Balney way*(*e*) 1579, 1606, 1625, 1679, 1709, 1720,
Balnwaye, *Balnwey* 1601, *Baulney way* 1674 (18), 1679, 1703, 1745, *Boulniway*
1697, *Balnow* 1579, *Baulney* 1657, *High* ~, *Nether Balney* 1606, *v.* **balne**, **weg**; it is
prob. that **ēg** is compounded in some forms with *balne*, a poss. early borrowing of
Lat *balneum* 'a place for bathing, a bath, a bath-house', here presum. denoting 'a
stream or pool suitable for bathing'; cf. Balne, YW **2** 14); Between the Hadlands
(*Between the Headlands* 1674 (18), 1703, 1745, *v.* **hēafod-land**; a furlong thus
called); Birles (1679, 1703, 1720, 1745, *Burles* 1579, 1656, *Byrles* 1601, 1606, *Birls*
1674 (18), *v.* **byrgels**; evidently a discovered Romano-British or pagan Anglo-Saxon
inhumation cemetery site; note also *Banlouwe* in f.ns. (b)); John Blackwell's Land
1781; Blakes Lowe (*Blaklow* 1467 × 84, 1601, *Blacklowe* 1579, *Blacklow* 1606,
Blakelowe 1606, 1656, *Blakelow* 1674 (18), 1703, 1709, 1720, 1745, *Blakloe* 1679,
v. **blæc**, **hlāw**); Breach Leyes (1745, *Breach Leayes* 1674 (18), ~ *Leays* 1679, ~ *Leys*
1703, *v.* **brēc**, **leys** and Breach Fm in Walton *supra*); Briskitt Balk (*Bisgate* 1467 ×
84, 1601, 1606, *Briskett* 1656, *Briskitt Baulk* 1674 (18), *Brisket Baulk*(*e*) 1679, 1703,
1745 (*v.* **balca**), *v.* **gata**; the first el. is uncertain; even in this Romano-British
survival countryside of Walton, a pre-English stream-name *Bis*, from Brit **bissi-* 'a
branch, a twig', perh. used to denote a tributary brook (cf. the river Bis (*Bis*, *Bys* 964
(14) BCS 1127 (S 727)) in Wiltshire (*v.* W **2** and RN 34)) seems unlikely
compounded with *gata*; poss. is an OE masc. pers.n. such as *Bisi* or *Bisa* as in Bisley
(Gl **1** 117) or even (**ge**)**bysce** or **busc**); Burgis (*Brydgys* 1467 × 84, *Burges* 1579,
1606, 1625 *et passim* to 1697, 1745, *Burgeys* 1579, (*on*) *Bridges* 1601, *Burgess* 1703,
1709, 1720, *v.* **brycg**); William Burrow's Land 1781 (note *Alfred Burrows* 1864
Census of Kimcote); The Rev. John Cant's Land 1781; Caudle ~ 1751, Cauldwell
Hill 1843 (*Cawldwell hill* 1601, 1606, *Caudle* ~ 1674 (18), 1703, 1709, 1745,
Caudell Hill 1679, *v.* **cald**, **wella**, **hyll**); Church way (1601, 1625 *et passim* to 1745,
Chirchewey(*e*) 1318, 1467 × 84, *Churchweye* 1606, *v.* **cirice**; earlier called *kirkeweye*
m.13, *kyrkeweye* m.13, l.13, *v.* **kirkja**, **weg** and All Saints' Church in Kimcote
supra); Cow Moore (1679, *Cowmore* 1579, *Cowmowre* 1697, *Cow Moor* 1703, 1745,
Cowmoore 1720, *v.* **cū**, **mōr**[1]); Croft Lands (1674 (18), 1703, 1745, *Croftlandes*
1579, 1601, 1679, *Craftlandes* 1606, *v.* **croft**, **land**); Dams Head (1656, 1674 (18),
1679, 1703, 1745, *Dames heade* 1579, 1601, *Damashad* 1697, *v.* **damme**, **hēafod**);
Lower ~, Docklands (1674 (18), 1679, 1703, 1709, 1720, 1745, *Doklandis* 1467 ×
84, *Docklandes* 1579, 1601, 1606, *Nether* ~, *Upper Docklands* 1656, *Docklands
leayes* 1679 (*v.* **leys**), *v.* **docce**, **land**); Dockleys (1674 (18), 1703, 1745, *Dockleies*

1625, *v.* **docce, leys**); Espid Slade (*East pitt slade* 1579, 1601, 1606, *Easpit* ~, *Espit Slade* 1674 (18), 1709, 1745, *Espitt slade* 1679, *Easpit Slade* 1697, 1703, *v.* **ēast, pytt, slǣd**); Long ~, Short Fernhill (1674 (18), 1697, 1703, 1709, 1720, *Longfernell, Schortfernell* 1467 × 84, *Long* ~, *Short Farnhill* 1606, 1625, 1656, *Longe fernehill, Short fernhill* 1679, *Long* ~, *Short Fernehill* 1745 (*v.* **lang**[1], **sc(e)ort**), *farnil* 1318, *fernehill* 1579, *fearnhill* 1601, *fernhill* 1679, *v.* **fearn, hyll**); Nether ~, Upper Fullwell (1709, *Nether* ~, *Upper Fulwell* 1656, 1703, 1720, *Neather* ~, *Upper Fullwell* 1674 (18), *Neither* ~, *Upper fullwell* 1679, *folewelle* l.13, *Fulwell* 1467 × 84, 1579, *Fullwell* 1601, 1606, 1625, cf. *Fulwell haden* 1606, 1656, *Fullwell Haden* 1709 (*v.* **hēafod**; note the archaic *-en* plural), *v.* **fūl, wella**); Grindle Haden (1606, 1625 *et passim* to 1745, *v.* **grendel, hēafod**; with the archaic *-en* pl.); Hadleys and Haggs (*the haggs* 1606, *Haggs* 1703, 1745, *Headleys and Haggs* 1674 (18), 1679, *v.* **hǫgg, headley**); the Haggs of Rylands (1674 (18), 1703, *the Haggs of the Rylands* 1679, *the Haggs of Rye Lands* 1745 (*v.* **hǫgg** and *Rylandes* in f.ns. (b)); Hanglands (1656, 1674 (18) *et passim* to 1745, *Hanglandys* 1467 × 84, *Hanglandes* 1579, 1601, 1606, 1625), Hanglands Way (1656, 1674 (18), 1679, 1703, 1745, *Hanglandes Waye* 1606) (*v.* **hangende, land**); Heath 1751, Kimcote Heath 1807 (*the heath* 1625, *Heath* 1703, 1745), Heath Brook ((*the*) *Heath Brook(e)* 1606, 1625 *et passim* to 1745, *v.* **brōc**) (*v.* **hȳð**); Heaway Brige (sic) (*v.* **brycg**) (*hayweye, heyway(e)* 1579, *Hea Waye* 1601, *Heye Waye* 1606, *Heiewaye* 1625, *Hay way* 1674 (18), 1679, *Heayway* 1745, *v.* **hēg, weg**); High Brinks (1674 (18), 1679, 1703, 1745, *Highbrynke* 1579, *Highbrinkes* 1606, 1625, *Hybrinks* 1697, 1709, *Hie Brinkes* 1720, *Short High Brinkes* 1679, *v.* **hēah**[1], **brink**); Home Hill (1674 (18), 1745, *Holme* 1467 × 84, 1579, (*on*) *Home* 1601, 1606, (*att*) *Home* 1709, *Home* 1720), Home Side (*v.* **sīde**) (*v.* **holmr**); the Homestead (1674 (18), 1709, *the Homested* 1745, *v.* **hām-stede**; i.e. of Kimcote's parsonage, *v.* The Rectory *supra*); Kimcote Green (1674 (18), *Kimcot(e)* ~ 1601, 1606, *Kimcott* ~ 1625, *Kimcot greene* 1679, *Kimcoate* ~ 1703, 1709, *Kimcott Green* 1745, cf. *al grene* e.13 (p), l.13 (p), *a le grene* l.13 (p), *atte Grene* 1392 (p) (*v.* **atte**), *v.* **grēne**[2]); Knaptoft Slough (1703, *Knaptofteslow* 1467 × 84, *Napton slowes* 1601, *Knaptough* ~ 1674 (18), *Knaptaugh Slough* 1679, 1745, *v.* **slōh**; Knaptoft parish adjoins to the north-east); Lantasse (1674 (18), 1745, *Langetas* l.13, 1335, *Langtasse* 1576, 1656, 1679, *langtas* 1606, *Lantass* 1697, *Lanctass* 1709, 1720; meaning uncertain, but poss. **langet** with **æsc**); Larliss (1674 (18), 1703, *Larlys* 1601, *Larles* 1606, *Larlasse* 1656, *Larless* 1709, *Larlisse* 1679, 1745; again of uncertain meaning; perh. **lāwerce** with **lǣs**); Long Bridge (1674 (18), 1703, 1745, *Longe Bridge* 1625, 1679, *Lon Brigg* (sic) 1709, *v.* **lang**[1], **brycg**); Thomas Lucas's Land 1781; Matfurlong (1674 (18), 1745, *Matte furlong'* 1467 × 84, *matforlonges* 1318, *Matt furlonge* 1576, 1601, 1606, ~ *furlong* 1656, 1703, 1709, *Matfurlonge* 1679, cf. *Mattefurlongeshadene* 1339 (*v.* **hēafod**; with an archaic *-en* pl.), *v.* **mǣte, furlang**); May Dike or Tilles Grave (*Meydik'* 1467 × 84, *Maydike* 1656, 1709, *May Dike or Till(e)ys Grave* 1674 (18), 1679, 1703, 1745, *v.* **mǣgðe, dík** and Tilles Grave *infra*); the Meadow (1674 (18), 1703, 1745, *the meddow(e)* 1606, 1709, *the meadowe* 1679, cf. *the Olde Meadowe* 1625 (*v.* **wald**), *v.* **mēd** (*mēdwe* obl.sg.)); Bottom ~, Top Meer 1843 (*v.* **(ge)mǣre**); Middle Fd (1656, 1674 (18) *et passim* to 1745, *Midulfelde* 1467 × 84, *Midle* ~, *Mydle Feild* 1579, *Middle feelde* 1601, 1606, ~ *Fielde* 1625, 1709, *Middel Feild* 1697, *v.* **middel, feld**; one of the great open-fields); Mill Haden (1674 (18), 1679, 1697, 1703, 1709, 1720, *mill hades* 1606, *v.* **myln, hēafod**; the majority of forms retain the archaic *-en* pl.); Millway (1656, 1674 (18), 1703, 1709, 1745,

Myll Waye 1601, (*the*) *Millwaye* 1606, 1625, *Milway* 1679, *v.* **myln, weg**); Mary Morpott's Land 1781; Morton Meer (1674 (18), 1709, 1745, *Mortonemere* 1318, *Morton meyre* 1467 × 84, *Moreton mere* 1579, *Moor*(*e*)*ton meere* 1601, 1606, *Moreton meer*(*e*) 1625, 1703, *Morton meere* 1679, *v.* (**ge**)**mǣre**; the parish boundary with Gilmorton which adjoins to the north-west); Musock (1745, *Mussock*(*e*) 1674 (18), 1679, 1703, cf. *Mussockes Waye* 1606, *Mussocks way* 1709 (*v.* **weg**), *v.* **mūs, hōc**); Musway (1679, 1745, *Musswaye* 1601, 1625, *Mussweye* 1606, *v.* **weg**; the spellings point firmly to **mūs** as the specific, although **mos** would sit more happily in the name of a track); Niddick way (1674 (18), 1679, 1703, 1745, *Needy*(*e*) *quey* (sic) 1601, *Niggate Way* (sic) 1625, *Niddike ~* 1679, *Nig*(*g*)*att way* 1709, *v.* **nīwe, dík, weg**); North Fd (1674 (18), 1679 *et passim* to 1745, *Northfelde* 1467 × 84, *the Northe feelde al's Mill feelde* 1606, *the North fielde* 1625, 1656, *~ ~ Feild* 1697, *v.* **norð, feld** and *Milnefeild* in f.ns. (b); one of the great open-fields); Parke Hill (1579, 1674 (18), 1679, 1745, *Park Hill* 1606, 1697, 1703, 1709, *v.* **park, hyll** and *Parkefelde* in f.ns. (b)); the Parsons Cl (1606, 1625, 1703, 1709, *the Parsones close* 1606; it is *the Parsonage close* 1745, *v.* **persone, personage**); Lower ~, Pessill (1679, 1703, *Pessell* 1326, *Pushull* 1359, *le Pessul* 1423, *Peshyll* 1428, *Peshill* 1469, *Peasehill* 1576, *Pessill* 1601, 1606, *Pesill* 1656, *Nether Pessill* 1606, *Middle Pessill* 1625, *Lower ~, Pesshill* 1674 (18), *Lower ~, Pessil* 1745, *v.* **pise, hyll**); Poultney Hedge (1601, 1674 (18), 1679, 1703, 1709, 1745, *Powltney hedg* 1606, *v.* **hecg**; the parish boundary hedge with Poultney which adjoins to the south-west); Short ~, Rushmeer(e) (1606, 1674 (18), 1679, 1703, *Ruschemere* 1467 × 84, *Rushemere* 1576, *Rushmeere* 1601, 1606, *Rishmeer* 1709, *Rushmear* 1745, *Over rishmere* 1625 (with **ōfer**[1] or **ofer**[3]), *Short Rishmeer* 1745, *v.* **risc, mere**[1]); Rylands (1674 (18), 1679, 1703, *Rylandes* l.13, *Ryelond'* 1318, *Ryelandes* 1601, 1606, *Rielands* 1709, *Rye Lands* 1745, *Nether ~, Upper Rielandes* 1625, *Lower Rylands* 1674 (18), 1679, 1703, 1745, *v.* **ryge, land**); Sallow pitts (1674 (18), 1709, 1745, *Salliepittes* 1625, *Salleypitts* 1656, *the Salloe pitts* 1679, *Sallowpits* 1703, *v.* **salh, pytt**); Saltergate way (1674 (18), 1679 *et passim* to 1745, *Saltergateweye* l.13, *Saltersgate waye* 1576, *Saltergate Way*(*e*) 1606 (*v.* **weg**), *Saltergate* 1318, *Saltersgate* 1656, *v.* **saltere, gata**); Seeds Cl 1843 (*v.* **sǣd**; used of grasses sown for one year's mowing or grazing); Sheele (1679, 1703, *Shale* 1674 (18), *v.* **scēla**); Shepard Board (1674 (18), 1745, *Sheppard ~* 1679, *Shepheard ~* 1703, *Shepperds Board* 1709, *v.* **scēp-hirde, bord**; a f.n. which occurs elsewhere in the eastern half of this county (as Lei **2** 223, 230 and Lei **3** 79, 149), evidently alluding to good grazing for sheep; OFr *bord* 'a cottage' may be discounted); Upper ~ ~, Small Doles (1674 (18), 1679, 1703, 1745, *Short ~ ~, Small Doles* 1601, *smaldole* m.13, *Small Doles* 1606, 1625, 1656, 1709, *Long Smalldoles* 1625, *v.* **smæl, dāl**); South Fd (1674 (18), 1679 *et passim* to 1745, *Sowthfeld* 1579, *Sowthfielde al's le park fielde* 1579, *the South feelde al's Park feelde* 1606, (*the*) *South Fielde* 1625, 1656, *v.* **sūð, feld**; one of the great open-fields, *v. Parkfelde* in f.ns. (b)); Sow Cl (1606, 1674 (18), 1703, 1745, *v.* **sūð**); Over Spittswell (1745 (*v.* **uferra**), *Spichewelle* m.13, l.13, *Spiceswell* 1467 × 84, *Spytchwell, Spitteswell, Spytteswell* 1579, *Spittes*(*s*)*well* 1601, 1606, 1674 (18), *Spithwell* 1697, *Spitswell* 1709, *Upper Spit*(*t*)*swell* 1709, 1703, *v.* **spic**[2], **wella**); Starmer Way (1674 (18), 1679, 1703, 1709, 1745, *Stermwtheueye* m.13, l.13, *Stermwortheweye* l.13, *Star*(*e*)*moore Waye* 1601, 1606, *Starmeer Waye* 1606, *v.* **weg**; the road to the lost *Stormsworth*, which lay 4 miles to the south in Westrill and Starmore parish); Stoniford (1679, *stonyforde* 1579, *Stony*(*e*) *foorde* 1601, 1606,

Stonie foord 1625, *Stoneyford* 1656, 1720, *Stony Foard* 1674 (18), *Stouniford* 1697, *Stony ford* 1703, *Stoney Foard* 1709, *Stonieford* 1745, *v.* **stānig, ford**); Stony Meers (1674 (18), 1703, *Stanymeyre* 1467 × 84, *Staneymere* 1601, *Stoonye Meere* 1606, *Stonimeeres* 1679, *Stoney Meer* 1709, *Stonimeers* 1745, *v.* **stānig, (ge)mǣre**); Theeves (1656, 1679, 1703, 1745, *Theyvis* 1467 × 84, *Theyves* 1579, *Theives* 1674 (18), 1709, cf. *theeves furlonge* 1601 (*v.* **furlang**), *v.* **þefa**); Thorpe Loe (1679, 1745, *Thorplowe* m.13, l.13, *Thorplow* 1467 × 84, *Thorpelowe* 1579, 1601, 1625, 1656, 1674 (18), *Thorpe Low* 1703, *v.* **þorp, hlāw**; bordering Bruntingthorpe parish which adjoins to the north-east); Nether ~ ~, Middle ~ ~, Upper Three Furlongs (1674 (18), 1703, 1709, 1745, *Threfurlonges* 1467 × 84, *threefurlonges* 1579, *Nether ~ ~, Over three furlonges* 1601, 1606 (*v.* **uferra**), cf. *three furlonge haden* 1606 (*v.* **hēafod**; with the archaic *-en pl.*), *v.* **þrēo, furlang**; this unit of three furlongs was part of *Parkfelde* (*v.* f.ns. (b)), but presum. detached in some way); Tibbits Haden (*Tibbates* ~ 1606, 1674 (18), 1679, 1709, 1745, *Tibbats Haden* 1703, *v.* **hēafod** (with the archaic *-en* pl.); the specific at first sight appears to be the surn. *Tibbatt* which developed both as an *-et, -ot* diminutive of *Tibb* (from the OFr masc. pers.n. *Tibald*, a variant of OFr *Theobald* (ContGerm *Theudobald*)) and also directly from a late weakening of *Tibald*; but the following f.n. Tibblecotes suggests that *Tibbat* in Tibbits Haden is the direct local development of the pers.n. *Tibald* rather than a surn.; it would be satisfying to include the pers.n. in Tabbermear's Fm (in Walton *supra*) with these two instances of *Tibald*, but the repeated survival of the vowel *e* in both elements of a dithematic pers.n. points to an unrelated OE masc. *Þēodberht* there rather than to another OFr *Tibald* (*Theobald*)); Tibblecotes (1606, 1625, 1745, *Tybbledecot'* c.1290, *Tyblecotes* 1579, *Tibble Coat(e)s* 1674 (18), 1679, 1703, *Tipple Coates* 1709, *v.* **cot**; with the OFr masc. pers.n. *Tibald* (OFr *Theobald*, ContGerm *Theudobald*)); Tilles Grave (*Till(e)ys Grave* 1674 (18), 1679, 1703, 1745, *v.* **græf** and May Dike *supra*; either with the surn. *Tilley*, or its source ME *tilie* 'a husbandman'; but note *Louisa Tilley* 1819 Census of adjacent Peatling Parva parish); Turnip Cl (*v.* **turnepe**); Turway (1674 (18), 1679, 1703, 1745, *Turfweye* l.13, *Turweye* 1601, *Tirway*, *Turwaye* 1606), Turway Huske (1625, 1679, 1745, *Turweye huske* 1606, *Turway Husk* 1674 (18), 1703 (with **hassuc** or **hyrst**) (*v.* **turf, weg**); Warlige Lands (*Wharlyche* 1467 × 84, *wharlitche, wharlytch, wharledge* 1579, *Wharlach(e)* 1606, 1703, 1745, *Whorlach* 1625, *Wharlich* 1656, 1674 (18), *Whorlig* 1697, *Whorlidge* 1709, 1720, cf. *Worlich furlonge* 1601 (*v.* **furlang**), *Whorlache side* 1625 (*v.* **sīde**), *v.* **hwerfel, lycce**); Washpitt Leyes (1745, *washpyttlayes* 1579, *Washpitt Leyse* 1601, *Washpit leyes* 1606, 1679, *Washpitt Lays, Whashpit leys* 1674 (18), *Washpit Leayes* 1679, *Washpitt Layes* 1703, *Washpit Leys* 1709, 1745, *v.* **wæsce, pytt, leys**); Long ~ ~, Short Water Thoroes (1679, 1703, 1745, *Long ~, Short Waterfurrowes* 1601, *Long ~, Short Waterthorowes* 1656, *Long ~, Short waterfurrows* 1674 (18), *waterfurwes* l.13, *Waterforowys* 1467 × 84, *Water furrowes* 1579, 1601, *Water thorowes* 1606, *Waterthorrowes* 1709, cf. *Waterforous furlonges* 1335 (*v.* **furlang**), *v.* **wæter, furh** and *Water furrowes* in Ashby Parva f.ns. (b)); Lord Willoughby's Land 1781; Willows Toft (*Willows Taft* 1674 (18), *Willowes* ~ 1679, 1703, *Willows Tauft* 1745, *v.* **wilig, toft**); Wowe (1606, 1625 *et passim* to 1745, *en le Wro* 1318 (p), *the wrowe, the wooue, Woowe* 1579, *Wooe* 1601, *Wow* 1656, 1709, *v.* **vrá**); Wronglands (1656, 1674 (18) *et passim* to 1745, *Wronglondes* e.13, m.13, l.13, *Wronglandes* 1579, 1601, 1606, 1625, *Wrongelandes* 1601), Wronglands Head (1674 (18), 1703, 1745, *v.* **hēafod**) (*v.* **wrang, land**); the Yards End (1679, 1703,

1745, *the yeardes end* 1625, cf. *Barkers Yard end* 1709 (with the surn. *Barker*), *v.* **geard, ende**).

(b) *the Arbour* 1601 (perh. with **erber**, but such names occasionally mask an earlier **eorð-burh**; note Short Arbour in adjoining Gilmorton f.ns. (a) which may refer to the same feature); *Bald Banke* 1709 (*v.* **balled, banke**); *Banlouwe* l.13, *Banlowe* 1318 (*v.* **hlāw**; prob. with **bān** 'bone' rather than with **bēan** in view of the early generic and poss. signifying a disturbed pagan Anglo-Saxon burial mound or an early inhumation cemetery; note Birles in f.ns.(a)); *beadehouse, the beadehowse* 1601, *the Beadhouse in the use of John Blockley, the Tenement of the Beadhouse of Leicester* (*v.* **tenement**) 1606, *the Beadhouse land*(*e*) (*v.* **land**) 1606 (*v.* **bede-hūs**; the property of the Hospital of the Blessed Virgin Mary (later called Trinity Hospital and the Newark Hospital) in Leicester (*v.* Lei **1** 100)); *Between the Townes* 1709 (*v.* **tūn**; a furlong thus called); *Vallentine Blockley hadland* 1606 (*v.* **hēafod-land**); *Bodlesmerebroc* 1333 (*v.* **brōc**), *Bodlismerebuttis* m.13, l.13 (*v.* **butte**) (*v.* Bridgemere Fm in Walton *supra*); *bonyforlong* 1344, *bonye furlonge* 1579 (*v.* **bony**, **furlang** and note *Banlouwe, supra*; **bony** here predates the earliest citation for this word in OED by nearly 200 years); *Bouetoune* 1634 ('(land) above the village', *v.* **bufan, tūn**); *Brech Furlonge* 1606 (*v.* **brēc, furlang** and Breach Fm in Walton *supra*); *Brodeslade* m.13, l.13, 1579, *Broadslade* 1579, 1709, *Broadeslade* 1606, *Broadslad* 1697 (*v.* **brād, slæd**); *the Brooke* 1679 (*v.* **brōc**); *Willm. Brownes hadland* 1606, *Brownes Hadland* 1656 (*v.* **hēafod-land**); *Bullhade* 1579, *Bullhad* 1697, *Bull haden* 1606, 1709 (with an archaic -*en* pl.), *bull hade furlonge* 1601 (*v.* **furlang**) (*v.* **bula, hēafod**); *the bullokes pasture* 1579, 1606 (*v.* **pasture**), *the olde Bullocke pen* 1625 (*v.* **ald, penn**) (*v.* **bulluc**); *Bunny furlonge hade* 1606 (*v.* **hēafod**), *Burney Furlong* 1656 (*v.* **bune, ēg, furlang**); *the buttes* 1606 (*v.* **butte**); *Butt Layes* 1709 (*v.* **leys**; with **butte** or **butt**²); *Fulk Buttones hadland* 1606 (*v.* **hēafod-land**), *Humfrie Buttons Ricksted* 1625 (*v.* **rickstead**) (cf. *Humphrey Button* 1653 PR, *Foulk Button* 1718 MI and the later *Mary Button* 1820 Census and *John Button* 1823 ib, all of Kimcote); *le Catchmane close* 1637 (poss. with the rare surn. *Catchman*, but in view of the date with its current religious sectarianism, perh. *catechumen* 'a learner of the faith' may be thought of, although the 1637 form suggests the palatal affricative of *catch* rather than the original velar stop of the Greek word which was adopted into English via Latin and French); *the Church meddoe* 1606, *Church medowe* 1679, *the Church meddow* 1709 (*v.* **mēd** (**mēdwe** obl.sg.) and All Saints' Church in Kimcote); *Coalepitt* 1720 (*v.* **cole-pytt**; for the manufacture of charcoal); *Coates pasture* 1703 (*v.* **cot, pasture**); *Cristemelehul* e.13 (*v.* **cristel-mǣl, hyll**); *the Cross* 1612 (*v.* **cros**); *the crosselandes* 1606 (*v.* **land**; with **cros** or **cross**); *Cuallhelleleys* 13 (*v.* **cwelle, hyll, lǣs**); *Dashes peice* 1674 (18), *Dashes* ~ 1703, *Dash's piece* 1745 (*v.* **pece**; with the surn. *Dash* (from ME *de Asche* '(dweller) by the ash-tree', the modern surn. retaining the French *de*); *East longe* 1606, ~ *Lange* 1656 (*v.* **lang**²); *Edricheslowebreche* 1328, *Edreslawbreche* 1344 (*v.* **hlāw, brēc**; with the OE masc. pers.n. *Ēadrīc*); *Edwardes Lowe* 1606, *Edwardsloe* 1709 (*v.* **hlāw**; perh. with the OE masc. pers.n. *Ēadweard*, but this f.n. may well be a development of the *Edreslaw* of the previous toponym); *elrestobslade, herlstobslade* l.13, *Erstubslade* 1318, *Esthopslade* 1467 × 84, *Eastuppslade* 1579 (*v.* **slæd**), *Esthophyll, Estuphyll* 1467 × 84 (*v.* **hyll**) (*v.* **ellern, stubb**); *Estoftes* 1467 × 84, *Eastoft* 1579 (*v.* **ēast, toft**); *Feldyngys* 1467 × 84 (*v.* **feld**; prob. with the OE noun suffix -**ing**¹, but because of the plural form, **eng** is poss.); *Feynys* 1467 × 84, *Fennes* 1601, 1606, *Fenns* 1709,

Fennes leyes 1625, *Fens Leays* 1674 (18), *Fenns Leyes* 1679, 1745, ~ *Leys* 1703 (v.
leys), *the Fenslade* 1606 (v. **slæd**) (v. **fenn**); *flaxlondes* m.13, 1.13 (v. **fleax, land**);
the For(e)dole 1606, 1709 (v. **fore, dāl**); *Gahewenescroft* 13 (v. **croft**; with the ME
masc. pers.n. *Gawain*); *the greene hedge* 1606 (v. **hecg** and Kimcote Green in f.ns.
(a)); *Grinley* ~, *Grynley hade* 1579 (v. **grēne**[1], **lēah, hēafod**); *the gutter in Mill slade*,
the gutter in the slade 1606, *the gutter* 1625 (v. **goter** and *Mill slade, infra*); *Gyrlow*
1467 × 84 (v. **gyr, hlāw**); *Halcroft'* 1467 × 84 (v. **croft**), *the hall close* 1606 (v. **hall**);
Thom' Halles hadland 1606 (v. **hēafod-land**), *Halls Towne end* 1709 (v. **tūn, ende**)
(cf. *Widow Hall* 1709 *Terrier*); *the Hempplecke* 1697, *the Hempleck, the Hemp pleck
in Walton* 1703 (v. **hænep, plek**); *Herningho* m.13, 1.13, *hernou* 1318, *nether* ~,
Harnow 1467 × 84 (v. **neoðera**), *le middelherwynhoue* e.13 (v. **middel**) (v. **hōh**; the
early 13th-cent. form indicates that the OE masc. pers.n. *Herewine* is the specific of
these reducing f.ns.); *Heyhul* m.13, 1.13, *Hyhil(l)* 1335, *Hyhul* 1343, *Highell, Highill*
1579, *Hichill* 1601, *Highsill* 1606, *Highshill* 1656, *Hisehill* 1674 (18), 1679 *et passim*
to 1745 (v. **hēah**[1], **hyll**; the *s* of the later forms appears intrusive and is unlikely to
represent *hys(s)e* 'a son, a youth' as of a separate name); *highill crosse* 1579 (v. **cros**;
perh. that on *Cristemelehul, supra*); *le Hill close* 1639; *Home brooke* 1601, 1606 (v.
brōc; prob. with **holmr** rather than with **home**); *Hyebanke* 1601 (v. **hēah**[1], **banke**);
Thomas Iliffes hadland 1606 (v. **hēafod-land**); *Jackleys close* 1639 (with the surn.
Jackley); *Kimcott bridge* 1601 (v. **brycg**); *Kimcot Townes end* 1606 (v. **tūn, ende**);
Knaptoft hedge 1606 (v. **hecg**; the parish boundary marker with Knaptoft parish
which adjoins to the north-east); *the knoles, the knowles* 1606 (v. **cnoll**); *Kylworth
meyre* 1467 × 84, *Killwoorth* ~ 1606, *Killworth Meere* 1625 (v. **(ge)mǣre**; North
Kilworth parish adjoins to the south-east); *Kyne hull* 1601, *Kanehull* 1625 (v. **hyll**;
prob. with **kine**, the archaic pl. of **cū** 'a cow'); *Kynstoneswell* 1318, *Kynstonswell*
1579, *Kingstones* ~ 1606, 1656, *Kingston* ~ 1679, *Kingstone Well* 1745 (v. **wella**;
with the OE masc. pers.n. *Cynestān*); *the lane meadowe* 1606; *le langelich* 1318,
langlytche 1579, *langlig* 1697, *Langlidge* 1720 (v. **lang**[1], **lycce**); *lavelayeslade* 1579
(v. **lǣfer, ley**[1], **slæd**); *Leueringdelesue* 1.13 (v. **lǣfer, -ing**[1], dell, **lǣs** (**lǣswe**
dat.sg.)); *the little meere* 1606, *litle mere hade* 1579, *little meere hade* 1606 (v.
hēafod) (v. **lȳtel**; with **mere**[1] or **(ge)mǣre**); *littulslade* 1.13, *little slade* 1709 (v. **lȳtel**,
slæd); *Longebanlondes* m.13, 1.13, *Longbanlondes* 1333, 1334, *Longbanlands* 1467
× 84 (v. **lang**[1], **bēan, land**); *the longe hadland* 1606 (v. **lang**[1], **hēafod-land**);
longeholm e.13, m.13, 1.13, 13, *longe home* 1579 (v. **lang**[1], **holmr**); *Lucas (his)
Headland* 1703, 1745 (v. **hēafod-land**; with the surn. *Lucas*, a surn. which is also
recorded in Kimcote from *Elizabeth Lucas* 1841 Census, *William Lucas* 1862 ib to
James Lucas 1879 ib; note also *Thomas Lucas* 1781 *Plan*); *Maywordeshom* 1318 (v.
mægðe, worð, hamm); *the meere hedge* 1606 (v. **(ge)mǣre, hecg**); *Middelmor*
m.13, 1.13 (v. **middel, mōr**[1]); *middilhaddone* 1335 (v. **middel, hēafod**; with a
surviving *-en* pl. rather than with *dūn* 'hill'); *Millwayslade* 1601 (v. **weg, slæd**),
Milnefeild, Mylnefeild 1579, *Mill feelde* 1601, 1606 (v. **feld**; one of the great open-
fields), *mylnefurlong* 1579 (v. **furlang**), *mylneslade* 1579, (*the*) *Mill slade* 1601,
1606 *et passim* to 1720, *milslade* 1625 (v. **slæd**), *Milslade ende* 1606, *Millslade End*
1709 (v. **ende**) (v. **myln**); *the Moores* 1606, *the moore dich* 1606 (v. **dīc**), *Morlaye*
1579 (v. **ley**[1]) (v. **mōr**[1]); *Mydul dole* 1467 × 84 (v. **middel, dāl**); *new breache* 1579,
Newbreach 1656 (v. **nīwe, brēc**); *the new hedge* 1606, *New Hedge* 1656 (v. **hecg**; the
'new' hedge kept its name at least 50 years after planting); *Ric' Niccolles ley-
hadlond* 1606 (v. **hēafod-land**; whether with **ley**[1] or **ley**[2] is uncertain);

northerneheyweye e.13 (*v.* **northerne**; with **hēg**, **weg** or **hēah-weg**); *the old brook* 1606 (*v.* **wald**, **brōc**); *le oldedam* 1321 (*v.* **ald**, **damme**); *the Olde meadow* 1606, *Oult Meadow* 1656 (*v.* **wald**); *the old mill* 1606, *Old Mill* 1720, *le oldemilneholm*(*e*) l.13 (*v.* **holmr**) (*v.* **ald**, **myln**); *the old pen*(*n*) 1606 (*v.* **ald**, **penn**); *parke* 1579, *Parkfelde* 1467 × 84, *Park Feild* 1579, 1601, 1606 (*v.* **feld**; one of the great open-fields, also called *Sowthfeld*, *supra*), *the Park knobs* 1709 (*v.* **knob**) (*v.* **park**); (*att*) *Parnells House* 1709 (with the surn. *Parnell*; a furlong thus called); *the Parsons pitt* 1601, 1606, *Parsones Pitt* 1625 (*v.* **persone**, **pytt**); *the partinge grasse* 1606 (*v.* **parting**, **græs**; poss. alluding to allocation by lot (*v.* Field 23)); *Paugell* 1601, 1697, *Pawgell* 1601, *Paugeill* 1606, *Paugill* 1606, 1709, 1720 (origin uncertain; perh. an OE masc. pers.n. *Paga* or *Pæga* with **wella** or **hyll**, but the medial *g* of the surviving forms appears to be plosive); *Peatlenge crosse* 1579, *Peatling*(*e*) *Crosse* 1601, 1606, 1625, 1656, *Peatling Cross* 1709 (*v.* **cros**), *Peatling Closen side* 1709 (*v.* **clos**(**e**), **sīde**; with an archaic *-en* pl. for *close*), *Petelyngeslowe* 1315 (*v.* **slōh**) (Peatling Parva parish adjoins to the north-west); *the Pikes*, *the Pykes* 1606 (*v.* **pīc**); *Pinfeld* 1606 (*v.* **pynd-fald**); *the Pittes* 1606, *le Pittesdale*, *le Puttisdale* 1339 (*v.* **pytt**, **dalr**); *Pultneymeyre* 1467 × 84 (*v.* (**ge**)**mǣre**; the boundary with Poultney which adjoins to the south); *Reyneshooke* 1579 (*v.* **hōc**; with the surn. *Reynes*, of a family originally from Rennes in south-west Normandy); *the Ricksteede* 1606 (*v.* **rickstead**); *Riggeweye* 1318, 1339, *Ridgeway* 1720 (*v.* **hrycgweg**); *Rydichewey* 1467 × 84 (*v.* **ryde**, **dīc**, **weg**); *Sadlers Headland* 1709 (*v.* **hēafod-land**; with the surn. *Sadler*); *scortestoft* e.13, *Schortestoft* m.13, l.13 (*v.* **toft**; with the surn. *Short*, an original by-name from OE *sc*(*e*)*ort* 'short', alluding to stature); *Scottes hadland* 1606 (*v.* **hēafod-land**; with the surn. *Scott*, cf. *Hugh Scott* 1606 *Terrier*); *Sedgmo*(*o*)*re* 1606, 1625 (*v.* **secg**[1], **mōr**[1]); *the Slade* 1674 (18), 1679, 1703, 1745 (*v.* **slæd**); *neyther* ~ ~ (*v.* **neoðera**), *Small Roodes* 1579 (*v.* **smæl**, **rōd**[3]); *le southecroft* 1321 (*v.* **sūð**, **croft**); *spichewellecrosforlong* m.13, l.13 (*v.* **cross**, **furlong** and Spittswell in f.ns. (a)); *stangrount* e.13, *stanground* l.13, 1335, *stangrund* l.13, *stonground* 1579, *Stonegroundes* 1606, *Stonegrounds* 1656, 1679, 1709, *Stonegrownds* 1720 (*v.* **stān**, **grund**); *Stone well* 1674 (18) (*v.* **stān**, **wella**); *stoneygrounde* 1579, *Stonye groundes* 1601, *Stony grounds* 1703 (*v.* **stānig**, **grund**); *Swynncoate* 1579, *Swynecoate* 1601, *Swincott* 1606, 1720, *Swincote* 1625, 1697 (*v.* **swīn**, **cot**); *Sydysmore* 1467 × 84 (*v.* **sīde**, **mōr**[1]); *Tebbermeere Rickstead* 1709 (*v.* **rickstead** and Tabbermear's Fm in Walton *supra*); *Thorpe meere* 1606 (*v.* (**ge**)**mǣre**; the boundary with Bruntingthorpe parish which adjoins to the north-west); *Thorpeweye* m.13, l.13 (*v.* **weg**; the road to Bruntingthorpe); *Three Thorns* 1709 (*v.* **þrēo**, **þorn**); (*the*) *Towne furlonge* 1601, 1606, 1679, *Town furlong* 1674 (18), 1703, 1745 (*v.* **tūn**, **furlang**); *Turweyslade* 1467 × 84 (*v.* **slæd** and Turway in f.ns. (a)); *Tuyseldeweye*, *Twyseldeweye* l.13 (*v.* **twisled**, **weg**); *Walton heath*(*e*) 1601, 1606, 1709 (*v.* **hǣð**); *Walton Townes ende* 1606 (*v.* **tūn**, **ende**); *Washpitt* 1601, 1625 (*v.* **wæsce**, **pytt** and Washpitt Leyes in f.ns. (a)); *the west pitt* 1703 (*v.* **west**, **pytt**); *Willowes*, *the Willowes bye Hey Waye* 1606 (*v.* **wilig** and Heaway Brige in f.ns. (a)); *Wintertons hadland* (*v.* **hēafod-land**), *the Tenement of Thomas Winterton* 1606 (*v.* **tenement**; note also *Edward Winterton* 1606 *Terrier* and *John Winterton* 1658 PR, both of Kimcote); (*the*) *Wire hole* 1606, 1703 (*v.* **hol**[1]), *Wollton where* 1679 (*v.* **weyour**); (*le*) *wodeweye* m.13, l.13, *Woodway* 1656 (*v.* **wudu**, **weg**); *Ric' Woolfes land* 1606 (*v.* **land**; a *Ricardus Wolfe* 1512 Ipm is also recorded for Kimcote); *Wouelond* m.13, l.13 (*v.* **wōh**, **land**); *Wytewold'* l.13 (*v.* **hwīt**, **wald**).

Knaptoft

Cnapetot 1086 DB, *Cnapetoft* 1156 (1318) Ch, 1196 GildR (p), 1200
Cur (p), e.13 *RTemple et passim* to 1220 × 50 *ib*, *Knapetoft* 1221,
1242 Fine, 1245 × 55 *RTemple et passim* to 1310 GildR (p), 1313
LCDeeds (p) *et freq* to 1338 Pat
Knaptoft(e) 1269, 1274 Ipm *et passim* to 1352 *LCDeeds* (p), 1335
Ipm *et freq*

Probably 'the curtilage of the servant(s)', *v.* **cnapa**, **toft**. Formally, the
OE masc. pers.n. *Cnapa* or the ON masc. pers.n. *Knappi* could constitute
the specific of this place-name, but the survival of a *Knaptofte* in Great
Glen (Lei **4** 85) suggests that this was a recurring appellative.

PINSLADE (lost)

Pynslad(e) 1154 × 89 Dugd, 1328 Banco, c.1530 *Dep*, 1535 VE,
1539 MinAccts, 1551 Pat
Pineslade 1156 (1318) Ch
Pinselade 1301 Ch, (*grangiam nostram de*) *Pinselade* 1467 × 84 *LTD*
Pinslade 1467 × 84 *LTD*, 1477 (e.16) *Charyte*, 1650 Nichols

Probably 'valley with an enclosure or pound', *v.* **pynd**, **slæd**, cf.
Pynslade in Thurmaston (Lei **3** 242). It is unlikely that the specific in
either case is **pinn** 'a peg, a pin', which A. H. Smith (Elements **2** 65)
suggests could refer to a particular type of fencing. That a grange of
Leicester Abbey was established at this location suggests that the *slæd*
here was a significant topographical feature such as a valley or a broad
stretch of grassland between woods rather than simply a breadth of
greensward in ploughed land. *Pinslade* lay at the boundaries of Knaptoft,
Husbands Bosworth and Mowsley (*v.* Lei **4** 125 and 200 for additional
forms presented in the Gartree Hundred parishes).

THE COTTAGE FM (KNAPTOFT COTTAGE 2½"). HALL FM (THE HALL 2½"), *the old Hall house* 1807 Nichols, *Knaptoft Hall* 1835 O, 1925 Kelly, *The Hall* 1846, 1863, 1877 White, *v.* **hall**. JANE BALL COVERT, *v.* **cover(t)**. JOHN BALL COVERT is *John Ball Gorse* 1835 O (*v.* **gorst**), *v.* **cover(t)**; local tradition names John Ball and his sister Jane as footpads who were hanged close to their home beside the road here. KNAPTOFT CHURCH, in ruins since the 17th cent.; it is early recorded as *ecclesie de Cnapetoft* 1235 RGros, *ecclesie de Knaptoft* 1379, 1441 *Pat* and locally is believed to have been dedicated to St Nicholas. KNAPTOFT GRANGE is *Knaptoft Lodge* 1807 Map, 1835 O (*v.* **loge**), *v.* **grange**. KNAPTOFT HO. KNAPTOFT LODGE, *v.* **loge**. TOPHOUSE FM is *Top House* 1925 Kelly, *v.* **topp**. WARREN FM, *le Warren* 1620 Ipm, *v.* **wareine**. WELFORD RD, Welford in Northants. lying 6 miles to the south.

FIELD-NAMES

In (a) forms dated 1858 are *TA*. Forms throughout dated 1374 are Inqaqd; those dated 1402 and 1406 are Cl; 1467 × 84 are *LTD*; 1482 are ISLR; 1483 are Banco; 1525, 1529, 1530, 1532, 1537, 1620 and 1629 are Ipm; c.1530 are *Dep*; 1536 are AAS; 1570 are Nichols; 1598 are *Deed*.

(a) Cance Mdw (sic) 1858 (unexplained, unless this is with a poor spelling of the surn. *Cant* in the possessive case; note *the Rev. John Cant* 1781 of adjoining Kimcote and Walton parish); The Grove 1858 (*le Grove* 1529, 1620 *v.* **grāf**).

(b) *Ashe close* 1620 (*v.* **æsc**); *Bradgate feld* 1506, 1525, 1629, *brodgate felde* 1529 (*v.* **feld**; an enclosure in the tenure of *Thomas Bradgate* 1506 Cl, *Thomas Brodegate* 1529 Ipm and *Richard Bradgate* 1572 ib); *le Corn close* 1620 (*v.* **corn**[1]); *Gallowe cloutes* or *Calow cloutes* 1570 (*v.* **calu**, **clūd**); *Gosse medow* 1525, 1529, *~ meadow* 1620, 1629 (*v.* **gorst**, **mēd** (**mēdwe** obl.sg.)); *of the hal* 1467 × 84 (p) (*v.* **hall**; with reference to a medieval hall, and judging by the surviving earthworks of early fishponds, it was on the same site as The Hall *supra*); *the Home feld* or *close* 1529 (*v.* **clos(e)**), *the Homefelde* 1536; *the Holm feld* 1530, *le Holmfeld* 1629 (*v.* **feld**; it is uncertain whether these all belong together in compound with **holmr**, or whether **home** is present in two instances); (*le*) *Inland* 1525, 1620, *Inland close* 1529, 1629 (*v.* **clos(e)**) (*v.* **in**, **land**); *Kenelfeld*, *Kenilfild* 1506, *Kennell feld* 1529, *~ feild* 1620 (*v.* **kennell**, **feld**; one of the great open-fields of the township); *Knaptoft hegge* c.1530 (*v.* **hecg**; a parish boundary hedge); *Knaptoft Pasture* 1482, 1483 (*v.* **pasture**); *le Ladie medow* 1529, *le Ladye meadow* 1620 (*v.* **ladi**, **mēd** (**mēdwe** obl.sg.); *Lane Bancks* (*v.* **banke**), *Lane close* 1620 (*v.* **lane**); *le Launde* 1529, 1620 (*v.* **launde**); *Little Bushey close* 1620 (*v.* **busshi**); *Medilfeld*, *le Medilfild* 1506, *Middelfeld* 1525, *midle felde* 1529, *Middle Feild* 1598, 1620 (*v.* **middel**, **feld**; one of the great open-fields); *Milnefeld* 1598, *Mill Feild* 1620 (*v.* **myln**, **feld**; another of the great open-fields); *Mowsley ~* 1598, *Moseley close* 1620 (Mowsley adjoins to the east); *Newclose* 1525, 1529, 1620, *le New close* 1629 (*v.* **nīwe**, **clos(e)**); *le Orcharde*

1529 (*v.* **orceard**); *Prestushadus* 1374 (*v.* **prēost, hēafod**); *Great* ~ ~, *Little Rammes close* 1620 (*v.* **ramm**); *Stubbiescroft close* 1554 (*v.* **croft, clos(e)**; either with the surn. *Stubbs* or with **stubb**); *le Thornehill* 1620 (*v.* **þorn, hyll**); *le Thorney close or Little Bushey close* 1620 (*v.* **þornig** and *Little Bushey close, supra*); *atte Welle* 1402 (p) (*v.* **atte, wella**).

Knighton

Knighton has been part of the Borough of Leicester since 1891.

KNIGHTON

> *Cnihtetone* 1086 DB, *Cnigtetuna* 1163 RegAnt, *Cnichtetun* c.1204 ib, *Cnihteton* 1215, 1218 ib, *Cnicteton* c.1215 ib (p), *Chnictheton* 1218 ib
>
> *Knict(t)eton* 1204, c.1215, 1258 × 79 RegAnt, *Knihteton* 1217 BodlCh, 1218 RegAnt
>
> *Cnichtingtunam* 1146 RegAnt, *Cnichtinthona* c.1200 *Sloane*, *Cnihtinton(e)* 1205 Dugd, 1205 ChR, *Cnicteton* 1231 Cur, *Cnichinton* 1318 Pat
>
> *Knictinton* 1200 Cur, 1258 × 79 RegAnt, *Knytinton* 1267 Cur
>
> *Cnicton* 1196 ChancR (p), *Chnictun* c.1215 RegAnt (p), *Cnithon* c.1215 ib
>
> *Knihtona* e.13 *Wyg* (p), *Knihtton* 1208 FF, *Knich(t)ton* 1269 Cl, 1293 OSut, *Knycton* 1288 *LCDeeds* (p), 1294 *RTemple*, *Knicton* c.1292 *LCDeeds*
>
> *Kniton* 1195 P, 1272 Cur, c.1278 *LCDeeds* (p), *Knytton* 1254 GildR (p) *et passim* to 1273 *LCDeeds*, *Knyton* 1267 Cur, 1277 RGrav, *Knitton* 1273 GildR (p) *et passim* to 1292 *LCDeeds*
>
> *Knygton* 1307 GildR (p), 1312 *Rut* (p), 1336, 1370 *Wyg*
>
> *Knyghton(e)* 1285 × 93 Hastings, 1297 Cl *et passim* to 1344 *LCDeeds et freq* to 1514, 1516 *Wyg et passim* to 1547 Chap, *Knighton* 1501 *Wyg*, 1547, 1551 Pat *et freq*

'The estate of the young warriors or retainers', *v.* **cniht** (**cnihta** gen.pl.), **tūn**. The DB form has a composition-joint in the gen.pl., but a range of early spellings suggests that there was an alternative **-ing-**[4] construction, hence 'the estate associated with the young warriors or retainers', *v.* **cniht**, **-ingtūn** (**-ing-**[4]). The exact sense of *cniht* in particular place-names is difficult to determine since its semantic range extended from small boy, youth, servant and soldier to the retainers of nobility and royalty. Such difficulty is compounded by the semantic range of *tūn* from farmstead and village to estate. Much depends on the date of a place-name's formation, in this case unknown.

ASHCLOSE SPINNEY, *v.* **æsc, clos(e), spinney**. ASHFIELD, cf. *Ashfield House* 1863, 1877 White, *v.* **æsc**. BROOKFIELD (lost), *Brookfield* 1846, 1877 White. BULL'S HEAD (P.H.) (lost), *Bull's Head* 1846 White. CHAPEL LANE. CLARENDON PARK. CRADOCK ARMS (P.H.), *Cradock-Hartopp Arms* 1863 White, *Cradock Arms* 1877 ib. *Sir Edmund Cradock Hartopp* is lord of the manor in 1807 Nichols and *Rev. Edward H. Cradock* of Brasenose College, Oxford, in 1877 White. DUN COW (P.H.) (lost), *Dun Cow* 1846 White. EASTFIELD (lost), *Eastfield* 1846, 1863 White. GOLDHILL FM (2½"). GOLDHILL SPINNEY, *v.* **spinney** and Goldhill in Aylestone *supra*; this is a parish boundary site. HOME FM, *v.* **home**. KNIGHTON BRIDGE. KNIGHTON FIELDS, 1877 White; cf. the early (*in*) *campis occidental'* 1477 (e.16) *Charyte* (with MLat *campus* 'a field' and *occidentalis* 'western'). KNIGHTON HAYES, *v.* **(ge)hæg**. KNIGHTON HALL, 1846, 1863, 1877 White; built in the early 18th cent., *v.* **hall**, but note the ancient *atte Halle* 1370 *Wyg* (p) in f.ns. (b). KNIGHTON HO., *Knighton House* 1863 White. KNIGHTON SPINNEY, *v.* **spinney**. PORTLAND HO. (lost), *Portland House* 1863 White; it is *Portland Lodge* 1877 ib, *v.* **loge**. SAFFRON BROOK, *Safforn* 1756 *EnclA*; a pre-English stream-name *Severne*, *v.* Lei **1** 226 *s.n.* ST MARY MAGDALENE'S CHURCH, *Church (St Mary Magdalene)* 1863, 1877 White; although recorded late, contains late 13th cent. masonry. SOUTH KNIGHTON. SPRINGFIELD HO. (lost), *Springfield House* 1846, 1863, 1877 White. STONEYGATE, 1835 O, 1846, 1863, 1877 White, *Stongate* 1515 VCHL, *v.* **stān, stānig, gata**; the Leicester end of the Roman *Via Devana* (later Gartree Road).

Street-names in urban development: note that it is uncertain whether those asterisked street-names *infra* represent continuity of some toponyms listed in f.ns. (a) and (b) in their original locations; they appear to be names retrieved by a Local Authority official from Nichols's excerpts from *Charyte*.

ABERDALE RD. ADDERLEY RD. ALEXANDER RD. ASHCLOSE AVE. ASHFIELD RD. ASQUITH BOULEVARD. AVENUE RD. BALDWIN RD. BARRINGTON RD. BEECHCROFT RD. BERESFORD DRIVE. BONINGTON RD. BRINSMEAD RD. BRIXHAM DRIVE. BURLINGTON RD. BURNS ST. CAIRNSFORD RD. CARISBROOKE RD. CECILIA RD. CENRAL AVE. CLARENDON PARK RD. COWPER ST. CRADDOCK RD. CROSS RD.

DEANCOURT RD. DOVEDALE RD. DUKES DRIVE. EAST AVE. EASTCOURT
RD. EDWARD RD. ELMFIELD AVE, ELMSLEIGH AVE. ELMS RD. FAIRHAM
RD. FERNDALE RD. FLEETWOOD RD. GAINSBOROUGH RD. GOLDHILL RD.
GREAT ARLER RD. GREENHILL RD. GRENFELL RD. GUILFORD RD.
HARTOPP RD. HEATHER RD. HEDDINGTON WAY. HERRICK RD. HIGHGATE
DRIVE. HOLBROOK RD*. HOLMFIELD RD. HOULDITCH RD. HOWARD RD.
HYLION RD. KEBLE RD. KINGSLEY ST. KINGSMEAD RD. KNIGHTON
CHURCH RD. KNIGHTON DRIVE. KNIGHTON FIELDS RD. KNIGHTON PARK
RD. KNIGHTON RD. LAMBORNE RD. LANDSEER RD. LEOPOLD RD. LINK
RD. LORNE RD. LYNHOLME RD. LYNMOUTH DRIVE. LYTHAM RD.
LYTTON RD. MEADVALE RD. MILFORD RD. MONTAGUE RD. MORLAND
AVE. NEWMARKET ST. NORTH AVE. NORTHCOTE RD. NORTHDENE RD.
NORTHFOLD RD. OAKDENE RD. OAKLAND RD. OVERDALE RD. OXFORD
RD. PALMERSTON BOULEVARD. PORTSDOWN RD. RAEBURN RD.
RAMSBURY RD. RATCLIFFE RD*. RIDGWAY RD*. RING RD. RYDE AVE.
SACKVILLE GARDENS. ST JOHNS RD. ST LEONARDS RD. SANDOWN RD.
SCOTT ST. SHACKERDALE RD*. SHANKLIN AVE. SHANKLIN DRIVE.
SHIRLEY AVE. SHIRLEY RD. SHREWSBURY AVE. SIDNEY RD. SKELTON
DRIVE. SOUTHERNHAY RD. SOUTH KNIGHTON RD. SOUTHLAND RD.
SPRINGFIELD RD. STANFELL RD. STOCKWELL RD*. STONEYGATE AVE.
STOUGHTON RD. SUTTON RD. THURLOW RD. TOLLER RD. VENTNOR RD.
VICTORIA PARK RD. WEST AVE. WESTBURY RD. WESTERNHAY RD.
WESTGATE RD. WIMBOURNE RD. WOODBANK RD. WOODCROFT AVE.
WOODLAND AVE. WORDSWORTH RD. WYNDALE RD.

FIELD-NAMES

In (a), forms dated 1756 are *EnclA*; those dated 1806 are *Deed*; 1852 are
TA. Forms throughout dated 1273, 1292, c.1292, 1584, 1620 and 1622
are *LCDeeds*; 1280 × 92 and 1336 are *Wyg*; 1294 are *RTemple*; 1332 and
1515 are VCHL; 1334 and 1589 are *Deed*; 1477 (e.16) are *Charyte*; 1606
and 1709 are MiscAccts; 1674 are *Terrier*; 1720 are LAS.

   (a) the Abbey Mdw (formerly the property of Leicester Abbey); the Breach Fd
1756 (*la Breche* 1332, *le Breche* 1477 (e.16), cf. *le Brechesik*(*e*) 1292, *Brechesyke*
1477 (e.16) (*v.* **sík**), *Brechesykefurlonge* 1477 (e.16) (*v.* **furlang**), *v.* **brēc**); Carbage
Cl 1806 (*v.* **cabache**); the Cow Pasture 1756 (*v.* **cū**, **pasture**); the Croft or Roundhill
Cl 1806 (*le Croft* 1334, *v.* **croft** and Roundhill Cl *infra*); Far Pasture (*v.* **feor**); Hill
Cl 1806 (*v.* **hyll**); Holbrooke Cl 1806 (cf. *Holbrook furlong* 1674 (*v.* **furlang**), *v.*
hol^2, **brōc**); Home Cl or Little Cl (*v.* **home**); Homestead 1806 (*v.* **hām-stede**); The
Lew 1852 (a meadow thus called; with ME **lewe** (ModEdial. **lew**) 'a shelter, a
sheltered place, a resting-place' (from OE *hlēo* 'a shelter')); Middle Mdw 1806,

1852; Near Mdw 1852; Upper ~ ~, Neather Ridgeway Cl 1806 (*Rygwey* 1477 (e.16), cf. *le Heyeriggeweye* c.1292 (*v.* **hēah**[1]), *Rygweyfurlong* 1477 (e.16) (*v.* **furlang**), *v.* **hrycgweg**); Roundhill Cl 1806 (*v.* **round, hyll**); Saffhurn otherwise Saffron Cl 1806 (*v.* Saffron Brook *supra*); Stockwell 1756 (*Stokwell* 1477 (e.16), cf. *Stocwellesike, Stokewellesike* c.1292 (*v.* **sík**), *v.* **stocc, well**); Townsend Cl 1806 (*v.* **tūn, ende**).

(b) *Bandall Siche* 1674 (*v.* **bēan, sīc**; with **dalr** or **deill**); *Banland* 1477 (e.16) (*v.* **bēan, land**); *Bird Catchers furlong* 1674 (*v.* **furlang**; prob. near the location of a cock-shoot, where nets were stretched in a woodland glade to catch woodcock); *Blackwell* 1674, *le Blakewelleforlong* 1273 (*v.* **furlang**), *le Blakewellesike* 1273 (*v.* **sík**) (*v.* **blæc, wella**); *Blakelond* c.1292 (*v.* **blæc, land**); *Broad Siche* 1674 (*v.* **brād, sīc**); *Upper Bullwell* 1674 (*v.* **bula, wella**); *in campis occident'* 1477 (e.16) (with MLat *campus* 'a field' and *occidentalis* 'western'); *le Clerkewell* 1334 (*v.* **clerk, wella**); *Crowethornhul* c.1292 (*v.* **crāwe, þorn, hyll**); *Elrenestubb', Elrenestubbis* c.1292, *Eldurstob* 1477 (e.16) (*v.* **ellern, stubb**); *Estmedewe* c.1292 (*v.* **ēast, mēd** (**mēdwe** obl.sg.)); *Fletcherland* 1589, *Fletchers Land(e)* 1606, 1709 (*v.* **land**; note *Samuel Fletcher* 1608 HP); *Folewellesike* c.1292 (*v.* **sík**), *Folewellewro* c.1292 (*v.* **vrá**) (*v.* **fūl, wella**); *Fulsiche* 1334 (*v.* **fūl, sīc**); *Gandertreyde* 1477 (e.16) (*v.* **gandra, trade**); *Gaseforlong* c.1292 (*v.* **gás, furlang**); *le Geldiswong* c.1292 (*v.* **geld, vangr**); *Goldhulfot* 1280 × 92 (*v.* **fōt** and Goldhill Fm *supra*); *Grenegate* 1477 (e.16) (*v.* **grēne**[1], **gata**); *Grimishul* c.1292 (*v.* **hyll**; prob. with the ON masc. pers.n. *Grímr*); *Grymlondes* 1334 (*v.* **land**; again presum. with the pers.n. *Grímr*, although lacking a composition-joint in the possessive case); *atte Halle* 1370 (p) (*v.* **atte, hall**), *de Aula* 1477 (e.16) (p) (with MLat *aula* 'a hall') (it is uncertain whether this hall was on the site of the later Knighton Hall *supra*); *Holgate* 1477 (e.16) (*v.* **hol**[1], **gata**); *le Horeston furlong* c.1292 (*v.* **furlang**), *Horstonpyt* 1477 (e.16) (*v.* **pytt**) (*v.* **hār**[2], **stān**); *Knighton Meere* 1620, ~ *Meare* 1622 (*v.* **(ge)mǣre**), *Knighton Slade* 1620 (*v.* **slæd**); *Littilhul* c.1292 (*v.* **lȳtel, hyll**); *le longforlong* c.1292, *Longfurlang, Schortlongfurlong* (*v.* **sc(e)ort**) 1477 (e.16) (*v.* **lang**[1], **furlang**); *the Long Lane end* 1674 (*v.* **lane, lane-ende**); *Middelesike* c.1292 (*v.* **middel, sík**); *Nether* ~, *Upper Millgate* 1674 (*v.* **myln, gata**); *molendinum aquaticum S. Leonardi* 1292 (with MLat *molendinum* 'a mill' and *aquaticus* 'worked by water'; the property of the Hospital of St Leonard in Leicester, *v.* Lei **1** 94); *Muggs house* 1709 (with the surn. *Mugg*, from an OE masc. pers.n. *Mugga*); *Mykylburgh* 1477 (e.16) (*v.* **micel, mikill, berg**); *at mylne* (p), *Attemylne* 1477 (e.16) (p) (*v.* **atte, myln**); *Nederthorp, Nedurthorp, Netherthorp, Nethyrthorp* 1477 (e.16) (*v.* **neoðera, þorp**); *Oldegate* 1334 (*v.* **ald, gata**); *radeclif* c.1292, *Radeclyue* 1294, *Radclyue* 1477 (e.16) (*v.* **rēad, clif**); *the Round Close* 1674 (*v.* **round**); *Schakersdale, Shakerestale* 1477 (e.16) (*v.* **scēacere, dæl**[1]); *Seggate* 1674 (*v.* **secg**[1], **gata**); *Shofell Nooke* 1674 (*v.* **scofl, nōk**); *Smaledolis* c.1292 (*v.* **smæl, dāl**); *le Smethehul* c.1292 (*v.* **smēðe**[1], **hyll**); *Sondwellesike* 1336 (*v.* **sand, wella, sík**); *Theuesgraue* 1477 (e.16) (*v.* **græf**; the specific with -*es* suggests **þēof**, but perh. **þēfa** 'brushwood, bramble' would sit more happily); *Nether Town Close* 1720 (*v.* **tūn**); *Trunland* 1477 (e.16) (*v.* **trun, land**); *the Vicaridge house* 1674 (*v.* **vikerage**); *Waterthirne* c.1292, *Waterthyrne* 1477 (e.16) (*v.* **wæter, þyrne**); *waterthorow* 1584 (*v.* **wæter, furh** and *Water furrowes* in Ashby Parva f.ns. (b) *supra*); *Wrangelondes* 1477 (e.16) (*v.* **wrang, land**).

Leire

Legre 1086 DB (×3)

Leire c.1130 LeicSurv, 1195 P (p), 1196 ChancR (p) *et passim* to
   1247 Ass, 1430 *Peake*, 1535 VE *et freq*, *Leirra* 1208 FF

Leghere 1176 P (p)

Leyr(*e*) 1221 Fine, 1236 Cur *et passim* to 1230 × 60 *Goodacre*, 1265
   Misc *et freq* to 1469 *Wyg et passim* to 1582 LEpis, *Leyra* 1220
   MHW, 1227 RHug *et passim* to l.13 *Goodacre*, e.14 *Wyg* (p)

Layer 1502 *MiscAccts*, *Layr*(*e*) 1510 Visit, 1517 AAS *et passim* to
   1546 MinAccts, 1723 LML

Most probably, the place-name Leire was in origin *Legra*, the pre-
English name of the stream on which the village stands, a name identical
with or related to that of the river Loire in France (Gaulish *Ligeris*,
perhaps from a root **lig* 'marsh', *v.* Bahlow 300 *s.n.* Lieg). This would
have given an OE river-name **Legor* (or **Ligor*). William of
Malmesbury, when writing c.1125, claimed that Leicester (*Ligoraceaster*
c.955, *Legraceastre* c.1000) was named *a Legra fluvio præterfluente*
'from the river Legra which flows past (the town)'. However, Leicester
stands on the river Soar of which *Legra* is a tributary. A more likely
explanation for Leicester's name is that an OE folk-name **Legora* or
(**Ligora*) 'the dwellers on the river Legor (or Ligor)' was given to those
people who lived around what was to become Leicester and some
distance to its south (including the Leire district) and that it was the folk-
name rather than the river-name which was used in forming the toponym
of their principal settlement, *v.* Leicester (Lei **1** 1–3). Note that the lost
Legham (with **hām** or **hamm**), which appears associated with the
holding of Hugo de Grentmaisnil in Leicester in the Domesday Survey
of 1086, may incorporate a reduced form of the river-name as its
specific. Thus for Leire, as perhaps for Great Glen (Lei **4** 79) and Glen
Parva *supra*, a pre-English river-name became attached to a riverine
settlement. See also Ekwall RN xlii and Forsberg 113.

AIREDALE FM. BACK LANE, 1786 *EnclA*, *v.* **back**. BALLY FM (local), *Bally farm* 1925 Kelly. BROUGHTON LANE, 1699 *Deed*; it is *Brauton way* 1601 *Terrier*, *Broughton waye* 1625 *ib*, *Broughton way* 1638, 1673 *ib*, 1698 *Deed*, *v.* **weg**; Broughton Astley lies 2 miles to the north. DUNTON LANE is *Dunton way* 1601 *Terrier*, *(the) Dunton Road* 1699 *Deed*, 1786 *EnclA*; Dunton Bassett lies one mile to the east. EAGLESFIELD FM, cf. *Mary Eaglesfield* 1846 White, of Leire. FAR HILL FM. GLEBE HO. (local), *v.* **glebe**. THE GREEN, *v.* **grēne**[2]. HALL FM, *The Hall* 1877 White, 1925 Kelly; an early hall is recorded in *ad Aulam* 1327 SR (p) (with MLat *aula* 'a hall') and *atte halle* 1332 ib (p) (*v.* **atte**), *v.* **hall**. HILLCREST FM. KIMBERLEY HO. (local), prob. named in celebration of the relief of Kimberley in 1900 during the Boer War in South Africa. LEIRE MILL, *(the Water Mill called) Leire Mill* 1786 *EnclA*, *Leir Mill* 1835 O, *v.* **myln**. LITTLE LANE. MAIN ST is the *Town Street* 1786 *EnclA*, *v.* **tūn**. METHODIST CHURCH. MOUNT PLEASANT, for the most part a complimentary name for a location, but occasionally may be given ironically. OLD BULL (P.H.) (lost), *Old Bull* 1846, 1863 White; it is *Bull's Head* 1877 ib. THE OLD RECTORY is *The Rectory* 1877 White, 1925 Kelly, *v.* **rectory**; earlier is *the Parsonage house* 1708 *Terrier*, *v.* **personage**. POPLAR FM. QUEEN'S ARMS (P.H.), *Queen's Arms* 1877 White, 1925 Kelly; it is *Queen's Head* 1846, 1863 White. THE RECTORY, *v.* **rectory**. ST PETER'S CHURCH, *Church (St Peter)*, 1846, 1863, 1877 White, 1925 Kelly; it is earlier recorded as *ecclesie de Leyra* 1220 MHW, *ecclesiam de Leir'* 1240 RGros, *ecclesie de Leyre* 1241, 1248 ib, 1294, 1324, 1334, 1349, 1350, 1386 *Pat*, *~ de Leire* 1334 *ib*. STATION LANE, leads to a former halt on the old *Midland Counties Railway* 1854 O. STEMBOROUGH LANE, *~ ~* FM, STEMBOROUGH MILL, *Steynesberwe* 1323 *MiD*, *molendinum de Steinesberue* 13 AD (with MLat *molendinum* 'a mill'), *Steyneborrowe Mill* 1616 Ipm, *Stenburrough ~*, *Stonburrough ~* 1699 *Deed*, *Stemborough ~* 1835 O, *Stembro' Mill* 1846 White, *v.* **myln**. What appears to be a genitival composition-joint in the early spellings suggests a pers.n. as the specific, perh. the ON masc. *Steinn*, but an ON pers.n. compounded with *berg* 'a hill' would be most unusual in the county. Possible would be an OE masc. pers.n. *Stān*, later Scandinavianized, but *Stān* is not recorded independently (it may occur in Stanesgate (Ess 227), in Stansfield (YW **3** 177) and in Stanshope (StH 508)). However, the soil of the hill is sandy and mixed with large pieces of sandstone, so it is possible that the common OE compound **stān-berg* (or **stānesberg* or **stānasberg*) 'stone(s) hill', with OE *stān* replaced by or influenced by its cognate ON *steinn*, is present in this instance. But there is no evidence for a lost ancient standing-stone here, *v.* **stān**,

steinn, **berg**. VALLEY VIEW FM. WELCOMB. WHITE HORSE (P.H.), *White Horse* 1846, 1863, 1877 White, 1925 Kelly.

FIELD-NAMES

In (a), forms dated 1762 are *Terrier*; those dated 1786 are *EnclA*. Forms throughout dated 1154 × 89 are Berkeley; those dated 1212 are Fine; e.13 are *Segrave*; Hy 3 are *Goodacre*; 1601, 1625, 1638, 1673, 1700, 1703, 1708 and 1724 are *Terrier*; 1616 are Ipm; 1698 and 1699 are *Deed*.

(a) Almeys Mdw 1786 (cf. *Mr Almeys hedge* 1699 (v. **hecg**); the surn. *Almey* is present in adjacent Broughton Astley parish, from *Thomas Almey* 1810 Census to *Annie Almey* 1879 ib); Ashby hedge 1762 (1601, 1638, 1708, *Ashby hedg* 1724, *Ashebie Hedg furlonge* 1601, *Ashby hedge Furlong* 1700, 1703 (v. **furlang**), v. **hecg**; the boundary hedge with Ashby Parva parish which adjoins to the south); Ashby Way 1762, (the) Ashby Road 1786 (*Ashby way* 1601, 1700, 1703, 1708, 1724, ~ ~ *furlong* 1638, 1673 (v. **weg**; land beside the road to Ashby Parva); Aukersdale 1762 (1601, 1673, 1700, 1703, 1708, 1724, *akersdall* 1601, *Akersdale* 1625, *Acres Dale* 1638, *Akersdale furlonge* 1625 (v. **furlang**); if the specific is the ON masc. pers.n. *Auðgeirr* (with AN interchange of *g* and *k*), then with **deill** or **dalr**; but if **æcer**, then with **dalr**); Bag Mdw 1786 (*bagnall medowe* 1601, *Bagmill meddow* 1638, (*in*) *bagnall*, *Bagnall hades* 1601, *Bagmill Heedes* 1638, 1673 (v. **hēafod**); v. *Baggemulne* in adjoining Ashby Parva f.ns. (b)); Blakelands 1786 (*Blaklandes* 1601, *Neather* ~, *Upper Blakland*(*e*)*s* 1625, 1638, 1673, v. **blæc**, **land**); Boggy Cl 1786 (v. **boggy**); Bracknell Cl 1786 (*braknell* 1601, cf. *Braknill furlong*(*e*) 1625, 1638, *Bracknell furlong* 1673 (v. **furlang**), v. **braken**, **hyll**); Bradfords Cl, ~ Mdw 1786 (*Bradford* 1601, 1699, v. **brād**, **ford**); Long ~, Short Breach 1762 (1703, 1708, 1724, *Long Breach* 1699, *Short Breach* 1700, v. **brēc**); Briery Hill 1762 (*Brier* ~ 1700, 1724, *Breer Hill* 1703, 1708, v. **brēr**, **brērig**); Broadarse 1762 (1638, 1673, 1724, *broad arsse* 1601, *Broadarse furlong*(*e*) 1625, 1700, 1703, *Brodarse furlong* 1708 (v. **furlang**), v. **brād**, **ears**; *ears* 'an arse, a buttock' is often transferred topographically as 'a rounded hill', but it is difficult to distinguish from **herse** 'a hill top' which may pertain here); Broughton Cl, ~ Mdw 1786 (bordering Broughton Astley parish which adjoins to the north); the Butts 1786 (*buts* 1601, *the Buttes* 1638, 1673, *the Butte furlong* 1625 (v. **furlang**), v. **butte**); Coats Cl 1786 (the surn. *Coates*, from OE *cot* 'a cottage' is poss. here, as is **cot** itself, but this may be a late form of *Carts Close* in f.ns. (b)); Collins Acre 1786 (v. **æcer**; with the surn. *Collin*(*s*), from *Colin*, an -*in* diminutive of *Col*, a pet-form of Nicholas; cf. *Colinus* 1196 RFL); Cow Cl 1786 (1699, v. **cū**); Cow Mdw 1786; Crisps Cl, ~ Mdw (cf. *John Crisps Plott* 1699 (v. **plot**); the surn. *Crisp* may be either from OE *crisp* 'curly-haired' (Lat *crispus*), or be a short form of the masc. pers.n. *Crispin*, originally a saint's name, also from Lat *crispus*); Under Dam Cl 1786 (*Underdam* 1699, v. **under**, **damme**); Far Cl 1786; Far Hill 1786 (v. **feor**); Fishpond Cl 1786 (v. **fisshe-ponde**); Four Acres Cl 1786 (v. **æcer**); Freeman's Cl 1762 (*Freemans Close* 1700, 1703, 1724, ~ ~

furlong (*v.* **furlang**), ~ ~ *side* (*v.* **sīde**) 1708; note *Thomas Freeman* 1699 *Deed* and *James Freeman* 1708 *Terrier*, both of Leire); Frolesworth ~, *Frowlesworth Way* 1762, Frolesworth Lane 1786 (*Throulesworth way* 1601, *Frowlesworth* ~ 1638, 1673, 1700, *Froolesworth* ~ 1703, *Frolesworth* ~ 1708, *Frolsworth* ~, *Froulesworth Way* 1724, *Frolesworth waye furlonge* 1625 (*v.* **furlang**); *v.* **weg**; the road to Frolesworth which lies one mile to the west); Gorsy Cl 1786 (*v.* **gorstig**); Gravel Pits 1762 (*gravill pitts* 1601, *Grauel pitts* 1638, 1673, 1708, 1724, *Gravell pitts* 1700, 1703, *grauell pittes furlonge* 1625 (*v.* **furlang**), *v.* **gravel, pytt**); Great Hill 1786 (*v.* **grēat**); Greens Cl 1786 (with the surn. *Green*); Hall Cl 1786; Hall Piece 1786 (1698, *the Hall piece furlong* 1698 (*v.* **furlang**), *v.* **pece** and Hall Fm *supra*); the Hayes 1786 (*v.* **(ge)hæg**); Highhorn Cl 1786 (*hyhorn* 1601, cf. *Highhorne furlong(e)* 1625, 1638, 1673 (*v.* **furlang**) and *horne end* 1601 (*v.* **ende**), *v.* **hēah**[1]; prob. with **horn**, but **þorn** is poss.); The Hill, Hill Cl 1786 (*Hill Close* 1699, *v.* **hyll**); The Hoke 1762, Hoke Cl, Hoke Lane 1786 (*the hoke* 1601, 1698, 1700, 1703, 1724, (*the*) *hocke, the hock, the hok* 1601, *the Hoag* 1699, *the Hoak* 1708, *the Further Hoake furlong(e)* (*v.* **furðra**), *the Hitherward Hoake furlong(e)* (*v.* **hiderweard**) 1625, 1638, 1673 (*v.* **furlang**), *v.* **hōc**); the Home Cl 1762, 1786 (1700, 1703, 1708, 1724; because of the name's longevity, perh. with **holmr** rather than with **home**); Jervis's Cl 1786 (*Gervise Close* 1699; with the surn. *Gervis, Jervis*, from the ContGerm masc. pers.n. *Gervas* (OFr *Gervais(e)*); Kettle Mdw 1786 (*Kettle* 1699, *v.* **cetel** and Green Kettle in adjoining Ashby Parva f.ns. (a); used topographically of a deep valley); Lammas Cl 1786 (*Lamas Close* 1699, *v.* **lammas**); Lane Cl 1786 (*v.* **lane**); Limsdale Hill 1762 (1724, *Linchdallhill* 1601, *Linshdale Hill* 1638, 1673, *Limsdale hill furlonge* 1625, *Linsdale Hill furlong* 1703, 1708 (*v.* **furlang**), *v.* **hlinc, deill**); Little Dale 1762 (1700, 1703, 1708, 1724, *Litledale* e.13, *Littelldale* 1601, *Littledale furlong* 1625 (*v.* **furlang**), *v.* **lȳtel, dalr**); Lynch 1762 (*Linch* 1601, 1698, 1724, *Linsh* 1638, 1673, *Linche furlonge* 1625, *Linch Furlong* 1700, 1703, 1708 (*v.* **furlang**), *v.* **hlinc**); Long Cl 1786; the Meadow 1762 (1708, 1724, *the meddow* 1625; cf. *the Meadow ground* 1700, 1703 (*v.* **grund**), *v.* **mēd** (**mēdwe** obl.sg.)); Middle Cl 1786; Middle Fd 1786 (*the midell fild* 1601, *Middle feild* 1673, 1700, 1703, *the Middle field or More hill field* 1698, *v.* **middel, feld**; one of the great open-fields of the township); the Mill 1762 (1724, *v.* Leire Mill *supra*); Mill Cl 1786; the Mill Dam 1786 (1625, 1700, 1703, *the Mill damm* 1708, *v.* **damme**; of Stemborough Mill *supra*); (the) Mill Fd 1762, 1786 (1698, 1724, *Mill Feilde* 1700, *the mill-feild* 1708, *v.* **myln, feld** and Stemborough Mill; one of the great fields, earlier called *the Lower feild* and *the Nether field*); Mill Holme 1786 (*v.* **holmr**); Mill Mdw 1786; Monk's Hill 1762 (*Monkeshill* 1724, *Monk(e)s Hill Furlong* 1700, 1703, 1708 (*v.* **furlang**); with the surn. *Monk*, cf. *John Monk* 1817 *Census* of adjoining Dunton Bassett parish); More Hill 1762 (1625, 1724, *morhill* 1601, *Moorehill* 1638, *Moor hill* 1699, *More Hill furlong* 1700, 1703, 1708 (*v.* **furlang**)), Morehill Fd 1762, Moor Hill Fd 1786 ((*the*) *Moore Hill feild* 1625, 1638, *Morehill Field* 1724, *v.* **feld** and Middle Fd *supra*; one of the great open-fields) (*v.* **mōr**[1], **hyll**); Old Dykes 1786 (*old dich* 1601, *olde dike furlonge* 1625 (*v.* **furlang**), *v.* **ald**; with **dīc** replaced by **dík**); the Orchard 1762 (1724, *v.* **orceard**); the Parsonage Land 1762 (1724, *v.* **personage, land**); Pauls Piece Furland (sic) 1762 (*Paules peece* 1625, *Pauls peice furlong* 1700, 1703, 1708, *Pauls pice Forland* (sic) 1724, *v.* **pece, furlang**; with the surn. *Paul, v.* Reaney *s.n.*); Poors Cl, ~ Mdw 1786 (*v.* **pouer(e)**; land administered by *the Trustees for Leire Poor* 1786 *EnclA*); Portway, Nether ~ ~, Upper Portway Cl 1786 (*port way* 1601, cf. *the portewaye end*

1625, *Portway end* 1638, 1673 (*v.* **ende**), *v.* **port-wey**; the road to the market town of Lutterworth, 4 miles to the south-east); Rail Mdw 1786 (*Raile meadow* 1698, 1699, *v.* **raile**); Red Doles Cl 1786 (*Redole* e.13, *Red dole* 1601, *Read Dole* 1625, *Reddoal* 1638, 1673, *v.* **rēad, dāl**); Reedmore 1762 (1625, 1638, 1673 *et passim* to 1724, *Redmor* 1154 × 89, *Redmore* e.13, *v.* **hrēod, mōr**[1]); Ruslbrough Leas 1762 (*rusulberow* 1601, *Rustleburrow laies* 1625, *Rusheborough leays* 1673, *Russell Burrough Leyes* 1698, *Rushleburrow* ~ 1703, *Russel Burrow* ~ 1708, *Russelburow Leas* 1724, *v.* **berg, leys**; **rust** and **wella** may be thought of as the protothemes, a 'rust-coloured spring or stream' resulting from the colour of local subsoil; but earlier forms are needed); Sheaf 1762 (1700, 1703, 1708, 1724, *sheaff(e)* 1601, *Sheafe* 1638, 1673, ~ *furlonge* 1625 (*v.* **furlang**); with **scēað** in its sense 'a boundary', cf. OHGer *skeida* 'a boundary'); Great ~, Little Skinsmoor, Skinsmoor Cl, ~ Mdw 1786 (*Skinsmore* 1601, 1673, 1699, *Skinsemore* 1625, *Skingsmore* 1638; 'the demon-haunted (wet) moorland' which Leire shared with adjacent Broughton Astley and Frolesworth *supra* (where local spellings are listed), *v.* **scinn, mōr**[1]; OE *scinn* has been Scandinavianized, with *sc* > *sk*); Sleaths Butts (*v.* **butte**), Sleath's Lane 1786 (cf. *Sleaths Close* 1699; with the surn. *Sleath*, from ON *slægr* 'sly, cunning'; note *John Sleath* 1786 *EnclA* and *Martha Sleath* 1829 Census, both of Leire); B. Smith's Cl 1762 (*v. Smiths Mill* in f.ns. (b)); Sowcraft 1762 (1708, 1724, *Sutcroft* 1212, *Sowcroft* 1638, 1700, *Socrafte* 1673, *Sowecroft* 1703, *v.* **sūð, croft**); the Spring Cl 1762, Watery or Spring Cl 1786 (*the Spring Close* 1700, 1703, 1708, 1724, *v.* **spring**[1] and Watery *infra*); Spinney Cl 1786 (*v.* **spinney**); Nether ~, Upper Stubway 1762 (1724, *stubway* 1601, *the lower* ~, *the upper stubway* 1625, 1638, 1673, *Neather* ~, *Upper Stub(b)way* 1700, 1703, 1708 (*v.* **neoðera**), *v.* **stubb, weg**; Swan's Nest Furland (sic) 1762 (*swan neast f.* 1673, *Swansnest Forland* (sic) 1724, *v.* **swan**[1], **nest, furlang**); Tafts Mdw 1786 (cf. *the tafte furlonge* 1625, *Tofts furlong* 1638, 1673 (*v.* **furlang**), *v.* **toft**); Thorps Cl 1786 (with the surn. *Thorpe*); Turnhades 1786 (*the Turne hades* 1699, *v.* **hēafod**; perh. with **þyrne**, but this may be a late form of *Thirden heades* in f.ns. (b)); Ullesthorpe Foot Road 1786 (*v.* **fōt**; Ullesthorpe lies 2 miles to the south-west); Understone 1762 (1625, 1638, 1673, 1698, 1699, 1724, *Understone* 1601, *Understone Forland* (sic) 1762 (1724, *Understone Furlong* 1700, 1703, 1708, *v.* **furlang**) (*v.* **under, stān**; it is uncertain whether this alludes to a lost standing stone or to stony ground); the Upper Fd 1762 (1673, 1698, 1724, *the Upper feild* 1673, 1700, 1703, 1708; earlier it is *the over fyld* 1601, *the Ouer feild(e)* 1625, 1638 (*v.* **uferra**), *v.* **upper, feld**; one of the great open-fields of Leire); Waklin 1762 (1724, *Wakelowe* 1154 × 89, *Waclauwe* 1212, *Wakeline* 1601, *Wakelowefurlong* Hy 3, *Wakelinge furlonge* 1625, *Wakeling* ~ 1700, 1703, 1708, *Wakelands furlong* 1708 (*v.* **furlang**), *v.* **wacu, hlāw**; note The Wakelins in adjoining Dunton Bassett f.ns. (a) and *Wakeley* in adjoining Ashby Parva f.ns (b); naming a major feature at the junction of three parishes); Watery 1762, 1786 (1708, 1724, *Wattery* 1699, *Watry* 1700, 1703, *watre furlonge* 1601 (*v.* **furlang**), *v.* **wæterig**); Wethersdale 1762 (1601, 1724, *Wetheresdalle* 1601, *Weathersdale* 1625, 1638, 1673, 1700, 1703, 1708, *v.* **weðer, dalr**); Whetstone Hill 1762 (1638, 1673, 1700, 1708, *Whetston* ~ 1601, 1625, *Whitstone Hill* 1724, *v.* **hwet-stān**); Wildmore 1762 (1638, 1673 *et passim* to 1724, *Wilemore* 1601, 1625, *Brodwildmor* 1154 × 89, *Brodewildmore* e.13, *Brodewildemor* 1212 (*v.* **brād**)), Great ~ ~, Wildmore Cl 1786 (*Wildmore Close* 1708), Wildmore Hole 1762 (1700, 1703, 1708, *Wilmore Hole* 1724, *v.* **hol**[1]), Nether ~ ~, Middle ~ ~, Wildmore Leas 1762 (*Wildmor(e)* ~ 1700, 1703, 1708, 1724,

Willmore Leas 1724, *v.* **leys**), Wildmore Mdw 1786, Wildmore Nether Foreland (sic) 1762 (*Wildmor neather furlong* 1703, 1708, *Wildmor Nether Forland* (sic) 1724, *v.* **neoðera, furlong**), Wildmore Spinney 1786 (*v.* **spinney**) (*v.* **wilde, mōr**[1]); Willow Cl 1786 (*v.* **wilig**); Withy Beds 1762 (1708, *withibed* 1601, *Withebed* 1625, *Withybed* 1625, 1638, *Weithy beds* 1724, *v.* **wīðig, bedd**); Woods Cl 1786 (with the surn. *Wood*).

(b) *Asby* ~, *Ashby meare* 1601 (*v.* **(ge)mǣre**; Ashby Parva parish adjoins to the south); *Ashdales* 1601, 1638, 1673, *Ashedales furlonge* 1625 (*v.* **furlang**), *Asedalebotme* e.13, *Assedalesbotme* 1212 (*v.* **botm**) (*v.* **æsc, dalr**); *the Balk* ~, *Baulk furlong* 1698 (*v.* **balca, furlang**); *barly hom(e)* 1601, *Barlye* ~ 1625, *Barley Home* 1638, 1673 (*v.* **bærlic, holmr**); *Bell dyke* 1638, 1673 (*v.* **dík**; the specific appears to be **belle** 'a bell', which was sometimes transferred topographically to 'a bell-shaped hill', but if so here, when compounded with *dík*, its implication is uncertain; if *dík* is taken to be a water-course rather than simply a ditch, then perh. *belle* in its sense 'a bubble which forms in a liquid' may pertain, as in *a belle in þe water* (1483) and *the bells which bubble up in the water* (1576), *v.* OED bell sb.[3]; Prof. R. Coates suggests as an alternative specific an OE **bel**, poss. here in a sense 'a piece of dry land in fen', *v.* VEPN *s.v.* ***bel**[1]); *belrops* 1601, *the Bell rope grasse* 1699 (*v.* **grǣs**), *the Bellrope piece* 1699 (*v.* **pece**) (*v.* **belle, rāp**; alluding to endowed land for the provision and maintenance of bell-ropes in the parish church); *Blacholm* e.13 (*v.* **blæc, holmr**); *bludacker* 1601, *Bloodacres* 1638, 1673, 1724, *bloodakeres furlonge* 1625 (*v.* **furlang**) (*v.* **blōd, æcer**; prob. referring to reddish (blood-coloured) soil; note what may be the similarly perceived **rust-wella* in Ruslbrough and the Red Doles *supra*); *the Brooke* 1625, 1638, 1673, 1698, 1699 (*v.* **brōc**); *Broughton foot way* 1699 (*v.* **fote-waye**), *Brauton hedg* 1601, *Broughton hedge* 1638, 1673 (*v.* **hecg**; a parish boundary marker), *Brauton mere*, ~ *town meare* (*v.* **tūn**) 1601 (*v.* **(ge)mǣre**) (Broughton Astley parish adjoins to the north); *browns mill* 1601 (*v.* **myln**; with the surn. *Brown*, alluding to Stemborough Mill *supra* and its miller); *Cadell* ~ 1601, *Caudle Home* 1638, 1673, *Cowdale home furlonge* 1625 (*v.* **furlang**) (*v.* **cald, wella, holmr**); *Mr Carts meadow* 1699, *William Carts Close* 1703, 1708 (the *Cart* family is also remembered in Leire in *John Cart* 1701 MI, *Dorothy Cart* 1715 ib, *Jane Cart* 1734 Nichols and *William Cart* 1744 MI); *the Colepit highe waye* 1625, ~~ *highway* 1638, 1673 (*v.* **col-pytt, hēah-weg**; one of the roads carrying pit coal from mines in the Bedworth area to the south and east of Leics.); *the Cow Common* 1698 (*v.* **commun**), *the cow pasture* 1638, 1673 (*v.* **pasture**), *the Cow Pasture Ground* 1698 (*v.* **grund**) (*v.* **cū**); *Cunstabuls balk* 1601, *the constable baulke* 1638, 1673, *Constables Balk* 1698 (*v.* **conestable, balca**); *Dalsende* 1638 (*v.* **dalr, ende**); *daslade* 1601, *Daw Slade* 1625 (*v.* **dawe, slæd**); *Dunton Hollowe* 1625, 1638, 1673 (*v.* **holh**; towards Dunton Bassett parish which adjoins to the east); *Mr Dysons meadow* 1699; *the Earle of Kents ground* 1699 (*v.* **grund**); *the enhads* 1601 (*v.* **hēafod**; prob. with **ende**); *Flaxlondes* 1212, *Flaxeland Furland* (sic) 1625 (*v.* **furlang**) (*v.* **fleax, land**); *4 lease* (sic) (*v.* **fēower, leys**; in compound with a numeral, *leys* represents grassland units of tenure corresponding to *lands* (i.e. selions or strips) similarly used of arable); *Fosters Mill* 1700, 1703, 1708 (*v.* **myln**; with the surn. *Foster* of the miller, but it is uncertain whether this is Stemborough Mill or Leire Mill, both *supra*; note *John Foster* 1630 Nichols, of Leire); *Freemans meadow* 1699 (in the possession of *Thomas Freeman* in 1699 Deed, *v.* Freeman's Cl in f.ns. (a)); *John Garretts Plott* 1699 (*v.* **plot**; cf. *Elizabeth Garrett* 1832 Census of adjoining Broughton Astley);

Goosy meadow, *Joseph Goozes plott* 1699 (*v.* **plot**; note *Joseph Goosey* 1687 Nichols and *Joseph son of Joseph Goosey* 1734 ib, both of Leire); *grumbols dich* 1601, *Grummills Dike furlonge* 1625, *Grummills dyke furlong* 1638 (*v.* **furlang**) (*v.* **dīc**, **dík**; with the surn. *Grumble, Grumell*, from the ContGerm masc. pers.n. *Grimbald*); *Hallesokyng* e.13 (*v.* **sōcn**), *hall ground* 1601 (*v.* **grund**), *the hall medowe* 1625 (*v.* **mēd** (**mēdwe** obl.sg.) (*v.* Hall Fm *supra*); *hen poolle* 1601, *Henpoole* 1625, 1638, 1673 (*v.* **henn**, **pōl**[1]); *hiewaye furlonge* 1625 (*v.* **hēah-weg**, **furlang**); *High Home* 1698 (*v.* **hēah**[1], **holmr**); *Higinsons Hedge* 1699 (*v.* **hecg**; with reference to *Nicholas Higginson* 1699 *Deed*), *Higusons lane end* 1601 (*v.* **lane-ende**, alluding to *John Higuson* 1601 *Terrier, John Higginson* 1625 *ib*; the family survived in Leire to *Richard Higginson* 1785 MI); *the holme* 1625, *the Holmes* 1638, 1673 (*v.* **holmr**); *the Homestall* 1708 (*v.* **hām-stall**; belonging to *the Parsonage house*, *v.* The Old Rectory *supra*); *the kinges highe waye* 1625, *the Kings High Way* 1638 (*v.* **hēah-weg**; with reference to King Charles I); *Long Holmes* 1699 (*v.* **holmr**); *the long med(d)ow* 1638, 1673 (*v.* **mēd** (**mēdwe** obl.sg.)); *Lord Barron Close* 1724 (*v.* **baroun**; alluding to part of *the Earle of Kents ground*, *supra*); *the Lower Feild* 1625, 1638, 1673 (*v.* **feld**; one of the great open-fields, later called *Mill Feilde*, alluding to Stemborough Mill *supra*); *Madridall* e.13, *Parva Madirdale* (with MLat *parva* 'little') e.13 (*v.* **mæddre**; with **deill** or **dalr**; *v. mother dolle, infra*); *Michelcroft* e.13 (*v.* **micel**, **croft**); *the Mill* 1625, *Against the Mill* 1638, 1673 (a furlong so called), *Before the Mill Dore* 1699 (*v.* **dor**; a furlong so called), *the mill end* 1601 (*v.* **ende**), *the Mill furlong(e)* 1601, 1625 (*v.* **furlang**), *the Mill way* 1699 (all referring to Stemborough Mill *supra*); *mother dolle* 1601, ~ *dole* 1638, 1673 (these forms may belong with *Madridall, supra*, despite the 400 year gap in survival; if not, they must be from **modor**, **dāl**, i.e., 'the share of land beside the bog'); *the Nether field* 1698 (*v.* **neoðera**, **feld**; one of the great open-fields, earlier called *the Lower Feild, supra* and later, Mill Fd *supra*); *Normanescroft* 1212 (*v.* **croft**; either with **Norðman** as a sb. or as a pers.n.; or, less likely at this date, with *Norman* as a surn.); *Oswardedole* e.13 (*v.* **dāl**; with the OE masc. pers.n. *Ōsweard*); *the overwhart peece* 1601 (*v.* **ofer-þwart**, **pece**); *Oxedaleput* 1154 × 89 (*v.* **oxa**, **dalr**, **pytt**); *the Parsons Hedge* 1699 (*v.* **persone**, **hecg**); *the parsons hokes* 1601 (*v.* **persone**, **hōc**); *the Parsonidge* ~ 1625, *the Parsonage Hookes* 1638, 1673 (*v.* **personage**, **hōc**; no doubt the same feature as of the previous name); *Pen Close* 1699 (*v.* **penn**); *the Pinfold furlong* 1698 (*v.* **pynd-fald**, **furlang**); *Reeves house* 1699 (at this date, prob. with the surn. *Reeve* (cf. *James le Reve* 1220 RFL) rather than with *reve* 'a reeve, a bailiff'); *the round peece* 1601 (*v.* **round**, **peece**); *the Shorte furlonge* 1625 (*v.* **sc(e)ort**, **furlang**; in *the Lower feild*); *the short meddow* 1601 (*v.* **sc(e)ort**, **mēd** (**mēdwe** obl.sg.)); *the slade* 1625 (*v.* **slæd**); *Smithey lane* 1699 (*v.* **smiðde**); *Smiths Mill* 1700, 1703, 1708 (*v.* **myln**; with the surn. *Smith* of the miller, but it is uncertain whether this was Stemborough Mill or Leire Mill, both *supra*; perh. of the family of *B. Smith* 1762 *supra* and *Susannah Smith* 1792 MI); *Stanfordsiche* e.13 (*v.* **stān**, **ford**, **sīc**); *the Stint* 1698 (*v.* **stynt**); *stockshill* 1601, *Stockhill furlonge* 1625, *Stockshill furlong* 1638 (*v.* **furlang**) (*v.* **hyll**; with **stoc** or **stocc**; note Stockshill in adjoining Dunton Bassett f.ns. (a)); *the Stone Meddow* 1625, 1638 (*v.* **stān**; either 'the stony meadow' or 'the stoned meadow', i.e., one having been cleared of stones to facilitate mowing, cf. *the stone middow* (1601), Lei **2** 19, and *the Stone Meadow* in Glen Parva f.ns. (b) *supra*); *Thirden heades, the Thirden head furlonge* 1625, *Thirden Heads furlong* 1638 (*v.* **furlang**) (*v.* **þridda** (**þriddan** nom.pl.), **hēafod**); *Throulsworth hedg* 1601,

Frolesworth hedge 1625 (*v.* **hecg**; the parish boundary hedge with Frolesworth parish which adjoins to the west); *the Towne bauke* 1625, *Town balk* 1700, 1703, 1708 (*v.* **tūn, balca**); *Tranemere* e.13 (*v.* **trani, mere**[1]); *Underhill* 1699 (*v.* **under, hyll**); *Waterfurrowes* 1673, *Waterfurrows* 1698 (*v.* **wæter, furh** and *Water Furrowes* in Ashby Parva f.ns. (b) *supra*); *Wellecroft(e)* 1212 (*v.* **wella, croft**); *welchmore* 1601, *Welchmore* ~ 1625, *Welshmore gap* 1638, 1673 (*v.* **gap**) (*v.* **wælisc, mōr**[1]); *winmill lease* 1601, *windemill laies* 1625, *windemille* ~, *windmill layes* 1638, *the Windmill Leyes* 1698 (*v.* **wind-mylne, leys**); *Wodeweye* e.13, *Woodway* 1638, 1673, *Woodwaye furlong* 1625 (*v.* **furlang**) (*v.* **wudu, weg**).

Lutterworth

Lvtresvrde 1086 DB

Luttreworth(*e*) 1202 Ass (p), 1220 MHW, 1275 Cl *et passim* to1347, 1355 Pat, *Luttrewrde* 1222 RHug, *Luttrewrth*(*e*) 1232 ib, 1258 Ch, 1286 OSut

Lutreworth(*e*) 1206 Ass (p), 1214 ChR, 1221 Seld, *Lutrewrth* 1243 Cl

Luterworth 1203 Ass (p), 1285 FA, *Luterwrde* 1222 RHug

Lutterworth(*e*) 1236 Fine, 1275 Cl, 1309 *Ferrers et freq*, *Lutterwrth*(*e*) 1231 Cur, 1254 Val, 1274 Ipm, *Lutterwurth* 1243 Fees, 1360 Ipm

Luchterwurth 1243 RGros (p), *Lucterworth* 1331 *Peake*, 1347 *LCDeeds* (p)

Luttirworth 1249 GildR (p), 1316 *LCDeeds*, 1324 Ipm, *Luttirwrthe* 1251 GildR (p)

Lutturworth(*e*) 1274 RGrav (p), 1276 RH *et passim* to 1401 Cl, 1435 Pap

Lytterworth(*e*) 1410 Pat, 1541 MinAccts, 1549 Pat, 1592 AD, *Litterworthe* 1577 LEpis, *Litturworth* 1594 AD

'The enclosure on the stream called the Hlutre', *v.* **worð**. **Hlūtre* ('the clear or pure one', from OE **hlūt(t)or** 'pure, clear, bright') is no doubt an older name for the river Swift whose earliest recorded form is *Swift* 1586 Camden.

INNS AND TAVERNS

ANGEL (lost), *Angel* 1846, 1877 White, *Angel Inn* 1863 ib. BOARD INN (lost), *Board Inn* Kelly 1925. BULL (lost), *Bull* 1846 White. BULL HEAD (lost), *Bull Head* 1699 *Deed*. COACH AND HORSES (lost), *Coach and Horses* 1846, 1863, 1877 White, 1925 Kelly. CROSSING HAND, 1807

Map, *Cross in Hand* 1835 O, 1925 Kelly; a garbled form of the early inn-name Cross Hands (i.e. clasping hands) from a traditional charge in chivalric heraldry, *v.* Cox[1] 24. It becomes Cross in Hand Fm *infra.* CROWN HOTEL (lost) is *the Old Crown Inn* 1830, 1832 *MB et passim* to 1838 *ib*, *Crown Hotel* 1846 White. DENBIGH ARMS, 1826, 1829, 1831 *MB*, 1846, 1863, 1877 White; the Feilding family, the Earls of Denbigh, were lords of the manor of Lutterworth. FOX, 1863, 1877 White, 1925 Kelly, *Fox Inn* 1846 White. GEORGE (lost), *the George* 1606 *Terrier.* GREYHOUND, 1828 *MB*, 1846, 1863, 1877 White, *Greyhound Inn* 1925 Kelly. HIND, *(the) Hind Inn* 1753 *Deed*, 1821 Sale, 1846, 1863 White, *Hind Hotel* 1925 Kelly. PEACOCK (lost), *Peacock* 1846, 1863 White, *Peacock Inn* 1877 ib. QUEEN'S HEAD (lost), *Queen's Head* 1846, 1863, 1877 White. RAM (lost), *Ram* 1846, 1863, 1877 White, 1925 Kelly. ROSE AND CROWN (lost), *Rose and Crown* 1846, 1863, 1877 White, 1925 Kelly. STAG AND PHEASANT (lost), *Stag and Pheasant* 1846, 1863 White. UNICORN (lost), *Unicorn* 1846, 1863 White, 1925 Kelly. VICTORIA (lost), *Victoria* 1846 White. WHEAT SHEAF (lost), *Wheat Sheaf* 1846 White. WHITE HART (lost), *White Hart* 1846, 1863, 1877 White. THE WINNING POST (lost), *the Winning Post* 1762 *Terrier*; a name listed with those from the great open Middle Fd presented in f.ns. (a); it may be that of an unrecorded hostelry on the Bitteswell Rd or record a furlong beside a lost 18th-cent. horse-racing track.

Miscellaneous late town buildings no longer extant:

Bishop Ryder's School 1846, 1863 White; founded in 1815 for poor girls by Henry Ryder, Bishop of Gloucester.

Ely Gate 1790 Nichols, 1846, 1863 White; a house on *Ely lane*, *infra.*

the Goal (sic) 1762 *Terrier*, *v.* **gaole**; the local lock-up.

Hill House 1863, 1877 White.

the Keepers house 1629 Nichols; earlier recorded as *the kepers house* 1557 Pat, *v.* **kepere**. The early Glebe Terriers for the parish indicate that James I held land in Lutterworth (as *the kinges ground* 1606 *Terrier*, *the kinges maiesties landes* e.17 *ib*). The Keeper may have been a royal park or woodland guardian. Note *le Parke* (1640) in f.ns. (b).

Sherrier's School and Almshouses 1846, 1863, 1877 White, *v.* **almeshous**; founded by Edward Sherrier in 1730.

Union Workhouse 1846, 1863, 1877 White, *v.* **workhouse**; a Poor Law institute. From about 1815, groups or unions of parishes combined to build workhouses for the poor, the aged and for orphaned children, hence here *Union* Workhouse.

The following names have not survived or have not been related with certainty to modern thoroughfares:

Ashby way c.1720 *Terrier*; the road to Ashby Parva which lies 2 miles to the north- west.

Back Lane 1863 White, *v.* **back**.

Bakehouse lane 1846 White, 1853 *Deed*, 1863, 1877 White, *v.* **bæc-hous**.

Beast Market 1846, 1863, 1877 White, *v.* **beste**, **market**.

the Coalepitt way 1679 *Terrier*, (*the*) *Colepitt way* 1703, c.1720, 1745 *ib*, *the Coal pitt way* 1721,1724 *ib*, *the Coal Pit Way* 1762 *ib*, *v.* **col-pytt**; a route for the transportation of pit coal from the Bedworth area of Warwks. Note its continuation as Coal Pit Lane across the county boundary in adjacent Willey parish.

Cow lane 1706 Nichols, *v.* **cū**.

Dead Lane 1704 *Deed*, *v.* **dēad**; prob. a lane with a dead-end, cf. Dead Lane, Lei 1 30 and Ru 104.

Dixon's Square 1863 White, *v.* **squar(e)**; with the surn. *Dixon*, cf. *Thomas Dixon* 1826 Census, *Elizabeth Dixon* 1828 ib and *Ada Dixon* 1875 ib of Lutterworth.

Ely lane 1679, c.1720 *Terrier et passim* to 1863, 1877 White, *Elelane* 1709 *Terrier*; this presumably contains the surn. *Ely* (derived from both OFr *Elie* 'Elijah' and the Cambridgeshire town of this name).

Greyhound lane 1846 White, the location of the Greyhound hostelry *supra*.

Hog lane 1674, 1709, 1724, 1745, 1762 *Terrier*, 1835 O, 1877 White, *the hogg lane* 1721 *Terrier*, *v.* **hogg**.

London road 1846, 1863 White.

Shambles lane 1863 White, *v.* **scamol**; a former butchers' quarter.

Shortes way 1601 *Terrier*; it is *Shorts lane* 1674, 1709 *ib et passim* to1762 *ib*; with the surn. *Short*.

Wickliff(e) terrace 1846, 1863, 1877 White, *v.* **terrace**; named after John Wycliffe, parish priest of Lutterworth 1374–84, cf. Wycliffe Fm *infra*.

Worship street 1846, 1863 White.

AUBURN PLACE, ~ ~ LODGE, *v.* **loge**; with the surn. *Auburn*, from Aubourn in Lincs. (cf. Auburn Rd in Blaby *supra*). BAKER ST. BANK ST, 1877 White. BITTESWELL RD, 1846, 1877 White; it is *Bitteswell waye* 1606 *Terrier*, *Bitchwell Way* 1674 *ib*, *Bitteswell Way* 1762 *ib*, *v.* **weg**; Bitteswell lies one mile to the north-west. BOUNDARY RD marks the eastern limit of the town's built-up area. CHURCH ST, *the Churche*

Street(*e*) 1601, 1606 *Terrier, the Chirch street* 1674 *ib, the Church Street*(*e*) 1709, 1721, 1724, 1745 *ib, Church Street* 1846, 1877 White, *v.* St Mary's Church *infra.* Note also *Church lane* 1846 White. COVENTRY RD, 1846, 1863, 1877 White; it is the principal road westwards, Coventry lying 12 miles to the south-west. CROSS IN HAND FM, *Cross-in-hand Farm* 1846, 1863 White, *v.* Crossing Hand (Inns and Taverns) *supra.* THE FIELDS, cf. *Lutterworth fields* 1846, 1863 White. GEORGE ST is *George's lane* 1804 Nichols, *George lane* 1846, 1863 White and *George street* 1877 ib; named from the former *George* (hostelry) *supra.* GILMORTON RD, Gilmorton lying 2½ miles to the north-east. GLADSTONE ST marks the north-eastward expansion of the town in the late 19th cent.; named from William Gladstone, prime minister 1868–74, 1880–5, 1886 and 1892–4. GLEBE FM, 1925 Kelly, *v.* **glebe**; it is *Lutterworth Lodge* 1835 O, *v.* **loge**. GLEBE FARM COTTAGE. HIGH ST, 1846, 1863, 1877 White, *High strete* 1589 AD, *v.* **hēah**[1], **strēt**. LEADERS FM, 1925 Kelly, cf. *Thomas Leader, farmer* 1863 White. LEICESTER RD is *Leic' way*(*e*) 1601, 1606 *Terrier, Leicestar way* 1674 *ib, Leicester Way* 1709, c.1720 *et passim* to 1762 *ib, v.* **weg**; Leicester lies 12 miles to the north. (Note the significance of *Leicester Lane End* as of a field-name type, in f.ns. (b) *infra.*) LODGE MILL SPINNEYS, *Lodge Mill* 1610 Nichols, 1835 O, *Lodge Mills* 1631 ib, 1846, 1863, 1877 White, *v.* **loge, myln, spinney**. LUTTERWORTH HALL, 1925 Kelly, *v.* **hall**. LUTTERWORTH HOUSE, 1863 White. MARKET ST. MILL FM, 1925 Kelly; at the site of *the Spittle Mills* 1631 Nichols, *Spittle Mill* 1863 White, *v.* **myln** and St John's Hospital *infra.* MILORD'S FM (LORD'S FM 2½"). MOORBARNS. *Morebarne* 1532 Nichols, 1601, e.17 *Terrier* 1610 Nichols, 1658 *Deed,* 1724 *Terrier, the Moorbarne* 1617 LML, 1629 Sale, *Moorebarne* 1663 *Deed,* 1674 *Terrier, Moore Barne* 1709 *ib, Morebarn* 1721, 1745 *ib, Morebarns* 1846, 1863, 1877 White, *Moorbarns* 1849 *TA; Morebarnfeildes* 1557 Pat, *Morebarne feilde* 1576 BM, *the Morebarne field* 1601 *Terrier, Moorebarnefield* 1629 Sale, *the Nether ~, the Upper Moorebarne field* 1629 ib (*v.* **feld**; one of the great open-fields of the township), *Moorebarne ground* e.17 *Terrier* (*v.* **grund**), *moorebarne pastures* 1606 *ib, Moorbarn Pastures* 1630 Nichols (*v.* **pasture**), *v.* **mōr**[1], **bern**. MOORBARNS FM, *Moorebarne Farm* 1878 Sale. MOORBARNS LANE. OAKBERRY FM. THE OAKS. OXFORD ST, 1846, 1863, 1877 White. PADGE HALL, *v.* **hall**; prob. with the surn. *Padge, Pagge,* cf. *Robert Pagge* 1872 Census, *Charles Pagge* and *Henry Pagge* 1873 ib, all of Lutterworth. THE RECTORY, 1877 White, 1925 Kelly, *v.* **rectory**; earlier is *the parsonage dwellinge house* 1601 *Terrier, the parsonage howse* 1606 *ib, the Parsonage House* c,1720, 1762 *ib, v.* **personage**. REGENT ST, 1877

White; the date of this street-name's origin is uncertain, but such names were given in honour of the Prince Regent (afterwards King George IV, who reigned from 1820 to 1830). With Oxford St *supra*, perhaps a transferred street-name from London. RIDDLESDEN FM, ~ ~ COTTAGES, probably with the surn. *Riddlesden*, from the Yorks. Riddlesden, *v.* YW **4** 172. RYE HILL, (*the*) *Rye hill* 1601, 1606 *Terrier et passim* to 1745 *ib*, 1835 O, 1925 Kelly, *Rie hill* 1606, 1745 *Terrier*, *the Righ Hill* 1674 *ib*, *Ryhill* 1709 *ib*, *the Royhill* c.1720 *ib*, cf. *Rye hill farm* 1925 Kelly, *v.* **ryge**, **hyll**. ST JOHN'S HOSPITAL, *St Johns Hospital* 1631 Nichols, *St Johns Hospital or St Johns Chapel* 1699 ib; it is *the Spittle* 1606 *Terrier*, *le Spittle* 1641 Nichols and is earlier recorded as *Hospitalis Sancti Johannis de Luthrewrth* 1242 RGros, *Hospitalis de Lutterwrth'* 1254 Val, *hospitalis Johannis Baptiste* 1341, 1350, 1391 *Pat*, *Hospitale de Lutterworthe*, *Hospitali Sancti Johannis iuxta Lutterworth* 1546 AAS, *v.* **hospital**. Minor earthworks are all that remain at the site of the hospital founded in the reign of King John (1199–1216) by Nicholas de Verdun. ST MARY'S CHURCH, *the Churche* 1606 *Terrier*, *the Church* c.1720, 1724, 1745 *ib*, *Lutterworth Church (St Mary)* 1846, 1863, 1877 White; earlier recorded as *ecclesie de Luttreworth* 1220 MHW, 1318 *Pat*, ~ *de Lutterworth* 1322, 1348, 1374 *ib*. SILVERSIDE. TOLL GATE HO., *v.* **toll-gate**; at the parish boundary on Bitteswell Rd. VICTORIA FM. WESTOVER. WOOD BRIDGE, ~ ~ FM, ~ ~ HILL (2½"), *Woodbrigge* 1601, 1606 *Terrier*, *the Wood Brigg* 1606, 1679 *ib*, ~ ~ *Bridg* 1674 *ib*, (*the*) *Wood Bridge* 1674, 1724, 1745 *ib*, 1925 Kelly, *v.* **wudu**, **brycg**; on the Coventry Rd *supra*. THE WOODEN BUNGALOW. WOODMARKET, *Wood market* 1785 *Deed*, 1846, 1863, 1877 White, 1925 Kelly, *Woodmarkett end* c.1720 (*v.* **ende**), *v.* **market**. WOODWAY RD, *Wood waye* 1601, 1606 *Terrier*, (*the*) *Wood Way* e.17, 1674 *ib et passim* to 1745 *ib*, 1790 *Map*, *v.* **wudu**, **weg**. WYCLIFFE FM, named from John Wycliffe (c.1330–84), religious reformer and producer of the first English translation of the Bible. He was the parish priest of Lutterworth from 1374 until his death.

Street-names in modern urban developments:

AVERY CL. CENTRAL AVE. CRESCENT RD. DENBIGH PLACE. DE VERDON RD. DUNLEY WAY. ELMHIRST RD. FEILDING WAY. FERRERS RD. GLEBE AVE. MAINO CRESC. MERITON RD. NEW ST. ORCHARD CL. RYDERWAY. ST MARY'S RD. SHERRIER WAY. SPENCER RD. STATION RD. SWIFT WAY. WICLIF WAY.

FIELD-NAMES

In (a), forms dated 1760 and 1807 are Nichols; those dated 1762 are
Terrier; 1790 are *Map*; 1835 are O; 1900 are Sale. Forms throughout
dated 1275 are Cl; those dated 1316, 1360 and 1640 are Ipm; 1403 are
ELiW; 1557 are Pat; 1601, 1606, e.17, 1674, 1679, 1709, c.1720, 1721,
1724 and 1745 are *Terrier*; 1629, 1664, 1674 and 1699 are Nichols.

(a) Bagshaw's Piece 1790 (*v.* **pece**; with the surn. *Bagshaw*); Ban Leys 1762,
1790 (1679, *Banleyes* 1709, *Bandleys* 1721, 1724, 1745; earlier it is *Bandlandes*
1601, 1606, e.17, *v.* **bēan**, **land**; the generic was replaced by **leys**); Between the
Brooks 1762, 1790 (*Betwene* ~ ~ 1601, *Betweene the Brookes* 1606, e.17, 1709,
c.1720, 1724, *Between(e) the Brooks* 1679, 1721, 1745, *Betwixt the Brokes* 1674, *v.*
betwēonan, **betwixt**, **brōc**; a furlong so called); Bitteswell Plank 1762, 1790
(*Bitteswell planke* 1606, (*at*) *Bichwell Planke* 1674, *v.* **planke**; Bitteswell parish
adjoins to the north-west); Bittsby Corner 1790 (*v.* **corner**; a small nook of
Lutterworth parish adjoins Bittesby parish beside Watling Street); Breach 1762
(1674, 1709 *et passim* to 1745, *le breache, the breach next to the towne* (*v.* **tūn**)
1601, *the breach* e.17, cf. *breach furlonge* 1606 (*v.* **furlang**)), Under Breach 1790
(1679) (*v.* **brēc**); Brier Furlong 1790 (*bryer* ~ 1606, *Bryar furlonge* e.17, *v.* **brēr**,
furlang); Butt Leys 1762 (c.1720, 1721, 1745, *Butleyes* 1709, 1724, *the Buttes* 1601,
1606, e.17, *Bitteswell buttes* 1601 (Bitteswell parish adjoins to the north-west), (*the*)
Butt Holes 1674, 1679, c.1720, 1721, 1724, 1745, *Butholes* 1709 (*v.* **hol**[1]), *v.* **butte**,
leys); Church Hadeland 1762, ~ Headland 1790 ((*the*) *Church hadland* 1601, 1606
et passim to 1745, *the Chirch Hadland* 1674, *the Church hadeland* c.1720, *the
Church hadley* 1721, 1724, *v.* **hēafod-land** (replaced late on occasion by **headley**),
Church Mdw 1790 ((*the*) *Churche meadowe* 1601, 1606, e.17, *the Chirche Meadow*
1674), Church Meadow Furlong 1762, 1790 (*v.* **furlang**), Church Slade 1762, 1790
(1601, 1606 *et passim* to 1745, *Church* ~ 1601, *the Chirche Slade* 1674, *v.* **slæd**) (*v.*
St Mary's Church *supra*); Cliper Pole (sic) 1790 (*Clippole* 1721, 1724, 1745, cf.
Cleypoole leyes 1601, 1606, *Cleypule* ~ e.17, *Clippol leyes* 1679, 1709, 1724, *Clipple*
~ 1709, *Clippole leys* 1745, *Clipwell Lease* 1674, *Clippwell Leys* c.1720 (*v.* **leys**), *v.*
clǣg, **pōl**[1]); Clippit Leys 1790 (*v.* **leys**) (*Clea Pitts* 1674, *v.* **clǣg**, **pytt**); Coal Pitt
Furlong 1762 (*v.* **furlang**), Coalpit Leys 1790 (*v.* **leys**) (*v.* **col-pytt**); the Common
1762 (c.1720, *the comon* 1606, 1674, *v.* **commun**); Cow Hades 1762, 1790, Little
Cowhade 1790 (*Cow hades* 1606, 1674 *et passim* to 1745, (*the*) *Cow haden* 1601,
e.17, *cowhadens* 1606 (with an archaic -*en* pl.), cf. *Cow(e) haden Gore* 1601, e.17
(*v.* **gāra**), *v.* **cū**, **hēafod**); Crabtree Corner 1762, 1790 (1679, 1709, c.1720, 1724,
Crabbtree Corner 1745, *v.* **crabtre**, **corner**); Cunnery 1762, Middle Cunnery 1790
(*le Connygree* 1601, *the Conerye* e.17, *Cunnigrye* 1606, *Cunery* 1674, *Connery*
1679, 1709, 1724, *Cunnery* c.1720, 1721, 1745), Cunnery Hades 1762 (c.1720, *v.*
hēafod), Cunnery Lands 1790 (*v.* **land**), Cunnery Leys 1790 (*v.* **leys**) (*v.* **coningre**);
Cunny Hills 1762 (*Cunny holes* 1606, 1674, *Cunny hills* c.1720, *v.* **coni**, **hol**[1]);
Dunford Hill 1762, 1790 (1601, e.17, 1674 *et passim* to1745, *Donford hill furlonge*
1606 (*v.* **furlang**), *v.* **dūn**, **ford**, **hyll**); Dunton Wound (sic) 1762 (1674, 1679 *et
passim* to 1745, *Dunton Woung* 1606, *v.* **vangr**; either with the rare surn. *Dunton* of
a family originally from Dunton Bassett which lies 3 miles to the north, or indicating

an unrecorded holding by Dunton township in Lutterworth); the Elms 1762 (*v.* **elm**); Ely Lane Fd 1762 (*v.* **feld**; one of the great open-fields of the township, earlier called *Thornborow Feild* and *Whitehill Feild*, *v. Ely lane*, *supra*); Fifteen Lands Piece 1762 (*v.* **land**, **pece**; an enclosure comprising 15 former 'lands' or selions of a former great open-field); Hawks Nest 1762 ((*the*) *Hawkesnest* 1601, 1606, 1674, (*the*) *Hawks Nest* 1629, 1679, 1721, 1724, 1745, *the Hawkes Nest* 1679, 1721, 1724, 1745, *Haukes nest* 1709, c.1720, *v.* **hafoc**, **nest**); the Heath Furlong 1762 (1679, 1709, 1721, 1724, 1745, *the Heath* 1606, 1679, 1709, 1721, 1724, 1745, cf. *del Heth* 1360 (p), *v.* **hǣð**, **furlang**); Hey Dykes 1762, Hay Dike 1790 (*Hey ditche* 1601, *Heydikes* 1606, *Hay Dikes* 1679, 1709, 1724, 1745, *v.* **(ge)hæg**, **dīc**, **dík**); The Hill 1900; Hog Lane End 1762 ((*the*) *Hog lane end* 1674, 1709, 1724, 1745, *the hogglane end* 1721 (*v.* **lane-ende** and *Hog lane*, *supra*); Home Cl 1762 (*v.* **home**); Langlands 1762, Longlands 1790 (*Longelandes*, *Longelondes* 1601, *Lange Landes* e.17, *Langlandes* 1606, *Langlands* 1674, 1679 *et passim* to 1745), Under Langlands 1762, Under Longlands 1790 (*v.* **under**), Langlands Head 1762 (1674, 1679, c.1720, *v.* **hēafod**) (*v.* **lang**[1], **land**); Leicester Lane End 1762 (1679, 1709 *et passim* to 1745, *Leic' lane end* 1606, *Lestar lane End* 1674, *Leicester lane* c.1720, 1721, 1724, 1745, *v.* **lane-ende**, **lane**; presum. not to be identified with *Leicester Way* (*v.* Leicester Rd *supra*), but a lane leading to it); Little Moore 1762 (1606, 1709, *litle more* 1601, *Littlemore* 1721, 1724, 1745, cf. *Litle more head* 1601, *Litle Moore Head* 1674, *Littlemoore Head* 1709 (*v.* **hēafod**), (*att*) *Litlemoore hedg*, *Little moore hedg* c.1720 (prob. with **hecg**; but *v. Wood Bridge Hedge* in f.ns. (b)), *Littlemore meadow* 1721, 1724, 1745), Little Moore Slade 1762 (*v.* **slæd**) (*v.* **lȳtel**, **mōr**[1]); Little Ward 1762 (1606, e.17, 1679 *et passim* to 1745, *the litle wade* 1557, *Litle Wade* 1601, *the Little Wade* 1629, *les Little Wades* 1640, *Litle warde* 1674), Littleward Furlong 1790 (*v.* **furlang**), Littleward Leys 1790 (*v.* **leys**), Little Ward Mdw 1762 (c.1720) (*v.* **lȳtel**, **(ge)wæd**); Long Furlong 1762 ((*the*) *Longe furlonge* 1601, 1606, *the long furlong* c.1720, 1721, 1724, 1745, *v.* **lang**[1], **furlang**; in *Whitehill Field*); Lugdole 1762 (*Luggloades* 1606, *Lugloades* e.17, *Lugdoles* 1674, cf. *Luglode Mead* 1623, 1629 (*v.* **mēd**), *v.* **(ge)lād** 'a ford, a passage over a river'; the specific appears to be a pre-English river-name borrowed into OE as **Lugge*, from the Indo-European base **lewk*- 'gleam, light' (cf. Greek *leukós* 'brilliant', Welsh *llug* 'light, radiance'), and since the OE name of the river Swift was **Hlūtre* 'the clear, pure, bright one' (from OE *hlūt(t)or* 'clear, bright), it is poss. that the Romano-British name of the river upon which Lutterworth stands was adopted and adapted by the Anglo-Saxons. The generic of the f.n. *Luglode* was either metathesized in the later 17th cent. (*lode* > *dole*) or *dole* represents **dāl** in a distinct compound with *Lugge*); the Middle Fd 1762 (1679, 1721, 1724, 1745, *the Middle Feild*(*e*) 1601, e.17, 1709, *the midle feild* 1606, *the Midell Feild* 1674, *the Middle Field* c.1720, 1724, *v.* **middel**, **feld**; one of the great open-fields of the township); Nelsons ~ 1762, Nelson's Cl 1790 (with the surn. *Nelson*); New Gate Furlong 1790 (*v.* **nīwe**, **furlang**; with either **geat** or **gata**); Newton Slade 1762 (1601, 1606 *et passim* to 1745, *Nuton Slade* 1674, *v.* **slæd**; *Newton* is prob. a surn. rather than representing a lost farmstead (as the latter, *v.* **nīwe**, **tūn**)); Old Slade 1762, 1790 (*the Old Slade* 1601, e.17 *et passim* to 1745, *the olde slade*, *tholde slade* 1606, *the oulde slade* 1674, *v.* **ald**, **slæd**); Lower ~, Middle ~, Road Paddock 1900 (*v.* **paddock**); Parsons Leys 1790 (1724, *the parsons leys* 1606, c.1720, *the parson leyes* e.17, *the Parson Lease* 1674, *the Parsons Leyes* 1709, *the Parson Leys* 1721, 1745), Parsons Leys Piece 1762 (*v.* **pece**), Parsons Leys Side 1762 (*v.* **sīde**) (*v.*

persone, **leys**); Pedlars Cross 1790 (*Pedlers Crosse* 1601, *the Pedlers Crosse upon Wood Way* e.17, *v.* **pedlere**, **cros** and Woodway *supra*; a site for pedlars' trade); Pole Ground 1790 (*v.* **pōl**[1], **grund**); Primrose Hill 1835 (*v.* **primerole**; this is poss. a transferred name from Camden in London, but the primrose is common in woodland and shady places); Long ~, Quinckoe 1762, Short ~, Quincux 1790 (*quynkote* 1601, *quinco*(*w*) 1606, *Quinkolme* e.17, *Quinco* 1679, *Quincoe* 1709, c.1720, 1721, 1724, 1745, *v.* **cwene**, **cot**); Rattlers Hedge 1762, ~ ~ Leys 1790 (*v.* **leys**) (with the surn. *Rattler*, from ME *ratyller* 'a stutterer'; *hedge* compounded with *leys* suggests **edisc** rather than **hecg**, *v. Wood Bridge Hedge* in f.ns. (b)); Redmore Pitt 1762, Redman's Pit 1790 (*Redmore* 1601, *Reedemoore* c.1720, *Redmore Pitt* 1606, 1724, 1745, ~ *Pit* 1679, *Redmoor*(*e*) *Pitt* 1709, 1721, cf. *Redmore furland* (sic) 1601, ~ *furlonge* e.17 (*v.* **furlang**), *v.* **hrēod**, **mōr**[1], **pytt**); Rush Pitts 1762 (*Thurspitte, Thurspittes* 1601, *Thrushpittes* 1606, *Rushpitts* 1674, 1709, c.1720, 1724, 1745, *Rushpits* 1721, *v.* **þyrs**, **pytt**); St John's Well 1807 (*v.* **wella** and St John's Hospital *supra*); Salter's Grave 1790 (*Salters Grave* 1679, 1709, 1721, 1745, cf. *Salters Meare* 1629 (*v.* **(ge)mǣre**); with **grāf** or **græf** and perh. with the surn. *Salter* rather than with **saltere**, although (*ge*)*mǣre* here may have been used in its sense 'boundary road' and so perh. part of a salters' route); Sand Piece 1790 (*v.* **sand**, **pece**); Short Furlong 1790 (*v.* **sc(e)ort**, **furlang**); Short's ~ ~, Shorts Lane End 1762 (*Shorts Lane End* 1674, 1721, 1724, 1745, *v.* **lane-ende** and *Shortes way, supra*); the Spital Fields 1760, Spittle Bridge 1835 (*v.* **brycg**), Spittle Leys 1790 (*v.* **leys**) (cf. *the Spittle ground* 1601, 1606, ~ ~ *groundes* e.17 (*v.* **grund**), *the Spittle Lands* 1699 (*v.* **land**), *v.* **hospital** and St John's Hospital *supra*); the Street Fd 1762 (1679, 1721, 1724, (*the*) *Streete feild*(*e*) 1601, 1606, 1709, c.1720, *the East feild commonly called the Street feild* e.17, *the Streat Feild* 1674, *v.* **feld**; one of the great open-fields), Street Furlong 1762, ~ Furlongs 1790 (*Street furlonge* 1601, (*the*) *Streete furlonge* 1606, e.17, *Street furlonge next unto the Streete* e.17, (*the*) *Street furlong* 1679, 1709, 1721, 1724, 1745, *v.* **furlang**) (*the Street*(*e*) 1601, 1606, e.17, *Streat* 1674, *v.* **strēt**; all alluding to Watling Street); Ten Lands 1790 (*v.* **tēn**, **land**; a close consisting of ten 'lands' or selions of a former great open-field); Ten Leys 1790 (*v.* **tēn**, **leys**; ten units of grassland), Ten Leys Furlong 1762 (*v.* **furlang**); Tenters 1790 (*v.* **tentour**; a close with frames for tenting cloth); Thurnborough 1762 (*Thurneborowe* 1601, *Thunborough*(*e*) 1606, 1679, *Thornborow* 1674, *Thunborrow* 1709, c.1720, 1721, *Thundborrow* 1724, *Thurnborow* 1745, *Thornborow Feild* 1674, *Thunborough Field* 1679 (*v.* **feld**; one of the great open-fields, earlier called *the East feild*, later *Whitehill Feild* and Ely Lane Fd), *Thunborough Field leyes* 1679 (*v.* **leys**), *v.* **þyrne**, **berg**); Townsend Furlong 1790 (*v.* **tūn**, **ende**, **furlang**); Turdills 1762, Turhill 1790 (*Turfe, Turfedale* 1601, *Turdale* e.17, *Turdales* 1606, 1674, *Turfill* 1679, *Turfield* 1721, 1724, 1745), Turdills Hill 1762 (*Turfeild hill* 1709, 1724, *Turfield hill* 1721, 1745, *v.* **hyll**), Turhill Leys 1790 (*v.* **leys**) (*v.* **turf**, **dalr**); the Tythe Yard 1762 (*v.* **tēoða**, **geard**; belonging to *the parsonage howse*); the Warren 1807 (1664, *v.* **wareine**); Wash Brook Furlong 1762 ((*the*) *Washbrook*(*e*) *furlong* 1709, 1721, 1745, *v.* **brōc**, **furlang**; with **wæsce** or **wæsse**); Water Laggs 1762, Far ~, Waterlag 1790 (*Waterlagges* 1601, 1606, e.17, *Wa*(*r*)*tar Lags* 1674, *Waterlaggs* 1679, c.1720, *Waterlags* 1721, 1724, 1745, *over waterlaggs* c.1720 (*v.* **ofer**[3]), *v.* **wæter**, **lagge**); Watery Pitt 1762 (*v.* **wæterig**, **pytt**); Middle ~ ~, White Hill 1762 (*Whighthill* 1606, *Whitehill* 1674, 1679 *et passim* to 1745, *Short whitehill* c.1720, *Whitehill Field* 1709, 1721, 1724, 1745 (*v.* **feld**; one of the great open-fields, earlier called *the East feild* and *Thornborow Feild*), *v.* **wiht**,

hyll); Willey Plank 1762 (*Willy plancke* c.1720, *v.* **planke**), Willey Way 1790 (Willey is the adjacent parish to the west, in Warwks. beyond Watling Street); Windmill Pool 1762 (*Winmill Poole* c.1720, *v.* **pōl**[1]; poss. with **wind-mylne**, but this f.n. may be a later development of *Wymonpoole, infra*, a pool not being usually associated with a windmill); (at) Wintertons Gate 1762 (*v.* **geat**; with the surn. *Winterton*; a furlong so called); Wood Bridge Slade 1760, 1790 (*v.* **slæd** and Wood Bridge *supra*); Wood Way Furlong 1762 (*v.* **furlang** and Woodway Rd *supra*).

(b) (*at*) *Barnaby Gate* 1721, 1724, 1745 (*v.* **geat**; with the surn. *Barnaby*, the English form of the pers.n. Barnabas); *Berne Meadow* 1601, *Barnmeadowe furlonge* e.17 (*v.* **furlang**), *Barnemeadowe Gate* 1606, *Barn Meadow Gate* 1674, 1709, ~ ~ *Yate* 1679 (*v.* **bern**, **mēd** (**mēdwe** obl.sg.), **geat**); *Bitteswell Brook*(*e*) 1709, 1724, 1745, *Bitchwell brooke* c.1720, *Bittiswel Brook* 1721 (*v.* **brōc**), *Bitteswell Towne End* 1679, *Bitteswell Towns end* 1709, 1721, 1724, 1745, *Bitchwell Townesend* c.1720 (*v.* **tūn**, **ende**), *Bitteswell towne side* 1606, *Bichwell Townes Side* 1674 (*v.* **sīde**) (Bitteswell parish adjoins to the north-west); *le Bonde end* 1403 (*v.* **bóndi**, **ende**); *le Buttocks* 1640 (*v.* **buttuc**; used here of a pair of rounded slopes); *Caves hadland* 1709, 1724, 1745 (*v.* **hēafod-land**; cf. *John Cave* 1674 *Terrier*, *Sir John Cave* 1713 Nichols); (*to*) *Chattins Gate* c.1720 (*v.* **geat**; with the surn. *Chetwin*); *the Church meadow* c.1720, *the Church slade* 1601, 1745 (*v.* **slæd**) (*v.* St Mary's Church *supra*); *Clarkes willowes* 1606 (*v.* **wilig**), *Clarks Close* 1629 (with the surn. *Clark*); (*upon*) *Cley* 1601 (*v.* **clǣg**); *the Common Baulk* 1721, 1724, 1745, *comon baulke end* 1606, *Comon Balke End* 1674 (*v.* **ende**) (*v.* **commun**, **balca**); *Cow broades* 1601 (*v.* **brode**), *the Cow Comon* 1709, ~ ~ *Common* 1721, 1724, 1745 (*v.* **commun**) (*v.* **cū**); *Coxe Furs* 1606 (*v.* **fyrs**; with the surn. *Cox*); *the Crosse* e.17 (*v.* **cros**; perh. to be identified with Pedlars Cross *supra*); *Crisp's Hadland* 1721 (*v.* **hēafod-land**; with the surn. *Crisp*, cf. *William Crisp* 1762 *Terrier*); (*the meadow called*) *Daynell or Dagnell* 1629 (perh. 'Dagga's spring', *v.* **wella**; with the OE masc. pers.n. *Dagga* (*Daggan* gen.sg.)); *Deanes* 1606, *Deane Furlong*(*e*) 1606, 1679, *Dane Furlong* 1709, 1721, 1724, 1745 (*v.* **furlang**) (*v.* **denu**); *the Great* ~, *the Little Dockey Dole* 1629 (*v.* **docce**, **-ig**[3], **dāl**); *the East feild* 1601, e.17, *the Easte feilde* 1606 (*v.* **ēast**, **feld**; one of the great open-fields, later called *Thornborow Field* and *Whitehill Field*); *Ely Lane Leyes* 1679, *Elelane leyes* 1709, *Ely Lane Leys* c.1720, 1721, 1745, *Eelylane Leyes* 1724 (*v.* **leys** and *Ely lane, supra*); *North flate* 1601 (*v.* **norð**), *the Over flat* 1601, *over Flatt next the Streete* e.17 (*v.* **uferra**; with reference to Watling Street) (*v.* **flat**); *flythill slade* 1601 (*v.* (**ge**)**flit**, **hyll**, **slæd**); *the foreyard* 1606 (*v.* **fore**, **geard**; of *the parsonage howse, v.* The Rectory *supra*); *the George yardes end* 1606 (*v.* **geard**, **ende**; the yard of the *George Inn, supra*); (*by*) *Gores hedge* 1709, 1721, 1724, 1745 (*v.* **hecg**; cf. *Thomas Gore* 1630 Nichols and *Mr Gore* 1724 *Terrier*); (*the*) *Gravell pittes* 1601, 1606, *Gravill pittes* e.17 (*v.* **gravel**, **pytt**); *the greate barne* 1606 (*v.* **bern**; the property of *the parsonage howse*); *the Hall Orchard*(*e*) 1557, 1629 (*v.* **hall**, **orceard**; with reference to an early hall); *Heath Slade* 1674 (*v.* **hǣð**, **slæd**); *Hie Thorne* 1606 (*v.* **hēah**[1], **þorn**); *the hogg hole* c.1720 (*v.* **hogg**, **hol**[1]); *le Hoppeyard* 1640 (*v.* **hop-yard**); *the Horse Common* 1679, 1709 *et passim* to 1745 (*v.* **hors**, **commun**); *Horse Faire Leyes* 1679 (*v.* **hors**, **feire**, **leys**); *Howbeck* 1679 (*v.* **bekkr**; prob. with **hol**[2] rather than with **hōh** or **haugr**); *Mr Inshleys Hedge* 1674 (cf. *Richard Insley* 1606 *Terrier*); *Jones* ~ 1679, *Joneses leyes* 1709, *Jones's ley*(*e*)*s* 1721, 1745, *Joaneses Leyes* 1724 (*v.* **leys**; with the surn. *Jones*); *Kerbyes hadland* 1709 (in the possession of *Tho. Kerby* 1709 *Terrier*), *Thomas Kerbyes hadeland* c.1720, *Jonath.*

Kerbys ~ 1721, *(Tho.) Kerby's* ~ 1724, *(Mr) Kerby's Hadland* 1745 (*v.* **hēafod-land**), *the Kerbys Pingell* 1674, *Kerbys Spindle* (sic) c.1720 (*v.* **pingel**) (note also *Thomas Kerby* 1630 Nichols); *the kinges ground* 1606, *the kinges maiesties landes* e.17 (*v.* **grund, land**; alluding to King James I); *the Kings Mills* 1724, 1745 (*v.* **myln**; with reference to King George I and King George II); *Loges* 1275 (*v.* **loge**); *the Long breache* 1601 (*v.* **lang**[1], **brēc**); *Longe forde* 1606, 1674 (*v.* **lang**[1], **ford**); *Longeleyes* 1316, 1360 (*v.* **lang**[1], **lǣs**); *the Lynche* 1601 (*v.* **hlinc**); *Malt mill* 1684 (*v.* **malt-mylne**); *the Meadows* c.1720; *the Middle path* 1601 (*v.* **middel, pæð**); *the Great Mill Meadow* 1629, *the Mill Meadow* 1674, *Mill piece* 1721, 1724, 1745 (*v.* **pece**), *Mylne hedland* 1601 (*v.* **hēafod-land**) (*v.* **myln**); *Moreknole* 1601 (*v.* **mōr**[1], **cnoll**); *Nottestone* 1601 (earlier forms are needed; perh. a lost farmstead (*v.* **tūn**), with the OE masc. pers.n. *Hnott* in the possessive case); *le Parke* 1640 (*v.* **park**); *Puleley* 1601 (*v.* **pōl**[1], **ley**[2]); *the Rams Close* 1629 (*v.* **ramm**); *Ratlifs Hedge* 1674 (*v.* **hecg**; with the surn. *Ratliff(e)*, *Ratcliff(e)* of a family poss. originally from Ratcliffe Culey, 16 miles to the north-west or Ratcliffe on the Wreake, 20 miles to the north); *the Ricke yard* 1606 (*v.* **reke-yard**); *Ryholm* 1601 (*v.* **ryge, holmr**); *Rylie lane ley*es 1606 (*v.* **lane, leys**; *Rylie* is either the surn. *Riley* or an early toponym meaning 'clearing where rye is grown', *v.* **ryge, lēah**); *Scotford slade* 1601, e.17 (*v.* **ford, slæd**; the prototheme could be **scot** ' a payment', indicating a ford available only by payment of a toll, or the OE masc. pers.n. *Scot(t)*, in either case with initial Scand *sk-*; OE **Scot(t)** 'a Scot' seems unlikely here, but note *Scotosyke* (Lei **4** 267)); *Sidmeadowe* 1606 (*v.* **sīde**); *the Slade* 1606 (*v.* **slæd**); *Smallowe, Smalley furlonge* 1601 (*v.* **furlang**) (these belong together, *v.* **smæl, hlāw**); *(at) Snayles gate* 1606, *Snealesgate furlonge* 1601 (*v.* **furlang**) (*v.* **geat**; with the surn. *Snail*, an original by-name from OE *snægel* 'a snail', once given to the slow or indolent); *the Stone meadowe in the East feild, the Stone meadowe in the Street feild* 1601 (*v.* **stān**; either 'stony meadow' or 'meadow cleared of stones'; by removing surface stones, the available area for grazing was greatly increased and allowed sunlight to reach the grass leaves; it encouraged the pasture to renew itself more rapidly for the cattle's all-important 'first bite' in spring and early summer, as well as facilitating mowing, *v. the stone middow*, Lei **2** 19); *the sydling bauck* 1601, *Sidling bauke* 1606 (*v.* **sīdling, balca**); *Weightmans Pool(e)* 1709, 1721, 1724, 1745 (*v.* **pōl**[1]; note *Ruth Weightman* 1707 Terrier, *William Weightman* 1721 *ib*, *Rich. Weightman* 1724 *ib* and *John Weightman* 1745 *ib*, all of Lutterworth); *Wood Bridge Hedge* 1606, *woodbridge hedge* c.1720 (compounded with a preceding surn., *hedge* in Glebe Terriers usually indicates a planted property-boundary, but here, the word may be a developed and disguised **edisc** (or even **etisc**), naming land beside the Wood Bridge *supra*); *Woodsgate* 1679, 1709, *(at) Woods Gate* 1721, 1724, 1745 (*v.* **geat**; a furlong so called), *Woods Yard* 1721, *Woods Yard(s) End* 1674, 1724, 1745 (*v.* **geard, ende**) (with the surn. *Wood*; perh. cf. *Elizabeth Wood* 1816 Census to *Emily Wood* 1855 ib of Lutterworth); *Wymonpoole* 1601, *Wineman(e) poole* 1606 (*v.* **pōl**[1]; with the surn. *Winman*, from the OE masc. pers.n. *Winemann*; cf. *Walterius Wyneman* 1250 Fees of neighbouring Northants.).

Misterton

1. MISTERTON

Minstreton(e) 1086 DB, 1231 RHug, 1243 Fees *et passim* to 1329
 Ipm, *Mynstreton* 1354, 1355 Cl
Menstreton(e) 1086 DB, 1229 Cl
Ministone 1086 DB
Ministerton c.1130 LeicSurv
Minsterton(e) 1189 Selby, 1226 Cur *et passim* to 1375 Cl, 1403 AD,
 Mynsterton c.1291 Tax, 1294 Pat, 1330 *Rut et passim* to 1353,
 1409 Pat
Minstirton 1271 Ipm, *Mynstirton* 1272, 1292 ib
Munesterton 1220 MHW, *Munsterton(e)* 1236, 1268 Fine *et passim*
 to 1348, 1349 Cl, *Munstreton* 1314 Ipm
Musterton(e) 1151 × 73 Selby, 1220 RHug, 1327 Banco, 1328 AD
Misterton 1236 Cur, 1264 Cl *et passim* to 1327 SR, 1330 Banco *et
 freq*, *Mysterton* 1465 Pat, 1497 *Braye*, 1517 *MktHPR et passim* to
 1594, 1596 AD

'The village or estate with a minster', *v.* **mynster, tūn**. Anglo-Saxon
minsters were religious communities, usually comprising a priest and a
group of monastic or secular assistants, which served as centres of
administration prior to the development of a system of ecclesiastical
parishes. They were usually established on royal estates and served large
territories. Little survives of the early village except St Leonard's Church
and the later Misterton Hall.

BUTTS FM, *v.* **butte**; in the narrow north-western angle of the parish.
COLD FM, 1925 Kelly, *v.* **cald**; an exposed site. DALE SPINNEY, *v.* **dalr**,
spinney. LEA BARN FM, *v.* **ley**[2]. THE LODGE is *Misterton Lodge* 1863
White, *v.* **loge**. MIDDLE FM. MISTERTON GORSE, 1835 O, *v.* **gorst**.
MISTERTON GRANGE, *v.* **grange**. MISTERTON HALL, 1804 Nichols, 1846,
1863 White, 1925 Kelly, *the hall house* 1796 EnclA, *The Hall* 1877
White, *v.* **hall**. OBACK FM is *Hoeback Barn* 1835 O, *Obacks farm* 1925
Kelly; *Holbecke* 1595 AD, 1600 Ipm, 1710 Deed, *v.* **hol**[2], **bekkr**. THE

147

RECTORY, 1877 White, 1925 Kelly, *v.* **rectory**; built c.1840, but earlier is *the Parsonage house* 1718 *Terrier*, *v.* **personage**. THE REEDS, *v.* **hrēod**. RYE CLOSE SPINNEY, *v.* **spinney** and Rye Cl in f.ns. (a). ST LEONARD'S CHURCH, *Church (St Leonard)* 1846, 1863, 1877 White, 1925 Kelly; it is earlier recorded as *ecclesie de Munesterton* 1220 MHW, ~ *de Minsterton* 1244 RGros; it was the mother church of the chapels at Poultney and Walcote, *v. cappellas de Pulteney et Walecote* in f.ns. (b). SHAWELL WOOD, 1835 O; bordering Shawell parish which adjoins to the south-west. SWINFORD RD, Swinford lying 3 miles to the south-east. THORNBOROUGH FM, ~ SPINNEY, *Thornborough Spinny* 1835 O (*v.* **spinney**); *Thorneborowe* 1595 AD, *Thornborowe* 1600 Ipm, *Thunborough* 1697 *Terrier*, *Thurnborough* 1710 *Deed*, *v.* **þorn**, **berg**; the specific is occasionally replaced by **þyrne**. WARREN FM, 1925 Kelly; *the Warren* 1595 AD, 1600 Ipm, *v.* **wareine**. WOOD FM, 1925 Kelly, *v.* **wudu**. WOOD FARM COTTAGES.

2. POULTNEY

> *Pontenei* (sic) 1086 DB
> *Pulteneia* l.12 AD, 1219 GildR (p), 1228 RHug (p), *Pulteney(e)* 1220 MHW, 1261 Cl *et passim* to 1379 ib *et freq* to 1594, 1595 AD, *Pultenay* 1285, 1329 Cl (p) *et passim* to 1384 (p), 1397 ib (p)
> *Poltenee* 1202 FF (p), *Polteneie* c.1300 AD, *Polteney(e)* 1314 Ipm (p), 1315 Cl *et passim* to 1331 *MiD*, 1339 Cl, *Poltenay* 1331 (p), 1333 Pap (p)
> *Poulteneye* 1322, 1339 Cl (p)
> *Poultney* 1593, 1598 AD

The generic of this toponym is OE **ēg** 'raised land in surrounding wet ground'. The specific is problematical. A large proportion of place-names with generic **ēg** have as a specific an OE pers.n. Poultney may have as the specific an unrecorded OE masc. pers.n. *Pulta*, as suggested for Poltimore (D 444). Alternatively, the ME verb *pulte* 'to thrust out' may have had an unrecorded OE word from the same stem, which if applied, would suit the location. The old village site at Great Poultney Fm stands on a low promontory which projects south-east into well-watered ground. Poultney medieval village was probably depopulated in the late 15th century to make way for sheep-farming. A famous son of the township was Sir John de Pulteney, Lord Mayor of London in 1312, 1330, 1331, 1333 and 1335.

3. WALCOTE

> *Walecote* 1086 DB (×2), 1166 RBE, 1176 P (p) *et freq* to 1278
> *Goodacre*, 1288 Pat *et passim* to 1316 Cl, 1322 Pat (p),
> *Wallecot*(*e*) 1166 LN, l.12 AD
> *Walcote* 1288 Ass, 1298 Banco *et freq*, *Walcot* 1520, 1524 Ipm *et*
> *passim* to 1535 Fine, 1616 AD
> *Wawcut* 1727 LML

'The cottage(s) of the Britons or (British) serfs', *v.* **walh** (**wala**
gen.pl.), **cot** (**cotu** nom.pl.). Walton ('the farmstead or village of the
Britons') lies some five miles to the north-east.

THE BELT (local), *v.* **belt**; a long, narrow plantation. BLACK HORSE
(P.H.), *Black Horse* 1846, 1863, 1877 White, 1925 Kelly. BRADGATE.
BROOK ST. BUCKWELL LODGE, *Buckwell* 1863 White, *v.* **loge** and
Buckwell Fd in f.ns. (a). BULL'S HEAD (P.H.) (lost), *Bull's Head* 1846,
1863, 1877 White. CHAPEL LANE, 1796 *EnclA*, *v.* **chapel**(**e**); the location
of two former nonconformist chapels. CROWN (P.H.) (lost), *Crown* 1877
White. FRANKS LANE, with the surn. *Franks*, cf. *Jacob Henry Franks*
who is *Lord of the Manor* 1796 *EnclA*. GLENFIELD FM, a transferred
name from Glenfield in Sparkenhoe Hundred. THE GRANGE, *v.* **grange**.
HANGLAND SPINNEY, *v.* **land**, **spinney**; with **hangol** or **hangende**.
HIGHFIELD FM is *Walcote Lodge* 1835 O, *v.* **loge**. HIGHFIELDS FM,
Highfield 1835 O. HILLCREST. HILL FM, 1925 Kelly. HILL TOP FM, cf.
Top of Hill 1792 *Deed*, *v.* **topp**. THE LODGE, 1925 Kelly, *v.* **loge**. LODGE
FM, 1925 Kelly. LONDON LODGE, 1925 Kelly, *v.* **loge**; it is *Walcote*
Lodge 1835 O; a 'remoteness' name for a site towards the parish
boundary (perh. cf. Melbourne Lodge *infra*, also towards the boundary).
LUTTERWORTH RD, Lutterworth lying one mile to the north-west.
MELBOURNE LODGE, *v.* **loge**; cf. London Lodge *supra*; the surn.
Melbourne, taken from the Derbys. p.n., occurs in Leics. very rarely, so
this is likely to be a 'remoteness' name also. ORCHARD FM, beside
extensive orchards; note *The Orchard* 1968 *Surv*, *v.* **orceard**. POPLARS
FM (is WALCOTEFIELD 2½"), *Walcote field* 1863 White. POULTNEY
GRANGE, *v.* **grange**. GREAT POULTNEY FM is *Poultney Lodge* 1835 O, *v.*
loge. MIDDLE POULTNEY FM is also *Poultney Lodge* 1835 O, *v.* **loge** and
Poultney *supra*. RASPBERRY SPINNEY, *v.* **resbery**, **spinney**. RED LION
(P.H.) (lost), *Red Lion* 1764 *Deed*, 1846, 1863, 1877 White, 1925 Kelly.
SHARRAG GROUNDS, (with ModE **ground** in its sense 'outlying
farmland'), cf. *Sharrag farm* 1925 Kelly; on the parish boundary and

thus if an ancient name, poss. 'boundary oak-tree', *v.* **sc(e)aru**, **āc**. STRAWFIELD HO., stands at the old boundary between Misterton and Walcote, so perh. a garbled *Sharfield*, *v.* f.ns. (a) *s.n.* Charfield Lane; but *straw* in later f.ns. was used in a derogatory sense indicating poorly productive land. TOWER FM, 1925 Kelly; named from a water-tower. WAKELEY FM, *Wakelow* c.1638 *Terrier*, cf. *Waklou weye* c.1400 AD (*v.* **weg**), *Wakely Meadow* 1712 *Deed*, *v.* **wacu**, **hlāw**. WALCOTE HO., *Walcote House* 1877 White. WALCOTE LODGE, *v.* **loge**. WEST VIEW FM. WINTERFIELD SPINNEY, *Winterfield Spinny* 1835 O (*v.* **spinney**); *Wynterfeild(e)* 1595 AD, *Wynterfeld* 1600 Ipm, *Winterfeild* 1637 Will, *Winterfield* 1670 Deed, 1968 *Surv*, *v.* **winter**[1], **feld**; the name suggests that this was not one of the great arable open-fields, but one used principally in the winter months, probably for livestock. WINTON FM, cf. *Lower ~ ~*, *Upper Winton Field* 1710 Deed; the location of the farm shows that despite the nearby name *Winterfield*'s having survived into the 20th cent., *Winton* is a developed or garbled form of *Winter*, possibly from local antiquarian knowledge that in 1296, part of Misterton was held in fee of the Honour of Winton (i.e. Winchester), *v.* Nichols **4** 1 306. WOOD'S FM, cf. *John Wood, farmer* 1846 White. WOODSIDE.

FIELD-NAMES

William Burton, writing in 1622, notes that 'this lordship hath long been inclosed ... affording large sheep-walks'. The surviving seven Glebe Terriers of St Leonard's Church, Misterton, date from 1638 to 1718 and list the Church's holdings in three great arable open-fields in the parish, namely *the West Feild*, *the Middle Feild* and *the North Feild* (otherwise called *Buckwell Feild*). These appear to be three open-fields which once belonged to the village of Walcote. It is difficult to place in the present extensive parish various other fields recorded from the late 16th, 17th and early 18th centuries and to be sure of their natures, notably *Hedg furlonge feild* and *Sharefield*. A will of 1637 assigns to Poultney a *Poultney High Feild*, a *Midlefeild* and a *Winterfeild*. The *Heighfeld* in f.ns. (b) may have been that of Poultney or one lying to the south of Walcote village where Highfields Fm (*Highfield* 1835 O) may still remember it. *Winterfeild*, as its name suggests, can hardly have been a great arable open-field, unless it was restyled and its function altered. As for the lost early great open-fields of Misterton (if, as an important ecclesiastical centre, it ever had them), nothing is certain. Because of such uncertainty, field-names for the greater parish (i.e. Misterton with Poultney and Walcote) are presented together.

In (a), forms dated 1792 are *Deed*; those dated 1796 are *EnclA*; 1835 are O; 1968 are *Surv*. Forms throughout dated l.12, 13, c.1360, c.1400, 1595, 1596 and 1598 are AD; those dated 1220 are MHW; 1261 and 1262 are Nichols; 1293 and 1298 are Banco; 1322 are Pat; 1327 are SR; 1547 are Fine; 1600 are Ipm; 1638, m.17, 1674, c.1680, 1697, 1709 and 1718 are *Terrier*; 1670, 1695, 1704, 1710 and 1712 are Deed.

(a) Six Acre, Seven Acres, Big ~ ~, Little Ten Acre, Eighteen Acre 1968 (*v.* **æcer**); Allens Lane 1796 (with the surn. *Allen*); Ant Banks 1968 (*v.* **æmette, banke**); Banker's 1968 (the surn. *Banker* in the possessive case, a surn. which is also found in adjoining North Kilworth); Banky Fd 1968 (*v.* **banke, -ig**³); Barn Fd 1968 (*v.* **bern**); Big Mdw 1968; Bonn (sic) 1968 (may allude to the use of bone-dust, phosphate manure obtained from bones, either burnt or ground; but note Little Bones in adjacent South Kilworth, so this may be the site of a pagan Anglo-Saxon inhumation cemetery, *v.* **bān**); Boveton 1792, Bufton 1968, 'Bove Town Leys 1796 (*v.* **leys**) (*Bufftown* 1638, m.17, 1709, 1718, *Bufton* 1674, *Buffton* c.1680, *v.* **bufan, tūn**); Branson's Cl, ~ Mdw 1968 (with the surn. *Branson* (from *Branston*, with the typical 17th- and 18th-century Leics. loss of *t* from the group *-ston*), cf. *Harriett Branson* 1839 Census of adjoining Gilmorton parish; prob. the surn. of a family originally either from Branston, 32 miles to the north-east or from Braunston, 12 miles to the north); Brick Cl 1792, 1796 (*the Brick Close* 1709, 1718; a site for the manufacture of bricks); Buckwell Fd 1796 (1709, *Bougwelle* c.1360, *Buckwell* 1718, *Buckwell Feild* 1638 (*v.* **feld**; one of the great open-fields, also called *the North feild towards Poultney Grounds* 1674, c.1680), cf. *Buckwell Furlong* 1638, 1674, 1709, 1718, *~ forlong* c.1680 (*v.* **furlang**), *v.* **wella**; either with **bucca** or with the OE masc. pers.n. *Bucca*); Bungalow Fd 1968; Caves Leys 1796 (*v.* **leys**; with the surn. *Cave*, prob. an original by-name from OFr *cauf* 'bald'; note *Thomas Caves hadland* 1674 (*v.* **hēafod-land**); also local to Misterton were *John Cave* 1726 MI, *John Cave* 1764 ib, *John Cave* 1791 ib and *Elizabeth Cave* 1796 *EnclA*); Charfield Lane 1796 (cf. *Sharefield* ~ 1709, *Sharfield Meadow* 1718, *v.* **sc(e)aru** and Strawfield Ho. *supra*); Cheatells Lane 1796 (with the surn. *Cheatell*, in origin the ON masc. pers.n. *Ketill*, anglicized to *Cytel*; note *Michael Cheatell* 1761 MI and *John Cheatell* 1767 ib; earlier in *Thomas Cattels hadland* 1674, *Thomas Cattles hadeland* c.1680 (*v.* **hēafod-land**), where the initial consonant of *Cattel* may have been a palatal, but if not, for another early 18th-cent. occurrence of the stop *k* > palatal *ch*, cf. *Caldwell* > *Chadwell*, Lei **2** 218); (the) Church Road 1796 (*v.* St Leonard's Church *supra*); Coal Pit Leys 1796 (*v.* **col-pytt, leys**; alluding to a charcoal-manufacturing site); Cotesbach Covan (sic) 1968 (Cotesbach parish adjoins to the south-west; perh. with **cofa** (**cofan** nom.pl.)); Cow Fd 1796, Cow Warren 1968 (*v.* **wareine**) (*v.* **cū**); Dinge Hill 1792, Dingehills 1796 (*Dingells* 1638, *Dingils* m.17, 1697, *Dingless* 1674, *Dingels* 1709, *Dingills East* ~, *Dingills West Furlong* 1718 (*v.* **furlang**); either **dingle** or **dynge** with **hyll** since the value of the medial *g* is uncertain); Middle ~, Top Doctors 1792 (*v.* **doctour**); Entry Fd 1968; Far Cl 1968; Filley Fd 1968 (poss. with **fillie** 'a young mare' or **fille** with **lēah**, but may represent the earlier *Finley Meadow* in f.ns. (b)); Frankie's 1968 (poss. remembers *Jacob Henry Franks* 1796 *EnclA*, who was Lord of the Manor, but the pet-form *Frankie* from Frank (from Francis) may pertain, *v.* Franks Lane *supra*); Gethins's 1968 (the surn. *Gethin* in the possessive case); Bottom ~, Top Hades 1968 (*v.* **hēafod**); Hand Cl, ~ Mdw 1968 (prob. with the surn. *Hand*, but otherwise may once have alluded to a finger-post or hand-post); Harborough Turnpike Road 1796 (*v.* **turnepike**; Market Harborough lies 12 miles to the east); Great Hedge Furlong 1792, Hedge Furlong 1796 (*the Hedge furlong* 1638, 1697, 1709, *hedg furlong* 1674, c.1680), Hedge Furlong Fd 1796 (*Hedg furlonge feild* 1674), Hedge Furlong Spinney 1835 (*v.* **spinney**; now a narrow stand of trees, one mile in length, along part of what must have been the former boundary between Misterton and Walcote, no doubt once a boundary hedge) (*v.* **hecg**, **furlang**); Great ~ ~, Little Hill Cl 1792; the Holt 1796 (*the Olt* 1638, 1709, *the Oult* 1674, c.1680, *the Olte* 1718, *v.* **wald**); First Home Cl, Home Fd 1968 (*v.* **home**); House Fd 1968; Jarmeny 1968 (presum. 'Germany', a transferred name for a remote field); Kilworth Stile 1796 (with **stīg** or **stigel**, North Kilworth and South Kilworth parishes adjoining to the east); Lankhorn Stile 1796 (*v.* **lang**[1]; with **horn** or **þorn** and **stīg** or **stigel**); Lay Cl 1968 (*v.* **ley**[1]); Light Land 1792 (*v.* **land**; alluding to an endowment to provide lamps for the parish church); Little Hills Furlong 1796 (*v.* **furlang**) (*Little Hill* c.1680, 1718, *Litle Hill* 1674, *v.* **lȳtel**, **hyll**); the Meadows 1792, 1968 (*Little Meadow, Long Meadow, Low Meadow* 1710, *Neather Meadow* 1712 (*v.* **neoðera**); the Middle Fd 1796 (1670, *Mydlefeld* 1547, *Midlefeild* 1637, *the Middle Feild* 1638, 1674, ~ *field* c.1680, 1718, *v.* **middel**, **feld**; one of the later great open-fields); the Great Moores 1796 (*the Moores* 1638, 1709, *the Moores* 1718, cf. *the Little Moor* 1638, 1709, *v.* **mōr**[1]); Oak Tree 1968 (*v.* **āc, trēow**; a close containing such a tree); Old Furlong 1796 ((*the*) *Old Furlong* 1674, c.1680, 1709, 1718, *v.* **furlang**; prob. with **ald**, but **wald** is poss.; note The Holt *supra*); Orams Cl 1796 (with the surn. *Oram*, from the ON masc. pers.n. *Ormr* (ODan *Orm*); cf. *Thomas Oram* 1842 Census of adjoining Lutterworth parish, with the surn. continuing there from *George Oram* 1860 ib to *Mary Oram* 1880 ib); The Paddock 1968 (*v.* **paddock**); Perry's Mdw 1968 (with the surn. *Perry*, an original locational surn. from OE *pirige* 'a pear-tree'); Great Pipes 1968 (*v.* **pīpe**); Pit Fd 1968 (*v.* **pytt**); Plough Fd 1968 (*v.* **plōg**); the Poultney Road 1796 (*v.* Poultney *supra*; at this date, no longer surviving as a township); Little Rams 1968 (*Little Ram Close* 1637, 1670), Rams Close Furlong 1796 (1718, *Ramscloss Furlong* 1638, *Ram(s) Close forlong* c.1680, *v.* **furlang**), Rams Close Gate 1796 (*v.* **geat**), Ramsclose Spinny 1835 (*v.* **spinney**) ((*the*) *Ram Close* 1637, *Rams Close* 1710, *v.* **ramm**); Road Fd 1968; Rye Cl 1968 (1637, 1655, 1670, 1710, *v.* **ryge**); Far ~, Near Sankey 1968 (prob. with the surn. *Sankey*, from the Cheshire (formerly Lancs.) place-name since there is no early evidence here for a pre-English stream-name *Sankey* (from Brit *Sancīo-*, perh. 'holy stream', *v.* RN 351)); Seeds 1968 (*v.* **sǣd**; used of grasses sown for one year's mowing or grazing as distinguished from permanent pasture); Slang 1968 (*v.* **slang**); South Kilworth Road 1796 (South Kilworth lies 2 miles to the south-east); South Mdw 1968; Spinney Fd 1968 (*v.* **spinney**); Stanford Gate 1792 (1718, *v.* **gata**), the Stanford Road 1796 (the road to Stanford on Avon, 3 miles to the south-east in Northants.); Nether ~ ~, Upper Starmore Leys 1792 (*Starmore Lays* 1638, 1709, ~ *Lease* m.17, ~ *leaves* 1674, ~ *leyes* c.1680, *v.* **leys** and the lost *Stormsworth* in Westrill and Starmore parish which adjoins to the south-east); Great Strawfield 1968 (*v.* Strawfield Ho. and Charfield Lane, both *supra*); Sussex Fd 1968 (presum. with the surn. *Sussex*; otherwise unexplained); Swinford Corner 1968 (*v.* **corner**), Swinford Gap 1796 (*v.* **gap**), Swinford Leys 1792 (*Swinford lease* m.17, ~ *leaves* 1674, ~ *leyes* c.1680, *v.* **leys**), Swinford Mdw 1792, the Swinford Road 1796

(Swinford parish adjoins to the south); First ~, Second Thistles 1968 (*v.* **þistel**); Lone Thorne Cl, ~ ~ Furlong (*v.* **furlang**) 1968 (*v.* **lone, þorn**); Far ~, Near Thorney 1968 (*v.* **þornig** and *Thorney Furlong* in f.ns. (b)); Townsend Lane 1796 (*v.* **tūn, ende**; with reference to Walcote); Wheat Cl 1968 (*v.* **hwǣte**).

(b) *Ansloe* 1638, 1709, *Anislow* 1718, *Anislowe leasse* m.17 (*v.* **leys**) (*v.* **hlāw**; with the OE masc. pers.n. *An(n)*; also appears at the western edge of adjoining North Kilworth parish, *v.* Ainsloe Spinney); *Askers Close* 1704 (either with the surn. *Asker* or with dial. *asker* 'a newt'); *Aukerly Hill* 1638, 1697, 1709 (prob. with **hlāw**, the reduction *low > ly* being common in Leics., cf. Wakeley (Fm) *supra*; perh. with the OE masc. pers.n. *Alca*, but earlier forms are needed); *Mr Armsons ricksted* 1674 (*v.* **rickstead**; the surn. *Armson* is from *Ermin*, a pet-form of names such as ContGerm *Ermenwald, Ermengot*; cf. *James Armson* 1813 Census and *Charles Armson* 1824 ib of adjoining Cotesbach parish); *Banforlongslade* m.17 (*v.* **bēan, land**); *Edward Barkers piece* 1674 (*v.* **pece**); *Benchwell Furlong* 1638, c.1680, 1697, 1709 (*v.* **benc, wella, furlang**); *Bernhanger* 1261, 1262 (*v.* **bern, hangra**); *Bogg Meadow* 1710 (*v.* **bog**); (*the*) *Breach* 1674, c.1680, (*the*) *Neather* ~ 1674, 1709, 1718, *Nether Breach* c.1680 (*v.* **neoðera**), *the Upper Breach* 1638, 1697, 1709, *Over Breach* 1718 (*v.* **uferra**), *Brechefurlong* 1293, *Breach furlong* 1718 (*v.* **furlang**), *Breach leayes* 1674, c.1680 (*v.* **leys**) (*v.* **brēc**); *Brexdale* l.12 (*v.* **dalr**; the specific appears to be **brēc** in the gen.sg. with Scand influence on its final consonant (*breck* is a well-attested variant of *breach*)); *Bryghteslowe furlong* 1298 (*v.* **hlāw, furlang**; with the OE masc. pers.n. *Briht* (*Beorht*)); *Bufton Moores* 1674, ~ *Moors* c.1680 (*v.* **mōr**[1] and Boveton in f.ns. (a)); *cappellas de Pulteney et Walecote* 1220 (with MLat *capella* 'a chapel'); *William Chapmans hadland* 1674 (*v.* **hēafod-land**); *Coltmans Close* 1704 (with the surn. *Coltman*, from OE *colt* with *mann*, hence 'a keeper of colts'); *Common furrs* 1674, *Comon forse* c.1680 (*v.* **commun, fyrs**); *Dockey Close* 1710 (*v.* **docce, -ig**[3]); *Ferrers Close* 1598 (*v.* **clos(e)**; with the surn. *Ferrer*, from OFr *ferreor* 'a smith, a worker in iron'; cf. *Henricus le Ferrur* 1196 Cur of Leics.); *Finley Meadow* 1712 (poss. **finn** with **lēah**, but earlier forms are needed; and note Filley Fd in f.ns. (a)); *Forshoots* ~ 1638, m.17, 1718, *foreshutes furlong* 1674, *forshutes forlong* c.1680 (*v.* **fore, scyte, furlang**); *Forsters* ~ 1638, *Fosters Furlong* 1709 (*v.* **furlang**; with the surn. *Forster, v.* Reaney *s.nn.* Forster, Foster); *Fryars* c.1680, *Great Friars* 1638, *Over or Great Fryers* 1718 (*v.* **uferra**), *Upper Fryers* 1709, *Nether* ~ 1638, *Neather Fryers* 1709, 1718 (with the surn. *Friar* in the possessive case; from OFr *frere* 'a friar'); *Frost Pitt Hill* 1638, *Frost-Pit* ~ 1674, 1709, *frospit hill* c.1680, *Frospitt Hill* ~ c.1680, *Frost Pitt Hill furlong* 1718 (*v.* **furlang**) (*v.* **frosc, pytt, hyll**); *fulon slade, bare fulon slade* 1674 (*v.* **bær**[1]), *Fat Forlong slade* m.17, *fat fulon slade* 1674, *Fat(t) furlong slade* c.1680 (*v.* **fatte**) (*v.* **furlang, slæd**); *the gravel pitt* 1718 (*v.* **gravel, pytt**); *Grindle* m.17, c.1680, 1697, 1718, *Grindel(l)* 1674, *Grundleswell* c.1400 (*v.* **wella**) (*v.* **grendel**); *hal-mark* 1674, *Hall Mark* 1709, 1718 (*v.* **mearc** and Misterton Hall *supra*); *le Halvidole* l.12, 13, *Upper Hovidoles* 1638, 1709, *Over Hovidoles* 1718 (*v.* **uferra**), *Hobbydoles* m.17, 1674, c.1680 (*v.* **half, dāl**); *hanging furlong(e)* 1674, c.1680 (*v.* **furlang**), *Hanging Hill* 1638, 1709, *hanging leayes* 1674 (*v.* **leys**) (*v.* **hangende**); *hattedamishinde* c.1400 (*v.* **atte, damme, ende**); *Heighfeld* 1547, (*the*) *Highe Feilde* 1595, 1596, (*the*) *Highfeild* 1600, 1670, 1674, *Upper High Field* 1704 (*v.* **hēah**[1], **feld**; one of the great open-fields, but whether of Poultney or of Walcote is uncertain); *High Feild Meadowe* 1569 (*v.* **mēd** (**mēdwe** obl.sg.)); *the high way* 1674, c.1680, *Highway Close* 1704 (*v.* **hēah-weg**); *Carter's* ~ (with the surn.

Carter), *Little ~, Middle Hoback* 1710 (*v.* Oback Fm *supra*); *the Homested* 1718 (*v.* **hām-stede**; belonging to *the Parsonage house, supra*); *horsslade* 1674, *horse slade* 1718 (*v.* **hors, slæd**); *in le Hurne* 1327 (p), *in le hyrne* 1332 (p) (*v.* **hyrne**); *Judges Meadow* 1710 (with the surn. *Judge*, from OFr *juge* 'a judge'); *The Long* 1638, 1709 (*v.* **lang**²); *Longfurland* 1293, *the Long Furlong* 1638, c.1680, 1709 (*v.* **lang**¹, **furlang**); *long hadland forlong* c.1680 (*v.* **lang**¹, **hēafod-land, furlang**); *Mill Meadow* 1710 (*v.* **myln**); *Minstreton Temple* 1322 (*v.* **temple**; in allusion to an otherwise unrecorded grange of the Knights Templar); *Munkslease* m.17 (*v.* **leys**; prob. with the surn. *Munk*, from OE *munuc* 'a monk', and not a popular allusion to the Knights Templar); *New Dike* 1674, c.1680, *~ ~ furlonge* 1674, *New Dyke forlong* c.1680 (*v.* **furlang**) (*v.* **nīwe, dík**); *the North feild towards Poultney Grounds* 1674, c.1680 (*v.* **norð, feld** and *Poultney Grounds, infra*; an alternative name for Buckwell Fd (*v.* f.ns. (a)); (*the*) *Park Close* 1709, 1718 (*v.* **park**); *Piffline Meadow, Lower ~ ~, Upper Pifflin Olders* 1710 (*v.* **alor**) (perh. 'the place with gravelly soil', *v.* **pofel, -ing**²; but if so, the change in the initial vowel is problematical); *Poultney Grounds* 1674, c.1680 (*v.* **grund** and Poultney *supra*); *the Great Rie Hill* 1638, m.17, *the Great Rye Hill* c.1680, *v.* **ryge**); *the Rickstede* 1709 (*v.* **rickstead**); *Round Meadow* 1710 (*v.* **round**); *Salters Way furlong* c.1680 (*v.* **saltere, weg, furlang**); *Sharpehill* 1595, *Sharphill* 1595, 1600, *~ hedg(e)* 1674, c.1680 (*v.* **hecg**) (*v.* **sc(e)arp, hyll**); *le Stonidole* c.1400 (*v.* **stānig, dāl**); *Thorney Furlong* 1638, 1674, c.1680, 1718 (*v.* **þornig, furlang**); *Thorowakeres* 1674, *Thorow Acres ~* 1638, c.1680, 1718, *Thorrowacres furlong* 1718 (*v.* **furlang**) (*v.* **furh, æcer**); *the Towne Moors* c.1680 (*v.* **tūn, mōr**¹; with reference to Walcote village); *Walcote Hill* 1712; *Washpit Meadow* 1710 (*v.* **wæsce, pytt**); *the West feild* 1638, m.17, 1674, c.1680, 1697 (*v.* **west, feld**; one of the great open-fields); *Wheat Furlong Slade* 1638, 1709, 1718 (*v.* **hwǣte, furlang, slæd**); *Wiggin Well* 1709, *~ ~ Furlong* 1638, 1709, 1718 (*v.* **furlang**), *Wiggin Well leaves* 1674, *Wiginwell Leyes* c.1680 (*v.* **leys**) (*v.* **wella**; either with **wigga** or with the OE masc. pers.n. *Wicga* (*Wicgan* gen.sg.)); *Willow Lays* 1638, 1709, *~ lease* m.17, c.1680, *~ leayes* 1674, *~ Leese* c.1680, *Willow Leays* 1718 (*v.* **wilig, leys**); *Wood Lane* 1638, m.17 *et passim* to 1718 (*v.* **wudu, lane**); *Wyarleese* m.17, *Ware leayes* 1674, *Wyar Lees* c.1680 (*v.* **weyour, leys**).

North Kilworth

Chivelesworde 1086 DB
Kivelingewurðe 1195 P, *Kivelingewurthe* 1208 Cur, 1226 RHug,
    Kivelingworth 1208 Cur, *Kivelingewrth* 1208 FF, 1295 Cl,
    Kyvelingewrthe 1236 RHug
Kevelingewurd 1196 ChancR, *Kevelingewrthe* 1212 RBE (p)
Kivelingwrde 1197 P, *Kivelingworth(e)* 1220 MHW, 1292 Coram,
    Kyvelingwrde 1226 RHug, *Kyvelyngworth* 1244 Cur, *Kyvelingworth*
    1293 Ipm, 1295 Cl, 1316 FA, 1322 Misc
Kevelingwrð 1197 P, *Kevelingworth* 1288 Cl, *Kevelingwurth* 1296
    OSut, *Kevelyngworth* 1322 Cl, 1328 Banco, 1341 Pat
Kylingwrth 1254 Val, *Killingworth* c.1291 Tax, 1393 Banco,
    Killyngworth 1395 Pat, 1396 Cl, 1399 Pat, *Kyllyngworth* 1383
    Goodacre, 1397 Cl *et passim* to 1470, 1473 *Wyg*, *Kylyngworth*
    1431 *ib*
Kelyngworth c.1291 Tax, 1327 SR, *Kelingworth* 1329 AD
Killeworth 1380 Banco, 1390, 1391 Cl, *Kylleworth* 1406 *LCh*
Kylworth 1412 Ass, 1416 Banco *et passim* to 1534 *Ct*, 1540
    MinAccts, *Kilworth* 1424 *Wyg*, 1482 Pat *et passim* to 1576 Saxton
    et freq

Affixes are added as:
~ *Rabaz* 1220 MHW, 1254 Val *et passim* to 1502 *MiscAccts*, 1510
    Visit
North(e) ~ 1288, 1295 Cl *et freq*

The earliest form indicates simply 'Cyfel's enclosure', *v.* **worð**.
However, a large number of early spellings with *-inge-* point to an
alternative early **-inga-** construction, hence 'the enclosure of the family
or followers of Cyfel', *v.* **-ingas** (**-inga-** gen.pl.), *v.* **worð**. But given the
simple genitival composition-joint of the DB form, 'the enclosure
associated with Cyfel' may rather pertain, *v.* **-ing-**[4], **worð**. The OE masc.
pers.n. *Cyfel* is unrecorded. Ekwall DEPN suggests that it is a derivative

155

of the recorded OE *Cufa*. The DB spelling with initial *Ch-* shows early AN usage for the voiceless stop [k]. Forms with *Ke-* are due to AN substitution of *e* for *i*.

The manor was held by *Ricardus Rabaz* in 1208 Cur, by *Robertus Rabaz* in 1244 ib and by *Stephanus Rabaz* in 1292 Coram. Forms with *North*(*e*) ~ distinguish this settlement from South Kilworth *infra*, *v.* **norð**.

AINSLOE SPINNEY, (*v.* **spinney**); *Anislo* 1625 *Terrier*, *Ansloe* 1638 *ib*, *Anislow* 1718 *ib*, cf. *Anisloo clos* 1550 Ipm, *Anislo Close* 1625 *Terrier* (*v.* **clos(e)**), *Anislow* ~ 1690, 1708, 1715 *ib*, *Anisloe gate* 1703 *ib* (*v.* **gata**), 'An's burial mound or hill', *v.* **hlāw**; with an unrecorded OE masc. pers.n. *An*(*n*) (cf. Annesley, Nt 112); the name also appears in Misterton f.ns. (b) *supra*. BACK ST, *v.* **back**. BOTTOM ROUND SPINNEY, *v.* **round**, **spinney**; with reference to shape. BULL (P.H.) (lost), *Bull* 1846, 1863 White. BUTLER'S SPINNEY, *v.* **spinney**; with the surn. *Butler*. CRANMER LANE, *Cranmeer* 1625 *Terrier*, *Cow Cramer* 1690, 1703 *ib*, ~ *Cranmer* 1700 *ib*, ~ *Crammer* 1708, 1715 *ib* (*v.* **cū**), *Long Crameer* 1625 *ib*, ~ *Crammer* 1690, 1708, 1715 *ib*, *Nether Cramer* 1550 Ipm (*v.* **neoðera**), *Cramer clos* 1550 ib (*v.* **clos(e)**), *Crameer leyes* 1625 *Terrier*, *Crammer Leies* 1690 *ib*, *Cranmere Leys* 1700 *ib*, *Cramer layes* 1703 *ib*, *Crammer Leys* 1715 *ib* (*v.* **leys**), *v.* **cran**, **mere**[1]. Note also *Cranmer House* 1925 Kelly. CHURCH ST is *Kirk*(*e*)*way* 1606, 1625, 1690, 1703, 1708, 1715 *Terrier*, *v.* **kirkja** and St Andrew's Church *infra*. CRICKET GROUND SPINNEY, *v.* **spinney**; with reference to the game of cricket. CROW SPINNEY, *v.* **crāwe**. DAIRY COTTAGES, *v.* **deierie**. FOX EARTHS SPINNEY, *v.* **fox**, **eorðe**, **spinney**. THE GRANGE (GRANGE FM 2½"), *the Graunge* 1553 Pat, *The Grange* 1925 Kelly, *v.* **grange**. THE GREEN (local), *v.* **grēne**[2]. HAWTHORNE RD. THE HAWTHORNS. HIGH ST. LUTTERWORTH RD, Lutterworth lying 5 miles to the west. NETHER HALL, *Netherhall*(*e*) 1392 Ass, 1394 Misc, 1395, 1399 Pat, *v.* **neoðera**, **hall**; more important townships often had two halls, *v.* Joan Turville-Petre, 'Overhall and Netherhall', JEPNS 31 (1999), 115–17. NORTH KILWORTH HO. is *Kilworth House* 1846, 1863 White, 1869 *Deed*, 1877 White. NORTH KILWORTH HOUSE COTTAGES. NORTH KILWORTH MILL FM (NORTH KILWORTH MILL 2½"), *North Kilworth Mill* 1789 *EnclA*, 1835 O, *The Mill* 1925 Kelly, *v.* **myln**. NORTH KILWORTH STICKS, perh. with ModE **stick** in its sense 'a timber tree' (*v.* OED stick sb.[1], 6 and 3), but ME **stykke** was used with the sense 'stick, twig', a resource important in medieval husbandry. OLD HALL, *The Hall* 1863 White, *v.* **hall**. PHEASANT SPINNEY, *v.* **phesant**, **spinney**. PINCET LANE, poss. with

pyncette 'tweezers, forceps'; this lane in the northern extremity of the parish splits into a Y-fork, echoing the shape of tweezers. The French surn. *Pincet* found esp. in Seine et Marne in the early 19th cent. is presum. to be discounted, no such surn. appearing in England in the 1881 Census. PINCET LODGE (THE FOLLY 2½"), takes its later name from its location on Pincet Lane, *v.* **folie**, **loge**. THE RECTORY, 1925 Kelly, *v.* **rectory**; earlier is *the Parsonage house* 1606, 1625, 1708 *Terrier, v.* **personage**. THE ROUND HO. ST ANDREW'S CHURCH, *Church (St Andrew)* 1846, 1877 White; it is earlier recorded as *ecclesie de Kiuelingworth Rabaz* 1220 MHW, *ecclesia de Northkilworth* 1559 *Pat.* Note also *the Church yeard* 1606 *Terrier, the Chirch Yard* 1625 *ib, the Church Yard* 1703, 1708, 1715 *ib, v.* **churchyerd**. SHOULDER OF MUTTON (P.H.) (lost), *Shoulder of Mutton* 1846, 1863, 1877 White, 1925 Kelly. SNOWDON LODGE, *v.* **loge**; with the surn. *Snowdon*, especially common in the north of Guthlaxton Hundred, as *William Snowden* 1824 Census of Knighton and *William Snowdon* 1829 ib of Wigston Magna. SOUTH KILWORTH RD, South Kilworth lying one mile to the south-west. SPARROW'S COTTAGE, cf. *John Sparrow* 1867 Census and *Elizabeth Sparrow* 1871 ib, both of North Kilworth. STATION FM. STATION RD, leading to the former Welford and Kilworth Station on the old Rugby and Stamford Branch Railway. SWAN (P.H.), *Swan* 1846, 1863, 1877 White, 1925 Kelly. UNION CHAPEL, 1877 White. VALLEY FM (HILL'S BARN 2½"), cf. *Wm. Hill, farmer* 1846 White. WATERWORKS COTTAGE. WESTERN COTTAGES. WHITE LION (P.H.), *White Lion* 1877 White, 1925 Kelly.

FIELD-NAMES

In (a), forms presented without dates are 1973 *Surv.* Forms throughout dated e.13 are *Harl*; those dated 1208 are Fine; 1322 and 1394 are Misc; 1327 and 1332 are SR; 1382 are Coram; 1392 are Ass; 1395 and 1399 are Pat; 1550 are Ipm; 1589 are AD; 1606, 1625, 1690, 1700, 1703, 1708 and 1715 are *Terrier*.

(a) Four Acre, Seven Acres, Seven Acre Cl (*v.* **æcer**); Ball Acre (land by a (boundary) mound, *v.* **ball**, **æcer**); Ballast Hole (a disused quarry which provided ballast in the construction of the former Rugby and Stamford Branch Railway, begun c.1840); Bankers Cl (poss. with the surn. *Banker*, but may refer to railway banking); Banky Cl (*v.* **banke**, **-ig**³); Barn Cl (*v.* **bern**); Berbidge (sic, but may be a miscopied Herbidge) (*Herbidg* ~ 1606, *Arbidge* ~ 1625, 1703, 1708, 1715, *Arbridge Hill* 1690, *Herbidg* ~ 1606, *Arbidge* ~ 1625, 1703, *Arbridge Way* 1690, *v.* **erbage**); Best Cl (*v.*

best; a complimentary name for very fertile land); Bottom ~, Middle ~, Top Bogs (*v.* **bog**); Bosworth Mdw (lying next to Husbands Bosworth parish which adjoins to the east); Bush Cl (*v.* **busc**); Buswells Cl, ~ Mdw (with the surn. *Buswell*, cf. *Edward Buswell* 1765 EnclA and *Mary Buswell* 1787 MI of North Kilworth); Camp Fd or The Seeds (*v. infra*) (poss. is the survival of OE **camp**, perh. in its sense 'enclosed land', but a modern temporary encampment of some sort may have given the name, while the continuity of **camp** in its early sense 'open land', a borrowing by the Anglo-Saxons of Lat *campus* from Romano-British inhabitants, seems unlikely here, *v.* Camp Cl, Lei **3** 49 and VEPN *s.v.* **camp**); Cheese Cake (1708, *chiscake* 1715, *v.* **chese-cake**); Church Cl (1703, 1708, 1715, *Church clos* 1550, *v.* **clos(e)** and St Andrew's Church *supra*); Clay Pits (*v.* **cley-pytt**); Common Mdw (*v.* **commun** and Kilworth Common *infra*); Corner Cl or Light Land (*v.* **corner** and Light Land *infra*); Cover Fd, ~ Mdw (*v.* **cover(t)**); Cows Fd (*v.* **cū**); Bottom ~, Top Cranmer, Cranmer Mdw (*v.* Cranmer Lane *supra*); The Croft or Craft (*v.* **croft**); Cross Cl or Cross Hill, Cross Hill Mdw (*atte Cros* 1322 (p), *at Cros* 1332 (p), (*ad crucem* 1327 (p) (with MLat *crux* (*crucem* acc.sg.) 'a cross'), *at the Crosse* 1606, 1690, *the Cros, at the Crose* 1625, *the Cross* 1703, 1708, 1715, *v.* **cros**); Crow Spinney Mdw (*v.* Crow Spinney *supra*); Dairy Cl (*v.* **deieirie**); Dorman's Fd or The Wassal (*v. infra*) (with the surn. *Dorman*, from the OE masc. pers.n. *Dēormann*; cf. *Jane Dorman* 1827 Census, *Thomas Dorman* 1858 ib and *Mary Dorman* 1861 ib, all of North Kilworth); Dutch Barn Cl; Fence Land (*v.* **fense** and Holliwell Hill *infra*); Fens Slade or Snipe (*v. infra*) (*Fen slade* 1625, 1703, 1708, 1715, *v.* **fenn**, **slæd**); First Fd; Flood Gate Hill North, ~ ~ ~ South, Flood Gate Hill Cl (*v.* **flodegate** and North Kilworth Mill *supra*; a water-mill); Bottom ~, Top Folly (*v.* The Folly *supra*, otherwise Pincet Lodge); Fords Home (*forwarde home* 1625, *Forward Holme* 1690, 1715, *v.* **foreward**, **holmr**); Fox Cover Cl (*v.* **fox**, **cover(t)**); Garden Fd or Hog Hole (*v. infra*) (*v.* **gardin**; land used for horticulture); Gravel Hole Cl (*v.* **hol**[1]), Gravel Pit or Ninety Nine Bumps (*v. infra*) (*v.* **pytt**) (*v.* **gravel**); Gripes Mdw (poss. with the surn. *Gripp* (if so, here prob. from the ON masc. pers.n. *Grípr*); otherwise *v.* **grȳpe**); Halls Cl (with the surn. *Hall*); Hardhill (1690, *nether* ~, *over Hardell* 1606, 1625 (*v.* **uferra**), *nether* ~, *Upper hardhill* 1690, 1703, *Nether* ~, *Upper Hardil* 1708, 1715, *v.* **heard**, **hyll**); Hardy's First ~, Hardy's Second Fd (with the surn. *Hardy*, cf. *Aderlain Hardy* 1876 Census of North Kilworth); Hill Piece (*v.* **hyll**, **pece**); Hills's Barn Cl (*v.* **bern**; with the surn. *Hill*, cf. *Robert Hill* 1641 SR and *Roger Hill* 1664 ib, both landowners in North Kilworth); Hirons Fd (with the surn. *Hirons*, cf. *Martha Hirons* 1820 Census of nearby Ullesthorpe; the more usual form of the surn. is *Irons*, cf. *Sarah Irons* 1823 ib of nearby Bitteswell; prob. from OE *hyrne* 'an angle, a corner', topographically 'a recess in the hills; a spit of land in a river-bend'); Hog Hole (1708, 1715, *v.* **hogg**, **hol**[1]); Holliwell Hill or Fence Land (*v. supra*) (*Hollowwell* ~ 1703, *Hollowell Hill* 1708, *v.* **hol**[1], **holh**, **wella**, **hyll**); Home Fd or Road Piece (*v.* **home**, **pece**); Homes Way (*Holmes way* 1703, cf. *holmes way* ~ 1690, 1708, *homes way furlong* 1703 (*v.* **furlang**), *the Holmes way field* 1708, 1715 (*v.* **feld**; a later name for Home Feild* 1625, *the Holme(s) Feild* 1690, 1703, one of the great open-fields, cf. *the Home feild leyes* 1625 (*v.* **leys**)), *v.* **holmr**, **weg**); Honeywell Lynch (*Lynch* 1708, 1715 *v.* **hlinc**; Honeywell is prob. a garbled form of Holliwell *supra* and appears nowhere else in records, but if an authentic, distinct f.n., then *v.* **hunig**, **wella**, naming a spring or stream where honey could be found); House Cl (*v.* Kilworth Ho. *supra*); Hut Cl (*v.* **hut**); Jenkins (the surn. *Jenkin* in the possesssive case, cf. *Thomas*

Jenkyn, rector of North Kilworth 1647 to 1652 Nichols); Kilworth Common (*the Common* 1703, 1715, *v.* **commun**); Lee's Fd (with the surn. *Lee*); Lettes Fd, ~ Mdw (with the surn. *Lett, Letts*, from *Lett*, a pet-form of the fem. pers.n. Lettice); Light Land, ~ Mdw (land endowed for the maintenance of various lamps in the parish church, *v.* Corner Cl *supra*); Linden Pit (*v.* **linden, pytt**); Little Cl; Little Dale, ~ ~ Mdw (*Litteldale* 1625, 1690, *Little Dale* 1703, 1708, 1715, cf. *Littledale* ~ 1625, *Littledale Hill* 1703, 1708, 1715, *v.* **lȳtel, dalr**); Little Fd; Long Close Bottom, ~ ~ Top; Long Mdw; Middle Fd; Mill Mdw 1846, 1863, 1877 White (*v.* North Kilworth Mill *supra*); Mushroom Fd (*v.* **musseroun**); Ninety Nine Bumps (another name for Gravel Pit *supra*, alluding to the uneven surface of land excavated for gravel); Osier Bed (*v.* **oyser, bedd**); Packwoods Big Fd, ~ First Fd, ~ Mdw (with the surn. *Packwood*, cf. *Elizabeth Packwood* 1822 Census and *William Packwood* 1824 ib of North Kilworth); The Park, North ~, South ~, West Park (*v.* **park**; belonging to Old Hall *supra*); Parlour (*v.* **parlur**; in later f.ns., used of a secluded piece of ground); Pieces (*v.* **pece**); Ploughed Fd; Ponies Fd (*v.* **pony**); Potato Fd (*v.* **potato**); Rabbit Fd (*v.* **rabet**); Randals Mdw (with the surn. *Randall*; the diminutive *Rand-el* of *Rand* (short for Randolph)); Road Piece (*v.* **pece**); Round Hill (1690, 1703, *Rownddill* 1625, *Roundhil* 1708, 1715, *v.* **round, hyll**); Rye East Hills (*Rastell clos* 1550 (*v.* **clos(e)**, *Ryeastell* 1625, *Ryeastil* 1708, *Ryeastile* ~ 1690, *Ryeastill Corner* 1715 (*v.* **corner**), *Ryeastile* ~ 1690, *Rye Astell* ~ 1700, *Ryastel* ~ 1708, *Ryeasthill Leys* 1715 (*v.* **leys**); if the earliest form *Rastell* belongs here, then the surn. *Rastall* may be thought of, from OFr *rastel* 'a rake, a mattock', and so metonymic for a maker of such agricultural implements; but the 1625 and 1708 forms, which appear to stand alone, suggest rather a toponym, hence perh., *v.* **ryge, ēast, hyll**, though this seems strained; but note the following f.n.); Far Rye Hills (*v.* **ryge, hyll**); Ryeland Cl (*v.* **ryge, land**); Second Mdw; Sedge Hill ((*on*) *Segould* 1625, *Seggolds* 1715, cf. *Seggoles putts* 1690 (*v.* **pytt**), *v.* **secg**[1], **wald**; with *hill* replacing *wold*); The Seeds (*v.* **sǣd** and Camp Fd *supra*); Slang Fd (*v.* **slang**); Slipe (*v.* **slipe**); Small Mdw; Small Thornes (*smalthornes* 1625, *smallthornes* 1690, *Small thorns* 1703, 1715, *v.* **smæl, þorn**); Smids Mdw (*Smith meadow* 1606, 1703, *Smeth medow* 1625, *Smidmedow* 1690, *Smiths meddow* 1708, 1715, *v.* **smēðe**[1]); Snipe (this is prob. **snæp** 'a boggy piece of land', later confused with the bird *snipe*; alternatively called Fens Slade *supra*); Spinney Mdw (*v.* **spinney**); Stoney Cl (*v.* **stānig**); Bottom ~, Top ~, First ~, Second Thacker (cf. *thacker leyes* 1625, 1690, ~ *leys* 1700, 1708, 1715, *Thacker Lays* 1703, *v.* **leys**; with the surn. *Thacker*, a medieval occupational name from *thakkere* 'a thatcher'); Toll Gate (*v.* **toll-gate**); Top Fd; Townsends Fd, ~ Mdw (*v.* **tūn, ende**); Wadbourne Mdw (poss. containing an old stream-name, with (**ge**)**wæd** and **burna**, but no early forms available and no evidence of such a surn. here); The Wassal (cf. *Wassoe Way* 1625, *v.* **wæsse, hōh**); First ~ ~, Second West Fd; First ~, Second Whale (with the surn. *Wale*, cf. *John Wale* 1857 Census and *Frances Wale* 1858 ib of North Kilworth); Witseys (the surn. *Whitsey* in the possessive case, cf. *Sarah Whitsey* 1827 Census of adjacent Misterton parish); Wooder Mdw, Little Wooder (*Woddoe* 1625, *Woodow* 1690, 1708, 1715, *Woodoe, Woodowe* 1703, *Widdow* 1715, *v.* **wudu, hōh**).

(b) *all wronges* 1625, *Allwongs* 1690, *allrangs* 1703, *alwrongs* 1708, *Allwrongs* 1708, 1715, *allrongs* 1715, *v.* **vangr**; with **hall** or **halh**, the generic influenced by **wrang, vrangr** 'twisted in shape'); *assewell* e.13 (*v.* **æsc, wella**); *Banburies* ~ 1690, *Banburys Hadland* 1703, 1708, 1715 (*v.* **hēafod-land**; note *Richard Banbury* 1703

Terrier); *Mr Belgraves Willowes* 1606, 1625 (*v.* **wilig**; the *Belgrave* family was no doubt originally from Belgrave, 12 miles to the north); *the blackepit* 1690, 1703, 1708, *Blackpitt* 1690, 1703, 1708, *black pit* 1715 (*v.* **blæc, pytt**); *Blakenhull* e.13 (*v.* **hyll**; either with **blæc** (**blacan** wk.obl.) or, much less likely, with the OE masc. pers.n. *Blaca* (*Blacan* gen.sg.)); *Boarsgore* 1708, 1715 (*v.* **gāra**; if this is an early survival, then poss. with the OE masc. pers.n. *Bār*, which is the specific of (Husbands) Bosworth, one mile to the north-east; *Boar* as a surn. does not occur); *Bosworth brook* 1703, 1708 (*v.* **brōc**), *Bosworth way* 1625, 1703, 1715, *Bowesworth way* 1690 (*v.* **weg**; the road to Husbands Bosworth); *branthowe* 1625, *Bratha* 1690, 1703, 1708, 1715, ~ *Baulk* 1703, 1708, 1715 (*v.* **balca**) (*v.* **brant, hōh**); *bridell* 1625, *Bridle* 1690, 1703, 1708, 1715, *bridel bottem* 1625, *Bridle bottom* 1700, 1703, 1708, 1715 (*v.* **botm**) (*v.* **brȳd, wella**; the name signifies a fertility spring or well, a place for newly-wed females to frequent); *the Brook(e) feild* 1625, 1690, 1703, ~ ~ *Field* 1708, 1715 (*v.* **brōc, feld**; one of the great open-fields of the township); *Brownes Close* 1589 (*v.* **clos(e)**), *Brownes dickes* 1606, 1625, *Browns Ditch* 1703 (*v.* **dík, dīc**; with the surn. *Brown*); *Bullocks pen* 1700 (*v.* **bulluc, penn**); *bullwell* 1690 (*v.* **bula, wella**; cf. Bulwell, Nt 141]; *Buttrill* 1625, *Butterhill* 1690, 1708, 1715, *butterill* 1703 (*v.* **butere, hyll**; a hillside pasture used in summer for the production of butter); *Catsacre* 1606, *Catsaker* 1625, *Catts Acre* 1703, 1708, 1715 (*v.* **æcer**; with the surn. *Catt*, an original by-name from OE *catt* 'a cat', *v.* Catthorpe *supra*); *Chiffurlonge* 1208 (*v.* **cis, furlang**; with assimilation *sf* > *ff*); *Chrismas pleck* 1625 (*v.* **plek**; with the surn. *Chris(t)mas*, originally of one born at Christmas); *Church Leys* 1708, 1715 (*v.* **leys** and St Andrew's Church *supra*); *Clusitch* 1625, 1690, *Cluse Sitch* 1690, 1700 (*v.* **clūs(e), sīc**); *Caudwell* 1606, *Codewell* 1625 (*v.* **cald, wella**); *the Common Pasture* 1708 (*v.* **commun, pasture**); *Coots* 1690 (*v.* **cot**); *(the) Crossedoles* 1625, 1690, *Cross doles* 1703, 1708, 1715 (*v.* **dāl**, with **cros** or **cross**; note Cross Hill *supra*); *neather* ~, *upper cuttle* 1625, *uper cuttle* 1703, *upper Cuttwell* 1708, ~ *Cuttwel* 1715 (*v.* **cutel**; *Daglane* 1382, 1715 (*v.* **dag, lane**; current in South Kilworth as Dog Lane, cf. *Daglane* in Market Harborough, Lei **4** 172]; *Davyes* 1589 (the surn. *Davy* in the possessive case; from a popular form of David); *Eberesmeeres* 1625, *Ebersmeers* 1690, 1700, 1708, 1715 (*v.* **mere**¹; with the OE masc. pers.n. *Ēadbeorht*); *Elstub* 1625, 1690, 1708, 1715, *Elstroup* 1703 (*v.* **ellern, stubb**); *Elverdale* 1625, 1708, 1715, *Eluerdale* 1690, 1703, *Eluerdale balke* 1625, ~ *baulk* 1703, *Elverdale baulk* 1708, 1715 (*v.* **balca**), *longe Eluerdale* 1625, *Long Eluerdale* 1690, 1703, ~ *Elverdale* 1708, 1715 (*v.* **dalr**; with the OE masc. pers.n. *Ælfhere*); *Fen balke* 1700 (*v.* **fenn, balca**); *fen hawthorn* 1625 (*v.* **fenn, hagu-þorn**); *fluslade* 1625, *Flewslade* 1690, 1700, 1703, 1715, *flue slade* 1708 (*v.* **flȳs, slæd**; perh. alluding to a valley producing good fleeces on its sheep); *Frankes hadland* 1625 (*v.* **hēafod-land**; with the surn. *Franks*, prob. from OFr, ME *franc* 'free', i.e. not a villein; note Franks Lane in adjoining Walcote *supra*); *the Furres* 1690, *The Furs* 1715, *the Common furs* 1708, 1715 (*v.* **commun**) (*v.* **fyrs**); *Gate Lands* 1690 (*v.* **gata, land**); *Gooseacre* 1700, 1703 (*v.* **gōs, æcer**); *goresbrode* 1625 (*v.* **garebrode, gorebrode**); *Grange craft hedge* 1690, 1708, 1715 (*v.* **croft, hecg** and The Grange *supra*); *Greenstede* 1606, *greenested* 1625, *Greenstead* 1690, 1703, 1715 (*v.* **grēne**¹, **stede**); *hall hedge* 1625, *Halls hedge* 1703, 1708, 1715 (*v.* **hecg**; with the surn. *Hall*, cf. Halls Cl *supra*); *the hallow* 1690, *Hallow hame* 1606, *holloham* 1625, *the Hollowham* 1708, 1715 (*v.* **hamm**), *hollow meadow* 1625, 1715, *Hallow meddow* 1690, *halow meade* 1703, *Hallow Meadow* 1708, 1715 (*v.* **holh, mēd (mēdwe** obl.sg.)); *Ham banks* 1606, 1703, 1708, 1715, *ham bankes* 1625 (*v.* **banke**), *hamlandes* 1690 (*v.* **land**) (*v.* **hamm**); *Hassockes* 1625, *Hassocks* 1690, 1703, 1715, *Hassacks* 1708, 1715 (*v.* **hassuc**); *the Hither Low* 1708, 1715 (*v.* **hider, hlāw**); *Hobwellebroc* e.13 (*v.* **wella, brōc**; if with **hob**, then a spring associated with a hobgoblin (*v.* B. Dickins, 'Yorkshire Hobs', *Transactions of the Yorkshire Dialect Society*, vii, 19–22), but less likely, if with **hobb(e)**, then a spring surrounded with high tufts of grass); *the holme* 1690, 1703, 1708, 1715, *the home* 1703 (*v.* **holmr**); *horneslade* 1625, 1690, *Horn Slade* 1703, 1708, 1715 (*v.* **horn, slæd**); *Huhehus* e.13 (*v.* **hūs**; with the OFr masc. pers.n. *Hue* (from ContGerm *Hugo*)); *Hulland* 1625, *Longe Huland* 1606, *Long hunlands* 1703, ~ *Hurlands* 1715, *Short hulland* 1606, 1625, ~ *hunlands* 1703, ~ *Hurlands* 1715 (*v.* **hyll, land**); *Kilworth path* 1703, 1708 (*v.* **pæð**; the footpath between North and South Kilworth); *the Kinges highe waye* 1606, *the kinges hie way* 1625 (*v.* **hēah-weg**; alluding to James I); *Knaptauft hedge* 1625, *Knaptoft Hedg(e)* 1690, 1703, 1708, 1715 (*v.* **hecg**; a parish boundary marker, Knaptoft adjoining to the north); *Lamcotes* 1625, 1690, 1700, *Lambcoats* 1708, 1715 (*v.* **lamb, cot**); *Langlands* 1625, 1708, 1715 (*v.* **lang¹, land**); *over langridge* 1625, *Offer Longledg* 1700 (*v.* **uferra**), *upper langledg* 1690, *uper Langlidge* 1703, *Upper Langledge* 1708, 1715 (*v.* **lang¹, hrycg**; the generic confused later with *ledge*); *Longehill* 1625, *Long hill* 1690, 1703, 1708, 1715 (*v.* **lang¹, hyll**); *Lukissis yardes end* 1625 (*v.* **geard, ende**; with the surn. *Lucas*, from the learned form of Luke); *Lusileslade* 1690, *Lassiles slade* 1700, *Lusiles slade* 1703, 1708, 1715 (*v.* **slæd**; with the surn. *Lascelles*, a Norman introduction from Lacelle in Orne); *Mallow* 1625, 1700, 1708, 1715, *Mollow* 1690, *Molow* 1703 (*v.* **malu**); *the milfeylde* 1606, *the Millfeyld* 1625, (*the*) *Milne Feild* 1690, 1703, *the Milne Field* 1708, 1715 (*v.* **feld**; one of the great open-fields), *the Milne Baulk* 1708, 1715 (*v.* **balca**), *the Mill furlong* 1690, 1703 (*v.* **furlang**), *the mill home* 1625 (*v.* **holmr**), (*the*) *Milway* 1606, (*the*) *Mill way* 1625, *the Milne way* 1703, 1708, 1715 (*v.* **weg**), *the Milne Willowes* 1690, *Mill Willows* 1703 (*v.* **wilig**), *the Milne Willows furlong* 1708, 1715 (*v.* **furlang**) (*v.* **myln**); *Mortons Penn* 1690, ~ *Pen* 1708, 1715 (*v.* **penn**; with the surn. *Morton*, perh. of a family originally from Gilmorton, 4 miles to the north-west); *Mosehill* 1606, *Mossill* 1625, *Mossels* 1690, 1715, *Mosels* 1708 (*v.* **mos**; ostensibly with **hyll**, but an altered **wella** would seem likelier); *Mousle way* 1625 (*v.* **weg**; the road to Mowsley, 4 miles to the north-east); (*the*) *Mutway* 1606, 1625, 1690, (*the*) *Mutt way* 1703, 1708, 1715 (*v.* **mote, weg**); *Nomans Leys* 1708, 1715 (*v.* **nān-mann, leys**); (*the*) *oat landes* 1625, *oatelands* 1703, *Oat Lands* 1708, 1715 (*v.* **āte, land**); *Old Land(s) Leyes* 1690, 1703 (*v.* **land, leys**; with **ald** or **wald**, note *Segould*, *supra*); *the parsons peece* 1625 (*v.* **persone, pece**); *Peaslandes* 1606, 1625, *Peaslands* 1690, *peaselands* 1703 (*v.* **land**), *Peshill* 1606, 1625, *Peashill* 1708, *Peshil* 1715 (*v.* **hyll**), *pessill leyes* 1625, *Peshill Leys* 1700, 1715, ~ *Layes* 1703, *Peshil Leys* 1708 (*v.* **leys**) (*v.* **pise**); *the plain* 1703, 1708, 1715 (*v.* **plain**); *Poultne hedg, Poultney hedge* 1625, *poltney hedg* 1703, *Pultney Hedge* 1708, 1715 (*v.* **hecg**; a parish boundary marker), *Poultney ~* 1625, *Poltney stile* 1700 (*v.* **stīg**), *Pultney ~~* 1690, 1708, 1715, *Poltney stile furlong* 1703 (*v.* **furlang**) (the depopulated village of Poultney lay 2 miles to the north-west); *the Queens highway* 1703, 1708, 1715 (*v.* **hēah-weg**; with reference to Queen Anne); (*the*) *Ridgeway* 1625, 1703, 1708, 1715, *Ridgway* 1690, *Ridg(e)way haden* 1625, 1690, 1703, 1708 (*v.* **hēafod**; with an archaic *-en* pl.) (*v.* **hrycgweg**); *Rixsted* 1625, *Rickstead* 1690, 1703 (*v.* **rickstead**); *Sixswathes* 1625, 1690, *Six swaths* 1708, 1715 (*v.* **six, swæð**); (*at*) *Stone* 1625, (*on*) *Stony* 1703, 1708, 1715 (*v.* **stān, stānig**); *Stone* *slade* 1703, *Stonyslade* 1708, *Stoney Slade* 1715 (*v.* **stān, stānig, slæd**); *Stoneway* 1625 (*v.* **stān, weg**); *Stonow* 1606, ~ *slade* 1690 (*v.* **slæd**) (*v.* **stān, hōh**); *tenteres* 1625, *Tenters* 1690, 1708, *tentars* 1703 (*v.* **tentour**); *Thomas Tawbuts hadle* 1625 (*v.* **headley**), *Talbuts hadeland* 1703, 1708, 1715 (*v.* **hēafod-land**) (with the surn. *Talbot*); *the Town Baulk* 1708 (*v.* **balca**), *the Towne grawnd* 1606, *the town(e) ground* 1625, 1703 (*v.* **grund**), *the town(e) hadland* 1625, 1703, 1708, 1715 (*v.* **hēafod-land**), *the Town Land* 1703, 1708, 1715 (*v.* **land**), *the Town side* 1703, 1715 (*v.* **sīde**) (*v.* **tūn**); *Wackefeld* e.13 (*v.* **wacu, feld**; alluding to an annual wake or festival, cf. Wakefield, YW **2** 163 and Wakefield, Nth 105; the recurring name negates the notion of the OE masc. pers.n. *Waca* as the specific); *Waltney furres* 1625, ~ *Furs* 1690, 1708, 1715, *Walton furse* 1703 (*v.* **fyrs**; with reference to Walton which lies 3 miles to the north-west); *Wasedale* 1625, *Wheasdale* 1690, 1708, *Whasedale* 1703, 1715 (*v.* **wāse, dalr**); *Waterforrowes* 1625, 1690, *Water Furrows* 1703, 1715, *waterfurreus* 1708, *v.* **wæter, furh** and *Water furrowes* in Ashby Parva f.ns. (b)); *the Well lane end* 1715 (*v.* **wella, lane-ende**); *neather* ~, *over wesmessoe* 1625 (*v.* **uferra**), *Nether* ~, *Upper Wessmiso* 1690, *Westmisso* 1700, *nether* ~, *uper westmister* 1703, *Nether* ~, *Upper Westminster* (*v.* **westmest, hōh**); *the West feild* 1625, 1690, ~ ~ *Field* 1708, 1715 (*v.* **west, feld**; one of the great open-fields); *Whatle* 1625, *Whatley* 1690, *Whatly* 1703, *Whatle stream*, *Whatley streame* 1690, *Whatly stream* 1703 (*v.* **strēam**) (*v.* **hwǣte, lēah**); *Whorne* 1625, 1700, 1708, 1715, *Whorn* 1703, 1708, *backeside whorne* 1625, *(the) Backside Whorne* 1700, 1703, 1708, 1715 (*v.* **bak-side**) (*v.* **cweorn**; either alluding to a mill or to a place where mill-stones could be obtained); *Widdowes Thornes* 1625, 1690, *Widdows* ~ 1703, *Woddows Thorns* 1715 (*v.* **þorn** and Wooder in f.ns. (a)); *Willowes* 1625, *(the) Willows furlong* 1690, 1700, 1703, 1708, 1715 (*v.* **furlang**), *wiles furres* 1625, *Willeis Furres* 1690, *Willows furs* 1708, 1715 (*v.* **fyrs**) (*v.* **wilig**); *Wlferescote* 1208 (*v.* **cot**; with the OE masc. pers.n. *Wulfhere*); *Woham* e.13 (*v.* **wōh, hamm**).

Oadby

Oldebi (sic) 1086 DB (×2)

Oudeby c.1130 LeicSurv, 1204 Cur (p) *et passim* to 1316 Banco,
1320 *Wyg et freq* to 1514, 1518 *ib et passim* to 1542 CoPleas,
1543 Fine, *Oudebi* 1209 × 34 *AllS*, 1367 *Wyg*

Outhebi 1199 FF, 1204 P, 1236 Fine, *Outhebia* e.13 *Wyg* (p),
Outhebya 1260 *ib*, *Outheby* 1220 MHW, 1223 Fine *et freq* to 1386
Banco, 1399 *Wyg*, *Owthebi* 1236 Fine

Houtheby 1219, 1220 Cur, 1221 RHug *et passim* to 1.13 *Wyg*,
Houdeby 1377 *LCDeeds*

Outebi 1203 P, *Outeby* 1226 Cur, 1254 Val *et passim* to 1393 *Wyg*,
1397 Pat

Owdeby 1404, 1412 *Wyg et passim* to 1528 Visit, 1535 VE, *Owdeby*
1440 Pat

Odeby 1443, 1508 Banco *et passim* to 1610 Speed, 1614 LML

Oteby 1465, 1467 *Wyg*, *Oteby alias dict' Oudeby* 1467 *ib*

Oadebye 1608 LML, *Oadby* 1629 *ib et freq*

Most probably 'the farmstead or village of a man called Authi', *v.* **bȳ**.
The masc. pers.n. *Auði* is ON (ODan *Øthi*) and appears as *Owði* in the
Liber Vitae of Thorney Abbey (*v.* D. Whitelock, 'Scandinavian personal
names in the Liber Vitae of Thorney Abbey', *Saga Book of the Viking
Society for Northern Research* 12, Pt 2, 137, 149) and cf. Oby, Nf **2** 42.
A possible alternative as the specific is OScand **auðr** 'wealth, riches',
since Oadby lies on easily worked and fertile glacial sand and gravel, *v.*
SSNEM 61.

The DB spelling has AN inverted *l* for pre-consonantal *u*.

ALBION ST, a popular name for new streets in the early 19th cent. Albion
was an old poetic name for Britain, once thought to be based on Lat
albus 'white', with reference to the colour of the southern coastal chalk
cliffs. It occurs in Pliny as early as the 1st cent. A.D.: *Albion ipsi nomen
fuit cum Britanniae vocarentur omnes*. Recent preference is for a name

from a Brit stem **albio-* meaning 'the land, the country', *v.* A. L. F.
Rivet and Colin Smith, *The Place-Names of Roman Britain*, 247–8.
BLACK DOG (P.H.), *Black Dog* 1846, 1863, 1877 White, 1925 Kelly.
BLACKTHORN LANE, *v.* **blakthorn**. BROCKS HILL, *Brockshill* 1635
Terrier, *Broxhill* 1635, 1661 *ib*, *Brock's Hill* 1925 Kelly, *Broxol*,
Broxole 1467 × 84 *LTD*, *Brocksall* 1697 *Terrier*, *Broxhol* 1700, 1708 *ib*,
Broxholl 1703 *ib*, *Brocksole hull*, *Brokisole hul* l.13 *Wyg*, *Brocksill hill*
1635 *Terrier*, *Brocksall* ~ 1697 *ib*, *Broxhol hill* 1638 *ib* (*v.* **hyll**), *Broxhill*
Feild 1661 *ib*, *brockhole* ~ l.17 *ib*, *brockole feelde* 1693 *ib*, *Broxhol(l)* ~
1700, 1703 *ib*, *the Brox-hill field* 1722 *ib* (*v.* **feld**; one of the township's
great open-fields, also described as *the Field towards Newton Harcoate*
1697 *ib*), *Broxhill hither* ~, *Broxhill nether furlong* 1661 *Terrier* (*v.*
furlang), *v.* **brocc-hol**. BROCKS HILL FM. BROOKSIDE FM, beside Wash
Brook *infra*. CHURCH ST, *v.* St Peter's Church *infra*. COTTAGE FM. THE
ELMS. FLAT SPINNEY, *v.* **flat**, **spinney**. FLUDES LANE, with the surn.
Flude, common in Leicester and nearby Arnesby throughout the 19th
cent., e.g. *John Flude* 1805 Census of Arnesby and *Samuel Flude* 1880
ib of Leicester. FOX (P.H.) (lost), *Fox* 1846 White. GALTREE SPINNEY,
cf. *Galtry* ~ 1661 *Terrier*, *Galtre* ~ 1693 *ib*, *Galtree* ~ 1708 *ib*, *the Galtry*
Close 1722 *ib*, *Galtree* ~ ~ 1638 *ib*, *Galtree Close hedge* 1708 *ib* (*v.*
hecg); poss. the site of an early gallows (*v.* **galg-trēow**), but uncertain
because of the proximity of Gartree Road and Gartree House *infra*,
which suggests a poss. 17th-cent. alteration by attraction of Gartree >
Galtree or even by script confusion of a long *r* with *l*. However, it is
close to Manor Fm on Manor Rd *infra*, which may be the site of the
medieval hall (note *atte Hall* l.13 *Wyg*, *v.* **atte**, **hall**) and thus may record
the former site of the manorial gallows. GARTREE HO. GARTREE ROAD,
the Roman *Via Devana*, whose later name was taken from the Gartree
Hundred, the moot-site of which lay a little north of Shangton, beside the
road, *v.* Lei **4** 1. GLEBE FM (local), *v.* **glebe**. GLEN HILL FM, Glen Hill
lying towards Great Glen, once some 2 miles to the south-east of Oadby.
GLEN RD is *Glengate* l.13 *Wyg*, 1467 × 84 *LTD*, 1625, 1638 *Terrier et*
passim to 1722 *ib*, *Glen(n) Gate* 1638, 1708 *ib*, *v.* **gata**. GORSE LANE, *v.*
gorst. HALF MOON SPINNEY, *v.* **spinney**; a D-shaped plantation. THE
GREEN (local), *The Green* 1877 White, *v.* **grēne**[2]. HARBOROUGH RD,
Market Harborough lying 10 miles to the south-east. HIGH CROFT, 1877
White, *v.* **croft**. HIGH ST is *the Streete* 1625 *Terrier*, *v.* **strēt**. HILL TOP
FM. KETTLESBOROUGH (2½"; extending into Stoughton parish, Gartree
Hundred, Lei **4** 259), *Katilbere hill*, ~ *hyll* 1467 × 84 *LTD*,
Kettleborough Hill 1625, 1638 *Terrier et passim* to 1722 *ib*,
Cettleborough ~, *Cettelborow(e) hill* 1635 *ib*, *Kettleborow* ~ 1661 *ib*,

Cattleborrow ~ 1674, 1.17 *ib*, *Cattelborrow hill* 1693 *ib*, *Kesborough Hill*
1845 *TA*, 1878 *PK*, 1906 *Surv*, 1907 *PK*, *v*. **berg**, **hyll**; with the ON
masc. pers.n. *Ketill*, an original by-name from *ketill* 'a cauldron, a
cauldron-shaped helmet'. The *a* spellings in the early forms of the name
are due either to AN scribal interchange between *e* and *a* or to monkish
latinization (cf. Lat *catillus* 'a small bowl'), their source being a register
of Leicester Abbey. An interpretation 'cattle byre' (with *cat*(*t*)*el* + *byre*),
may be discounted, OE *ȳ* rarely giving *e* in ME in Leics., more usually
i, *u* or *y*. That said, an ON masc. pers.n. as a specific with *berg* is very
rare in the county. Stemborough (*Steinesberue* 13, *Steynesberwe* 1323)
in Leire *supra* may be the only other instance recognized to date. The
very late appearance of a genitival medial *s* in Kettlesborough may be
due to local antiquarian interest. KNIGHTON GRANGE, 1863 White, 1925
Kelly, *v*. **grange**. KNIGHTON GRANGE RD, Knighton parish adjoining to
the west. LEICESTER RACE COURSE. LEICESTER RD is *Leicester way* 1625,
1635 *Terrier et passim* to 1708 *ib*, *v*. **weg**. LONDON RD. MANOR FM, cf.
Old Manor House 1877 White, *v*. **maner**. MANOR RD. MODEL FM, *v*.
Model Fm in Catthorpe *supra*. NEW INN, 1877 White, 1925 Kelly. NEW
ST. OADBY FRITH (local), *Oadby Frith* 1877 White, 1925 Kelly, *v*. **fyrhð**.
OADBY GRANGE, ~ ~ FM, *The Grange* 1877 White, *v*. **grange**; it is
Oadby Lodge 1835 O, *v*. **loge**. OADBY HILL HO., *Oadby hill* 1925 Kelly,
cf. *super le Hil* 1280 *Wyg* (p), *del Hul* SR (p), *de la Hull* 1332 ib (p),
(*super montem* c.1247 *Wyg* (p), with MLat *super* 'on', *mons* (*montem*
acc.sg.) 'a hill'), *v*. **hyll**. OADBY LODGE FM (OADBY LODGE 2½"), *v*.
loge. THE OAKS FM. THE PANTILES, a building with pantiles, a pantile
being a roofing tile whose transverse section is a flattened S-shape.
RINGER'S SPINNEY (2½"), *The Ringers Spinny* 1835 O, *v*. **spinney**; prob.
refers to endowed land for the payment of bell-ringers in the parish
church, since the surn. *Ringer* (either from ME *ringere* 'a bell-ringer' or
from the OFr masc. pers.n. *Rainger* (*v*. Reaney *s.n.*)) is not found in
Leics. ST PETER'S CHURCH, *Church (St Peter)* 1846, 1863, 1877 White,
1925 Kelly; it is recorded earlier as *ecclesie de Outheby* 1220 MHW,
1370 *Pat*, ~ *de Oudebi* 1223 *ib*, *ecclesiam de Otheby* 1250 RGros, ~ *de
Oudeby* 1445 *Pat*; note also *the Church Yard* 1638, 1693, 1700, 1703,
1708 *Terrier*, *v*. **churchyerd** and *the Vicarage house* 1638, 1693, 1700,
1703 *ib*, *the vicaridge house* 1689, 1709, 1730 ChAccts, *the Vicarige
house* 1708 *Terrier*, *the Viccaridge House* 1751 *ib*, *the Vicarage house*
1772, 1793, 1814, 1835 ChAccts, *v*. **vikerage**. SHADY LANE, *v*. **shady**.
STACKYARD SPINNEY, *v*. **stackyard**, **spinney**. STOUGHTON GRANGE FM
(GRANGE FM 2½"), *Stoughton Graunge* 1554 AILR, 1560 Pat, ~ *Grange*
1562 Ipm, 1595 Nichols, 1604, 1705 LML, 1724 LeicW, ~ *Grainge* 1765

HB, *v.* **grange**; at the parish boundary with Stoughton which adjoins to the north-east. STOUGHTON RD is *Stowtongate* 1467 × 84 *LTD* (*v.* **gata**), *Stoughton way* 1638, 1661, 1697, 1700, 1703, 1708 *Terrier, Stoton* ~ 1674, 1693, l.17 *ib, Stouton way* 1722 *ib* (*v.* **weg**). WASH BROOK, *the Brook(e)* 1700, 1703, 1708 *Terrier, v.* **brōc**; either with **wæsce** or **wæsse**. WHITE HORSE (P.H.) (lost), *White Horse* 1846, 1863, 1877 White, 1925 Kelly. WIGSTON RD is *Wigston Gate* 1722 *Terrier, v.* **gata**; Wigston Magna lies 1½ miles to the south-west. WOODSIDE FM.

Street-names in recent urban developments:

ASH TREE RD. BANKART AVE. BEAUMONT ST. BRAMBLING WAY. BRABAZON RD. BRIAR WALK. BROCKS HILL DRIVE. CARFAX AVE. CARTWRIGHT DRIVE. COOMBE PLACE. COOMBE RISE. COVERT CL. CROSS ST. DRURY LANE. ELIZABETH DRIVE. FAIRFIELD RD. FOXHUNTER DRIVE. FREEMANTLE RD. GARDEN CL. GLEN WAY. GRANVILLE AVE. GREENBANK DRIVE. GROSVENOR CRESC. HALF MOON CRESC. HIDCOTE RD. HIGHCROFT RD. HIGH LEYS DRIVE. HILL WAY, INTREE CRESC. KENDRICK DRIVE. KILBURN AVE. KING ST. KNIGHTON RISE. LAUNDE RD. LYNDON DRIVE. MEADOWCOURT RD. MERCIA DRIVE. MILTON GARDENS. MOUNT RD. ORCHARD CL. PARK CRESC. POWYS AVE. PRIMROSE HILL. PRINCE DRIVE. QUEEN ST. REGENT ST. ROSEMEAD DRIVE ST ANDREW'S DRIVE SEAGRAVE DRIVE. SIBTON LANE. SOUTHFIELDS AVE. SOUTHMEADS RD. SPENCER ST. STOUGHTON DRIVE. THE BROADWAY. THE FAIRWAY. THE OVAL. TUDOR DRIVE. UPLANDS RD. VANDYKE RD. WAYSIDE DRIVE. WESTMINSTER RD. WOODFIELD RD. WOODSIDE RD.

FIELD-NAMES

In (a), names dated 1806 are Map; those dated 1814 are ChAccts; c.1830 and 1871 are *Terrier*; 1835 are O. Forms throughout dated l.13, c.1247, 1280, 13, 1379, 1396 (1473) and 1484 are *Wyg*; those dated a.1238 are Hastings; 1330 are Coram; 1332 are SR; 1467 × 84 are *LTD*; 1629 are *QH*; 1689, 1709 and 1730 are ChAccts; 1625, 1635, 1638, 1661, 1668, 1674, l.17, 1693, 1697, 1700, 1703, 1708 and 1722 are *Terrier*.

(a) Barn Cl c.1830, Barn Fd or First Barn Cl, Far Barn Fd or Second Barn Cl 1879 (*v.* **bern**); Bottom ~, Middle ~, Top Bradshaw 1879 (with the surn. *Bradshaw,* cf. *James Bradshaw* 1845 Census, *George Bradshaw* 1871 ib and *John Bradshaw* 1880 ib, all of Oadby); Largest Cl by Brook (*v.* **largest**), Least Cl by Brook (*v.* **lǣst**)

c.1830 (*the Brooke* 1635, 1638, 1661, 1697, 1722, *the Brook* 1708, *v.* **brōc**); Far Cl
c.1830 (*v.* **feor**); Great Mdw c.1830; House Cl c.1830; Little Cl c.1830; Little Mdw
c.1830 (*Litulmedow* 1467 × 84, *Little meadow*(*e*) 1635, 1638 *et passim* to 1722, *Littel
middow* l.17, *~ medow* 1693, *v.* **lȳtel, mēd** (**mēdwe** wk.obl.)); Marshall's Lands 1814
(*Marshalls Land* 1689, 1709, 1730, *v.* **land**; with the surn. *Marshall*, cf. *Mary
Marshall* 1832 Census); Middle Cl c.1830; New Bridge Cl, New Bridge Mdw or
Salters Nook c.1830 (*v.* Salters Nook *infra*); New Covert 1806 (*v.* **cover(t)**); New
Pool Bank 1879 (*v.* **banke**) (*the new poole* 1722, *v.* **nīwe, pōl**¹); Oadby Toll Gate
1835 (*v.* **toll-gate**); Salters Nook c.1830 (*v.* **saltere, nōk** and *Salt Riggewey* in f.ns.
(b)); Smalley's Piece 1879 (*v.* **pece**) (cf. *John Smalleys hadland* 1722 (*v.* **hēafod-
land**), *John Smalleys pen* 1722 (*v.* **penn**); note *William Smalley* 1826 Census and
George Smalley 1829 ib, the family still living in Oadby as late as *Harry Smalley*
1881 ib); Little ~ ~, Thorney Fd c.1830 (*v.* **þornig**); Moore's Thorney Pit Fd (with
the surn. *Moore*, cf. *John Moore* 1834 Census, *Thomas Moore* 1842 ib and *Eunice
Moore* 1872 ib, all of Oadby), Thorney Pit Mdw c.1830 (*v.* **þornig, pytt**).

(b) *Abrahams Pen* 1697 (*v.* **penn**; an enclosure unusually known at this date by
a pers.n., that of *Abraham Goodaker* 1697 *Terrier*); *John Andrews hadland* 1722 (*v.*
hēafod-land; earlier in Oadby is *Richard Andrewes* 1544 Nichols); *badfordale* l.13,
Bedforddale 1467 × 84, *Badfordaleouerende* l.13 (*v.* **uferra, ende**) (*v.* **ford, dalr**; the
prototheme is prob. the OE masc. pers.n *Bad*(*d*)*a*, with **badde** 'bad, poor' less
likely); *the Ball Cross* 1722 (*v.* **ball, cros**; *ball* could refer to part of a stone cross's
particular construction or to a hillock on which the cross was sited); *Bannefurlong*
1467 × 84, *Banner ~* 1635, 1661, 1674, 1697, *Banny furlong* 1722 (*v.* **furlang**; the
base of this name is uncertain; since the earliest form may be erratic in the cartulary
copy, something as prosaic as **bēan** or **bān** is poss., but **baner** 'a flag', which was
sometimes applied to a more permanent boundary marker, is doubtful; the name may
eventually have become associated with *bannering*, the custom of beating the parish
bounds while carrying flags, although at what period this custom began is unknown);
Thos. Bates hadland 1722, *v.* **hēafod-land**); *Black pittes* 1625, *~ pitts* 1635, 1638 *et
passim* to 1722, *black pites* l.17, 1693 (*v.* **blæc, pytt**); *Blakemylys* 1467 × 84 (*v.*
blæc, mylde); *Tho. Brandards hadland* 1722 (*v.* **hēafod-land**); *brodesike* l.13, 1379,
Braddesyke, Bradsyke, Brod(*e*)*seke, Brodesyke, ~ nether ende* (*v.* **neoðera, ende**)
1467 × 84, *Broadsick* 1625, 1635 *et passim* to 1722, *broade sick* 1638, *broad sicke*
1661 (*v.* **brād, sík**); *Brokefurlong, Brukfurlong* 1467 × 84 (*v.* **brōc, furlang**); *Brooke
fyeld* 1635, *the brook field* 1674 (*v.* **feld**; one of the great open-fields of the township,
otherwise called *brockhole feelde*, *v.* Brocks Hill *supra*; it is uncertain whether this
alternative name is the result of a reduction of *brocc-hol* to *brōc*); *John Browns
hadland* 1697, 1722 (*v.* **hēafod-land**; *Jane Brown* 1831 Census and *Joseph Brown*
1840 ib of Oadby may have been John's descendants, but the surn. is common);
bullocks pen 1661 (*v.* **bulluc, penn**); *the butes* l.17, 1693 (*v.* **butte**); *Caluerlesure,
Caluerleysure, Calfurleysure furlong* (*v.* **furlang**) 1467 × 84, *calver leyes* 1674,
Caluer ~ l.17, *Calver Lease* 1693, *Couerleys* 1700, 1703, *Couerles* 1708 (*v.* **calf**
(**calfra** gen.pl.), **lǣs** (**lǣswe** dat.sg.)); (*in*) *campo austral'* l.13 (with MLat *campus*
'a field' and *australis* 'southern'; i.e., *Brooke fyeld, supra*), (*in*) *campo borial'* l.13
(with MLat *borialis* 'northern'; i.e., *Mill fyeld, infra*), (*in*) *campo oriental'* l.13 (with
MLat *orientalis* 'eastern'; i.e., *Hill fyeld, infra*); *the Cankwell* 1668 (*v.* **canc** 'a steep,
rounded hill'; **wella** may have replaced **hyll**, a common later substitution); (*in*) *Carr*
1674, 1708, (*in*) *Car* l.17, 1693, *Long Carr* 1708 (*v.* **kjarr**); *John Cartwrights Close*

1722, ~ ~ *Hadland* 1697 (*v.* **hēafod-land**), ~ ~ *Leys* 1722 (*v.* **leys**), *Matthew Cartwrights hadley* 1722 (*v.* **headley**) (note *Elizabeth Cartwright* 1739 MI and *John Cartwright* 1766 ib of Oadby); *Cawdewelle* 1467 × 84, *Cadewell Poole* 1638, ~ *Pool* 1700, 1703, 1708 (*v.* **pōl**[1]) (*v.* **cald, wella**); *the Church*(*e*) *hadland* 1625, 1638 *et passim* to 1722, *the church headland* 1674 (*v.* **hēafod-land** and St Peter's Church *supra*); *Clerks close* 1629, *William Clarkes hadland* 1635, *John Clarks hadland* 1722 (*v.* **hēafod-land**) (cf. *William Clarke* 1630 Nichols and *John Clarke* 1759 EnclA); *the Colepitt way* 1635, *Colepit* ~ 1661, *Coalpitt nooke* 1722 (*v.* **nōk**) (*v.* **col-pytt**; while those forms with *nooke* refer to a place where charcoal was made, the first may refer rather to a route by which pit coal was transported); *Henry Colsons yard end* 1722 (*v.* **geard, ende**; the surn. *Colson* here may be a patronymic from the ODan masc. pers.n. *Kol* or *Koli*, an original by-name *kol* 'coal', hence 'dark-skinned, swarthy'; otherwise with typical Leics. -*ston* > -*son* development of a surn. from the Notts. p.n. Colston (~ Bassett and Car ~), respectively 20 and 28 miles to the north); *the Commons* l.17 (*v.* **commun**); *the Cow*(*e*) *pasture* 1625, 1638 *et passim* to 1722 (*v.* **pasture**), *Cow slade* 1635 (*v.* **slæd**) (*v.* **cū**); *the Craft* l.17, 1693, (*at*) *the croft gate* 1674 (*v.* **geat**) (*v.* **croft**); *Cromborousike* l.13, *Cromber syke* 1467 × 84 (*v.* **berg, sík**; the prototheme may be **crumbe** 'a bend' rather than the adj. **crumb** 'twisted, bent'); *william dauinport close* l.17, *Thomas Davenports grass hadley* 1697 (*v.* **græs, headley**), *Ann Davenports Close* 1722, *John Davenports hadley*, ~ ~ *Shield* 1722 (*v.* **sceld**, used of a hut or a shelter of some kind; but *a rood called a sheild in broad sick* 1635 may be rather from **sceldu** 'a shallow place'); *le dedemor* l.13 (*v.* **dēad, mōr**[1]; in Leics., commonly used of infertile moorland); *Doo planke* 1467 × 84 (*v.* **planke**; a plank bridge across a stream), *Doue Acres* 1638, 1700, 1703, 1708, ~ *akers* l.17 (*v.* **æcer**) (*Dove* is a Brit stream-name from *dubo*- 'black, dark', *v.* RN 134); *Flanniers* 1661, 1697, ~ *head* 1697 (*v.* **hēafod**), *Flanners peece* 1722 (*v.* **pece**) (the surn. *Flanner* in the possessive case; from OFr *flaunier* 'a maker of custard confections', cf. *Ricardus le Flaunier* 1211 RFL); *Foxholes* 1625, 1635 *et passim* to 1722, *fockholes* 1693 (*v.* **fox-hol**); *foxlondsik* l.13, *Foxlondsyke* 1467 × 84 (*v.* **fox, land, sík**); *John Freestones Side land* 1722 (*v.* **sīde, land**; the Freestone family continued in Oadby from *John Freestone* 1834 Census and *Enos Freeestone* 1841 ib to *Fanny Freestone* 1876 ib); *Galltree* ~ ~ 1638, *Galtree Close hedge* 1708 (*v.* **hecg** and Galtree Spinney *supra*); *Gamulshadland* 1467 × 84 (*v.* **hēafod-land**; with the ON masc. pers.n. *Gamall*, an original by-name *gamall* 'old'); *Gegecros* l.13 (*v.* **cros**; with ME **gegge**, a contemptuous term for beggars, hence the cross was a place where the indigent gathered; perh. explains *le Scheld ad le Cros* in Cosby f.ns. (b), as a shelter for the poor beside a roadside cross); *Glen Cross* 1635, 1661, 1697, 1722 (*v.* **cros**; poss. at the parish boundary), *Glengate boske* l.17, ~ *bouske* 1693 (*v.* **buskr** and Glen Rd *supra*), *Glenside* 1635, 1661 (*v.* **sīde** and Great Glen, Lei **4** 79); *Grange mere* 1467 × 84 (*v.* **(ge)mǣre** and Knighton Grange *supra*); *the Grauill holes* 1722 (*v.* **gravel, hol**[1]); *Grease Nooke* 1722 (*v.* **nōk**; perh. with **græs** (cf. *Greshadland, infra*), but OE **smeoru** and ON **smjǫr**, both meaning 'grease, fat, butter', were used of rich pasturage where such foodstuffs were produced; hence perh. the specific is indeed **grease**, which in 18th-cent. dialect may have been used in a similar way as *smeoru, smjǫr* in earlier f.ns.); *the Great ground* 1722 (*v.* **grēat, grund**); *Green sick* 1674, *Lytelgrenesyke* 1467 × 84 (*v.* **lȳtel**) (*v.* **grēne**[1], **sík**); *Greshadland* 1467 × 84 (*v.* **græs, hēafod-land**); *grimes hill* 1635, 1661, *Grimshill* 1697, 1722 (*v.* **hyll**; either with the surn. *Grimes*, from the ON masc. pers.n. *Grímr* (ODan *Grim*), or with the pers.n. itself); *at Hall* 1396 (1473) (p), *atte Halle Wal* l.13 (*v.* **atte**, **wall**), (*the*) *Hall leyes* 1635, 1638, 1700, 1708, *the hall leas*(*e*) 1661, l.17, 1693, ~ ~ *leyse* 1674, ~ ~ *leys* 1697 (*v.* **leys**) (*v.* **hall**); (*into*) *hard* 1635, *Hard Galles* 1708 (*v.* **galla**), *Hard Gutter* 1638, 1700, 1703 (*v.* **goter**), *Hardepolis* 1467 × 84, (*att*) *Hard poole* 1635, 1661, 1697, *the hard poole* 1722 (*v.* **pōl**[1]) (*v.* **heard**; the adj. 'hard' is here used as a sb., perh. 'firm, rough ground'); *Hede medow* 1467 × 84 (*v.* **hīd**, **mēd** (**mēdwe** obl.sg.); cf. Hide Mdw in Claybrooke Magna f.ns. (a)); *Hedghill* 1635, 1661 (*v.* **ecg**, **hyll**; cf. Edge Hill, Wa 12, the site of the first major battle of the English Civil War in 1642); *Hengyn hadland* 1467 × 84 (*v.* **hangende**, **hēafod-land**); *Hill fyeld* 1635, (*the*) *Hill Field* 1638, 1674 *et passim* to 1708, *the Hill Feild* 1661, 1722, ~ ~ *feelde* l.17, 1693 (*v.* **hyll**, **feld**; one of the great open-fields); *Holbroc* l.13, *Holbrok*(*e*) 1467 × 84, *Hobroke* 1635, *Hoobrooke* 1635, 1661, 1697, *Howbrook*(*e*) 1697, *Hobrooke* 1722, *Holbrocouerende* l.13 (*v.* **uferra**, **ende**), *Holbrokehill* 1467 × 84, *Hoobrook hill* 1638, 1708, *Hobroke* ~, *Hoobroke hill* 1661, *hobrock hill* 1674, *Hoebrooke* ~, *Howbrooke hill* 1697, *Hoobrooke Hill* 1700, 1703, 1722 (*v.* **hyll**), *Hoebrooke Leys* 1697 (*v.* **leys**) (*v.* **hol**[2], **brōc**); *the homestall* 1625 (*v.* **hām-stall**); *Horsharde* 1330 (*v.* **hors**, **heard** and (*into*) *hard*, *supra*); *horstonsikenethirende* l.13 (*v.* **neoðera**, **ende**), *Whorston syke* 1467 × 84 (*v.* **hār**[2], **stān**, **sík**; the stone was prob. a boundary marker); *Robt. Ilyffes* ~ 1661, *Mr Ilyffes* ~ 1697, *John Ilifes Hadland* 1722 (*v.* **hēafod-land**), *Mr Ilyffes Yard end* 1697 (*v.* **geard**, **ende**) (the *Iliffe* family continued to live in Oadby as, for example, *John Iliffe* and *Mary Iliffe* 1759 EnclA, *Thomas Iliffe* 1829 Census); *Instys hadland* 1467 × 84 (*v.* **hēafod-land**; with **in**, **stīg**, **stígr**); *Robert Jordains hadley* 1722 (*v.* **headley**; the surn. *Jordain* is from the river Jordan in Israel, which was used as a christian name by returning crusaders who brought back with them water from the river for the baptism of their children); *Kettleborough sick* 1638, 1722, *Kettleborow sicke* 1661, *Cattleborrow sick*(*e*) 1674, l.17, *Cattelborrow* ~ 1693, *Kettleborrow sick* 1697 (*v.* **sík** and Kettlesborough *supra*); *Knighton dayle* 1635 (*v.* **dalr**), *Knytongate* 1467 × 84, *Knighton gate* 1625, 1635 *et passim* to 1722, *Kniton geat*(*e*) l.17, 1693 (*v.* **gata**), *Knytonemere* 1467 × 84, *Knighton meare* 1635, 1661 (*v.* (**ge**)**mǣre**) (Knighton parish adjoins to the north-west); *Kyrkehadland* 1467 × 84 (*v.* **kirkja**, **hēafod-land** and St Peter's Church *supra*); *Langemor* 13, *Longmore* 1467 × 84, 1625, 1635 *et passim* to 1722, *Long Moore* 1638, 1661, 1674, 1700, 1703, ~ *Moor* 1722 (*v.* **lang**[1], **mōr**[1]); *Lechpittes* a.1238 (*v.* **lǣce**[2], **pytt**); *Littlyng*, *Lytlyng furlong* 1467 × 84 (*v.* **furlang**), *v.* **lȳtel**, **líttil**, **eng**); *the Lott Meadow* 1638, *the Lot medow* 1693, ~ ~ *Meadow* 1700, 1703, 1722 (*v.* **hlot**); *Magott* (sic) 1467 × 84 (this may be an incompletely-copied ecclesiastical register form (having lost *hill*?) and prob. represents **magotte** 'a grub, a maggot' rather than either *Magg-ot*, a diminutive of *Magge*, a pet-form of Margaret or a reduced *maggot-pie* 'a magpie'; for the peasant, maggots such as the red maggot, the larva of the wheat-midge which seriously damaged ripening ears of corn and were therefore important, may well have given rise to a locational name; *v.* the following f.n.); *Mattock Hill* 1635, (*upon*) *Mattock* 1661, 1697, *Mattack* 1722 (this f.n. may be a later form of *Magott* (*hill*?) *supra*; if so, ME **maðek** 'a maggot' (either from an unrecorded OE *maðuc* or ON *maðkr*) has replaced **magotte** 'a maggot' (poss. through some metathetic process); ME **mattok**, the agricultural tool for loosening hard ground and grubbing up trees etc., seems much less likely as a simplex); *the Meadow* 1661, *the Middow* 1693, (*the*) *Meadow End* 1661, 1697, 1722 (*v.* **ende**), *the Meadow*(*e*) *hedge* 1635, 1638, 1700, 1703, 1708 (*v.* **hecg**), *the meddowe side* 1674, *the Middou* ~ l.17, (*the*) *Meadow Side*

1697, 1722 (*v.* **sīde**) (*v.* **mēd** (**mēdwe** obl.sg.)); *John Meadows hadland* 1722 (*v.*
hēafod-land); *Mettcalfes* ~ 1661, *Medcalfes* ~ 1674, *Medcafs hadland* 1722 (with
the surn. *Metcalfe*, cf. *William Meatecalf* 1560 RFL; the surn. is from ME *mete-calf*
'a calf to be fattened up for eating', hence disparaging of a person 'fat as a prize
calf'); *michildic* l.13 (*v.* **micel, mikill, dík**); *middilhul* l.13, *Middulhul* 1379 (*v.*
middel, hyll); *Midulfurlong, Mydulfurlong* 1467 × 84 (*v.* **middel, furlang**); *the Mill*
1661, 1697, 1722, *the mill bridge* 1674, *the Mill brig* l.17, 1693 (*v.* **brycg**), *Mill fyeld*
1635, *the Mill feild* 1661, 1693, 1722, ~ ~ *field* 1674, 1697, 1700, 1703, 1708, ~ ~
Feelde l.17 (*v.* **feld**; one of the great open-fields, earlier called *Northfelde, infra*),
Milnfurlong 1467 × 84 (*v.* **furlang**), *Milnehill* 1467 × 84, (*the*) *Mill hill* 1661, 1708,
1722 (*v.* **hyll**), *Milnewey, Mylnewey* 1467 × 84, (*the*) *Mill Way* 1635, 1638 *et passim*
to 1722 (*v.* **weg**) (*v.* **myln**; *Milnehill* and *the mill bridge* suggest that Oadby once
possessed both a windmill and a water-mill); *Millin hill* 1635, 1661, l.17, *Milling* ~
1638, 1700, 1703, 1722, *Millon* ~ 1674, l.17, *Millen hill* 1687 (the specific may be
the vb.sb. **milling** 'the action of grinding in a mill' or 'the process of milling' as in
fulling cloth; but forms of **myln**, as *myline* and *myllen*, survived in literature into the
15th cent. and *mylne* into the 17th cent., although there is already a *Mill hill* here in
1661); *Rich. Monks Leys* 1722 (cf. *John Monk* 1759 EnclA of Oadby and *Susanna
Monk* 1814 Census of adjoining Wigston Magna parish); *Netteshard* 1467 × 84 (*v.*
heard and (*into*) *hard, supra*; the specific is prob. **nēat** 'cattle' but the surn. *Neat,
from *nēat* and thus metonymic for 'a cowherd', does occur); *the New feelde* 1693,
(*the*) *New field* 1697, ~ ~ *feild* 1722, *New field hedge* 1638, 1700, 1703, 1708 (*v.*
hecg), (*at*) *New field gate* 1697 (*v.* **geat**), *new field meadow* 1697, *the New feild
meadow* 1722 (*v.* **nīwe, feld**); (*the*) *New lane end* 1697, 1722 (*v.* **nīwe, lane, lane-
ende**); *Newton hill*(*s*) 1635, 1661, 1697, 1722 (Newton Harcourt adjoins to the south-
east); *Noones Bridg* 1635, ~ *bridge* 1661, 1722 (*v.* **brycg**), *John Noones hadland*
1722, *Thomas Noones hadland* (*v.* **hēafod-land**) (cf. *Roger Noone* 1630 Nichols,
1635 *Terrier, Thomas Noone* 1661 *ib, John Noone sen*ʳ 1697 *ib*); *Northfelde* 1467 ×
84 (*v.* **norð, feld**; one of the great open-fields, later called *Mill fyeld, supra*); *Odebie*
~ 1661, *Odeby thornes* 1697, *Thornes* 1722 (*v.* **þorn**); *the ould Mill stoumpe* l.17, ~
~ ~ *stompe* 1693, (*at*) *old Mill stump* 1697, (*at*) *the Mill Stump* (*v.* **stump**; the
surviving wooden base pillar of a former windmill); *Palmers hadland* 1697 (*v.*
hēafod-land), *Palmers pen* 1697 (*v.* **penn**) (with the surn. *Palmer*; cf. *Esther Palmer*
1853 Census, *Joseph Palmer* 1854 *ib, William Palmer*1879 *ib* and *Evelyn Palmer*
1880 *ib*, all of adjoining Wigston Magna parish); *Parsonage close* 1629 (*v.*
personage); *the pasture* 1635, 1661, l.17, 1722, *the paster* 1693 (*v.* **pasture**); (*the*)
Pen close 1629, 1693, *Penn Close* 1638, 1700, 1703, 1708 (*v.* **penn, clos(e)**); *John
Perkins grasse hadland* 1635 (*v.* **græs**), *Perkins hadland* 1697 (*v.* **hēafod-land**) (the
Perkins family continued in Oadby from *Samuel Perkins* 1837 Census, *John Perkins*
1849 *ib* to *Ernest Perkins* 1877 *ib* and *Lilian Perkins* 1880 *ib*); *Robert Picks yard end*
1697 (*v.* **geard, ende**; note *Samuel Pick* 1815 Census of Oadby); (*at*) *Pindars House*
1638, 1693, 1700, 1703, 1708, *Pinders house* l.17 (*v.* **pyndere**); *Richard Plummers
hadland* 1625 (*v.* **hēafod-land**; cf. *Osbertus le plummer* 1225 RFL and *William
Plummer* 1630 Nichols); *Redys nok'* 1467 × 84 (*v.* **nōk**; prob. with the surn. *Reed,
an original by-name from OE *rēad* 'red', alluding to complexion or to hair; otherwise
v. **hrēod**); *Rugeweyus* 1379, (*the*) *Ridgway* 1635, 1661, 1708, *Ridgeway* 1638, 1697,
1700, 1703, *Cokys rygeway* 1467 × 84 (with a surn., prob. *Cock* or *Cox*), *þest
rygeway* 1467 × 84, *East Ridgway* 1625, *yest regway* l.17, 1673 (*v.* **þe, ēast**), *le*

mideliste riggewey l.13, *Mydulrygeway* 1467 × 84 (*v.* **middel**; the earlier form appears to present an otherwise unrecorded superlative *middlest*), *Ouerrygeway* 1467 × 84, *the over Ridgway* 1722 (*v.* **uferra**), *Upper ridgway* 1661, *Salt Riggewey* l.13, *Saltrigewey, Saltrygewey* 1467 × 84, *Salt Ridgeway* 1625, 1638 *et passim* to 1708, (*the*) *salt ridgway* 1635, 1661, 1672, *Salt ridg way* 1674, *saltregway* l.17, 1693 (*v.* **salt**[1]; alluding to a salt-merchants' route on the ridgeway), *Short Rigew'* l.13 (*v.* **sc(e)ort**), *Smoresladrygeway* 1467 × 84, *Smore Slade Ridgway* 1722 (*v. Smorslade, infra*) (*v.* **hrycgweg**); *Sand hill* 1722 (*v.* **sand**); *Sandland'* 1467 × 84 (*v.* **sand**, **land**); *Seyves thing* 1467 × 84 (*v.* **thing**; with the surn. *Sayve*, from the OE fem. pers.n. *Sægifu*); *Sir Johns Pen* 1697 (*v.* **penn**), *Sir John Lambs Land* 1700, 1703 (*v.* **land**) (note *Sir John Lamb* 1607 Nichols); *the farr ~, the heither slade* 1625, *the far ~, the hether slade* 1635, *far ~, hither slade* 1638, 1697, 1722, *the farther ~, the hether slade* 1661, l.17 (*v.* **farder**), *the hither ~* 1674, 1700, 1703, 1722, *the heather ~, the hether slade* 1693 (*v.* **feor**, **hider**, **slæd**); *Smorehull* l.13, *Smorehyll* 1467 × 84, *Smore hill* 1635 (*v.* **smeoru**, **hyll**); *Smorslade* 1379, *Smoreslade* 1467 × 84, 1635, 1661, 1697, 1722, *~ hades* 1697 (*v.* **hēafod**), *~ haggs* 1697 (*v.* **hǫgg**), *~ hyll* 1467 × 84, *~ hill* 1635, 1661, 1697, 1722 (*v.* **hyll**), *~ nooke* 1661 (*v.* **nōk**), *~ way* 1635 (*v.* **weg**) (*v.* **smeoru**, **slæd**); *Sowslade* 1379, 1467 × 84 (*v.* **sūð**, **slæd**); *Sowthfelde* 1467 × 84 (*v.* **sūð**, **feld**; one of the great open-fields, later called *the Brooke fyeld, supra*); *Spelthorn* a.1238 (*v.* **spell**, **þorn**; a moot site); *the Spinny* 1674, *the spinne* l.17 (*v.* **spinney**); *stoton hedg* 1674, l.17 (*v.* **hecg**; a parish boundary marker), *Stoctonemer', Stoutonemer'* l.13, *Stowton mere* 1467 × 84, *Stoughton Meere* 1625, 1635, *~ meare* 1638, 1661 *et passim* to 1722, *stoton meare* 1693 (*v.* **(ge)mǣre**) (Stoughton parish in Gartree Hundred adjoins to the north-east); *stoophill* 1635, *Stoope hill* 1661 (*v.* **hyll**), *Stowpyng* 1467 × 84 (*v.* **eng**) (*v.* **stolpi**); *Stretton gate* l.13, 1467 × 84, 1625, 1635 *et passim* to 1722, *~ yate* 1635, *Streton geate* l.17, 1693, *Stretton gate baulke* 1661, 1722 (*v.* **balca**) (*v.* **gata**; the road to Stretton Magna which lies 2 miles to the east; also called *Stretton way* 1697); *Syke greynes, ~ grenis* 1467 × 84 (*v.* **sík**, **grein**); *Thykleyes* 1467 × 84 ('clearings amid dense undergrowth', *v.* **þicce**[1], **lēah**); *timhull, timhyl, tymhyl* l.13 (*v.* **hyll**; with the OE masc. pers.n. *Tima*, cf. *Timan hyll* 963 (13) BCS 1111 (S 1307)); *Tinwillowes* 1661, *Tinwillows* 1674, 1693, *tinwillouse* l.17 (*v.* **wilig**; prob. with **tēn**); *Mr Toolyes ~* 1635, *John Tooleys hadland* 1661 (*v.* **hēafod-land**), *Edward Tooleys Hade* 1708 (*v.* **hēafod**) (note *Thomas Tooley* 1630 Nichols, of Oadby); (*the*) *Town hill* 1635 (*v.* **tūn**, **hyll**); *the townsend* 1661, *the Townesend* 1674, *the Town End* 1722 (*v.* **ende**), *Townesend close* 1629 (*v.* **clos(e)**), *the townside* 1661 (*v.* **sīde**) (*v.* **tūn**); *Tymwell* 1467 × 84, 1638, 1700, 1703, 1708 (*v.* **wella**; with the OE pers.n. *Tima*, cf. *timhull, supra*); (*the*) *vicars hadland* 1661, 1697 (*v.* **vikere**, **hēafod-land**); *George Wal(l)drams Land* 1700, 1703 (*v.* **land**; with the surn. *Waldram, Waldron*, from the ContGerm masc. pers.n. *Waleran* (OFr *Galeran*), cf. *Walran* 1154 × 89 Dane of Leics.; also in Oadby were once *Thomas Waldron* 1544 Nichols, *John Waldron* 1559 ib, 1607 Fine and *Gregory Waldron* 1630 Nichols); *Warwick leys* 1697 (*v.* **leys**; either with the surn. *Warwick* (as in *Warwick Hill, ~ Spinney* in Saddington, Lei **4** 226) or lying alongside the old road to Warwick); *Warwykeway* 1467 × 84, *Warwick(e) way* 1635, 1661, 1722 (*v.* **weg**; Warwick lies 30 miles to the south-west); *Waterthorows* 1638, 1703, *water furrowse* 1674, *the waterforrows* l.17, *the water thorrows* 1693, (*the*) *Waterthorowes* 1700, 1708 (*v.* **wæter**, **furh** and *Water furrowes* in Ashby Parva f.ns. (b)); *þe Wattri, þe Watt'* l.13, *the Wattre* 1467 × 84, *watrie* 1625, *watre, Watree* 1635, *Wattery* 1638, 1700, 1703,

1708, *Wattrie* 1661, *Wattry* 1661, 1722, *wattere* 1693, *Watterre* l.17, *Watry* 1697 (*v.*
þe, **wæterig**; with the adj. used as a sb. 'a wet place, a watery place'); *the*
Wellsprings 1661, 1697, 1722, *the hether well spring* 1635, *hither wellsprings* 1638,
1674, 1700, 1703, 1708, *the hether welspring* l.17 (*v.* **hider**), *uestewellespringes* l.13
(*v.* **west**), *Constabul Welspryng furlong* (*v.* **conestable**), *welspryng furlong* (*v.*
furlang) 1467 × 84 (*v.* **wella**, **spring**[1]); *Wells yard end* 1697 (*v.* **geard**, **ende**; with
the surn. *Wells*); *West close* 1629 (*v.* **west**, **clos(e)**); *Westhaued* 1467 × 84 (*v.* **west**,
hēafod); *Wigston Corner* 1661, 1697, 1722 (*v.* **corner**), *Wygston* ~, *Wykeston forth*
1467 × 84, *Wigston Ford* 1635, 1722, ~ *foord* 1635 (*v.* **ford**), *Wigston hedge* 1722
(*v.* **hecg**; a parish boundary marker), (*next*) *Wigston Meadow* 1638, 1708, *Wyxton*
mere 1467 × 84, *Wigston(e) Meere* 1625, 1635, *Wigston Meare* 1661 (*v.* **(ge)mǣre**),
Wigston nooke 1635 (*v.* **nōk**) (Wigston Magna parish adjoins to the south-west); *Wild*
Willows 1638, 1700, 1703, 1708 (*v.* **wilde**, **wilig**); *Wlrichegate* l.13 (*v.* **gata**; with the
OE masc. pers.n. *Wulfrīc*); *Wresls close* 1629 (*v.* **clos(e)**; with the surn. *Wressle*, cf.
Stephanus Wresel' 1327 SR of Leics.).

Peatling Magna

Petlinge 1086 DB (x6), 1190 P *et passim* to 1283 Pat (p), 1299 Ipm
Petling c.1130 LeicSurv, 1166 RBE, 1205 Cur *et freq* to 1317 *Rey*,
   1319 Pat *et passim* to 1369 *Wyg* (p), 1457 *Ct*, *Petlinga* 1190 P,
   Petlyng(*e*) 1236 Fine (p), 1239 Cur *et passim* to 1277 Hastings,
   1284 Pat (p) *et freq* to 1400 ib, 1428 FA *et passim* to 1535 VE
Petlingis c.1131 Ord, *Petlinges* c.1160 Dane (p), 1166 LN (p), 1203,
   1225, 1227, 1233 Cur, 1236 Cl (p), 1247 FineR, *Petlinguis* 1190
   × 1204 France, *Petlynges* 1327 SR (p)
Pedling(*e*) 1193 (p), 1195 P (p), 1196 ChancR (p), 1205 P (p), 1243
   Fees (p)
Pedlynges 1196 ChancR (p), 1197 (p), 1198 (p), 1199 (p), 1200 P (p),
   Pedlinges 1237 RGros, *Pethling* 1199 GildR (p), e.Hy 3 Derby
   (p), *Pethlyng*(*e*) 1317 Ipm, 1342 *LCDeeds* (p)
Petelyng 1247 Ass, c.1291 Tax *et passim* to 1550, 1564 Fine,
   Peteling 1510, 1518 Visit
Peatlyng 1412 Banco, 1507 Ipm, 1576 Saxton, 1594 Fine, *Peatling*(*e*)
   1576 LibCl *et freq*, *Peatelyng* 1528 Visit, *Peatelinge* 1617 LML
Peytlyng 1517 AAS, *Peytling* 1526 ib, 1592 ISLR

Affixes are variously added as:
Magna ~ 1224 RHug, 1243 Fees *et passim* to 1428 FA, 1467 *Wyg*,
   Magne ~ 1220 MHW
~ *Magna* 1241 Cur, 1247 Ass *et passim* to 1592 ISLR, 1617 LML *et*
   freq
Mykyll ~ 1431 × 42 *MiD*
Much(*e*) ~ 1499 *MiD*, c.1500 ECP, *Moche* 1507 Cl
Great(*e*) ~ 1610 Speed, 1708 *Terrier*

'(The settlement of) the family or followers of a man called Peotla',
v. **-ingas**. **Pēotlingas* is a folk-name which survives also in adjoining
Peatling Parva *infra*. The OE masc. pers.n. *Pēotla* is unrecorded but is
presumably a diminutive of the recorded OE *Pēot*. It is uncertain whether

the earlier surviving plural forms refer to the two settlements of Peatling Magna and Peatling Parva or represent the original *Pēotlingas*, although spellings such as *Parva Petlinges* 1225, 1226 Cur, *Parva Pedlinges* 1237 RGros incline to the latter.

Affixes are MLat *magna* 'great', **micel (muche)**, **mikill** and **grēat** *q.v.*

ALL SAINTS' CHURCH, *Church (All Saints)* 1846, 1863, 1877 White, 1925 Kelly; it is earlier recorded as *ecclesie de Magne Pedling* 1220 MHW, ~ *de Magna Pethlyng* 1369 Pat, ~ *de Petlyng Magna* 1400 *ib.* Note also *the church yeard* 1703 *Terrier* (*v.* **churchyerd**) and *the Vicaridge house* 1606 *ib*, *The vicarage house* 1703 *ib* (*v.* **vikerage**). BROMLEY HO., remembers Elizabeth Jervis ('Beloved Tetty'), the second wife of Dr Samuel Johnson, who is buried at Bromley in Kent. She was born and grew up in Peatling Magna where the Jervis family were lords of the manor for some two hundred years in the 17th and 18th centuries. BROOKHILL FM. COCK INN, 1863 White, *The Cock* 1877 ib, 1925 Kelly, *The Cock Inn* 1928 *Deed*. CORNER LODGE FM, *v.* **corner**, **loge**; at the south-east corner of the parish. FOLLY BRIDGE, *v.* **folie**. GATE COTTAGES, at a Y-junction of two principal roads north-east of the village and thus poss. a toll-gate site; *v.* **cotage**, with either **gata** or **geat**. GREAT PEATLING COVERT is *Peatling Gorse* 1835 O, *v.* **gorst**, **cover(t)**. GREAT PEATLING LODGE, 1835 O, *Peatling Lodge* 1863, 1877 White, *v.* **loge**. HOME FM (×2), *v.* **home**. LODGE COTTAGE, beside Peatling Lodge Fm *infra*. LOWER BROOKHILL FM. MAIN ST is *the common street* 1606 *Terrier*, *v.* **commun**, **strēt**. MANOR FM, 1877 White, *v.* **maner**. MERE RD, *v.* **(ge)mǣre**; the road forms the long western boundary of the parish. NEW FM. PEATLING HO. PEATLING LODGE FM (PEATLING LODGE 2½"), *v.* **loge**. THE PLANTATION, *v.* **plantation**. SCHOOL LANE. STAG INN (lost), *Stag Inn* 1846 White. STRAW HALL (JUBILEE FM 2½"), *Straw Hall* 1925 Kelly; cf. Straw Hall, Nt 55; evidently a term of contempt, perh. a derogatory name for land which produced straw rather than ear in the corn. The jubilee commemorated in the alternative name of the farm was either the Golden (1887) or the Diamond Jubilee (1897) of Queen Victoria. TITHE BARN LODGE (PEATLING LODGE 2½"), *v.* **tēoða**, **loge**. WESTDALE FM (WESTDALE HO. 2½"), *Westerdale* 1606, 1625 *Terrier*, *v.* **wester**, **dalr**. WESTERN FM is *Great Peatling Lodge* 1835 O, *v.* **loge**. WHITEHOUSE FM.

FIELD-NAMES

In (a), forms presented without dates are 1968 *Surv*; those dated 1755 and 1889 are *Plan*; 1843 are *Paget*. Forms throughout dated 1259 and 1401 are Fine; those dated 1386 and 1412 are Banco; 1572 are LeicW; 1606, 1625, 1674, 1679, 1697, 1700, 1703 and 1708 are *Terrier*; 1614 are Ipm; 1681 are LAS.

(a) Three Acre Fd, Three Acres 1968, Five Acre Cl 1889, Five Acres 1968, Six Acre 1843, Top Six Acre 1968, Six Acre Mdw 1843, Six Acres 1843, 1968, Seven Acre, Long Nine Acre, Nine Acres, Far Ten Acre 1968, Ten Acres 1843, 1968, Eleven Acres 1968, Twelve Acre Mdw 1843, Twelve Acres, Thirteen Acres, Twenty Acre, Twenty-four Acre(s), Thirty Acres, Forty Acres 1968 (*v.* **æcer**); Top ~, Allotments (*v.* **allotment**); Arnesby Fd (Arnesby parish adjoins to the east); Arthur's Cl (with the surn. *Arthur*); Attfields Second Fd (with the surn. *Attfield*; cf. *Ann Attfield* 1826 Census, *Elizabeth Attfield* 1854 ib, with family members recorded through to *Albert Attfield* 1868 ib, all of nearby Ashby Magna parish); Back Fd (*v.* **back**); Barley Hill 1889, 1968 (*v.* **bærlic**); Barn Cl 1889, 1968, ~ Fd 1968 (*v.* **bern**); Bents Cl, ~ Mdw (prob. with the surn. *Bent* rather than with **beonet**); Big Mdw; Bottle Cl, Bottle Ploughed Fd (*v.* **bōtl**); Bottom Cl 1843, ~ Mdw 1968 (*v.* **bottom**); Brakespeare's (the surn. *Brakespeare* in the possessive case); Bull's Piece (*the bull peece* 1625, *v.* **bula, pece**); Butts Cl, ~ Mdw (*v.* **butte**); Carters Cl, ~ Mdw, ~ Ploughed Cl (with the surn. *Carter*); Chapman's (the surn. *Chapman* in the possessive case; cf. *Thomas Chapman* 1807 Census and *William Chapman* 1821 ib, the Chapman family resident in Peatling Magna to *Anne Chapman* 1880 ib); Corner Fd (*v.* **corner**); Cottage Fd (*v.* **cotage**); Crabtree (*v.* **crabtre**); The Craft (*v.* **croft**); Corralls Cl, Little ~ ~, Corralls Mdw 1843, Curells (sic) 1968 (with the surn. *Corrall*); Eales Fd, ~ Mdw (with the surn. *Eales*; cf. *William Eales* 1823 Census and *Ellen Eales* 1853 ib, the Eales family living in adjoining Arnesby parish to *Thomas Eales* 1880 ib); The Elbow (an L-shaped field, *v.* **elnboga**); Elliot's, Second Elliot's Mdw (with the surn. *Elliot*); Fallow Cl (*v.* **falh**); Far Fd 1968, Far Hill 1843, 1968, Far Mdw 1968 (*v.* **feor**); Flat Cl 1843, ~ Fd 1968, ~ Mdw 1843, 1968 (*v.* **flat, flatr**); The Foley (sic) 1968, Second Folly Mdw 1889 (*v.* Folly Bridge *supra*); Fourth Mdw; Fox Covert 1843 (*v.* **fox, cover(t)**); Front Fd (*v.* **front**); Fulling Mill 1889 (*v.* **fulling**; on the stream to the east of the village, *v.* Mill Bank *infra*); Gravel Hole 1968, Gravel Pit Cl 1843 (*v.* **gravel**); Great Mdw 1843; Greenlands 1889, 1968 (*v.* **grēne**[1], **land**); Gutter Cl (*v.* **goter**); Bottom High Grounds 1889, 1968 (*v.* **grund**); Holme Cl 1843, 1968 (*v.* **holmr**); Big Home Cl 1889, By Home Cl 1968 (poss. with **bī**, but more likely a later form of the previous f.n.; however, note *Byholme* in Aylestone f.ns. (b)), Second Home Cl, Home Fd 1968 (*v.* **home**); Homestead (*v.* **hām-stede**); House Cl; Hovel Fd (*v.* **hovel**); Humpty Dumpty (a field containing humped earthworks relating to the early manor house and prob. medieval house platforms; its humps attracted, through doubling, the name of the nursery rhyme character, *v.* Gerhard Bendz, 'English Word Pairs', *Otium et Negotium: Studies in Onomatology and Library Science presented to Olof von Feilitzen*, Stockholm 1973, 1–12); Jarvis's Cl (with the surn. *Jarvis, Jervis*; cf. *William Jervis* 1597 MI, *William Jervais* 1614 ib (who held the manor of Peatling Magna in 1609 Nichols), *Elizabeth Jervis* 1708 PR, *Samuel*

Jervis 1772 ib, *William Jervis* 1780 MI; the most well-known of this family is Elizabeth Jervis (born 1708) who married Dr Samuel Johnson in 1735, *v.* Bromley Ho., *supra*); Little Cl, ~ Mdw 1843, Little Fd, ~ Hill 1968; Long Cl 1843, ~ Mdw 1968; Lowes Cl (with the surn. *Lowe*, cf. *Sarah Lowe* 1833 Census, *Mary Lowe* 1845 ib and *Helen Lowe* 1859 ib, all of Peatling Magna); Mear Cl, ~ Mdw 1755 (*v.* (ge)mǣre and Mere Rd *supra*); Middle Cl 1843, 1889, 1968, ~ Fd 1968; Mill Bank 1889 (*v.* banke), Mill Mdw 1968, Little Mill Mdw 1889 (*v.* myln and Fulling Mill *supra*); Bottom ~ ~, Top ~ ~, Second Mount Pleasant (a complimentary name, but sometimes given ironically); Musson's Cl (with the surn. *Musson*, cf. *John Musson* 1827 Census, *William Musson* 1854 ib and *Edward Musson* 1872 ib of Peatling Magna; the family originally from Muston, 32 miles to the north-east, the surn. with typical 17th-cent. Leics. loss of *t* from the group *-ston*, here also with assimilation *st* > *ss*); Nether Grounds (*v.* grund); New Piece (*v.* pece); Old Orchard (*v.* orceard); Old Plough (*v.* plōg); Old Seeds (*v.* sǣd; in modern f.ns., used of grasses sown for one year's mowing or grazing as distinguished from permanent pasture); Open Fd (in some sort unenclosed, perh. lacking fencing, or hedges or fixed gates); The Paddock (*v.* paddock); The Great Pasture Cl 1755 (*v.* pasture); Peatling Cl; Penneyfords (with the surn. *Pennyford* in the possessive case); Pinks Cl, ~ Mdw (with the surn. *Pink*); Far Ploughed Cl 1889; Plummers, Far ~, First ~, Second Plummers (with the surn. *Plummer*); Pollards (the surn. *Pollard* in the possessive case; cf. *Josiah Pollard* 1830 Census, *Peter Pollard* 1837 ib, *Mary Pollard* 1866 ib and *Horace Pollard* 1880 ib, all of Peatling Magna); Poor's Cl 1843 (*v.* pouer(e); land endowed for poor-law relief or charity); Pump Fd (*v.* pumpe); Ram Fd 1968, Big ~ ~, Little Ram Pen 1889, 1968 (*v.* penn) (*v.* ramm); Red Brinks (a streamside enclosure, *v.* brink; prob. with hrēod rather than rēad (alluding to the colour of the soil)); Reynolds Cl (with the surn. *Reynolds*; cf. *George Reynolds* 1852 Census and *John Reynolds* 1856 ib of Peatling Magna); Road Fd (a close beside a major road); Rough Cl (*v.* rūh); Second Mdw; Side Cl (*v.* sīde); The Slade (*v.* slæd); Bottom ~, Top Soddoms (prob. with the surn. *Soden* in the possessive case (from OFr *soudan* 'a sultan'), a pageant-name from the Soldan of the Saracens; here attracted to the biblical Sodom); Stackyard 1968, ~ Cl 1843, 1968 (*v.* stackyard); Spring Cl, ~ Fd (*v.* spring¹); Stevens Cl, ~ Mdw (with the surn. *Stevens*, cf. *Sarah Stevens* 1831 Census); Stonebridge (*v.* stān, brycg); Tank Fd (presum. with reference to a water tank); Thistley Cl (*v.* thist(e)ly); Three Corner Cl 1843 (*v.* three-corner); Top Cl; Undlin Mdw (unexplained; but perh. a reduced *underling* in its sense 'small'); Whales Mdw (with the surn. *Wale*, cf. *James Wale* 1840 Census); Willeys (the surn. *Willey* in the possessive case; cf. *Thomas Willey* 1813 Census and *Emma Willey* 1840 ib); Williamsons (the surn. *Williamson* in the possessive case); Windmill Hill (1606, *v.* wind-mylne); Far ~, Wyatts, ~ Cl 1968, ~ Mdw 1889 (with the surn. *Wyatt*; *Mary Wayte* 1832 Census of Peatling Magna may be a poor spelling of this).

(b) *atte Aleynes* 1412 (p) (*v.* atte; with the OFr masc. pers.n. *Alein*); *Beggars Bush Close* 1681 (*v.* beggere, busc; a common f.n. which appears to denote poor or unproductive land (perh. cf. EDD *beggar* 'to impoverish land, to exhaust soil of its nutrients')); *Broadgates close* 1614 (most prob. with the surn. *Bradgate* of the family which held extensive lands in adjoining Peatling Parva, from *Willielmus Bradgate* 1474 Deed, *Thomas Bradgate* 1518 ib and *Ricardus Bradgate* 1553 Comp to *William Bradgate* 1775 Nichols); *the brooke* 1606 (*v.* brōc); *bullies lane* 1625 (*v.* lane; with the surn. *Bull(e)y*, *v.* Reaney *s.n.*); *Burdets close* 1625 (held by *William Burdet* 1625

Terrier); *Caudwel gappe* 1606 (*v.* **cald**, **wella**, **gap**); *Colepitwaye* 1606 (*v.* **col-pytt**; a route for the transportation of pit coal from the Bedworth area of Warwks.); *Ernesby way* 1625 (the road to Arnesby which lies 1½ miles to the east); *Estfeld* 1259, *Eastfeild* 1606, *the East feilde* 1625, *Great East Field* 1681 (*v.* **ēast**, **feld**; one of the great open-fields of the township); *the Forest* 1572 (*v.* **forest**; unenclosed woodland); *Foston Bridge* (*v.* **brycg**), *Foston Gate* 1681 (*v.* **gata**) (Foston lies 1½ miles to the north-west); *Foxeholes* 1606, *Foxholes* 1625, *the Damm of Foxeholes* 1606, *the Dam of Foxholes* 1625 (*v.* **damme**) (*v.* **fox-hol**); *the furres* 1625 (*v.* **fyrs**); *Horse pasture* 1606, 1625 (*v.* **hors**, **pasture**); *Hungarland* 1625 (*v.* **hungor**, **land**); *land well leyes* 1606 (*v.* **land**, **wella**, **leys**); *the lesser close* 1674, 1679, 1697 (*v.* **lesser**); *Little Peatling way* 1625 (the road to Peatling Parva which lies 2 miles to the south-west); *little slade* 1625 (*v.* **slæd**); *Longlands* 1681, *the south longlandes* 1674, 1679, 1697, *South Longlayes* (sic) 1700 (*v.* **lang**[1], **land**); *Micklehooke slade* 1625 (*v.* **micel**, **mikill**, **hōc**, **slæd**); *the Milne baulke* 1606 (*v.* **myln**, **balca**); *Nicholeswell* 1305 (*v.* **wella**; either with the ME masc. pers.n. *Nicol* (from Lat *Nicolaus*) or, less likely, with the surn. *Nichol(s)* which developed from it); *Northbroke* 1606, *Norbrooke* 1625, *Narbrooke Meadow* 1681 (*v.* **norð**, **brōc**); *Nortfeld* 1259 (*v.* **norð**, **feld**; one of the early great open-fields); *atte Parsones* 1401 (p) (*v.* **atte**), *the parsons close* 1703, *the Parsons great Close*, *the Parsons house Close* 1708 (*v.* **persone**); *the Pen close* 1625 (*v.* **penn**); *the port waye* 1606 (*v.* **port-wey**; the road to Leicester, originally 7 miles to the north); *Ridgewaye* 1625 (*v.* **hrycgweg**); *Sheles furlong* 1625 (*v.* **scēla**, **furlang**); *South brooke* 1625 (*v.* **sūð**, **brōc**); *Stockhill* 1606, 1625, ~ *furlong* 1625 (*v.* **furlang**) (*v.* **stocc**, **hyll**); *Sudfeld* 1259, *the Southfeild* 1606, *the South feilde* 1625 (*v.* **sūð**, **feld**; one of the great open-fields); *Thebotes place* 1386 (*v.* **place**; with the surn. *Tebbut*, from the OFr masc. pers.n. *Thiebaut*, *Tibaut* (Theobald)); *the Thornes* 1674, 1679, 1697, *the Thorns* 1700 (*v.* **þorn**); *Thorpe waye* 1606, 1625 (the road to Bruntingthorpe which lies 2 miles to the south-east); *the Vicars greater plot* 1674, 1679, 1697, 1700 (*v.* **plot**), *Vicars Meddowes or Vicars Closes* 1606 (*v.* **mēd** (**mēdwe** obl.sg.)) (*v.* **vikere**); *the West close* 1625; *Westfeild* 1606, *the West feilde* 1625 (*v.* **west**, **feld**; one of the great open-fields); *Wormedale* 1606, 1625 (*v.* **dæl**[1]; either with the OE masc. pers.n. *Wyrma* or with **wyrm** 'a serpent', but if the latter, whether the allusion is to the dragon of folk-lore (as in *Beowulf* 2287) is uncertain; cf. Wormdale in Kent).

Peatling Parva

For forms and interpretation, *v.* adjoining Peatling Magna *supra*.

Affixes are variously added as:
Alia ~ 1086 DB, 1166 RBE
Parva ~ 1225, 1226 Cur *et freq* to 1325 *Wyg et passim* to 1535 VE
~ *Parva* 1431, 1432 *Wyg et passim* to 1576 Saxton *et freq*
Litle ~ 1546 AAS, 1549 Pat, *Lyttell* ~ 1558 AAS, *Little* ~ 1610 Speed

With MLat *alia* 'the other (of two)', MLat *parva* 'little' and **lȳtel** *q.v.*

ASHBY RD is *ashbie gate* 1625 *Terrier*, *Ashby Yate* (sic) 1638 *ib*, *v.* **gata**; Ashby Magna lies some 1½ miles to the north-west. ASHBY ROAD COTTAGES. BRUNTINGTHORPE RD, Bruntingthorpe lying one mile to the east. CEDAR HOUSE FM. DAIRY FM, cf. *Dairy Close* 1828 *Terrier*, *v.* **deierie**. DOG AND GUN (P.H.) (lost), *Dog and Gun* 1846 White, 1850 *TA*, 1863, 1877 White, *Dog and Gun Inn* 1925 Kelly. GLEBE FM, *v.* **glebe**. HALL FM, *v.* Peatling Hall *infra*. HALL FARM COTTAGES. IVY COTTAGE. THE LAURELS. MAIN ST. MILL DAM SPINNEY, *Mill Dam Spinny* 1835 O, *v.* **myln**, **damme**, **spinney**; a stream is dammed here to form a mill-race. THE OLD RECTORY, cf. *the Parsonage House* m.18 *Terrier*, *v.* **personage**. ORCHARD COTTAGE, cf. *Biggs's* ~ 1843 *Paget*, *Bigg's Orchard* 1850 *TA*, *v.* **orceard**; with the surn. *Biggs*. PEATLING HALL, 1831 Curtis, 1835 O, 1925 Kelly, *The Hall* 1846, 1863, 1877 White, *v.* **hall**. PEATLING LODGE, *v.* **loge**. PEATLING PARVA LODGE is *Peatling Lodge* 1835 O, *v.* **loge**. ST ANDREW'S CHURCH, *Church (St Andrew)* 1846, 1863, 1877 White, 1925 Kelly; it is earlier recorded as *ecclesie de Parve Pedling* 1220 MHW, *ecclesiam de Parva Pedlinges* 1237 RGros, ~ *de Parva Petling* 1242 *ib*, *ecclesia Parve Petlynge* 1477 (e.16) *Charyte*. Note also *the church yard* m.18 *Terrier*, *v.* **churchyerd**.

FIELD-NAMES

In (a), forms dated 1754 and 1788 are *Deed*; those dated 1807 are
Nichols; 1828 are *Terrier*; 1843 are *Paget*; 1846, 1863 and 1877 are
White; 1850 are *TA*. Forms throughout dated 1327 are SR; those dated
1400 are Pat; 1567 and 1573 are Ipm; 1601, 1625, 1638, 1690 and m.18
are *Terrier*; 1702 and 1729 are *Deed*.

(a) The Two ~, The Four ~, The Six ~, North ~ ~, South Forty Acres 1843, 1850
(*v.* **æcer**); Anpits 1850 (*v.* **pytt**; either with **ān** 'solitary, lonely' or, less likely, with
the OE masc. pers.n. *Anna*); Bottom Barn Cl 1850, Top ~ ~, Barn Cl 1843, 1850 (*v.*
bern); The Breaches 1850 (*Breach* 1625, *v.* **brēc**); Bristlings 1850 (no continuity of
forms survive, but this is prob. the earlier *Prestinges* 1625, *v.* **prēost, eng**); Browns
Cl 1843, 1850 (with the surn. *Brown*); Burdetts Cl 1843, 1850 (with the surn.
Burdett; cf. *Samuel Burdett* 1850 *TA* of Peatling Parva); Caves Cl 1843, 1850 (with
the surn. *Cave*); Clover Cl 1828, Great ~ ~, Little Clover Cl 1850 (*v.* **clāfre**; a fodder
crop); Cottage Piece 1846, 1863, 1877 (*v.* **cotage, pece**); Near ~ ~, Cow Cl 1843,
1850, Cow Close Mdw 1850, Cow Mdw 1843 (*v.* **cū**); Bottom ~ ~, Cow Sedge, ~ ~
Mdw (*cowsitch* 1625, 1638, *v.* **cū, sīc**); The Croft, Croft Mdw 1843, 1850 (*v.* **croft**);
Far Cl, ~ Mdw 1850 (*v.* **feor**); Farrenleys 1843, 1850 (*far*[…]*en leas* 1601, *farraine
leies* 1625, *Farraigne Leas* 1638, *v.* **leys**; with the surn. *Farran, Farren*); Fenn ~
1843, Fen Cl 1850 (cf. *nether* ~, *over fenne* 1601, *over fennes* 1625 (*v.* **uferra**), *longe
fenns* 1601, *v.* **fenn**); Bottom ~, Middle ~, Top ~, Little ~, South Fulpits 1850
(*fulpites* 1625, *Full Pitts* 1638, *v.* **fūl, pytt**); Gilmorton Cl 1850, ~ Mdw 1843
(Gilmorton parish adjoins to the south-west); Gravel Pit Cl 1843, 1850 (*v.* **gravel**,
pytt); Great Cl 1850; The Hall Cl 1843, 1850 (*v.* Peatling Hall *supra*); Little ~ ~,
Great Home Cl (*v.* **home**); Hop Yard Mdw 1843, 1850 (*v.* **hop-yard**); House Cl
1843, 1850; Hut Cl 1843, 1850 (*v.* **hut**); Intake 1850 (*v.* **inntak**); Kimcote Way 1850
(1625, *Kimcote waye* 1601, *v.* **weg**; Kimcote lies 2 miles to the south-west); The Leys
1850 (*v.* **leys**); Long Cl, ~ Mdw 1843, 1850; Martins Yard 1850 (*v.* **geard**; with the
surn. *Martin*); Mawsons Mdw 1843, 1850 (with the surn. *Mawson*); Mill Bank 1843,
1850 (*v.* **myln, banke**), Milldam Fd 1895 (*v.* Mill Dam Spinney *supra*); The Moors
1843, 1850 (*v.* **mōr**[1]); Upper ~ ~, New Cl 1850; New Grounds 1850 (*v.* **grund**); The
Noorbrooke 1843, Norbrook 1850 (*norbrooke* 1601, *narbroke, narbrooke* 1625, cf.
norbrooke syde 1601, *narbroke side* 1625, *Narbrooke Side* 1638 (*v.* **sīde**), *v.* **norð,
brōc**); Orchard Cl 1843, 1850 (*v.* **orceard**); Over Cl 1843, 1850 (*v.* **uferra**); Parsons
Cl 1850 (*v.* **persone**); Peatling Cl, ~ Mdw 1843, 1850; Peatling Cross Cl 1754, 1788
(*v.* **cros**); Pinfold 1850 (*v.* **pynd-fald**); Far ~ ~, Old Ploughed Cl 1843, 1850; Poor
Allotments 1850 (*v.* **pouer(e), allotment**; land endowed for poor-law relief or
charity); The Road Mdw (land beside a major roadway); Rough Cl 1850, ~ Mdw
1843, ~ Pasture 1843, 1850 (*v.* **pasture**) (*v.* **rūh**); Scotts Cl, ~ Mdw 1850 (with the
surn. *Scott*); Skinners Mdw 1843, 1850 (with the surn. *Skinner*); The Slade, Far Slade
1850 (*fare slade* 1625 (*v.* **feor**), *v.* **slæd**); Spinney Cl 1843, 1850 (*v.* Mill Dam
Spinney *supra*); Spring Cl 1843, 1850 (*v.* **spring**[1]); Square Piece 1828 (*v.* **squar(e),
pece**); Star Pits 1807 (*starpits* 1625, *v.* **storr**[2], **pytt**); Stone Pits 1850 (*v.* **stān, pytt**;
poss. an error for the previous f.n.); Top Cl 1828, 1843, 1850, ~ Mdw 1850;
Townsends Cl 1850 (*the towne ende* 1625, *The Town End* 1638, *v.* **tūn, ende**); Vales

Cl 1843, 1850 (with the surn. *Vale*); Waldrams Cl, ~ Mdw 1843, 1850 (with the surn. *Waldram*, from the ContGerm masc. pers.n. *Waleran* (OFr *Galeran*); note *Walran* 1154× 89 Dane of Leics.); Walton Poors Land 1850 (*v.* **pouer(e)**; endowed land for the benefit of the poor of Walton which lies 2 miles to the south-east); Willoughby Hill 1828, 1850 (cf. *Willoughby Hill Close* 1690; Willoughby Waterleys parish adjoins to the north-west); Little ~ ~, Windmill Hill 1843, 1850 (*v.* **wind-mylne**).

(b) *allerdes* ~, *allordes way* 1625 (*v.* **weg**; with the surn. *Allard*, prob. from the OE masc. pers.n. *Æðelheard*, but may be also from the ContGerm masc. pers.n. *Adelard*); *arnesbie hedge* 1625 (*v.* **hecg**; a parish boundary marker), *arnsby way* 1625 (*v.* **weg**) (Arnesby lies 2½ miles to the north-east); *Ashbie hedge* 1601 (*v.* **hecg**; a parish boundary marker), *ashbie meare* 1625 (*v.* **(ge)mǣre**) (Ashby Magna parish adjoins to the west); *Mr Ashers close* m.18 (cf. *Thomas Asher* 1781 MI, *Elizabeth Asher* 1786 ib of Peatling Parva); *begmans* ~, *beggemans waye* 1601, *begmans way* 1625, *Beakemans Way* 1638 (the first word is obscure; no medieval occupation or occupational surn. is obvious, so perh. eModE **bagman** in an unattested sense 'a packman, a pedlar' is present, influenced by *beggere* 'a beggarman' to account for the initial *a*; a reduced OE masc. pers.n. *Bēagmund* may explain the name but if so, one would not have expected the later plosive medial *g*, *v.* **weg**); *betwene the wayes* 1625 (*v.* **betwēonan**; a furlong so called); *Broad Close* 1729 (*v.* **brād**); *broadwaye* 1601, *brod(e)way* 1625, *Under* ~, *Broadway* 1638, *brodway hedge* 1625 (*v.* **hecg**) (*v.* **brād**, **weg**); *brodwelhole* 1625, *Bradwell Hole* 1638 (*v.* **brād**, **wella**, **hol**[1]); *the brood* 1601 (*v.* **brode**); *the brooke* 1625 (*v.* **brōc**); *br*[..]*nt* ~ 1601, *burnt hill* 1625, 1638 (*v.* **hyll**; either with **brant** 'steep' or with **brend** 'burnt'); *chesters way* 1625 (in Leics., long-distance routes are invariably compounded with *weg* rather than with *gata*; here, because of the plural form, perh. rather with **ceaster**, but whether alluding to undiscovered local Romano-British remains (cf. Road Chesters, Lei **3** 81) or whether to a long-distance route to Chester is uncertain; but note *Chestreway* (1397) in Cosby *supra* and *Chesterwey* in Leicester from 1381 (*v.* Lei **1** 27)); *church landes* 1601, 1625, *Churchlands* 1638 (*v.* **land**), *Church leyes* 1625 (*v.* **leys**) (*v.* St Andrew's Church *supra*); *colepite dale* 1601 (*v.* **col-pytt**, **dalr**; the reference is to a charcoal-burning site); *the common grounde* 1601 (*v.* **grund**), *the common* 1625 (*v.* **commun**); *cragdale* 1625 (*v.* **cragge**, **dalr**; a f.n. also recorded later in adjoining Bruntingthorpe parish); *the lease of William Davy* 1625 (*v.* **leys**); *the easte filde* 1625, *East Field* 1638 (*v.* **ēast**, **feld**; one of the great open-fields of the township); *fearne furlonge* 1601, *ferny forlonge* 1625, *Fearney furlong* 1638 (*v.* **fearnig**, **furlang**); *fennslade* 1625 (*v.* **fenn**, **slæd**); *the fowerteene Acres* m.18 (*v.* **fēowertēne**, **æcer**); *the galls* 1601, *Galles* 1625, 1638 (*v.* **galla**); *galney* 1601, *gawnie* 1625, *Gawney* 1638 (*v.* **galla** (**gallan** dat.sg.), **ēg**; the name appears also in Gawney Lane and Gurney Lane in adjoining Kimcote and Walton parish and in adjoining Gilmorton parish); *Gilmorton meare* 1625, ~ *meere* 1638 (*v.* **(ge)mǣre**); *gossecrafte* 1625, *Gossecroft* 1638 (*v.* **croft**; either with **gōs** 'goose' or with dial. **goss(e)** 'gorse'); *grangia de Parva Peatlinge* 1567 (with MLat *grangia* 'a grange'); *hampit furlonge* 1601, ~ *forlonge* 1625, *Hampitt Furlong* 1638 (*v.* **furlang**), *hampit hole* 1601, 1625, *Hampitthole* 1638 (*v.* **hol**[1]), *hampit way* 1625 (*v.* **weg**) (*v.* **hamm**, **pytt**); *harrow slade* 1601, *harrolde* ~, *har(r)oulde* ~, *harrowlde slade* 1625, *Harrow Slade*, *Harroodslade* 1638 (*v.* **slæd**; perh. with **hǫrgr** 'a heap of stones'; the surn. *Harrold* (in Leics. prob. from the ON masc. pers.n. *Haraldr* (ODan *Harald*)) may have influenced the forms, cf. *Thomas Harrold* 1821 Census, *John Harrold* 1855 ib and *Ada Harrold* 1879 ib of adjoining Willoughby Waterleys parish; but note *Harrow akers* in adjoining Bruntingthorpe parish and *v.* Harrow Cl in Broughton Astley f.ns. (a)); *The Homestale* 1625 (*v.* **hām-stall**); (*the*) *Lammas Close* 1690, 1707 (*v.* **lammas**); *in the Lane* 1327 (p), *the Lane* 1625 (*v.* **lane**); *longe hil* 1601, *longe hull* 1638 (*v.* **lang**[1], **hyll**); *The Meadow* 1690; *the mill lane end* 1601 (*v.* **lane-ende** and Mill Dam Spinney *supra*); *morrowes* 1625 (*v.* **mōr**[1], **hōh**); *morton hill* 1625 (a hill towards the Gilmorton parish boundary to the south); *the North Close* 1690, m.18; *the North feilde* 1625, ~ ~ *Field* 1638 (*v.* **norð**, **feld**; one of the great open-fields); *okeyard* 1601 (*v.* **āc**, **geard**; the name appears later in adjoining Bruntingthorpe as The Oak Yard, a boundary feature); *the overwhorte forlonge* 1625, *the Overthwarte Furlong* 1638 (*v.* **ofer-þwart**, **furlang**; in *the easte filde*, *supra*); *Peaks akar* 1601, *peakseacre* 1625 (*v.* **æcer**; with the surn. *Peak*); *Peatlinge corner* 1625 (*v.* **corner**), *Peatlinge hedge* 1601, 1625 (*v.* **hecg**; a parish boundary marker), *Peatling(e) way* (*v.* **weg**; the road to Peatling Magna which lies 2 miles to the north); *atte persones* 1400 (p) (*v.* **atte**, **persone**); *the ridge way* 1625 (*v.* **hrycgweg**); *salemorrowes* 1625 (*v.* **salh** and *morrowes*, *supra*); *sevenacre* 1601, *seaven acres* 1625, *Seaven acre* 1638 (*v.* **seofon**, **æcer**); *Shepegate* 1573 (*v.* **scēp**, **gata**); *short butts* 1601, 1638, *shorte buttes* 1625 (*v.* **sc(e)ort**, **butte**); *Shugbyes Close* 1729 (with the surn. *Shugby*, that of a family originally from Shuckburgh (*Shugborough* 1547), 18 miles to the south-west in Warwks.); *Siddlinges* 1601 (*v.* **sīdling**); *the South Close* 1690, m.18; *the south filde* 1625 (*v.* **sūð**, **feld**; one of the great open-fields); *Stinckley* 1601, *Stinkley* 1601, 1638, *stinckeley* 1625 ('the foul-smelling pool', *v.* **stinck**, **ley**[1]); *Stockhil* 1601 (*v.* **stocc**, **hyll**); *stockewellheade* 1625, *Stockwell Head* 1638 (*v.* **stocc**, **wella**, **hēafod**); *the Stone* 1601, (*uppon*) *stoune* 1625, *Stone* 1638 (*v.* **stān**; whether used of a boundary stone or used as 'stony ground' is uncertain); *taftes* 1625, *toftes* 1625, 1638 (*v.* **toft**); *thorp(e) hedge* 1601, 1625, 1638 (*v.* **hecg**; a parish boundary marker), *thorp meare* 1625 (*v.* **(ge)mǣre**), *thorp(e) slade* 1625, 1638 (*v.* **slæd**) (the forms refer to Bruntingthorpe parish which adjoins to the east); *Throwlesworth furlonge* 1601, *frolesworth forlonge* 1625 (*v.* **furlang**; Frolesworth lies 5 miles to the west, so unless the township name is used here as a surn. (but as such is unrecorded), the nature of the allusion is obscure (perh. cf. (*on*) *Peatling* in Claybrooke Parva parish, some 6 miles to the south-west)); *Walton way(e)* 1601, 1625 (*v.* **weg**; the road to Walton which lies 2 miles to the south-west); *washpit* 1625, *Washpitt* 1638, *washpit furlonge* 1601 (*v.* **furlang**), *washpit way* 1625, *Washpitt Way* 1638 (*v.* **weg**) (*v.* **wæsce**, **pytt**; presum. a sheep-dip); *Willougby parke* 1601, *Willow Parke* (sic) 1625, 1638 (*v.* **park**; the later forms represent a repeated copying error in the Glebe Terriers), *willowebie meare* 1625 (*v.* **(ge)mǣre**), *Willougbie* ~ 1601, *willow(e)bie* ~ 1625, *Willoughby Slade* 1638 (*v.* **slæd**) (Willoughby Waterleys parish adjoins to the north-west); *winterhill* 1625, *Winter Hill* 1638 (*v.* **winter**[1], **hyll**; land used (for livestock?) in winter).

Shawell

SHAWELL

Sawelle 1086 DB, 1205 FF, *Sawell* 1233 Cur, 1235 Cl
Sewell 1203, 1230 Cur
Scawell 1220 MHW, *Schawelle* 1232 RHug
Schadewell(*e*) 1224 RHug, 1241 Cur, c.1291 Tax, *Shadewell* 1338
    Hosp
Shathewell(*e*) 1270 RGrav, 1316 FA *et freq* to 1424 Banco, 1428 FA
    et passim to 1497 *Braye*, 1517 Hastings, 1533 Fine, *Shathwell*
    1518 *Braye*
Shawell 1507 Ipm, 1510, 1518 Visit *et freq*

'The boundary stream', *v.* **scēað, wella**. The stream on which the settlement developed crosses the county boundary (here formed by Watling Street) at right angles. Its name seems unlikely to refer to this particular boundary therefore. Possibly the stream once divided the territory of Cotesbach from that of Swinford at some time prior to the growth of Shawell.

ALL SAINTS' CHURCH, *Church (All Saints)* 1846, 1863, 1877 White, 1925 Kelly; it is earlier recorded as *ecclesie de Schawell* 1220 MHW, ~ *de Schadewell* 1241 Cur, ~ *de Shathewell* 1400 *Pat*. Note also *the Church yard* 1708 *Terrier*, *v.* **churchyerd**. BARN FM. CASTLE MOUND, cf. *Mount furlong*(*e*) 1606, 1631 *Terrier*, *v.* **munt**(**e**), **furlang**; land beside the earthworks of a motte and bailey castle. CAVE'S INN, 1807 Nichols; named from an 18th-cent. landlord, Edward Cave, and stands beside Watling Street at the site of the important Romano-British settlement of *Tripontium* ('(the place of) three bridges'), *v.* A. L. F. Rivet and Colin Smith, *The Place-Names of Roman Britain* (1979), 476. CATTHORPE RD, Catthorpe lying 2 miles to the south-east. CEDAR FM. GIBBET LANE. GIBBET HILL on Watling Street is called *Loseby's Gibbet* 1729 Bei, *v.* **gibet**; a gibbet was an upright post with an arm for hanging the bodies of already executed criminals, here on a principal route as a very evident example to others. Whether Gibbet Hill is to be identified with *Gallow Hill* 1842 *TA* is uncertain, since strictly, a gallows (**galga**) was the instrument for execution by hanging rather than a means to exhibit the executed, so that rather than being from *galga*, Gallow Hill may be an instance of the common 'bare hill', *v.* **calu**. GREENACRES. GREEN LANE SPINNEY, *v.* **grēne**[1], **spinney**. GREEN SPINNEY. HILLCREST. HILL FM. LUTTERWORTH RD, Lutterworth lying 3 miles to the north. MIDDLE FM. THE MOUNT, a modern house on a small hill. THE OLD RECTORY is *The Rectory* 1877 White, 1925 Kelly, *v.* **rectory**; earlier is *the parsonage howse* 1606 *Terrier*, *The Parsonage House* 1700, 1708 *ib*, *v.* **personage**. SHAWELL GRANGE is *The Grange* 1925 Kelly, *v.* **grange**. SHAWELL HALL, cf. *Hall Farm* 1925 Kelly, *v.* **hall**. SHAWELL LODGE FM (SHAWELL LODGE 2½"), *v.* **loge**. SHAWELL MANOR is *the manor house* 1807 Nichols; cf. *Manor Farm* 1925 Kelly, *v.* **maner**. SHOULDER OF MUTTON (P.H.) (lost), *Shoulder of Mutton* 1846 White. SPINNEY FM, 1925 Kelly, *v.* **spinney**. SWAN (P.H.) (lost), *Swan* 1863, 1877 White, *White Swan Inn* 1925 Kelly.

FIELD-NAMES

In (a), forms presented without dates are 1842 *TA*; those dated 1756 and 1807 are Nichols; 1790 are Ct; 1821 are *Terrier*; 1835 are O; 1846 and 1863 are White; 1868 are *Deed*. Forms throughout dated 1205 are FF; those dated 1279 are Ipm; 13 are *Combe*; 1325 are Pat; 1546 are AAS; 1606, 1625, 1631, 1674, l.17, 1700, 1708, 1742 and 1745 are *Terrier*.

(a) The Acre 1821, One Acre, Two Acres, Seven ~, Eight ~, Ten Acres 1842, Twelve Acres 1842, 1868 (*v.* **æcer**); The Anterfield 1821, Far ~, First ~, Antifield, ~ Mdw 1842 (*Anterfeild* l.17, *Auntherfield* 1700, *Aunterfield* 1708, *Anterfield* 1742, 1745, cf. *Anterfield Close* 1674, *the Auntherfield Close* 1700 (*v.* **aunter** 'a venture, an enterprise'); Far ~ ~ 1842, Bank(e)y Ground 1842, 1868 (*v.* **banke**, **-ig**[3], **grund**); Barn Cl 1842, 1868 (*v.* **bern**); Billings Mdw, ~ Ploughed Cl (with the surn. *Billing* of a family originally from the township of this name, 20 miles to the south-east in Northants.; cf. *Hannah Billing* 1836 Census of adjoining Swinford parish); Bit Mdw (*v.* **bit**); Brick Kiln Cl 1842, 1868 (*v.* **brike-kiln**); Bridge Cl 1821 (*the Bridg Close* 1708, *v.* **brycg**); Browns Cl (with the surn. *Brown*); Bull Cl (*Bulcloase* 1625, *v.* **bula**, **clos(e)**); *Bullocks Orchard* (*v.* **orceard**; with the surn. *Bullock*); Calves Cl (1674, *v.* **calf**); Cave's Inn Bank 1842, *v.* **banke** and Cave's Inn *supra*; the Common 1790 (1606, 1625, *v.* **commun**); the Corner Cl 1843, 1868 (*v.* **corner**); Cosland (sic) (earlier forms are presum. *Colslade* 1606, 1625, ~ *furlong* 1606, 1631 (*v.* **furlang**); *v.* **cald**, **slæd**); Cottagers Cl (*v.* **cotager**); Cross Leys, ~ ~ Mdw (*crosse leas* 1606, cf. *Crosleys hades* 1625 (*v.* **hēafod**), *crosse leas furlong(e)* 1606, 1631 (*v.* **furlang**) (*v.* **leys**; with **cros** or **cross**); Dairy Cl (*v.* **deierie**); Middle ~, Three Cornered ~ (*v.*

three-cornered), Debdale 1842, Debdale Mdw 1790 (*depdale* 1606, 1625, *deepdale furlong* 1631 (*v.* **furlang**), *v.* **dēop, dalr**); The Elms, Little Elms (cf. *Elme feilde* 1606, *Elmefield* 1625, *Elme feild* 1631 (*v.* **feld**; one of the great open-fields of the township), *Elme furlonge* 1606, 1631 (*v.* **furlang**), *the farther Elme furlong* 1606 (*v.* **farder**), *the Elme way, the way to the Elme* 1606 (*v.* **weg**) (*v.* **elme**; apart from in the final form, an original elm wood is indicated rather than a single elm-tree (**elm**)); Bottom ~, Top ~, Enslade (*Inslade* 1606, 1625, *~ close* 1708), Enslade Mdw (*Inslade meddow* 1708, *v.* **in, slæd**); Far Cl (*v.* **feor**); Flax Leys, ~ ~ Banks (*v.* **banke**) (*flaxleas* 1606, 1631, *Flaxleys* 1625, *v.* **fleax, leys**); Far Gallow Hill, Gallow Hill Mdw (*v.* Gibbet Hill *supra*); Bottom Grass Cl (*v.* **græs**); Great Cl; Green Mdw (*v.* **grēne**[1]); Grove Mdw (*v.* **grāf**); (the) Hallfield 1821, Far ~ ~, Middle ~ ~, Hall Fd 1842 ((*the*) *Hallfeild* 1606, 1631, *the Hall field* 1700, 1708, cf. *Hallfeild stile* 1631 (*v.* **stigel**)), Hallfield Mdw 1821 (*Halfield meddow* 1625) (*v.* Shawell Hall *supra*); Hipwells Cl (with the surn. *Hipwell*; cf. *Henry Hipwell* 1817 Census of adjoining Catthorpe parish, *Eli Hipwell* 1817 ib and *Maud Hipwell* 1879 ib of adjoining Swinford parish); Holywell Fd 1846, 1863 (*Halywell* 1279, *Haliwell* 13, *the chapel of Halywell by the high way of Watlyngstrete* 1325; cf. *Holy Well furlong* 1606, *Holywell hill* 1631, *Holywell hill furlong* 1606 (*v.* **furlang**), *v.* **hālig, wella**; the lost small Holywell Priory lay on Watling Street at Cave's Inn at the site of Roman *Tripontium* and took its name from this sacred spring); Home Cl, ~ Mdw (*v.* **home**); Hovel Cl (*v.* **hovel**); Humphry Hill (with the surn. *Humphrey*, from the ContGerm masc. pers.n. *Humfrid* (via OFr *Humfrid*); Jenkins Cl (cf. *Jenkins peece* 1606, *v.* **pece**; note *Tho. Jenkins* 1606 Terrier); Kings Ground, ~ Mdw (*v.* **grund**; prob. with the surn. *King*, although the king was patron of Shawell parish church from 1696 to 1809 and may have held land here); Long Mdw; Long Slade 1756, 1807, 1842 (1606, 1625, *Longslade furlong* 1606, 1631 (*v.* **furlang**), *v.* **lang**[1], **slæd**); Lucks Mdw (with the surn. *Luck*, from the popular form of the masc. pers.n. *Lucas*; cf. *William Luck* 1791 Ct of Shawell); Martins Cl (with the surn. *Martin*); Middle Ground 1842, 1868 (*v.* **grund**); New Mdw; Old House Ground; Old Orchard (*v.* **orceard**); Over Ground 1790, 1842 (*v.* **uferra**); Parsons Ground, ~ Mdw, ~ Far Mdw (*v.* **persone, grund**); Pen Cl, ~ Mdw (*v.* **penn**); Percivals Top Mdw (with the surn. *Percival*); Pindell (*v.* **pingel**); Plot, ~ Mdw (*v.* **plot**); First ~ ~, Second ~ ~, Third Ploughed Cl, Far ~ ~, Bottom ~ ~, Middle ~ ~, Top Ploughed Cl; Poors Plot 1835 (*the Poors Plott* 1742, 1745, *v.* **pouer(e), plot**; land endowed to support the township's poor); Ram Cl 1821, 1842 (*Rams Close* 1700, 1708, *Ram close syde* 1631 (*v.* **sīde**), *v.* **ramm**); Rantipole (sic) (whether this is the adj. *rantipole* 'wild, disorderly' and thus a disparaging name for an unproductive field is uncertain; poss. also is 'boundary pool' (with **rand** and **pōl**[1]), but early forms are lacking); Round Hill 1807 (the mound of a motte and bailey castle, *v.* Castle Mound *supra*); School Leys (*v.* **leys**); Sedgleys Cl (with the surn. *Sedgley*; the family was of long standing in the parish, from *James Sedgeley* 1790 Ct, *Thomas Sedgeley* 1790 ib, *Elizabeth Sedgley* 1829 Census, *James Sedgley* 1830 ib to *John Sedgley* 1857 ib and *Alfred Sedgley* 1873 ib); Shawell Brook 1756 (*the brooke* 1606, *the Brook* 1708, *v.* **brōc**); Skinners Cl (with the surn. *Skinner*; cf. *Thomas Skinner* 1790 Ct, *William Skynner* 1790 ib and *Mary Skinner* 1788 MI of Shawell); Spinney Cl (*v.* **spinney**); Starveall Mdw (with a derogatory name for unproductive land); Far ~, Stoneleighs Mdw (with the surn. *Stoneleigh* of a family originally from the township of this name, 14 miles to the south-west in Warwks.); Top ~, Stubble (*v.* **stubbil**; land on which stubble was allowed to remain for a long period, prob. as grazing for sheep); Three Cornered Cl (*v*. **three-cornered**); Top Cl; Top Ground (*v*. **grund**); Far ~ ~ 1842, 1868, Townsends Ground 1790, 1842 (*v*. **tūn, ende**); Top ~, Townside (*the townesyde* 1606, *Towneside* 1625, *townesyde furlong* 1631 (*v*. **furlang**), *v*. **tūn, sīde**); Top ~, Wood ~, Twenty (*the Twentie* 1606, *v*. **twēntig**; here alluding to twenty units of grassland, cf. *the fowrteene* in f.ns. (b)); Bottom ~ ~, Middle ~ ~, Top ~ ~, Two Hedges (with **edisc** or **etisc**); Waltons Cl (with the surn. *Walton*, cf. *Sarah Walton* 1848 Census, *Henry Walton* 1855 ib and *Anne Walton* 1879, all of adjoining Swinford parish; the family prob. originally came from Walton, 5 miles to the north-east); White Leys (*v*. **hwīt, leys**; dial. *white* often referred to dry, open pasture); Whitemans Cl, ~ Mdw, ~ Orchard (*v*. **orceard**) (with the surn. *Whiteman*, from the OE masc. pers.n. *Hwītmann*; cf. *William Whiteman* 1790 Ct and *Elizabeth Whiteman* 1790 ib of Shawell).

(b) *Alstertune* 1205 (*v*. **tūn**; a solitary form, but perh. a contracted **ald** with **ceaster**, referring to the Roman *Tripontium* may be thought of, or else the OE masc. pers.n. *Ealdstān* as the specific); *Apesface furlong* (sic) 1606 (*v*. **æpse, fæs, furlang**); *barly crofte*, ~ ~ *furlong* 1631, *Barley croft(e) furlonge* 1606, *Barlicroft furlong* 1625 (*v*. **furlang**), *v*. **bærlic, croft**); *Brockhurst hollow* 1606, *Brocage hollow(e)* 1631 (*v*. **hyrst, holh**; with **brōc** or **brocc**); *the bull baulk* 1606, ~ ~ *balke* 1606, 1631 (*v*. **balca**), *Bullcroft, Bole Crofte* 1546 (*v*. **croft**) (*v*. **bula**); *Butchers Close* 1700 (with the surn. *Butcher*); *Bykesacre* 1606, *Bikesacre* 1625, ~ *field* 1625, *Bykesacre feild* 1631 (*v*. **feld**; one of the great open-fields), *Bykesacre furlong* 1631 (*v*. **furlang**), *Bykesacre syde* 1606 (*v*. **sīde**) (*v*. **æcer**; the specific is uncertain, but **byxe** 'a box-tree' with metathesis may pertain, or else **bica** 'a point, a beak-like projection' accorded a ME gen.sg.); *the churchills, the 2 Churchills* 1606, *both Churchhills* 1631, *over* ~, *neather church(h)ills* 1606 (*v*. **uferra, neoðera**), *Upper* ~ ~, *Neather Church hils* 1631 (*v*. **hyll** and All Saints' Church *supra*); *Mr Clarkes peece* 1606 (*v*. **pece**), *Ric. Clarke his headland* 1606 (*v*. **hēafod-land**) (note also *Edward Clarke* 1790 Ct of Shawell); *colepit way* 1631, *Colepitt way* 1708 (*v*. **col-pytt, weg**; a route for the transportation of pit coal from the Bedworth area of Warwks. to southern and eastern Leics.); *the common pasture* 1606 (*v*. **commun, pasture**); *Cottesbych hedg* 1625 (*v*. **hecg**; a parish boundary marker), *Cotsbitch meere*, ~ ~ *furlonge* 1606, *Cotsbatch meare furlong* 1631 (*v*. **furlang**) (*v*. **(ge)mǣre**; Cotesbach parish adjoins to the north-west); *Cuttedwong* 1205 (*v*. **cutted, vangr**); *Eathring Syde furlonge* 1606 (*v*. **sīde, furlang**; the first word is of uncertain meaning and additional forms are needed; perh. 'wasteland ridge' with **ēðe** with **rind(e)** or **ēðe** with -ing[2], with intrusive *r*); *Thom. Elkintons headland* 1606 (*v*. **hēafod-land**), *John Elkingtons land* 1625 (*v*. **land**) (note *Richard Elkington* 1607 Will, *Thomas Elkington* 1630 Nichols, *James Elkington* 1739 MI and *Thomas Elkington* 1754 ib, all of Shawell; the family originally came from Elkington, 5 miles to the south-east in Northants.); *Feneldoale* 1625, *fennill dole* 1631, *Fennill dole furlonge* 1606 (*v*. **furlang**) (*v*. **fenol, dāl**); *findale* 1606, *Findale feilde* 1606, *Findall field* 1625, *Finden feild* 1631 (*v*. **feld**; one of the great open-fields), *Findale* ~, *fyndale furlong* 1606, *Finden furlong* 1631 (*v*. **furlang**) (*v*. **dæl**[1]; the specific may be **finn** 'coarse grass' or even the masc. pers.n. *Fin(n)*; the name of *Finn*, king of the East Frisians, who appears in *Beowulf* and *Widsith*, may have been used in England prior to the Scandinavian incursions with their ON *Finnr* (ODan *Fin*); and note in comparison the poss. influence of the name of *Scēafa*, king of the Langobards in the poem *Widsith*, on the township name Shearsby, *infra*); *the fowrteene* 1606 (*v*. **fēowertēne**; here alluding to 14 units of grassland; cf. Twenty in f.ns. (a)); *4 thornes* 1631 (*v.* **fēower, þorn**); *the Furze* 1700 (*v.* **fyrs**); *the gleabe land* 1625 (*v.* **glebe, land**); *gullsons lane end* 1631 (*v.* **lane-ende**; with the surn. *Gulson*, from the OE masc. pers.n. *Goldstān*); *Halcloase, Halclose, Halcloase brook* 1625 (*v.* **brōc**), *Hall close stile* 1631 (*v.* **stigel**) (*v.* **clos(e)** and Shawell Hall *supra*); *Wm. Hall his headland* 1606 (*v.* **hēafod-land**; a *William Hall* is recorded in Shawell in 1630 Nichols); *Edw. Hands his headland* 1606 (*v.* **hēafod-land**); *Harlotts way* 1606 (*v.* **weg**; presum. with the surn. *Arlott*, from OFr *harlot* 'a lad, a young fellow'; in the 13th cent., the noun *harlot* was also used of 'a vagabond, a beggar' and in the 14th cent., of 'an itenerant tumbler, jester or juggler', any of which may pertain here, but a surn. is preferable); *Heavy furlong(e)* 1631 (*v.* **heavie, furlang**; alluding to the nature of the ground); *the highe way* 1606 (*v.* **hēah-weg**); *the Home Ground* 1700 (*v.* **home, grund**); *Lester haden* 1606, *Leicester Hades* 1625 (*v.* **hēafod**; note the archaic *-en* plural of the earlier form; land beside the highway to Leicester); *Litchslade* 1606, *litslade* 1625, *lichslade* 1631, *farsyde* ~, *homeward lichslade* 1631 (*v.* **hāmweard**), *Litchslade furlong* 1606 (*v.* **furlang**) (*v.* **līc, slæd**; prob. alluding to a place where ancient burials were discovered); *the Litle Furlonge* 1606 (*v.* **lȳtel**); *longcroft, greate longcrofte* 1606 (*v.* **grēat**), *neather* ~, *over lancrofte* 1631 (*v.* **neoðera, uferra**), *Lancroft Close* 1674, *Longcrofte furlong* 1606 (*v.* **furlang**) (*v.* **lang¹, croft**); *(the) long goars* 1606 (*v.* **gāra**); *the Meddowe* 1606, 1631, *meadowe* ~, *the Meddowe furlonge* 1606, *meddow furlonge* 1631 (*v.* **furlang**) (*v.* **mēd (mēdwe** obl.sg.)); *the mill way* 1606, *Milway* 1625 (*v.* **myln, weg**); *the myres* 1631 (*v.* **mȳrr**); *Overmeere* 1625, *ouer meere, ouer mere furlong* 1631 (*v.* **furlang**) (*v.* **ofer³, (ge)mǣre**); *the owld* 1606, *the olte* 1631, *the Owld furlong* 1606 (*v.* **wald**); *Parsonage Close* 1708, *the Parsonage headland* 1606 (*v.* **hēafod-land**), *the parsonage land* 1606 (*v.* **land**) (*v.* **personage**); *Mr Porters headland,* ~~ *peece* 1606 (*v.* **pece**), *Will. Porters land* 1625 (note *Wm. Porter* and *Gabriell Porter* 1606 *Terrier*); *Reddhurst* 1606, *redhurst* 1606, 1625 (*v.* **hyrst**; with **rēad** or **hrēod**); *Sherman slade* 1606 (*v.* **slæd**; with the surn. *Sherman*, from the ME occupational name *shereman* 'a cloth shearer'; cf. *Rogerius Sereman* 1207 RFL); *the Slade* 1606 (*v.* **slæd**); *Smalewalt* 1205 (*v.* **smæl, wald**); *Stony Lands furlong* (*v.* **furlang**), ~ ~ *peece* (*v.* **pece**) 1606 (*v.* **stānig, land**); *stony leas* 1631 (*v.* **stānig, leys**); *Streete* ~ 1606, *street furlonge* 1631 (*v.* **strēt, furlang**; land abutting Watling Street); *the street way* 1606, *Streetway* 1625 (*v.* **strēt, weg**; it is uncertain whether this is a road leading to Watling Street or is the Roman road itself, since *watling streete* is accorded its particular name in the 1606 Terrier); *Thorp(e) meere* 1606, 1625, ~ ~ *furlong(e)* 1606, 1625, 1631 (*v.* **furlang**) (*v.* **(ge)mǣre**; Catthorpe parish adjoins to the southeast); *Tomley peece* 1606 (*v.* **pece**; adjacent to Tomley in Catthorpe *supra*); *(the) Towne furlong(e)* 1606, 1625, *the towne way* 1606 (*v.* **tūn**); *the water lane end* 1606 (*v.* **wæter, lane, lane-ende**); *Windmill hill* 1625, *wyndmill hill furlonge* 1631 (*v.* **furlang**), *wyndmill way* 1606 (*v.* **weg**) (*v.* **wind-mylne**); *Wm. Woodd his headland* 1606 (*v.* **hēafod-land**); *Woods lane end* 1606 (*v.* **lane-ende**; with the surn. *Wood*).

SHEARSBY

Sevesbi 1086 DB, Seuesbi 1195 P (p), 1196 ChancR (p), 1204 Cur
  (p), Seuesby e.13 Wyg (p), e.13 Rey (p), Sevesby 1208 Fine, 13
  Wyg (p)
Svevesbi 1086 DB
Svesbi 1086 DB
Seuebi 1197 P (p), 1190 × 1204 France, 1205 ClR
Shevysby 1220 MHW, Shevesby 1236 Fine (p), 1247 Ass (p) et
  passim to 1288 Banco, 1301 Ass (p) et freq to 1339 Coram et
  passim to 1455 Fine, 1524 CoPleas, Sheuesby e.14 Wyg, 1327 Pat
  et passim to 1416 Cl, Shevisbye 1537 MinAccts, Shevesby alias
  Shethesby c.1547 ECP
Schevesby 1276 RH, Scheuesby 1292 Ipm, Scheveby 1306 Pat
Shethesby 1436 Banco, 1502 MiscAccts et passim to 1551, 1590 Fine,
  Shethisby 1510 Visit, Sheathesby 1614 Ipm
Shewesby 1488 Ipm, Shewysby(e) 1549 ib, 1571 BM
Sheavesby 1639 Fine, 1675, 1702, 1717 LML
Sheresby 1541 MinAccts, Shersbie 1626 LML, Sheareshie 1678 ib
Shesbye alias Shethesbye 1560 Fine, Sheasby 1576 Saxton, 1610
  Speed, 1621, 1691 LML, Sheas(e)bey 1614, 1619 ib, Sheesbey
  1631 ib
Shearsby 1639 Fine, 1721 LML et freq

This is a difficult name. A possible meaning is 'the farmstead or
village of a man called Skeif', v. **bȳ**. The ON masc. pers.n. Skeifr is a by-
name, cf. ON skeifr 'askew, crooked' (Feilitzen 356). In this case, the
original initial Scand sk would have undergone anglicization in an area
of only light Scandinavian settlement. Perhaps there was an early
association with the OE name Scēafa, that of the legendary king of the
Langobards in the poem Widsith. Ekwall DEPN suggests the OE masc.
pers.n. Swǣf as the specific (as in Swæfes heale 940 (13) BCS 762 (S
461)), based on the form Svevesbi, one of the disparate DB spellings.

Fellows-Jensen (SSNEM 68) tentatively proposes that the specific is OE *scēaf* 'a sheaf', perhaps used metaphorically of the steep hill on which Shearsby stands; and Watts CDEPN also offers OE *scēaf* as a possible specific, translating the place-name as 'the village of the sheaf'. But neither of these suggestions is clearly explained in application. If OE *scēaf* is indeed the first element of the name, it may be that with its splay of four minor promontories to the west, the hill formation beneath which Shearsby stands reminded the early farmers of the upper spread of a sheaf of corn. Such a topographical shape appears quite striking as presented on the O.S. 1st edn map of the area, but whether it would have been obvious to men on the ground rather than as when seen as from above on this particular map is open to question.

BACK LANE, *v.* **back**. BATH HOTEL is *Baths Inn* 1846 White, *Baths Hotel* 1863, 1877 ib, *Bath Hotel* 1925 Kelly; at the former Shearsby Spa *infra*. BEAN HILL FM, *v.* Bean Hill in f.ns. (a) *infra*. BRANT HILL FM, *v.* Brant Hill in f.ns. (a). BRUNTINGTHORPE RD, Bruntingthorpe lying one mile to the south-west. CHANDLERS' ARMS (P.H.), *Chandlers' Arms* 1846 White, 1925 Kelly, *Chandler's Arms* 1863 White, *Chandlers Arms* 1877 ib; mine host *Richard Bottrill* is designated *inn-keeper and chandler* 1846 ib. CHURCH LANE, *v.* St Mary Magdalene's Church *infra*. JOHN BALL FM. JOHN BALL HILL, 1835 O, *v.* John Ball Covert in Knaptoft *supra*. LIME TREE COTTAGE. MAIN ST. MILL LANE. NEW INN FM is *New Inn* 1846, 1863, 1877 White. OLD CROWN (P.H.) (lost), *Old Crown* 1863 White, 1921 Sale, 1925 Kelly, *Crown* 1877 White. ROWLEY FIELDS, *v.* Rowley Fd in f.ns. (a). SADDINGTON RD, Saddington lying 2 miles to the north-east. ST MARY MAGDALENE'S CHURCH, *Church (St Mary Magdalene)* 1846, 1863, 1877 White; earlier recorded is *capellam de Shevysby* 1220 MHW, *Schevisby capella* 1467 × 84 *LTD* (with MLat *capella* 'a chapel'), *The Chapel* 1804 Nichols. Note also *the Churchyard* m.18[1] *Terrier*, *v.* **churchyerd**. SHEARSBY LODGE, *v.* **loge**. SHEARSBY SPA, 1846, 1863, 1877 White; it is *Shearsby Bath* 1835 O, the site of a mineral spring which was developed as a spa in the early 19th cent. WELFORD RD, Welford in Northants. lying 7 miles to the south-east. WHEATHILL FM, *v.* Wheathill in f.ns. (a).

FIELD-NAMES

In (a), forms presented without dates are 1968 *Surv*; those dated 1752 and 1753 are *Deed*; 1770, 1771 and 1828 are *ConstR*; 1774 are *EnclA*;

1843 and 1889 are *Paget*. Forms throughout dated 1606, 1638, 1745, m.18¹, m.18² and 18 are *Terrier*; those dated 1732 and 1736 are *ConstR*.

(a) The Three Acre, First Three ~, Second Three ~, The Five ~, First Five ~, Second Five ~, Third Five ~, The Six ~, The Seven ~, The Ten ~, The Thirteen Acre (*v.* **æcer**); Arnesby Cl 1752 (abutting Arnesby parish which adjoins to the north-west); First ~ ~, Second ~ ~, Back Fd (*v.* **back**); Top ~ ~, Jane Ball (*v.* Jane Ball Covert in Knaptoft parish *supra*); Bank Mdw (*v.* **banke**); Banky Cl 1889, 1968 (*v.* **banke, -ig**³); Barn Cl 1843, ~ Fd, ~ Mdw 1968 (*v.* **bern**); Bath Mdw (*v.* **bæð**; the site of a mineral spring, developed as a spa, *v.* Shearsby Spa *supra*); Bean Hill 1968, Short Bean Hill 1774, Bean Hill Cl 1843 (*Beanhill* 1638, *Long* ~, *Short Beanehill* 1601, 1606, 1638, *Long* ~, *Short Beanhill* 1745, m.18¹, m.18², *v.* **bēan, hyll**); Betty's Fd (with the fem. pers.n. *Betty*, a pet-form of Elizabeth; whether referring to an owner or to a favoured horse is uncertain); Big Cl, ~ ~ Mdw, Big Fd, The Big Mdw; Bog Mdw 1889, 1968 (*v.* **bog**); Branthill 1774, ~ Mdw 1968 (*Long Branthill* 1638; *Brantwood feilde* (sic) 1601, *Brantwell Feild* (sic) 1638, *Brantell field* 1745, *Brantill* ~ m.18¹, *Branthill field* m.18² (*v.* **feld**; one of the great open-fields of the township); despite the 1601 form which deceives into a 'burnt wood' interpretation, this is prob. 'steep hill', *v.* **brant, hyll**); Brickyard Fd (*v.* **brike-yard**); Bull Hooks (*Bullhoke* 1732, *Bullhuks* 1736, *v.* **bula, hōc**); The Burrow Fd (perh. with the surn. *Burrows*, cf. *Thomas Burrowes* 1744 *EnclA*, but ME **borow** 'an animal burrow' is poss.; if with **burh**, one would have expected earlier forms to survive); Caudell Furlong 1753 (*v.* **furlang**) (*Caudwell* 1638, *Caudel* 1745, *Caudell* m.18¹, m.18², *v.* **cald, wella**); Churchill Mdw (*Church hill* 1606, m.18², *Churchill* 1638, 1745, m.18¹, *v.* **hyll**; St Mary Magdalene's Church *supra* (a chapel until the 19th cent.) stands on a steep hillside, so while the specific of the f.n. may be **cirice**, it could be PrW **crŭg**); Clay Pits (*v.* **cley-pytt**); Club Fd or Club Land (belonging to the fraternity of Oddfellows, founded in the 18th cent.); Cook's Cl (with the surn. *Cook*); Cooper's Cl, ~ Mdw (with the surn. *Cooper*); Copnor Bridge 1828, Copman's Bridge Mdw 1968 (*v.* **brycg**; a ford preceded the bridge, hence *Cokmore ford* 1601, *v.* **mōr**¹; with **cocc**¹ or **copp** (each in the sense 'a small hill'); *Copman* (ON *kaupmaðr* 'a chapman, a merchant') replaced *Copnor* (< *Cokmore*)); Copper Cl (presum. with a reduced *Copnor* (with assimilation of *pn* > *pp*)); Cornbrook 1753 (1745, *Cornebrooke* 1601, *Cornbrooke* 1638, *Corne bruck* m.18¹, *Cornbruck* m.18², *v.* **corn**², **brōc**); Corner Fd (*v.* **corner**); Cotton's Cl 1843 (with the surn. *Cotton*); Covert Fd (*v.* **cover(t)**); Cow Cl 1752, Cow Pasture 1771 (*the Cowpasture* m.18¹, *v.* **pasture**) (*v.* **cū**); Crab Tree Mdw (*v.* **crabtre**); Crook Tree Mear 1771 (*v.* **trēow, (ge)mǣre**; either with a reduced **croked** 'crooked, twisted' or with **krókr** 'a bend, land in the bend of a stream'; the name appears from 1601 (as *Crooktree*) in adjoining Arnesby where the later forms are *Crooked Tree*); The Croft (*v.* **croft**); Far Cl 1843 (*v.* **feor**); Flat Mdw (cf. *The Flat of the Moores* 1638, *v.* **flat, flatr**); Lower ~, Upper Foxenhill 1753 (*Foxen hill* 1601, 1606, *foxnill* m.18², *Nether* ~ ~, *Upper foxes hill* 1638, *nether* ~, *upper foxnill* 1745, m.18¹), Foxenhill Cl 1752 (*foxnill close* m.18²) (*v.* **fox, hyll**; *foxen* appears to be a plural alternating with *foxes*, although it may be approximating to the fem. form *vixen* (ME *fixen*), cf. *Foxennoles*, Lei **4** 144); Front Fd (*v.* **front**); Furnival's (the surn. *Furnival* in the possessive case; originally the family name of Normans from Fournival (that either in Oise or in Orne)); First ~, Second Gate (*v.* **gata**; roadside closes); Glover's Fd, Bottom Glover's Cl 1889, 1968 (with the surn.

Glover); Goode's Cl (with the surn. *Goode*; cf. *Mary Goode* 1793 MI of Shearsby); Gospel Cl, Bottom Gospel Cl or Gospel Mdw (cf. (*the*) *Gospell tree* 1606, m.18¹, m.18², 18, (*at*) *Gospel tree* 1745, *Gospell Tree Furlong* 1638 (*v.* **furlang**), *gospell tree way* m.18¹, 18 (*v.* **weg**), *v.* **godspel, trēow**; a place where a passage from the gospel was read when the parish bounds were beaten); Big ~ ~, Little Gravel Holes (*v.* **gravel, hol**¹); Great Mears 1771 (*v.* **grēat, (ge)mǣre**); Halfyard Lands (sic) (*v.* **half, yerdland**); Hanger Spinney 1774 (*v.* **hangra, spinney**); Hawkshill Spinney 1774, ~ Cl 1968 (*Hawkeswell* 1606, *Hawkswell* 1638, m.18¹, m.18², *haukswell* 1745, *Hawkswell Mires* 1638 (*v.* **mýrr**); it is uncertain whether **wella** or **hyll** was the original generic, but *Mires* suggests *wella*; for the specific, either an OE masc. pers.n. *Hafoc* or **hafoc** 'a hawk' or even a ME metonymic surn. *Hawk* for 'hawker', depending on the generic); Holbrook, Bottom ~, Top Holbrook (*hoebroke* 1606, *Hobrooke* 1638, *hobrook* 1745, *howbruck* m.18¹, m.18², *hobruck* 18, cf. *hoebroke end* 1606 (*v.* **ende**)), Holbrook Hill Cl (*hoebroke hill* 1606, *hobrook* ~ 1745, *howbruck* ~ m.18¹, *hobruck hill* 18) (*v.* **brōc**; prob. with the common **hol²** as specific, although the early forms suggest **hōh**); Home Cl 1752, 1843, 1968, ~ Fd 1968 (*v.* **home**); Horningholds or Horneygolds 1968 (*Horningold slade* 1638, 1745, m.18¹, 18, *horn(e)ingold slade* m.18², *v.* **slæd**; with the surn. *Horningold* in the possessive case of a family originally from Horninghold, 12 miles to the north-east); House Cl; Hunger Hill, ~ ~ Mdw (*v.* **hungor, hyll**); Lammas Cl 1752, ~ Pastures 1770 (*v.* **pasture**) (*v.* **lammas**); Langthorne Furlong 1753 (*v.* **furlang**), Langthorn Mear 1771 (*v.* **(ge)mǣre**) (*Langhorne* 1606, *Langthorne* 1638, m.18¹, m.18², *langthorn* 1745, *v.* **lang**¹, **þorn**); The Limes Paddock (*v.* **paddock**); The Little Fd; The Little Mdw; Long Cl 1889, 1968, Far Long Cl 1843; Long Lands (*v.* **land**); Marshalls Cl 1752, 1968 (with the surn. *Marshall*); Martin's (the surn. *Martin* in the possessive case); The Meadow; Middle Fd; Mitchell's First ~, Mitchell's Second Cl (with the surn. *Mitchell*); Mud Hovel Fd (*v.* **mudde, hovel**); New Inn Paddock (*v.* **paddock** and New Inn Fm *supra*); Nicholls' Big ~, Nicholls' Little Fd (with the surn. *Nicholls*); Osier Cl 1843, 1968 (*v.* **oyser**); Oswin's 1774, Ossin's 1968 (the surn. *Oswin* in the possessive case; from the OE masc. pers.n. *Ōswine*, cf. *James Oswin* 1791 Nichols of Shearsby); The Paddock, Top Paddock (*v.* **paddock**); Peatling Cl (presum. with the surn. *Peatling* of a family originally from Peatling Magna or Peatling Parva, 2 miles to the north-west and south-west respectively; perh. cf. (*on*) *Peatling* and *Peatlin thorne* in Claybrooke Parva f.ns. (b)); Pen Cl (*v.* **penn**); The Pieces (*v.* **pece**); Pit Fd (*v.* **pytt**); Pump Cl (*v.* **pumpe**); Ring Cl (*v.* **hring**; a circular enclosure); Rowley Fd 1774, 1968 (*Rowloe* 1601, 1606, 1638, *Rowlow* 1601, 1745, m.18¹, m.18², 18, *Rowloe feilde* 1606, *Rowlow field* 1745, m.18¹, m.18², 18 (*v.* **feld**; one of the great open-fields), cf. *Rowlow way* m.18¹, 18 (*v.* **weg**)), Short Rowlow Mear 1770 (*v.* **(ge)mǣre**) (*Short Rowlow* 1745, cf. *Long Rowlow* 1745, m.18¹, m.18², 18) (*v.* **rūh, hlāw**); The Seeds (*v.* **sǣd**; in modern f.ns., used of grasses sown for one year's mowing or grazing); Shearsby Cl; Shortditch Furlong 1753 (*v.* **sc(e)ort, dīc, furlang**); The Slang (*v.* **slang**); Smart's (the surn. *Smart* in the possessive case); Smithall Mear 1770 (*v.* **(ge)mǣre**) (*Smytholde* (×2) 1606, *Smithel* 1745, *Smithell* m.18¹, *Smithill* m.18² (of uncertain meaning; if the generic is **wald**, then the specific is perh. **smēðe**¹ 'smooth. level'; if the generic is **hald**¹ 'a shelter', then perh. with **smið**); Spinney Mdw (*v.* **spinney**); Spring Cl (*v.* **spring**¹); Stable Cl (*v.* **stable**); Near Thorpe Hill, Far Thorpe Hill or Upper Thorpe Hill, Thorpe Hill Cl, ~ ~ Mdw 1968, Thorpe Hill Fds 1774 (*thorp hill* 1606, 1745, *Tharphill* m.18¹, m.18², *nether* ~, *upper* *thorphill* 1745, m.18¹, cf *Thorpehill Meer* 1732 (*v.* **(ge)mǣre**) (*v.* **þorp, hyll**; with reference to Bruntingthorpe parish which adjoins to the south-west); Three Cornered Cl (*v.* **three-cornered**); Bottom ~, Top Tilley's 1889, 1968 (with the surn. *Tilley*, cf. *John Tilley* 1793 MI of Shearsby and *Tilles Grave* in Kimcote); Top Cl, ~ Fd, ~ Mdw; Townsend 1968, ~ Cl 1752, 1843, 1968 (*the townes end* 1601, *the townend* 1745, *Townesend* m.18¹, *South townes end* 1638), Townsend Slang (*v.* **slang**) (*v.* **tūn, ende**); Warren Fd (*v.* **warrein**); Wheathill 1774, 1968, Top Wheathill, Wheathill Mdw 1968 (*Wheathill* 1601, 1606, 1638, 1745, m.18¹, m.18², *Nether* ~, *Upper Wheathill* 1638, 1745, m.18¹, m.18²) Wheathill Mear 1771 (*Wheathill mear*(*e*), ~ *meer* 1745, *v.* **(ge)mǣre**) (*v.* **hwǣte, hyll**); Willow Ford 1774 (*v.* **wilig, ford**; perh. *the ford* 1606 belongs here); Wistow Hill 1753, ~ ~ Cl 1753, 1865 (*Wistoe* ~ 1638, *Wistow Hill* 1745, m.18¹, m.18²; cf. *Wistoe Slade* m.18² (*v.* **slæd**), *Wistoe* ~ ~ 1638, *Wistow Slade Head* 1745, m.18¹ (*v.* **hēafod**); Wistow lies 3½ miles to the north-east; if the f.ns. do not contain the surn. *Wistow* from the township of this name, then any other relationship of Shearsby with Wistow is unrecorded, but an endowment of land for the ancient pilgrim's church of St Wistan in Wistow is poss.).

(b) *Abbottes Leyes* 1601, 1606, *Abbots leys* 1745, m.18¹, ~ *leays* m.18² (*v.* **leys**), *Abbots pits* 1638 (*v.* **pytt**) (with the surn. *Abbot*, cf. *Thomas Abbot* 1601 *Terrier* of Shearsby); *Amerlandes* 1606, *Amberlands* 1745, m.18¹, m.18² (*v.* **amer, land**); *Arnesbye Brooke* 1606 (*v.* **brōc**), *Arnesbie mere* 1601, *Arnesby meare* 1606 (*v.* **(ge)mǣre**) (Arnesby parish adjoins to the north-west); *Asgates* 1745 (*v.* **gata**), *Ashe medowe* 1601, *Ash Meadow* 1638, *Asmeadow* m.18¹, m.18², 18 (*v.* **æsc**); *Blackwell pittes* 1606, *Blakewell Pitt* 1638 (*v.* **blæc, wella, pytt**); *Blakenil* 1745, *blacknill* m.18¹, *Blackenill* m.18², 18 (*v.* **blæc** (**blacan** wk.obl.), **hyll**); *the brake* 1606 (*v.* **bracu**); *Brier furlonge* 1601, *Bryar* ~ 1638, *Brear* ~ 1745, *Brier furlong* m.18¹, m.18², 18 (*v.* **brēr, furlang**); *Brincks* 1606 (*v.* **brink**); *Bryans willows* 1745 (*v.* **wilig**; with the surn. *Bryan*, a Breton name introduced by the Normans and found in ON as *Brján*); *burgesse* ~ 1606, *bergis way* 1638 (*v.* **weg**; with the surn. *Burgess*, from OFr *burgeis* 'a freeman of a borough'; cf. *Phillipus Burgis* 1199 RFL); *the butts* 1745, ~ *buts* m.18¹ (*v.* **butte**); *the Cheescake piece* 1745, *Chiscake piece* m.18¹, m.18² (*v.* **chese-cake, pece**; a wedge-shaped field resembling a piece of the tart called a cheesecake); *Crownest* 1638, m.18¹, (*on*) *cronest* 1745 (*v.* **crāwe, nest**; sometimes used to denote the highest point in a district); *deadford* 1745, *dead foord* m.18¹, m.18² (*v.* **dēad, ford**; presum. the site of a death); *Dead Man* 1638 (*v.* **dede-man**); *Dormans Close* (with the surn. *Dorman*, from the OE masc. pers.n. *Dēormann*); *the fourteen lands* 1745 (*v.* **fēowertēne, land**); *long* ~, *old flaxlondes* 1601 (*v.* **fleax, land**); *fullwell* 1601, 1606, 1638, m.18¹, m.18², 18, *fulwell* 1745 (*v.* **fūl, wella**); *the gawles* 1601, *The Galls* 1638, *the Gauls* 1745, *the gaules* m.18¹, *the gales* m.18², 18 (*v.* **galla**); *the gravell pittes* 1601 (*v.* **gravel, pytt**); *Harpehill* 1638 (*v.* **hyll**; the specific is either **hearpe**, which may refer to an instrument for winnowing corn, or more likely, a reduced **here-pæð** 'a military road, a highway', alluding to a designated ridgeway route); *Hyngnoe* 1606, *Hingnoe* 1638, *hingnay* 1745, *hingnah* m.18¹, *hingnough, hinghnough* m.18², *hingnah hags* m.18¹ (*v.* **hǫgg**), *v.* **hōh**; the specific is either **hengen** 'a gallows, a cross' or **henge** (**hengan** obl.sg.) 'steep'); *Knaptoft hedge* 1601 (*v.* **hecg**; the boundary marker of Knaptoft parish which adjoins to the south); *Lady medow* 1601 (*v.* **ladi, mēd** (**mēdwe** obl.sg.); often referring to a dowager or to a female proprietor or to the lady of the manor; but Our Lady, the Virgin Mary, may be alluded to, esp. with reference to rents for the upkeep of a

chapel); *Langettes balke* 1606, *language balk* (sic) 1745, ~ *baulk* m.18¹ (*v.* **langet,**
balca); *London way* m.18² (the main route to London); *longe dole* 1606, *long dole*
1638, 1745, m.18¹, m.18², 18 (*v.* **lang**¹, **dāl**); *Long lane end* 1745, m.18¹, 18 (*v.* **lane,**
lane-end); *mesfurlong* 1745, m.18¹, 18 (*v.* **mēos, furlang**); *mildiche, myldyche* 1606,
Milditch 1638, 1745, m.18¹, *Millditch* m.18² (*v.* **dīc**), *Milfeilde* 1606 (*v.* **feld**), *Mill*
hill 1638 (*v.* **myln**); *the Moore feilde* 1601, *Moore Feild* 1638, *the Moore field* 1745,
m.18¹, m.18² (*v.* **feld**; one of the great open-fields); *Neathill* 1638, *Meathill* (sic)
1745, m.18¹, m.18², *Meathill gutter* 1745 (*v.* **goter**) (*v.* **nēat, hyll**; perh. later
confused with **mete** 'a boundary'); *New furlong* 1638 (*v.* **nīwe, furlang**); *Old feilde*
1601, *Old Field* 1638, 1745, m.18² (*v.* **feld**; prob. with **wald** and one of the great
open-fields of the township); *the parsons hookes* 606 (*v.* **persone, hōc**); *the pinfold*
banke 1601 (*v.* **pynd-fald, banke**); *Portslade* 1638, 1745, m.18¹, *port slad* m.18² (*v.*
port², **slæd**); *Rinksoe* 1638, *Ringsaw* 1745, m.18¹, 18, *rincsey* m.18² (*v.* **hōh**; either
with **rinc** 'a warrior' or less likely with the OE masc. pers.n. *Hring*, cf. *Rynkso*, Lei
4 200); *Sadington Mere* 1601 (*v.* **(ge)mǣre**; Saddington parish adjoins to the north-
east); *Sand furlong* 1638, 1745, m.18¹, m.18², 18 (*v.* **sand, furlang**); *Shitterlye* 1606,
Chitterley 1638, 1745, m.18¹, m.18², 18, *Chitterly* 1745 (prob. **scytere** with **lēah**,
scitere with **ley**¹ being less likely because of the longevity of the name); *Stamford*
way(e) 1601, 1745, m.18¹, m.18², 18 (the road to Stamford on Avon, 7 miles to the
south-west in Northants.); *Street thorn(e)* 1745, m.18¹, m.18², 18 (*v.* **strēt, þorn**); *the*
towne syde 1601 (*v.* **tūn, sīde**); *verges* ~ 1745, *varges way* m.18¹ (*v.* **verge**); *water*
furrowes 1601, *waterfurrows* 1745, *waterthorowes* m.18¹, m.18² (*v.* **wæter, furh** and
Water furrowes in Ashby Parva f.ns. (b)); *watergalls* 1606 (*v.* **wæter, galla**);
Whorleditch 1638, *whirlditch* 1745, *Whirleditch* m.18¹, m.18² (*v.* **hwerfel, dīc**); *at*
the willowe m.18² (*v.* **wilig**; a furlong so called); *Wyattes hadland* 1606 (*v.* **hēafod-**
land), *Wyattes* ~ 1606, *Wyats Pen* 1638, m.18², *nether* ~ ~, *upper Wyatts pen* 1745,
m.18¹ (*v.* **penn**; with the surn. *Wyatt*; the family is recorded in Shearsby from *Mary*
Wyatt 1693 MI, *John Wyatt* 1721 ib, *Elizabeth Wyatt* 1762 ib to *George Wyatt* 1793
ib).

South Kilworth

For principal forms and interpretation, *v.* adjacent North Kilworth *supra*. The settlement is recorded independently in the Domesday Survey of 1086 by the garbled spelling *Cleveliord* (×2). The development of the name is otherwise as for North Kilworth.

Affixes are variously added as:
Alterius ~ 1220 MHW
Alia ~ 1209 × 35 RHug
Australis ~ Hy 3 BM
~ *Rogeri* 1249 RGros, ~ *Rog'* 1254 Val, 1285 FA, ~ *Roger* 1344 Nichols
Suth ~ 1237 RGros, 1268 Cur *et passim* to 1285 Banco *et freq* to 1328 ib *et passim* to 1370 ib, *South*(*e*) ~ 1309 *Ferrers*, 1316 FA *et passim* to 1376 *Wyg*, 1383 *Goodacre et freq*, *Sowth* ~ 1526 LWills, 1553 Pat
~ *South* 1309 *Ferrers*, 1376 *Wyg*, 1502 *MiscAccts*
~ *Regis* (sic) 1428 FA, 1510 Visit

Rogerus de Suthkiuelingworth is recorded in 1285 Banco and held the manor from the mid 13th century as the affixes ~ *Rogeri* and ~ *Rog'* indicate. The later use of ~ *Regis* 'of the king, belonging to the king' is doubtlessly an error arising from misreadings of the abbreviated ~ *Rog'* as ~ *Reg'*. South Kilworth was never a royal manor. A similar mistake may well have created a Studley Royal from Studley Roger, *v.* YW **5** 190, 192.

Note MLat *alterius*, MLat *alia* 'another, the other (of two)', MLat *australis* 'southern'; and *v.* **sūð**.

ASH LEIGH. THE BELT, *v.* **belt**. BOTNEY LODGE, *v.* **loge**; at the western extremity of the parish and thus presum. a 'remoteness' name, one transferred from Botany Bay in New South Wales, Australia, where Captain James Cook landed in 1770 and where his companion, Sir

Joseph Banks, collected a large variety of previously unknown plants which gave the bay its name and where, later, a penal colony was established. CALDICOTE SPINNEY, *Caldicote Spinny* 1835 O, *v.* **spinney**; it is uncertain whether the first word is a surname or a place-name. *Caroline Caldecote* 1815 Census is recorded in nearby Bitteswell and *Clare Caldecott* 1877 ib in Knighton. Place-names in Caldecote are usually associated with former Roman roads, for which there is no evidence here (*v.* P. Tallon, 'What was a Caldecote?', JEPNS 31 (1998–9), 31–54); *v.* **cald**, **cot**. CHURCH SPINNEY, *v.* **spinney**; at the parish's northern boundary away from the church and thus poss. endowed land. CORDALS (local), *caldewelle, chaldewelle* 1200 AAS, *Cawdells* 1601 *Terrier, Cawdles* 1638, 1674, 1708 *ib, Cawdels* 1724 *ib, Top ~, Middle ~, Low Caudle* 1821 *ib,* cf. *Cawdleyes* 1701, 1733 *ib, Caudwell leys* c.1715, 1724 *ib, Cawdleys* 1781, 1784 *ib, Cawdwell Lays* 1781 *ib* (*v.* **leys**), *Cawdle springe* 1638, 1674 *ib, Cawdles Spring* 1708 *ib, Cawdels ~, Cawdley's ~* 1765, 1781 *ib, Cawdleys Spring* 1784 *ib* (*v.* **spring**[1]), *v.* **cald**, **wella**. DOG LANE, *v.* **dag** 'moisture; mire'; recorded as *Daglane* 1382 in North Kilworth (cf. Dag Lane, Lei **4** 172); Dog Lane in Burton Lazars (Lei **2** 63) is interpreted as with *dogge* 'a dog' but may well conceal *dag*. THE ELMS. HIGHFIELDS FM, *Highfield* 1925 Kelly. HIGH LEIGH. THE HOLLIES. HOME FM, *v.* **home**. LITTLE BONES, *bone* (sic) 1606 *Terrier,* cf. *bones hawx(e)low* 1601, 1606 *ib, Bone Hoxlow* 1703 *ib, Bone Hawxlow* 1708, 1724, 1733, 1765, 1781 *ib* (*v.* Hawxlow in f.ns. (a)), *Bone Leyes* 1703 *ib, ~ Leys* 1708 *ib, ~ Layes* 1733 *ib, ~ Lays* 1724, 1765, 1781, 1784 *ib* (*v.* **leys**), *Bone Nook(e)* 1703, 1708, 1724, 1733, 1765, 1781, 1784 *ib* (*v.* **nōk**), *Bone spring* 1756 Nichols (*v.* **spring**[1]); evidently with **bān** 'bone' and poss. referring to an unearthed Anglo-Saxon inhumation cemetery. Note Bonn in adjacent Misterton f.ns. (a). MALT SHOVEL is *Maltshovel Farm* 1937 Sale; on Walcote Rd and no doubt a former inn. MANOR HO., *Manor House* 1877 White, *v.* **maner**. THE MOATS were medieval fish-ponds belonging to the early manor house and gave *the Mutt Field,* one of the great open-fields of the township, its name, *v.* **mote** and Mutt Fd in f.ns. (a). NEW COVERT, *v.* **cover(t)**. NORTH KILWORTH RD, North Kilworth lying one mile to the north-east. OAK LEIGH. OLD COVERT, *v.* **cover(t)**. THE ORCHARD. THE RECTORY, 1925 Kelly, *the Rectory house* 1821 *Terrier, v.* **rectory**; earlier is *the Parsonage house* 1606 *ib, v.* **personage**. RESERVOIR COTTAGE, beside Stanford Reservoir. ROYAL OAK (P.H.) (lost), *Royal Oak* 1846, 1863, 1877 White, *Oak* 1925 Kelly. RUGBY RD, Rugby in Warwks. lying 8 miles to the south-west. ST NICHOLAS'S CHURCH, *Church (St Nicholas)* 1846, 1863, 1877 White, 1925 Kelly; it is earlier recorded as *ecclesie alterius Kiuelingworth* 1220 MHW (with MLat *alterius* '(the) other, another'), *ecclesiam de Suthkivilingworth* 1237 RGros, ~ *de Kyuelingwrth Rogeri* 1249 ib, *ecclesie de Kyvelyngworth* 1322 *Pat*, ~ *de Southkelyngworth* 1348 *ib*. Note also *the Church yard* 1733, 1781, 1821 *Terrier*, *v.* **churchyerd**. SOUTH KILWORTH GRANGE, *The Grange* 1925 Kelly, *v.* **grange**. SOUTH KILWORTH LODGE, *v.* **loge**. TALBOT (P.H.) (lost), *Talbot* 1846 White. WALCOTE RD is *Walcote Gate* 1789 *EnclA* (*v.* **gata**), Walcote lying 2 miles to the north-west. WELFORD RD, Welford in Northants lying 2 miles to the south-east. WHITE HART (P.H.), *White Hart* 1846, 1863, 1877 White, 1925 Kelly.

FIELD-NAMES

In (a), forms dated 1756 are Nichols; those dated 1765, 1781, 1784 and 1821 are *Terrier*; 1789 are *EnclA*. Forms throughout dated 1200 are AAS; those dated 1376 are *Wyg*; 1383 and 1384 are *Goodacre*; 1414 are Coram; 1553 are *Pat*; 1601, 1606, 1638, 1674, 1703, 1708, c.1715, 1724 and 1733 are *Terrier*; 1625 are Ipm.

(a) Six Acres 1765, 1781, 1784 (1638, 1674, 1708, *sixe acres* 1601, *Six Acers* 1703, 1724, *Six Acurs* 1733), Twelve Acre Cl 1821 (*v.* **æcer**); Annislow 1781 (1708, c.1715, 1724, *v.* **hlāw**; with the OE masc. pers.n. *An(n)*; the toponym also appears in adjoining Misterton and North Kilworth parishes); Ballong Corner 1789 (*v.* **corner**) (*Ballong* 1606, *v.* **ball**; with **lang²** or **vangr**); Bann Lands 1765, 1781, 1784 (*banlandes* 1601, 1606, *Bannlands* 1703, 1733, *Bandlands* 1708, *Banlands* 1724, *v.* **bēan, land**); Barn Cl 1821 (*v.* **bern**); Barslade Furlong 1765, 1781, 1784 (1638, 1674, 1703, 1724, 1733 (*v.* **furlang**), *Barslade* 1601, 1606, 1708, 1724), Braislade ~ 1764, Barslaid Ford 1781 (*Barslaid* ~ 1674, 1708, *Barslade ford* 1703, *Braslaid forde* 1733, *v.* **ford**) (*v.* **bær¹, slæd**); Beggars Baulk 1781 (1708, c.1715, *beggars balke* 1601, *Beggers baulk* 1724, *v.* **beggere, balca**); Bickleys Cl 1789 (with the surn. *Bickley*); Blakenell 1765, 1781, 1784 (*Blakenill* 1601, 1638, 1674, *Blaknill* 1606, *Blakenel* 1708, *Blackenell* 1733, *v.* **hyll**; either with **blæc** (**blacan** wk.obl.) or, much less likely, with the OE masc. pers.n. *Blaca* (*Blacan* gen.sg.); the form *Blakenhull* (e.13) is listed in North Kilworth f.ns. (b)); Bradgate Haden 1765, Breadgit ~ 1781, Bradgit Haden 1784 (*Broadgit haden* 1638, 1674, *Bradget headen* 1703, *Bradgate* ~ 1708, 1724, *Bradgit Haden* 1733, *v.* **hēafod**; either with the surn. *Bradgate* of a family originally from Bradgate, 19 miles to the north-west or with a toponym 'broad road' (*v.* **brād, gata**); note the archaic -*en* plural of *haden*); (*the*) *Breach* 1765, 1781, 1784 (*Breche* 1200, *Breach* 1606, 1638 *et passim* to 1733, *v.* **brēc**); Bricklin (sic) 1821 (*v.* **brike-kiln**); Bridewell 1765, Bridwell 1781, 1784 (*Bridell* 1601, 1724, *Bridewell* 1638, 1674, 1708, *Bridwell* 1703, 1733, *v.* **brȳd, wella**; also appears in forms listed in North Kilworth f.ns. (b)); Brook Fd 1765, 1781, 1784, 1789 (1708, 1724, *the Bruk Field* 1638, *the Brook filde* 1674, *the Brook(e) Field* 1703, c.1715, 1724, 1733, *v.* **brōc, feld**; one of the great open-fields of the township; earlier called *the nether feilde*, *v.* f.ns. (b)); Budewell Furlong 1789 (*v.* **furlang**; this may be a late or a poor form of Bridewell *supra*, but if not, then *v.* **wella**; and either with the OE masc. pers.n. *Budda* or, less likely, with **budda**); Sir Tho. Caves Grounds 1781 (c.1715, 1724, cf. *Sir Roger Caves Ground* 1708, *v.* **grund**); Church Hades Furlong 1781 (*v.* **furlang**), Nether ~ ~, Upper Church Hades 1781 (*Nether* ~ ~, *Middle* ~ ~, *Upper Church Hades* 1708, c.1715, 1724), (the) Over Church Hades 1765, 1781, 1784 (1658, 1674, 1703, 1708, 1733, *v.* **uferra**) (*v.* **hēafod** and St Nicholas's Church *supra*); the Church Lays 1765, 1781, 1784, Church Leys 1821 (*Church Leys* 1606, 1708, 1724, *the Church Lays* 1638, ~ ~ *Leyes* 1733, *v.* **leys**); Cockmaydame Lays 1781 (*Copperdown* 1708, 1724, *Coperdown* c.1715, *Cockmaydame leyes* 1733, *v.* **copped**[1], **dūn**, **leys**); Colepitt ~ 1765, 1781, Colepit Hill 1784 (*Colepit* ~ 1638, 1674, 1724, *Coalpit Hill* 1708, *v.* **col-pytt**; a place where charcoal was made); Cottmore 1765, 1781, 1784 (1703, 1708, 1724, 1733, *Cotmore* 1601, 1606, *Cotmoore* 1638, 1674, *v.* **cot**, **mōr**[1]); the Cow Pasture 1789 (*v.* **cū**, **pasture**); The Croft 1789 (*v.* **croft**); Dancing Mire 1781 (*v.* **dauncing**, **mýrr**; presum. quake-fen); Dowells 1765, 1781, 1784 (1601, 1606, 1708, 1733, *dufwell* 1200, *Dowills* 1703, *Dowels* 1724, *v.* **dūfe**, **wella**; cf. *douewell* in Croxton Kerrial, Lei **2** 106); Dunsacre 1765, 1781, 1784 (*Dunz acres* 1606, *Dunzacre* 1638, 1674, 1708, 1733, *Dunz Acer* 1703, 1724, *Donzacer* 1724, *v.* **dyncge**, **æcer**); Fallow How 1765, 1781, Follow How 1784 (*Phaleweslow* 1200, *Followslow* 1606, 1638, 1674, 1703, *Fellow How* 1733, *v.* **hlāw**; perh. with **fealu**, whose gen.sg. **fealwes** here may represent a substantive use of the adj. and denote 'something fallow, pale-brown', perh. 'the fallow deer', cf. Fawsley, Nth 23 (*fealuwes lea* 956 (14) BCS 944 (S599)) and prob. Fawley, Brk 298; 18th-cent. forms have been influenced by **hōh** 'a spur of land'); Full Pit Hill 1765, 1781, Fulpithill 1784, Pulpit Hill (sic) 1821 ((*the*) *Fullpitt* ~ 1606, 1638, 1674, 1703, 1733, *Fulpit hill* 1708, 1724, *v.* **fūl**, **pytt**, **hyll**); (the) Goss Green Furlong 1765, 1781, 1784 (1703, 1708, 1724, 1733, *gosse greene furlong* 1606, *Gowse green furlong* 1638, 1674, *v.* **gōs**, **grēne**[2], **furlang**); (the) Grange Furlong 1765, 1781, 1784 (1703, 1708, 1733, *v.* **furlang** and South Kilworth Grange *supra*); The Great Cl 1789; the Grove 1781, 1784 (1703, 1708, 1733, *the Groue* 1724, cf. *the Grove end*(*e*) 1601, 1733 (*v.* **ende**), *v.* **grāf**); Hall Land 1756 (*v.* **hall**, **land**; belonging to Stanford Hall in adjoining Westrill and Starmore parish); Hanghome Baulk 1781 (1708, c.1715, 1724, *Hangholme* 1703, 1733, *Hanghome* 1703, 1724, *v.* **hangende**, **holmr**, **balca**); Hangland 1765, 1781, 1784 (*Hangendelond*, *Hangingdel'* 1200, *Hangland* 1606, 1638, 1674, 1703, *hanglong* 1606, *Hanglands* 1708, 1724, 1733), Hangland Furlong 1781 (c.1715, 1724, *Hanglands furlong* 1708, *v.* **furlang**), Hanglands Sitch 1765, 1781, 1784 (*hanglong seeche* 1601, ~ *sitch* 1606, *hanglangsitch* 1638, 1674, *Hanglands Sitch* 1703, 1724, 1733, *Hangland sich* 1708, *v.* **sīc**) (*v.* **hangende**, **land**); Hang Woong 1765, 1781, 1784 (1733, *Hangwong* 1601, 1606, 1638, 1674, 1703, *v.* **hangende**, **vangr**); Hauxlow, Hoxlow 1765, 1781, 1784 (*hawxelow* 1601, *Hawxlow* 1606, 1708, 1724, 1733, *Hoxlow* 1638, 1674, 1703, 1733, *Haxlow*, *Hoxlo* 1724, *v.* **hlāw**; either with **hafoc** or with the OE masc. pers.n. *Hafoc*); Hay Furlong 1765, 1781, 1784 (1703, 1708, 1724, 1733, *v.* **furlang**; with **hēg** or **hege**); Hogshole 1765, 1781, 1784 (1601, 1638, 1674, 1703, 1708, 1733, *hoges hole* 1606, *Hogghole*, *Hoggshole* 1724), Hogs Hole Furlong 1781 (1708, c.1715, *Hoghole furlong* 1724, *v.* **furlang**), Hogs Hole North Piece, ~ ~ South Piece 1781 (1708, c.1715, 1724, *v.* **pece**) (*v.* **hogg**, **hol**[1]); Holme Hill 1765, 1781, 1784 (1601, 1606, 1638, 1674, 1703, 1733, *Home hill* 1708, c.1715, 1724, *Holm* 1200, *v.* **holmr**, **hyll**); the Home Cl 1789 (*v.*

home); the Homestead 1781 (*v.* **hām-stede**); Howards Cl 1789 (with the surn. *Howard*); Iron Way 1765, 1781, 1784 (1703, 1708, 1733, *Iron waye* 1601, 1638), Iron Way Furlong 1765, 1784 (1703, 1733, *Iron ways Furlong* 1708, 1724, *v.* **furlang**), Ironways End 1765, 1781 (1708, 1724, (*on*) *Iron Wayes end* 1703, 1733, *Iron Way End* 1724, *v.* **ende**) (*v.* **hyrne, weg**); Key Furlong 1765, 1781 (1606, 1703, 1708, 1724, *v.* **key, furlang**; beside the river Avon); Kilworth Cross 1765, 1781, 1784 (1708, (*at*) *Kilworth crosse* 1601, 1606, (*at*) *Killworth Cross*(*e*) 1638, 1674, 1703, 1724, 1733, *Kilworth Crose* 1724, *v.* **cros**); Kilworth Way Baulk 1781 (c.1715, 1724, ~ ~ *bauk* 1708, *v.* **balca**); Lake 1821 (*v.* **lake**; the river Avon broadens into a large lake on the parish boundary); Lane End Furlong 1765, 1781, 1784 (1703, 1708, 1724, 1733, *v.* **lane-ende, furlang**); Langlands 1765, 1781 (1638, 1674, 1703, 1708, 1724, 1733, *langelond'* 1200, *Langlandes* 1601, 1606, *v.* **lang¹, land**); Linslade 1765, 1781, 1784 (1724, *Lenchslade* 1601, 1606, *Lenslade* 1638, 1674, 1708, 1733, *Leneslade* 1703), Linslade End 1781 (1724, *Leneslade End* 1703 (*v.* **ende**), cf. *Leneslade* ~ 1703, *Linslade head* 1724 (*v.* **hēafod**)) (*v.* **hlenc, slæd**); Little Cliffe 1765, 1781, 1784 (1638, 1674, *Luttelclif* 1414, *Little Clif* 1703, 1708, *Littelclif* 1724, *Little Cleffe* 1733, *v.* **lȳtel, clif**); Lockstead 1765, 1781, 1784, Locksted 1784 (*locstede* 1200, *Lockstedd* 1601, *locksted* 1606, *Loxtid* 1724, *Lockstead* 1703, 1708, 1733, *v.* **loc, loca, stede**); Longet Baulk 1781 (1708, *v.* **langet, balca**); Long Furlong 1765, 1781, 1784 (1703, 1708, 1724, 1733, *longe furlonge* 1601, *v.* **lang¹, furlang**); Longlands 1765, 1781, 1784 (1703, 1708, *Long Land* 1638, 1674, *v.* **lang¹, land**; a separate feature from Langlands *supra*); Long Row 1765, 1781, 1784 (1703, 1708, 1724, 1733, *v.* **lang¹**; with **rāw** or **ræw**); the Meare ~ 1765, 1781, the Mere Furlong 1784 ((*the*) *Meare* ~ 1601, 1638, 1674, 1733, *the Mear* ~ 1703, (*the*) *Meer furlong* 1708, 1724, *v.* **furlang**), Meer Fd 1789, Mere Cl, ~ Mdw 1821 (*v.* (**ge**)**mǣre**); Middle Ground Hades 1781 (*v.* **grund, hēafod**); Mill Wakefield 1765, 1781, ~ Wakefeild 1784 (*millwakefeild* 1606, *Millwakefield* 1703, 1708, 1724, 1733, *v.* **myln, wacu, feld**; note Wakelow *infra*); Minslow 1765, 1781, 1784 (1703, 1733, *Memslow* 1708), Neither Mimslow Furlong 1781 (*v.* **neoðera, furlang**) (*Nether Mimslow* c.1715, 1724) (*v.* **hlāw**; prob. with (**ge**)**mǣnnes**); Moor's ~ 1765, 1781, Moors Butts 1784 (*Meare butts* (sic) 1638, 1674, *Moore* ~ 1703, 1733, *Moor* ~ 1708, *More Butts* 1724 (*v.* **butte**; poss. with **mere¹** replaced by **mōr¹**); (the) Mutt Fd 1765, 1781, 1784 (1703, 1708, c.1715, 1733, *Mutt Fielde* 1638, ~ *filde* 1674, *the Mut Field* 1708, 1724, *v.* **mote, feld** and The Moats *supra*; one of the great open-fields, earlier called *the North feilde*); the Nursery 1789 (*v.* **nursery**); the Old Pen 1789 (*v.* **ald, penn**); Padock Hole 1765, 1781, 1784 (1703, 1708, 1724, 1733, *paddock* ~ 1601, 1606, *Paddocke hole* 1638, 1674, *v.* **padduc, hol¹**); Port Hill 1781 (1606, 1708, 1724), Porthill Lays 1781 (*Porthill leys* 1708, 1724, *v.* **leys**) (*v.* **port², hyll**; a hill beside a *port-wey*, poss. a shortening of **Port-way hill, v.* Cox² 81, *s.n.* Port Hill), Port Way 1765, 1781, Porteway 1784 (*Port Way* 1703, 1708, 1724, *portwayes end* 1601, 1703, *Portway end* 1724, *Porte-wayes End* 1733 (*v.* **ende**), *Porte Way head* 1733 (*v.* **hēafod**) (*v.* **port-wey**; either the road to Market Harborough which lies 8 miles to the north-east or to Lutterworth, 4 miles to the north-west); Purchase Pit 1765, 1784, ~ Pitt 1781 (*Purchase Pitt* 1703, 1724, ~ *Pit* 1708, *Purchas* ~, *Purches Pitt* 1733, *v.* **purchas, pytt**); Rickstead 1765, 1781, Ricksted 1784 (*Rickstead* 1638, 1674, 1703, 1708, *Rixted* 1724, *Ricksted* 1733, *v.* **rickstead**); Small Brook 1765, 1781, 1784 (1601, 1708, 1724, *Small brooke* 1606, 1703, *v.* **smæl, brōc**); Smeeth ~ 1765, 1781, Smeth Mdw 1784 (*Smethemede* 1200, *Smeeth* ~ 1606, 1638, 1703, 1733, *Smith* *meadow* 1708, *Smithsmeddo* 1724, *v.* **smēðe**[1], **mēd** (**mēdwe** obl.sg.)); Stanford Way Baulk 1781 (1708, c.1715, 1724, *Stanford way* 1606, *v.* **balca**; land beside the road to Stanford on Avon which lies 2 miles to the south-west in Northants.); Starmore Lays 1765, 1781, Starmor ~, Stormour lays 1784 (*Stormsworth* ~ 1606, *Stormworth leys* 1638, 1674, *Stormer Leyes* 1703, ~ *Leys* 1708, *Starmorlays* 1724, *Starmer* ~, *Stormer Leyes* 1733, *v.* **leys**; adjoining Starmore (formerly *Stormsworth*) in adjacent Westrill and Starmore parish); (at) the Stones 1781 (*the Stones* 1724, *v.* **stān**); Stork's ~ 1765, 1781, Storkes Nest 1784 (*Storkes Nest* 1638, 1674, 1703, 1733, *v.* **storc, nest**); Stow Corner (sic) 1765, 1781, Stone Corner 1784 (*Stone Corner* 1606, 1638, 1674, 1724, 1733, *v.* **stān, corner**); Tenter Piece 1781 (1708, 1724, *Tenter peice* c.1715, *v.* **tentour, pece**); (at) Thacker 1765, (on) Thacker 1784 (*thachere* 1200, cf. *thacker hedge* 1601, 1638, 1674, 1708, *Thackers Hedge* 1703, 1733, *v.* **hecg**), Thacker Mdw 1781, 1821 ('the thatch place', *v.* **þæc, -er**; with influence from Scand **þak**); Thistledown Baulk 1781 (1708, c.1715, *v.* **thistledown, balca**); Tolegate Cl 1821 (*v.* **toll-gate**); the Town Side 1765, 1781, 1784 (*the Towne Side* 1601, 1703, 1708, 1733, *v.* **tūn, sīde**); The Town Street 1789 (*v.* **tūn, strēt**); Wakelow 1765, 1781, 1784, Wakerlough 1821 (*Wakelow* 1601, 1606 *et passim* to 1733), Wakelow Fd 1765, 1781, 1784, 1789 (1703, 1708, c.1715, 1724, 1733, *Wakelowe Feild* 1638, *Wakelow fild* 1674, *v.* **feld**; one of the great open-fields, formerly *the West feilde*) (*v.* **wacu, hlāw**); Water Furrows 1765, 1781, 1784 (1708, 1724, *Waterfurrowes* 1601, 1606, 1703, *Watter Furrowes* 1733, *v.* **wæter, furh** and *Water furrowes* in Ashby Parva f.ns. (b)); Welford Bridge 1764, 1781, 1784, 1789 (1601, 1606, 1703, 1708, 1724, *Wellford Bridge* 1733; the bridge across the river Avon into Welford parish in Northants., Welford lying one mile to the south-east); Well Lane End 1781, 1789 (1708, c.1715, 1724, cf. *Well Lane Furlong* 1708 (*v.* **furlang**), *v.* **wella, lane, lane-ende**); Westerhill 1765, 1781, 1784, Westrill 1781 (*Westerhill* 1601, 1703, 1708, *Westrill* 1724, *Nether Westerhill* 1708, ~ *Westrill* 1724, *Westrill hill* 1733, cf. *Westerhill gate* 1601 (*v.* **gata**), *v.* **wester, hyll**; Westrill and Starmore parish adjoins to the south-west); Whorn 1765, 1781, 1784 (*whoorne* 1606, *Whorne* 1638, 1674, 1703, *the whorne* 1733), Nether ~, Upper Whorn 1765, 1781, 1784 (*over whoorne* 1606 (*v.* **uferra**), *Ne(a)ther* ~, *Upper Whorn(e)* 1703, 1708, c.1715, 1724, 1733, *Under whorn* 1708 (*v.* **under**)) (*v.* **cweorn**; either alluding to a mill or to a place where quernstones were obtained; forms of this toponym are also present in North Kilworth f.ns.); Woolcott 1765, 1781, 1784 (*Wolscott* 1601, *Wolcote* 1638, 1674, *Wollcot* 1703, *Woolcote* 1724, *Woollcott* 1733), Woolcot Furlong 1781 (*Wolcot* ~ 1708, *Woolcot furlong* c.1715, 1724, *v.* **furlang**) (*v.* **cot**; with the OE masc. pers.n. *Wulfhere*, an early form (*Wlferescote* 1208) is listed in North Kilworth f.ns. (b)); Wow 1765, 1781, 1784 ((upon) *Wow* 1601, *Wow* 1638, 1674, (on) *Wow* 1703, 1708, 1724, 1733), Wow Furlong 1781 (1708, c.1715, *v.* **furlang**) (*v.* **wōh** 'twisted'; perh. used as a stream-name, but more likely simply to be a shortened form of *Woham* (e.13) (with **hamm**) listed in North Kilworth f.ns. (b)); Youngfield 1765, Youngfeild 1784 (*yong feild* 1606, *Youngfield* 1703, 1708, *Youngfeild* 1733), Youngfield ~, 1765, 1781, Youngfeild Side 1784 (*Youngfield* ~ 1703, 1708, *Youngfeild Side* 1733 (*v.* **sīde**, cf. *Young Field Top* 1724 (*v.* **topp**) (*v.* **yonge, feld**).

   (b) *le Barlycornes* 1553, *Barleycorns* 1625 (*v.* **barlicorn**); *Barnecroft* 1625 (*v.* **bern, croft**); *Broadgrene* 1638, *Broadgreene haden* 1606 (*v.* **hēafod**; note the archaic *-en* pl.) (*v.* **brād, grēne**[2]); *the church hill* 1601 (*v.* **hyll** and St Nicholas's

Church *supra*); *corvenlond* 1200 (*v*. **corven**, **land**); *eggeslades* 1200 (*v*. **slæd**; prob. with **ecg**, but the OE masc. pers.n. *Ecga* is poss.); *fullen seeche* 1601, ~ *sitch* 1606, 1724 (*v*. **sīc**, perh. with **fuglung** 'fowling, bird-catching'; **fulling** is unrecorded before 1688 OED, while **fūlan** (wk.obl. form of **fūl**) is unlikely in so minor a name); *le Grange land* 1625, *Grange Lays* 1724 (*v*. **leys**) (*v*. South Kilworth Grange *supra*); *othe grene* 1376 (p), *atte grene* 1383 (p), 1384 (p) (*v*. **atte**) (*v*. **grēne**²); *Greenes land* 1625 (*v*. **land**; with the surn. *Green*); *le Ham* 1553, *le Hame* 1625 (*v*. **hamm**); *hereshaker* 1200 (*v*. **æcer**; either with the OE masc. pers.n. *Here*, a short form of names such as *Herefrið* or with the surn. *Here*, an original by-name from OE *hēore*, ME *here* 'gentle, mild'); *the Kings Highway* 1708 (*v*. **hēah-weg**; a careless copying of a Glebe Terrier, since at this date Queen Anne was on the throne); *Littelhil* 1200 (*v*. **lȳtel**, **hyll**); (*upon*) *long* 1606 (*v*. **lang**²); *Lutterworth bushes* 1606 (*v*. **busc**), *Lytterworth way* 1601 (*v*. **weg**) (Lutterworth lies 4 miles to the north-west); *Madame Croft* 1625 (*v*. **madame**, **croft**; alluding to the wife of the landowner, *v*. Field 174); *Marchewell*, *Marcheswell* 1200 (*v*. **mearc**, **wella**); *Meredich* 1200, *meyre dytch* 1606 (*v*. (**ge**)**mǣre**, **dīc**); *middelslade* 1200 (*v*. **middel**, **slæd**); *mill furlong* 1606 (*v*. **myln**, **furlang**); *the nether feilde* 1601 (*v*. **neoðera**, **feld**; one of the great open-fields of the township, later Brook Fd *supra*); *the North feilde* 1601, ~ ~ *Field* 1708 (*v*. **norð**, **feld**; one of the great open-fields, otherwise Mutt Fd *supra*); *ortons myres* 1601 (*v*. **mýrr**), *Ortons townes end* 1601 (*v*. **tūn**, **ende**) (with the surn. *Orton*, cf. *Robert Orton* 1601 *Terrier* of South Kilworth); *Pinfold furlong* 1606 (*v*. **pynd-fald**, **furlong**); *Pit forlong* 1200 (*v*. **furlang**), *Pit hill* 1733 (*v*. **pytt**); *the Sandpitt* 1601, *Sandpitt ley* 1606 (*v*. **ley**²) (*v*. **sand-pytt**); *scardelowe* 1200 (*v*. **sc(e)ard**, **hlāw**; cf. Shardlow, Db 501); *sinderlond* 1200, *Synderlandes* 1606, *Cunderland* (sic) 1638 (*v*. **sundor-land**); *Stoneslade* 1638, 1674 (*v*. **stān**, **slæd**); (*the*) *Town(e) ground* 1601, 1703, 1724 (*v*. **tūn**, **grund**); *Waud* 1200 (*v*. **wald**); *the West feilde* 1601 (*v*. **west**, **feld**; one of the great open-fields, later Wakelow Fd *supra*); *Wethercliuemere* 1200 (*v*. **weðer**, **clif**; with (**ge**)**mǣre** or **mere**¹).

Swinford

Svineford 1086 DB, *Suineford* 1175 (p), 1184 (p), 1199 P (p),
   Suineforda c.1155 Dane, *Suinefort* c.1200 ib
Svinesford 1086 DB, *Swinesforde* 1166 RBE, *Sueinesford* 1185 (p),
   1190 P (p), *Swynesford* 1341, 1344 Cl
Svinford 1086 DB (×4), *Suinford* 1176 (p), 1177 P (p) *et passim* to
   1193 ib, *Suinforda* Hy 2 Dane, *Sueinford* 1175 ChancR (p), 1176
   P (p) *et passim* to 1181 ib (p)
Swineford c.1130 LeicSurv, 1166 LN *et passim* to 1315 AD (p), 1333
   Cl, *Swyneford*(e) 1225 RHug, 1226 Fine *et freq* to 1370, 1373
   Banco
Swynford 1229 Selby, 1273 Coram (p) *et passim* to 1347 Banco, 1348
   Cl *et freq* to 1551, 1555 Fine, *Swinford* 1561 Ipm, 1576 Saxton *et
   freq*

'Swine ford', *v.* **swīn**[1] (**swīnes** gen.sg., **swīna** gen.pl.), **ford**. The
reference is to domestic pigs. Occasional spellings with *Sueines-* and
Suein- may show attraction to ON *sveinn* 'a young man, a servant'.

ALL SAINTS' CHURCH *Church (All Saints)* 1846, 1863, 1877 White, 1925
Kelly; it is earlier recorded as *ecclesie de Suyneford* 1220 MHW,
ecclesiam parochialem de Swynford 1489 *Pat* (with MLat *parochialis*
'parochial'), *ecclesiam Omnium Sanctorum de Swynford* 1548 *ib*; and in
ecclesiarum de Swineford et Walcote 1560 *ib*. Note also *the Church yard*
1803 *ib*, *v.* **churchyerd**. CATTHORPE BARN, *v.* **bern**; at the parish
boundary with Catthorpe which adjoins to the south-west. CAVE'S ARMS
(P.H.), 1846, 1863, 1877 White, *Cave Arms* 1925 Kelly; *Sarah Otway
Cave, Baroness Braye* of neighbouring Stanford Hall is *Lady of the
Manor* 1846 White. CHEQUERS (P.H.), *Chequers* 1846, 1863 White, 1925
Kelly, *Chequers Inn* 1877 White. CROSS KEYS (P.H.) (lost), *Cross Keys*
1846, 1863 White, 1925 Kelly, *Cross Keys Inn* 1877 White. DENYER'S
BARN, *v.* **bern**; with the surn. *Denier, Denyer*, cf. *Stephen Denier* 1839
Census of Leicester; a surn. either from Denier (Pas-de-Calais) or an

occupational surn. from French *denier* 'money' (from Lat *denarius*, a small Roman silver coin). LUTTERWORTH RD, Lutterworth lying 3 miles to the north-west. SWINFORD CORNER, 1835 O, *v.* **corner**; a road junction at a northern angle of the parish. SWINFORD COVERT, *v.* **cover(t)**. SWINFORD LODGE, 1835 O, *The Lodge* 1925 Kelly, *v.* **loge**. THE VICARAGE, 1925 Kelly; earlier is *the Vicarage House* 1606, 1751, 1803 *Terrier*, *v.* **vikerage**.

FIELD-NAMES

Forms in (a) presented without dates are 1968 *Surv*; those dated 1751 and 1803 are *Terrier*; 1792 are *Deed*; 1835 are O; 1886 and 1900 are *Map*. Forms throughout dated e.13 are AD; those dated 1327 and 1332 are SR; 1348 are Cl; 1453 are Pap; 1546 are AAS; 1548 are Pat; 1601, 1606, 1674, 1679, 17 and m.18 are *Terrier*; 1614 are Deed; 1638 are Ipm.

(a) Two Acre, Four Acre Ploughing, Six Acre, ~ Acres, Ploughed 6 Acres, 8 Acre, 8 Acre Church Piece (*v.* All Saints' Church *supra* and **pece**) 1968, Nine Acres 1792, 9 Acre, 9 Acre Church Piece, Ten Acres, The 10 Acres or Second Webster's (with the surn. *Webster*, *v.* Webster's Cl *infra*), 11 Acre, The Fir Tree 11 Acre (*v.* **firr**), The 13 Acre, 16 Acre, Top 17 Acre 1968 (*v.* **æcer**); Allotments (*v.* **allotment**); Bottom ~, Top Ashbrook (*v.* **æsc**, **brōc**); Ashby Way (land beside the road to Ashby Magna, 7 miles to the north); Bankey Mdw (*v.* **banke, -ig³**); Banks (*v.* **banke**); Little ~~, Old ~~, Barn Cl 1792, 1968, Barn Fds 1968 (*v.* **bern**); Benn's Cl (with the surn. *Benn*); Black Mans Dyke (*v.* **dík**; no early forms survive, but the generic suggests an old f.n., either with the OE masc. pers.n. *Blæcmann*, an original by-name for 'a dark or swarthy man', a pers.n. which was common into the 13th cent., or with its surn. issue *Blackman*); Brick Kiln Cl or Brittle Cl (*v.* **brike-kiln**); The Brickyard (*v.* **brike-yard**); Bridge Fd, The Bridge Mdw (*v.* **brycg**); Brookside (*v.* **brōc**, **sīde**); Bullock Fd (*v.* **bulluc**); Bush Cl 1792, 1968 (prob. with **busc**, but *v.* Widow Bushes East, ~ ~ West *infra*); Calves Cl (*v.* **calf**); Cockshut (*v.* **cocc-scēte**); Cogington Hollow (*v.* **tūn**, **holh**; Cogington is presum. an early p.n., perh. cf. Smockington Hollow, 9½ miles to the north-west on Watling Street in Wigston Parva parish); Coopers Cl (with the surn. *Cooper*); Cotton Fd (*v.* **cot, cote (cotan** nom.pl.) (**cotum** dat.pl.), cf. Cotton Cl in Wistow, Lei **4** 296); First ~ ~, Dairy Cl (*v.* **deierie**); Drain Fd (*v.* **drain**); East Mdw; First Fd; The Flags (*v.* **flagge**); The Flats (*v.* **flat**); Floyds Mdw (with the surn. *Floyd*); Foalyard 1886 (*v.* **fola, geard**); First ~ ~, Second Ford Fd (*v.* **ford**); The Fox Cover (*v.* **fox**, **cover(t)**); Fulsidge (*Fulsike* e.13, *fulsidg* 17, m.18, *fulsage* 1674, *v.* **fūl, sík, sīc**); Gadget Fd (obscure; *gadget* is usually used of a small mechanical device); Garner's Mdw (with the surn. *Garner*; cf. *William Garner* 1821 Census of Swinford); The Glebe (*v.* **glebe**); Gorse Fd (*v.* **gorst**); The Granell (poss. with **grendel**; earlier forms are needed); Greenbank (*v.* **grēne¹, banke**); Hall's Cl 1886 (with the surn. *Hall*); Long Hangings (*v.* **hangende**); Harris's (the surn. *Harris* in the possessive case, cf. *Henry Harris* 1826 Census and *Ellen Harris* 1850 ib of

Swinford); Holly Furlong (*v.* **holegn, furlang**); Home Cl, ~ Fd (*v.* **home**); The Hooks (*v.* **hōc**); House Cl; Top ~ ~, Hovel Mdw (*v.* **hovel**); Bottom ~, Top Hull (*v.* **hyll**); Middle ~, Top Islands (*v.* **ēa-land**; used of land by water, but also of fields surrounded by other fields); Knight's Fds (with the surn. *Knight*, cf. *Berry Knight* 1838 Census, *Jane Knight* 1851 ib and *John Knight* 1862 ib, all of Swinford); Lallystone (again, earlier forms are needed; perh. with **lǽl**, used of willow); Lamcote Hill (*v.* **lamb, cot**); Langlands or Longlands (*v.* **lang**[1], **land**); Lee's Mdw (with the surn. *Lee*); The Leys (*v.* **leys**); Little Hill 1968, ~ ~ East, ~ ~ South, ~ ~ West 1886; Little Mdw; The Long Fd or First Webster's (*v.* Webster's Cl *infra*); Lukes Cl 1900 (with the surn. *Luke*, from the popular form of Lucas); Martin's Mdw (with the surn. *Martin*); The Meadow, First ~, Second Mdw; Mere Fds (*v.* **(ge)mǣre**; closes at the parish boundary); Milestone Mdw 1886 (*v.* **mīl-stān**; land beside the road to Shawell); Mill Cl (*v.* **myln**); Moor Fd 1968, Moorpit Mdw 1886 (*v.* **pytt**), The Moors 1968 (*v.* **mōr**[1]); Narrow Piece (*v.* **nearu, pece**); The Old Mill 1835 (cf. *mil furlong* 17, *Millforlong* m.18, *over mil furlong* 1679 (*v.* **uferra**), *v.* **myln**); The Paddock, Bottom Paddock, Ingram's Paddock (with the surn. *Ingram*, from the ContGerm masc. pers.n. *Ingelram, Engelram*) (*v.* **paddock**); Park Furlong (*v.* **park, furlang**; abutting the park of Stanford Hall, Westrill and Starmore parish *infra*); Parson's Cl 1803, Parson's Top Cl, First ~ ~, Second Parson's Mdw 1900 (prob. with the surn. *Parsons*, cf. *John Parsons* 1679, 1700 Deed, *Thomas Parsons* 1717 ib of Swinford; but note *Parson Holme* in f.ns. (b)); Pen Cl (*v.* **penn**); First ~, Ploughed Penfolland (perh. **pynd-fald, land**; otherwise **penn** with **furlang**, cf. *Rackly forland, infra*); Percival Mdw 1900 (with the surn. *Percival*); The Pines, Near the Pines (*v.* **pyne**); Little Ploughed Fd; The Polo Fd (for the game of polo); Porter's Bit 1792 (*v.* **bit**), Porter's Piece 1968 (*v.* **pece**) (with the surn. *Porter*, cf. *Charles Porter* 1806 Census, *Timothy Porter* 1814 ib, *Thomas Porter* 1833 ib, *Sam Porter* 1863 ib and *George Porter* 1872 ib, all of Swinford); The Quicks, Far Quicks (*v.* **quyk**); Bush Rackley (prob. with **busc**) (*Rackley* 1674, cf. *Rackly forland* 1679, ~ *furlong* 17 (*v.* **furlang**), *v.* **lēah**; most likely with **racu**, and referring to a straight stretch of the river Avon; the name also appears in adjoining Catthorpe f.ns. (a)); Long Rick-Stead 1751, Ricksted 1968 (*Ricksted* m.18, *v.* **rickstead**); Rickyard (*v.* **reke-yard**); The Roadside (land beside a road); Rose Cl (prob. with the surn. *Rose*); Rush Furrow (*v.* **risc, furh**); School Fd; Sedgleys (the surn. *Sedgeley* in the possessive case, cf. *Ellen Sedgeley* 1801 Census of Swinford); Seed Fd, Seeds (×2) (*v.* **sǣd**; in modern f.ns., used of grasses sown for one year's mowing or grazing as distinguished from permanent pasture); Side Hook Mdw (*v.* **sīd, hōc**; a long, irregular-shaped piece of land beside the river Avon); The Slade (*v.* **slæd**); Spencer's Bottom, ~ Top (with the surn. *Spencer*, cf. *Ellen Spencer* 1801 Census of Swinford); The Spinney (*v.* **spinney**); Stallion Cl (*v.* **stallion**); The Stone Plank (*v.* **stān, planke**); 1st ~ ~, 2nd Street Furlong (*v.* **strēt, furlang**); (The) Swimmings (*nether Swiminge* 1601, *swimming forland* 1679 (*v.* **furlang**), *v.* **swīn, svín, eng**); Tea Kettle Cl 1900 (alluding to the fancied shape of the enclosure); Thorn Furlong Middle, ~ ~ North, ~ ~ South 1886 (*Thorn furlong* 1674, 1679, 17, *Thorne Furlong* m.18, *v.* **þorn, furlang**); Far ~, Middle ~, Near Thorpe 1968, Thorp-Hill 1751 (*Torphul* e.13, *Tharphill* m.18, *v.* **hyll**) (towards Catthorpe parish which adjoins to the south-west); The Tin Hut Fd, Tin Hut Mdws (*v.* **hut**); Top Cl 1900, First ~ ~, Second Top Fd, Top Mdws; Town Cl (*v.* **tūn**), Bottom ~, Top Track (*v.* **trak**); Walker's (the surn. *Walker* in the possessive case); Water Furrows (*v.* **wæter, furh** and *Water Furrowes* in

Ashby Parva f.ns. (b) *supra*); Webster's Cl (with the surn. *Webster*, cf. *William Webster* 1816 Census, *Laura Webster* 1868 ib and *William Webster* 1871 ib, all of Swinford); West Mdw; Weston's Cl (with the surn. *Weston*, cf. *William Weston* 1798 Census, *Joseph Weston* 1839 ib, *Lettie Weston* 1875 ib and *Joseph Weston* 1879 ib of Swinford); Wheat Hill (*v.* **hwǣte**); Widow Bushes East, ~ ~ West 1886 (it is uncertain whether these were fields which belonged to a woman called Widow Bush, since no family with the surn. *Bush* is recorded for Leics. in the 1881 Census or earlier; but *Widow* here may represent the surn. *Widdow*(*s*) (cf. Leicester's *William Widders* 1576 RFL) or simply represent ME **widewe**, both 'widow' and 'widower'; in which case, *v.* **busc** and note Bush Cl and Bush Rackley *supra*; a further complication is the possibility of early OE **widu** with **hōh**); Woodford's Mdw (with the surn. *Woodford*, cf. *John Woodford* 1698 Nichols of Swinford).

(b) *Banlond* e.13 (*v.* **bēan**, **land**); *the Brooke* m.18 (*v.* **brōc**); *le Chauntre hous*, *le Chaunterye hous* 1546, *le Chaunterye Howse* 1548 (*v.* **hūs**), *the Chantry Land* 1614 (*v.* **chaunterie**); *Crosforlong* e.13 (*v.* **cross**, **furlang**); *the east field* 1601, *the East feild* 1679 (also called *the field towards Stanford* 1674, 17) (*v.* **ēast**, **feld**, one of the great open-fields and referring to Stanford on Avon which lies 1¼ miles to the east in Northants.); *the Farme* 1638 (*v.* **ferme**); *Hatchelles* 1546 (*v.* **ēcels**); *Holdehole* e.13 (*v.* **hold**, **hol**[1]; alluding to a shelter for animals); *the homstall* 1606 (*v.* **hām-stall**; belonging to the early *Vicarage House*); *Langesachedole* e.13 (*v.* **lang**[1], **sacu**, **dāl**; presum. land subject to dispute or bargaining in some sort, cf. *Sachdole* in Ashby Parva f.ns. (b)); *Marchesakerdene* e.13 (*v.* **mearc**, **æcer**, **denu**); *Medweaker* e.13 (*v.* **mēd** (**mēdwe** obl.sg.), **æcer**); *the north field* 1601, 17, ~ ~ *feild* 1679 (*v.* **norð**, **feld**; one of the great open-fields); *Ouerdale* e.13 (*v.* **ofer**[3], **dalr**); *Parson Holme, le person holme* 1453 (*v.* **persone**, **holmr**); *the South field* 1679 (also called *the field* (*lying*) *towards Lilborn* 1674, 17) (*v.* **sūð**, **feld**; one of the great open-fields and alluding to Lilbourne which lies 1½ miles to the south-west in Northants.); *Stotfold* e.13 (*v.* **stōd-fald**); *the weast field* 1601, *the west feild* 1606 (*v.* **west**, **feld**; one of the great open-fields, to be identified with the later *South field* which lay south-west in the parish towards Lilbourne); *atte Well* 1327 (p), 1332 (p), 1348 (p), (*ad Fontem* 1327 (p), with MLat *fons* (*fontem* acc.sg.) 'a spring, a well') (*v.* **atte**, **wella**); *Wrongelond* e.13 (*v.* **wrang**, **vrangr**, **land**).

Ullesthorpe

ULLESTHORPE

> *Vlestorp* 1086 DB
> *Olestorp* 1190 P (p), John BM, 1243 Fees, 1261 RGrav, l.13 (p), 13
>   Goodacre (p), *Olesthorp(e)* 1233 Fees, Hy 3 RBE, 1278 Ipm *et*
>   *passim* to 1414 *LCDeeds*, 1424, 1440 Pat, *Olsthorp(e)* 1231 Cur,
>   1285 FA, 1369 Ipm
> *Holestorp* 1129 × 46 France, 1236 Fees, *Holesthorp* 1285 FA
> *Olvestorp* 1278 Ipm
> *Oulesthorp* 1325 (1449) *WoCart, Oulsthorpe* 1429 Cl
> *Ulvesthorp(e)* 1285 Abbr, 1311 Banco (p), *Ulvesthrope* 1610 LML
> *Ullesthorp(e)* 1278 Cl, 1306 Banco, 1428 FA *et passim* to 1541 Ipm,
>   1622 LML *et freq, Ullisthorpe* 1524 Ipm, *Ullesthropp* 1631 LML
> *Ulsthorp(e)* 1439, 1453 Pat, 1535 VE, 1610 Speed, *Ulstropp* 1627
>   LML
> *Wollesthrop alias Ollersthrop* 1512 BM, *Wolstroppe, Woulstropp*
>   1536 AAS

'The outlying farmstead belonging to a man called Ulf', *v.* **þorp**. The ON masc. pers.n. *Ulfr* (ODan *Ulf*) is an original by-name 'wolf'. It was common in Norway, Denmark and Iceland throughout the medieval period. Spellings with initial *o* are due to AN substitution of *o* for *u* (*v.* Feilitzen §17); occasionally *o* with prosthetic *h*.

With the exception of Ullesthorpe, Bittesby and Catthorpe, the township names which line Watling Street and those to its north-east in this region are predominantly English in origin. Ullesthorpe and Bittesby parishes appear once to have been a single land unit from which the small parish of Bittesby was later carved out. Ullesthorpe, which presumably was originally a dependent of Bittesby, now has a narrow reach of land to its west which runs to Watling Street. It is in this general area that the lost *dunninc wicon* of the Claybrooke Anglo-Saxon charter of 962 seems to have been situated. (For discussion of this name, *v.* note 5 to An Anglo-Saxon Woodland Estate at Claybrooke, appended to Claybrooke Parva parish names *supra*). Whether the Ullesthorpe/

Bittesby land unit was originally that of a *wīchām* related to Romano-British *Venonis* is uncertain but a direct route, principally as a pathway, still runs from Ullesthorpe through Claybrook Parva parish to the High Cross site of *Venonis*. Although clearly Ullesthorpe in name is a late-comer when compared with Bittesby, whether it lies on a former Anglo-Saxon habitation site is unknown. It is worthy of note that while Ullesthorpe has both Scandinavian specific and generic, Bittesby's specific is English and that of Catthorpe is a feudal affix, all of which would indicate only slight Scandinavian settlement hereabouts.

LILINGE (lost)

Lilinge 1086 DB

'(The settlement of) the family or followers of a man calle Lilla', *v.* **-ingas**; with the OE masc. pers.n. *Lilla*. *Lilinge* appears in the Domesday Survey listed between Ullesthorpe and Bitteswell. But a case may be made for its location in Westrill and Starmore parish *infra* which lies adjacent to Lilbourne ('Lilla's stream'), *v.* Nth 72. According to the Domesday Survey, Ullesthorpe, *Lilinge*, Bitteswell and Starmore (*Stormsworth*) were all held by Goisfridus de Wirce.

AMOS LODGE, *v.* **loge**; with the common Leics. surn. *Amos*, cf. *Caroline Amos* 1854 Census of nearby Lutterworth. ASHBY RD, Ashby Magna lying 4 miles to the north-east. BALDWIN'S SPINNEY, *v.* **spinney**, with the surn. *Baldwin*; note Baldwin's Green in adjacent Claybrooke Parva. BLACK HORSE (P.H.) (lost), *Black Horse* 1843 *TA*. BREACH BARN, cf. *Breach farm* 1925 Kelly, *v.* **brēc**. CHEQUERS (P.H.) (lost), *The Chequers* 1843 *TA*, *Chequers* 1846, 1863 White, *Chequers Inn* 1877 ib. CHUCKEY HALL FM (CHUCKEY HALL 2½"), *Chuckey Hall farm* 1925 Kelly; no early forms, but prob. with dial. *chucky* (as in the nursery-style *chucky-hen*), from ME *chukken* 'to make a clucking noise like a hen calling its chicks'. Locally (in 2010) it is Chuckney Hall Fm, with intrusive *n*. COLLEGE ST, tithes in Ullesthorpe once pertaining to Trinity College, Cambridge. COURT FM, *v.* Ullesthorpe Court *infra*. CROWN INN, 1846, 1877 White, 1925 Kelly, *Crown* 1863 White. THE DAIRY FM, cf. *Dairy House Close* 1843 *TA*, *v.* **deierie**. THE ENGINE (P.H.) (lost), *The Engine* 1877 White; relating to the former Midland Counties Railway. FROLESWORTH RD, Frolesworth lying 2 miles to the north. HALL LANE, *v.* **hall**. HAPPY VALLEY COTTAGE. HILLCREST. HILLSIDE. HOME BARN, cf. *The Home* 1843 *TA*; prob. with **holmr** rather than with **home** because

it stands at the parish's northern limits. LUTTERWORTH RD, Lutterworth
lying 3 miles to the south-east. MAIN ST. MANOR HO., *Manor House*
1863 White, cf. *Manor farm* 1925 Kelly, *v.* **maner**. MILL HO. (local),
Mill house 1925 Kelly, *v.* **myln**. MILL RD. NORMANTON HOUSE FM.
STATION RD, leading to the disued Ullesthorpe Station *infra*. SWAN INN,
1846, 1877 White, 1925 Kelly, *Swan* 1863 White. ULLESTHORPE COURT,
v. **court**. ULLESTHORPE GRANGE, 1925 Kelly, *v.* **grange**. ULLESTHORPE
LODGE, 1843 Census, 1877 White, *v.* **loge**. ULLESTHORPE STATION, on
the former Midland Counties Railway.

FIELD-NAMES

In (a), forms presented without dates are 1843 *TA*; those dated 1807 are
Nichols.

(a) Four ~, Ten Acres (*v.* **æcer**); Alms Cl (*v.* **almes**; the property of Frolesworth
Almshouses); Ball's Spinney (*v.* **spinney**; with the surn. *Ball*); Far ~ ~, Barn Cl (*v.*
bern); Bayley's Cl (with the surn. *Bayley*); Big Cl, ~ Mdw; Short ~, Bittell (*v.* **byttel**;
the stumpy hill here gave its name to adjacent Bittesby); Blockley's Bog (*v.* **bog**), ~
Cl (with the surn. *Blockley*, cf. *John Blockley* 1798 Nichols of Ullesthorpe, *Elizabeth
Blockley* 1801 Census of adjoining Claybrooke Parva and in adjoining Claybrooke
Magna, *Thomas Blockley* 1806 ib, *Ann Blockley* 1818 ib and *Alfred Blockley* 1844
ib); Boggy Mdw (*v.* **boggy**); First ~ ~, Second ~ ~, Third Brass Piece (sic) (*v.* **pece**;
either with a transmission error for *grass* (*v.* **græs**) or with a reduced **brēost**, alluding
to a piece of land rounded and swelling like a breast); Bottom ~ ~, Top ~ ~, Side
Breach (*v.* **sīd**) (*v.* **brēc**); Brick-kiln Cl, ~ ~ Mdw (*v.* **brike-kiln**); Bridleway Cl (*v.*
brigdels); Bullgoar (*v.* **bula**, **gāra**); Cawdel well 1807, Cordlewell Mdw 1843 (*v.*
cald, **wella**); Chapel well 1807 (*v.* **chapel(e)**, **wella**); Clover Cl (*v.* **clāfre**; a fodder
crop); First ~ ~, Second ~ ~, Top ~ ~, Cow Cl (*v.* **cū**); Crabtree Cl (*v.* **crabtre**);
Croft's Cl (with the surn. *Croft*); Culvert Piece (*v.* **culvert**, **pece**); Dead-fallow (*v.*
dēad, **falh**; presum. alluding to poor ground); Den Furlong (*v.* **denu**, **furlang**);
Dumbleton Cl (with the surn. *Dumbleton*); Far ~ ~, Near Easnill (*v.* **ēastan**, **hyll**); Far
Cl; Far Furlong (*v.* **furlang**); Farm Piece (1725, *v.* **ferme**, **pece**); Gravel Holes (*v.*
gravel, **hol**[1]); Great Mdw; Harry's Cl, ~ Big Mdw, ~ Little Mdw (prob. with the surn.
Harry; from the regular pronunciation of the masc. pers.n. *Henry* in the Middle
Ages); Heals Big Fd, ~ Long Fd, ~ Top Fd (with the surn. *Heales*, cf. *Charles Heels*
1861 Census, *Mary Heels* 1862 ib and *Annie Heels* 1871 ib of Ullesthorpe); Hill Cl;
First Holt, Second ~, Bottom ~, Middle ~, Side ~, Top Holt, Wells Holt, ~ Little Holt
(with the surn. *Wells*) (no early forms, but because of the extent of the fields, prob.
from **wald** rather than **holt**); Home Cl (*v.* **home**); Horse Cl (*v.* **hors**); Little ~ ~, Hut
Cl (*v.* **hut**); Jelley's Cl, ~ Mdw (with the surn. *Jelley*, from a late form of the masc.
pers.n. *Giles*; cf. *William Jelley* 1857 Census and *Mary Jelley* 1865 ib of
Ullesthorpe); Bottom ~, Top Lands (*v.* **land**); The Lawn (*v.* **launde**); Far ~ ~, Near
~ ~, Leicester Hill (beside the road to Leicester); Little Cl, ~ Mdw; Long Cl, ~ Mdw,
~ Close Mdw; Long Lands (*v.* **land**); Lord's Cl, ~ Second Cl, ~ Railway Piece (*v.*

pece; adjacent to the now dismantled Midland Counties Railway) (with the surn. *Lord*); Manton's Cl, ~ Mdw (with the surn. *Manton* of a family poss. originally from Manton, 26 miles to the north-east in Rutland); Middle Cl; First ~ ~, Top Martin's Mill Fd (with the surn. *Martin*, cf. *Embrey Martin* 1845 Census and *Emily Martin* 1856 ib, both of adjoining Bitteswell), Mill Field Mdw (*Mill field* 1725) (*v.* **myln**); Near Furlong (*v.* **furlang**); New Cl; The Orchard (*v.* **orceard**); Part Acres (*v.* **æcer**; land prob. allocated by lot); Paynes Cl, ~ Little Cl (with the surn. *Payne*, cf. *Ann Payne* 1812 Census, *George Payne* 1826 ib, *John Payne* 1832 ib and *Henry Payne* 1834 ib, all of adjoining Claybrooke Magna parish); Great ~ ~, Little ~ ~, Pen Cl (*v.* **penn**); Portway Mdw (*v.* **port-wey**; a former road to Lutterworth); Priest's Barn Cl, ~ Far Barn Cl. ~ Top Cl, ~ Great Cl, ~ Great Mdw, ~ Little Mdw (with the surn. *Priest*); Proctors Cl (with the surn. *Proctor*, cf. *Caroline Procter* 1819 Census and *John Proctor* 1820 ib of neighbouring Lutterworth); Far ~ ~, Railway Piece (*v.* **pece** and Lord's Railway Piece *supra*); Ralph's Bit (*v.* **bit**; with the surn. *Ralphs*, cf. *Joseph Ralphs* 1821 Census and *John Ralphs* 1862 ib of adjoining Ashby Parva parish); Big ~ ~, Little Redham (*v.* **hrēod, hamm**); Far ~ ~, Rickyard Cl (*v.* **reke-yard**); Road Mdw (a roadside close); Great ~ ~, Little ~ ~, Rollo Mdw (with the surn. *Rollo*, a latinization of the ON masc. pers.n. *Hrólfr* (ODan *Rolf*)); Great ~, Little Saunt (*v.* **sand**); Second Cl; Sedgeley's Cl, ~ Mdw (with the surn. *Sedgeley*); Slade, Near ~ ~, Middle ~ ~, Top Slade Cl, Slade Gutter (1725, *v.* **goter**) (*v.* **slæd**); Spinney Mdw (*v.* Baldwin's Spinney *supra*); Swithams or Smithams (*v.* **smēðe**[1], **hamm**); Third Cl; Top Cl; Big ~ ~, Little Town Hill, Town's End Cl (*v.* **ende**) (*v.* **tūn**); Ward's Cl, ~ Far Cl (with the surn. *Ward*, cf. *Ann Ward* 1832 Census and *Thomas Ward* 1836 ib, both of adjoining Ashby Parva); Wharf Piece (*v.* **wharf, pece**; beside the former Midland Counties Railway); Wright's Cl, ~ Mdw (with the surn. *Wright*, cf. *Martha Wright* 1811 Census of adjoining Bitteswell parish, *Thomas Wright* 1820 ib, *Sarah Wright* 1846 ib and *Walter Wright* 1867 ib, all of adjoining Ashby Parva parish).

Westrill and Starmore

There is no longer a village in this parish. *Stormsworth* probably ceased to exist in the sixteenth century as the result of an unrecorded enclosure.

STARMORE (earlier *Stormsworth*)

> *Stormeorde* 1086 DB
> *Stormode* 1086 DB
> *Stormesworth(e)* 1156 × 73, a.1250 Selby (freq.), 1276 RH *et freq* to 1424 *Wyg et passim* to 1578 *Braye, Stormesword* 1229, a.1250 Selby, *Stormysworth(e)* 1497, 1518 *Braye*, 1530 CoPleas, 1536 *Braye, Stormsworth* 1559 Ipm, 1606 *Terrier*
> *Stormeworth* 1239 Cur (p), a.1250 Selby, 1316 Banco, 1352 *Peake* (p)
> *Stormworth* 1208 Cur (p), a.1250 Selby, 1497 *Braye*, 1519 *Wyg*, 1638, 1674 *Terrier, Stormwurth* 1243 Fees
> *Stormysworth alias dict' Stormore* 1518 *Braye, Stormore alias Stormysworth* 1518 *ib*
> *Stormer* 1703, 1733 *Terrier*
> *Starmer* 1733 *Terrier, Starmor* 1724 *ib, Starmore* 1765, 1781 *ib*

'The enclosure belonging to a man called Storm', *v.* **worð**. The OE masc. pers.n. *Storm* is unrecorded. It is probably an original by-name, cf. OE *storm* 'storm, tempest, attack' which may be compared with the OScand masc. pers.n. *Styrmir*, itself a by-name meaning 'one who storms forward in battle; the impetuous one' (SPNLY 269). The lost settlement lay in the north of the modern parish where it is still remembered in the field-name *High Starmore*.

There is little record of moorland hereabouts to suggest late influence of *mōr* on the form of the generic. The development of the name may be presented simply as: *Stormesworth* > *Stormsworth* > *Stormworth* > **Stormorth* > *Stormore* > *Starmore*.

BOG SPINNEY, 1968 *Surv, v.* **bog, spinney**. EDGELL SPINNEY, 1968 *Surv*; with the pers.n. and surn. *Edgell*, cf. *Rev. Edgell Wyatt Edgell* (sic) 1877

White and *Capt. Edmund Verney Wyatt Edgell*, both of Stanford Hall *infra*. GRAVEL HILL, 1835 O, 1968 *Surv*, *v*. **gravel**. HOVEL HILL, 1835 O, *v*. **hovel**. MICHAEL SPINNEY, with the masc. pers.n. *Michael*. NEW ~ ~ ~, OLD GRAVEL HILL SPINNEY, 1968 *Surv*, *v*. Gravel Hill *supra*. PARK BELT, *v*. **belt** and Stanford Park *infra*. PORTER'S BARN, with the surn. *Porter*, cf. *Timothy Porter, farmer and grazier* 1877 White of adjacent Swinford, the barn being at the Swinford parish boundary. THE ROOKERY, *v*. **rookery**; the name of planted woodland in Stanford Park. RUGBY RD, Rugby in Warwks. lying 6 miles to the south-east. SERPENTINE, a transferred name (from London's Hyde Park) for an elongated, sinuous, snake-like lake formed in Stanford Park by the damming of a brook. THE SHRUBBERY, *v*. **shrubbery**; a park feature. STANFORD HALL, 1807 Map, 1846, 1863, 1877 White, 1925 Kelly, *v*. **hall**; a replacement begun in 1697 by Sir Roger Cave for the early hall in Stanford on Avon across the river in Northants. STANFORD PARK, 1807 Nichols, *the Park* 1846, 1863, 1877 White, *v*. **park**. VERNEY SPINNEY, 1968 *Surv*; with the surn. *Verney* (as pers.n.), cf. *Capt. Edmund Verney Wyatt Edgell* 1877 White of Stanford Hall. WESTRILL, ~ SPINNEY, *Westerhyll* 1578 *Braye*, *Westerhill* 1601, 1708, 1765, 1781, 1784 *Terrier*, *Westrill* 1724, 1733, 1781 *ib*, 1807 Nichols; 'the western hill', *v*. **wester**, **hyll** and Westerhill in South Kilworth f.ns. (a) *supra*.

FIELD-NAMES

In (a), forms presented without dates are 1968 *Surv*; those dated 1792 are *Deed*; 1807 are Nichols. Forms throughout dated 1200 × 50 are Selby; those dated 1384 are Cl; 1453 are Pap; 1464 and 1481 are Deed; 1480, 1487 and 1561 are Ipm; 1578 are *Braye*.

(a) Four Acres, 5 Acre, Eight ~, Knight's 8 ~, Porter's Ten ~, Top ~ ~, Eleven Acre, The Fourteen ~, Nineteen ~, The Twenty Acre (*v*. **æcer**); Addison's (the surn. *Addison* in the possessive case; cf. *Thomas Addison* 1807 Census of adjoining Swinford parish); Old Allotments (*v*. **allotment**); Asplin's Cl, ~ Mdw 1792 (with the surn. *Asplin*); Badger Hole Fd (*v*. **bagger**, **hol**[1]); Lower ~ ~, Upper Banking Mdws (*v*. **banking**; meadows protected from flooding by embankments); Barn Mdw, Old Barn Cl, ~ ~ Mdw (*v*. **bern**); Bert's Cl, ~ Mdw (*Bert* is usually the familiar shortened form of the masc. pers.n. Herbert, although Reaney *s.n.* also lists it as a surn. from the OFr fem. pers.n. *Berte* (ContGerm *Ber(h)ta*)); Binion's (the surn. *Binion* in the possessive case); Bliss's Corner (*v*. **corner**; with the surn. *Bliss*); The Borough Ground, Barnett's Borough Ground (with the surn. *Barnett*, cf. *Henry Barnett* 1843 Census, *William Barnett* 1867 ib and *Edwin Barnett* 1880 ib, all of adjoining Swinford parish), Borough Ground Mdw (*v*. **berg**, **grund**); Burge or Birds [Bridge]

Close Lane (sic) 1807 (cf. *Brig Close* 1561, *the Brydge Close* 1578, *v.* **brycg, clos(e)**); Colds Cl (sic) (either with an error in transmission for the surn. *Cole* or referring to bleak, cheerless land); Conduit Grounds (*v.* **cundite, grund**); Cooks Mdw (with the surn. *Cook*); Corbetts, ~ Mdw (with the surn. *Corbett*); The Corners (*v.* **corner**); Cowslip (land growing with *Primula veris* 'the cowslip'); Dorothy's Spinney (*v.* **spinney**; a number of the names of spinneys in the parish are compounded with pers.ns., as Edgell ~, Michael ~, Verney Spinney *supra* and Simon's Spinney *infra*); Durrants Mdw (cf. *Durants Close* 1578; with the surn. *Durrant*, from the OFr masc. pers.n. *Durant*); Far Spinney 1792 (*v.* **spinney**); Harris's (the surn. *Harris* in the possessive case); The House Cl (*Howse Close* 1578, *v.* **hūs, clos(e)**); Hovel Cl, ~ Mdw (*v.* **hovel**); Top Knight's (with the surn. *Knight*); Little Field Mdw (cf. *Lyttlefyeld Quarter* 1578 (*v.* **quarter**), *v.* **lȳtel, feld**); Little Side (*v.* **sīde**); Lord Spark (sic) (*v.* **park**; with the surn. *Lord* in the possessive case; adjoining Stanford Park and with the name as the result of modern misdivision (metanalysis)); Mayo's (the surn. *Mayo* in the possessive case, from the OFr masc. pers.n. *Mahieu*, a Norman form of Matthew; note *Maheo de Charun* 12 Dane of Leics.); Near Spinney 1792 (cf. Far Spinney 1792 *supra*); The Ploughed Ground; Porter's (the surn. *Porter* in the possessive case; cf. *Charles Porter* 1806 Census, *Thomas Porter* 1833 ib, both of adjoining Swinford and *v.* Porter's Barn *supra*); Pudding Mdw (a fanciful name for soft, sticky land); Bottom ~ ~, Top Red Hut, Red Hut Cl (*v.* **hut**); Reservoir Fd (adjoining Stanford Reservoir); The Rickyard (*v.* **reke-yard**); Road Cl (a roadside field); The Rough Piece (*v.* **rūh, pece**); Simon's Spinney (*v.* **spinney**; with the masc. pers.n. *Simon*); Bottom ~ ~, Spencers Cl 1792, Top Spencers 1968 (with the surn. *Spencer*, cf. *John Spencer* 1799 Census and *Ellen Spencer* 1801 ib, both of adjoining Swinford); Spinney Cl; Spring Piece (*v.* **spring**[1], **pece**); High Starmore (in the north of the parish in the area of former *Stormsworth*); Straw Mdw (*v.* **strēaw**; sometimes used as a derogatory name for poor land); Thorny (*Thorney Close* 1578, *v.* **þornig**); Ward's Ground (*v.* **grund**; with the surn. *Ward*); Watts Ground (with the surn. *Watt(s)*, from *Watt*, the pet-form of Walter); Westrill Mdw (*v.* Westrill *supra*); Little Woad Ground (*v.* **wād, grund**).

(b) *Barley Close* 1578 (*v.* **bærlic, clos(e)**); *Barnehyll Close*, ~ *medowe* 1578 (*v.* **bern, hyll** and **mēd (mēdwe** obl.sg.)); *le Blakedole* 1200 × 50 (*v.* **dāl**; with **blāc** or **blæc**); *Bunforlonk'* 1200 × 50 (*v.* **bune, furlang**); *Burnhill close* 1561 (*v.* **hyll, clos(e)**; either with **brend** or **burna**); *Childfurlang'* 1200 × 50 (*v.* **cild, furlang**); *Crokiswell* 1200 × 50 (*v.* **wella**; the genitival composition-joint suggests an OE masc. pers.n. with *wella* (and this is common) rather than **crocc** 'a pot, a crock, a vessel (of some sort)', perh. an OE *Crōc* (from ON *Krókr* (ODan *Krōk*)); *Dene* 1200 × 50 (*v.* **denu**); *Dutu'* 1200 × 50 (*v.* **tūn**; a lost farmstead, poss. that of an Anglo-Saxon male called *Dudda*); *Fillefurlang'* 1200 × 50 (*v.* **fille, furlang**); *Filleshou* 1200 × 50 (*v.* **fille, hōh**); *Fraternity Land* 1464 (*v.* **fraternite**; no doubt land once belonging to Selby Abbey which held property here in the 13th cent.); *Fullepit* 1200 × 50 (*v.* **fūl, pytt**); *le Halledam* 1348 (*v.* **damme**), *le hallane* 1453 (*v.* **lane**) (*v.* **hall**; with reference to a medieval hall of *Stormsworth*); *Hefurlang'* 1200 × 50 (*v.* **furlang**; with **hēah**[1] or **hēg**); *Henhou, Henhowe* 1200 × 50 (*v.* **henn, hōh**); *ad Hogam* 1200 × 50 ('at the mound, at the how'; with MLat *hoga* (*hogam* acc.sg.)); *Hokedick, Hoggedik* 1200 × 50 (*v.* **hōcede, dík**); *Ingrames Close* 1578 (*v.* **clos(e)**; with the surn. *Ingram*, from the ContGerm masc. pers.n. *Enge(l)ram, Inge(l)ram, Ingram* (OFr *Engerran*)); *Littlehille* 1200 × 50 (*v.* **lȳtel, hyll**); *le Lotforlonck* 1200 × 50 (*v.* **hlot, furlang**);

Luffes mill 1481 (*v.* **myln**; with the ME surn. *Luffe* (ModE *Luff*), from the OE masc. pers.n. *Luffa*); *Merfurlang'* (*v.* (**ge**)**mǣre**, **furlang**); *the Old Myll Holmes* 1578 (*v.* **ald**, **myln**, **holmr** and *Luffes mill*, *supra*); *Patchis Land* 1464 (*v.* **land**; with the surn. *Patch* (from *Pache*, a ME form of *Pasches* 'Easter')); *Peseburne* 1200 × 50 (*v.* **burna**; here **pise** presumably refers to some wild plant resembling pease, such as marsh-trefoil); *Portway* 1200 × 50 (*v.* **port-wey**; prob. the road to Lutterworth); *Rayle Close*, *Rayles medowe* 1578 (*v.* **raile**); *Spornefurlang'* 1200 × 50 (*v.* **spurn**, **furlang**); *Springewelle* 1200 × 50 (*v.* **spring**[1], **wella** and note Spring Piece *supra*); *Stepingakyr* 1200 × 50 (*v.* **steepyng**, **æcer**); *Steynes Land* 1464 (*v.* **land**; with the surn. *Steyn*, from the ON masc. pers.n. *Steinn*); *Stormefeld* 1480, 1487 (*v.* **feld**; with the OE masc. pers.n. *Storm* as present in *Stormsworth*); *Swynford Quarter* 1578 (*v.* **quarter**), *Swynfordway* 1200 × 50 (*v.* **weg**) (Swinford lay some 2½ miles to the south-west of *Stormsworth*); *Walcot* ~ 1561, *Walcott Quarter* 1578 (*v.* **quarter**; land towards Walcote in adjoining Misterton parish *supra*); *Walleton Waye* 1200 × 50 (*v.* **weg**; the road to Walton which lay some 4 miles to the north of *Stormsworth*); *Wauda* 1200 × 50 (*v.* **wald**); *Westerhyll Quarter* 1578 (*v.* **quarter** and Westrill *supra*); *Wulframhilheiland* 1200 × 50 (*v.* **hyll**, **hēah**[1], **land**; with the OE fem. pers.n. *Wulfrūn*); *Wythebed*, *Wythibed* 1200 × 50 (*v.* **wīðig**, **bedd**).

Whetstone

Westhā (sic) 1086 DB
Wetstan l.12 Dane, 1225 Fine, 1255 Cl, *Wethstan* p.1204 Hastings,
  1220 × 35 Berkeley
Hwetstan 1220 Cur, 1255 Ipm, *Whetstan* 1156 (1318) Ch
Westan p.1204 Hastings, 1205 ClR, c.1250 BM, 1277 Hastings
Wetston 1220 MHW, 1280 × 92 *Wyg*, 13 *Peake* (p)
Wheston(*e*) e.13 *GarCart* (p), 1226 RHug, 1255 Cl *et passim* to 1295
  Wyg, 1313 *Win* (p), 1326 *Fisher* (p) *et freq* to 1550 Pat *et passim*
  to 1578 LEpis, 1607 LML
Weston(*e*) 1254 Val, 1277 Hastings, 1292 *Wyg et passim* to 1502
  MiscAccts, 1537 MinAccts
Wiston 1280 × 92 (p), c.1300 *Wyg*, *Wyston* 1280 × 92 (p), 1295 (p),
  1298 *ib* (p)
Whetston 1576 Saxton, 1585 LibCl, 1610 Speed, *Whetstone* 1642
  LML *et freq*

Literally, 'Whetstone', *v.* **hwet-stān**. The name may refer to an
ancient standing stone (as nearby Humberstone, Lei **3** 133) used for the
honing of large agricultural implements such as scythes, but likelier,
there may have been a local source of materials suitable for use as
whetstones. Indeed, cropping out at intervals in this region are several
small bosses of a very fine-grained syenite, such as in adjoining Cosby
and Narborough parishes. Soft sandstones and clays are otherwise
dominant.

ARCHWAY COTTAGE, near an arch carrying a road through the
embankment of the dismantled Midland Counties Railway. BAMBURY
LANE, forms part of the south-eastern parish boundary and thus may
contain an early place-name, but nothing as such survives; otherwise
with the surn. *Bambury*, cf. *Ada Kate Bambury* 1862 Census of Leicester.
BOTTOM END BRIDGE, *v.* **ende**; at the southern end of the township,
crossing Whetstone Brook. THE BROOKLANDS. BROOKSIDE. BROOK ST,
v. Whetstone Brook *infra*. BULL'S HEAD (P.H.), 1846, 1863 White, 1925

Kelly. CAMBRIDGE RD. COLLEGE RD, *v.* Trinity Rd *infra*. THE COTTAGE is *Whetstone Cottage* 1835 O, *v.* **cotage**. COUNTESTHORPE RD, Countesthorpe lying one mile to the south-east. CROSSWAYS FM, *the Crossway* 1696 *Terrier*, *v.* **cross**, **weg**; near the crossing of Countesthorpe Rd by Springwell Lane *infra*. DICKEN BRIDGE, with the surn. *Dicken*, from an -*en* diminutive of *Dick*, a pet-form of Richard. DOG AND GUN LANE, leading to the former Dog and Gun Inn in Blaby. THE ELMS (2½"). ENDERBY BRIDGE, crosses the river Soar at the parish boundary with Enderby. ENDERBY RD, Enderby originally lying 2 miles to the north-west. HIGH ST. KAFFIR INN, 1925 Kelly, (still current 2010); a hostelry name prob. dating from the period of the Boer War, it is a surprising survival in these days of sensitivity concerning racial and ethnic slurs, since nowadays *kaffir* is an offensive term for a black person, after its use from the 16th cent. in English and Dutch (and later in Afrikaans) as a general term for various peoples of southern Africa. Originally from Arabic *kafir* 'unbeliever, infidel', it is still used with this meaning in the Muslim world. THE LODGE, *v.* **loge**. THE NOOK (local), *The Nook* 1925 Kelly *v.* **nōk**. PARK FM. ST PETER'S CHURCH, *Church (St Peter)* 1846, 1863, 1877 White, 1925 Kelly; it is recorded earlier as *capella*(*m*) *de Wetston* 1220 MHW, 1253 × 58 RTAL, *capella de Wheston* 1549 *Pat* (with MLat *capella* 'a chapel'). Still a chapel in 1807, Nichols records its dedication to St Matthew. SPRINGWELL, 1745 *Terrier*, *v.* **spring**[1], **wella** and *Springwell furze* in f.ns. (b). SPRINGWELL LANE. STATION ST, leading to the former Whetstone Station. TRINITY RD, with Cambridge St and College Rd *supra*, named from Trinity College, Cambridge, a landholder in the parish. THE VICARAGE, 1877 White, 1925 Kelly; earlier is *The Vic*(*c*)*arage House* 1724, 1745 *Terrier*, *The Old Vicarage* 1863 White, *v.* **vikerage**. VICTORIA RD, prob. named from one of Queen Victoria's jubilees (of 1887 and 1897). WARWICK RD. WESTGATE HO. WHEATSHEAF (P.H.), *Wheat Sheaf* 1846, 1863, 1877 White, *Wheatsheaf Inn* 1925 Kelly. WHETSTONE BROOK, *the Brooke* 1709, 1724 *Terrier*, cf. *ad Brock* 1340 Ch (p) (with MLat *ad* 'at'), *v.* **brōc**. WHETSTONE GORSE, ~ ~ EAST, ~ ~ WEST, *Whetstone Gorse* 1806 Map, 1835 O, *The Gorse* 1877 White, *v.* **gorst**. WHETSTONE GORSE COTTAGES. WHETSTONE GORSE LANE. WHETSTONE GRANGE, 1877 White, *The Grange* 1863 ib, *v.* **grange**. WHETSTONE HO. WHETSTONE LODGE (×2), *v.* **loge**. WHETSTONE PASTURES, 1877 White, *The Pastures* 1863 ib, *v.* **pasture**. WILLOUGHBY RD, Willoughby Waterleys lying 3 miles to the south-east.

FIELD-NAMES

In (a), names dated 1764 are EnclA. Forms throughout dated 1340 are Ch; those dated 1477 (e.16) are *Charyte*; 1630 are Letter; 1696, 1709, 1724 and 1745 are *Terrier*.

(a) Thatchcroft 1764 (*Thack croft* 1709, 1724, *Thatch croft* 1745, *v.* **þak, þæc, croft**); Westernholme 1764 (*Westerholm* 1709, 1724, *v.* **vestr, holmr**).

(b) *Alfledeweye* 1477 (e.16) (*v.* **weg**; with the late OE fem. pers.n. *Alfled*, from either *Ælfflǣd* or *Æðelflǣd*); *James Allens ~* 1709, *Ralph Allens ~* 1724, *Edward Allens Hadland* 1745 (*v.* **hēafod-land**), *Thomas Allens close* 1724 (the *Allen* family continues on record in Whetstone as *Edward Allen* 1748 MI, *William Allen* 1764 EnclA, *Frances Allen* 1775 MI); *Andrew Furze* 1709, 1724 (*v.* **fyrs**; if not with the surn. *Andrew*, then belonging to *Andrew King* 1724 *infra*); *Ashby Stye* 1709, 1724 (*v.* **stīg**), *Ashbystie furlong* 1630, *Ashby Stye forlong* 1709, *~ ~ Furlong* 1724, 1745 (*v.* **furlang**) (Ashby Magna lies 4 miles to the south); *Ashes furlong* 1745 (*v.* **æsc**); *de Aula* 1477 (e.16) (p) (with MLat *aula* 'a hall'); *Ayleston ~* 1709, 1724 *Ailston hedge* 1745 (*v.* **hecg**; the parish boundary marker with Aylestone which once adjoined to the north); *Tho. Barkers hadland* 1724 (*v.* **hēafod-land**); *Bare Leys* 1709, 1724, 1745 (*v.* **bær¹, leys**); *John Bents hadland* 1724; *Biches* 1696, *Byches* 1724, *~ furlong* 1745 (*v.* **furlang**) (*v.* **bēce²**); *Blaby mear* 1709, *~ meer* 1724, 1745 (*v.* **(ge)mǣre**; Blaby parish adjoins to the east); *Bodycotts Close, John Bodycotts hadland* (*v.* **hēafod-land**), *Bodycotts land* 1709, *Tho. Bodycoats close, ~ ~ hadland* 1724 (the surn. is that of a family presum. in origin from Bodicote in Oxfordshire (*v.* Ox 395)); *bootling* 1724 (*v.* **bōtl**; with **-ing²** or **eng**); *longe ~, shorte brannteley* 1630, *Long ~, Short Bransley* 1709, *~, ~ Brancel(e)y* 1724, *~, ~ Bransly* 1745 (*v.* **lēah**; with **brend** or **brant**); *Break forlong* 1709, *Brake ~* 1724, *Break furlong* 1745 (*v.* **furlang**), *Break forlong haggs* 1709, *Brake ~ ~* 1724, *Break furlong haggs* 1745 (*v.* **hogg**) (*v.* **bracu**); *Brisey* 1696, *Brizie* 1709, 1745, *Brizzie* 1709 (*v.* **brīosa, ēg**); *Broad ~* 1709, 1745, *brode hook* 1724 (*v.* **brād, hōc**); *Browns lane end* 1709, 1724 (*v.* **lane-ende**; cf. *Tho. Brown* 1724 *Terrier* of Whetstone); *Brucke furlong* 1696, *Brooke forlong* 1709, 1724, *Brook furlong* 1709, 1724, 1745 (*v.* **furlang** and Whetstone Brook *supra*); *nether ~, ouer bulley* 1709 (*v.* **uferra**), *upper bulley* 1709, *neather ~, upper bulley* 1724, *Nether ~, Over Bully* 1745 (*v.* **bula**; with **ēg** or **lēah**); *John Burgesses headland* 1745 (*v.* **hēafod-land**; with the surn. *Burgess*, cf. *Philippus Burgis* 1199 RFL); *John Butlers Close* 1745 (note *George Butler* 1738 MI and *John Butler* 1764 EnclA of Whetstone); *Carres Closs* 1696 (*v.* **clos(e)**; with the surn. *Carr*, cf. *John Carr* 1816 Census, *James Carr* 1835 ib and *Fred Carr* 1845 ib, all of Whetstone); *Caudill ~, Cordall ~* 1696, *Cawdywell ~* 1724, *Cowdywell Meadow* 1745 (*v.* **cald, wella**); *Church hadland* 1696, 1709, 1724, *~ Hadeland* 1745 (*v.* **hēafod-land** and St Peter's Church *supra*); *Clay forlong* 1724, *~ furlong* 1724, 1745 (*v.* **clǣg, furlang**); *Coatgreene* 1696 (*v.* **cot, grēne²**); *the Common cartway* 1709 (*v.* **commun, carte-wey**); *the Common Cow pasture* 1709, 1724, *the Cow paster* 1709, *~ ~ pasture* 1709, 1724, 1745 (*v.* **cū, pasture**); *the Common ground* 1745; *the Common Haggs* 1709, 1724, 1745 (*v.* **hogg**); *Copply green* 1709, *Coply Greene* 1745 (*v.* **grēne²**), *Coplee hole* 1724 (*v.* **hol¹**) (*v.* **copp**; prob. with **lēah**, but perh. with **hlāw** as in Copley, Ca 100); *Cosby mear* 1709, *~ Meer* 1724, 1745 (*v.* **(ge)mǣre**; Cosby parish adjoins to the west); *Countistharp mear* 1709, *Countisthorp* ~ 1724, *Countesthorpe Meer* 1745 (*v.* (**ge**)**mǣre**; Countesthorpe parish adjoins to the north-east); *Damdicke* 1696, *dam dike forlong* 1709, ~ ~ *furlong* 1724, *Dam dikes furlong* 1745 (*v.* **furlang**) (*v.* **damme, dík**); *Deadmore leyes* 1696, ~ *leys* 1709, ~ *leas* 1724, *Deadmoor leys* 1745 (*v.* **leys**), *Deadmore* ~ 1709, 1724, *Deadmoor stones* 1745 (*v.* **stān**) (*v.* **dēad, mōr**[1]; a common Leics. term to describe infertile moorland); *Dough bank* 1745 (*v.* **dogh, banke**; the fanciful transference of the notion of a sticky mass of dough to describe an embankment or an awkward slope); *fern(e) hedge* 1709, 1724 (*v.* **fearn**; with **edisc** or **hecg**); *Thomas Findleys headland* 1745 (*v.* **hēafod-land**); *Robert Foremans close* 1745 (cf. *Robert Forman* 1758 MI and *Mary Forman* 1758 ib (sic) of Whetstone; the occupational surn. *Foreman* means 'swineherd', from OE *för* 'pig', with *mann*); *(the) foxholes closs* 1696 (*v.* **clos(e)**), *Foxall forlong* 1709, *foxhill* ~ 1724, *Foxall furlong* 1745 (*v.* **furlang**), *Foxall way* 1709, 1724, 1745 (*v.* **fox-hol**); *Furr Leys* 1724 (*v.* **feor, leys**); *the Furzes* 1696 (*v.* **fyrs**); *(the top of) Gib white* 1709, 1724, *Gibwhite* 1745 (also as *Gibwhite Hill* 1846 *TA* in adjoining Willoughby Waterleys parish; of uncertain meaning, but poss. are (i) 'gibbet hill' (*v.* **gibet**), (ii) with the surn. *Giberd* (from the ContGerm masc. pers.n. *Gibard* (via OFr *Gibard*), cf. *Alicia Giberd* 1327 SR of Leics.), (iii) with the name of an owner called *Gib White*, with *Gib*, a pet-form of Gilbert; the value of the initial *g* is unknown, although a back consonant seems prob.); *the Glebe Land* 1696 (*v.* **glebe**); *gramerhill* 1709, *Grammerhill* 1724, *Gramer hill* ~ 1724, *Grammerhill furlong* 1745 (*v.* **furlang**), *gramere sick* 1709, *Grammer Sick(e)* 1724, 1745 (*v.* **sík**) (*v.* **grauntmoder**; alluding to dower land, land assigned to the support of the widow of a late owner); *John Grants Dam* 1709, 1724 (*v.* **damme**); *de la Grene* 1340 (p) (*v.* **grēne**[2]); *Grindhill* 1697, *Grindel* 1724, *Grindell forlong* 1709, ~ *furlong* 1709, 1724, *Grindhill furlong* 1745 (*v.* **furlang**), *grindill* ~ 1630, *Grindell* ~ 1709, 1724, *Grindhill Slade* 1745 (*v.* **slæd**) (*v.* **grindel**); *Little halley tafts* 1709, ~ *hallitafts* 1724, *Little Holy Tofts furlong* 1745, *Long halley tafts* 1709, ~ *hallitafts* 1724, *Long Holy Tofts* 1745, *Long halley tafts forlong* 1709, *Long Holy Tofts Upper Furlong* 1745 (*v.* **furlang**) (*v.* **halh, lēah, toft**; in a remote valley in the south of this extensive parish, 2 miles from Whetstone village); *Harton far leys* 1745 (*v.* **feor, leys**), *Harton field* 1696, 1709, 1745 (*v.* **feld**; one of the later great open-fields of Whetstone township), *Harton meadow* 1709, 1724, 1745, *Harton side* 1696 (*v.* **sīde**) (*v.* **tūn**, either with **hār**[2] in its sense 'boundary' or with **hær**; a lost settlement, recorded also in neighbouring Countesthorpe f.ns. (a) and in Willoughby Waterleys f.ns. (a); the pronounced eastward bulge in the south of the present elongated parish of Whetstone may be the original territory of *Harton*); *hawthorn dike forlong* 1709, ~ ~ *furlong* 1724, *hawthorn dike close furlong* 1724 (*v.* **hagu-þorn, dík, furlang**); *hea brook(e)* 1630 1709, 1724, *hay brooke* 1709, *Hay Brook* 1745, *hea brook forlong* 1709, *hea brooke* ~ 1724, *Hay brook Furlong* 1745 (*v.* (**ge**)**hæg, brōc**); *Hell hole* 1709, 1724, 1745, *Hellhole Gate* 1696 (*v.* **gata**) (*v.* **hell-hole**, a derogatory name for a very poor patch of land; appearing also in adjoining Countesthorpe parish); *Hencrofts* 1696 (*v.* **henn, croft**); *hobgoblins pit forlong* 1709, *Hobgobling Pit fur'* 1724, *Gobling Pitt furlong* 1745 (*v.* **hobgoblin, pytt, furlang**; *hobgoblin* was another name for *Robin Goodfellow*, 'the drudging goblin', who threshes corn and does domestic chores while the farmer and his household are asleep, otherwise called *Robin-a-Tiptoe, v.* E. M. Wright, *Rustic Speech and Folklore* (Oxford 1913), 201, B. Dickins, 'Yorkshire Hobs', *Transactions of the Yorkshire Dialect Society*, vii, 19–22, Robin-a-Tiptoe Hill, Lei **3** 245 and (The) Hobgoblin, Lei **4** 155); *the homestall* 1709 (*v.* **hām-stall**; of *the Vicarage House, supra*); *House hollow* 1745 (*v.* **hūs, holh**); *under how* 1696, 1709, 1724, *Underlow* (sic) 1745, *under how furlong* 1724, *Underlow furlong* 1745 (*v.* **furlang**) (*v.* **under, hōh**); *howgates forlong* 1709, *~furlong* (*v.* **hōh, gata**); *Andrew Kings* ~ 1724, *Edgar Kings hadland* 1724 (*v.* **hēafod-land**); *Kirkhill* 1709, 1724, 1745 (*v.* **kirkja, hyll** and St Peter's Church *supra*); *Kitling furzes* 1724 (*v.* **fyrs**), *Kittling slade* 1709, 1724, 1745 (*v.* **slæd**) (with the surn. *Kitling*, a double diminutive of *Kit* (as *Kit-el-in*), a pet-form of Christopher); *Ladywell hill forlong* 1709, *~ ~furlong* 1724 (*v.* **furlang**) (*v.* **ladi, wella**; a holy well, sacred to Our Lady, the Virgin Mary); *Langdike* 1696, *Lang ditch* 1709, 1724, 1745, *Lang Dikes* 1724, *Langditch furlong* 1745, *Lang ditch haggs* 1709, 1724, 1745 (*v.* **hǫgg**) (*v.* **lang**[1], **dík, dīc**); *Larkehead* 1696, *Larkhead* 1724, 1745 (*v.* **lāwerce, hēafod**); *Little Leek bed* 1709, 1724, 1745, *Leekbed haggs* 1709, 1724, 1745 (*v.* **hǫgg**) (*v.* **lēac, bedd**); *Lester* ~ 1709, *Leicester way* 1724 (*v.* **weg**; the road to Leicester); *Litterworth* ~ 1709, 1724, *Lutterworth way* 1745 (the road to Lutterworth); *the Little Field* 1745; *London road* 1696, *London high way* 1709, 1724, 1745 (*v.* **hēah-weg**); *Long Doles* 1696 (*v.* **lang**[1], **dāl**); *Longlands furlong* 1745 (*v.* **lang**[1], **land, furlang**); *March* 1709, 1724, *Marches Close* 1709, *March meadow* 1745 (*v.* **mearc**); *John Martins Close* 1709, 1724, 1745, *~~hadland* 1709, 1724, 1745 (*v.* **hēafod-land**), *John Martins Normans ground* 1724 (*v. Normans land, infra*) (cf. *John Martin* 1764 EnclA of Whetstone); *William Masons Close* 1745; (*the*) *Mill Field* 1696, 1709, 1745 (*v.* **feld**; one of the great open-fields), *Mill forlong* 1709, *~ furlong* 1724, 1745 (*v.* **furlang**), *Mill furlong haggs* 1724, 1745 (*v.* **hǫgg**), *Mill furlong peece* 1696 (*v.* **pece**), *Mill hill* 1696, *Mylne holme* 1477 (e.16), *Mill Home* 1696, *~ holm* 1724, 1745 (*v.* **holmr**); *Millway* 1696, *the miln way* 1709, *Mill Way* (*v.* **myln**); *Moltmill furlong* 1696 (*v.* **malt-mylne**); (*the*) *Moor* 1709, 1724, *More furlong* 1696, *Moor forlong* 1709, 1724, *~ furlong* 1745 (*v.* **furlang**), *moor forlong haggs* 1709, *~ furlong haggs* (*v.* **hǫgg**), *moor stones* 1724 (*v.* **stān**) (*v.* **mōr**[1]); *Narmeadow* ~ 1696, *North Meadow Furlong* 1724, 1745, *~ ~ hades* 1709, 1724, 1745 (*v.* **hēafod**) (*v.* **norð, mēd** (**mēdwe** obl.sg.)); *the new pen* 1709, 1724 (*v.* **penn**); *Normans land* 1709 (*v.* **nān-mann, land**); *North field* 1696; *Long oho* 1709, 1724, 1745, *Long ohoe* 1724 (*v.* **wōh, hōh**); *Old field* 1696, 1709, 1724, 1745 (*v.* **ald**); *Owse* ~ 1709, *Ouze acers* 1724 (*v.* **æcer**), *Ouze acre furlong* 1745 (*v.* **furlang**), *Owse acers* ~ 1709, *Ouze acers* ~ 1724, *Ouze acre haggs* 1745 (*v.* **hǫgg**) (*v.* **wāse, æcer**); *the parting meadows* 1724 (*v.* **parting**; meadowland for dividing and sharing); *Peatling field mear* 1709, *~ ~ meer* 1724, *Peatling Meer* 1724, 1745 (*v.* (**ge**)**mǣre**; Peatling Magna parish adjoins to the east); *the pen* 1709, 1724, *~ ~ way* 1709, 1724, 1745 (*v.* **penn**); *John Pratts Hadeland* 1745 (*v.* **hēafod-land**), *John Pratts Tythe free piece* 1745 (*v.* **tēoða, frēo, pece**) (note *John Pratt* 1764 EnclA of Whetstone); *the Punders balke* 1696 (*v.* **pyndere, balca**); *Redcross leys* 1709, 1724, *~ Leas* 1724 (*v.* **leys**; ostensibly with **rēad** and **cros**, but may be identical in origin with Redcross in Wigston Magna f.ns. (a)); *the roundhill* 1696 (*v.* **round, hyll**); *St Mary holm* 1709, *St Marys holm* 1724, 1745 (*v.* **holmr**; presum. relating to an endowment for a chapel to St Mary Magdalene or to the Virgin Mary in the parish church here; there is no indication of a connection with St Mary's Mill or St Mary's Holmes, 3 miles downstream on the river Soar (*v.* Lei **1** 152, 201)); *Tho. Sandersons hadland* 1724 (*v.* **hēafod-land**), *Sanderson piece* 1709, *Tho. Sandersons piece* 1724 (*v.* **pece**), *Sanderson sheepcoat* 1709 (*v.* **scēp-cot**) (an earlier *Thomas Sanderson* of Whetstone is recorded for 1609 Nichols); *Siborn* ~ 1724, *Syborn Leys* 1745; with the

surn. *Siborne*, from the OE masc. pers.n. *Sæbeorn*); *Smith fur hill* 1709, 1724 (*v.*
feor; with the surn. *Smith*); *Sore hill* 1709, 1724 (overlooking the river Soar);
Sowfeild 1630, *Sow field* 1709, 1724, 1745 (*v.* **feld**; one of the great open-fields),
Sowfield hill 1745, ~ *meadow* 1709, 1724, ~ *side* 1696 (*v.* **sīde**), ~ *thorns* 1745 (*v.*
þorn) (*v.* **sūð**); *Springwell furze* 1745 (*v.* **fyrs**), *Springwells* ~ 1696, *Springwell head*
1709, 1745 (*v.* **hēafod**) (*v.* Springwell *supra*); *Willm. Standlys* ~ 1709, *William
Stanleys hadland* 1745 (*v.* **hēafod-land**; cf. *Thomas Stanley* 1764 EnclA of
Whetstone); *Staniforthe* 1477 (e.16) (*v.* **stānig, ford**); *stone doles* 1709, *Stony Doles*
1724 (*v.* **stān, stānig, dāl**); *stonie forlong* 1709, *Stony* ~ 1724, *stoney furlong, Stoney
Lands furlong* 1745 (*v.* **stānig, furlang**); *Swang* ~, *Swang hill* ~, *Swangland(s)
furlong* 1724 (*v.* **swang**); *Swinie* ~ ~, *Swynie hill forlong* 1709, *Swiney hill Furlong*
1745, *Swynie lands forlong* 1709 (*v.* **swīn, hyll, furlang**; it is uncertain whether
Swinie contains an **ēg** or **-ig**[3] in compound); *Tafts* 1724, *tafts forlong* 1709, *Taffts* ~,
Tafts furlong 1745 (*v.* **toft**); *Tharp Meare* 1696, ~ ~ *forlong* 1709, *Thorp meer
furlong* 1724 (*v.* **(ge)mǣre**; Countesthorpe parish adjoins to the north-east); (*on*)
Three forlongs 1724, ~ *furlongs* 1745 (*v.* **þrēo, furlang**); *Peter Throsbury's Close*
1745 (the surn. appears to be a late development of the township name Thoresby (*v.*
L **4** 165 and Nt 92)); *the Town balke* 1696 (*v.* **balca**), *the Townside* 1709 (*v.* **sīde**) (*v.*
tūn); (*on*) *Two furlongs* 1696, 1724, *Two forlong haggs* 1724 (*v.* **hǫgg**) (*v.* **tū,
furlang**); *the Ty(e)th free land* 1709, 1745 (*v.* **tēoða, frēo, land**); *Vales lane end*
1745 (*v.* **lane-ende**; with the surn. *Vale*); *the Vicars Square* 1745 (*v.* **vikere,
squar(e)**; presum. alluding to the shape of a close); *Water forrows* 1709, ~ *furrows*
1709, 1724, 1745, *Water furrows furlong* 1724, 1745 (*v.* **furlang**) (*v.* **wæter, furh**
and *Water furrowes* in Ashby Parva f.ns. (b)); *Webster furze* 1709, 1745, ~ *Furrs*
1724 (*v.* **fyrs**), *John Webster hadland* 1724 (*v.* **hēafod-land**), *Webster leys* 1709,
1724, 1745 (*v.* **leys**); *wellsicke* 1696, *Well Sick* 1724, 1745, ~ ~ *forlong* 1709, ~ ~
furlong 1724, 1745 (*v.* **furlang**) (*v.* **wella, sík**; *Widow Whitmores hadland* 1745 (*v.*
hēafod-land; cf. *Elizabeth Whitmore* 1748 MI); *Willoughby Meare* 1696,
Willowby(e) mear 1709, *Willo(w)by* ~ 1724, *Willoughby meer* 1745 (*v.* **(ge)mǣre**;
Willoughby Waterleys parish adjoins to the south); *Wood Way* 1709, 1724, 1745 (*v.*
wudu, weg).

Wigston Magna

Wichingestone 1086 DB (×3), *Wichingest'* 1109 × 1122 (1358) Ch,
  Wichingestun 1205 Pap, *Wichingestonia* 1199 × 1216 Dugd,
  Wychingestona c.1155 (1316) Ch
Wikingeston(e) 1191, 1193 P *et passim* to 1309, 1324 *Wyg*,
  Wikingestona 1223 BM, *Wyking(g)eston(e)* 1220 MHW, 1247 Ass
  et passim to 1335 *Wyg*, 1376 Banco, *Wykyng(g)eston(e)* 1271
  Wyg, 1274 Ass *et passim* to 1508, 1509 *Wyg*, *Wykyngestona*
  a.1189 (15) *ib*
Wikingston 1247 Ass, 1208 × 92 *Wyg*, *Wykingston(e)* 1247 × 60,
  1280 × 92, 1298 *ib et passim* to 1328 *Rey*, *Wykyngston* 1345, 1352
  Pat *et passim* to 1511 *Wyg*
Wikinston 1247 × 60 *Wyg*, *Wykinston* c.1280 × 92 *ib*, *Wikynston* 1348
  LCDeeds, *Wykenston* 1431, 1443 *Wyg*, *Wykynston* c.1291 Tax,
  1351 Fine, 1428 FA, 1503 *LCDeeds*
Wykeston 1456 *Wyg*
Wixton 1401 *Wyg*, *Wyxton* 1553 *ib*
Wiggeston 1410 *Wyg*, 1416 Fine *et passim* to 1515 *Wyg*, 1535 VE,
  Wyg(g)eston 1418 Cl, 1419 ELiW *et passim* to 1515 *Wyg*, 1517
  CoPleas
Wygston 1457, 1473 *Wyg et passim* to 1543 *ib*, 1550 Fine, *Wigston*
  1491, 1493 *Wyg et passim* to 1550 Pat, 1576 Saxton *et freq*

Affixes are variously added as:
~ *with too steples* c.1545 ECP, ~ *with the two steeples* 1558 × 79 ib,
  ~ *two-Steeples* 1846 White
Great ~ 1610 Speed, 1687 LML
~ *Magna* 1630, 1693 LML *et freq*

Probably 'the village or estate named from or belonging to a man
called Wicing or Viking', *v.* **tūn**. Four instances of an OE masc. pers.n.
Wicing are listed in *Prosopography of Anglo-Saxon England*
(www.pase.ac.uk), those of moneyers from coin evidence dated between

218

1029 and 1066. Mills (DBPN 498) suggests an OE masc. pers.n. *Wīcing* as a possible specific for the place-name, but the length of the initial vowel of such a pers.n. is uncertain, as is that of the OE sb. **wīcing**, **wicing** 'a pirate, a viking'. It is possible, though much less likely, that the specific of Wigston (Magna) is the Scand **víkingr** 'a viking' (perhaps the source of the ON pers.n. *Víkingr*, although Feilitzen 405 regards such a source as doubtful), or even the OE **wīcing**, **wicing**. For the ON masc. pers.n. *Víkingr* (ODan *Viking*), *v.* Feilitzen 405. And further to these pers.ns., note the discussion of OE *wicing* and ON *víkingr* in Professor Christine Fell's 'Old English *wicing*: a question of semantics', *Proceedings of the British Academy*, vol. 72 (1986), 295–316.

Only in the 16th cent. did confusion arise between forms for Wigston Magna and Wigston Parva, for the latter has a different etymology and development (*v.* Wigston Parva *infra*), hence the late addition of MLat *magna* 'great' and ~ *with too steples* (*v.* **tū**, **stēpel**). Wigston Magna possessed two medieval churches. That of St Wistan was pulled down in the early 17th cent. but its tower with spire remained standing and the church was rebuilt in 1853.

STREETS, ROADS AND LANES

ALBION ST, *v.* Albion St in Oadby *supra*. AYLESTONE LANE, Aylestone originally lying 2½ miles to the north-west. BELL ST, 1846, 1863, 1877 White, 1925 Kelly, *v.* Bell in Inns and Taverns *infra*. BLABY LANE is *blabygathe* 1247 × 60 *Wyg*, *blabie gate* 17 *Terrier*, *v.* **gata**, Blaby lying 2½ miles to the south-west. BLUNT'S LANE, 1925 Kelly, cf. *Edward Blunt* 1841 Census, *George Blunt* 1848 ib, *Thomas Blunt* 1848 ib and *Arthur Blunt* 1852 ib, all of Wigston Magna. BULL HEAD ST (sic), *Bullhead Street* 1766 *Wyg*, *Bull's Head Street* 1846, 1863, 1877 White, *v.* Bull's Head in Inns and Taverns *infra*. BURGESS ST, 1877 White. COOKS LANE, 1877 White; with the surn. *Cook*. GAS LANE, leading to a gasworks. GLADSTONE ST, named after William Gladstone, prime minister 1868–74, 1880–5, 1886, 1892–4. HORSEWELL LANE, *Horswell* 1348 *Wyg*, *Horsewell* 1686 *ib*, cf. *Horsewell close* 1766 *ib*, *v.* **hors**, **wella**. LEICESTER RD, 1846, 1863, 1877 White. LONG ST, 1766 *Wyg*, 1846, 1863, 1877 White, 1925 Kelly. MOAT ST, 1846, 1863, 1877 White, 1925 Kelly. NEWTON LANE is *Neutonegate* 1280 × 92, 1342, 1347 *Wyg*, *Neutongate* 1393 *ib*, *Newtongate* 1393, 1417 *ib*, *v.* **gata**; the road to Newton Harcourt which lies 2½ miles to the south-east. OADBY RD is *Outhebygate* c.1306 *Wyg*, *Oudeby gate* 1417 *ib*, *v.* **gata**; Oadby lying 1½ miles to the north-east. PADDOCK ST. SAFFRON RD, *v*. Saffron Brook, *v*. Lei **1** 226. SHACKERDALE RD, *v*. Shackerdale Fm *infra*. SPA LANE, 1925 Kelly, *v*. **spa**. STATION RD, 1877 White, 1925 Kelly, leading to the former *Wigston Station* 1854 O. VICTORIA ST, named in honour of Queen Victoria (1837–1901). WELFORD RD in its Wigston Magna reach was formerly *Kylebygate* c.1306 *Wyg*, *Kylbygate* 1395, 1417 *ib*, *Kilbye gate* 1635, 1656, 17 *Terrier*, *Kilby gate* 1639 *Wyg*, 1656, 1661 *Terrier*, 1731 *Wyg*, *v*. **gata**; the road to Kilby, 2½ miles to the south-east. Welford in Northants. lies 12 miles to the south-east.

The following names either have not survived or cannot be related with certainty to the lines of modern streets:

Balldike street 1766 *Wyg*, *v*. **ball**, **dík** and Balldike Cl in f.ns. (a) *infra*.

Bushloe road 1925 Kelly; it is *Bysselowstrett* 1422 Hastings, *Byslowstrete* 1443 *Wyg*, *v*. **strēt** and *Bussclowe* in f.ns. (b) *infra*.

Colepitway 17 *Terrier*, *Coale pitt way* 1709 *Wyg*, *Colepitt way* 1736, 1744 *ib*, *v*. **col-pytt**; a route for the transportation of pit coal.

Fostongate 1393 *Wyg*, 1661, 17 *Terrier*, 1704 *Wyg*, *Foustongate* 1635 *Terrier*, *v*. **gata**; the early road to Foston, 2 miles to the south.

Foursladegate, *Fowrsladegate* 1348 *Wyg*, *v*. **gata** and *Fourewelleslade* in f.ns. (b) *infra*.

Fulewellegate 1273 *Wyg*, *Folewellegate* 1280 × 92 *ib*, *v*. **gata** and *Fullewelle* in f.ns. (b) *infra*.

Glengate 1280 × 92, 1347, 1395 *Wyg*, 1656, 17 *Terrier*, *Glenngate* 1639, 1731 *Wyg*, *Glenway* 1635 *Terrier* (*v*. **weg**), *Glen Lane* 1766 *Wyg*, *v*. **gata**; the early road to Glen Parva, 2 miles to the west.

le Grenegate c.1306 *Wyg*, *v*. **grēne**[1], **gata**.

Hawethorngathe 1240 × 60 *Wyg*, *Hauthurngate*, *Hawethorngate* 1280 × 92 *ib*, *Hawthorngate* 1442 Hastings, *v*. **hagu-þorn**, **gata**.

Hoctonegate 1247 × 60 *Wyg*, *Houtonegate* 1273, 1280 × 92, c.1306 *ib*, *Houctonegate* 1280 × 92 *ib*, *Outonegate* c.1306 *ib*, *Howtongate* 1348 *ib*, *Hoghtonegate* 1395 *ib*, *Houghton gate* 1656, 1661 *Terrier*, *v*. **gata**; the road to Houghton on the Hill which lies 5½ miles to the north-east.

Mill lane 1863 White, *v*. **myln**.

Mouse lane 1877 White, *v*. **mūs**

Neugate 1347, 1393 *Wyg*, *v*. **nīwe**, **gata**.

Portgate 1271, 1280 × 92 *Wyg*, 1635, 1656 *Terrier*, *Portegate* 1348, 1393 *Wyg*, *Poortgate* 1661, 17 *Terrier*, *v.* **port-gate**; it is also *Porteweye* 1417 *Wyg*, *v.* **port-wey**; the early road to Leicester.

Sandpitt lane 1766 *Wyg*, *v.* **sand-pytt**.

Spowtewell Strete 1424 *Wyg*, *v.* **spoute**, **wella**, **strēt**.

Stoughton waye 1639 *Wyg*, *v.* **weg**; the road to Stoughton, 3 miles to the north-east.

Wharf road 1877 White, *v.* **wharf**.

le Wodegate 1273 *Wyg*, *Wodegate* 1280 × 92, c.1306, 1393 *ib*, *Wodgate* 1348 *ib*, *Woodgate* 1635, 1656, 1661 *Terrier*, *v.* **wudu**, **gata**.

Wyndmill gate 1635 *Terrier*, *Windmill gate* 1656, 1661, 17 *ib*, *v.* **wind-mylne**.

Bushley End 1766 *ib*, *Bushloe End* 1846, 1863 White, 1925 Kelly (*v.* **ende**), *Busley Townsend* 1661, 17 *Wyg*, *Busloe Townes End* 1705 ib (*v.* **tūn**), *v. Bussclowe* in f.ns. (b).

Church End 1846, 1863 White, *v.* **ende** and All Saints' Church *infra*.

Mowsley End 1846, 1863 White, 1925 Kelly, *v.* **ende**; Mowsley lies 7 miles to the south-east, so it is difficult to accept it as the first word in this name. Perh. to be related to *Mouse lane*, *supra*.

Newgate End 1766 *Wyg*, 1846, 1863, 1877 White, 1925 Kelly, *v.* **ende** and *Neugate*, *supra*.

Street-names in recent urban developments:

AISNE RD. ALFRETON RD. ASHBOURNE RD. AVONDALE RD. BAKEWELL RD. BALDWIN RD. BASSETT ST. BLABY RD. BRAMCOTE RD. BRIGHTON AVE. BRIXHAM DRIVE. CANAL ST. CARLTON DRIVE. CASTLETON RD. CEDAR AVE. CHEDDAR RD. CHELLASTON RD. CHERRY ST. CLARKES RD. CLEVELAND RD. CLIFFORD ST. CORONATION AVE. COTTAGE RD. CROSS ST. DALE AVE. DENMEAD AVE. DUNTON ST. ESTORIL AVE. EXETER RD. FAIFIELD ST. FARLEIGH AVE. FINSON CL. FREDERICK ST. GARDEN ST. GRANGE RD. GRANGE ST. GRANVILLE RD. HARCOURT RD. HAYES RD. HAZELWOOD RD. HEALEY ST. HIGHFIELD DRIVE. HINDOOSTAN AVE. HOLMDEN AVE. INGLEBY RD. IRLAM ST. JUNCTION RD. KENILWORTH RD. KINGS DRIVE. KINGSTON AVE. LANDSDOWNE GROVE. LEOPOLD ST. MAGNA RD. MANOR ST. MAPLETON RD. MARSTOWN AVE. MERE RD. MILVERTON DRIVE. NAMUR RD. NORTH ST. NORTHFIELD AVE. ORSON DRIVE. OWSTON DRIVE. PARK RD. PULLMAN RD. QUEENS DRIVE. REPTON RD. ROEHAMPTON DRIVE. ROLLESTON RD. SANDOWN RD.

SANDY RISE. STATION ST. THIRLMERE RD. TIMBER RD. WARWICK RD.
WATERLOO CRESC. WELDON RD. WEST AVE. WESTCOTES DRIVE.
WESTFIELD AVE. WILLOW PARK DRIVE. WILTSHIRE RD. WISTOW RD.

INNS AND TAVERNS

BELL, 1846, 1863, 1877 White, *Bell Inn* 1925 Kelly. BULL'S HEAD (lost),
Bull's Head 1846, 1863, 1877 White, *Bull's Head Inn* 1925 Kelly.
DURHAM OX (lost), *Durham Ox* 1846, 1863, 1877 White, 1925 Kelly.
HORSE AND TRUMPET, 1846, 1863, 1877 White, 1925 Kelly. KING
WILLIAM IV (lost), *King William IV* 1846, 1863, 1877 White.
NAVIGATION, 1846, 1863, 1877 White, 1925 Kelly. OLD CROWN, 1846,
1863, 1877 White, *Old Crown Inn* 1925 Kelly. PLOUGH, 1846, 1863,
1877 White. QUEEN'S HEAD, 1846, 1863 White, 1925 Kelly. RAILWAY
HOTEL (lost), *Railway Hotel* 1925 Kelly. ROYAL OAK, 1877 White, 1925
Kelly. SHOULDER OF MUTTON (lost), *Shoulder of Mutton* 1846, 1863
White. STAR AND GARTER, 1925 Kelly. SWAN (lost), *Swan* 1846 White.

DOMESTIC BUILDINGS

BUSHLOE HO. (lost), *Bushloe House* 1704 *Wyg*, 1863 White, *v.*
Bussclowe in f.ns. (b) *infra*. CROW LODGE, *v.* **loge** and *Crow Mill*, *infra*.
HIGHFIELD HO. HUNGERTON HO., 1877 White, *v. Hungertonhill* in f.ns.
(b) *infra*. IVY COTTAGE. MANOR HO., 1877 White, 1925 Kelly, *v.* **maner**.
NORWOOD HO. RAILWAY COTTAGES, beside the former *Midland Railway*
1853 O. SPRING COTTAGE (~ LODGE 2½"), *v.* **spring**[1], **loge**. TYTHORN
LODGE (2½"), *v.* **loge** and Tythorn Hill *infra*. THE VICARAGE, *the*
Vicarage house 1606 *Terrier*, *the Vicaridge house* 18 *ib*, *v.* **vikerage**.
WIGSTON GRANGE (2½"), 1835 O, 1875 *Map*, 1925 Kelly, *The Grange*
1863 White, *v.* **grange**. WIGSTON HALL, 1846, 1863, 1877 White, 1925
Kelly, *v.* **hall**.

BRIDGES

CLIFTON'S BRIDGE, crosses the Grand Union Canal; with a local surn.
Clifton, cf. *Ann Clifton* 1810 Census and *William Clifton* 1841 ib of
Wigston Magna. CROW MILL BRIDGE, *Crow Bridge* 1686, 1766 *Wyg*,
Croobridg 1687 *ib*; a shortened form of Crow Mill Bridge, itself related
to *Crowewell'* 1395 *Wyg*, *v.* Crow Mill *infra*. HAWTHORN BRIDGE (lost),
Hawthorn Bridg 1687 *Wyg*, *v. Hawthorngathe* in Streets, Roads and
Lanes *supra*. KILBY BRIDGE, 1686 *Wyg*, 1835 O, 1846, 1863, 1877

White, 1925 Kelly, *Kilby bridg* 1661 *Terrier*; on the road to Kilby which lies 2½ miles to the south-east. KILBY CANAL BRIDGE, crosses the Grand Union Canal. KNIGHT'S BRIDGE, crosses the Grand Union Canal; with a local surn. *Knight*, cf. *Sharrett Knight* 1846 Census and *Arthur Knight* 1877 ib of Wigston Magna. LANGHAM'S BRIDGE, crosses the Grand Union Canal; with a local surn. *Langham*, cf. *Josiah Langham* 1822 Census, *William Langham, farmer* 1846 White. POCHIN'S BRIDGE, crosses the Grand Union Canal; with a local surn. *Pochin*; cf. *James Pochin, farmer* 1846 White and *John Pochin, farmer* 1846 ib. STONEBRIDGE (lost), *Stanbrig* 1280 × 92 *Wyg*, *Stanebrygge* c.1306 *ib*, *Stanebrigge* 1318, 1321 *ib*, *Stanbrigge* 1393, 1395 *ib*, *Stonbrige* 1635 *Terrier*, *Stonebridge* 1639, 1661, 17, 1709 *ib*, *Stonbrige* 1656 *ib*, *le Brodestanibrig* 1280 × 92 *Wyg* (*v.* **brād**, **stānig**), *v.* **stān**, **brycg**. TAYLOR'S BRIDGE, crosses the Grand Union Canal; with a local surn. *Taylor*, cf. *John Taylor* 1854 Census and *Charles Taylor* 1865 ib. TOWNSEND BRIDGE (lost), *Townsend Bridge* 1687 *Wyg*, *v.* **tūn**, **ende**. TURNOVER BRIDGE, crosses the Grand Union Canal; a bridge which allowed a horse to cross the canal while still drawing a barge, without the need to unhitch the towrope. TYTHORN BRIDGE, crosses the Grand Union Canal, *v.* Tythorn Hill *infra*. VICE'S BRIDGE, crosses the Grand Union Canal; with a local surn. *Vice*, cf. *Samuel Vice* 1828 Census and *John Vice* 1856 ib, both of adjoining Blaby parish.

MILLS

Bodicotes mill 17 *Terrier*, *v.* **myln**; with the surn. *Bodicote* of a family originally from Bodicote in Oxfordshire (*v.* Ox 395).

Clays Mill 17 *Terrier*; with the surn. *Clay*.

Crowmilne 1467 × 84 LTD, *Crow Mill* 1766 *EnclA*, 1806 Map, 1846 White; names such as *Crowewell* 1395 *Wyg* and *Crowe willowes* 1635 *Terrier* suggest that the base of each is either **crōh**[2] 'a nook, a corner of land' or **crūw** 'a bend' (as of the river Sence), *v.* f.ns. (b) *s.nn.*, *infra*.

Lanktons mill 1656 *Terrier*; with the surn. *Langton*.

Union mill, 1835 O, 1863 White; named from *Union Canal* 1835 O.

(*The*) *Watermill* 1635 *Terrier*, 1639 *Wyg*, 1661 *Terrier*, *v.* **water-mylne**.

The Wyndmill 1635 *Terrier*, *Wind Mill* 1863 White, *v.* **wind-mylne** and *Wyndmill gate*, *supra*.

ABINGTON, another instance of the name found in Hallaton (Lei **3** 95); poss. a transferred name from Abington in Northants. (*v.* Nth 132) or Cambs. (*v.* Ca 51 and 99) or a surn. taken from the p.n.; otherwise of uncertain significance. ALL SAINTS' CHURCH, *Church (All Saints)* 1846, 1863, 1877 White; it is earlier recorded as *ecclesie de Wykingeston* 1220 MHW, 1301, 1339 *Pat*, ~ *de Wykyngeston* 1323, 1337, 1338, 1339, 1344, 1349, 1359 *ib*, *ecclesiam de Wykynston* 1331 *ib*, ~ *de Wichingeston* 1333, 1505 *ib*, ~ *de Wikyngeston* 1339, 1379 *ib*, ~ *de Wykenestyon* 1339 *ib*, *ecclesiam Omnium Sanctorum* 1352, 1355 *ib*, *ecclesie de Wikynston* 1355 *ib*, ~ *de Wykynston* 1355 *ib*, ~ *de Wygeston* 1388 *ib*, ~ *de Wyggeston* 1399 *ib*, ~ *de Wyguston alias Wygguston* 1410 *ib*. Note *All Saints' churchyard* 1595 Nichols, *v.* **churchyerd**. AYLESTONE LANE PARK, *v.* Aylestone Lane *supra*. THE BARN. BUSH LOCK, *v.* **lock**; on Grand Union Canal, as are Double Rail Lock, Ervin's Lock and Kilby Bridge Lock *infra*. DOUBLE RAIL LOCK, *v.* **lock**. ERVIN'S LOCK, with the surn. *Ervin*, *v.* **lock**. GLEBE FM (WIGSTON LODGE 2½"), *v.* **glebe**, **loge**. HIGHFIELD FM. KILBY BRIDGE FM, *v.* Kilby Bridge *supra*. KILBY BRIDGE LOCK, *v.* **lock**. LITTLE HILL, 1877 White. LODGE FM, *v.* **loge**. MERRYMEAD. OLD MERE, *v.* **(ge)mǣre**. RUSKINGTON LODGE FM, *v.* **loge**; named from Ruskington in Lincs., but there is no local evidence for a surn. pertaining to that township. ST WISTAN'S CHURCH, *St Wiston Church* 1639 PR, *St Wolstan's Church* 1756 MiscAccts, 1846, 1863, 1877 White, *Church (St Wolstan)* 1925 Kelly; the original dedication of the church is earlier evidenced in f.ns.: *Seintwistoneshauedlond* 1308 *Wyg*, *St Wolfstans hadelond* 1656 *Terrier*, *St Wistons hadland*, *St Woolstanes Headland* 1661 *ib*, *St Wistans hadland*, *St Wolston's headland* 17 *ib* (*v.* **hēafod-land**), *Wystons corner* 1635 *ib*, *Saint Wolfstans corner* 1656 *ib* (*v.* **corner**). The confusion between the early saints Wigstan (*v.* Wistow, Lei **4** 295) and Wulfstan (c.1009–95, Bishop of Worcester) evidently occurred in the 17th cent. SHACKERDALE FM (2½"), *Shackresdale* 1342 *Wyg*, *Shakerdale* 1393 *ib*, 1635, 1661 *Terrier*, *Shakadale* 1656 *Wyg*, 1661, 17 *Terrier*, *v.* **scēacere**, **dæl**[1], **dalr**; found also as *Shackadale* in adjoining Aylestone f.ns. (b) and as *Shakersdal* in adjoining Knighton f.ns. (b). SOUTH WIGSTON. TYTHORN HILL, TYTHORN HILL FM, *Thythorne* 1656, 1661, 17 *Wyg*, *Thytorne* 1661 *ib*, *Thythornhull* 1305 *ib*, *Thithernehul* 1348 *ib*, *Theythornhull* 1376 *ib*, *Thikthornhill* 1393 *ib*, *Thythornhill* 1393 *ib*, 1635, 1656, 1661, 17 *Terrier*, *Thytornhill* 1667, 17 *ib*, *Thytorne hill* 1709 *Wyg*, *Thythorne Hill* m.18 *ib*, *Thykthornhill felde* 1417 *ib*, *Thythorn(e)hill feylde* 1635 *Terrier*, *Thythorne hill Feild* 1656, 17 *ib*, *Thytorn(e)hill Feild* 1661, 17 *ib*, *Thythorn Hill Field* 17 *ib* (*v.* **feld**; one of the great open-fields of the township), *v.* **þicce**[2], **þorn**, **hyll**; on the parish boundary with Newton Harcourt. The interpretation 'boundary hill' (from *tēo* 'boundary') given in Lei **4** 298 is shown to be incorrect by this additional evidence. WIGSTON CEMETERY. WIGSTON FIELDS, 1877 White, 1925 Kelly, *Wigston field* 1863 White. WIGSTON JUNCTION, WIGSTON CENTRAL JUNCTION, WIGSTON SOUTH JUNCTION and WIGSTON SIDINGS each relate to the major railway complex west of the town.

FIELD-NAMES

Forms presented in (a) dated 1761, 1766 and 1786 are *Wyg*; those dated 1846, 1863 and 1877 are White; 1861 and 1884 are *Deed*; l.19 are *Map*. Forms throughout dated 1247 × 60, 1250 × 60, 1269, 1271, 1272, 1273, 1280 × 88, 1280 × 92, 1292, 1298, 1304, 1305, c.1306, 1308, 1309, 1318, 1319, 1320, 1321, 1324, 1338, 1342, 1347, 1348, 1354, 1376, 1393, 1395, 1405, 1412, 1417, 1418, 1443, 1453, 1455, 1463, 1464, 1491, 1514, 1591, 1624, 1639, 1687, 1698, l.17, 1704, 1705, 1709, 1710, 1731, 1736 and 1744 are *Wyg*; those dated 1606, 1635, 1656, 1661 and 17 are *Terrier*.

(a) Anchor Cl 1766 (poss. with a lost inn or tavern name, but if so, unrelated to the Union Canal which the form predates by some 30 years, though *Anchor* as an inn name is recorded from 1682, *v.* Cox[1] 19 *et passim*; a memory of a hermit (**ancre**) is more likely, cf. *del Ermytage* 1455 (p), 1463 (p), *v.* **ermitage**); Balldike Cl 1766 (*Balldyke close* 1591, *v.* **ball, dík, clos(e)**); Bottom Cl l.19 (*v.* **bottom**); Brick Kiln Cl 1861, 1884, l.19 (*v.* **brike-kiln**); Bridge Mdw 1766 (*v.* **brycg**); Broad Mdw l.19 (*Brademedwe* c.1306, *Bradmedou* 1342, *Bradmedow* 1412, *Broad meadow(e)* 1635, 1661, 1704, *Brode meadowe* 1639, *Broadmeddowe* 1656, cf. *Brademedweharde* 1305 (*v.* **heard**; prob. in the sense 'firm, rough ground'), *v.* **brād, mēd (mēdwe** obl.sg.)); Brook Slade l.19 (*Brokeslade, Brokkeslade* 1393, *Brokslade* 1417, *Brockslade* 1635, 1656, 1661, 17, *Brookslade* 1704, *Brooke Slade* 1709, cf. *Brook Slade Baulk* 1736 (*v.* **balca**), *v.* **brōc, slæd**); Church Nook 1766 (*v.* **nōk** and St Wistan's Church *supra*); Crowhill Cl 1766 (ostensibly from **crāwe** with **hyll**, but this may be a late form of *Crowewell*, *v. Crow Mill, supra*); Crowson's Cl 1786 (with the surn. *Crowson*, a late Leics. form of Croxton, the family prob. originally from either South Croxton, 8 miles to the north-east or from Croxton Kerrial, 24 miles to the north-east); Little ~ ~, Double Gorse (sic) l.19 (*double gore* 17, *v.* **duble, gāra**); Faux Cl 1766 (*Fawkes closse* 1635, cf. *Faulks Close Corner* 17 (*v.* **corner**); with the surn. *Fawcus, Fawkes*, *v. Faucoussty* in f.ns. (b)); Flatt Cl 1766 (*v.* **flat, flatr**); Gaol Cl 1846, 1863, 1877 (l.17, *v.* **gaole**; a site used as a temporary prison in the English Civil War of 1642–8); Goodwins Cl l.19 (with the surn. *Goodwin*, cf. *Mahalia Goodwin* 1818 Census, *Martha Goodwin* 1826 ib and *John Goodwin* 1880 ib, all of Wigston Magna); Gravel Hill l.19 (*Gravel* ~, *Gravill hills* 17, *v.* **gravel**); The Green 1766 (*v.* **grēne**[2]); Hilly Meadow Cl 1766 (*Hullimedwe* c.1306, *Hillymedou* 1342, *Hyllymedowe* 1393, *Hilly(e) meadowe* 1635, 1639, *hilley* ~, *hillye meddowe* 1656, *Hilly me(a)dow* 1661, *Hillo(w) Meadow* 17, *v.* **hyllig, mēd (mēdwe** obl.sg.)); Holwell Cl 1766 (poss. with a late form of *Holywell* in f.ns. (b); otherwise, *v.* **hol**^{2}, **wella**); Little Hill 1766 (*little hills* 1656); Long Cls 1766; Long Mdw 1766 (*Longemedwe* 1305, *Long*(*e*) *meadow*(*e*) 1635, 1639, 1661, 17, ~ *meddowe* 1656, cf. *Long meadow close* 1709, *Long meadow end* 1635 (*v.* **ende**), *v.* **lang**^{1}, **mēd** (**mēdwe** obl.sg.)); the Meer 1766 (*the meere* 1656, *the Mere* 1707, *v.* (**ge**)**mǣre**); Bottom ~, Top Navigation l.19 (fields beside Grand Union Canal); Near Mdw 1761 (this may be a late form of *Northmedwe, infra*, where locally *north* > *narr* (> *near*?)); New Close Mdw 1766 (*new closse* 1591, *New Close* 1635, 1656, 17, 1710, *v.* **nīwe**, **clos**(**e**)); Pinder's Cl 1846, 1863, 1877 (with the surn. *Pinder*, cf. *William Pinder* 1613 MiscAccts of Wigston Magna); Redcross 1761 (*Radegres* c.1306, *Redgrass* 1661, 1709, *v.* **hrēod**, **grǣs**; prob. identical with *Redcross* in Whetstone f.ns. (b) *supra*); Slaters Cls 1766 (with the surn. *Slater*); Spring Well l.19 (*v.* **spring**^{1}, **wella**; perh. a late inversion of *Wellespring* (1304) in f.ns. (b)); Square Cl l.19 (*v.* **squar**(**e**)); Stockhill Holme Cl 1766 (*Stokwelleholm* 1320, *Stockwellholme* 1635, *Stokelhome* 1661, *v.* **stocc**, **wella**, **holmr**; cf. *Joh' de Stockwell* 1348 *Wyg* of Wigston Magna); the Tithe Piece 1766 (*the tyth peece* 1658, *v.* **tēoða**, **pece**).

(b) *Abbots close* 1661, *Abbotts hadland* 1635 (*v.* **hēafod-land**) (with the surn. *Abbott*, cf. *William Abbott* 1831 Census, *Clara Abbott* 1860 ib and *Alfred Abbott* 1866 ib of Wigston Magna); *Ailstonemere* 1348 (*v.* (**ge**)**mǣre**), *Aylestone crosse* 1635 (*v.* **cros**), *Aylestone* ~ 1661, *Elson gap* 17 (*v.* **gap**; used of openings for roads through parish boundary hedges; Aylestone parish adjoins to the north-west); *Algerystoft* 1341 (*v.* **toft**; either with the ME surn. *Alger* or a masc. pers.n. source which could be OE *Æðelgār* or OE *Ælfgār* or ON *Álfgeirr* (ODan *Alger*)); *Allhallows* ~ 1661, *all hallo hadland* 17 (*v.* **hēafod-land**; with the popular form for All Saints' (Church) (with **hālga** 'a saint') *supra*); *Baily Pieces* 1698 (*v.* **pece**; with either **baillie** or the surn. *Bailey*, as *Eli Bailey* 1823 Census, *John Bailey* 1856 ib and *Geoffrey Bailey* 1880 ib of Wigston Magna); *le bankende* c.1306 (*v.* **banke**, **ende**); *barrowsteades* 1635, *Barrowstead* 1661, *barrowsted, the Barrowsteds* 17 (*v.* **burh-stede**); *bastardley* 1661 (*v.* **bastard**, **ley**^{2}; *bastard* was used in a derogatory way for land of low yield or abnormal shape); *Bear pitt* 1709 (an arena for bear-baiting); *Becke tenement* 1338 (*v.* **tenement**; with the surn. *Becke*, cf. *Joh' Becke* 1247 × 60 *Wyg* of Wigston Magna); *Beggar hadland* 1635, *Beggers hadeland* 1656, *Beggars hadland* 1704, 1709 (*v.* **hēafod-land**; poss. with **beggere**, but this f.n. may be a survival of *bulgarishauidlond* (1273) *infra*; if so, its longevity would be unusual); *First Berry Peece* 1661 (*v.* **pece**; with **burh** or **berige**); *Blabygate dikes* 1661, 17 (*v.* **dík** and Blaby Lane *supra*); *blakemilde* 1280 × 92, *Blakemylde* 1305, *Blakemyld'* 1376 (*v.* **blæc**, **mylde**); *Blakewellesike* 1269, *Blacwellesyke, Blacwelsick', Blagwellesyke* 1280 × 92, *Blacwellesike* 1280 × 88, c.1306, 1318, *Blakwellesike, Blakwelsike* 1393, *Blackwell Sick* 1635, 1656, 1661, 17, *Blacwellesikenethirend'* 1347 (*v.* **neoðera**, **ende**) (*v.* **blæc**, **wella**); *Bloxoms hadland* 1661 (*v.* **hēafod-land**; with the surn. *Bloxam*, cf. *Thomas Bloxam* 1868 Census and *Charles Bloxam* 1870 ib, a family prob. in origin from Bloxholm, 44 miles to the north-east in Lincs.); *Bodicoates hadland* 1661 (*v.* **hēafod-land**; with the surn. *Bodicote, v. Bodicotes mill, supra*); *Boones yardes end* 1635 (*v.* **geard**, **ende**; with the surn. *Boon*); *Boyteresyke, Boytersyke* 1280 × 92, *Boydersike* 1393, *Butersick*(*e*) 1635, 1656, 1661, *butar* ~, *butter sick* 17, *Boytersikeouerende* c.1306 (*v.* **uferra**, **ende**), *Beuter sick furlonge* 1639 (*v.* **furlang**) (*v.* **butere**, **sík**; referring to rich pasture which yielded good butter); *Bowling leyes* 1635, *Bowleing leayes* 1661 (*v.* **bowling**, **leys**); *Wm. Brabsons* *had*(*e*)*land* 1656, 17 (*v.* **hēafod-land**; cf. *Robert Brabson* 1635 *Terrier* of Wigston Magna, the surn. *Brabson, Brabazon* from AFr *Brabançon* 'a native of Brabant'); *the Breach* 1656, 1661, 17 (*v.* **brēc**); *Bretterhul* 1280 × 92, 1347, *Bretterhill* 1393 (*v.* **hyll**; the specific is either ON **Bretar** 'Britons' or OE **Bretta** (gen.pl. of **Brettas** 'Britons')); *the brig* 1635, *the bridge* 17 (*v.* **brycg**); *broadgreene* 1635, *Broad greene pasture* 1639 (*v.* **pasture**) (*v.* **brād, grēne**[2]); *Brochilslade* 1273, *Brochulslade* 1280 × 92, c.1306, *Brokhulslade* c.1306, *Brochilslade ouerende* 1273, *Brockelisslade ouereende* 1273, *Brochulslade ouerende* 1280 × 92 (*v.* **uferra, ende**) (*v.* **brōc, hyll**); *far~, midle brokenbackes* 1635, *Far brockenbackes* 1656, *far brokenbacks* 1661, 17, *Middle~, Brokenbacks* 1709 (alluding to land back-breaking to till); *Broomhill* 1661, 17 (*v.* **brōm, hyll**); *Browneplace* 1453 (*v.* **place**; with the surn. *Brown*); *bulgarishauidlond* 1273, *bulgereshauedlond* 1280 × 92 (*v.* **hēafod-land**; prob. with the common surn. *Bulger*, from OFr *boulgier* 'a maker of leathern bags' (giving ME *bulge* 'a leathern bag, a wallet'); but Prof. R. Coates wonders if the specific originally may rather have referred to a heretic, 'a Bulgar' (into ME from OFr *boulgre*), a name given to a religious sect which came from Bulgaria in the 11th cent., that was later applied to other heretics (esp. the Albigensians) and then to usurers. The 'unnatural' practices of these heretics gave rise to the notion of buggery. As a surn., *Bulgar* is very rare in England, but if this is an early instance of the surn. (or even of the sb.), it would sit more happily with the 17th-cent *Beggar hadland, supra*, if related); *Bussclowe* 1454, 1455, *Buslo Closes* 17 (*v.* **busc, hlāw**); *les Buttes* 1405 (*v.* **butte**); *Cakeforlang'* c.1306 (*v.* **cak, furlang**); *Caldewelle* c.1306 (*v.* **cald, wella**); *Calulese* 1305 (*v.* **calu, læs**); *Caluerelesewe* 1280 × 92, *Caluirlese* 1376 (*v.* **calf** (**calfra** gen.pl.), **læs** (**læswe** dat.sg.)); *Cappehauitland* 1247 × 60, *Cappehauidland* 1250 × 60, *Cap hadland* 1635, 1661, 17, ~ *hadeland* 1656 (*v.* **hēafod-land**; the specific is prob. **cape** 'a look-out place'; less likely because of the early date of the f.n. is the surn. *Capp*, metonymic for ME *cappere* 'a cap maker'); *Carr* 1656, *Carebanke* 1661, *Carr Banke* 1709 (*v.* **banke**), *Car* ~ 1635, *Carr hill* 1661, *Carehill* 17 (*v.* **kjarr**); *Church corner* 1709 (*v.* **corner** and All Saints' Church *supra*); *Clayes headland* 17 (*v.* **hēafod-land**; with the surn. *Clay*; note *Clays Mill, supra*, and cf. *Ethel Clay* 1878 Census and *John Clay* 1880 ib of Wigston Magna); *Cleyhilsike* 1273, *Cleyelesike* 1280 × 92, *Cleylesike* c.1306, *Cleylesikebrode* c.1306 (*v.* **brād**) (*v.* **clǣg, hyll, sík**); *Cleysike* 1393 (*v.* **clǣg, sík**); *Cobaldeswong* c.1306, *kobaldeswong* 1348 (*v.* **vangr**; either with the surn. *Cobbald* or with its source, the OE masc. pers.n. *Cūðbeald*); *Cockpitt leyes* 1704 (*v.* **cock-pit, leys**; a venue for cock-fighting); *Colpit* 1393 (*v.* **col-pytt**; a place where charcoal was made); *Coltmans yard*(*e*) 1661, 17 (*v.* **geard**; with the surn. *Coltman*, cf. *Thomas Coltman* 1806 Census and *Annie Coltman* 1839 ib of Wigston Magna); *Cokkesyert* 1393 (*v*, **geard**; with the surn. *Cock*(*e*)); *Crossfurlong* 17 (*v.* **cross, furlang**); *Crowewell* 1395 (*v.* **wella**), *Crow*(*e*) *willowes* 1635, 1656, *Crow Willows* 1709 (*v.* **wilig**) (prob. with **crōh**[2] rather than with **crāwe**; cf. *Crow Mill, supra*); *Dog foard* 1661, 17 (*v.* **ford**; prob. with **docce** rather than with **dogga**); *Evans* ~ 1661, *Evins close* 17 (with the surn. *Evans*); *Eyl, Heyl* 1247 × 60, *Eyel* c.1306, 1324, 1348, *Eyle* 1393, *under oyle* 17, *Oyle hill* 1635, 1661, 17, *Oyl Hill* 17, *Oyle hill side* 1709, *Oile Hill Side* 1724 (*v.* **sīde**) (*v.* **ēl** (< **ēg** + **-el**[3]); a small area of dry ground in fen); *Faucoussty* 1309 (with **stīg** or **stig**), *Faukeslond* 1443 (*v.* **land**), *Fawkes meadow close* 1624 (with the surn. *Fawcus, Fawkes*, from the ContGerm masc. pers.n. *Falco* (via OFr *Fauques*); cf. *Joh' Faucous* 1309 *Wyg* of Wigston Magna and note Faux Cl in f.ns. (a)); *firkinhole*

17 (*v.* **fyrkin, hol**[1]; presum. a small water-filled pit likened to a firkin, a small cask for liquids); *Folepit* 1280 × 92, *Folepyth* 1292, *Fulpit* 1321 (*v.* **fūl, pytt**); *Fotdolis* 1348 (*v.* **fōt, dāl**; land at the foot of a hill); *Fourewelleslade* 1269 (*v.* **wella**), *Foureslade* 1324, 1393, *Fower slade* 1639, *Foardslade* 1661, *Foureslade side* 1635 (*v.* **sīde**) (*v.* **slæd**; it is assumed that the forms from 1324 represent a shortening of that of 1269 and this would suggest that the first el. is **fōr** 'a pig', which would sit happily in the forms with *slæd* without *wella*; otherwise with **fēower**, describing a slade with four springs, *v. Foursladegate, supra*); *Fox closse* 1656 (*v.* **clos(e)**), *Fox meadow close* 1661, *Foxes hadland* 17 (*v.* **hēafod-land**) (with the surn. *Fox*, cf. *Mary Fox* 1835 Census and *Thomas Fox* 1855 ib of Wigston Magna); *Isack Fryers closse* 1635, *William Fryes closse* 1656, *Wm. Freers Close* 1661, 17 (*v.* **clos(e)**; the surn. is *Freer, Fryer* from OFr *frere* 'a friar'; later in Wigston Magna are recorded *Samuel Freer* 1827 Census, *Frederick Freer* 1852 ib and *Annie Freer* 1864 ib); *Fullewelle*, *Fulwell'* 1393, *Fulwell* 1661, 17, *Fullwell* ~ 1635, 1656, 1705, *Fulwell Head* 17 (*v.* **hēafod**), *Fullwell* ~ 1635, *Fulwell path* 1656 (*v.* **pæð**), *Fulwell Willowes* 1731 (*v.* **wilig**) (*v.* **fūl, wella** and *Fulewellegate, supra*); *Gesseliniswong* c.1306 (*v.* **vangr**; with the surn. *Gesling* (from ON *gæslingr* 'a gosling')); *the gleab* 17, *the Gleebe hadland* 17 (*v.* **hēafod-land**), *the Glebe grass hadeland* 1756 (*v.* **græs**) (*v.* **glebe**); *Glengap* 1635 (*v.* **gap**), *Glensick* 1635, 1656, 1661, 17, *Glenn Sick* 1709 (*v.* **sík**), *Glensicke planke* 1687 (*v.* **planke**) (Glen Parva parish adjoins to the west); *Golden medou* 1342, *Goldene Medwe* 1324 (*v.* **gylden, mēd** (**mēdwe** obl.sg.); alluding to meadowland, golden with flowers in season); *Goldehil* 1273, *Goldewhel* 1348, *Goldhill* 1635, 17, *Gouldhill* 1639, 1656, 1709, *Gold Hill* 1731, *Goldhill close* 1661, *Goldhill Feyld* 1635, *Gould hill Feild* 1656, *Goldhill Field* 1661, ~ *Feild* 1661, 17 (*v.* **feld**; one of the great open-fields of the township, lying towards Aylestone), *Goldhulfot* 1280 × 92, *goldhill foot* 17 (*v.* **fōt**), *Goldhill side* 1635 (*v.* **sīde**) (*v.* Goldhill in adjoining Aylestone parish); *Gonewarehil, Gunewarehul* 1269, *Gonwarhull* 1342, *Gunwarhill* 1417 (*v.* **hyll**; with the ON fem. pers.n. *Gunnvǫr* (ODan *Gunwǫr*)); *le Gore* 1280 × 92, 1298 (*v.* **gāra**); *Goseholm* c.1306, *Goose holme* 1661, ~ *Home* 17 (*v.* **gōs, holmr**); *gravill pitts* 1635 (*v.* **gravel, pytt**); *le Grescroft* c.1306 (*v.* **græs, croft**); *the grips* (in *Portgate*) 1635 (*v. Portgate, supra*), *the Gripps* 1656, 1709 (*v.* **grȳpe**); *the Gutter* 17 (*v.* **goter**); *Halcroft* 1443 (*v.* **croft**), *Hall close* 1591 (*v.* **hall** and Wigston Hall *supra*); *Halls hadland* 1661 (*v.* **hēafod-land**; with the surn. *Hall*); *Halteresslade* 1319, *Halterslade* 1324, 1393, 1635, 1639, 1656, 1661, 17, *haliter slade* 1661, *haltarslade* 17 (*v.* **slæd**; either with the ME occupational surn. *Haltrere*, from *haltrere* 'a maker or seller of halters for horses' (from OE *hælftre* 'a halter') or with **hælftre** and alluding to a strip of greensward where horses were tethered); *le Hankende* c.1306, *le Hangend'* 1395, *Hinging* ~ 1635, *Hanging hills* 1661, 17 (*v.* **hangende**); *Hauthernehil, Hauthernehul* 1280 × 92, *Hawethornhul* c.1306, *Hawethornhill* 1395, 1417, *Hawthorn(e)* 1635, 1661, 17 (*v.* **hagu-þyrne, hyll**; **þyrne** replaced by **þorn**); *Hecroft* 1247 × 60 (*v.* **hēg, croft**); *the Hempe lands* 1656, *hemp place* (sic) 1661, *hemp layes* 17 (*v.* **land**) (*v.* **hænep**); *Herburgh Hull* 1376, *Harborow* ~ 1661, 17, *Harbrough Hill* 17 (*v.* **eorð-burh, hyll**); *Hericks hedg(e)* 1661, 17 (*v.* **hecg**; with the surn. *Herrick*, from the ON masc. pers.n. *Eiríkr* (ODan *Erik*), cf. *Clara Herrick* 1853 Census of Wigston Magna); *Holywell* 1417, 1635, *hollywell closse* 1656, *Holywell Close* 1709 (*v.* **clos(e)**) (*v.* **hālig, wella**); *le Hountheng* 1272, *Houndheng* 1280 × 92, *Houndyng* 1393 (*v.* **hund, eng**); *The Homestall* 1606 (*v.* **hām-stall**; of *the Vicarage house, supra*); *Hungertonhill* 1280 ×

92, 1393, *Hungertonehull* 1305, *Hongertonehul* c.1306, *Hungirtonhull* 1342, *Hungirton' Hull* 1376, *Hungerton hill* 1635, 1656, 1661, 17 (*v.* **hyll**), *Hungertonesike* 1280 × 92, *Hungertonsike* 1393, *Hungerton sick* 1635, 1661, 17 (*v.* **sík**), *Hungertonesikeouerende* c.1306 (*v.* **uferra, ende**) (*v.* **hungor, tūn**; a lost failed farmstead, sited on unproductive soil, cf. Hungarton, Lei **3** 144); *Thos. Jacksons hadland* 1656, 17 (*v.* **hēafod-land**; *Dennys Jackson* 1635 *Terrier* was presum. Thomas's forebear); *le ker* 1269, *le kerresheued* c.1306 (*v.* **hēafod**) (*v.* **kjarr**); *Kilnes* 1635, 1661, *Killnes* 1656, *Kills* 1661, 1736, *Kilns* 17 (*v.* **cyln**); *Kirkdale Meer* 1709 (*v.* **kirkja, dalr, (ge)mǣre**); *Knighton Meere* 1635, 17 (*v.* **(ge)mǣre**; Knighton parish adjoins to the north); *Lamas close* 1709 (*v.* **lammas**); *Lambecotes* c.1306, 1393, 1395 (*v.* **lamb, cot**); *Lepwing leyes* 1635, *leapinge ~* 1656, *Leaping leyes* 1661, ~ *Leys* 17 (*v.* **hlēapewince, leys**; alluding to the lapwing or peewit (*Vanellus vulgaris*) which was named from the manner of its flight (from OE *hlēapan* 'to leap' and **winc-* 'to totter, to waver')); *Lesemylde* 1393, *Leyesmyles close* 1635 (*v.* **mylde**; with **lǣs** in an early sense 'land that has remained untilled for some time'); *Long Feild* 17 (*v.* **feld**; a later replacement name for *Muklowe felde, infra*); *Long lane stile* 1706 (*v.* **stigel**); *Luttledale* c.1306, *litteldale* 1308, 1393, *Littledale* 1635, 1639, 1656, 1661, 17, *Little Dale Flatt* 1731(*v.* **flat**) (*v.* **lȳtel, dalr**); *the marlepitts* 1656 (*v.* **marle-pytt**); *Maudes balke* 1635, 1656 (*v.* **balca**), *Moulds hadland* 17 (*v.* **hēafod-land**), *Moulds pen* 1661, 1704, *Moldspen* 17 (*v.* **penn**) (with the surn. *Maud, Mould*, from the ContGerm fem. pers.n. *Mahthild* (which gave the learned form *Matilda* (as that of the wife of William the Conqueror) and the common vernacular *Mahald, Mahalt*), cf. *Mahald* 1172 × 80 Dane of Leics.; the surn. is found in Wigston Magna as early as *Elizabeth Molde* 1569 PR and later from *Ann Mould* 1805 Census, *Joseph Mould* 1815 ib to *Albany Mould* 1880 ib); *the mill forlonge* 1656 (*v.* **myln, furlang**); *Mokilhow* 1280 × 92, *Mokelow* 1393, *Muckley* 1635, 1661, *Mucklow(e)* 1656, 17, 1731, *Muckloe* 17, 1704, 1736, *Muklowe felde* 1417, *Muckley Feyld* 1635, *Mucklowe Feild* 1656, *Mucklow Field* 1661, 17, *Muckley ~, Mucklowe ~* 1661, *Muckloe Feild* 17 (*v.* **feld**; one of the great open-fields of the township) (*v.* **micel, mikill, hōh, haugr**); *le Moriwong* 1273, *moriwong'* 1280 × 92 (*v.* **mōrig, vangr**); *Moseho* 1443 (*v.* **mos, hōh**) *the narroe layes* 17 (*v.* **nearu, leys**); *Neprotis* 1273, *Neprodes* 1280 × 92, *Neperotes* 1417 (*v.* **hnæpp, rōd**³; the allusion may well be to roods of land lying in a bowl-shaped depression rather than to turnips (Angl **nēp**)); *New Clos(s)e* 1591, 1710 (*v.* **clos(e)**); *Newgate Hill* 1635, 1661, 1731, *Neugate lane end* 1635, 1687 (*v.* **lane-ende**) (*v.* *Neugate* and *Newgate End, supra*); *new meddowe* 1656 (*v.* **mēd** (**mēdwe** obl.sg.)); *Newton gap* 1635, 17, ~ *gapp* 1656 (*v.* **gap**; Newton Harcourt lies 2½ miles to the south-east); *Nomans bush* 1661 (*v.* **nān-mann, busc**); *Northmedwe* 1271, 1280 × 92, c.1306, *Northmedowe* 1393, *North Meadow* 1635, 1661, 17, *nare meadow* 1639, *Northemedowefurlong'* 1417, *North meadow furlong* 1635, *Narr meadowe furlong* 1639, *the nare meddowe furlong* 1656 (*v.* **furlang**) (*v.* **norð, mēd** (**mēdwe** obl.sg.); for *north > nar(r)*, cf. nearby Narborough); *Odeby ~* 1635, 1661, 17, *Oadby corner* 1656, 17 (*v.* **corner**), *Outebymere* 1393 (*v.* **(ge)mǣre**) (Oadby parish adjoins to the north-east); *Palletes house* 1635 (with the surn. *Pallett*, cf. *Fanny Pallett* 1815 Census and *Benjamin Pallett* 1833 ib of Wigston Magna); *the Parsonage ground* 1606 (*v.* **personage, grund**); *Parsons pikes* 1661 (*v.* **persone, pīc**); *Francis Pawleys grasse headland* 17 (*v.* **græs, hēafod-land**; with the surn. *Pawley*, cf. *Elizabeth Pawley* 1800 Census, *Thomas Pawley* 1805 ib, the surn. recurring in Wigston Magna to *Charles Pawley* 1880 ib and *Minnie Pawley* 1881 ib);

Pease furlong 17 (*v.* **pise, furlang**); *Pegshooke* 1656 (*v.* **hōc**; with the surn. *Pegg*); *Personesmedow* 1393 (*v.* **persone, mēd** (**mēdwe** obl.sg.)); *le Pitt* 1273 (*v.* **pytt**); *Prestesthirne* 1393, *Preist Thyrne* 1709 (*v.* **prēost, þyrne**); *Raggs grass* 17 (*v.* **græs**), *Rags hadland* 17 (*v.* **hēafod-land**) (with the surn. *Ragg*, prob. here from the ODan masc. pers.n. *Wraghi* (which also gave the surn. *Wragg*)); *Malkeyn Randull' croft* 1464, *Adam Randelles croft or Swetynges* 1491, *Mawde Randylles Croft* 1514 (*v.* **croft** and *Swetynges, infra*); *Reddeleiz tofth* 1464 (*v.* **toft**), *Redlys Crofte* 1514 (*v.* **croft**) (*v.* **hrēod, lǣs**); *Ridgway* 1661 (*v.* **hrycgweg**); *roundford* 1661, *round foard* 17 (*v.* **ford**; a compound of uncertain meaning, but poss. with **hrung** 'a pole', indicating a ford marked by a pole or poles, cf. the common Stapleford (with OE *stapol* 'a post')); *Scabhome* 1635, 17 (*v.* **scabbe, holmr**; a water-meadow where livestock infections such as sheep-scab were prevalent); *Seuenacres* 1393 (*v.* **seofon, æcer**); *Sherpol* 1342 (*v.* **scearpol**); *Shipplands* 1656, *Sheeplands* 1661, 17 (*v.* **scēp, land**); *Shoueldale* 1348 (*v.* **scofl, dalr**); *Sinderland*(*s*) 1656, 17, *Synderland gapp* 1656 (*v.* **gap**) (*v.* **sundor-land**); *Smalehulles* 1321, *Smalhull'* 1348, *Smalehilles* 1393 (*v.* **smæl, hyll**); *Sotdoles* 1348 (*v.* **sōt, dāl**); *Spring leyes* 1635 (*v.* **spring**[1], **leys**); *Squires* ~ 1661, *Squiars hadland* 17 (*v.* **hēafod-land**; with the surn. *Squire*(*s*)); *Stony leyes* 1635, 1656, 1661, ~ *layes* 17, *Stoney Leys* 1704 (*v.* **stānig, leys**); *le styes* 1280 × 92, *lez Styes* 1417 (*v.* **stig**); *Stye wayes* 1656, 17, *Stywayes* 1661, *Styway* 1704, 1709, 1724, *middle stye wayes* 1656, *Midle Styways* 17, *neather* ~ 1635, *nether stywayes* 17, *uper stywayes* 17 (*v.* **sty-way**); *Swetynges* 1491, *Swetyngges* 1514 (a croft so called), *Swetttynges Croft* 1464 (*v.* **croft**) (either with the surn. *Sweeting*, from the OE masc. pers.n. *Swēting*, or with **swēte**, with **-ing**[2] or **eng**); *Taselhill* c.1306, 1393, *Tasilhulsty* c.1306, 1393 (*v.* **stīg**) (*v.* **tæsel, hyll**); *Taylliholm* 1319 (*v.* **tægl, holmr**); *Thackyrhil* 1273, *Thackerhul* 1280 × 92, *Thakkerhull* 1342, *Thakkerhill* 1395, *Thackerhill* 1635, 1656, 1661, 17, *Thatcher hill* 17 (*v.* **hyll**), *Thackeresike* c.1306, *Thackeresik'* 1354, *Thakkersike* 1393, *Thacher* ~ 1661, *Thatcher Sick* 1709 (*v.* **sík**), *Thackersikeouerende* 1280 × 92 (*v.* **uferra, ende**) (in both f.ns. the specific is the ME occupational surn. *Thacker* (*thakkere* 'a thatcher'), anglicized late to *Thatcher* (*thacchere* 'a thatcher'); *Toftis* 1273, *Tofftis* 1347, *Toftes* 1393, *Tauftes* 1635, *Toft*(*e*)*s* 1661, 1704, *Taufts* 17, *far tofts* 17 (*v.* **toft**); *the town pound peece* 17 (*v.* **tūn, pund, pece**); *Townsend* 1661 (*v.* **tūn, ende**); *Twobrokes* 1393, *Tobrokes feld* 1417 (*v.* **feld**; one of the early great open-fields) (*v.* **tū, brōc**); *Watermill hill* 1635, 1639, 1656, 1661 (*v.* (*The*) *Watermill, supra*); *le Wattrie* 1324, *Wattry* 1393 (*v.* **wæterig**); *watrey leyes* 1635, *Watery Leys* 1639, *Watry leyes* 1704 (*v.* **wæterig, leys**); *atte Welle* 1417 (p), 1418 (p) (*v.* **atte, wella**); *Wellespringhul* 1304, *Wolspringehill* 1395, *Wellesprynghill* 1417, (*the*) *welspring hill* 1635, 1661, *Wellspring hill* 1639, 1656, 1661, *Well Spring Hill* 1709 (*v.* **wella, spring**[1], **hyll** and Spring Well in f.ns. (a)); *the white ours headland* (sic) 17 (obscure, *v.* **hēafod-land**; no hostelry called The White Horse is recorded for Wigston Magna (but this name is found from the early 16th cent., *v.* Cox[1] 85), while a 'white house' here at this date seems unlikely); *witchgraue* 1635, 1656, *Witchgrave* 1661, 17, 1709, 1731 (*v.* **wice**; with **grāf** or **græf**); *Wolfil* c.1306, *Wolfhilmylne* 1393 (*v.* **myln**) (*v.* **wulf, hyll**); *Wrthegraue* c.1306, *Worthegraue* 1348, *Wortegrauehouerend'* 1347 (*v.* **uferra, ende**) (*v.* **worð, græf**); *Wronglandes* 1393 (*v.* **wrang, land**); *wyndmill furlong* 1635, *Windmill Forlong* 1656 (*v.* **furlang**), *windmill haggs* 17 (*v.* **hogg**) (*v.* The *Wyndmill, supra*); *wyer arme* 1656, *Wire Arm* 17 (*v.* **weyour, earm**; alluding to a branch or arm of a pool).

Wigston Parva

Wicgestane 1002 × 04 (11²) Bu 29 (S 1536), 1004 (11²) Bu 28 (S 906)
Wiggestane 1002 × 04 (11²) Bu 29 (S 1536)
Wicestan 1086 DB
Wigestan 1148 × 54 Reg, 1188 P (p) *et passim* to 1202 Ass (p)
Wiggestan 1196 ChancR (p), 1198 P (p)
Wiggestain 1195 (p), 1197 P (p), *Wichestain* 1202 Ass (p)
Wigeston 1200 Cur (p), 1202 Ass (p), *Wygeston* 1261 RGrav, 1310
  Pat (p) *et passim* to 1394 Banco
Wiggeston 1316 FA, 1536 *Ct et freq* to 1627 LML, *Wyggeston* 1327
  SR, 1392 Banco, 1399 Pat, 1445 Ipm
Wigston 1576 Saxton, 1610 Speed, *Little Wigston* 1610 Speed, 1627
  LML, 1807 Nichols, *Wigston Parva* 1843 *TA et freq*

Probably 'Wicg's stone', *v.* **stān**. An OE masc. pers.n. *Wicg* is
unrecorded, but it would be a side-form of the common OE masc. pers.n.
Wicga. Nichols records the late form *Wiggenston* (1445) which appears
to contain the possessive case (*Wicgan*) of *Wicga*, but this is most
probably erratic. A few early spellings with *-stain* indicate Scand
influence from *steinn* 'stone' on the generic *stān*. The southern boundary
of the parish is formed by Roman Watling Street and the village is some
half-mile from the Romano-British settlement of *Venonis* at High Cross.
Whether the stone which gave Wigston its name was already in situ at
the period of settlement or was placed later as a boundary marker is
unknown (perh. compare the nature of 'Guthlac's Stone' of Guthlaxton
Hundred *supra*). Ekwall DEPN suggests as an alternative interpretation
of the name that the specific may be rather OE **wigga** 'a beetle' (as in
ModE *earwig*) in a more original sense 'that which moves' (as retained
in ModE *wiggle*), hence denoting 'a wiggling stone, a logan-stone', as
perh. does Stanwick (reversed as **stān-wigga*) in Northants. If so, such
a rocking stone has not survived here. The late affixes of ~ *Parva* and
Little ~ distinguish the village from Wigston Magna in the same
Hundred.

Wigston Parva parish is today a small island of Guthlaxton Hundred territory within that of Sparkenhoe Hundred, separated from it by fields of Sparkenhoe's Sharnford parish to its east. That it should remain as part of the later Guthlaxton Hundred after the Sparkenhoe Hundred was carved out of the extensive old Guthlaxton Wapentake suggests its significant early relationship with the parishes to its immediate east. It may be that Wigston Parva parish, with those of Sharnford, Claybrooke, Ullesthorpe and Bittesby, formed that part of the *territorium* of *Venonis* which lay on Watling Street and later, perhaps, the *parochia* of an early Anglo-Saxon minster located at Claybrooke (Parva). For an extended discussion of these possibilities, *v.* Charles Phythian-Adams, *Continuity, Fields and Fission: the Making of a Midland Parish*, Leicester 1978. For *Venonis* 'the place of the tribe', *v.* A. L. F. Rivet and Colin Smith, *The Place-Names of Roman Britain* (1979), 491–2.

THE BUNGALOW. GREYHOUND INN (lost), *Greyhound Inn* 1843 *TA*, *Greyhound* 1863 *Deed*; earlier it was called *George and Dragon* 1790 *ib*. LODGE FM, *v.* **loge**. MANOR FM, *v.* **maner**. ST MARY'S CHURCH is *The Chapel* (dedicated to *the Assumption of Our Lady*) 1807 Nichols, *Chapel (St Mary)* 1846, 1863, 1877 White, *Chapel (St Mary the Virgin)* 1925 Kelly; earlier is recorded (*duas*) *capellas Wikinston et Wibetoft* 1220 MHW (with MLat *capella* 'a chapel'). SHADE COTTAGES, named from The Shade (*v.* **scadu**) in adjoining Sharnford parish, Sparkenhoe Hundred. SMOCKINGTON HOLLOW, 1807 Nichols, 1835 O, *v.* **holh**; Smockington lies in adjoining Hinckley parish in Sparkenhoe Hundred. WIGSTON HALL (local), *Wigston Parva Hall* 1843 *TA*, *Wigston Hall* 1846 White, 1925 Kelly, *The Hall* 1863, 1877 White, *v.* **hall**.

FIELD-NAMES

Forms presented in (a) are 1843 *TA*.

(a) Ash Hill (*v.* **æsc**); Aston Bank (*v.* **banke**; towards Aston Flamville parish which adjoins to the north-west); Barn Cl (*v.* **bern**); Bilson's Fd (cf. *William Bilson* 1843 *TA*); Brick-kiln Cl (*v.* **brike-kiln**); Calves Fd (*v.* **calf**); Carters Cl, ~ Mdw (with the surn. *Carter*, cf. *Samuel Carter* 1842 Census, *Henry Carter* 1849 ib, *Annie Carter* 1867 ib and *Samuel Carter* 1870 ib, all of adjoining Sharnford parish); Coney Hill (*v.* **coni**); Crab-tree Fd (*v.* **crabtre**); Little ~, Long ~, Cromwell (*v.* **cran, cron, wella**); East Cl; Ephraims Cl, ~ Mdw (either with the masc. pers.n. *Ephraim* or with a surn. taken from it; from Ephraim whose tribe once occupied the central mountainous district of Israel around Mount Ephraim (*v.* The Holy Bible, Joshua 17:15, 19:50 and 20: 7)); Far Cl; Four Acres, Four Acre Cromwell (*v.* **æcer** and

Cromwell *supra*); Gate Cl (a roadside field, *v.* **gata**); Godfrey's Fd (with the surn. *Godfrey*, cf. *John Godfrey* 1821 Census, *Emblin Godfrey* 1823 ib and *Jane Godfrey* 1842 ib, all of Sharnford parish; and later *Rosie Godfrey* 1861 ib, *George Godfrey* 1863 ib and *Julia Godfrey* 1865, all of Wigston Parva parish); Great Mdw; The Green (*v.* **grēne**²); Home Croft (*v.* **home, croft**); House Cl (prob. with reference to Wigston Hall *supra*); Intake (*v.* **inntak**); Kings Far ~, Kings Upper Fd (with the surn. *King*); Far ~ ~, Near Licetto Cl (sic) (an oddity; if this is not a fanciful spelling of the English surn. *Lycett*, then *Licetto* appears to be a surn. imported from Corsica); Little Mdw; Little Park (*v.* **park**); Long Leys (*v.* **leys**); Marl Cl (*v.* **marle**); Martin's Garden (*v.* **gardin**; with the surn. *Martin*, cf. *William Martin* 1807 Nichols of Wigston Parva parish and *Henry Martin* 1856 Census, *James Martin* 1861 ib and *Louisa Martin* 1864 ib of adjoining Sharnford parish; the land is described as meadow in the Tithe Apportionment); The Meadow; Middle Cl, ~ Fd; Nether Ground Fd, ~ ~ Mdw (*v.* **grund**); North Fd; Pinfold (*v.* **pynd-fald**); Plough Croft (*v.* **plōg, croft**); Far ~ ~, Saintfoin Fd (*v.* **sainfoin**; named from a fodder plant); Sharnford Cl (Sharnford parish adjoins to the east and north-east); Short Lane (*v.* **sc(e)ort**); South Fd; Spires Mdw (either with dial. *spire* 'reeds, rushes' or with the surn. *Spires*, cf. *Thomas Spiers* (sic) 1831 Census of adjoining Sharnford); Towns End Cl, ~ ~ Piece (*v.* **pece**) (*v.* **tūn, ende**); Walkers Cl, ~ Mdw (with the surn. *Walker*, cf. *John Walker* 1807 Nichols of Wigston Parva, *James Walker* 1822 Census, another *James Walker* 1861 ib and *Louise Walker* 1864 ib, all of Sharnford parish); Well Lane Cl (*v.* **wella**); Far ~, Middle ~, Near Whitmore (*v.* **hwīt, mōr**¹; in eModE, *white* was used of dry, infertile land); Wigston Fd; Wigston Hill.

Willoughby Waterleys

Wilebi 1086 DB, 1183, 1185 P (p), 1197 × 1207 Dugd, 1208 P (p), 1230 ChancR, *Willebi* 1190 × 1204 France, *Wilubi* c.1130 LeicSurv, *Wiluby* 1253 GildR (p), *Wileby* 1205 RotNorm, 1280 Banco, *Wyleby* 1212 FF, 1260 Cur *et passim* to 1295, 1296 *ShR*, *Wyluby* 1248 RGros *et passim* to 1306 *LCDeeds* (p), 1329 Ipm
Wileweby 1243 GildR (p), 1338 Pat, *Wyleweby* 1301 Ipm
Wyl(l)ughby 1278 Banco, 1304 Ipm (p) *et passim* to 1352, 1359 Pat, 1411 Banco, *Wylugby* 1305 *LCDeeds* (p), 1315 GildR (p), 1317 *LCDeeds* (p), *Wilughby* 1305, 1341 Banco, 1346 Pat, 1390 Banco
Wilouby 1345 *LCDeeds* (p), *Wilougby* 1352 *ib* (p)
Wylloby 1448 *RTemple*, 1477 (e.16) *Charyte*, *Willoby* 1518 Visit, 1526 AAS
Willoughby(e) 1507 Ipm, 1510 Visit, 1535 VE *et freq*

Affixes are added as:
~ *Waterles* 1420 Fine, 1430 Pat *et passim* to 1579 LEpis, ~ *Waterlesse* 1518 Visit, 1539 MinAccts, ~ *Waterlies* 1535 VE, 1623 LeicW, ~ *Waterleys* 1559 Pat, 1610 LeicW, 1925 Kelly, ~ *Waterleas* 1628, 1629 LML, ~ *Waterless* 1807 Nichols

'The farmstead or village at the willows', *v.* **wilig**, **bȳ**. Ekwall DEPN notes the common occurrence of this hybrid place-name and suggests that in most cases it is a Scandinavianized form of OE **wiligtūn* 'farmstead or village where willows grow', *v.* **wilig**, **tūn**. Some of the names of this type may conceal an OE **wiliga-bēag* 'a circle of willow-trees', *v.* **wilig**, **bēag**.

As its name indicates, Willoughby is a well-watered parish. The settlement lies on gravel and clay between two arms of Whetstone Brook and has numerous large pools in its immediate vicinity. *Waterless* is a corrupted version of *Waterleys*, the ending *-leys* being from **lǣs** 'meadow land', *v.* **wæter**. Willoughby may have been afforded this affix to distinguish it from Willoughby on the Wolds just beyond the Nottinghamshire boundary to the north.

BROADVIEW. CHURCH FM, *v*. St Mary's Church *infra*. COSBY LANE, Cosby lying 2 miles to the north-west. FLUDE LODGE, 1835 O, 1846 White; cf. *Daniel Flude, landowner* 1846 ib. The Flude family of adjacent Arnesby is recorded from *John Flude* 1805 Census to *Ephraim Flude* 1842 ib. GENERAL ELLIOTT (P.H.), *General Elliott* 1846, 1863, 1877 White, 1925 Kelly; named from the defending officer of Gibraltar against the Spanish 1779–81. GILMORTON LANE, Gilmorton lying 3 miles to the south. GRANGE FM, *v*. **grange**. HILL FM. THE LIMES, a house dated 1702 and thus poss. providing an allusion to early local flora; note *Lynbe land* in f.ns. (b). LODGE FM, *v*. **loge**. MAIN ST is *the Town Streete* 1708 *Terrier*, *v*. **tūn, strēt**. MANOR FM, cf. *Manor House* 1877 White, 1925 Kelly, *v*. **maner**. MERE RD, cf. *Meare Closse* 1674 *Terrier, Mear* ~ 1829 *Surv, Mere Close* 1846 *TA*, *v*. **(ge)mǣre**; an ancient ridgeway, the road forms the entire eastern parish boundary. METHODIST CHURCH. NENE HOUSE FM, 1925 Kelly. NICHOLLS FM, *Nichols farm* 1925 Kelly; with the surn. *Nicholls*, cf. *John Nicholls* 1820 Census, *James Nichols* 1862 ib of adjacent Whetstone parish. OLD HALL is *The Hall* 1925 Kelly, *v*. **hall**. THE RECTORY, 1877 White, 1925 Kelly, *v*. **rectory**; earlier is *The Parsonage House* 1700, 1703, 1821 *Terrier*, *v*. **personage**. RETREAT FM. ST MARY'S CHURCH, *Church (St Mary)* 1846, 1863, 1877 White, 1925 Kelly; it is earlier recorded as *ecclesie de Wleweb'* 1220 MHW, *ecclesiam de Wyluby* 1248 RGros, *ecclesie de Wylughby* 1352 *Pat*. Note also *the Church Yard* 1821 *Terrier*, *v*. **churchyerd**. THISTLE HALL is a disparaging name for a site just to the east of Main St, *v*. **þistel**. No early forms, but this may once have been a name with **halh** in its sense 'a water meadow', since a large mere lies 400 yards to its east; cf. Straw Hall in Peatling Magna *supra*. WEST END FM, *v*. **ende**. WILLOUGHBY LODGE FM (HUNT'S LODGE 2½"), *Willoughby Lodge* 1835 O, *v*. **loge**; cf. *Elizabeth Hunt, farmer* 1846 White, *William Hunt, farmer* 1863 ib; also *Thomas Hunt* 1854 Census and *Edwin Hunt* 1856 ib, all of Willoughby parish.

FIELD-NAMES

In (a), forms dated 1751, 1764, 1770, 1774, 1778, 1784, 1788, 1790, 1793, 1795, 1800[1], 1802, 1807, 1809, 1816, 1835 and 1848 are *Deed*; those dated 1800[2] are *Map*; 1829 and 1968 are *Surv*; 1846 are *TA*. Forms throughout dated 1555 are Ipm; those dated 1658, 1670, 1699, 1704, 1706, 1710, 1711, 1712, 1720, 1721, 1724, 1729, 1732, 1733, 1734, 1735, 1738, 1739, 1742, 1745 and 1748 are *Deed*; 1674, 1703 and 1708 are *Terrier*.

(a) The Two Acres 1846, (The) Four ~ 1829, 1846, (The) Five ~ 1829, 1846, 1968, Six Acres 1829, 1846, Six Acre Mdw 1829, (The) Seven Acres 1846, Nine ~ 1846, Ten ~ 1829, Eleven ~ 1829, Nineteen Acres 1770, 1829, Bottom ~ ~, Top Nineteen Acres 1829 (v. **æcer**); Aldermans Long Cl, Aldermans Mdw 1846 (with the surn. *Alderman*); Bottom ~, Top Allotments, Pratt's Allotments (with the surn. *Pratt*) 1968 (v. **allotment**); Ashby Brook Mdw 1790, Far ~ ~ ~, Near Ashby Brook Furlong 1829 (v. **furlang**) (v. **brōc**; alluding to a principal stream flowing from Ashby Magna parish which adjoins to the south-west); Middle ~, Top 'Arton 1968 (with the p.n. *Harton* which occurs earlier in Countesthorpe and Whetstone parishes, v. **tūn**; either with **hær** or with **hār**[2]); First ~, Second Bandings 1829, Far ~, Banglings 1968 (v. **bān**, **-ing**[1], **-ling**; poss. the site of a pagan Anglo-Saxon inhumation cemetery; a specific **bēan** seems less likely); Far ~, Near Bandylands 1846 (v. **bēan**, **land**); Barn Cls 1751, (The) Barn Cl 1835, 1846, 1968, Far ~ ~, Near Barn Cl 1829, 1846, Middle Barn Cl 1829, Barn Mdw 1968 (v. **bern**); Bell Cl 1784 (v. **belle**; alluding to endowed land, either for the provision and maintenance of church bells or for the payment of bell-ringers); Benskin's Mdw 1829 (with the surn. *Benskin*); Big Mdw 1829; Biggin Cl 1816 (1735, *Biggings* 1734, *Biggans* ~ 1711, *Bigging Close* 1733, *Vann's Biggin Close* 1711 (with the surn. *Vann*, v. Vann's Cl *infra*), Willey's Biggin 1816 (*Willeys Biggin* 1699, 1734; with the surn. *Willey*, cf. *Sophia Willey* 1816 Census and *Mary Willey* 1829 ib of Willoughby parish) (v. **bigging**); Birdie's Cl 1968 (with a local popular form of the surn. *Burdett*, v. Top Burdetts *infra*); Bottom ~ ~, Great ~ ~, Top Blakesley's Cl 1829, Blakesley's Barn Cl 1829 (v. **bern**), Blakesley's Mdw 1829, 1846 (with the surn. *Blakesley* of a family originally from the township of this name, 28 miles to the south in Northants.); The Bog 1968 (v. **bog**); Bottom Cl 1829, 1846, ~ Fd 1968, ~ Mdw 1846 (v. **bottom**); Breach Cl 1764 (v. **brēc**); Brick Kiln Cl 1829, Top ~ ~ ~, Brick-Kiln Cl 1846, Top Brittle 1968 (v. **brike-kiln**); Brier's Cl 1800[2], 1846 (*Bryer's Close* 1710), Briar's ~ 1800[1], Brier's Mdw 1835, 1846 (with the surn. *Briers*, cf. *John Briers* 1866 Census and *Thomas Briers* 1869 ib of adjoining Whetstone parish); Bridge Cl 1846, 1968, Brig ~ 1829, Bridge Mdw 1846, Great ~ ~, Little Bridge Mdw 1800[1], 1800[2], 1835 (1710) (v. **brycg**); Brook Mdw 1846 (v. **brōc**); The First ~, The Top Browns 1968, Big ~ ~ ~, Little ~ ~ ~, Top Brown's Hill Cl 1829, Bottom ~, Top Brownsill 1968 (v. **hyll**; with the surn. *Brown*); Top Burdetts 1968 (with the surn. *Burdett* in the possessive case, cf. *William Burdett* 1834 Census, another *William Burdett* 1851 ib and *Richard Burdett* 1859 ib, all of Willoughby; *Hugo Burdet* 1086 DB was a major landholder in Leics.); The Burning Cl 1968 (an enclosure for the regular burning of agricultural waste); Bushey Cl 1770, Bushey or Bushby Cl 1968 (v. **busshi**); Calliborough Cls 1788 (1729, 1739), Calliborough Cl 1848 (1738, 1739) (*Calliborough* 1729, v. **calu**, **berg**); Calverslade 1790, 1793 (v. **calf** (**calfra** gen.pl.), **slæd**); Cemetery Fd 1968 (land adjacent to a burial ground); Bottom ~ ~, Top Church Leys (v. **leys** and St Mary's Church *supra*); Copleys 1790 (either the surn. *Copley* in the possessive case, or **copp** with **leys** or an earlier **lǣs**); Corn Cl 1770 (v. **corn**[1]); The First ~, The Second Corporation 1968 (land owned by the Local Authority); Cottyers, Thythorne Cottyers Pastures 1793 (v. **pasture** and Thythorne Cl *infra*) (v. **cottere**); Cow Cl 1968 (v. **cū**); The Crabtree 1968 (v. **crabtre**); Crisp's Mdw 1829 (with the surn. *Crisp*); Croft 1829, Croft Leys 1793 (v. **leys**) (v. **croft**); Cross Leys 1829 (v. **cross**, **leys**); The Dale 1784, 1846, The Dales 1751, Great Dale 1829, Little Dale 1784, 1829, Dale Cl 1784, 1788, 1829 (1732, 1739), Dale End 1795 (v. **ende**), Dale Mdws 1751, 1793, ~ Mdw 1829, 1835 (v.

dalr); Exon's ~ 1829, Hexton's Cl, ~ Big Cl 1846, The Exons 1968 (with the surn. *Exton* of a family originally from the township of this name, 24 miles to the north-east in Rutland; note *Robertus de Exton* 1327 SR of Leics.); Far Cl 1829, 1846, ~ Mdw 1829, 1846, 1968, Top Far Leys 1829, Far Leys 1846 (*v.* **leys**) (*v.* **feor**); First Cl 1829, 1846, ~ Mdw 1846; Bottom ~ ~, Fish Pit 1968 (*v.* **fisc, pytt**); Flat Mdw 1829, 1968 (*v.* **flatr, flat**); Far ~, Near Flatman's, The Flatman's Fd 1968 (with the surn. *Flatman*, signifying a dweller on level ground; from ON *flat*); Floating Mdw 1968 (a meadow through which river water was diverted in channels; usually flooded twice a year, in winter to ensure an early bite for livestock and in late spring to produce a good crop of hay); The Ford 1968 (*v.* **ford**; land beside a river crossing); Fourth Cl 1829; Frett's ~ 1770, 1968, Fred's Cl (sic) 1846 (with the surn. *Frett*, metonymic for ME *fretter* 'a maker of jewelled interlace work'); The Front Fd 1968; Furlongs 1846, Fullongs 1968 (*v.* **furlang**); Lower Garden Cl 1829 (*v.* **gardin**); Far ~ ~, Near Gibwhite Hill 1846 (*v.* *Gib white* in Whetstone f.ns. (b) *supra*); Gorsey Cl 1829, 1846, Little Gorsey Cl 1846 (*v.* **gorstig**); The Glebe, Glebe Fd 1968 (*v.* **glebe**); Gravel Hole Cls 1829, The Gravel Hole Fd or Bent's 1968 (with the surn. *Bent*), Gravel Pit Cl 1829, Gravelpit 1846 (*v.* **gravel**); Great Cl 1790, 1846, ~ Mdw 1751, 1790, 1846; Hall Leys 1829 (this may belong with *halley tafts* in Whetstone f.ns. (b); otherwise, *v.* **hall, leys**); Hangman's Mdw 1829 (presum. the site of a gallows); Happyland 1968; Hempit Cl 1800[1], 1835, ~ Mdw 1835, North ~ ~, South Empty Cl, Empty Mdw 1829 (*Hempitt Close, ~ Meadow* 1710, *v.* **hænep, pytt**); Hemp Hill Cl, ~ ~ Mdw 1800[2] (*v.* **hænep**); Higgs Cl, ~ Mdw 1829, 1846 (with the surn. *Higgs*); High Cl 1793 (*v.* **hēah**[1]); Hill Cl; Home Cl 1770, 1790, 1829, 1846, 1968, Bottom ~ ~, Top Home Cl 1829, 1846, First ~ ~, Second Home Cl 1829 (*The Home Closse* 1674, ~ ~ *Close* 1703, 1708, 1710), The Home Fd 1968, Home Leys 1829, 1846 (*v.* **leys**) (*v.* **home**); Hut Cl 1846 (*v.* **hut**); The House Cl 1968; Iliff's Cl 1751 (with the surn. *Iliffe*, cf. *Ann Iliffe* 1814 Census of adjoining Whetstone parish); Lane End Cl 1829 (*v.* **lane-ende**); Far Lawrence's Cl 1829 (with the surn. *Lawrence*); The Leys 1846 (*v.* **leys**); Little Cl 1829, 1846; Far ~ ~, Near Little Fd 1846, Little Field Cl 1968; (the) Little Mdw 1751, 1790, 1829, 1846, 1968; Lodge Fd 1968 (*v.* Willoughby Lodge *supra*); Long Bit 1846 (*v.* **bit**); Top ~ ~, Long Cl 1829; The Long Fd 1968; Long Mdw 1770; Long Slang 1968 (*v.* **slang**); Lower Cl 1829; Lowes Mdw 1968 (with the surn. *Lowe*, cf. *Sarah Lowe* 1833 Census, *Mary Ann Lowe* 1845 ib, *Helen Lowe* 1859 ib and *William Lowe* 1862 ib, all of adjoining Peatling Magna parish and *Mary Lowe* 1850 ib of adjoining Whetstone); Lutterworth Way Furlong 1790 (*v.* **furlang**); Lutterworth lies 5 miles to the south-west); The Meadow 1829, 1846, Meadow Cl 1770; Middle Cl 1751, 1826, 1846 (*Middle Closse* 1674, *the Middle Close* 1703, 1708); Neal's Fd 1968 (with the surn. *Neal*); Near Mdw 1829 (*v.* **nēah**); Nether Cl formerly known as Iliff's Cl 1751 (*v.* Iliff's Cl *supra*); Newton's Paddock 1826 (*v.* **paddock**; with the surn. *Newton*); Nicholl's Bottom ~, Nicholl's Top Cl 1829 (*v.* Nicholls Fm *supra*); North Holme 1774, 1788, 1848 (1748, *v.* **norð, holmr**); Oak Tree Mdw 1829, 1846 (*v.* **āc, trēow**); Old Barn Cl 1846 (*v.* **bern**); Old Cl 1829, 1846, Odd Cl (sic) 1968 (*v.* **ald**); Old Plough Cl 1846 (*v.* **plōg**); Orchard Cl 1846 (*Orchard Closes* 1719, *v.* **orceard**); Page's Upper Cl 1751 (with the surn. *Page*, cf. *Sophia Page* 1818 Census, *Matilda Page* 1836 ib and *William Page* 1841 ib, the family recorded in Willoughby parish until *Frederick Page* 1858 ib); The Parks 1829 (*v.* **park**); Parlour Cl 1829, The Parlour 1846, 1968 (*v.* **parlur**); Parnell's Mdw 1800[1], 1800[2], 1835 (1710; with the surn. *Parnell*); Pear Tree Lane Mdw 1829 (*v.*

pertre); Peatling Cl 1829, 1968, ~ Mdw 1829, 1846, Bottom ~ ~ ~, Top Peatling
Lane Cl 1829 (Peatling Magna parish adjoins to the east); Permin's Brook Cl 1846
(*v.* **brōc**; with the surn. *Permin*); Bottom ~ ~, Top ~ ~, Perry's Cl 1829 (with the
surn. *Perry*; perh. cf. *Mary Parry* 1811 Census and *James Parry* 1816 ib of adjoining
Peatling Magna); The Pig Fd 1968 (*v.* **pigga**); Bottom ~ ~, Top Pit Cl 1829, Pit Cl
1846, Pit Fd 1968 (*v.* **pytt**); Far ~ ~, Near ~ ~, Ploughed Cl, Bottom ~ ~ ~, Old
Ploughed Cl 1829; Pond Fd 1968 (*v.* **ponde**); Poor's Mdw 1829 (*v.* **pouer(e)**; land
dedicated to poor-law relief or charity); Railway Mdw 1968 (beside a railway line,
now dismantled); Rath Hades 1968 (*v.* **hēafod**; perh. with **wraðu**, cf. *Long Rathes*
in nearby Countesthorpe f.ns. (b)); The Road Fd 1968 (a roadside close); The Rough
Cl 1968 (*v.* **rūh**); Second Cl 1829; Seed Cl 1829 (*v.* **sǣd**; alluding to grass sown for
one year's mowing or grazing as distinguished from permanent pasture); Sheep Cl
1793, 1835, Sheep or High Cl 1793 (*v.* **scēp**); The Slang (*v.* **slang**); Spinney Cl 1829,
The Spinney Mdw 1968 (*v.* **spinney**); Spring Mdw 1829, 1846, 1968 (*v.* **spring**[1]);
Square Cl 1829 (*v.* **squar(e)**); Stack Mdw 1829, ~ Cl 1846 (*v.* **stakkr**); Stackyard Cl
1968 (*v.* **stackyard**); Stonebridge Mdw 1764, 1802, 1846, 1968, Stone Brig Mdw
1829 (*v.* **stān, brycg**); Taylor's ~ 1800[1], 1800[2], 1968, Tayler's Mdw 1835 (*Tayler's
Meadow* 1710; with the surn. *Taylor*, cf. *Ann Taylor* 1749 MI and *William Taylor*
1751 ib of Willoughby parish); Third Cl 1829; Thornton's Cl 1846, Thornton Spring
Cl 1829 (*v.* **spring**[1]) (with the surn. *Thornton*, cf. *Betsey Thornton* 1835 Census,
Eliza Thornton 1840 ib, *Saloma Thornton* 1842 ib, the family continuing in
Willoughby to *George Thornton* 1868 ib; poss. a family originally from Thornton,
12 miles to the north-west); Three Cornered Cl 1829, ~ ~ Fd 1968 (*v.* **three-
cornered**); Neather Thyhorn 1751, Nether Thyhorne ~ 1790, Nether Thythorne Cl
1793, Thythorns Cl 1799, Far Lower ~, Far Upper Thyorne, Near Lower ~, Near
Upper Thyorne 1829 (*Thyhorne* 1658, 1704, *Thythorne* 1706, *Thyhorn* 1721,
Thyhorne Close 1670, 1710, 1712, *v.* **þorn**; perh. with **þicce**[2], as in what appears to
be the parallel name Tythorn (Hill) in Wigston Magna *supra* for which 14th-cent.
forms survive); Thyon Mdws, Nether ~, Over Thyon, Nether ~ ~, Over Thyon Mdw
(*v.* **uferra**) 1770, Bottom ~, Top Thyine 1846, Bottom ~, Top Thynes 1968 (*v.*
þyrne; these forms are taken to be distinct in origin from the previous group,
although apparently attracted to them); Far ~ ~, Near ~ ~, Top Cl 1846, Top Fd 1968
(*v.* **top**); Townsend Cl 1778, 1802, 1809, Bottom Townsend Cl or Bell Cl (*v.* Bell Cl
supra), Top Townsend Cl 1784, 1816, Townsend Bottom ~, Townsend Top Cl, First
~ ~, Second Townsend Cl 1829, Far ~ ~ ~, Near Town's End Cl 1846 (*v.* **tūn, ende**);
The Trespass 1968 (*v.* **trespas** 'encroachment', cf. *Trespasesike*, Ru 256); Upper Cl
1829 (*the Upper Close* 1703, 1708); Vann's Cl 1778, 1816 (1724; with the surn.
Vann, cf. *Thomas Vann* 1822 Census, *Hannah Vann* 1851 ib, the family continuing
in adjoining Whetstone parish to *Rebecca Vann* 1881 ib; note *Vann's Biggin Close*
1711 *supra*); Ward's Cl, ~ Mdw 1829, 1846 (with the surn. *Ward*, cf. *Elizabeth Ward*
1810 Census of adjoining Peatling Parva); Washbrook Cl 1829 (*v.* **brōc**; with **wæsce**
or **wæsse**, the former more likely); Water Furrows 1829, 1846 (*v.* **wæter, furh** and
Water furrowes in Ashby Parva f.ns. (b) *supra*); Whinney ~ 1774, 1848, Winney
Doles 1788 (*v.* **whinney, dāl**); Willey's Home Cl, ~ Top Cl, ~ Mdw 1846 (*v.*
Willey's Biggin *supra*); Willoughby Cl 1829, 1846, First ~, Second Willoughby
Mdw 1846, Willoughbies, Willoughby Mdw 1968; Bottom ~, Top Willows 1968 (*v.*
wilig).

(b) *Gore's Close otherwise Biggings* 1734 (*v.* Biggin Cl *supra*; either with the surn. *Gore* or with **gāra**); *Lynbe land* 1555 (*v.* **land**; this may be with a surn. *Linby* from the Notts. township of this name (*v.* Nt 122), but such a surn. is unrecorded; otherwise 'the farmstead at the lime-tree(s)', *v.* **lind**, **bȳ** and note The Limes *supra*); *Pudwell Close* 1720, 1742, 1745 (*v.* **wella**; with the OE masc. pers.n. *Puda*).

THE ELEMENTS, OTHER THAN PERSONAL NAMES, IN GUTHLAXTON HUNDRED'S PLACE-NAMES, FIELD-NAMES AND STREAM-NAMES.

This list includes the elements in uncompounded and compounded place-names, field-names and stream-names. The names quoted in each entry are arranged in alphabetical order, with no distinction between uncompounded and compounded names. Names which survive on modern maps and also lost major names are listed first, followed by a summary of use of the elements in field-names and stream-names. Although a concise translation of each element is provided, for fuller discussion of its significance and use, reference should be made to *English Place-Name Elements* (EPNS, vols. 25 and 26, amended in JEPNS 1), *The Vocabulary of English Place-Names* (EPNS, in progress), M. Gelling, *Place-Names in the Landscape*, 1984 and M. Gelling and A. Cole, *The Landscape of Place-Names*, 2000.

The elements are often given in an OE, ON, OFr or ME form, but it should be remembered that many of these elements continued as common nouns in the English language and that many of the names of Leicestershire's Guthlaxton Hundred are of more recent origin than the periods represented by the lexical head-forms used. Many terms are included which are not listed in the above-mentioned volumes, but it has not been felt necessary to distinguish these. Those elements marked * are not independently recorded in the head-forms cited or are hypothetical reconstructions from the place-name evidence.

A field-name which is common to a series of townships is sometimes quoted in a form which may have alternative spellings in those townships and which may appear for an individual township in either list (a) or list (b), depending on date. Where this occurs, the particular list in which the field-name features is not specified.

abbey ME, 'an abbey'. *Abbethirne* (f.n. Kilby).

above eModE, prep., 'above, over'. *Aboueriggewey* (f.n. Bitteswell), *above the gaytes* (f.n. Littlethorpe).

āc OE, 'an oak-tree'. Kibbled Oaks, Oak Spinney, ?Sharrag Grounds. Oak Cl (f.n. Ashby Parva), Oak Tree (f.n. Misterton), Oak Tree Cl (f.n. Broughton Astley, Dunton Bassett), Oak Tree Ground, the Old Ark (f.ns. Bitteswell), The Oak Yard (f.n. Bruntingthorpe), *okeyard* (f.n. Peatling Parva).

ald OE (Angl), adj., 'old, long-used; disused'. Common in f.ns., esp. describing land units, e.g. Old Cl (Foston), Old Furlong (Misterton), Old Home Cl (Broughton Astley), Old Slade (Lutterworth); or with structures, e.g. Old Bridge Cl, *Ould Mill Hill* (Countesthorpe), *le oldemilneholme, the old pen* (Kimcote), *Old Milfeild* (Gilmorton).

allotment ModE, 'a portion of land assigned to a particular individual', esp. in f.ns. recording the redistribution of land at Enclosure; and later, 'a small portion of land let out to an individual (e.g. by a town council) for cultivation'. The Allotment (Dunton Bassett), Allotment Fd, Garden Allotments (Broughton Astley), Allotment Fd (Cosby), Allotment Ground (Foston), (The) Allotments (Bitteswell, Swinford), Back Allotment, Crooked Tree Allotment (Arnesby), Old Allotments (Westrill and Starmore), Poor Allotments (Peatling Parva), Top Allotments (Peatling Magna, Willoughby Waterleys).

almes ME, 'charitable relief of the poor, charity'; applied esp. to the material substance of the relief. Alms Cl (f.n. Ullesthorpe).

almes-hous ME, 'an almshouse, a house founded by a private charity for the reception and support of the aged poor'. The Almshouses.

alor OE, 'an alder-tree'. *Pifflin Olders* (f.n. Misterton).

amer OE, a bird, prob. 'a bunting'. ?Amberdale Spinney. *Amerlandes* (f.n. Shearsby).

ān OE, adj., 'lonely'. ?Anpits (f.n. Peatling Parva).

ancre ME, 'a hermit, a recluse'. ?Anchor Cl (f.n. Wigston Magna).

anstig OE, 'a steep path'. *Anstye way* (f.n. Frolesworth).

āte OE, 'oats'. Oat Fd (f.n. Ashby Parva), *the oat landes* (f.n. North Kilworth), Oat Mdw (f.n. Bittesby), Top Oat Ground (f.n. Cotesbach).

atte, atten ME, prep. with masc. or neut. def.art., 'at the'. Common in f.ns. and often used for ME toponymic surns. Examples in f.ns. are *atte Forth'* (Aylestone), *hattedamishinde* (Misterton), *?Nygunholmes* (< *atten innome*) (Blaby); toponymic surns. include *atte Barr* (Bitteswell), *atte Grene* (Kimcote), *atte Welle* (Knaptoft).

aunter ME, 'a venture, an enterprise'. The Anterfield (f.n. Shawell).

æcer OE, 'a plot of cultivated land; an acre, a specified measure of ploughland'; originally the unit of land which a yolk of oxen could plough in a day. The OE el. is generally indistinguishable from ON **akr** 'a plot of arable land'. Six Acres, Two Acre Spinney. Very freq. in f.ns.: as a simplex, e.g. *les Acres* (Cosby); with a numeral indicating size, e.g. Two acre (Ashby Parva), Four Acre, The Ten Acre Mdw (Arnesby), *twelue acres* (Cotesbach), Twelve Acre Wood (Bitteswell); with a surn., e.g. *Butchers acre* (Blaby), Collins Acre (Leire); with reference to livestock, e.g. *Cowakars* (Ashby Magna), *Gooseacre* (North Kilworth), *goose acres* (Kilby); to the nature of the soil, e.g. Clay Acres (Blaby), Dunsacre (South

Kilworth), *the rowe acres* (Catthorpe); to location, e.g. Ball Acre (North Kilworth), *Breake acre* (Aylestone), Dale Acre (Countesthorpe). Recurring is *thorough acres* (Cotesbach, Misterton).

æmette OE, 'an ant'. Ant Bank (f.n. Arnesby), Ant Banks (f.n. Misterton), Ant Hills (f.n. Ashby Parva).

æppel-trēow OE, 'an apple-tree'. *Apiltrefurlong* (f.n. Bitteswell), *Applebystub furlong* (sic) (f.n. Aylestone).

æsc OE, 'an ash-tree'. Ashby Magna, Ashby Parva; Ashclose Spinney, Ashfield, Ash Pole Spinney, Ash Spinney. Freq. in f.ns.: identifying individual closes, e.g. *Ashe close* (Knaptoft); roads, e.g. Ashgates (Arnesby, Shearsby); springs and streams, e.g. Ashbrook (Swinford), Ashwell (Ashby Parva, North Kilworth). Distribution of ash-trees in f.ns. in the Hundred is principally marked in its eastern parishes.

back ModE, adj., 'lying behind, hindmost'. Back Lane (Leire, Shearsby), Back St. Common in f.ns.: e.g. Back Allotment (Arnesby), Back Cl (Bitteswell, Catthorpe, Dunton Bassett, Glen Parva), Back Croft (Cotesbach), Back Fd (Peatling Magna, Shearsby), Back Garden Cl (Claybrooke Parva), Back Lane (Cosby, Lutterworth).

*badde ME, adj., 'bad, worthless'. ?*badfordale* (f.n. Oadby).

*bagger ME, 'a badger'. Badger Hole Fd (f.n. Westrill and Starmore).

baillie ME, 'a bailiff'. ?*Baily Pieces* (f.n. Wigston Magna).

bak-side ME, 'property behind a dwelling; the back, the rear'. Back Side. *backeside whorne* (f.n. North Kilworth).

balca OE, 'a ridge, a bank; a ridge of ploughed land that marked the boundary between adjacent strips of a common field'. Baulk Lane. Common in f.ns.: compounded with the title of a township functionary, e.g. *Constables balk* (Bruntingthorpe, Leire), *the neatheards Baulk* (Bruntingthorpe), *the Punders balke* (Whetstone); esp. with reference to location, e.g. *Eluerdale balke, Fen balke* (North Kilworth), *Swallowgore bauke* (Claybrooke Parva), *the Sydling bauck* (Lutterworth).

*ball OE (Angl), 'a ball'; topographically, 'a rounded hill; a mound of earth set up as a boundary marker'. Ball Acre (f.n. North Kilworth), *the Ball Cross* (f.n. Oadby), Balldike Cl (f.n. Wigston Magna), Ballong Corner (f.n. South Kilworth).

balled ME, adj., 'bald'; topographically, 'bare, lacking in vegetation'. *Bald Banke* (f.n. Kimcote).

balne ME, 'a bath', perh. also 'a place for bathing'. Balney way (f.n. Kimcote).

bān OE, 'a bone'. Little Bones. Bandings (f.n. Willoughby Waterleys), ?*Banlouwe* (f.n. Kimcote), ?*Bannefurlong* (f.n. Oadby), ?Bonn (f.n. Misterton).

baner OFr, ME, 'a banner, a flag'; perh. applied topographically to some more permanent boundary marker. ?*Bannefurlong* (f.n. Oadby).

banke ODan, 'a bank, a slope of a hill or ridge'. Laurel Bank. Freq. in f.ns.: as a simplex, e.g. The Banks (Catthorpe, Claybrooke Magna), (The) Banks (Broughton Astley, Cosby, Swinford); with an indication of place, e.g. Aston Bank (Wigston Parva), Mill Bank (Peatling Magna), New Pool Bank (Oadby), *the pinfold banke* (Shearsby); the nature of the bank may be described, e.g. *Bald Banke* (Kimcote), *Dough bank* (Whetstone), Greenbank (Swinford), *Red Bank* (Aylestone). Recurring are Ant Bank(s) (Arnesby, Misterton), Banky Cl (Countesthorpe, North Kilworth, Shearsby) and Banky Mdw (Cotesbach, Shearsby, Swinford).

banking ModE, 'an embankment'. Banking Mdws (f.n. Westrill and Starmore).

bark-milne ME, 'a tannery'. *the bark milne holme* (f.n. Blaby).

barlicorn ME, 'barley', and its grain. *le Barlycornes* (f.n. South Kilworth).

barn-yard ModE, 'a farm yard'. Hulses Barn Yard (f.n. Broughton Astley).

barre OFr, ME, 'a bar, a barrier'. *atte Barr* (p) (Bitteswell).

barro- Brit, 'a top, a summit, a hill'. Barom Hill (f.n. Gilmorton).

bastard OFr, adj., sb., '(a) bastard'; toponymically, used of fields of abnormal shape or poor yield and occasionally of selions of former great fields not completely swarded over. *Bastard Lees* (f.n. Bruntingthorpe), *bastard ley* (f.n. Wigston Magna).

bataille OFr, **batail** ME, 'a battle'; also 'a juridical battle'. Battle Flat (f.n. Frolesworth).

bæc-hūs OE, 'a bakehouse'. *Bakehouse lane* (Lutterworth).

bær[1] OE, adj., 'bare, without vegetation'. *barearsse furlong* (f.n. Claybrooke Parva), *bare fulon slade* (f.n. Misterton), Bare Leys (f.n. Whetstone), Barslade (f.n. South Kilworth).

bærlic OE, **barlich** ME, 'barley'. *Barley Close* (f.n. Westrill and Starmore), *barly crofte* (f.n. Shangton), Barley Hill (f.n. Peatling Magna), Barley Home (f.n. Leire), Barley Mdw (f.n. Bittesby), *Barlyhull* (f.n. Catthorpe, Kilby).

bæð OE, 'a bath, a bathing place; a pool, a pond'. Bath Cl (f.n. Cotesbach), Bath Mdw (f.n. Claybrooke Parva, Shearsby).

bēag OE, 'a ring, a circle'; prob. in a topographical sense 'the circular bend of a stream', or in allusion to things of ring-like form. ?Willoughby Waterleys. ?*Bewcroft* (f.n. Littlethorpe).

bēan OE, 'a bean'. Freq. in f.ns.: in the compound *bean-lands* (with various spellings in Ashby Parva, Bitteswell, Cosby, Kimcote, Misterton, South Kilworth, Sutton in the Elms, Willoughby Waterleys), *Banebut*, Bean Fd (Bitteswell), *Banforlongslade* (Misterton), Ban Leys (Lutterworth), *Banlouwe* (Kimcote), ?*Bannefurlong* (f.n. Oadby), Bean Hill (Shearsby).

bece[1], **bæce** OE, 'a stream, a stream valley'. Cotesbach. ?*Kerbidge* (f.n. Arnesby).

bece[2] OE, 'a beech-tree'. *Biches* (f.n. Whetstone).

bedd OE, 'a bed, a plot of land for growing plants'. *Leeke bedys* (f.n. Littlethorpe), *Leekbed haggs* (f.n. Whetstone), Osier Bed (f.n. Blaby, Claybrooke Magna, Littlethorpe, North Kilworth), Willowbeds (f.n. Gilmorton), *Wythy beddes* (f.n. Broughton Astley, Cosby, Leire, Westrill and Starmore).

bede-hūs OE, 'a prayer-house, a chapel, an oratory'; in ME, sometimes used of an almshouse. *beadehouse* (Kimcote).

begen OE, adj., 'growing with berries'. ?Binger's Hill (f.n. Arnesby).

beggere ME, 'a beggar'. *Beggar hadland* (f.n. Wigston Magna), *Beggars Baulk* (f.n. South Kilworth), *Beggars Bush Close* (f.n. Peatling Magna).

bekkr ON, 'a stream'. Oback Fm. *þe Beke* (f.n. Kilby). This ON el. is notable for its virtual absence from Guthlaxton Hundred. OE **brōc** 'a brook, a stream' is dominant, *v.* Lei **2** 311, Lei **3** 287 and Lei **4** 305.

belle OE, 'a bell'. ?Bell Paddock. Bell Cl (f.n. Willoughby Waterleys), *Bell dyke*, *belrops* (f.ns. Leire).

belt ModE, 'a belt (of woodland), a screen of trees'. The Belt (South Kilworth, Walcote), Park Belt. Belt Cl (f.n. Bitteswell).

benc OE, 'a bench'; topographically, 'a shelf of land, a bank'. *Benchwell* (f.n. Misterton).

benethe ME, prep., 'beneath, under, below'. *Binetheriggewey* (f.n. Bitteswell).

bēo OE, 'a bee'. Bee Fd (f.n. Bitteswell).

beonet OE, 'bent grass'. Benting Holme Cl (f.n. Aylestone), Bents Cl (f.n. Peatling Magna).

berc OE (Angl), 'a birch-tree'. The Barks (f.n. Frolesworth).

bere ME, 'a bier; a framework for carrying a corpse'. *the beere balke* (f.n. Gilmorton).

bere-tūn OE, 'a barley enclosure, a barley farm'. *Barton poole* (f.n. Blaby).

berg OE (Angl), 'a hill, a mound, a burial mound', **berg** ON, 'a hill'. Kettlesborough, Stemborough Mill, Thornborough Fm. *barefote* (f.n. Frolesworth), The Borough Ground (f.n. Westrill and Starmore), Calliborough Cl (f.n. Willoughby Waterleys), *Cromborousike* (f.n. Oadby), *Halebergh* (f.n. Kilby), Leyborough, Littleborough Leys, Little Fordborough (f.ns. Dunton Bassett), Ruslbrough Leas (f.n. Leire), *Scalboro* (f.n. Blaby, Countesthorpe), *Thorneborrow* (f.n Claybrooke Parva), *Thurnborow* (f.n. Broughton Astley, Gilmorton, Lutterworth, Sutton in the Elms), *Towborrowe* (f.n. Broughton Astley).

berige OE, 'a berry'. ?*First Berry Peece* (f.n. Wigston Magna).

bern OE, 'a barn'. Catthorpe Barn, Denyer's Barn, Moorbarns, Throne's Barn. Freq. in f.ns.: recurring are Barn Cl (in Ashby Parva, Bitteswell, Blaby, Bruntingthorpe, Catthorpe, Claybrooke Parva, Cosby, Dunton Bassett), with an owner's name, e.g. Burbages Barn Cl (Broughton Astley), Harrolds Barn Cl (Ashby Parva); and Barn Mdw (in Ashby Parva, Bittesby, Cotesbach, Dunton Bassett), *Berne Meadow* (Lutterworth). Note also Hay Barn Cl (Dunton Bassett), Old Barn Cl (Ashby Parva), Red Barn Fd (Arnesby), Morebarns (Bitteswell).

best ModE, adj., 'best'; used in f.ns. of very fertile ground. Best Cl (f.n. North Kilworth).

beste OFr, 'a beast'; by the 16th cent., generally restricted to livestock, esp. cattle. *Beast market* (Lutterworth).

betwēonan OE, prep., 'between, amongst', usually in compound p.ns. with the elliptical sense 'the place between'. Between the Brooks (f.n. Lutterworth).

betwixt eModE, prep., 'between'; in p.ns., used as **betwēonan** *supra*. *Betwixt the Brokes* (f.n. Lutterworth).

bī OE, prep., 'by, near'. ?By Home Cl (f.n. Peatling Magna).

***bica** OE, of uncertain meaning, poss. 'a point; a beak-like projection'. ?*Bykesacre* (f.n. Shawell).

bigging ME, 'a building'; later also 'an outbuilding'. Biggin Cl (f.n. Willoughby Waterleys), *Biggin Field* (f.n. Catthorpe), Biggin Mdw (f.n. Glen Parva).

birce OE (Angl), 'a birch-tree'. Big Birches (f.n. Blaby).

bit ModE, 'a bit'; topographically, 'a small piece of land'. Bit Mdw (f.n. Shawell), the Bits (f.n. Bitteswell), *Byte* (f.n. Ashby Parva), Long Bit (f.n. Glen Parva, Willoughby Waterleys), Porter's Bit (f.n. Swinford), Ralph's Bit (f.n. Ullesthorpe), Short Bit, Three Corner Bit (f.ns. Blaby), Triangle Bit (f.n. Broughton Astley).

bjúgr ON, 'a river bend'. ?*Bewcroft* (f.n. Cosby).

blāc OE, adj., 'pale, bleak'. ?*Blakedole* (f.n. Cosby, Westrill and Starmore).

blacksmith ModE, 'a blacksmith'. Blacksmith's Cl (f.n. Broughton Astley).

blæc (blacan wk.obl.) OE, **blak(e)** ME, **black** ModE, adj., 'black, dark'; in eModE, also 'fertile' as against *white* 'infertile'. Blakenhall Fm. Freq. in f.ns.: principally with an el. signifying soil, e.g. *Blackelandes* (Ashby Parva, Cosby, Leire, Littlethorpe), *Blakmyle* (Blaby, Oadby, Wigston Magna); or with an el. indicating a hill, e.g. *Black Hill* (Aylestone, Claybrooke Parva, Gilmorton); or a stream or spring, e.g. *Blackwell* (Ashby Magna, Broughton Astley, Shearsby); or a pit, e.g. *the blackpit* (North Kilworth, Oadby). Recurring also is Black Holme (Dunton Bassett, Leire). The weak oblique form **blacan** survived in *Blakenil* (Shearsby) and poss. in *Blakenell* (South Kilworth).

blakthorn ME, 'a blackthorn, a sloe-tree'. Blackthorn Lane. Blackthorn Bottom (f.n. Arnesby).

blindman ME, 'a blind man'. *blindemans wong* (f.n. Frolesworth).

blōd OE, 'blood'; topographically, may refer to the colour red. *bludacker* (f.n. Leire).

blōma OE, 'a lump or ingot of metal'. ?Bloomhills Fm.

bog ME, 'a bog, a marsh'. Bog Spinney. Blockley's Bog (f.n. Ullesthorpe), Bottom Bogs (f.n. North Kilworth), The Bog(s) (f.ns. Dunton Bassett, Littlethorpe, Willoughby Waterleys), Bog Cl (f.n. Foston), Bog Fd (f.n. Bitteswell, Cosby), Bog Mdw (f.n. Ashby Parva, Misterton, Shearsby), Bog More (f.n. Ashby Parva).

boga OE, 'a bow; something curved or bent (as a curved valley or river bend); an arch or arched bridge'. Bowbrook (f.n. Ashby Parva).

boggy ModE, adj., 'boggy'. *Boggy Brays* (f.n. Ashby Parva), Boggy Cl (f.n. Leire), Boggy Mdw (f.n. Bittesby, Broughton Astley, Claybrooke Magna, Cotesbach, Frolesworth, Ullesthorpe).

*boi(a) OE, 'a boy, a servant' ?Boyam (f.n. Gilmorton), *Boycroftes* (f.n. Cosby).

bóndi ON, **bunde** ODan, 'a peasant landowner', **bōnda** OE, 'a freeman'. ?The Bundards (f.n. Bruntingthorpe).

bony ME, adj., 'full of bones'. ?*Bannefurlong* (f.n. Oadby), *bonyforlong'* (f.n. Kimcote).

bord OE, 'a table, a board'. Shepard Board (f.n. Kimcote).

borow ME, 'a burrow'. ?The Burrow Fd (f.n. Shearsby), Rabbit Burrow Cl (f.n. Dunton Bassett).

bōðl, bōtl OE, 'a dwelling, a house'. Bridgemere Fm. *bootling* (f.n. Whetstone), Bottle Cl, Bottle Ploughed Fd (f.ns. Peatling Magna).

botm OE, 'a bottom'; in p.ns., esp. 'the floor of a valley'. *Asedalebotme* (f.n. Leire), Blackthorn Bottom (f.n. Arnesby), ?Bottom Fd, Bottoms (f.ns. Dunton Bassett), Bottom Hill (f.n. Claybrooke Magna, Cosby), Bottom of the Orchard (f.n. Cosby), *bridel bottem* (f.n. North Kilworth).

bottom ModE, adj., 'bottom, lowermost' (by extension from **botm**). Bottom Cl (f.n. Peatling Magna), ?Bottom Fd (f.n. Dunton Bassett), Bottom Mdw, Bottom Orchard, Harrolds Bottom Cl (f.ns. Ashby Parva), Bottom Piece (f.n. Ashby Magna, Ashby Parva).

boundary ModE, 'a boundary, a border'. Boundary Fd (f.n. Bitteswell).

bowling eModE, vbl.sb., ppl.adj., 'the playing at bowls, the action of rolling a ball'. *Bowling closes* (f.n. Foston), *Bowling leyes* (f.n. Aylestone, Wigston Magna).

bowling-alley eModE, 'an alley or long enclosure for playing bowls or skittles'. Bowling Alley (f.n. Bitteswell).

box OE, 'a box, a receptacle'; used topographically of a small (hedged?) enclosure. Haybox (f.n. Bitteswell).

bracu OE, 'a thicket, a clump, a patch of brushwood'; also prob. 'bracken, fern'. *Brachou* (f.n. Blaby), *the brake* (f.n. Shearsby), *Breake acre* (f.n. Aylestone), *Break forlong* (f.n. Whetstone).

brād OE, adj., 'broad, spacious'. Common in f.ns.: e.g. *Broadarse*, *Brodeacre*, *Brodgreynys* (Blaby), Broadwell (Arnesby, Ashby Magna, Cotesbach, Gilmorton), *Brodeslade* (Kimcote), *Brode water* (Kilby), *Broodcrofte* (Ashby Parva) etc.

braken ME, 'bracken, fern'. Bracknell Cl (f.n. Leire), *brackney* (f.n. Dunton Bassett), *Brakenholm* (f.n. Cosby), *Breaknel* (f.n. Frolesworth).

brant OE, adj., 'steep, steep-sided'. *Branhowstyes* (f.n. Cosby), ?*brannteley* (f.n. Whetstone), Brant Hill (f.n. Arnesby, Shearsby), *branthowe* (f.n. North Kilworth), ?*burnt hill* (f.n. Peatling Parva).

*bræsc OE, 'brushwood'. ?Braceford (f.n. Bruntingthorpe).

brēc OE (Angl), **breche** ME, 'land broken up for cultivation, newly broken-in ploughland'. Breach Barn, Breach Fm. Common in f.ns.: e.g. (The) Breach (Dunton Bassett, Lutterworth, South Kilworth), Breach Leyes, *new breache*, *Edricheslowebreche* (Kimcote), the Breach Fd (Knighton), *the breches* (Cosby), Breeches Mdw (Glen Parva), *le Longbrech*, *le Schortbreche* (Bitteswell).

brēg OE (Angl), **breu** ME, 'an eyebrow'; prob used topographically for 'the brow of a hill'. *Boggy Brays* (f.n. Ashby Parva).

breiðr ON, adj., 'broad'. ?Braceford (f.n. Bruntingthorpe), *Bratherne hill* (f.n. Blaby), *Bretlong* (f.n. Cosby).

brend OE, pa.part., 'burnt, cleared by burning, destroyed by fire'. ?The Brindles. ?*branntteley* (f.n. Whetstone), ?*burnt hill* (f.n. Peatling Parva).

brēost OE, 'a breast'; prob. used topographically of 'a rounded slope or hill'. ?Brass Piece (f.n. Ullesthorpe).

brēr OE (Angl), 'a briar, a wild rose'. Briar Furlong (f.n. Dunton Bassett, Shearsby, Lutterworth), *Brier Hill* (f.n. Blaby, Leire).

ƀrērig OE (Angl), adj., 'growing with or overgrown with briars'. Briery Hill (f.n. Leire).

Bretar (**Breta** gen.pl.) ON, 'Britons'. ?*Bretterhul* (f.n. Wigston Magna).

bretheren ME, 'brothers, brethren'. Brethren Cl (f.n. Dunton Bassett).

Brettas (**Bretta** gen.pl.) OE, 'Britons'. ?*Bretterhul* (f.n. Wigston Magna).

brigdels, **brīdels** OE, 'a bridle', used in the sense 'fit for riding, fit for the passage of horses, but not vehicles'. Bridle Road Cl (f.n. Blaby), Bridle Road Fd, ?*Breddles* (f.ns. Arnesby), Bridleway Cl (f.n. Claybrooke Magna, Ullesthorpe).

brike-kiln ME, 'a brick-kiln'. Brick Kiln, Brickhill Mdw (f.ns. Bitteswell), Brickhill Cl (f.n. Blaby), Brick Kiln Cl (f.n. Claybrooke Magna, Claybrooke Parva, Gilmorton, Shawell, Swinford, Wigston Magna, Wigston Parva, Willoughby Waterleys), Brick Kiln Road Cl (f.n. Cotesbach), Brickkiln Spinney, Richardsons Brick Kiln Cl (f.ns Broughton Astley), Bricklin (f.n. South Kilworth).

brike-yard ME, 'a brick-works, a yard where bricks are made'. Brickyard Fm, Brickyard Lane. The Brickyard (f.n. Swinford), Brickyard Cl (f.n. Broughton Astley), Brickyard Fd (f.n. Shearsby), Old Brickyard (f.n. Bitteswell).

brimme ME, 'a bank, an edge'. *brimsiche* (f.n. Dunton Bassett).

brink ME, 'a brink, an edge', esp. the edge of water or of a steep place. *Brincks* (f.n. Shearsby), High Brinks (f.n. Kimcote), Near Brinks (f.n. Claybrooke Magna).

brīosa OE, 'a gadfly'. *Brisey* (f.n. Whetstone), ?*Brisway* (f.n. Sutton in the Elms).

bro ME, 'a steep slope'. *Brograss* (f.n. Bruntingthorpe).

brōc OE, 'a brook, a stream'. Broughton Astley, Claybrooke (Magna and Parva); Rushbrook Fm, Wash Brook, Whetstone Brook, Willow Brook Fm. Freq. in f.ns.: as a simplex, e.g. *Broke* (Blaby), *the brooke* (Ashby Parva); with the names of enclosures, as Brook Fd (Arnesby, Bitteswell, Cosby); with flora, e.g. Ashbrook (Swinford); with an el. indicating location, e.g. *Carbrook* (Bruntingthorpe), *Holbrooke*, Millbrook (Gilmorton); in compound with a township name and thus prob. identifying a more major stream, as *Westonbroke* (Blaby), *Willowby brooke* (Ashby Magna). Recurring is Washbrook (Arnesby, Lutterworth, Willoughby Waterleys).

brocc OE, 'a badger'. ?*Brockhurst* (f.n. Shawell), ?Broxwell End (f.n. Gilmorton).

brocc-hol OE, 'a badger-sett'. Brocks Hill.

brode ME, 'a broad stretch of land'. *Cow broades* (f.n. Lutterworth).

brōm OE, 'broom'. *Broomhill* (f.n. Wigston Magna).

brooder ModE, 'a device or structure for rearing young chickens or other birds'. Brooder Fd (f.n. Bitteswell).

bryce OE, 'a breach, a breaking'; used topographically of 'land newly broken up for cultivation'. *la Brouce* (f.n. Broughton Astley).

brycg OE, 'a bridge, a causeway'. Bransford Bridge, Clifton's ~, Crow Mill ~, Dow ~, Folly ~, Kilby ~, Kilby Canal ~, Knight's Bridge (Glen Parva, Wigston Magna), Langham's ~, Pochin's ~, Simpkin's ~, Stoney ~, Stult ~, Taylor's ~, Turnover ~, Vice's ~, Wood Bridge. In f.ns., recurring is Stonebridge (Arnesby, Peatling Magna, Wigston Magna). Location is often indicated, as *the church brigg* (Claybrooke Parva), *gonnelesbrige* (Dunton Bassett), *Severne bridg* (Aylestone), *Townsend Bridge* (Wigston Magna).

brȳd OE, 'a bride, a wife, a young woman'; in compound with **wella** may denote a fertility spring. Bridewell (f.n. North Kilworth, South Kilworth).

bū OE, 'a dwelling', **bú** ON, 'a farmstead' *Bewcroft* (f.n. Littlethorpe).

bucca OE, 'a buck, a male deer; a he-goat'. ?Buckwell Fd (f.n. Misterton).

budda OE, 'a beetle, a weevil'. ?*Budewell Furlong* (f.n. South Kilworth), ?*Budmore* (f.n. Claybrooke Magna).

bufan OE, prep., 'above, over'. *Buueton* (f.n. Foston, Kimcote, Misterton).

bula OE, 'a bull'. Common in f.ns.: e.g., *the bull close* (Catthorpe, Shawell), Bull Furlong (Cosby, Gilmorton), Bull Gore (Claybrooke Parva, Ullesthorpe), *the Bull Peice* (Blaby, Dunton Bassett, Littlethorpe, Peatling Magna, Sutton in the Elms).

bulluc OE, 'a bullock'. *the bullockes pasture*, *the olde Bullocke pen* (f.ns. Kimcote), Bullock Fd (f.n. Swinford), *Bullocks pen* (f.n. North Kilworth, Oadby).

bune OE, 'a reed'. *Bunforlonk'* (f.n. Westrill and Starmore), *Bunny furlong hade* (f.n. Kimcote).

burh (**byrig** dat.sg.) OE, 'a fortified place'. ?*burdich* (f.n. Arnesby), ?*First Berry Piece* (f.n. Wigston Magna).

burh-stede OE, 'the site of a stronghold'. *barrowsteades* (f.n. Wigston Magna), *Buristede* (f.n. Dunton Bassett).

burna OE, 'a stream'. *Peseburne* (f.n. Westrill and Starmore), *the Shelbourne meadow* (f.n. Ashby Magna), ?*Wadbourne Mdw* (f.n. North Kilworth).

busc OE, **bush** ME, 'a bush, a thicket; ground covered with shrubs'. *Beggars Bush Close* (f.n. Peatling Magna), ?Briskitt Balk (f.n. Kimcote), Bush Cl (f.n. Ashby Parva, Glen Parva, North Kilworth, Swinford), ?Bush Rackley (f.n. Swinford), *Bussclowe* (f.n. Wigston Magna), *Mussel Bush* (f.n. Arnesby), *peaseland busshe* (f.n. Aylestone), Shepherd's Bush (f.n. Dunton Bassett), Thorn Bush Cl (f.n. Bitteswell), *Thurnborough bush* (f.n. Broughton Astley).

*buskr ON, 'a bush, a thicket'. *Glengate boske* (f.n. Oadby), *Heyman buskys* (f.n. Cosby).

busshi ME, adj., 'growing with bushes'. Bushy Cl (f.n. Willoughby Waterleys), Little Bushey Broadwell (f.n. Cotesbach), *Little Bushey close* (f.n. Knaptoft).

butere OE, 'butter'; often referring to rich pasture used in the preparation of butter. *Boyteresyke* (f.n. Wigston Magna), *Buttrill* (f.n. North Kilworth).

búð ON, 'a temporary shelter'. *Bowthe* (f.n. Ashby Parva).

butt² OFr, ME, 'a mound; an archery butt'. ?*but leyes* (f.n. Catthorpe, Kimcote), Butway Hedge (f.n. Dunton Bassett).

butte ME, 'a short strip of arable land'. Butts Fm. Common in f.ns.: as *Banebut'* (Bitteswell), *Bodlismerebuttis* (Kimcote), *the Butt close* (Claybrooke Parva, Countesthorpe, Peatling Magna), *the buttes* (Kimcote, Leire), *Gilbert Buttes* (Cotesbach), *gildenebutes*, Gilliams Butts (Countesthorpe), Moors Butts (South Kilworth), *Short buttes* (Bruntingthorpe), Sleaths Butts (Leire).

buttuc OE, 'the buttock'; used topographically of a rounded slope. *le Buttock* (f.n. Lutterworth).

bȳ ODan, 'a farmstead, a village'. Arnesby, Ashby Magna, Ashby Parva, Bittesby, Blaby, Cosby, Kilby, Oadby, Shearsby, ?Willoughby Waterleys.?*Lynbe land* (f.n. Willoughby Waterleys).

byge¹ OE, 'a corner, an angle, the bend of a river'. *Byholme* (f.n. Aylestone).

byrgels OE, 'a burial place, a tumulus'. Birles (f.n. Kimcote).

*(ge)bysce OE (Angl), 'a copse of bushes'. ?Briskitt Balk (f.n. Kimcote).

bytme, byðme OE, 'the floor of a valley'. Bitteswell.

*byttel OE, 'a stumpy hill'. Bittesby. Bittell (f.n. Ullesthorpe).

*byxe OE, 'a box-tree'. ?*Bykesacre* (f.n. Shawell).

cabache ME, 'cabbage'. Cabbage Cl (f.n. Knighton), *Cabbage Croft* (f.n. Broughton Astley), Cabbage Piece (f.n. Frolesworth).

*cak ME, 'cack, excrement'. *Cakeforlang'* (f.n. Wigston Magna).

calc OE (Angl), 'limestone'; also used of coarse sand mixed with pebbles. ?Cork Lane.

cald OE (Angl), **cald**, **cold** ME, adj., 'cold; exposed, wind-swept'. ?Caldecote Spinney, Caudle Hill, Cauldwell Fm, Cauldwell Lane, Cold Fm, Cordals. In f.ns., often compounded with **wella**, as in *Cadell home* (Leire), *Caldwell Close* Bruntingthorpe), *Caudell* (Shearsby), *Caudel slade* (Claybrooke Parva), *Cawdewelle* (Oadby), *Cordwell Hole* (Ashby Parva), Cowdale Mdw (Arnesby). Note also Cold Slade (f.n. Cotesbach, Shawell).

calf (**calfra** gen.pl.) OE, 'a calf'. *Caluerelesewe* (f.n. Wigston Magna), *Caluerlesure* (f.n. Oadby), *Calver pastur* (f.n. Littlethorpe), Calverslade (f.n. Willoughby Waterleys), Calves Cl (f.n. Broughton Astley, Frolesworth, Shawell, Swinford), Calves Fd (f.n. Wigston Parva), *Glencaluerley fen* (f.n. Blaby).

calu OE, adj., 'bare, lacking in vegetation'. Calliborough Cl (f.n. Willoughby Waterleys), *Calow cloutes* (f.n. Knaptoft), *Calulese* (f.n. Wigston Magna), ?*Gallow Hill* (f.n. Shawell).

camp OE, 'open land'. Camp Barn.

***canc** OE, 'a rounded hill'. *the Cankwell* (f.n. Oadby).

canon OE, 'a canon, a clergyman living under canonical rule'; in p.ns., often alluding to land belonging to and supporting clergy. *Canonesholm* (f.n. Aylestone).

***cape** OE, 'a look-out place'. ?*cappehauitland* (f.n. Wigston Magna).

cat(t) OE, 'a cat, a wild-cat'. Cattern (f.n. Bitteswell), ?*Cattyshyll* (f.n. Blaby).

ceaster OE, 'a walled town, an old fortification'. ?*Alstertune* (f.n. Shawell), ?*chesters way* (f.n. Peatling Parva).

cetel OE (Angl), 'a kettle'; topographically, 'a hollow'. Green Kettle (f.n. Ashby Parva), Kettle Mdw (f.n. Leire).

chain ModE, 'a chain'. The Chain.

chanel ME, 'a watercourse, a gutter, a channel'. *Chanel syke* (f.n. Kilby).

chapel(e) OFr, ME, 'a chapel'. Baptist Chapel, Chapel Lane. Chapel well (f.n. Ullesthorpe).

chaunterie ME, 'a chantry'. *the Chantry Land* (f.n. Swinford), *le Chauntre hous* (Swinford).

cheker ME, 'a chequer'; topographically, usually referring to land with a chequered appearance.?*Cecesslade* (f.n. Bitteswell).

chese-cake ME, 'a cheesecake'; used topographically of a wedge-shaped field, alluding to a slice of the tart so called. Cheese Cake (f.n. North Kilworth), Cheesecake Cl (f.n. Frolesworth), Cheese Cake Mdw (f.n. Countesthorpe), *the Cheescake piece* (f.n. Shearsby).

chike ME, 'a chick, a young chicken'. ?*Cecesslade* (f.n. Bitteswell).

churchyerd ME, 'a churchyard'. Freq.: some earlier instances recorded are those of the parish churches of Wigston Magna (All Saints') 1595, Ashby Magna 1601, Aylestone 1605, Bitteswell, Dunton Bassett, Gilmorton, Lutterworth, North Kilworth 1606 and Oadby 1638. Rarely in f.ns., e.g. Churchyard Croft (Ashby Magna).

cīcen OE, 'a chicken'. Chicken Fd (f.n. Bitteswell).

cild OE, 'a child, a young person, a young nobleman'. *Childfurlang'* (f.n. Westrill and Starmore). ?*Kill Well Hedg* (f.n. Arnesby).

cirice OE, **chirche**, **churche** ME, 'a church'. ?Church Hill Fm. ?Churchill Mdw (f.n. Shearsby), Church way (f.n. Kimcote).

***cis** OE, 'gravel'. *Chiffurlonge* (f.n. North Kilworth).

clāfre OE, 'clover'. *Claver leyes* (f.n. Countesthorpe), Clover Cl (f.n. Bittesby, Broughton Astley, Claybrooke Magna, Claybrooke Parva, Cosby, Cotesbach, Countesthorpe, Dunton Bassett, Foston, Glen Parva, Peatling Parva, Ullesthorpe), Clover Fd (f.n. Bitteswell), Clover Grass Cl (f.n. Aylestone), *Littelclarouhull* (f.n. Bitteswell).

clǣg OE, 'clay'; in p.ns., often 'clayey soil'. Claybrooke Magna, Claybrooke Parva. Clay Acres (f.n. Blaby), Clay Furlong (f.n. Gilmorton), *Cleyhilsike* (f.n. Wigston Magna), *Cleylond* (f.n. Littlethorpe), *Cleypoole* (f.n. Lutterworth), *the fare cley* (f.n. Aylestone).

clerk ME, 'a cleric; a scholar, a scribe'. *le Clerkewell* (f.n. Knighton).

cley-pytt ME, 'a clay-pit'. Clay Pits (f.n. North Kilworth, Shearsby), *Cleypittes* (f.n. Cosby, Littlethorpe).

clif OE, 'a cliff, a steep slope'. Clifts (f.n. Gilmorton), *Little Cliffe*, *Wethercliuemere* (f.ns. South Kilworth), *Little Cliffe* (f.n. Bruntingthorpe).

*clinc OE, 'a crevice, a small crack'. *þe clincis* (f.n. Kilby).

clos(e) ME, 'an enclosure'. Ashclose Spinney. Very freq. in f.ns.: early examples are *Church ~*, *Cramer ~*, *Rastell clos* 1550 (North Kilworth), *Gibbet ~*, *Great Close* 1590, *New closse* 1470, *the Round Close* 1590 (Aylestone), *Inland close* 1529, *Newclose* 1525 (Knaptoft), *Seusbys croft close* 1554 (Arnesby). Note the archaic pl. form in *Peatling Closen* (Kimcote).

clūd OE, 'a mass of rock, a cliff, a hill'. *Calow cloutes* (f.n. Knaptoft), *Cludhils* (f.n. Arnesby).

clump ModE, 'a cluster of trees'. Clump Hill.

clūs(e) OE, 'an enclosure' and also 'a dam, a sluice'. *Clusitch* (f.n. North Kilworth).

cnapa OE, 'a boy, a young man, a servant'. ?Knaptoft.

cniht OE, 'a youth, a servant'; in late OE, it developed the sense of 'a retainer of a royal or noble personage, a soldier'. Knighton.

*cnocc[2] OE, 'a hillock'. *knockstone* (f.n. Gilmorton).

cnoll OE, 'a hill top, the summit of a large hill'; later 'a knoll, a hillock'. Ashby Path Noles, *michilhil knowles* (f.ns. Dunton Bassett), *the knoles* (f.n. Kimcote), *le knolles*, *Robynetisknolle* (f.ns. Bitteswell), *Moreknole* (f.n. Lutterworth), *Porty knoale* (f.n. Broughton Astley).

*cocc[1] OE, 'a heap, a hillock'; difficult to distinguish from **cocc**[2]. *?cocesleyes* (f.n. Dunton Bassett), ?Cock Hill Cl (f.n. Cosby), *?Cokmore ford* (f.n. Shearsby).

cocc[2] OE, 'a cock'; esp. of a wild bird such as a woodcock. ?Cock Hill Cl (f.n. Cosby), *?Cokmore ford* (f.n. Shearsby).

*cocc-scēte OE (Angl), 'a cock-shoot, a woodland glade where nets were stretched to catch woodcock'. Cockshut (f.n. Swinford).

cock-pit ModE, 'a cock-pit, an enclosure in which game-cocks were set to fight for sport'. *Cockpitt leyes* (f.n. Wigston Magna).

cofa (**cofan** dat.sg., nom.pl.) OE, 'a shelter, a hut; a recess in the steep side of a hill'. ?Cotesbach Covan (f.n. Misterton).

col[1] OE, 'coal'; especially 'charcoal'. Colelane Fd. ?*Cole Corner* (f.n. Ashby Parva), ?*Coslade* (f.n. Cotesbach).

college ME, 'a fraternity, a religious fellowship; a university college'. *the Colledge land* (f.n. Blaby).

col-pytt OE, 'a coalpit, i.e. a place where charcoal was made'. In the names of roads and tracks, the allusion is sometimes to routes from places where pit coal was dug. *Coalepitt* (f.n. Kimcote, Wigston Magna), *colepite dole* (f.n. Peatling Parva), Coal Pitt Furlong (f.n. Lutterworth), Coalpit Leys (f.n. Lutterworth, Misterton), Colepitt Hill (f.n. South Kilworth); *the Coal Pit Way* (Claybrooke Parva, Lutterworth, Oadby, Peatling Magna, Shawell, Wigston Magna), *the Colepit highe way* (Leire), *Colepitt Road* (Arnesby).

colt OE, 'a colt'. *colt slade* (f.n. Kilby).

commun ME, used both as a sb. meaning 'common land' and as an adj. 'shared by all, of a non-private nature'. Freq. in f.ns.: *the Common* (Ashby Parva, Bruntingthorpe, Frolesworth, Shawell), *the Cow Common*, *the Horse Common* (Lutterworth), Kilworth Common (North Kilworth), *moore haden common* (Bruntingthorpe); *the Common Balke* (Ashby Parva, Gilmorton), *the Common ground* (Blaby, Gilmorton), *the common brooke* (Broughton Astley), *the comon* *cowe pasture* (Dunton Bassett), Common Mdw (North Kilworth), *le Communpitt'* (Cosby), *the Common streete* (Countesthorpe), *the Common waie* (Claybrooke Parva), (*Queenes high way called*) *common street* (Ashby Parva).

conestable ME, 'a constable'. *Constables balk* (f.n. Bruntingthorpe, Leire), Constables Cl (f.n. Ashby Parva), *the constables peece* (f.n. Aylestone, Claybrooke Parva), *Constabul Welspryng* (f.n. Oadby).

coni ME, 'a rabbit'. Coney Hill (f.n. Wigston Parva), Cunny Hills (f.n. Lutterworth).

coningre, coninger ME, a rabbit-warren'. Conery (f.n. Broughton Astley), *conningrye* (f.n. Dunton Bassett), Cunnery (f.n. Lutterworth), Cunnery Mdw (f.n. Foston), *Cunningre close* (f.n. Blaby).

copis ME, 'a coppice'. The Coppice, Lattice Coppice.

copp OE, 'a summit, a hill or ridge which has a narrow, crest-like top'. ?Copleys (f.n. Willoughby Waterleys), *copmores slade* (f.n. Aylestone), Copnor Bridge (f.n. Shearsby), *Copply green* (f.n. Whetstone), Copwell Mdw (f.n. Claybrooke Parva).

copped[1] ME, adj., 'having a peak'. Cockmaydame Lays (f.n. South Kilworth), *Coppedhill* (f.n. Bitteswell), Coppidmoore (f.n. Gilmorton).

copped[2] ME, pa.part., adj., 'pollarded; with the head removed'. Copthorne (f.n. Catthorpe), *Copthorne* (f.n. Broughton Astley).

corn[1] OE, 'corn, grain'. ?*Corlond* (f.n. Bitteswell), Corn Cl, *Cornelandes* (f.ns. Cotesbach), Corn Cl (f.n. Willoughby Waterleys), *le Corn close* (f.n. Knaptoft).

corn[2] OE, 'a crane' (the bird). Cornbrook (f.n. Shearsby).

corner ME, 'a corner, a nook'. Corner Lodge Fm, Crabtree Corner, Swinford Corner (Misterton, Swinford). Common in f.ns.: *Ashbies corner* (Cotesbach), Ballong Corner, Stow Corner (South Kilworth), Bittesby Corner, Crabtree Corner (Lutterworth), Bliss's Corner, The Corners (Westrill and Starmore), *Cole Corner* (Ashby Parva), Corner Brinks (Claybrooke Magna), Corner Cl (Bittesby, Broughton Astley, North Kilworth, Shawell), Corner Fd (Shearsby, Peatling Magna), *Cornerwylow* (Littlethorpe), *Faulks Close Corner*, *Wystons corner* (Wigston Magna), Lilbourne Corner (Dunton Bassett), *the Parke corner* (Broughton Astley), *Peatlinge corner* (Peatling Parva), Snipes Corner (Arnesby), *Witcham corner* (Aylestone).

cot neut. (**cote** dat.sg., **cotu** nom.pl.), **cote** fem. (**cotan** dat.sg., nom.pl.) (**cotum** dat.pl.) OE, **cotes** (nom.pl.) ME, 'a cottage, a hut, a shelter'. Cotes de Val, Kimcote, Walcote; ?Caldicote Spinney, West Cote. Common in f.ns.: *Coates pasture*, Tibblecotes (Kimcote), Coats Cl (Leire), *Coatgreene* (Whetstone), *Coots* (North Kilworth), Cottmore, Woolcott (South Kilworth), Cotton Fd (Swinford), Great Cotes (Dunton Bassett), Hawcott Mdw (Foston), Lambcote(s) (Dunton Bassett, Frolesworth, North Kilworth, Swinford, Wigston Magna), Quinckoe (Lutterworth), *Sharcutt hyll* (Bitteswell), *Swynncoate* (Kimcote), *Wlferescote* (North Kilworth).

cotage ME, 'a cottage, a hut, a shelter'. Archway Cottage, The Cottage, Cottage Fm, Cottage Lane, Gate Cottages. Bates Cottage, Judds Cottage (Ashby Magna), Bilstons ~ ~, Burdetts Far ~ ~, Harris ~ ~, Marvins ~ ~, Phillips Cottage Cl (f.ns. Broughton Astley), Cottage Cl (f.n. Peatling Magna), Cottage Far Pasture (f.n. Frolesworth), Cottage Fd (f.n. Arnesby), Cottage Piece (f.n. Peatling Parva).

cotager eModE, 'one who lives in a cottage'; used esp. of the labouring population of rural districts. Cottagers Close. Cottagers Cl (f.n. Shawell), *the Cottagers close* (f.n. Catthorpe).

cottere OE, 'a cottar, a cottager'. *Cottiers Close* (f.n. Aylestone), *Cottyers* (f.n. Willoughby Waterleys), *Cottyers pasture* (f.n. Frolesworth).

court ME, 'a large house, a manor house'. Ullesthorpe Court.

court-hous ME, 'a house where manorial courts were held, a manorial dwelling'. ?Corthouse Cl (f.n. Blaby).

cover(t) ME, 'a covert, a shelter for game'. Diamond Jubilee Covert, Fox ~, Great Peatling ~, Jane Ball ~, John Ball ~, Jubilee ~, New Covert (Cotesbach, South Kilworth), Old ~, Swinford Covert. Cover Fd, ~ Mdw (f.ns. North Kilworth), Covert Fd (f.n. Shearsby), The Fox Cover (f.n. Swinford), Fox Cover Cl (f.n. North Kilworth), Fox Covert (f.n. Peatling Magna).

crabbe ME, 'a crab-apple-tree'. ?Crabbies (f.n. Cosby).

crabtre ME, 'a crab-apple-tree'. Crabtree Corner. Crab Tree (f.n. Arnesby, Peatling Magna, Willoughby Waterleys), Crabtree Cl (f.n. Ashby Parva, Bruntingthorpe, Ullesthorpe), Crabtree Corner (f.n. Lutterworth), Crab-tree Fd (f.n. Wigston Parva), Crabtree Mdw (f.n. Catthorpe, Shearsby).

cragge ME, 'a rock, a crag'. Cragdale (f.n. Bruntingthorpe), *cragdale* (Peatling Parva).

cran, cron OE, 'a crane, a heron'. Cranmer Lane. Cromwell (f.n. Wigston Parva).

crāwe OE, 'a crow'. Crow Spinney. *Crowethorne* (f.n. Bitteswell), *Crowethornhul* (f.n. Knighton), *Crowewell* (f.n. Wigston Magna), *Crownest* (f.n. Shearsby), *Crothorne*, Crow Trees (f.ns. Ashby Parva), Crow Spinney (f.n. Blaby).

cristel-mǣl OE, 'a cross, a crucifix'. *Cristemelehul* (f.n. Kimcote).

crocc OE, 'a crock, an earthenware pot'. ?*Crokiswelle* (f.n. Westrill and Starmore).

croft OE, 'a small enclosed field, a small enclosure near a house'. Croft, High Croft, Stokes Croft. Very freq. in f.ns.: esp. with pers.ns. and surns., e.g. *Archers crofte*, *Fyssherscroft* (Aylestone), *Gahewenescroft* (Kimcote), *Malkeyn Randull' croft* (Wigston Magna), *Martines Croft*, *Wilkynescrofte* (Cosby); with crops, e.g. *barly crofte* (Shawell), Cabbage Croft (Broughton Astley), *le Grescroft'* (Wigston Magna), *Heycroft* (Aylestone, Blaby), Lincroft (Ashby Parva); with livestock, e.g. Cows Croft (Broughton Astley), *Gossecroft* (Peatling Parva), *Hencrofts* (Whetstone); with township structures, e.g. Hallcroft (Countesthorpe, Gilmorton, Kimcote), Mill Croft (Ashby Parva, Dunton Bassett); with an adj. of size or shape, e.g. *Broodcrofte*, *Shorte Crofte* (Ashby Parva), *longcroft* (Shawell); with an indicator of location, e.g. Churchyard Croft (Ashby Magna), Hill Path Croft (Claybrooke Magna), *Innecrofte* (Aylestone), North Croft (Blaby), Sowcraft (Leire), West Croft (Bitteswell); and often appears as a simplex, e.g. The Croft (Ashby Magna, Catthorpe, Gilmorton, Knighton, North Kilworth, Peatling Magna). Recurring is Croftlands (Gilmorton, Kimcote).

*crōh[2] OE, 'a nook, a corner'. ?*Crowmilne*, ?*Crowewell*, ?*Crowe willowes*, (f.ns. Wigston Magna).

croked ME, adj., 'crooked, twisted'. ?Crooked Tree Cl (f.n. Arnesby), Crook Tree Mear (f.n. Shearsby), *crucked tree* (f.n. Kilby).

cros late OE, ME, 'a cross'; difficult to distinguish from **cross** when acting as a specific. High Cross. Common in f.ns.: *Ashehill Crosse* (Ashby Parva), *Aylestone crosse* (Wigston Magna), *the Ball Cross*, *Gegecros*, *Glen Cross* (Oadby), *Cattes crosse*, *Stonie crose* (Aylestone), *the Crosse* (Cosby, Kimcote, Lutterworth), *Crosse hill* (Cotesbach, North Kilworth), Kilworth Cross (South Kilworth),

Peatlinge crosse (Kimcote), Peatling Cross Cl (Peatling Parva), Pedlars Cross (Lutterworth), Poor Cross (Gilmorton).

cross ME, adj., 'athwart, lying across, crosswise'. Crossways Fm. ?*Crosfelde*, ?*Crosspit* (f.ns. Blaby), *Crosfurlong* (f.n. Bitteswell), ?*Croslands* (f.n. Cotesbach, Kimcote), ?*Crossedoles* (f.n. North Kilworth), ?*Cross Leys* (f.n. Shawell).

crūg PrW, 'a hill'. ?Church Hill Fm. ?Churchill Mdw (f.n. Shearsby).

crumb OE, adj., '?*Cromborousike* (f.n. Oadby), *Crum dike* (f.n. Frolesworth).

***crūw** OE, 'a bend'. ?*Crowmilne*, ?*Crowewell*, ?*Crowe willowes* (f.ns. Wigston Magna).

cū OE, 'a cow'. Freq. in f.ns.: as Cowage, Cowhead (Bitteswell), *Cowakars* (Ashby Magna), Cow Cl (Arnesby, Ashby Parva, Bittesby, Bitteswell, Broughton Astley, Bruntingthorpe, Claybrooke Magna, Cosby), Cow Leys (Bruntingthorpe), Cow Pasture (Broughton Astley), *Cow lane* (Lutterworth), Cow Moore (Kimcote).

cuccu ME, 'the cuckoo'. Cuckoo Cl (f.n. Blaby).

culvert ModE, 'a channel, a conduit, a tunnelled drain of masonry or brickwork'. Culvert Piece (f.n. Ullesthorpe).

cundite eModE, 'a conduit, an aqueduct'. Conduit Grounds (f.n. Westrill and Starmore), Conduit Spinney (f.n. Ashby Magna).

cuntesse OFr, ME, 'a countess'. Countesthorpe.

cutel OE, ME, 'an artificial water-channel'. *cuttle* (f.n. North Kilworth).

cutted ME, ppl.adj., 'cut short, shortened'; poss. also, 'provided with a channel'. *Cuttedwong* (f.n. Shawell).

***cwelle** OE (Angl), 'a spring, a well'. *Cuallhelleleys* (f.n. Kimcote).

cwene OE, 'a woman'. Quinckoe (f.n. Lutterworth).

cweorn OE, 'a quern, a hand-mill'. *Whorne* (f.n. North Kilworth, South Kilworth).

cyln OE (Angl), 'a kiln'. *Kilne close* (f.n. Ashby Magna, Frolesworth), *Kilnes* (f.n. Wigston Magna), Upper Kiln Cl (f.n. Cotesbach), *the Kylne yard* (f.n. Sutton in the Elms).

cȳta OE (Angl), 'a kite' (the bird *Milvus milvus*). the Quitall (f.n. Bruntingthorpe).

dag ME, 'moisture; ?mire' (from ON *dǫgg* 'dew'). Dog Lane. *Daglane* (f.n. North Kilworth).

dag-lock eModE, 'lock(s) of wool clotted with dirt at the rear end of a sheep'. Daglock Cl (f.n. Frolesworth).

dāl OE, **dole** ME, 'a share, a portion; a share in a common field'. Freq. in f.ns.: with a pers.n., e.g. Ansdoles (Gilmorton), *Oswardedole* (Leire); with indicators of shape, size, e.g. *Longdoles* (Countesthorpe, Dunton Bassett), Small Doles (Kimcote), *Wrongedole* (Glen Parva); with flora, e.g. *Dockey Dole* (Lutterworth), *Feneldoale* (Shawell); with minor locational names, e.g. *Kitehill doles, Tongue doles* (Bruntingthorpe), *Rigdole* (Littlethorpe), *le Sladole* (Bitteswell); with indications of soil quality, e.g. *le Blakedole, Sourdole* (Cosby), Red Doles Cl (Leire), *le Stonidole* (Misterton), Recurring is *Fordoles* (Blaby, Frolesworth, Kimcote).

dalr ON, 'a valley'; in later spellings, very difficult to distinguish from **deill** 'a share, a portion of land'. Amberdale Spinney, Westdale Fm. Freq. in f.ns.: recurring are *Debdale* (Ashby Parva, Broughton Astley, Shawell) and *Langdale* (Aylestone, Blaby); wild flora features, as *Fernedale, Thurnedale* (Kilby), *Thefedayle* (Blaby) and crops, e.g. *Flaxdale* (Aylestone), *Madridall* (Leire); livestock occurs, e.g. *Oxedale, Wethersdale* (Leire), while pers.ns. are rare, e.g. *Elverdale* (North Kilworth).

damme ME, 'a dam', usually created for use at mills or for watering livestock. Mill
Dam Spinney. *le Milnedam* recurs (f.n. Aylestone, Blaby, Claybrooke Magna,
Dunton Bassett, Leire), as do Dam Cl (f.n. Bitteswell, Leire) and Dam Mdw (f.n.
Bitteswell, Broughton Astley). Private ownership is indicated, as
Baggemulnedam (f.n. Ashby Parva), *John Grants Dam* (Whetstone); and
location, e.g. *The Damm of Foxeholes* (f.n. Peatling Magna), *Glendame* (f.n.
Blaby). Note *fishedame* (f.n. Dunton Bassett).

dauncing ME, vbl.sb., ppl.adj., 'dancing; rhythmical movement'. Dancing Mire (f.n.
South Kilworth).

dauði ON, 'death'. ?*Dawthames* (f.n. Ashby Parva).

dauðr ON, adj., 'dead'. ?*Dawthames* (f.n. Ashby Parva).

dawe ME, 'a jackdaw'. *Daw Slade* (f.n. Leire).

dæl[1] OE, 'a hollow, a valley'. Shackerdale Fm. *findale* (f.n. Shawell), *Hodale*,
Shackadale (f.ns. Aylestone), *Schakersdale* (f.n. Knighton), *Wormedale* (f.n.
Peatling Magna).

dēad OE, adj., 'dead'; often used in p.ns. with reference to a site of violent death or
to the discovery of human bones; but also may indicate infertile moorland. *Dead
Lane* (Lutterworth). Dead-fallow (f.n. Ullesthorpe), *deadford* (f.n. Shearsby),
deadhurst (f.n. Sutton in the Elms), Dead Lane (f.n. Bruntingthorpe), Deadmer
(f.n. Dunton Bassett), *le dedemor* (f.n. Oadby, Whetstone).

deakne ME, 'an ecclesiastical deacon'. *the Deacon cloase* (f.n. Broughton Astley).

dede-man ME, 'a dead man, a corpse'. *Dead Man* (f.n. Shearsby), *dead mans piece*
(f.n. Bruntingthorpe).

deierie ME, 'a dairy'. Dairy Cottages, Dairy Fm, The Dairy Fm. *Dayrie close* (f.n.
Ashby Magna), Dairy Cl (f.n. Ashby Parva, Claybrooke Magna, Countesthorpe,
Dunton Bassett, North Kilworth, Shawell, Swinford), Dairy Ground (f.n.
Catthorpe), Dairy Leys (f.n. Claybrooke Parva).

deill ON, 'a share, a portion of land'; in later spellings, very difficult to distinguish
from **dalr** 'a valley', but pl. forms with -*dales* are sometimes indicators of *deill*.
Hole dale, *Longdale* (f.ns. Bruntingthorpe), Limsdale Hill (f.n. Leire),
?*Ouergreyndall'* (f.n. Littlethorpe), *Thorpdalys* (f.n. Blaby).

denn OE, 'a den, a pit'. ?*Paddocksden* (f.n. Countesthorpe).

denu OE, 'a valley'. *the Deane* (f.n. Aylestone, Blaby, Westrill and Starmore),
Deanes (f.n. Lutterworth), Den Furlong (f.n. Ullesthorpe), ?*Hoden Haggs*,
?*Paddocksden* (f.ns. Countesthorpe), *Marchesakerdene* (f.n. Swinford).

dēop OE, adj., 'deep'. *Debdale* (f.n. Ashby Parva, Broughton Astley, Shawell),
Deepslade (f.n. Ashby Parva).

dēor OE, 'an animal, a beast', **deer** ME, 'deer'. ?*Darleys Cl* (f.n. Claybrooke Parva).

derne OE (Angl), adj., 'hidden, obscure'. *Derneslade* (f.n. Catthorpe).

dew-pond ModE, 'an artificial pond used for watering livestock'. Dew Pond Fds
(f.n. Cosby).

dīc OE, 'a ditch'. *Browns Ditch* (f.n. North Kilworth), *burdich*, *Langedich* (f.ns.
Arnesby), *Dastels* (f.n. Ashby Parva), *Ditch furlong*, *the old ditch* (f.ns.
Cotesbach), *Hey ditche* (f.n. Lutterworth), *John Clarkes Ditch*, *the Meadow
Ditch*, *Wiggeston ditch* (f.ns. Blaby), *mildiche*, Shortditch, *Whorleditch* (f.ns.
Shearsby), *the moore dich*, *Rydichewey* (f.ns. Kimcote), *old dich* (f.n. Leire), *Rye
Hill ditch* (f.n. Frolesworth).

dík ON, 'a ditch'; the el. varies with OE **dīc** in some f.ns. Ash Dikes, ?Dikes Cl (f.ns. Bruntingthorpe), *Brownes dickes* (f.n. North Kilworth), *Lituldykes*, *Medodyke*, Pye Dyke (f.ns. Blaby), *le Medudykys* (f.n. Cosby), *New Dike* (f.n. Misterton), Niddick way (f.n. Kimcote), *the Moore dykes* (f.n. Broughton. Astley), *le Roudik* (f.n. Glen Parva), *Thurspitt dike* (f.n. Catthorpe), *wide dickes* (f.n. Dunton Bassett).

dingle ME, 'a deep hollow'. ?Dingle Hill (f.n. Misterton).

docce OE, 'a dock-plant'; poss. also 'a water-lily' when combined with words denoting water. *Docepittewey*, *le Docestile* (f.ns. Cosby), *Dockey Close* (f.n. Misterton), *Dockey Dole* (f.n. Lutterworth), Docklands (f.n. (Kimcote), ?*Dog foard* (f.n. Wigston Magna).

doctour ME, 'a medical practitioner'. Doctors Cl (f.n. Claybrooke Parva), Top Doctors (f.n. Misterton).

dogga late OE, **dogge** ME, 'a dog'. ?*Dog foard* (f.n. Wigston Magna).

dogh ME, 'dough'. *Dough bank* (f.n. Whetstone).

donke ME, adj., 'wet, watery, dank'. *Donkkesteles* (f.n. Aylestone).

dove-cot(e) ME, 'a dove-cote'. Dovecote Cl (f.n. Claybrooke Parva).

drāf OE, 'a herd, a drove; a drove-way'. *the Drove* (f.n. Aylestone).

drain ModE, 'a drain'. Drain Fd (f.n. Swinford).

drȳge OE, adj., 'dry, dried-up; well-drained'. Dry House (f.n. Gilmorton), *Dryland* (f.n. Bruntingthorpe).

duble ME, adj., 'double'. Double Fence (f.n. Frolesworth), Double Gate Cl (f.n. Broughton Astley), Double Gorse (f.n. Wigston Magna).

dūfe OE, **dúfa** ON, 'a dove'; prob. also 'a pigeon'. ?Dow Bridge. Dowells (f.n. South Kilworth)

dūn OE, 'a tract of hill country, an upland expanse; upland pasture'. Dunton Bassett. Cockmaydame Lays (f.n. South Kilworth), Dunford Hill (f.n. Lutterworth), Warden (f.n. Frolesworth).

dunt ME, 'a hollow, an indentation, a dent'. ?*Dunting* (f.n. Cosby).

*****dus** OE, 'a heap', *****dus** ODan, 'a heap, a grave mound'. ?Dust Furlong (f.n. Gilmorton).

dūst OE, 'dust'. ?Dust Furlong (f.n. Gilmorton).

dyncge OE, 'manured land'. ?Dinge Hill (f.n. Misterton), Dunsacre (f.n. South Kilworth).

ēa-land OE, 'land by water or by a river; an island'; very difficult to keep apart from *ēg-land* OE (Angl), 'an island', with which it is confused in ME. Top Islands (f.n. Swinford).

earm OE, 'an arm'; used topographically of a branch of something. *wyer arme* (f.n. Wigston Magna).

earn OE, 'an eagle'. *Arnest feld* (f.n. Aylestone).

ears OE, 'an arse, a buttock', transferred topographically to 'a rounded hill'; difficult to distinguish from *****herse**, 'a top, a hill-top'. *Broadarse* (f.n. Blaby, Leire), Dry House (f.n. Gilmorton).

ēast OE, adj., 'eastern, east'. Common in f.ns.: e.g. *Astewell'* (Frolesworth), *Eastfeld* (Arnesby, Bruntingthorpe), *Estmedow* (Blaby), *Estoftes* (Kimcote).

ēastan OE, adv., 'east, east of'; used in p.ns. elliptically, '(place) east of'. Easnill (f.n. Ullesthorpe).

*ēcels OE (Angl), 'an addition, land added to an estate'. *Eychuls* (f.n. Ashby Magna).

ecg OE, 'an edge; the edge of a hill, an escarpment', a steep slope'. ?*eggeslades* (f.n. South Kilworth), *Hedghill* (f.n. Oadby).

edisc OE, 'an enclosure'. Cowage (f.n. Bitteswell), ?*ferne hedge* (f.n. Whetstone), Kelmidge, Micklidge, Sowledge, Stullidge, *Whorelidge* (f.ns. Gilmorton), ?*Kill Well Hedg* (f.n. Arnesby), ?Two Hedges (f.n. Shawell), ?Wood Bridge Hedge (f.n. Lutterworth).

ēg OE (Angl), 'an island, a piece of raised ground in wetlands, land partly surrounded by water'. Poultney; Gawney Lane, Gurney Lane. ?Balney, *Bunny* (f.ns. Kimcote), *Brisey*, ?*bulley*, ?*Swinie hill* (f.ns. Whetstone), ?*Ely lane* (f.n. Lutterworth), *Ferey* (f.n. Gilmorton), *galney* (f.n. Peatling Parva), *le Redy* (f.n. Aylestone), *Reedye* (f.n. Sutton in the Elms).

*ēl OE (Angl), 'a small island'. *Eyl* (f.n. Wigston Magna).

-el[3] OE, noun suffix. ?The Bindles.

elevyn ME, numeral, 'eleven'. *Ellevyn rodes* (f.n. Aylestone).

ellern OE, 'an alder-tree'. *Elrenestubb'* (f.n. Knighton), *elrestobslade* (f.n. Kimcote), *Elrynstub* (f.n. Bitteswell), *Elstub* (f.n. North Kilworth).

elm OE, 'an elm-tree'. the Elms (f.n. Lutterworth).

*elme OE, 'an elm wood'. The Elms (f.n. Shawell).

elnboga OE, 'an elbow'; transferred topographically to a feature with the shape of an elbow. The Elbow (f.n. Peatling Magna).

ende OE, 'an end; the end of a district or quarter of a village or town'. Bottom End Bridge, Town End Fm, West End Fm (Bitteswell, Willoughby Waterleys). Freq. in f.ns.: e.g. *Blaby End, Sweets End* (Countesthorpe), *le Brokesende* (Oadby), *Bushley End, Church End, Mowsley End, Newgate End* (Wigston Magna), *butwaie hedge ende* (Dunton Bassett); and recurring in the compound *town(s)end* (with various spellings in Ashby Parva, Aylestone, Broughton Astley, Claybrooke Parva, Dunton Bassett, Gilmorton, Sutton in the Elms).

eng ON, 'a meadow, a pasture'. ?Little End. Common in f.ns.: e.g. *bootling* (Whetstone), Bristlings (Peatling Parva), *Dunting'*, *le Westing'* (Cosby), Englands (Arnesby), *Feldyngys* (Kimcote), Greeping (Dunton Bassett), *Horsein Hylles, Reddinge End* (Ashby Parva), *le Hountheng, Swetynges* (Wigston Magna), *Littlin, Thrallyn* (Aylestone), *Littlyng, Stowpyng* (Oadby), *Muklyng'* (Kilby), *Northeng* (Foston), The Swimmings (Swinford).

eorð-burh OE, 'an earthwork, a fortification built of earth'. ?*the Arbor* (f.n. Kimcote), ?Short Arbour (f.n. Gilmorton), *Herburgh Hull* (f.n. Wigston Magna).

eorðe OE, 'earth, soil, ground'; later, 'an animal's den dug into the ground'. Fox Earths Spinney. *Blackearth* (f.n. Claybrooke Parva).

-er OE, noun suffix. Thacker (f.n. South Kilworth).

erbage ME, 'herbaceous growth or vegetation'; usually applied to grass and other low-growing plants covering a large extent of ground, esp. as used for pasture. Berbidge (f.n. North Kilworth).

erber OFr, ME, 'a grass-covered piece of ground, a garden'.?*the Arbor* (f.n. Kimcote), Harbour Cl (f.n. Dunton Bassett), ?Short Arbour (f.n. Gilmorton).

erewygge ME, 'the earwig' (*Forficula auricularia*), so called because it was thought to penetrate into the head through the ear. *Erewygfurlong'* (f.n. Bitteswell).

ermitage OFr, ME, 'a hermitage'. *Armitage* (f.n. Arnesby), *del Ermytage* (p) (Wigston Magna).

ersc OE, 'a ploughed field, a stubble field'. ?Usher Fm.

esce OE, 'a stand of ash-trees'. In forms for ?Ashby Magna, ?Ashby Parva.

eski ON, 'a place growing with ash-trees'. In forms for ?Ashby Magna, ?Ashby Parva.

ēðe OE, 'wasteland'. ?*Eathring Syde* (f.n. Shawell).

*etisc OE, 'a plot of land' (prob. 'pasture land'), ?Two Hedges (f.n. Shawell), ?Wood Bridge Hedge (f.n. Lutterworth).

faggot ME, 'a bundle of sticks or twigs bound together for use as fuel'. Faggot Fd (f.n. Bitteswell).

falh OE (Angl), 'land broken up for cultivation, ploughed land'; later, 'ploughed land left uncultivated for a year, fallow land'. Dead-fallow (f.n. Ullesthorpe), Fallow Cl (f.n. Peatling Magna), Great North Fallow (f.n. Claybrooke Magna).

*(ge)fall OE (Angl), 'a felling, a place where something falls'; in p.ns., usually 'a felling of trees, a woodland clearing'. *Falstedes* (f.n. Cosby).

farder eModE, adj., 'at a greater distance'. *the farther Elme furlong* (f.n. Shawell), *the farther slade* (f.n. Oadby).

fatte ME, adj., 'fertile, rich'. *Fat Forlongslade* (f.n. Misterton).

fealu OE, adj., 'pale brown or reddish yellow'. ?Fallow How (f.n. South Kilworth).

fearn OE, 'a fern'. *Fernedale* (f.n. Kilby), *ferne hedge* (f.n. Whetstone), Fernhill (f.n. Kimcote), *the upper fernes* (f.n. Sutton in the Elms).

feeding ModE, vbl.sb., ppl.adj.; for agriculture, 'feeding ground, pasturage'. Feeding Cl (f.n. Broughton Astley), Feeding Mdw (f.n. Frolesworth).

feire, faire ME, 'a fair, a gathering of merchants'. *Horse Faire Leyes* (f.n. Lutterworth).

feld OE, 'open country', **felde** ME, 'land for pasture or cultivation; a common or great open-field of a township', **field** ModE, 'an enclosed or fenced-in plot of ground'. Of Guthlaxton Hundred's 44 townships which are assumed to have had open-field systems of their own, 35 have the names of their great fields surviving in records, while Littlethorpe has two certain names extant and Knighton one (plus one uncertain). Frolesworth, Peatling Magna, Peatling Parva and Swinford had fields which were designated by combinations of the simple directional adjectives *north*, *south*, *east*, *west*. There are 11 townships which had an early Middle Fd, while 10 had a Mill Fd. Recurring also are 6 great open-fields with **wald** (disguised variously as *wold*, *owlte*, *olte*, *old*). Otherwise the great fields were in general named from topographical features, as e.g., in Ashby Magna (*Ingesicke*, *Therne*, *Westbrook*), in South Kilworth (*Bruk*, *Mutt*, *Wakelow*) and in Wigston Magna (*Goldhill*, *Muklowe*, *Tobrokes*). Changes in the names of a township's open-fields may or may not indicate the reorganization of their arable, but such changes of names or alternative names for great fields are evidenced for Arnesby, Aylestone, Bitteswell, Blaby, Bruntingthorpe, Countesthorpe, Dunton Bassett, Gilmorton, Kilby, Leire, Peatling Magna, South Kilworth, Walcote and Walton.

felging OE (Angl), 'ploughed or fallow land'. ?*Fellings* (f.n. Bruntingthorpe).

*felling OE (Angl), 'a felling of trees, a clearing'. ?*Fellings* (f.n. Bruntingthorpe).

fenn OE, 'a fen, a marsh, marshland'; also 'mud, mire'. *Fen balke, fen hawthorn,* Fens Slade (f.ns. North Kilworth), Fen Cl (f.n. Cosby, Peatling Parva), *fenn* *hades* (f.n. Frolesworth, Sutton in the Elms), *Feynys* (f.n. Kimcote), *Glencaluerley fen* (f.n. Blaby).

fennig OE, adj., 'dirty, muddy, marshy'. First Fenny (f.n. Claybrooke Magna).

fenol OE, 'fennel'. *feneldoale* (f.n. Shawell).

fense eModE, 'a railing, a fence'. Double Fence (f.n. Frolesworth), Fence Lands (f.n. North Kilworth).

feoh OE, 'wealth, property', **fee** ME, 'payment; a perquisite allowed to a village official'. *Fee Furlong* (f.n. Gilmorton).

feor OE, adj., 'far, distant'. Far Cl (f.n. Ashby Parva, Blaby, Broughton Astley), Far Mdw (f.n. Arnesby, Ashby Parva, Bitteswell, Broughton Astley), *the fare cley*, *the farr Stanehill* (f.ns. Aylestone), *Farmoor Leases* (f.n. Countesthorpe), Ferey (f.n. Gilmorton), *Furr leyes* (f.n. Aylestone, Whetstone).

fēower OE, numeral, 'four'. ?*Fourewelleslade* (f.n. Wigston Magna), *4 lease* (f.n. Leire), *4 thornes* (f.n. Shawell).

fēowertēne OE, numeral, 'fourteen'. *the fourteen lands* (f.n. Shearsby), *the fowerteene Acres* (f.n. Peatling Parva), *the fowrteene* (f.n. Shawell).

ferme OFr, ME, 'rent', eModE, 'land held on lease, an agricultural tenement, a farm'. Common in modern minor p.ns. In earlier instances, sometimes prefixed by a surn., e.g. *Brooksbyes farme* (Ashby Magna), *Goddards Farm* (Cotesbach); also *the Farme* (Swinford), *Hall Farme* (Arnesby, Ashby Magna), *Pippinwell Farme* (Arnesby), Saffron Farm (Aylestone). Note *Fermforlang'* (f.n. Cosby).

fille OE, 'thyme', or some such plant (*v.* OED *s.v.* fill). *Fillefurlang'*, *Filleshou* (f.ns. Westrill and Starmore), Fillow Mdw (f.n. Ashby Parva), ?Filley Fd (f.n. Misterton).

fillie ME, 'a young mare, a female foal'. ?Filley Fd (f.n. Misterton).

finger-post ModE, 'a guide post, a post with one or more arms, often terminating in the shape of a finger, set up at a road-junction to indicate direction, distance or destination'. Finger Post Cl (f.n. Dunton Bassett, Frolesworth), Finger Post Fd (f.n. Arnesby).

*finn OE, ON, 'coarse grass'. ?*findale* (f.n. Shawell), *Finland* (f.n. Cosby).

firr ME, 'a fir-tree'. The Fir Tree 11 Acre (f.n. Swinford).

fisc OE, 'fish'. *fishedame* (f.n. Dunton Bassett), Fish Pit (f.n. Willoughby Waterleys).

fiscere OE, 'a fisherman'. ?*Fyssher mydo* (f.n. Littlethorpe).

fisshe-ponde ME, 'a fish-pond'. Fish Pond (f.n. Bitteswell), Fish Pond Cl (f.n. Frolesworth, Leire).

flagge ME, 'a reed, a rush'. *Flaggefurlong*, *flagspitt* (f.ns. Bitteswell), The Flags (f.n. Swinford).

flask ODan, 'swampy grassland, a swamp'. ?*Flaxknorrs* (f.n. Cosby), *Flaxstaves* (f.n. Aylestone).

flasshe ME, 'a swamp'. The Flashes (f.n. Cosby).

flat ON, 'a piece of flat, level ground'. Flat House Fm, Flat Spinney. Battle Flat (f.n. Frolesworth), The Flats (f.n. Swinford), Flat Side (f.n. Gilmorton), *the Flatt*, *Shepehusflatte* (f.ns. Ashby Magna), *Little Dale Flatt* (f.n. Wigston Magna), *the Over flat* (f.n. Lutterworth), Stonebridge Flat (f.n. Arnesby); ?Flat Cl (f.n. Broughton Astley, Peatling Magna, Wigston Magna), ?Flat Fd (f.n. Peatling Magna), ?Flat Mdw (f.n. Peatling Magna, Wigston Magna, Willoughby Waterleys).

flatr ON, adj., 'flat, level'; difficult to distinguish from **flat** when acting as a specific. ?Flat Cl (f.n. Broughton Astley, Peatling Magna, Wigston Magna), ?Flat Fd (f.n. Peatling Magna), ?Flat Mdw (Peatling Magna, Wigston Magna, Willoughby Waterleys).

flaxe OE, 'a wooden vessel for liquids'. ?*Flaxstaves* (f.n. Aylestone).

fleax OE, **flax** ME, 'flax'. Flaxhill. *flaxbrokeleyes* (f.n. Dunton Bassett), *Flaxdale* (f.n. Aylestone), ?Flaxknorrs (f.n. Cosby), *Flaxlandes* (f.n. Blaby, Cosby, Kimcote, Leire, Shearsby), *Flaxyard* (f.n. Cosby), *Flax leyes* (f.n. Blaby, Glen Parva, Shawell).

flēot OE, **fljót** ON, 'a small stream, a rivulet'. Fleet Slade (f.n. Gilmorton), *Flotegras* (f.n. Cosby).

(ge)flit OE, 'dispute'. ?Flitters pit (f.n. Gilmorton), *flythill slade* (f.n. Lutterworth).

flodegate ME, 'a flood-gate, a sluice'. *Blabye Mylne fludgate* (f.n. Blaby), *le Flodegates* (f.n. Cosby), Flood Gate Hill (f.n. North Kilworth), Floodgate Mdw (f.n. Broughton Astley).

flȳs OE, ' fleece'. *fluslade* (f.n. North Kilworth).

fola OE, 'a foal'. *Foale close*, *Folehouse* (f.ns. Aylestone), Foalyard (f.n. Swinford).

folie ME, 'an extravagant or foolish building'. The Folly, Folly Bridge.

fōr OE, 'a hog, a pig'. ?*Foureslade* (f.n. Wigston Magna).

ford OE, 'a ford'. Swinford. Freq. in f.ns.: common are locations, e.g. *Barslaid Ford* (South Kilworth), *Cokmore ford* (Shearsby), Dunford (Lutterworth); the nature or appearance of the ford may feature, e.g. *badford* (Oadby), *Gilford* (Aylestone), *Myrye foarde* (Sutton in the Elms), *Stanford* (Leire); the use of the ford may be indicated, e.g. *le Waynford* (Aylestone). Recurring is *Bradeford* (Aylestone, Leire, Sutton in the Elms). Spellings with -*forth*(*e*) (arising from late ME -*rd* > -*rth* in unstressed syllables which occurs only in the Danelaw and may be due to Scand influence) are recorded occasionally, e.g. *Alforth* (Littlethorpe), *atte Forth'* (Aylestone), *Wigston forth* (Oadby).

fore OE, prep., 'in front of, before'; elliptically, '(land, place, thing) in front of, lying or standing before something'. *le fordoles* (f.n. Blaby, Frolesworth, Kimcote), *Drylands forelands* (f.n. Bruntingthorpe), *long foreland* (f.n. Bitteswell), *le Formedewe* (f.n. Cosby), *the foreyard* (f.n. Lutterworth), *Forshoots* (f.n. Misterton).

forest OFr, ME, 'a large tract of woodland or of hunting country'. *the Forest* (f.n. Peatling Magna), *Foryste of Annurdale* (f.n. Kilby), Great Forest (f.n. Cotesbach).

foreward OE, 'a bargain, an agreement'. Fords Home (f.n. North Kilworth).

foss[1] OE, 'a ditch'. Fosse Fm (relating to the Roman Fosse Way).

fōt[1] OE, ' a foot'; topographically, 'the foot or bottom of something; the bottom of a hill'. *barefote* (f.n. Frolesworth), Bridge Foot Cl (f.n. Glen Parva), *Fotdolis*, *Goldhulfot* (f.ns. Wigston Magna), *Goldhulfot* (f.n. Knighton); Foot Road Fd (f.n. Cosby), Ullesthorpe Foot Road (f.n. Leire).

fote-brydge ME, 'a foot-bridge'. *at the footbrigg* (f.n. Countesthorpe).

fote-path ME, 'a footpath'. Footpath Fds (f.n. Dunton Bassett).

fote-way(**e**) ME, 'a footpath'. *Washpitt footway* (f.n. Gilmorton).

fox OE, 'a fox'. Fox Earths Spinney. *Foxall way* (f.n. Broughton Astley), The Fox Cover (f.n. Swinford), Fox Cover Cl (f.n. North Kilworth), Fox Covert (f.n. Peatling Magna), Foxenhill (f.n. Shearsby), *foxlondsik* (f.n. Oadby).

fox-hol OE, 'a fox's earth, a fox-hole'. ?Foxenhill (f.n. Shearsby), Foxhall (f.n. Claybrooke Magna), *Foxholes* (f.n. Gilmorton, Oadby, Peatling Magna, Whetstone).

fraternite ME, 'a fraternity, a brotherhood'. *Fraternity Land* (f.n. Westrill and Starmore).

frēo OE, adj., 'free'. *Freewells* (f.n. Bruntingthorpe).

front ME, adj., 'situated at the front'. Front Cl (f.n. Glen Parva), Front Fd (f.n. Bitteswell, Dunton Bassett, Peatling Magna, Shearsby), Front Orchard (f.n. Ashby Parva).

frosc OE, 'a frog'. *Frost Pitt Hill* (f.n. Misterton).

fuglung OE, 'fowling, bird-catching'. ?*fullen seeche* (f.n. South Kilworth).

fūl (fūlan wk.obl.) OE, adj., 'foul, dirty, filthy'. *Fowlewells* (f.n. Aylestone), ?*fullen seeche* (f.n. South Kilworth), Fullmore Mdw (f.n. Cosby), *Fullpittes* (f.n. Ashby Parva, Peatling Parva), Fulsidge (f.n. Swinford), *fullwell* (f.n. Catthorpe, Kimcote, Littlethorpe).

fulling ModE, vbl.sb., 'the process of cleansing and thickening cloth by washing and beating'. Fulling Mill (Peatling Magna).

furh OE, 'a furrow, a trench'; in ME, also used of 'a piece of arable land'. Rush Furrow (f.n. Swinford), *Schortforrou* (f.n. Blaby, Frolesworth), *smale thorowes* (f.n. Dunton Bassett), *Thorowe acres* (f.n. Catthorpe, Cotesbach, Misterton). *Water furrowes* recurs (f.n. Ashby Parva, Aylestone, Blaby, Claybrooke Parva, Cosby, Kilby, Kimcote, Knighton, North Kilworth, Swinford).

furlang OE, 'the length of a furrow, a furlong, a piece of land the length of a furrow (esp. in a great open-field)'; in ME, 'a division of a great field cultivated as a unit'. Very freq. in f.ns.: e.g. *Benting home furlong*, *Elleridges Furlong*, *Haliwell furlong*, *Reede forlong* (Aylestone), *Couhauedinfurlong*, *Dam furlong*, *Erewygfurlong'*, *Flaggefurlong'*, *Pasfurlong*, *Sand furlong*, *le Strykfurlong* (Bitteswell), *Fulpit furlonge*, *Green Kettle furlonge*, *Langefurlong*, *Wolte Furlonge* (Ashby Parva). Many of the so-called 'field-names' in ME sources are furlong names.

furðra OE, adj., 'more distant'. Further Cl, Further Ground (f.ns. Cotesbach), *the Further Hoake furlonge* (f.n. Leire).

fyrhð OE, 'a wood, woodland, wooded countryside'. Oadby Frith.

fyrkin ME, 'a small cask for liquids'. *firkinhole* (f.n. Wigston Magna).

fyrs OE, 'furze'. *Common furrs* (f.n. Misterton), *Coxe Furs* (f.n. Lutterworth), *the furrs* (f.n. Broughton Astley, North Kilworth, Peatling Magna, Shawell, Whetstone), *the furres of Thomas Beale* (f.n. Ashby Parva), *Pikefurres* (f.n. Catthorpe), *Port fyrsse* (f.n. Blaby), *Shackits furs* (f.n. Bitteswell), *waltney furres* (f.n. North Kilworth), *Webster furze* (f.n. Whetstone). Later spellings are easily confused with plural forms of **furh**.

***fyrsig** OE, adj., 'growing with furze'. *the Furry close* (f.n. Frolesworth).

galga OE, **galgi** ON, 'a gallows'. ?Gallaway (f.n. Countesthorpe).

galg-trēow OE, **gálga-tré** ON, 'a gallows-tree, a gallows'. ?Galtree Spinney.

galla (gallan dat.sg.) OE, 'a sore'; in p.ns., prob. 'a barren or wet spot in a field'. Gawney Lane, Gurney Lane. *gaales*, *Watergall Closes* (f.ns. Ashby Parva), *the galls*, *galney* (f.ns. Peatling Parva), *the gawles*, *watergalls* (f.ns. Shearsby), Hard Galles (f.n. Oadby).

gandra OE, 'a gander, a male goose'. *Gandertreyde* (f.n. Knighton).

gaole ME, 'a gaol'. Gaol Cl (f.n. Wigston Magna), *the Goal* (f.n. Lutterworth).
gap ON, 'a gap, an opening', **gappe** ME, 'a breach or opening in a wall or fence'. Guthlaxton Gap, Swinford Gap. *Caudwell gappe* (f.n. Peatling Magna), Lincroft Gap (f.n. Ashby Parva), Ullesthorpe Gap (f.n. Bitteswell), *Welchmore gap* (f.n. Leire).
gāra OE, 'a point of land, a triangular plot of ground'. *Boarsgore* (f.n. North Kilworth), Bull Gore, *Swallowgore* (f.ns. Claybrooke Parva), Bullgoar (f.n. Ullesthorpe), *Cow haden Gore* (f.n. Lutterworth), *Dudwell Goore* (f.n. Ashby Parva), *le Gore* (f.n. Bitteswell, Wigston Magna), ?*Gore's Close* (f.n. Willoughby Waterleys), Hog's Gore (f.n. Blaby), *the long goars* (f.n. Shawell), *le Oldgore, Wadgorslade* (f.ns. Cosby), *Pedlers goare* (f.n. Sutton in the Elms), *waie gore syde* (f.n. Dunton Bassett).
gardin ME, 'a garden, an enclosed plot used for cultivation of fruit, vegetables etc.'. Back Garden Cl (f.n. Claybrooke Parva), Bottom Garden (f.n. Claybrooke Magna), Garden Allotments (f.n. Broughton Astley), Garden Cl (f.n. Catthorpe), Garden Fd (f.n. Arnesby), Lower Garden Cl (f.n. Willoughby Waterleys), Martin's Garden (f.n. Wigston Parva).
garebrode, gorebrode ME, 'a broad triangular piece of land'. *Gorebroade* (f.n. Cotesbach, North Kilworth, Sutton in the Elms), Sutton Garbage (f.n. Cosby).
gás ON, 'a goose', a wild-goose'. *Gaseforlong* (f.n. Knighton).
gata ON, 'a way, a road, a street'. Stoneygate. It may be prefixed by a township name (as destination), e.g. *asby gate* (Dunton Bassett), Coates Gate (Gilmorton), *Foxton Gate* (Arnesby), *Glengate* (Oadby); several early names of this type are recorded for Wigston Magna, as *blabygathe, Kylebygate, Neutonegate* and *Outhebygate*. Recurring is *Grenegate* (Cosby, Knighton). Note Saltersgate way (Kimcote). Many of these road-names have survived as furlong-names, even when not specifically designated as such.
geard OE, 'an enclosure; a yard, a courtyard'. Freq. in f.ns.: esp. with a surn., e.g. *Boones yardes end, Coltmans yard* (Wigston Magna), Dysons Yard (Broughton Astley), Martins Yard (Peatling Parva), *Pallmers yearde* (Dunton Bassett), *Pycrofts yard* (Frolesworth); with a minor township building, e.g. *the George yardes end* (Lutterworth), *the Parsonage Yard* (Blaby, Catthorpe), *le Spitelyerd* (Cosby). Recurring are The Oak Yard (Bruntingthorpe, Peatling Parva), *Pooleyard* (Aylestone, Blaby). Note the unusual Parish Yard (Claybrooke Magna).
geat OE, 'a gate'; difficult to distinguish from **gata**. ?Gate Cottages. *Fludes gate*, Mr Grundy's Gate (f.ns. Dunton Bassett), *hallesgate* (f.n. Cotesbach), *Lammas cloase gate* (f.n. Broughton Astley), *(at) New field gate* (f.n. Oadby), *Snealesgate*, Wintertons Gate, *Woodsgate* (f.ns. Lutterworth).
gegge ME, 'a beggar'. *Gegecros* (f.n. Oadby).
geld OE, 'tax, payment'. *le Geldiswong* (f.n. Knighton).
gibet ME, 'a gibbet, a gallows'. Gibbet Hill, Gibbet Lane. *Gibbet Close* (f.n. Aylestone, Cotesbach), ?Gibwhite (f.n. Whetstone).
gilden OE, adj., 'golden'; also 'wealthy, splendid, rich'. Gilmorton.
glebe ME, 'glebe', i.e. land belonging to an ecclesiastical benifice. Glebe Fm (Bitteswell, Blaby, Broughton Astley, Countesthorpe, Lutterworth, Oadby, Peatling Parva, Wigston Magna); Glebe Ho., Glebe Rd. *the Glebe* (f.n. Bruntingthorpe, Swinford), *the glebe hadlande* (f.n. Ashby Parva), *the gleabe*

land (f.n. Shawell), Twin Glebe (f.n. Arnesby).

godspel OE, 'the gospel'. Gospel Cl (f.n. Shearsby).

gold OE, 'gold; gold treasure'. ?Goldhill. ?Goldpit (f.n. Claybrooke Parva).

golde OE, 'a marigold, a marsh marigold'. ?Goldhill. ?Goldpit (f.n. Claybrooke Parva).

gonele ME, 'a channel, an artificial course for running water'. *gonnelesbrige* (f.n. Dunton Bassett).

gorst OE, 'gorse, furze'; freq. in modern minor names and in f.ns. in the sense 'a piece of ground covered with gorse, a fox-covert of gorse bushes'. Gorse Lane, Gwens Gorse, Misterton Gorse, Walton Holt Gorse, Whetstone Gorse. Aylestone Gorse (f.n. Aylestone), Dunton Gorse (f.n. Dunton Bassett), Gorse Cl (f.n. Cosby, Dunton Bassett), *Gorsehurst*, Gorse Pit (f.ns. Blaby), *Gostill* (f.n. Catthorpe), Harris Gorse Cl (f.n. Broughton Astley), *Peatling Gorse* (f.n. Peatling Magna). Note the dial. form *goss(e)* in *Gosse medow* (f.n. Knaptoft) and perh. in ?*Gosmore* (f.n. Aylestone) and ?*Gossecroft* (f.n. Peatling Parva); but difficult to distinguish in the dial. form from **gōs**.

*gorstig OE, adj., 'overgrown with gorse'. Gorsy Cl (f.n. Leire, Willoughby Waterleys).

gōs OE, **gás** ON, 'a goose'. *goose acres* (f.n. Kilby, North Kilworth), *Goose holmes* (f.n. Foston, Wigston Magna), ?*Gosmore* (f.n. Aylestone), ?*Gossecroft* (f.n. Peatling Parva), Goss Green Furlong (f.n. South Kilworth).

goter ME, 'a gutter, a water channel'. *the gutter* (f.n. Kimcote), Gutter Cl (f.n. Peatling Magna), *Kitehill guttor* (f.n. Bruntingthorpe), *langesladegutter* (f.n. Dunton Bassett), *Meathill gutter* (f.n. Shearsby), *myrye gutter* (f.n. Sutton in the Elms), Slade Gutter (f.n. Ullesthorpe), Winter Gutter (f.n. Catthorpe), *Wollandes gutter* (f.n. Ashby Parva).

grāf OE, 'a grove, a copse'. The Grove (f.n. Arnesby, Knaptoft, South Kilworth), Grove Mdw (f.n. Shawell), ?Salter's Grave (f.n. Lutterworth), ?*Witchgrave* (f.n. Wigston Magna).

grange OFr, ME, 'a grange', originally 'a granary, a barn', later 'a farm'; also 'an outlying farm belonging to a religious house or to a feudal lord, where crops were stored'; often used in modern p.ns., usually with an older p.n. prefixed to convey a pretence of antiquity. Aylestone ~, Bitteswell ~, Claybrooke Grange, The Grange (Claybrooke Magna, North Kilworth, Walcote), Kilby ~, Knaptoft ~, Misterton ~, Poultney Grange, *Pynselade Grange*, Shawell ~, South Kilworth ~, Stoughton ~, Ullesthorpe ~, Walton ~, Whetstone ~, Wigston Grange; Grange Fm (Arnesby, Ashby Magna, Broughton Astley, Bruntingthorpe, Sutton in the Elms, Willoughby Waterleys), Grange Spinney. Grange Mdw (f.n. Ashby Parva).

grauntmoder ME, 'a grandmother'. *Grammerhill* (f.n. Whetstone).

gravel ME, 'gravel'. Gravel Hill. Gravel Cl (f.n. Arnesby), Gravel Hill (f.n. Arnesby, Blaby), Gravel Hole (f.n. Arnesby, Bitteswell, Countesthorpe, Dunton Bassett), Gravel Hole Cl (f.n. Frolesworth, North Kilworth), Gravel Pit (f.n. Arnesby, Misterton), Gravel Pit Cl (f.n. Broughton Astley, Frolesworth), Gravel Pits (f.n. Ashby Parva, Leire, Lutterworth).

græf OE, 'a digging, a pit, a trench; a grave'. ?Salter's Grave (f.n. Lutterworth), *Theuesgraue* (f.n. Knighton), Tilles Grave (f.n. Kimcote), ?*Witchgrave*, *Wrthegraue* (f.ns. Wigston Magna).

græs OE, 'grass, pasture'. *The Bell rope grasse* (f.n. Leire), *Brograss* (f.n. Bruntingthorpe), *Clover Grass Close* (f.n. Aylestone), *Flotgres*, Grass Cl, *le Swetegres* (f.ns. Cosby), *Grasfeelde* (f.n. Bitteswell), Grass Cl (f.n. Shawell), *Grass plots* (f.n. Gilmorton), ?*Grease Nooke*, *Greshadland* (f.ns. Oadby), *the Horsegrasse* (f.n. Broughton Astley), *the partinge grasse* (f.n. Kimcote), Redcross (f.n. Wigston Magna), *Reydgreys* (f.n. Blaby), *Sutton horsegrass* (f.n. Sutton in the Elms), *Whyte gresse* (f.n. Kilby).

grease ModEdial. 'grease, fat'; perh. used of rich pasture. ?*Grease Nooke* (f.n. Oadby).

grēat OE, adj., 'bulky', **great** ME, 'big in size'. *Greate bridge* (f.n. Aylestone), Great Cl (f.n. Ashby Parva, Aylestone, Catthorpe, Claybrooke Parva), Great Hill (f.n. Leire), *greate longecrofte* (f.n. Shawell), Great Mdw (f.n. Catthorpe), *greate more feylde* (f.n. Dunton Bassett).

greeneswarth ModE, 'greensward'. *the green swerd* (f.n. Bruntingthorpe).

grein ON, 'a branch, a fork; a small valley forking off from another'. ?*Brodgreyns* (f.n. Blaby), ?*Grenestokysmere* (f.n. Cosby), ?*Ouergreyndall'* (f.n. Littlethorpe), *Syke greynes* (f.n. Oadby).

***grendel** OE, 'a gravelly place or stream'. *Caldewellegrindil* (f.n. Bitteswell), ?The Granell (f.n. Swinford), *grindle* (f.n. Cotesbach), *Grindle Haden* (f.n. Kimcote), *Grundleswell* (f.n. Misterton).

grēne[1] OE, adj., 'green, grass-grown'. Green Lane. *Greenwell Haggs*, *Greene Yard*, *Green Hill* (f.ns. Aylestone), Green Kettle, Green Lane (f.ns. Ashby Parva), Greenlands (f.n. Peatling Magna), Greenleys (f.n. Arnesby), Greensitch (f.n. Dunton Bassett), Greenway (f.n. Frolesworth), *Greensty* (f.n. Blaby), *Grinley hade* (f.n. Kimcote), *Grinway* (f.n. Gilmorton).

grēne[2] OE, 'a grassy spot, a village green'. The Green (Bitteswell, Leire, North Kilworth, Oadby). Baldwin's Green, The Green (f.ns. Claybrooke Parva), *Broadgrene*, *Goss green Furlong* (f.ns. South Kilworth), ?*Brodgrenys* (f.n. Blaby), *Broughton Green* (f.n. Broughton Astley), *Coatgreene*, *Copply green* (f.ns. Whetstone), the Green (f.n. Arnesby, Wigston Magna), Green Furlong (f.n. Claybrooke Magna), Kimcote Green (f.n. Kimcote), *Ridgeway Greene* (f.n. Sutton in the Elms).

***grindel** OE, 'a mill, a grind-stone, a thing for grinding with'. *Grindhill* (f.n. Whetstone).

grund OE, 'ground; a stretch of land', **grund** ON, 'earth, a plain'; later also 'an outlying farm, outlying fields' and 'a piece of land enclosed for agricultural purposes'. Sharrag Grounds. Allotment Ground, Foston Grounds, Peatling Grounds (f.ns. Foston), Barn Ground, Dairy ~, Dove Bridge ~, Hill ~, Langhams ~, Middle Ground (f.ns. Catthorpe), Hill ~, Middle Ground (f.ns. Bittesby), *Kirbie grownd* (f.n. Arnesby), Kings ~, Middle ~, Old House ~, Parsons Ground (f.ns. Shawell), *Lubsthorp grounds* (f.n. Aylestone), *the middle ground* (f.n. Ashby Parva), *Katherine Moors Grounds*, Mr Wigley's Grounds (f.ns. Dunton Bassett), Oak Tree Ground (f.n. Bitteswell), Potatoe Ground (f.n. Claybrooke Parva), Sir Tho. Caves Grounds (f.n. South Kilworth), *stanground* (f.n. Kimcote), Top Oat Ground (f.n. Cotesbach).

grȳpe OE, **gryppe** ME, 'a ditch, a drain'. Greeping (f.n. Dunton Bassett), Gripes Mdw (f.n. North Kilworth), *the grips* (f.n. Wigston Magna).

***gylde** OE, 'a golden flower'. *Gilford Low* (f.n. Aylestone).

gylden OE, adj., 'golden'; in p.ns., often alluding to golden-coloured flowers. *gildenebutes* (f.n. Countesthorpe), *gilden furlong*, *gilden roodes* (f.ns. Catthorpe), *Golden medou* (f.n. Wigston Magna).

gyr OE, 'mud, filth; a marsh'. *Gyrlow* (f.n. Kimcote).

hafoc OE, 'a hawk'. ?Hawkswell Spinney (f.n. Shearsby), Hawks Nest (f.n. Lutterworth), Hawxlow (f.n. South Kilworth).

haga[1] OE, 'a hedge, an enclosure', **hagi** ON, 'a grazing enclosure, a pasture'. ?Usher Fm. Hawcott Mdw (f.n. Foston).

hagu-þorn, **hagu-þyrne** OE, 'the hawthorn, the whitethorn'. *fen hawthorn* (f.n. North Kilworth), *Hawthorne hill*, *Neyther Hawthorne bush* (f.ns. Aylestone), *hawthorn dike* (f.n. Whetstone), *Hawthorngathe*, *Hauthernehil* (f.ns. Wigston Magna).

hald[1] OE (Angl), 'protection', **hald**, **hold** ME, 'a shelter, a refuge'. *Holdehole* (f.n. Swinford), ?*Holdingsik* (f.n. Cosby), ?*Smytholde* (f.n. Shearsby).

half OE (Angl), adj., 'half, a half part'. Halfyard Lands (f.n. Shearsby), *le Halvidole* (f.n. Misterton).

hālga (**hālgan** nom.pl.), OE, 'a saint'. All Hallows Church (Wigston Magna), *Allhollen Lane* (Gilmorton).

halh OE (Angl), 'a nook, a corner of land, a hollow, a secluded valley'. ?Thistle Hall. ?*all wronges* (f.n. North Kilworth), *bagnall medewe* (f.n. Leire), *Cauldwell Hole* (f.n. Bitteswell), Cordwell Hole, *Springale hill* (f.ns. Ashby Parva), *Halebergh* (f.n. Kilby), *the halles* (f.n. Sutton in the Elms), *halley tafts* (f.n. Whetstone), *Foxall way*, Hall Hay Mdw, *the Haul* (f.ns. Broughton Astley), ?Oxhall (f.n. Arnesby).

hālig OE, adj., 'holy'. Holowell Fd (f.n. Arnesby), *Holywell* (f.n. Wigston Magna), Holywell Fd, ~ Hill (f.ns. Shawell).

hall OE (Angl), 'a hall, a manor house'. Aylestone ~, Bitteswell ~, Blaby Hall, *Bruntingthorpe Hall*, Catthorpe ~, Claybrooke ~, Cotesbach Hall, Foston Hall Fm, Knighton Hall, Lutterworth ~, Misterton ~, Peatling ~, Shawell ~, Stanford ~, Tomley ~, Wigston Hall (Wigston Magna, Wigston Parva), The Hall (Broughton Astley, Claybrooke Magna, Cosby, Knaptoft, Walton), (The) Hall Fm (Ashby Magna, Frolesworth, Leire, Peatling Magna), Hall Lane, Nether Hall, Old Hall (North Kilworth, Willoughby Waterleys). ?*all wronges* (f.n. North Kilworth), *Hall baulk* (f.n. Bruntingthorpe), Hall Cl (f.n. Ashby Parva, Claybrooke Parva, Dunton Bassett), *Halcroft* (f.n. Kimcote), Hallcroft (f.n. Countesthorpe, Gilmorton), *le Hall land* (f.n. Claybrooke Parva, Foston), *the hall mere* (f.n. Arnesby).

hām OE, 'a village, an estate; a homestead'. ?*Legham*. ?*Dawthames* (f.n. Ashby Parva), ?*Hennams Cl*, Tilbram Cls (f.ns. Cosby).

hamer ME, adj., comp., 'nearer home, nearer the village'. *Hammer meadow* (f.n. Blaby).

hamm OE, 'a water meadow, land hemmed in by water or marsh, wet land hemmed in by higher ground'. Barom Hill, Boyam, Peasom, *sotham* (f.ns. Gilmorton), ?Collum Mdw (f.n. Glen Parva), ?*Dawthames*, Langham, Redham (f.ns. Ashby Parva), *Hallow hame* (f.n. South Kilworth), *hampit* (f.n. Peatling Parva), The Hatcham, South Hams (f.ns. Littlethorpe), ?Hennams Cls (f.n. Cosby), Langhams Ground (f.n. Catthorpe), ?*Legham* (?Leire), Lingham's (f.n. Frolesworth), *Longams* (f.n. Blaby), Redham (f.n. Ullesthorpe), ?*Sealom*, *Witcham corner* (f.ns.

Aylestone), Sizeham, *Usom* (f.ns. Bitteswell), Sweetham (f.n. Claybrooke Magna).

hām-stall OE (Angl), '(the enclosure of) a homestead'; surviving as **homestall** ModEdial., 'a farmyard'. *the Homestall* (f.n. Ashby Magna, Bruntingthorpe, Claybrooke Parva, Dunton Bassett, Leire), *the parsonage homestall* (f.n. Catthorpe), *Richard Burroughes's Homestall* (f.n. Ashby Parva).

hām-stede OE, 'a homestead, the site of a dwelling', surviving as **homestead** ModE, 'the home buildings'. (The) Homestead (f.n. Ashby Parva, Blaby, Broughton Astley, Claybrooke Parva, Frolesworth, Kimcote, Knighton, Misterton, Peatling Magna), Kimbles Homestead, Walls Homestead (f.ns. Catthorpe), Snelson's Homestead(f.n. Gilmorton).

hāmweard OE, adj., 'towards home, towards the village'. *the homeward forlonge* (f.n. Gilmorton), *homeward lichslade* (f.n. Shawell).

hand-post ModE, 'a guide-post', i.e. one with hands terminating the direction boards, cf. **finger-post** *supra*. The Hand Post (f.n. Glen Parva).

hangende OE, **hengjandi** ON, pres.part., ppl.adj., 'hanging'; used in p.ns. of places on a steep slope or hillside. ?Hangland Spinney. *le Hangend'* (f.n. Wigston Magna), Hanghome Baulk, Hangland, Hang Woong (f.ns. South Kilworth), Hanging Barom (f.n. Gilmorton), *hanging furlonge*, *Hanging Hill*, *hanging leayes* (f.ns. Misterton), *Hanginhill* (f.n. Aylestone, Claybrooke Magna), Hanglands (f.n. Kimcote), *Hengyn hadland* (f.n. Oadby), Long Hangings (f.n. Swinford).

*hangol OE, adj., 'sloping'. ?Hangland Spinney.

hangra OE, 'a wood on a steep hill-side'. *Bernhanger* (f.n. Misterton), ?Binger's Hill, *Hangarshull'* (f.ns. Arnesby), Hanger Spinney (f.n. Shearsby), Hungerlands (f.n. Dunton Bassett).

hār² OE, adj., 'grey, hoar', esp. 'grey through being overgrown with lichen'; prob. came to mean 'boundary' because of its freq. use with features forming boundary marks or lying on boundaries. ?*Hareland* (f.n. Cosby), ?*Harestiles* (f.n. Ashby Parva), ?*Harton* (f.n. Countesthorpe), ?*Harton field* (f.n. Whetstone), Horston Hill (f.n. Dunton Bassett), *Horstonpyt* (f.n. Knighton), *horstonsikenethirende* (f.n. Oadby), ?Top 'Arton (f.n. Willoughby Waterleys).

hara OE, 'a hare'; difficult to distinguish from **hār²**. ?Harestiles (f.n. Ashby Parva).

hassuc OE, 'a clump of coarse grass'. Hassockes (f.n. North Kilworth), Hussucky Cl, Near Husks (f.ns. Broughton Astley), ?*Turway Huske* (f.n. Kimcote).

haugr ON, 'a hill, a hill-top; a burial mound'; sometimes difficult to distinguish from OE **hō(e)** (dat.sg. of **hōh**). ?*Brachou* (f.n. Blaby), *Hechow*, ?*Mowshow* (f.ns. Littlethorpe), ?*Mokilhow* (f.n. Wigston Magna), ?*Warhthou* (f.n. Ashby Magna).

hæc(c) OE (Angl), 'a hatch, a sluice, a flood-gate'. The Hatcham, *Hechow* (f.ns. Littlethorpe).

(ge)hæg OE, **hay** ME, 'a fence, an enclosure'. Knighton Hayes. Hall Hay Mdw, Town Hay (f.ns. Broughton Astley), the Hayes (f.n. Leire), Hey Dikes (f.n. Lutterworth), *Russcheheye*, *Walteresheye* (f.ns. Aylestone), *stodyhill* (f.n. Dunton Bassett).

hælftre OE, 'a halter'. ?*Halteresslade* (f.n. Wigston Magna).

hænep OE, 'hemp'. Empty Cl, Empty Mdw, Hemp Hill Cl (f.ns. Willoughby Waterleys), *Hempbrookes* (f.n. Ashby Parva), *the Hempe lands* (f.n. Wigston Parva), *the Hempplecke* (f.n. Kimcote).

*hær OE, 'a rock, a heap of stones, a tumulus'. ?*Hareland* (f.n. Cosby), ?Harton (f.n. Countesthorpe), ?*Harton field* (f.n. Whetstone), ?Top 'Arton (f.n. Willoughby Waterleys).

*hæs OE (Angl), 'brushwood'. ?*Hastye* (f.n. Broughton Astley).

hæsel OE (Angl), 'a hazel'. Hazlewood (f.n. Ashby Parva).

hǣð OE (Angl), 'a heath, heather'. *Mr Bradgate his heath* (f.n. Ashby Magna), The Heath, Kimcote Heath, Mill Heath (f.ns. Gilmorton), *heath furlong* (f.n. Frolesworth), the Heath Furlong, *Heath Slade* (f.ns. Lutterworth), Kimcote Heath, *Walton heathe* (f.ns. Kimcote).

hæt(t) OE, 'a hat'; used topographically to allude to a hat-shaped hill. *Hat, Hatthill* (f.ns. Aylestone).

headley ModEdial., '?a swarded-over or grass headland; ?an end unit of grassland'. Hadleys and Haggs (f.n. Kimcote), *Phillipes hadley* (f.n. Kilby), *Robert Jordains hadley, Thomas Davenports grass hadley* (f.ns. Oadby), *Thomas Tawbuts hadle* (f.n. North Kilworth).

hēafod OE, 'a head; the (top) end of something, a headland, unploughed land at the end of the arable where the plough turns', cf. **hēafod-land**. Freq. in f.ns. and very often in the pl. referring to headlands at the end of the arable, e.g. *the Arrow hades* (Bruntingthorpe), *Brademeereheuedes* (Cosby), *Estmedohaddis* (Blaby), *Fen hades* (Sutton in the Elms). Sometimes in the sg. alluding to a large physical feature, e.g. *Bullhade*, Dams Head (Kimcote), Cowhead (Bitteswell). In Guthlaxton Hundred, the archaic pl. form -*en* often survives, e.g. Bradgate Haden (South Kilworth), *michillhaden* (Dunton Bassett), *Morehaden* (Bruntingthorpe), *Ridgeway haden* (North Kilworth), Tibbits Haden (Kimcote).

hēafod-land OE, 'a strip of land at the head of a furlong left for turning the plough'. Freq. in f.ns.: usually with a villager's name prefixed, e.g. *Mr Ashbys hadland* (Blaby), *brownes haidlande* (Dunton Bassett), *John Burneys Hadland, gregories hedland* (Aylestone), *Thomas Killpacks headland* (Catthorpe); the parish church appears regularly, e.g. *Church Hadland* (Ashby Parva, Aylestone, Blaby, Bruntingthorpe), *Kyrkehadland* (Blaby), *Marymawdelyn hadeland* (Kilby).

hēah[1] (**hēan** wk. obl.), **hēh** (Angl), **high** ModE, adj., 'high, tall; important; lying high up, standing in a high place'. High Cross. Hennams Cls (f.n. Cosby), High Leys (f.n. Ashby Parva, Blaby), *hie Tomley* (f.n. Catthorpe).

hēah-weg OE, 'a highway, a main road'. Common is *the Kinges highway* (with various spellings in Ashby Parva, Aylestone, Blaby, Broughton Astley, Leire), *the Queens highway* (Ashby Parva, Aylestone, Gilmorton). Note *the Colepit highe waye* (Leire) and *the Fosse high way* (Broughton Astley).

heard OE, adj., 'hard, hard to till'. Hardhill (f.n. North Kilworth), Hard Mdw (f.n. Cotesbach); also used as a sb. for 'hard standing-ground; dry rough pasture'. *Brademedweharde* (f.n. Wigston Magna), *hard, Horsharde, Netteshard* (f.ns. Oadby).

hearpe OE, 'a harp', used topographically for something resembling a harp in shape. *the Harpe* (f.n. Catthorpe), ?*Harpehill* (f.n. Shearsby).

hearpere OE, 'a harper'. ?*harpston* (f.n. Aylestone).

heavie ModE, adj., 'heavy'; in f.ns., in allusion to weighty, sticky soil. *Heavy furlonge* (f.n. Shawell).

hecg OE, 'a hedge'. Freq. used in f.ns. with reference to boundary hedges between townships, e.g. *Ashby magna hedge, Ashby parva hedge* (Dunton Bassett), *Glen* *hedge* (Blaby), *peateling hedge* (Gilmorton), Poultney Hedge (Kimcote), *Shawell hedge* (Cotesbach). A surn. may be prefixed indicating hedges of private property, e.g. *Duckettes hedge* (Broughton Astley), *Goddins Hedge* (Countesthorpe), *John Lords hedge* (Bitteswell). Topographical features may be prefixed, e.g. *Butway Hedge* (Dunton Bassett), *the meere hedge* (Cotesbach). Some modern forms with *hedge* may conceal an original **edisc** or **etisc** (*q.v.*), as ?*ferne hedge* (Whetstone), ?*Kill Well Hedg* (Arnesby).

hēg OE (Angl), 'hay, mowing grass'; in late forms, sometimes difficult to distinguish from **hēah**[1] when compounded with **weg**. Hay Barn Cl (f.n. Dunton Bassett), Haybox (f.n. Bitteswell), the Hay Croft (f.n. Aylestone, Blaby), ?Hay Furlong (f.n. South Kilworth), ?*Hefurlang'* (f.n Westrill and Starmore), Heaway, *northerneheyweye* (f.ns. Kimcote).

hege OE, 'a hedge, a fence'. ?Hay Furlong (f.n. South Kilworth).

heiward ME, 'an officer in charge of fences and enclosures'. *the Haywardes peece* (f.n. Catthorpe).

hell-hole ModEdial., 'a dark haunted nook; a wretched place (for cultivation)'. *Hell hole* (f.n. Countesthorpe, Whetstone), *Hellhole Gate* (f.n. Whetsone).

henge** (hengan** obl.sg.) OE, adj., 'steep, precipitous'. ?*Hyngnoe* (f.n. Shearsby).

hengen OE, 'a gallows'. ?*Hyngnoe* (f.n. Shearsby).

henn OE, 'a hen', esp. of wild birds, as a water-hen. *Hencrofts* (f.n. Whetstone), *Henhou* (f.n. Westrill and Starmore), *Henmeere* (f.n. Cotesbach), *Henpoole* (f.n. Leire).

heorde-wīc OE, 'a herd farm'. *hardwicke way* (f.n. Aylestone), *Hardwyke* (f.n. Ashby Parva).

here-pæð OE, 'a military road, a highway'. ?*Harpehill* (f.n. Shearsby), ?*harpston* (f.n. Aylestone).

***herse** OE, 'a top, a hill-top. ?*Broadarse* (f.n. Blaby, Leire).

heyrek ME, 'a hayrick'. ?The Yerricks (f.n. Bitteswell).

hīd OE, 'a hide of land, an amount of land for the support of one free family and its dependants'. *Hede medew* (f.n. Oadby), Hide Mdw (f.n. Claybrooke Magna).

hider ME, adj., 'nearer'. *the hither cley* (f.n. Aylestone), *the Hither Low* (f.n. North Kilworth).

hiderweard OE, adj., 'towards this place'. *the Hitherward Hoake furlonge* (f.n. Leire).

hlāw OE, 'a mound, a hill'. Ainsloe Spinney, Tomley Hall, Wakeley Fm. Annislow, Fallow How, Hawxlow, Minslow, *scardelowe* (f.ns. South Kilworth), *Ansloe, Aukerly Hill, Bryghteslowe* (f.ns. Misterton), *Banlouwe*, Blakes Lowe, *Edricheslowebreche, Edwardes Lowe, Gyrlow*, Thorpe Loe (f.ns. Kimcote), Fillow Mdw, *Wakeley* (f.ns. Ashby Parva), *Gilford Low, Ruelowe* (f.ns. Aylestone), *the Hither Low* (f.n. North Kilworth), *Hornlowe, Stotfoldlow* (f.ns. Bitteswell), Rowley Fd (f.n. Shearsby), *Shardelowe* (f.n. Ashby Magna), *Smallowe* (f.n. Lutterworth), The Wakelins (f.n. Dunton Bassett), Wakelin (f.n. Leire).

hlēapwince OE, 'the lapwing'. *Lepwing leyes* (f.n. Wigston Magna).

***hlenc** OE, 'a hill-side'. Linslade (f.n. South Kilworth).

hlinc OE, 'a ridge, a bank'. Honeywell Lynch (f.n. North Kilworth), *Linches* (f.n. Aylestone), Limsdale Hill, Lynch (f.ns. Leire), *the Lynche* (f.n. Lutterworth).

hlot OE, 'a lot, a share, an allotment'. *le Lotforlonck* (f.n. Westrill and Starmore), *the Lott Meadow* (f.n. Oadby).

hnæpp OE, 'a bowl'; used topographically of 'a hollow'. ?*Neprodes* (f.n. Wigston Magna).

hob, **hobbe** ME, 'a hobgoblin'. ?*Hobwellebroc* (f.n. North Kilworth).

*hobb(e) OE, 'a tussock, a hummock'. ?*Hobwellebroc* (f.n. North Kilworth).

hobgoblin ME, 'a hobgoblin, a mischievous sprite; a bogey'. *hobgoblins pit* (f.n. Whetstone).

hōc OE, 'a hook, a bend in a river, a spit of land in a river bend, a corner or bend in a hill'. *austenhuke*, Joiner's Hook (f.ns. Dunton Bassett), *the Bulhooke*, *the Parsons hooke* (f.ns. Blaby), Bull Hooks (f.n. Shearsby), The Hoke, *the parsons hokes*, *the Parsonidge Hookes* (f.ns. Leire), *hookesickmiddo* (f.n. Gilmorton), The Hooks, Side Hook Mdw (f.ns. Swinford), *Mallens hooke* (f.n. Broughton Astley), *Micklehooke slade* (f.n. Peatling Magna), Musock (f.n. Kimcote), *Osemondeshoke* (f.n. Glen Parva).

hōcede OE, adj., 'having a hook or corner; curved'. *Hokedick* (f.n. Westrill and Starmore).

hogg OE, 'a hog'. (*at*) *hogges wateringe* (f.n. Aylestone), Hog Lane, *the hogg hole* (f.ns. Lutterworth), Hog Hole (f.n. North Kilworth), Hogshole (f.n. South Kilworth).

hǫgg ON, 'a cutting or felling of trees'. Common in f.ns.: *Blackwell haggs*, *Ratley hagges* (Broughton Astley), Bloomhills Haggs (Dunton Bassett), *Break forlong haggs*, *the Common* ~, *Leekbed* ~, *moor furlong* ~, *Two forlong haggs* (Whetstone), *Bull Meadow hagges*, *the haggs*, *Ridgeway hagges* (Sutton in the Elms), *Glen haggs*, *Greenwell Haggs* (Aylestone), Hadleys and Haggs, the Haggs of Rylands (Kimcote), *Hagg* (Cosby), The Hagg, *Hoden Haggs* (Countesthorpe), Haggs Fd (Blaby), *hingnah hags* (Shearsby), *Smoreslade haggs* (Oadby), *windmill haggs* (Wigston Magna).

hogghirde ME, 'a swineherd'. *Hoggheards goar* (f.n. Blaby).

hōh OE, 'a hill; a hill-spur'; in the Danelaw, difficult to distinguish from **haugr**. Common in f.ns.: ?*Brachou*, *Branhowstyes*, ?*Hechow*, *Marlhowey*, Wadders (Cosby), *branthowe*, The Wassal, *Westmisso*, Wooder Mdw (North Kilworth), *Filleshou*, Henhou (Westrill and Starmore), *Herningho* (Kimcote), *Hodale* (Aylestone), ?*homedow* (Gilmorton), *howgates forlong*, *Long oho*, *under how* (Whetstone), *Hyngnoe* (Shearsby), ?*Larow Hill* (Broughton Astley), *Littelclarouhull* (Bitteswell), ?*Mokilhow*, *Moseho* (Wigston Magna), *Mowshow* (Littlethorpe), *Rinksoe* (Shearsby), ?*Warthou* (Ashby Magna).

hol¹ OE, **hol** ON, 'a hole, a hollow'. Common in f.ns.: *Boyom hole*, Broadwell Hole (Gilmorton), *Butt Holes*, Cunny Hills, *the hogg hole* (Lutterworth), ?*Cauldwell Hole*, Gravel Hole (Bitteswell), ?*Cordwell Hole* (Ashby Parva), *firkinhole* (Wigston Magna), Gravel Hole (Dunton Bassett), Gravel Hole Cl, Hog Hole (North Kilworth), Hogshole, Padock Hole (South Kilworth), *Holdehole* (f.n. Swinford), ?*Oxhall*, Wiggins Hole (Arnesby), *Wildmore Hole* (Leire).

hol² OE, **holr** ON, adj., 'lying in a hollow, running in a hollow; sunken (esp. in stream-names)'. Oback Fm. Hobrook (f.n. Gilmorton), Holbrooke Cl (f.n. Knighton), ?*Hole dale* (f.n. Bruntingthorpe).

holegn OE, 'holly'. Holly Walk Spinney. Holly Furlong (f.n. Swinford).

holh OE, 'a hollow, a hole'. Smockington Hollow. Broadway Hollow (f.n. Bruntingthorpe), *Brockhurst hollow* (f.n. Shawell), Cogington Hollow (f.n. Swinford), *Dunton Hollowe* (f.n. Leire), *godscroft hollow* (f.n. Frolesworth), *the hallow*, Holliwell Hill (f.ns. North Kilworth), *the Hollow* (f.n. Cotesbach), Hollow Fd (f.n. Countesthorpe), Hollows, *Holoughtherne* (f.ns. Cosby), *Whitehill Hollow* (f.n. Arnesby).

holmr ON, 'a water meadow; a piece of drier ground amid marsh'. Very freq. in f.ns.: with prefixed surn. or pers.n., e.g. Colemans Home, Spillmans Home (Gilmorton), *Coulmans Holme* (Claybrooke Parva), *Guttulmesholm* (Kilby); with wild flora, e.g. *Brakenholm* (Cosby), *Lyngholmsyke* (Frolesworth), *Redholme, le thisteliholm* (Aylestone), *Thacheholme* (Littlethorpe); with crops, e.g. *Barley Home* (Leire) *Ryholm* (Lutterworth). Recurring are Mill Holme (Aylestone, Blaby, Catthorpe, Claybrooke Magna), *Goose holmes* (Foston, Wigston Magna), Holme Cl (Bruntingthorpe, Peatling Magna) and *the Holm feld* (Knaptoft, North Kilworth). The el. may occur as the specific of a minor name, e.g. Home Hill (Kimcote, South Kilworth), Home Side (Kimcote). As a simplex, it occurs both in sg. and pl. form, e.g. *le Holme* (Ashby Magna, Aylestone) and Holmes (Ashby Parva, Cotesbach, Littlethorpe).

holt OE, ON, 'a small wood'. Aylestone Holt, The Holt.

home ModE, adj., 'near home'. Home Fm (Ashby Parva, Knighton, South Kilworth), Home Farm Lodge. Recurring is Home Cl (f.n. Arnesby, Bittesby, Bitteswell, Blaby, Broughton Astley, Peatling Magna) and Home Fd (f.n. Arnesby, Bitteswell, Broughton Astley, Peatling Magna).

hop-yard ModE, 'a hop-yard, a hop-garden, an enclosure where hops grow'. Hop Yard (f.n. Claybrooke Parva), Hop Yard Mdw (f.n. Peatling Parva).

horgr ON, 'a heap of stones, a cairn'. ?*Arrow furlong*, ?Harrow Cl (f.ns. Broughton Astley), ?*Harrow akers* (f.n. Bruntingthorpe), ?*harrow slade* (f.n. Peatling Parva).

horh OE, 'dirt'. ?*hourding hags* (f.n. Countesthorpe).

horn OE, ON, 'a horn; a projecting piece of land'. ?Highhorn Cl, ?*horne end* (f.ns. Leire), *horneslade* (f.n. North Kilworth), *Hornlowe* (f.n. Bitteswell), ?Lankhorn Stile (f.n. Misterton).

hors OE, **hross** ON, 'a horse'. Horsewell Lane. Horse Cl (f.n. Arnesby, Bitteswell, Blaby, Broughton Astley, Claybrooke Parva, Cotesbach), Horse Close Mdw (f.n. Bittesby), *the Horse Common, Horse Faire Leyes* (f.ns. Lutterworth), *the horsegrasse* (f.n. Broughton Astley), *Horsein Hylles* (f.n. Ashby Parva), *Horseharde* (f.n. Oadby), *Horselandis* (f.n. Blaby), *horsslade* (f.n. Misterton), *Sutton horsegrass* (f.n. Sutton in the Elms).

hospital ME, 'a hospital, a hospice'. St John's Hospital, *Frolesworth Hospital* (The Almshouses).

hovel emodE, 'a hovel, a shed, a frame or stand on which a stack of corn is built'. Hovel Hill. Ducketts Hovel Cl, Hovel Mdw (f.ns. Broughton Astley), Hovel Cl (f.n. Bitteswell, Broughton Astley, Frolesworth), Hovel Fd (f.n. Blaby, Peatling Magna), Hovel Mdw (f.n. Swinford), Mud Hovel Fd (f.n. Shearsby).

hræfn OE, **hrafn** ON, 'a raven'. ?Rangmore Slade (f.n. Dunton Bassett), ?Ravens Hill (f.n. Claybrooke Magna), ?*Raven Willow Leyes* (f.n. Claybrooke Parva).

hrēac OE, 'a rick'. *the ricke place* (f.n. Aylestone), Straw Rick Cl (f.n. Bitteswell).

hrēod OE, 'a reed, a rush', prob. also 'a reed-bed'; sometimes difficult to distinguish from OE **rēad** 'red'. The Reeds, Reed Pool. ?*Red Bank, Redholme, Reede forlonge* (f.ns. Aylestone), Redcross, *Reddeleiz tofth* (f.ns. Wigston Magna), *Reddhurst* (f.n. Shawell), *Reddinge End, Reddwombe*, Redham (f.ns. Ashby Parva), ?*Redehull* (f.n. Glen Parva), Redham (f.n. Ullesthorpe), ?*Redhill* (f.n. Sutton in the Elms), Redmore Pitt (f.n. Lutterworth), ?*Redys nok* (f.n. Oadby), Reedfield (f.n. Foston), Reedmore (f.n. Leire), Reed Pool Cl (f.n. Countesthorpe), *Reydgreys* (f.n. Blaby), Rodmore Mdw (f.n. Claybrooke Magna).

hrēodig OE, adj., 'reedy, growing with reeds'. ?*le Redy* (f.n. Aylestone), ?*Reedye* (f.n. Sutton in the Elms).

hrōc OE, **hrókr** ON, 'a rook'. Rooks Church (f.n. Gilmorton).

hrung OE, 'a pole'.?*roundford* (f.n. Wigston Magna).

hrycg OE, 'a ridge'. *langridge* (f.n. North Kilworth), Seven Ridges (f.n. Gilmorton).

hrycgweg OE, 'a ridgeway'. *Aboueriggewey* (f.n. Bitteswell), *Ridgeway* (f.n. Claybrooke Parva, Gilmorton, Glen Parva, Kimcote, Littlethorpe, North Kilworth, Oadby, Peatling Magna), Ridgeway Cl (f.n. Knighton), *Ridgeway Greene, Ridgeway hagges* (f.n. Sutton in the Elms).

hryggr ON, 'a ridge'. *Rigdole* (f.n. Littlethorpe), Top Riggs (f.n. Cosby).

*****hrynge** OE, 'a pole'. ?Range Mdw (f.n. Foston).

hund OE, **hundr** ON, 'a hound'. ?Houndsacre (f.n. Bitteswell), *le Hountheng* (f.n. Wigston Magna).

hundred OE, numeral, 'one hundred'; sb., 'an administrative division of a county, prob. consisting originally of 100 hides of land'. Guthlaxton Hundred.

hungor OE, 'hunger', usually an allusion in f.ns. to 'barren ground'. *Hungarland* (f.n. Peatling Magna), Hunger Hill (f.n. Cosby, Shearsby), *Hungertonhill* (f.n. Wigston Magna).

hungrig OE, adj., 'hungry, poor'. *Hongrye Fielde* (f.n. Sutton in the Elms).

hunig OE, 'honey'; in p.ns., usually alluding to places where honey was found or produced, or perh. to 'sweet land'; but sometimes also used of sites with sticky soil. Honey Bags (f.n. Blaby), Honey Pot (f.n. Catthorpe), *honey rushes* (f.n. Kilby), Honeywell (f.n. North Kilworth).

hūs OE, 'a house', usually a dwelling house, but sometimes used of a building for a special purpose. *Catshouse, Folehouse, Hallehouse* (Aylestone), *Huhehus* (North Kilworth), *Reynoldes howse* (Blaby); *Husland slade* (f.n. Aylestone), *Usom, Wolfoushull* (f.ns. Bitteswell).

hut eModE, 'a hut, a shed'. Hut Cl (f.n. Arnesby, Ashby Parva, Claybrooke Magna, Claybrooke Parva, North Kilworth, Peatling Parva, Willoughby Waterleys), Hut Mdw (f.n. Ashby Parva, Bitteswell), Red Hut Cl (f.n. Westrill and Starmore), Tin Hut Cl (f.n. Cosby), Tin Hut Mdws (f.n. Swinford).

hwǣte OE (Angl), 'wheat'. ?Great Wheatly (f.n. Claybrooke Parva), *Whatley* (f.n. North Kilworth), Wheat Cl (f.n. Ashby Parva, Blaby, Cotesbach), Wheat Fd (f.n. Ashby Parva), *Wheat Furlong Slade* (f.n. Misterton), Wheathill (f.n. Shearsby, Swinford).

hwerfel OE (Angl), 'a circle', used in p.ns. to denote a physical feature which wheels around. Warlige (f.n. Kimcote), *Whorelidge* (f.n. Gilmorton), *Whorleditch* (f.n. Shearsby).

hwet-stān OE, ' whetstone'; prob. alluding in p.ns. to places where stone for such implements was to be found. Whetstone. Whetstone Hill (f.n. Leire).

hwīt OE, **hvítr** ON, adj., 'white'; in ModEdial., *white* 'infertile' may be contrasted with *black* 'fertile', while dial. *white* may refer to dry open pasture. Limestone or chalky soil may also be alluded to: *white hill* (f.n. Arnesby), White Leys (f.n. Shawell), Whitemore (f.n. Wigston Parva), *Whytston* (f.n. Sutton in the Elms), *Wytewold'* (f.n. Kimcote).

hyll OE, 'a hill'. ?The Brindles, Church Hill Fm, Cosby Hill, Elwells Fm, Flaxhill, Frolesworth Hill, Rye Hill, Westrill. Very freq. in f.ns.: geology/soil quality may feature, e.g. *Cludhils* (Arnesby), Hardhill (North Kilworth), *Sand hill* (Arnesby, Broughton Astley, Claybrooke Magna, Oadby), *Stanehill* (Arnesby, Aylestone), *white hill* (Arnesby); wild flora may be indicated, e.g. Bracknell (Leire), *Bromhill* (Wigston Magna), Fernhill (Kimcote), Sedge Hill (North Kilworth), Thistle Hill (Cosby), *le Thornehill* (Knaptoft); hill sites were common for crops, e.g. Bean Hill (Shearsby), *Barlyhull* (Catthorpe, Kilby), *Peshull'* (Ashby Parva, Frolesworth, Kimcote), Rye Hill (Bruntingthorpe, Catthorpe, Dunton Bassett, Kilby), Wheathill (Shearsby); early owners may feature, e.g. *Gonewarehil* (Wigston Magna), *inkereshill* (Dunton Bassett); or husbandry, e.g. *Buttrill* (North Kilworth), *winterhill* (Peatling Parva); the appearance of a hill may be described, e.g. *Coppedhill* (Bitteswell), *Hanginhill* (Aylestone), *Langhull* (Frolesworth), *Sharpe hill* (Misterton). Windmills were constructed on hill sites, hence, e.g., Mill Hill (Ashby Parva, Aylestone, Blaby, Kilby). Note the rare *Cristemelehul* (Kilby).

hyllig OE, adj., 'hilly'. *Hilliforlang* (f.n. Cosby), Hilly Meadow Cl (f.n. Wigston Magna).

hyrne OE (Angl), 'an angle, a corner; a recess in a hill, a corner in a valley, a spit of land in a river-bend'. *in le Hurne* (p) (Misterton), Iron Way (f.n. South Kilworth).

hyrst OE (Angl), 'a hillock, a wooded hill'. *Bradefordehurst* (f.n. Aylestone), Broad Hurst, *Gorsehurst* (f.ns. Blaby), *Brockhurst hollow*, *Reddhurst* (f.ns. Shawell), *le Hurst* (f.n. Catthorpe), *deadhurst* (f.n. Sutton in the Elms), ?Turway Huske (f.n. Kimcote), *wileardes hyrste* (f.n. Claybrooke Parva).

īfig OE, 'ivy'. Ivy House Fm.

-ig[3] OE, suffix, mostly adj., **-i(e)**, **-y(e)** ME, **-y** ModE, adj. suffix. Banky (f.n Claybrooke Parva), Banky Cl (f.n. Countesthorpe, North Kilworth), Banky Fd (f.n. Misterton), Banky Ground (f.n. Shawell), Banky Mdw (f.n. Cotesbach, Swinford), *Dockey Close* (f.n. Misterton), *Dockey Dole* (f.n. Lutterworth), Hussocky Cl (f.n. Broughton Astley), *Stocky Lands* (f.n. Aylestone), ?*Swinie hill* (f.n. Whetstone).

in OE, prep., 'in, into, upon, at, among', sometimes with the adj. force 'inner'. Enslade (f.n. Shawell), *le Inland* (f.n. Knaptoft), *le Inmedewe*, *Innecrofte* (f.ns. Aylestone), *Intstys hadland* (f.n. Oadby).

-ing[1], **-ling** OE, noun-forming and diminutive-forming suffixes. Bandings (f.n. Willoughby Waterleys), ?*Feldyngys*, *Leueringdelesue* (f.ns. Kimcote), Sharlings (f.n. Gilmorton).

-ing[2] OE, place-name-forming suffix. Benting Holme Cl (f.n. Aylestone), ?*bootling* (f.n. Whetstone), ?*Dunting'*, ?*Holdingsik* (f.ns. Cosby), ?Greeping, *torningsway* (f.ns. Dunton Bassett), ?*Pifflin Olders* (f.n. Misterton), ?*Swetynges* (f.n. Wigston Magna).

-ing-[4] OE, connective particle, linking a first el., which may be a pers.n. or a significant word, to a final el. ?North and South Kilworth. ?*dunninc wicon* (f.n.

Ullesthorpe).

-ingas OE nom.pl., **-inga-** gen.pl.; in compound p.ns., denoting associations or groups of people. *Lilinge*, ?North and South Kilworth, Peatling Magna, Peatling Parva. ?(*on*) *Peatling* (f.n. Claybrooke Parva).

-ingtūn OE, added to an el. or pers.n. to denote an estate belonging to a person or to a group. Knighton.

innām OE, **innám** ON, 'a piece of land taken in or enclosed'. ?*Nygunholmes* (f.n. Blaby).

inntak ON, 'a piece of land taken in or enclosed'. Intake (f.n. Peatling Parva, Wigston Parva).

island eModE, 'a piece of land completely surrounded by water, a piece of elevated land surrounded by marsh'; also 'a piece of woodland surrounded by open country'. Island Pit Cl (f.n. Broughton Astley), Island Mdw (f.n. Claybrooke Magna).

kennel ME, 'a watercourse'. *Kenelfeld* (f.n. Knaptoft), Short Kennell (f.n. Dunton Bassett).

kepere ME, ' a guardian, a warden'. *the Keepers house* (Lutterworth).

key ME, 'a quay, a wharf'. Key Furlong (f.n. South Kilworth).

kine ME, 'cows'. ?*Kyne hull* (f.n. Kimcote).

kirkja ON, 'a church'. *Kirkdale* (f.n. Glen Parva), *Kirkdale Meer* (f.n. Wigston Magna), *Kirkeway* (North Kilworth), *kirkeweye* (Kimcote), *Kirkhill* (f.n. Whetstone), *Kyrkehadland* (f.n. Blaby).

kjarr ON, 'brushwood', **ker** ME, 'a bog, a marsh, esp. one overgrown with brushwood'. *Carbrook* (f.n. Bruntingthorpe), *Carr* (f.n. Oadby), *le ker* (f.n. Wigston Magna), *Kerbidge* (f.n. Arnesby).

knob ME, 'a knob', whence topographically 'a knoll'. *the Park knobs* (f.n. Kimcote).

knorre ME, 'a knot; rough, gnarled ground'. Flaxknorrs (f.n. Cosby).

kollr ON, 'a hill, a top, a summit'. ?*Lancoldale* (f.n. Blaby).

konungr ON, 'a king'. ?*Conston* (f.n. Frolesworth).

krókr ON, 'a bend, a crook', usually denoting 'land in the bend of a river'; but later also 'a nook, a secluded corner of land'. ?Crooked Tree Cl (f.n. Arnesby), ?Crook Tree Mear (f.n. Shearsby).

(ge)lād OE, 'a watercourse'. *Luggloades* (f.n. Lutterworth).

ladi ME, 'a lady'; often referring to a dowager or to a female proprietor or to the lady of the manor. Our Lady, the Virgin Mary, may be alluded to, esp. with reference to rents for the upkeep of a chapel. *le Ladie medow* (f.n. Foston, Knaptoft, Shearsby), Lady Cl, Lady Leys (f.ns. Cosby), *Ladywell hill* (f.n. Whetstone).

***lagge** OE, prob. 'a marsh'; dial. **lag** 'a marshy meadow by a stream'. Water Laggs (f.n. Lutterworth).

lamb OE, 'a lamb' Lambcote (f.n. Dunton Bassett), *lambcoates* (f.n. Frolesworth, North Kilworth, Wigston Magna), Lamb Fd, *Lambhill* (f.ns. Bitteswell), Lambs Cl (f.n. Ashby Parva), Lamcote Hill (f.n. Swinford).

lambing eModE, vbl.sb., 'the parturition or yeaning of lambs'. Lambing Mdw (f.n. Cosby), *the Laming Close* (f.n. Catthorpe).

lammas eModE, 'Loaf Mass'; the 1st of August, in the early English Church observed as a harvest festival at which loaves of bread made from the first ripe corn were consecrated. In f.ns., referring to land which was under cultivation until harvest and reverted to common pasture from Lammas-tide until the following Spring. Lammas Cl (f.n. Ashby Parva, Broughton Astley, Catthorpe, Claybrooke Parva, Dunton Bassett, Gilmorton, Leire, Shearsby), Lammas Mdw (f.n. Bruntingthorpe), Lammas Piece (f.n. Littlethorpe).

land, lond OE, **land** ON, 'land', either in the general sense 'ground, part of the earth's surface' or 'an estate or small tract of land' or 'a selion, a strip of arable in a great open-field'. The Leyslands. Very freq. in f.ns.: crops may be alluded to, e.g. Banlands (with various spellings in Ashby Parva, Bitteswell, Cosby, Kimcote, Lutterworth, Sutton in the Elms), *Flaxlandes* (Cosby, Kimcote, Leire), *peasseland* (Arnesby, Aylestone, Bruntingthorpe, Cosby), Ryland (Aylestone, Cosby); and wild flora, e.g. Docklands (Kimcote), Sallands, Starlands (Ashby Parva); the colour and nature of the soil may be specified, e.g. *Blackelandes* (Ashby Parva, Cosby, Leire), *Dryland* (Bruntingthorpe), *Hungarland* (Peatling Magna), *Sandelands* (Aylestone, Kilby), *stanlands* (Countesthorpe); shape and extent are freq. specified, e.g. *Brodelandes* (Cotesbach), *Langlond* (Bitteswell, Catthorpe), *Ranglands*, *Wranglandes* (with various spellings in Aylestone, Cosby, Dunton Bassett, Glen Parva, Kilby, Kimcote, Knighton); ownership or tenure may be noted by a surn., e.g. *Barbereysland*, *Simondis Landis* (Frolesworth), *Bloxam's Land*, *Chapman's Land*, *Woodcock's Land* (Gilmorton), *Kynseman land* (Cosby).

lane OE, 'a lane, a narrow road'. Common in f.ns.: earlier examples are *Daglane* (North Kilworth), Dead Lane (Bruntingthorpe), *le hallane* (Westrill and Starmore), *le Pollelane* (Aylestone), *Rylie lane* (Lutterworth), *Smythlane* (Blaby). As the specific of a f.n.: *Lane Bancks* (Knaptoft), Lane Cl (Bitteswell), Lane Piece (Claybrooke Magna).

lane-ende ME, 'a lane-end; land at the end of the lane' (*v.* Löfvenberg 117 and Ch 5 (1.ii), 262–3). Ashby Lane End (f.n. Dunton Bassett), *Browns lane end*, *Vales lane end* (f.ns. Whetstone), *Frolesworth Lane End* (f.n. Ashby Parva), *gullsons lane-end* (f.n. Shawell), *Higusons lane end* (f.n. Leire), Hog Lane End, Leicester Lane End, Short's Lane End (f.ns. Lutterworth), *the Long Lane End* (f.n. Knighton), *the New lane end* (f.n. Oadby), *Pawmers lane end* (f.n. Aylestone), *Smythlanesende* (f.n. Blaby), *the water lane end*, *Woods lane end* (f.ns. Shawell), (*the*) *Well lane end* (f.n. North Kilworth, South Kilworth); Lane End Cl (f.n. Willoughby Waterleys), Lane End Furlong (f.n. South Kilworth).

lang¹ OE, **langr** ON, adj., 'long'. Freq. in f.ns. with a range of aspects of agricultural land, e.g. *Langedich* (Arnesby), *Langefurlong*, Long roods (Ashby Parva), Longdole (Bruntingthorpe), Longlands (Bitteswell, Catthorpe), *the long leys* (Ashby Magna); compounded in the names of topographical features, e.g. *langdale moore* (Aylestone), Langham (Ashby Parva), *Langhull* (Frolesworth).

lang² ME, sb., 'a long strip of land'. ?Ballong (f.n. South Kilworth), *Bretlong* (f.n. Cosby), *East longe* (f.n. Kimcote), *The Long* (f.n. Misterton), (*in*) *longe* (f.n. Ashby Parva).

*langet OE, 'a long strip of land'. *Langettes balke* (f.n. Shearsby), ?Lantasse (f.n. Kimcote), Longet Baulk (f.n. South Kilworth).

largest ModE, superl.adj., 'most spacious, widest, greatest'. Largest Cl by Brook (f.n. Oadby).

latis ME, 'a lattice, a structure made of wood with open spaces left between the laths, often used as a screen'. Lattice Coppice.

launde OFr, ME, 'an open space in woodland, a forest glade, woodland pasture'. *le Launde* (f.n. Knaptoft), The Lawn (f.n. Ullesthorpe).

lāwerce OE, 'the lark'. *Larkhead* (f.n. Whetstone), ?Larliss (f.n. Kimcote).

lǣce[2] OE, 'a leech'. *Lechpittes* (f.n. Aylestone, Oadby).

lǣfer, lēfer OE, 'a rush, a reed, levers'; prob. also 'a reed bed'. *lavelayeslade, Leueringdelesue* (f.ns. Kimcote).

lǣl OE, 'a twig'; prob. used of withies or the like. ?Lallystone (f.n. Swinford).

lǣs (lǣswe dat.sg.) OE, 'pasture, meadow'; very difficult to distinguish from the pl. of **lēah (lǣh (lǣs** nom.pl.) (Angl)) to which some of the following may belong. Willoughby Waterleys; The Leyslands. *Caluerelesewe, Calulese, Lesemylde, Reddeleiz* (f.ns. Wigston Magna), *Caluerlesure* (f.n. Oadby), ?*Copleys* (f.n. Willoughby Waterleys), *Cuallhelleleys*, ?Larliss, *Leueringdelesue* (f.ns. Kimcote), *Lese hadland* (f.n. Blaby).

lǣst OE, superl.adj. (of **lȳtel**), 'smallest'. Least Cl by Brook (f.n. Oadby).

lēac OE, 'a leek, garlic'. *Leekbed haggs* (f.n. Whetstone), *Leeke bedys* (f.n. Littlethorpe).

lēah OE, **lǣh (lǣs** nom.pl.) (Angl), 'woodland, a woodland glade, a clearing in a wood'; later, 'pasture, meadow'. ?*bulley*, ?*Copply green, halley tafts* (f.ns. Whetstone), ?*Darleys* Cl, ?*Great Wheatly* (f.ns. Claybrooke Magna), ?*Finley Meadow* (Misterton), ?*Frankley Mdw*, ?*Midgley Mdw* (f.ns. Bruntingthorpe), *Glencaluerley fen* (f.n. Blaby), *Grinley hade* (f.n. Kimcote), *Magsley* (f.n. Kilby), *Rackley* (f.n. Catthorpe, Swinford), *Ratley* (f.n. Broughton Astley), ?*Rylie lane* (f.n. Lutterworth), ?*Shitterlye* (f.n. Shearsby), *Thykleyes* (f.n. Oadby), *Whatley* (f.n. North Kilworth).

lesser ME, comp.adj., 'smaller'. *the lesser close* (f.n. Peatling Magna).

lewe ME, **lew** ModEdial., 'a shelter, a sheltered place, a resting-place'. The Lew (f.n. Knighton).

ley[1] ME, 'a pool'. *lavelayeslade* (f.n. Kimcote), Lay Cl (f.n. Misterton), *Morlaye*, ?*Ric' Niccolles ley-hadland* (f.ns. Kimcote), ?*Shitterlye* (f.n. Shearsby), *Stinckley* (f.n. Peatling Parva).

ley[2] ModE, 'a meadow, a pasture', *v.* **leys**. Lea Barn. *bastardley* (f.n. Wigston Magna), *Bosse his lea*, The Ley (f.ns. Broughton Astley), Church Lea, The Ley (f.ns. Claybrooke Magna), *Puleley* (f.n. Lutterworth), *Ric' Niccolles ley-hadland* (f.n. Kimcote), *Sprinkley* (f.n. Bruntingthorpe), Stony Lea (f.n. Claybrooke Parva).

leys ModE, 'meadows, pastures; grassed-over selions of a great open-field (lying fallow)'. F.ns. with *leys* (spellings in Guthlaxton Hundred also in *leas, lease, leases, lees, leese, leyes*) may have developed variously from the pl. of **lēah (lǣh (lǣs** nom.pl.) (Angl)) in its later sense 'pasture, meadow' and from the early **lǣs** 'pasture, meadow' and it is very difficult to assign with confidence an individual name to either source, except where forms in this Hundred with *lesewe, lesure* (from **lǣswe** gen.sg., dat.sg. of the latter) survive. Professor Kenneth Cameron has argued that most later f.ns. with *leys* (*ley* sg.) are prob. from **lēah**, *v.* L **2** 66 *s.n.* Carr Leys Wood. However, the modern sg. form *ley* may also be the result of the reduction of *leys* (from **lǣs** 'pasture, meadow') as a perceived plural. Lady Leys. Very freq. in f.ns.: esp. with locations, e.g. *Blackwell leyes* (Ashby Magna), *Church leyes* (Ashby Parva), *flaxbrokeleyes* (Dunton Bassett), *Farmoor Leases, Hell hole leases* (Countesthorpe), *Raven Willow Leyes, streete leas* (Claybrooke Parva); with wild flora, e.g. *Claver leyes* (Countesthorpe), *Rush leyes* (Blaby).

Recurring are Long Leas (Arnesby, Ashby Magna), Short Leys (Broughton Astley, Claybrooke Parva), Highleys (Ashby Parva, Blaby), *the holmes leese* (Ashby Magna, Ashby Parva). In compound with a numeral, *leys* represents grassland units of tenure corresponding to *lands* (i.e. selions or strips) similarly used of arable, e.g. *4 lease* (Leire), *Six Leys Close* (Ashby Parva). A note of disparagement is indicated in *Bastard Lees* (Bruntingthorpe) and *Woefull Lees* (Ashby Parva).

līc OE, 'a body, a corpse', alluding to places where corpses had been found or old burial places had been unearthed. *Litchslade* (f.n. Shawell).

līn OE, lín ON, 'flax'. Lincroft (f.n. Ashby Parva).

lind OE, ON, 'a lime-tree'. ?*Lynbe land* (f.n. Willoughby Waterleys).

linden OE, adj., 'growing with lime-trees'. Linden Ho., Linden Lodge. Linden Pit (f.n. North Kilworth).

*lisc OE, 'reeds, reedy marsh'. *Lysslade* (f.n. Ashby Parva).

loc OE, 'a lock, a bolt; a fold', loca OE, 'an enclosure'. Lockstead (f.n. South Kilworth), *Over Locke* (f.n. Cotesbach).

lock ModE, 'an enclosed section of a waterway which has gates at each end and in which the water level can be raised or lowered to move boats from one level to another, a canal lock'. Aylestone Mill Lock, Bush ~, Double Rail ~, Dunn's ~, Ervin's ~, Gee's ~, Kilby Bridge ~, King's Lock.

loge OFr, log(g) ME, 'a hut, a small house'; later, 'a house in a forest for temporary use (as a forester's house or a hunting-lodge), a house at the entrance of a park'. Freq. in modern house-names as a pretentious term for a country villa, often prefixed by an older p.n by analogy with names of genuine hunting-lodges, forest houses or manorial estate-houses. Amos Lodge, Arnesby ~, *Aylestone* ~, Bittesby ~, Bitteswell ~, Boston ~, Botney ~, Broughton Astley ~, Buckwell ~, Cosby ~, Crow ~, Dunton ~, Fir Tree ~, Flude ~, Foston ~, Frolesworth ~, Frowlesworth ~, Gilmorton ~ (Ashby Magna, Gilmorton), Glen Hill ~, Glen Parva ~, Great Peatling ~, Hill Top ~, Home Farm ~, Inkersall ~, Kilby ~, Linden ~, Littlethorpe Lodge, The Lodge (Bitteswell, Whetstone), Oadby Lodge, Peatling ~, Peatling Parva ~, Pincet ~, Shawell ~, Shearsby ~, Snowdon ~, Spinney ~, Spring ~, Sutton ~, Swinford ~, Tithe Barn ~, Tythorn ~, Ullesthorpe ~, Walcote ~, Walton ~, Whetstone ~, White ~, Wigston Lodge; Claybrooke Lodge Fm, Corner ~ ~, Cotesbach Lodge Fm, Lodge Fm (Blaby, Littlethorpe, Wigston Magna, Wigston Parva, Willoughby Waterleys), Peatling Lodge Fm, Ruskington ~ ~, Soars ~ ~, Walton ~ ~, Willoughby Lodge Fm; Lodge Mill Spinneys, Lodge Plantations.

lone ME, adj., 'solitary'. Lone Thorne Cl (f.n. Misterton).

*lort(e) OE, 'dirt, mud, a muddy place, a swamp'. *Lortewelle* (f.n. Cosby).

lowsy ME, adj., 'lousy, infested with lice or other insects'. Lowsy Mdw (f.n. Foston).

*lycce OE, 'an enclosure'. *langelich*, Warlige (f.ns. Kimcote).

lyng ON, 'ling, heather'. Lingham's, *Northling* (f.ns. Frolesworth).

lȳtel, litel OE, lítill ON, adj., 'little, small'. Littlethorpe. *Littell brooke, Littelwell, the Little Feild, Little Home, le lytel end* (f.ns. Aylestone), Little Hill (f.n. Bitteswell), Littlemore (f.n. Ashby Parva).

madame ME (< OFr *ma dame* 'my lady'); a mode of address to a woman of rank. *Madame Croft* (f.n. South Kilworth).

magotte ME, 'a worm or a grub'; possibly referring in f.ns. to the larva of the wheat-midge which is destructive to corn. ?*Magott* (f.n. Oadby).

ELEMENTS

malt-kylne emodE, 'a malt-kiln'. Maltkiln Orchard (f.n. Broughton Astley).

malt-mylne emodE, 'a mill for grinding or crushing malt'. *Malt mill* (Lutterworth), *Moltmill furlong* (f.n. Whetstone).

*malu (***malwe** dat.sg.) OE, 'a gravel ridge'. *Mallow* (f.n. North Kilworth).

maner ME, 'a manor (house), a mansion'. The Manor, Shawell Manor; Manor Fm (Arnesby, Ashby Parva, Broughton Astley, Claybrooke Magna, Cosby, Frolesworth, Kimcote, Oadby, Wigston Parva, Willoughby Waterleys), Manor Ho. (Aylestone, Bitteswell, Bruntingthorpe, Cosby, Cotesbach, Dunton Bassett, South Kilworth, Ullesthorpe).

mangere OE, 'a trader, a merchant, a monger'. ?*Mongereswelle* (f.n. Cosby).

mansion-house emodE, 'the house of a lord of the manor; an official residence, esp. that belonging to the benefice of an ecclesiastic'. *the mansion house* (The Rectory, Bruntingthorpe).

market ME, 'a market, a market-place'. *Beast market*, Woodmarket (Lutterworth).

marle ME, 'marl'. Marl Cl (f.n. Wigston Parva), Marl Hill Cl (f.n. Cosby).

marle-pytt ME, 'a marl-pit'. *Marle-pitt* (f.n. Aylestone, Bruntingthorpe, Countesthorpe), *the marlepitts* (f.n. Wigston Magna), Marlpit Cl (f.n. Broughton Astley).

manig OE, adj., 'many'. *Many Banks* (f.n. Arnesby).

maðek ME, 'a maggot'. ?*Mattock hill* (f.n. Oadby).

mattock ME, 'a mattock' (an agricultural tool for loosening hard ground, grubbing up trees etc.). ?*Mattock hill* (f.n. Oadby).

mæddre OE, 'madder'; a plant from the root of which a red dye was obtained. *Madridall* (f.n. Leire).

mægð[1] OE, 'a maiden'. ?*Maidethorne* (f.n. Cosby).

mǣgð[2] OE, 'folk, people'. ?*Maidethorne* (f.n. Cosby).

mægðe OE, 'may-weed'. May Dike, *Maywordeshom* (f.ns. Kimcote).

(ge)mænnes OE, 'community', used of 'common land, a common holding'. *Mansemore* (f.n. Claybrooke Parva), ?*Minsloe* (f.n. South Kilworth).

(ge)mære OE, 'a boundary, a border; a strip of land forming a boundary'; often difficult to distinguish from **mere**[1]. Mere Barn, Mere Rd (Peatling Magna, Willoughby Waterleys), Tabbermear's Fm. Freq. in f.ns.: most often with the name of an adjoining township, e.g. *Bitswell meere* (Ashby Parva), *Cosby Meare* (Sutton in the Elms), *Dunton Meare* (Broughton Astley), *Glen Meeare*, *Knighton Meeare* (Aylestone); occasionally with a pers.n. or surn., e.g. *Aþelnodes gemære* (Claybrooke Parva), *Woolmans meire* (Broughton Astley).

mæte OE, adj., 'poor, bad'. *Matfurlong* (f.n. Kimcote).

mearc OE, 'a march, a boundary', and when used as a final el., 'a boundary mark'. *Hall Mark* (f.n. Misterton), *March* (f.n. Whetstone), *Marchesakerdene* (f.n. Swinford), *Marchewell* (f.n. South Kilworth).

mēd (**mēdwe** obl.sg.) OE (Angl), 'a meadow'. Examples of f.ns. from the nom.sg. are very few in Guthlaxton Hundred's records, e.g. *Meadwellgate* (Countesthorpe), *Ryemede* (Aylestone), but very freq. in the obl.sg.: early instances are *Estmedow*, *Medodyke* 1467 × 84 (Blaby), *Houeresinthemedue* 13, *Smethemedewe* 1467 × 84 (Bitteswell), *le Inmedewe*, *le Nortmedowe* c.1250 (Aylestone), *Gosse medow* 1525 (Knaptoft).

meg ModEdial., 'a halfpenny'. ?*Winneymeg* (f.n. Cotesbach).

mēos OE, 'a marsh, a bog'. *mesfurlong* (f.n. Shearsby).

mere[1] OE, 'a pool, a lake', also 'wetland'; difficult to distinguish from **(ge)mǣre**. Bridgemere Fm, Cranmer Lane. *Ebersmeeres* (f.n. North Kilworth), Fullmore Mdw (f.n. Cosby), *Henmeere* (f.n. Cotesbach), *Rushmeere* (f.n. Kimcote), *Skinsmeere* (f.n. Broughton Astley, Frolesworth), *Tranemere* (f.n. Leire), *Wainsford meare* (f.n. Aylestone), Waterley Meer (f.n. Arnesby).

mete ME, 'a boundary; a boundary mark or stone'. ?*Meathill* (f.n. Shearsby).

micel OE, **mikill** ON, adj., 'big, great'; the OE el. is much influenced by the ON el. in the Danelaw and is difficult to distinguish. *Mickle Meddow* (f.n. Arnesby).

middel OE, adj., 'middle'. Freq. in f.ns.: e.g. the *Midelfilde* (Aylestone, Blaby, Bitteswell, Countesthorpe), the *middle ground* (Ashby Magna), *Middle Hills* (Arnesby), *Mydulheynams* (Cosby), *Mydulrygeway* (Oadby).

milling eModE, vb.sb., 'the action of grinding (esp. corn) in a mill'. ?*Millin hill* (f.n. Oadby).

mīl-stān OE, 'a mile-stone'. Milestone Fd (f.n. Bitteswell), Milestone Mdw (f.n. Swinford).

***modor** OE, 'mud, bog'. ?*mother doll* (f.n. Leire).

molda OE, 'the crown of the head', used topographically of a hill. Moult Thorne Leys (f.n. Gilmorton).

moneye ME, 'coin, money'. *Money Balk* (f.n. Arnesby).

mōr[1] OE, **mór** ON, 'a moor; marshland, barren wasteland, barren upland'. Gilmorton; Moorbarns. Freq. in f.ns.: e.g. Assemore, Coppidmoore, Throwsmoore (Gilmorton), Bogmore, Broadmore, *Learemoore*, Littlemore (Ashby Parva), Budmore, Rodmore (Claybrooke Magna), *Gosmore* (Aylestone), *Mansemore* (Claybrooke Parva), Rangmore (Dunton Bassett), Redmore (Lutterworth), Reedmore, Wildmore (Leire), *Sedgmoore* (Kimcote), Skinsmore (Broughton Astley, Leire). Recurring are le *dedemor* (Dunton Bassett, Oadby, Whetstone) and *Walschemore* (Cosby, Leire).

mōrig OE, adj. 'swampy, marshy'. le *Moriwong* (f.n. Wigston Magna).

mos OE, **mosi** ON, 'moss, lichen'; also 'a bog, a swamp'. *Moseho* (f.n. Wigston Magna), *Mosshill* (f.n. North Kilworth), *Mussel Bush* (f.n. Arnesby), ?Musway (f.n. Kimcote).

mote ME, 'a moat, a protective ditch filled with water around a building'. The Moats, Moat Spinney. Moat Furlong (f.n. Claybrroke Magna), Mott Cl (f.n. Claybrooke Parva), Mutt Fd (f.n. South Kilworth), the *Mutway* (f.n. North Kilworth).

muche ME, adj., 'great'. As an early affix for Ashby Magna.

mudde ME, 'mud'. Mud Hovel Fd (f.n. Shearsby).

mug eModE, 'a mug, a cylindrical drinking vessel'. ?*Mug pitt* (f.n. Cotesbach).

munt(e) ME, 'a mount, a hill'. *Mount furlonge* (f.n. Shawell).

mūs OE, 'a mouse'. *Mouse lane* (Wigston Magna), *Mowshow* (f.n. Littlethorpe), Musock, ?Musway (f.ns. Kimcote).

musseroun ME, 'a mushroom'. Mushroom Fd (f.n. North Kilworth).

mycg OE, 'a midge, a gnat'. ?Midgley Mdw (f.n. Bruntingthorpe).

***mylde** OE (Angl), 'soil, earth'. *blakemilde*, *Lesemylde* (f.ns. Wigston Magna), *Blakemylys* (f.n. Oadby), *Blakmyle* (f.n. Blaby).

myln OE, 'a mill'; also *v.* **water-mylne** and **wind-mylne**. Aylestone Mill Lock, Blaby Mill, Claybrooke Magna ~, Dunton ~, Leire ~, North Kilworth ~, Soar ~, Stemborough Mill; Lodge Mill Spinneys, Mill Dam Spinney, Mill Fd, Mill Ho.,

Mill Lane (Blaby, Gilmorton). Surviving only in f.ns. are: *Baggemulne* (Ashby Parva), *Cosby Mill* (Cosby), *Countesthorpe Mill* (Countesthorpe), *Crowmilne* (Wigston Magna), Fawkes Mill (Claybrooke Magna), *Hawysmylle* (Aylestone), *Luffemilne* (Catthorpe). Note the range *Bodicotes* ~, *Clays* ~, *Lanktons* ~, *Union Mill* (Wigston Magna). Mill Fd recurs (Aylestone, Bitteswell, Blaby, Catthorpe, Cosby, Cotesbach), as does Mill Hill (Ashby Parva, Aylestone, Blaby, Bruntingthorpe, Cosby, Kilby) and Mill Holme (Aylestone, Blaby).

mynster OE, 'a major church served by a priest, and with monks or secular clergy'. Misterton.

mýrr ON, 'a mire, a bog, swampy ground'. Chitmans Mires (f.n. Claybrooke Parva), Dancing Mire (f.n. South Kilworth), *Hawkswell Mires* (f.n. Shearsby), *the mires* (f.n. Cotesbach, Shawell).

myry ME, adj., 'miry, muddy'. ?*Maryroodes* (f.n. Countesthorpe), *Myrye foarde*, *myrye gutter* (f.ns. Sutton in the Elms).

nām OE, 'a taking (of land)'. ?Hennams Cl (f.n. Cosby).

nān-mann OE, 'no man, nobody'. *Nomans bush* (f.n. Wigston Magna), *Nomans Leys* (f.n. North Kilworth), *Normans land* (f.n. Whetstone).

nearu OE, adj., 'narrow'. Narrow Piece (f.n. Swinford).

nēat OE, 'cattle'. *Neathill* (f.n. Shearsby), *Netteshard* (f.n. Oadby).

neetherd ME, 'a cowherd'. *the Neatheards Baulk* (f.n. Bruntingthorpe).

neoðera OE, adj., 'lower'. Nether Hall. *Blacwellesikenethirend'* (f.n. Wigston Magna), *horstonsikenethirende* (f.n. Oadby), *Neather Hollywell*, *nethirmylnholm* (f.ns. Aylestone), *Neddrewong* (f.n. Ashby Magna), *Nedurfurlong*, *Nedertoftes* (f.ns. Kilby), *the Neither feild* (f.n. Claybrooke Parva), *Nether Blackelandes*, *Nether Throwlesworthe waye* (f.ns. Ashby Parva), *the Nether Fielde*, *Nether holmes* (f.ns. Sutton in the Elms), *le Netherwold* (f.n. Bitteswell).

nēp OE (Angl), 'a turnip'; difficult to distinguish from **hnæpp**. ?*Neprodes* (f.n. Wigston Magna).

nest OE, 'a nest'. *Arnest feld* (f.n. Aylestone), *Crownest* (f.n. Shearsby), Hawks Nest (f.n. Lutterworth), Paddy's Nest (f.n. Blaby), Podocks Nest (f.n. Gilmorton), Stork's Nest (f.n. South Kilworth), Swans Nest (f.n. Arnesby, Blaby, Leire).

netel(e) OE, 'a nettle'. Nettle Mdw (f.n. Cosby).

nighe ME, prep., 'near to, close to'. An early affix of Walton.

nigon OE, num., 'nine'. ?*Nygunholmes* (f.n. Blaby).

nīwe OE, adj., 'new'. *Neugate* (f.n. Wigston Magna), *new breache*, Niddick way (f.ns. Kimcote), *New closse* (f.n. Aylestone, Knaptoft, Sutton in the Elms), *New Dike* (f.n. Misterton), *Newetoft* (f.n. Aylestone), *New furlong* (f.n. Blaby), New Gate Furlong (f.n. Lutterworth), New Pool Bank (f.n. Oadby).

nōk ME, 'a nook (of land), a triangular plot of ground'. The Nook (Bitteswell, Cosby). Ashby Nook (f.n. Frolesworth), *Bone Nook* (f.n. South Kilworth), *Church nook* (f.n. Wigston Magna), *Colepit nooke*, *Grease Nooke*, *Redys nok'*, Salters Nook, *Smoreslade nooke*, *Wigston nooke* (f.ns. Oadby), Hall Nook Cl (f.n. Cosby), *Noke medow* (f.n. Kilby), The Nook (f.n. Broughton Astley), *Shofell Nooke* (f.n. Knighton).

norð OE, ON, adj., 'northern, north'. North Kilworth. *Northbroke*, *Nortfeld* (f.ns. Peatling Magna), *Northeng* (f.n. Foston), *Northfeld* (f.n. Arnesby), *le Nortmedewe* (f.n. Aylestone).

norðan OE, sometimes with the prep. **bī**, '(lying) north of'. *Northentowne* (f.n. Aylestone).

northerne emodE, adj., 'lying to the north'. *Northern* Cl (f.n. Foston), *northerneheywey* (f.n. Kimcote).

Norðman late OE, 'a Norwegian'. ?*Normanescroft* (f.n. Leire).

norðmest OE, adj., 'northernmost'. *Nortmest* (f.n. Bitteswell).

nursery emodE, 'a piece of ground in which young plants or trees are reared until fit for transplantation; a nursery garden'. Glen Hills Nursery. Big Nursery (f.n. Frolesworth), the Nurseries (f.n. Dunton Bassett), the Nursery (f.n. South Kilworth).

odde ME, adj., 'odd, single'; may be confused with **ald**. Odd House Cl (f.n. Broughton Astley).

*ofer² OE, 'a slope, a hill, a ridge'. *Houeresinthe medue* (f.n. Bitteswell).

ofer³ OE, prep., 'over, above'; difficult to distinguish from **uferra**. *Overmeere* (f.n. Shawell), ?*Overplus* (f.n. Ashby Parva), *over waterlaggs* (f.n. Lutterworth).

ofer-þwart ME, adj., 'across, lying across'. *the Overthwarte Furlong* (f.n. Peatling Parva), *the overwhart peece* (f.n. Leire).

orceard OE, 'a garden'; later in OE, 'an orchard'. Orchard Cottage, Orchard Fm (Cotesbach, Walcote). Common in f.ns.: e.g., Bottom ~, Clarks ~, Coventry ~, Front ~, Little ~, Lower ~, Top Orchard (Ashby Parva), (The) Old Orchard (Blaby, Cotesbach), Orchard Cl (Countesthorpe, Dunton Basset, Peatling Parva). Occasionally with an owner's surn. prefixed, e.g., Dutton's Orchards (Dunton Bassett), Hubbards Orchard (Countesthorpe), Sutton's Orchard (Broughton Astley). Early instances are *the Hall Orcharde* 1557 (Lutterworth), *le Orcharde* 1529 (Knaptoft).

oxa OE, 'an ox'. *Oxedaleput* (f.n. Leire), *oxemeere*, Ox House (f.ns. Frolesworth), Oxhall (f.n. Arnesby).

oyser, osyer ME, 'osier, willow'. Osier Bed (f.n. North Kilworth), Osier Bed Cl (f.n. Blaby), Osier Cl (f.n. Shearsby), Osiers Beds (f.n. Littlethorpe), Ozier Bed (f.n. Claybrooke Magna).

packeman ME, 'a pedlar'. ?Packman (f.n. Countesthorpe).

paddock emodE, 'a small field or enclosure; a plot of pasture land usually adjoining a house or stable'. Bell Paddock (f.n. Arnesby), Bitteswell House Paddock, Temple Cottage Paddock (f.ns. Bitteswell), The Paddock (f.n. Arnesby, Bitteswell, Blaby, Countesthorpe, Dunton Bassett, Misterton), The Paddocks (f.n. Kimcote), Road Paddock (f.n. Lutterworth), Two Acre Paddock (f.n. Cosby).

*padduc OE, **paddok** ME, 'a frog'. Paddocksden (f.n. Countesthorpe), Paddy's Nest (f.n. Blaby), Padock Hole (f.n. South Kilworth), Podocks Nest (f.n. Gilmorton).

pāl OE, **pole** ME, 'a pole, a long slender piece of wood'; later, 'a pole of definite length used as a measure'. Ash Pole Spinney.

paradis ME, 'a garden, an enclosed pleasure ground'. Paradise (f.n. Broughton Astley).

park ME, 'an enclosed tract of land for beasts of the chase'; later also, 'an enclosed plot of ground, a field'. Aylestone Park, Bitteswell Hall Park, The Park (Cotesbach), Stanford Park. Paled Park, Pegs Park, Walled Park (f.ns. Foston), The Park (f.n. Cosby, North Kilworth), *parke*, Parke Hill (f.ns. Kimcote), *le Parke* (f.n. Lutterworth), The Parks (f.n. Willoughby Waterleys), Pink's Park (f.n. Ashby Parva), Stevenson's Park (f.n. Bitteswell), *Willoughby parke* (f.n. Peatling Parva), Park Cl, Park Mdw (f.ns. Frolesworth), the Park Fd (f.n. Broughton Astley), Park Seeds (f.n. Blaby).

parlur ME, 'a private room'; in later f.ns., 'a secluded piece of ground'. (The) Parlour (f.ns. Bitteswell, Broughton Astley, North Kilworth), Parlour Cl (f.n. Willoughby Waterleys).

part ME, 'a part, a portion'. Clear Close Part (f.n. Blaby).

parting ModE, ppl.adj.; in f.ns., prob. meaning 'that which may be divided or shared'. *the partinge grasse* (f.n. Kimcote).

pasture ME, 'pasture, a piece of pasture land'. Whetstone Pastures. *Calver pastur* (f.n. Littlethorpe), *the common cow pasture*, Upper Pasture (f.ns. Dunton Bassett), Cottage Far Pasture (f.n. Frolesworth), *Knaptoft Pasture* (f.n. Knaptoft), Meadow Pastures (f.n. Blaby), the Pasture (f.n. Aylestone), The Pastures (f.n. Catthorpe), Spencers Pasture (f.n. Claybrooke Parva), *Sutton Pasture* (f.n. Sutton in the Elms).

patche eModE, 'a patch; a small piece of ground'. *the Paches* (f.n. Sutton in the Elms).

*pæsc(e) OE, prob. 'a muddy place'. ?*Pasfurlong* (f.n. Bitteswell).

pæð OE (Angl), 'a path, a track'. Ashby Path Noles (f.n. Dunton Bassett), *Fulwell path* (f.n. Wigston Magna), Hill Path Croft (f.n. Claybrooke Magna), *Kilworth path* (f.n. North Kilworth), *the Middle path* (f.n. Lutterworth), *le Patthes* (f.n. Cosby), *path lands* (f.n. Claybrooke Parva), *loofspath* (f.n. Catthorpe), Path Cl (f.n. Ashby Parva).

pece ME, 'a piece; a piece or plot of land'. Freq. in f.ns.: with a surn. indicating ownership, e.g. Bagshaw's Piece (Lutterworth), *Fishers piece* (Ashby Parva), Lewis's Piece (Glen Parva), *Mr Porters peece* (Shawell); with township buildings, e.g. Hall Piece (Blaby, Leire), *Milne peece*, *St Andrews peece* (Aylestone), Windmill Piece (Broughton Astley); with farm animals, e.g. *the Bull peice* (Blaby, Countesthorpe, Dunton Bassett, Littlethorpe, Peatling Magna, Sutton in the Elms); with village notables, e.g. *the constables peece* (Aylestone, Claybrooke Parva), *the Haywardes peece* (Catthorpe), (the) Parsons Piece (Aylestone, Bruntingthorpe, Cotesbach, Dunton Bassett, Gilmorton, Glen Parva), *the Vicars peice* (Arnesby). Recurring is *the tithe peece* (Ashby Parva, Aylestone, Catthorpe, Claybrooke Parva, Dunton Bassett). Note *dead mans piece* (Dunton Bassett) and unexplained *The Priors Peeces* (Claybrooke Parva).

pedlere ME, 'a pedlar'. Pedlars Cross (f.n. Lutterworth), Pedlar's Well Cl (f.n. Bruntingthorpe), *Pedlers goare* (f.n. Sutton in the Elms).

penn OE, 'a small enclosure, a fold'. Pen Close. *Bullocks pen* (f.n. North Kilworth, Oadby), *the olde Bullocke pen* (f.n. Kimcote), Pen Broadwell (f.n. Cotesbach), Pen Cl (f.n. Ashby Parva, Blaby, Broughton Astley, Claybrooke Magna, Cotesbach), ?*Penfolland* (f.n. Swinford), The Ram Pen (f.n. Foston), *the Sheep Pen* (f.n. Blaby), *Wyattes Pen* (f.n. Shearsby).

personage ME, 'a parsonage'. *The Parsonage* (Aylestone), *the Parsonage House* (Ashby Parva, Blaby, Broughton Astley, Bruntingthorpe, Catthorpe, Cotesbach, Foston, Frolesworth, Gilmorton, Kimcote, Lutterworth, Misterton, North Kilworth, Shearsby, South Kilworth). *the Parsonage close* (f.n. Kimcote, Oadby, Shawell), *the parsonage hedge*, *the parsonage homestall*, *the parsonage yards end* (f.ns. Catthorpe), *the Parsonidge Hookes* (f.n. Leire), *Parsonage lays*, *the*

Parsonage peece (f.ns. Bruntingthorpe), *the Parsonage Pykes* (f.n. Broughton Astley), *the parsonage willowes* (f.n. Frolesworth), *the Parsonage Yard* (f.n. Blaby).

persone ME, 'a parson, a beneficed cleric'. *atte Parsones* (p) (Peatling Magna), (the) Parsons Cl (f.n. Kimcote, Peatling Parva), *the Parsons Closses* (f.n. Gilmorton), *the Parsons hadland* (f.n. Bruntingthorpe), *the Parsons Hedge* (f.n. Leire), *Parson Holme* (f.n. Swinford), *the Parsons hooke* (f.n. Blaby, Leire), Parsons Leys (f.n. Kilby, Lutterworth), Parsons Mdw (f.n. Catthorpe, Foston, Wigston Magna), Parsons piece (f.n. Aylestone, Bruntingthorpe, Cotesbach, Dunton Bassett, Gilmorton, Glen Parva), *Parsons pikes* (f.n. Broughton Astley, Wigston Magna), *the Parsons pitt* (f.n. Kimcote), *the Parsons Townsend close* (f.n. Aylestone).

pertre ME, 'a pear-tree'. Pear Tree Lane (f.n. Willoughby Waterleys).

phesant ME, 'a pheasant'. Pheasant Spinney.

pīc OE, 'a point; a pointed piece of land, a pointed hill'. *the Parsonage Pykes, the parsons pykes* (f.ns. Broughton Astley), *Parsons pikes* (f.n. Wigston Magna), Pike Cl, Pike Mdw (f.ns. Claybrooke Magna), *Pikefurres* (f.n. Catthorpe), *the Pikes* (f.n. Kimcote).

pīe[1] OE, 'an insect, a parasite of somekind'. ?Pye Dyke (f.n. Blaby).

pīe[2] ME, 'a magpie'. ?Pye Dyke (f.n. Blaby).

pigeon ME, 'a pigeon'. Pigeon Cl (f.n. Bittesby).

***pigga** OE, **pigge** ME, 'a young pig'. ?Piggins Fd (f.n. Cosby).

***pīl-āte** OE, 'pill-oats'. *Pillit land* (f.n. Bruntingthorpe).

pingel ME, 'a small plot of ground'. *the Kerbys Pingell* (f.n. Lutterworth), Pindell (f.n. Shawell), *the Pingle* (f.n. Blaby, Claybrooke Parva).

pīpe OE, 'a conduit'. Great Pipes (f.n. Misterton), *Pipendeput* (f.n. Glen Parva).

pise OE, 'pease'. *Pease close* (f.n. Ashby Parva), *Pease furlong* (f.n. Catthorpe, Wigston Magna), *Peshull'* (f.n. Ashby Parva, Frolesworth, Kimcote, North Kilworth), *Peselond* (f.n. Bruntingthorpe, Cosby, North Kilworth), *peaseland busshe* (f.n. Aylestone), *peasseland way* (f.n. Arnesby), Peasom (f.n. Gilmorton), *Peseburne* (f.n. Westrill and Starmore).

place ME, 'an area surrounded by buildings'; later, 'a plot of land' and 'a residence'. *Brantingthorpe Hall place* (f.n. Bruntingthorpe), *the ricke place* (f.n. Aylestone), *Thebotes place* (f.n. Peatling Magna).

plain ME, 'a great open tract of land'; also 'a piece of flat meadow-land'. *the plain* (f.n. North Kilworth).

planke ME, 'a plank, a plank bridge; a bridge'. Bitteswell Plank, Willey Plank (f.ns. Lutterworth), *Glensicke planke* (f.n. Wigston Magna), The Stone Plank (f.n. Swinford).

plantation ModE, 'a wood of planted trees'. The Plantation, Lodge Plantations.

plat[2] ME, 'a plot, a small piece of ground'. Platt Ho. Big Platt, Cow plat, Little Platt, Six Acres Platt, Tobins plat, Top plat (f.ns. Broughton Astley).

***plæsc** OE, 'a pool'. Plash (f.n. Claybrooke Magna), The Plash (f.n. Dunton Bassett).

plek ME, 'a small plot of ground'. *the Hempplecke* (f.n. Kimcote), *Hounsplack*, Pleck (f.ns. Broughton Astley).

plōg OE, **plógr** ON, 'a plough'. Old Plough (f.n. Peatling Magna), Old Plough Cl (f.n. Willoughby Waterleys), Plough Cl (f.n. Ashby Parva, Claybrooke Magna, Dunton Bassett), Plough Croft (f.n. Wigston Parva), Plough Fd (f.n. Misterton).

plot late OE, ME, 'a small piece of ground'. *Church-Land Plot* (f.n. Ashby Parva), *Grass plots* (f.n. Gilmorton), *John Crisps Plott, John Garvatts Plott, Joseph Goozes plott* (f.ns. Leire), Plot Cl (f.n. Cotesbach), The Poor's Plot (f.n. Claybrooke Magna), *the Vicars greater plot* (f.n. Peatling Magna), *Waddonesykeplot* (f.n. Frolesworth).

*plysc OE, 'a pool'. Overplus (f.n. Ashby Parva).

*pofel OE, prob. 'a small piece of land'. ?*Pifflin Olders* (f.n. Misterton).

pōl[l] OE, 'a pool'. Reed Pool. Common in f.ns.: *Barton poole, Poole yard* (Blaby), *Cadewell Poole* (Oadby), Cliper Pole, Pole Ground, *Puleley, Weightmans Poole,* Windmill Pool, *Wymonpoole* (Lutterworth), *hen poolle* (Leire), *New-found-pool close* (Gilmorton), *le Pollelane,* ?*pooles headlond, Poole yard* (Aylestone), ?*Polwelthirne* (Cosby), Pool Cl (Foston), ?Rantipole (Shawell), Reed Pool Cl (Countesthorpe).

ponde ME, 'a pond, an artificial or natural pool'. Pond Cl (f.n. Bitteswell), Pond Fd (f.n. Willoughby Waterleys).

pony ModE, 'a horse of any small breed'. Ponies Fd (f.n. North Kilworth).

port[2] OE, 'a market town, a market'. Port Hill. Poor Cross (f.n. Gilmorton), Port Hill (f.n. South Kilworth), *Portslade* (f.n. Shearsby).

port-gate ME, 'a road to a (market) town, a road to a market'. *Portgate* (Wigston Magna).

port-wey ME, 'a road to a (market) town, a road to a market'. ?Port Hill. *le Portwey* (with various spellings in Bitteswell, Frolesworth, Leire, Peatling Magna, South Kilworth, Westrill and Starmore, Wigston Magna), Portway Cl (f.n. Claybrooke Parva), Portway Mdw (f.n. Ullesthorpe), ?Porteys Piece (f.n. Broughton Astley).

potato eModE, 'the potato'. Potatoe Ground (f.n. Claybrooke Parva), Potato Fd (f.n. North Kilworth).

pot(t) late OE, 'a pot'. Honey Pot (f.n. Catthorpe).

pouer(e) ME, adj., 'poor'; in modern f.ns., 'poor' (for 'the poor') alludes to land dedicated to poor-law relief or charity. Poor Allotments, Walton Poors Land (f.ns. Peatling Parva), Poor Cl (f.n. Cotesbach), Poor Cross (f.n. Gilmorton), Poors Cl (f.n. Leire, Peatling Magna), Poor's Mdw (f.n. Willoughby Waterleys), The Poor's Plott (f.n. Claybrooke Magna, Shearsby).

prēost OE, 'a priest'. Bristlings (f.n. Peatling Parva), *Prestesthirne* (f.n. Wigston Magna), *Prestushadus* (f.n. Knaptoft).

primerole ME, 'the primrose' (*Primula vulgaris*). Primrose Hill (f.n. Arnesby).

pumpe ME, 'a pump'. Pump Cl (f.n. Countesthorpe, Shearsby), Pump Fd (f.n. Cosby).

pund ME, 'a pound, an enclosure into which stray cattle were put'. The Pound (f.n. Broughton Astley), *the town pound peece* (f.n. Wigston Magna).

purchas ME, 'that which is purchased or acquired'. Purchas Pit (f.n. South Kilworth).

pyncette eModE, 'tweezers, forceps; ?something bifurcated'. ?Pincet Lane.

pynd OE, 'a pound, an enclosure'. *Pinslade*.

pyndere ME, 'a pinder, an officer of a manor or township who impounded stray beasts'. (*at*) *Pindars House* (f.n. Oadby), *the Punders balke* (f.n. Whetstone).

*pynd-fald OE, 'a pinfold'. Pinfold (f.n. Kimcote, Peatling Parva, Wigston Parva), *the pinfold banke* (f.n. Shearsby), *the Pinfold furlong* (f.n. Leire, South Kilworth), ?Penfolland (f.n. Swinford).

pyne ME, 'a pine-tree'. The Pines (f.n. Swinford).

pytt OE (Angl), 'a pit, a natural hollow, an excavated hole'. Freq. in f.ns.: with wild flora, e.g. *Ashpitt* (Arnesby), *Docepitte* (Cosby), *flagspitt* (Bitteswell), Gorse Pit, Willow Pits (Blaby), *Sallowe pitte* (Ashby Magna, Kimcote); with ownership specified, e.g. *Dunspitt*, Wards Pit (Countesthorpe), *the Parsons pitt* (Kimcote); or with folklore denizens, e.g. *hobgoblins pit* (Whetstone), Rush Pitts (Lutterworth), *Thurspitt* (Catthorpe). Recurring are Washpit (Arnesby, Bruntingthorpe, Frolesworth, Gilmorton, Misterton, Peatling Parva) and Gravel Pit (Broughton Astley, Leire, Lutterworth, Misterton).

quarter ME, 'a division of or locality in a larger area'. *Lyttlefyeld Quarter*, *Swynford Quarter*, *Walcott Quarter*, *Westerhyll Quarter* (f.ns. Westrill and Starmore).

quarterne ME, 'a quarter, a fourth part, a division of a larger area'. *Seares quarterne of yardland* (f.n. Cosby).

quyk ME, 'a hedge planted with one species, esp. whitethorn'. *little Quicks hills* (f.n. Bitteswell), The Quicks (f.n. Swinford).

rabet ME, 'a rabbit'. Rabbit Burrow Cl (f.n. Dunton Bassett), Rabbit Fd (f.n. North Kilworth), Rabbit Warren (f.n. Cosby).

***racu** OE, 'a hollow, the bed of a stream'. Rackley (f.n. Catthorpe, Swinford).

rād-weg OE, 'a riding-way (as distinct from a footpath), a road broad enough for riding along'. *the red way* (Frolesworth), *?þone rodweg* (Claybrooke Parva).

raile ME, 'a fence, a railing'. Draw Rails (f.n. Arnesby), Rail Mdw (f.n. Leire), *Rayle Close*, *Rayles medowe* (f.ns. Westrill and Starmore).

ramm OE, 'a ram'. Ram Cl (f.n. Shawell), Ram Fd (f.n. Peatling Magna), Ram Mdw (f.n. Bittesby), *The Ram Pen* (f.n. Foston), *Rammes close* (f.n. Arnesby, Ashby Magna, Knaptoft, Lutterworth).

rand OE, 'an edge, a border'. *?Rantipole* (f.n. Shawell).

ranke ME, adj., 'vigorous or luxurious of growth'. *Ranke slade* (f.n. Sutton in the Elms).

rāp OE, 'a rope'. *belrops* (f.n. Leire).

rāw OE, 'a row', esp. 'a row of houses'. ?Long Row (f.n. South Kilworth), ?Upper Row, *?Wastrow* (f.ns. Blaby).

ræsn OE, 'a plank', prob. in the sense 'a plank bridge'. *?Rason land* (f.n. Cosby).

rǣw OE, 'a row, a row of houses'. ?Long Row (f.n. South Kilworth), ?Upper Row, *?Wastrow* (f.n. Blaby).

rēad OE, adj., 'red', in allusion to the colour of soil, rocks, water (esp. peat-stained); in f.ns., often difficult to distinguish from **hrēod**. ?Ratley (f.n. Broughton Astley), *?Red Bank* (f.n. Aylestone), *?Redcross leys* (f.n. Whetstone), *?Reddhurst* (f.n. Shawell), Red Doles (f.n. Leire), *?Redehull* (f.n. Glen Parva), *?Redhill* (f.n. Sutton in the Elms), ?Rodmore (f.n. Claybrooke Magna).

rectory ModE, 'the residence pertaining to a rector'. The Old Rectory (Leire, Shawell), The Rectory (Ashby Parva, Blaby, Broughton Astley, Catthorpe, Cotesbach, Foston, Frolesworth, Gilmorton, Kimcote, Leire, Lutterworth, Misterton, North Kilworth, South Kilworth, Willoughby Waterleys).

rein ON, 'a boundary strip'. ?Reins Mdw (f.n. Littlethorpe).

reke-yard ME, 'an enclosure containing ricks, a stackyard'. (The) Rickyard (f.n. Broughton Astley, Lutterworth, Swinford, Westrill and Starmore), Rickyard Cl (f.n. Bitteswell, Cotesbach, Frolesworth, Ullesthorpe), Rickyard Fd (f.n. Arnesby).

*resbery ME, 'a raspberry (bush)'. Raspberry Spinney (f.n. Walcote).

rickstead ModE, 'an enclosure containing ricks, a stackyard'. *Mr Armsons rickstead* (f.n. Misterton), *Humfrie Buttons Ricksted, the Ricksteede, Tebbermeere Rickstead* (f.ns. Kimcote), Long Rick-Stead (f.n. Swinford), Rickstead (f.n. South Kilworth), *Rixsted* (f.n. North Kilworth).

rinc OE, 'a warrior'. ?*Rinksoe* (f.n. Shearsby).

*rind(e) OE, 'a hill, a ridge'. ?*Eathring Syde furlonge* (f.n. Shawell).

risc, *rysc OE, 'a rush'. Rushbrook Fm. *honey rushes* (f.n. Kilby), *the Rushes* (f.n. Broughton Astley, Dunton Bassett), Rush Furrow (f.n. Swinford), *Rush leyes* (f.n. Blaby), Rushmeere (f.n. Kimcote), *Russcheheye* (f.n. Aylestone).

*riscig OE, **rushy** ModE, adj., 'growing with rushes'. Rushy Cl (f.n. Frolesworth), Rushy Piece (f.n. Broughton Astley).

rise ModE, 'a piece of rising ground'. The Rise.

rīðig OE, 'a small stream'. (*andlang*) *riþiges* (f.n. Claybrooke Parva).

rōd[3] OE, 'a rood of land, a rood measure'. Black Roods (f.n. Claybrooke Magna), *Ellevyn rodes, six roode peece, Threthen rodes* (f.ns. Aylestone), *gilden roodes* (f.n. Catthorpe), Long roods, *Shorte Roodes* (f.ns. Ashby Parva), *Maryroodes* (f.n. Countesthorpe), *Neprodes* (f.n. Wigston Magna), *Smalerodes* (f.n. Bitteswell, Kimcote), the 3 Rood Land (f.n. Dunton Bassett).

rookery ModE, 'a colony of rooks'. The Rookery. Rookery (f.n. Claybrooke Parva).

round ME, adj., 'round'; in modern f.ns., sometimes describing fields not necessarily circular, but equilateral rather than oblong or irregular polygons. Bottom Round Spinney, The Round Ho. *the Round Close* (f.n. Aylestone), Round Cl (f.n. Broughton Astley, Cosby, Frolesworth, Glen Parva), Round Hill (f.n. North Kilworth, Shawell, Whetstone), Roundhill Cl (f.n. Knighton), Round Mdw (f.n. Catthorpe, Misterton), *the round peece* (f.n. Leire).

rūh OE, adj., 'rough'. *le Roudik* (f.n. Glen Parva), Rough Cl (f.n. Frolesworth, Peatling Magna, Peatling Parva, Willoughby Waterleys), The Rough Piece (f.n. Westrill and Starmore), *rowhill* (f.n. Dunton Bassett), Rowley Fd (f.n. Shearsby), *Ruelowe* (f.n. Aylestone).

rūm[1] OE, **rúm** ON, 'an open space, a clearing'. *þe Ryme* (f.n. Blaby).

rust OE, 'rust, rust-colour'. ?Ruslbrough Leas (f.n. Leire).

*ryde OE (Angl), 'a clearing'. *the Rud Closse, Rydesholme* (f.ns. Aylestone), *Rydichewey* (f.n. Kimcote).

ryge OE, 'rye'. Rye Close Spinney. *Mariots risich* (f.n. Cosby), Rye Cl (f.n. Ashby Parva, Catthorpe, Frolesworth, Misterton), Rye Crofts, Rye Sharlings, Rye Tofts (f.ns. Gilmorton), ?Rye East Hills (f.n. North Kilworth), Rye Hill (f.n. Bruntingthorpe, Catthorpe, Dunton Bassett, Frolesworth, Gilmorton, Glen Parva, Kilby, Lutterworth, North Kilworth), *Ryholm* (f.n. Lutterworth), *Ryland* (f.n. Aylestone, Corby, Kimcote, North Kilworth), *Ryemede* (f.n. Aylestone), *Rye more* (f.n. Cotesbach), ?*Rylie lane leyes* (f.n. Lutterworth).

sacu OE, 'dispute'. *Langesachedole* (f.n. Swinford), *Sachdole* (f.n. Ashby Parva).

safron ME, 'saffron'. ?*Safforn Furlong* (f.n. Gilmorton).

sainfoin ModE, 'the fodder plant sainfoin'. Saintfoin Cl (f.n. Wigston Parva).

salh OE, 'a willow, a sallow'. *salemorrowes* (f.n. Peatling Parva), Sallands (f.n. Ashby Parva), *Sallowe pitte* (f.n. Ashby Magna), Sallow pitts (f.n. Kimcote).

salt[1] OE (Angl), 'salt'. *Salt Riggewey* (f.n. Oadby).

salt[2] OE (Angl), adj., 'salty, brackish'. ?*Shaltwells* (f.n. Bruntingthorpe).

saltere OE (Angl), 'a salt-merchant'. *Saltersgate way* (f.n. Kimcote), ?Salter's Grave (f.n. Lutterworth), Salters Nook (f.n. Oadby), *Salters Way* (f.n. Misterton).

sand OE, **sandr** ON, 'sand'. ?Sanvey Lane. *Sand furlong* (f.n. Bitteswell, Shearsby), Sandhill (f.n. Arnesby, Broughton Astley, Claybrooke Magna, Frolesworth, Oadby), *Sand Landes* (f.n. Aylestone, Kilby, Oadby), Sand Piece (f.n. Lutterworth), *Sondwellesike* (f.n. Knighton).

sand-pytt OE, 'a sand-pit'. Sandpit Cl (f.n. Ashby Parva, Claybrooke Magna), *the sandpitt* (f.n. South Kilworth), Sand Pits (f.n. Gilmorton), *Sandpitt lane* (Wigston Magna).

saw-pytt ME, 'a sawpit'. Sawpit Cl (f.n. Broughton Astley).

sǣd OE, 'seed; sowing'; in modern f.ns., used of grasses sown for one year's mowing or grazing as distinguished from permanent pasture. Park Seeds (f.n. Blaby), Seed Cl (f.n. Arnesby, Broughton Astley, Claybrooke Magna), Seed Mdw (f.n. Cotesbach), (The) Seeds (f.ns. Cosby, North Kilworth), Seeds Cl (f.n. Dunton Bassett, Kimcote), Street Seed Cl (f.n. Ashby Parva).

scabbe ME, 'a cutaneous disease in animals, esp. sheep'. *Scabhome* (f.n. Wigston Magna).

scacol OE, 'a shackle', in p.ns. used esp. in the sense 'a place where animals are tethered or shackled'; but note that **shackle** ModEdial., 'quaking-grass' may have a long history (*v.* Elements **2** 98-9). *Schakulwade* (f.n. Blaby).

scadu OE, 'a shadow, shade, a shady place'. Shade Cottages.

scamol OE, 'a shamble, a bench, a stall for displaying goods for sale'; in ME, 'a stall for the sale of meat'. *Shambles lane* (Lutterworth).

scēacere OE, 'a robber'. Shackerdale Fm. *Schakersdal* (f.n. Knighton), *Shackadale slade* (f.n. Aylestone).

scēaf OE, 'a sheaf, a bundle'. ?Shearsby.

sc(e)ald OE, adj., 'shallow'. ?*Shaltwells* (f.n. Bruntingthorpe), ?Showell (f.n. Ashby Parva).

sc(e)alu OE, adj., 'shallow'. *the Shelbourne meadow* (f.n. Ashby Magna), ?Showell (f.n. Ashby Parva).

sc(e)ard OE, 'a cleft, a gap'; also as adj., 'notched'. *scardelowe* (f.n. South Kilworth), *Shardelowe* (f.n. Ashby Magna).

sc(e)arp OE, adj., 'sharp, pointed'. Sharpland. *Sharpehill* (f.n. Misterton).

*****scearpol**, *****scerpel** OE, 'a pointed hill; a pointed feature'. *Sherpol* (f.n. Wigston Magna).

sc(e)aru OE, 'a share, a share of land'; also 'a boundary'. Charfield Lane, ?Sharrag Grounds. *Sharcutt hill* (f.n. Bitteswell), Sharlings (f.n. Gilmorton), *Sharwood* (f.n. Countesthorpe).

scēað OE, 'a boundary'. Shawell. Sheaf (f.n. Leire).

*****scēla** OE (Angl), **schele** ME, 'a temporary hut, esp. a shepherd's hut on the summer pastures, a summer pasturage, a hovel'. Sheele (f.n. Kimcote), *Sheles furlong* (f.n. Peatling Magna).

sceld OE (Angl), 'a shield, protection'; prob. used in p.ns. of 'a shelter of some kind'. *le Scheld* (*ad le Cros*) (f.n. Cosby).

*****sceldu** OE (Angl), 'shallowness; a shallow place'. ?*Second Shallow*, ?*Shallow Thistles* (f.ns. Arnesby), ?*the Shoulder peice* (f.n. Aylestone).

scēne OE (Angl), adj., 'bright, beautiful'. ?Sheen Mdw (f.n. Broughton Astley).

sc(e)ort OE, adj., 'short'. Common in f.ns.: *Schortacres, Schortmorsikes, Schort Ryggus* (Cosby), *le Schortbreche, Schortgatetunge, Schortgathyll* (Bitteswell), *Schortehechowe* (Littlethorpe), *Schortfernell* (Kimcote), *Schortforrou, Schortfostonwey* (Blaby), *Short buttes* (Bruntingthorpe), Short Cl, Short Leys (Broughton Astley), *Shorte Crofte, Shorte Roodes* (Ashby Parva), *Shortekirkedale* (Glen Parva), *Short Leys* (Claybrooke Parva), *Short meadow* (Sutton in the Elms), *Short Rigew'* (Oadby).

scēp OE (Angl), 'a sheep'. Sheep Cl (f.n. Ashby Parva), Sheep or High Cl (f.n. Willoughby Waterleys), *the Sheep Pen* (f.n. Blaby), *Shipplands* (f.n. Wigston Magna).

scēp-cot OE (Angl), 'a shelter for sheep'. *Sanderson sheepcoat* (f.n. Whetstone), *Schepcotes* (f.n. Kilby).

scēp-hirde OE (Angl), 'a shepherd'. Shepard Board (f.n. Kimcote), Shepherd's Bush (f.n. Dunton Bassett).

scēp-hūs OE (Angl), 'a shelter for sheep'. *Shepehusflatte* (f.n. Ashby Magna).

scinn OE, 'a phantom, a spectre'. *Skinsmeere* (f.n. Frolesworth), Skinsmoor (f.n. Leire), Skinsmore Cl (f.n. Broughton Astley).

***scitere** OE, poss. 'a sewer, a stream used as an open sewer'. ?*Shitterlye* (f.n. Shearsby).

scofl OE, 'a shovel'; in p.ns., it may denote something resembling the hollow blade of a shovel, or something the width of a shovel. *Shofell Nooke* (f.n. Knighton), *Shoueldale* (f.n. Wigston Magna).

scot ME, 'a tax, a payment'. ?*Scotford* (f.n. Lutterworth).

Scot OE, 'a Scot'. ?*Scotford* (f.n. Lutterworth).

scyte OE, 'shooting'; prob. used like dial. *shute* 'a steep hill, a steep slope', and later, 'a steep channel of water, a mill-shoot'. *Forshoots furlong* (f.n. Misterton).

***scytere** ME, 'a shooter, an archer'. ?*Shitterlye* (f.n. Shearsby).

secg[1] OE, 'sedge, a reed, a rush'. Sedge Hill (f.n. North Kilworth), *Sedgmoore* (f.n. Kimcote), *Segbrygfurlong'* (f.n. Littlethorpe), *Seggate* (f.n. Knighton).

seofon OE, num., 'seven'; perh. considered a lucky number. *sevenacre* (f.n. Peatling Parva), *Seuenacres* (f.n. Wigston Parva), Seven Furlongs (f.n. Cosby), Seven Ridges (f.n. Gilmorton), ?*Showell* (f.n. Ashby Parva).

shady ModE, adj., 'affording shade'. Shady Lane.

shrubbery ModE, 'a plantation of shrubs, shrubs in a mass'. The Shrubbery.

sīc OE, 'a small stream' (often used of a stream forming a boundary), **siche** ME, 'a piece of meadow along a stream'. *Bandall Siche, Broad Siche, Fulsiche* (f.ns. Knighton), Blacksitch (f.n. Ashby Parva), *brimsiche*, Greensitch (f.ns. Dunton Bassett), *Clusitch* (f.n. North Kilworth), Cow Sedge (f.n. Peatling Parva), *Fulsidge* (f.n. Swinford), Hanglands Sitch (f.n. South Kilworth), *Langhams sich* (f.n. Frolesworth), *Mariots risich* (f.n. Cosby), *Ryelandesiche* (f.n. Aylestone), The Sitch, Sitch Cl, Sitch Mdw (f.ns. Broughton Astley), *Stanfordsiche* (f.n. Leire).

sīd (**sīdan** wk.obl.) OE, adj., 'large, extensive, long'. Side Hook Mdw (f.n. Swinford), ?Siden Cl (f.n. Frolesworth).

sīde OE, 'a side, the long side of a slope or hill, a hill-side, the land alongside a stream, a road, a wood etc.'. *the brooke side* (f.n. Broughton Astley), Coats Side, Flat Side (f.ns. Gilmorton), *Foston way side* (f.n. Blaby), Home Side (f.n. Kimcote), *Leicester way side*, Side Cl (f.ns. Frolesworth), Little Side (f.n.

Westrill and Starmore), *London way side* (f.n. Arnesby), The Long Sides, *the Town Side* (f.ns. Bruntingthorpe), *old waie side* (f.n. Dunton Bassett), Side Cl (f.n. Bitteswell), *Wigston Way side* (f.n. Aylestone), *Woodway side* (f.n. Claybrooke Parva).

*sīdling OE, 'a strip of land lying alongside a stream or some other piece of land'. *Siddlinges* (f.n. Peatling Parva), Sidlings (f.n. Gilmorton), *the sydling bauck* (f.n. Lutterworth), *Sydlinges* (f.n. Claybrooke Parva).

sík ON, 'a ditch'; later, 'a piece of meadow along a stream'. *Blakesick* (f.n. Ashby Parva), *le Brechesike* (f.n. Knighton), *Chanel syke* (f.n. Kilby), *Fulsike* (f.n. Swinford), *Holdingsik, Schortmorsikes, le Sikefurlonges* (f.ns. Cosby), *hookesickmiddo* (f.n. Gilmorton), *Inggesickefeld* (f.n. Ashby Magna), ?Sickle Hill, *Stockwell sick Field* (f.ns. Glen Parva).

sikel ME, 'a reaping hook'. ?Sickle Hill (f.n. Glen Parva).

sinder OE, 'cinder, slag'; prob. in allusion to where cinders were dumped. *Syndurs* (f.n. Blaby).

six OE, numeral, 'six'. Six Acres (f.n. South Kilworth), *Six Leys Close* (f.n. Ashby Parva), *six roode peece* (f.n. Aylestone), *Sixswathes* (f.n. North Kilworth).

skalli ON, 'a bald head', used topographically of 'a bare hill'. *Scalboro* (f.n. Blaby), Scalborough (f.n. Countesthorpe).

skeið ON, 'a track between fields, a boundary road, a boundary'. ?*Skatescroft* (f.n. Aylestone).

slang eModE, 'a long narrow (sometimes sinuous) piece of land; the ground beside a (winding) stream'. Long Slang (f.n. Willoughby Waterleys), (The) Slang (f.n. Arnesby, Bitteswell, Broughton Astley, Cosby, Misterton, Shearsby, Willoughby Waterleys), Slang above Mill Dam (f.n. Claybrooke Magna), Slang Fd (f.n. Blaby, North Kilworth), Townsend Slang (f.n. Shearsby).

slæd OE (Angl), 'a valley, a hollow, a breadth of greensward in ploughed land'. *Pinslade*. Very common in f.ns.: e.g. *brimsiche slaid, broughton slade, craftslaid, michilhaden slade, olteslaide* (Dunton Bassett), *copmores slade, Husland slade, Saffron Slade, Shackadale slade, Well Slade* (Aylestone), Deepslade, *Lysslade* Thrush Slade (Ashby Parva), *fluslade, horneslade, Lusileslade* (North Kilworth), *Derneslade*, Gents Slade, *Thurspitt slade, Wallslade* (Catthorpe).

slidor OE, adj., 'slippery'. *Slithers* (f.n. Aylestone, Cotesbach).

slipe ME, 'a slip. a long narrow piece of ground'. Slipe (f.n. North Kilworth), Slipes (f.n. Cotesbach).

slōh OE, 'a slough, a mire'. Knaptoft Slough (f.n. Kimcote), Slowes (f.n. Dunton Bassett), *Wrensloes* (f.n. Cosby).

smæl OE, adj., 'narrow, thin', **smal(r)** ON, adj., 'small'. *Smalegrendale* (f.n. Cosby), *Smalehulles* (f.n. Wigston Magna), *le smalemedewefurlong* (f.n. Catthorpe), *Smale old* (f.n. Cotesbach), *Smalerodes, Smalthorn* (f.ns. Bitteswell), *Smale Roudik* (f.n. Glen Parva), *Smale thorne* (f.n. Ashby Parva), *smale thorowes, small thorn* (f.ns. Dunton Bassett), *Smalewalt* (f.n. Shawell), Small Doles (f.n. Kimcote), *Smallowe* (f.n. Lutterworth), Small Thornes (f.n. North Kilworth).

smeoru OE, 'grease, butter'. *Smorehull, Smorslade* (f.ns. Oadby).

smēðe¹ OE, adj., 'smooth'. ?The Smee (f.n. Bruntingthorpe), Smeeth Mdw (f.n. South Kilworth), *le Smethehul* (f.n. Knighton), *Smeythe Meddowe* (f.n. Ashby Parva), *Smetholme* (f.n. Aylestone), Smid's Mdw (f.n. Bitteswell, North Kilworth), ?Smithall Mear (f.n. Shearsby), Smithams (f.n. Ullesthorpe), Smiths

Mdw (f.n. Catthorpe).

smið OE, **smiðr** ON, 'a smith, a worker in metal'. ?Smithall Mear (f.n. Shearsby), *le Smythesacre* (f.n. Aylestone), ?*Smythlanesende* (f.n. Blaby).

*snæp OE, prob. 'a boggy piece of land'. ?Snipe (f.n. North Kilworth).

sneið ON, 'a slice, a piece cut off, a detached piece of land'. *snayth* (f.n. Dunton Bassett).

sōcn OE, **soke** ME, 'the district over which a right of jurisdiction was exercised, an estate'. *Hallesokyng* (f.n. Leire).

*sōg OE, 'a bog, a swamp'. Sough Cl (f.n. Broughton Astley).

sōt OE, 'soot'; poss. in allusion to charcoal burning or the like, or to the colour of the soil. *Sotdoles* (f.n. Wigston Magna).

spa emodE, 'a spa, a mineral medicinal spring'. Spa Lane.

spang OE, 'a clasp, a buckle'; prob. used topographically of 'a long narrow strip of land'. Spanglands (f.n. Countesthorpe).

spell OE, 'speech, discourse'; used in p.ns. esp. where speeches were made in assemblies and thus freq. denotes a Hundred moot-site or other meeting place. *Spelthorn* (f.n. Oadby).

*spic[2] OE, 'brushwood' or the like. Spittswell (f.n. Kimcote).

spinney ME, 'a copse, a small plantation, a spinney'. Ainsloe Spinney, Amberdale ~, Ash ~, Ashclose ~, Baldwin's ~, Bittesby ~, Black ~, Bog ~, Bottom Round ~, Butler's ~, Button's Hill ~, Caldicote ~, Catherine ~, Church ~, Clarke's Spinney, Cosby Spinneys, Cricket Ground Spinney, Crow ~, Edgell ~, Flat ~, Fox Earth's ~, Galtree ~, Gilmorton ~, Goldhill ~, Grange ~, Green Lane Spinney, Greenspinney, Hangland Spinney, Holly Walk ~, Home ~, Jeremy's Ground ~, Knighton Spinney, Lodge Mill Spinneys, Long Spinney, Low ~, Michael ~, Mill Dam ~, Moat ~, New Gravel Hill ~, Oak ~, Old Gravel Hill ~, Pheasant ~, Raspberry ~, Reed Pool ~, Ringer's ~, Rye Close ~, Stackyard ~, Thornborough ~, Two Acre ~, Verney ~, Westrill ~, Winterfield Spinney; Spinney Fm. Common in f.ns.: e.g., Aylestone Spinney (Aylestone), Balls Spinney, The Spinney (Claybrooke Parva), Back Close and Spinney, Small Spinny (Catthorpe), Brickkiln Spinney (Broughton Astley), Crow Spinney (Blaby), Fourteen Acre Spinney, Poole's Spinney Cl, Spinney Piece (Bittesby), Little Spinney Fd, the Spinnies (Cosby), *Ramsclose Spinney* (Misterton), Spinney Cl (Ashby Parva, Bitteswell), Spinney Mdw (Bitteswell. Claybrooke Magna).

spitel ME, 'a hospital, a religious house'. *le Spitelwong, le Spitelyerd* (f.ns. Cosby).

splash ModE, 'a shallow pool'. the Splash (f.n. Cosby).

spoute ME, 'a spout, a gutter'. *Spowtewell Strete* (Wigston Magna).

spring[1], **spryng** OE, 'a spring, a well, the source of a stream'. Spring Cottage, Spring Hill Fm, Springwell. *Bone spring, Cawdle springe* (f.ns. South Kilworth), Broadwell-hole Spring (f.n. Gilmorton), *Springale hill* (f.n. Ashby Parva), Spring Cl (f.n. Catthorpe, Claybrooke Magna, Foston, Leire), Springes (f.n. Frolesworth), Spring Fd (f.n. Bitteswell), Spring Mdw (f.n. Willoughby Waterleys), Spring Piece, *Springwelle* (f.ns. Westrill and Starmore), Springwell Cl, ?*Sprinkley* (f.n. Bruntingthorpe), *the Wellspringe* (f.n. Oadby).

*spurn ME, 'a spur, a projecting piece of land'. *Spornefurlang'* (f.n. Westrill and Starmore).

squar(e) ME, adj., 'square', **square** ModE, also sb., 'a town square'. Square Cl (f.n. Wigston Magna, Willoughby Waterleys), Square Fd (f.n. Arnesby, Bitteswell),

Square Mdw (f.n. Ashby Parva, Claybrooke Magna), Square Piece (f.n. Peatling Parva), *the Vicars Square* (f.n. Whetstone); *Dixon's square* (Lutterworth).

stable ME, 'a building in which horses are kept'. Stable Cl (f.n. Blaby, Shearsby), Stable Fd (f.n. Bitteswell).

stackyard ModE, 'an enclosure for ricks'. Stackyard Spinney. Stackyard (f.n. Arnesby), Stackyard Cl (f.n. Willoughby Waterleys).

stakkr ON, 'a stack, a rick'. Stack Mdw (f.n. Willoughby Waterleys).

stall OE (Angl), 'a place', esp. 'a standing place, a stall for cattle etc.'. Stullidge (f.n. Gilmorton).

stallion ME, 'an uncastrated male horse'. Stallion Cl (f.n. Swinford).

stān OE, 'a stone'; when used as a first el., often has the adj. function 'stony', esp. in the names of roads, streams, fords and plots of ground; or may refer to something stone-built. Wigston Parva; ?Stemborough Mill, Stoneygate. *Bradstone* (f.n. Broughton Astley), *at newton stone, the farr Stanehill*, ?*harpston* (f.ns. Aylestone), *at Stone* (f.n. North Kilworth), Horston Hill (f.n. Dunton Bassett), *horstonsikenethirende* (f.n. Oadby), *knockstone*, Pultney Stones (f.ns. Gilmorton), Stonebridge Flat, Stonehill (f.ns. Arnesby), Stone Hill (f.n. Bruntingthorpe), *the Stone Meadow* (f.n. Glen Parva, Leire, Lutterworth), ?Stonetree (f.n. Gilmorton), *Stonys* (f.n. Littlethorpe), *Stounemore pitt* (f.n. Bitteswell), *Tweyston'* (f.n. Cosby), *Whytston* (f.n. Sutton in the Elms).

stānig OE, adj., 'stony, made of stone'. Stoney Bridge, Stoneygate, Stony Lea. *Stanydolis* (f.n. Littlethorpe), Stanymere (f.n. Claybrooke Magna), *Stanywelfurlong', Stony furlong* (f.ns. Bitteswell), Stony Cl (f.n. North Kilworth), *stoneygrounde* (f.n. Kimcote), *le Stonidole* (f.n. Misterton), *Stonie crose* (f.n. Aylestone), *Stony leyes* (f.n. Wigston Magna), *Stounie hill* (f.n. Claybrooke Parva).

*stān-pytt OE, ***stan(e)pytt** ME, **stone-pit** ModE, 'a stone-pit, a quarry'. Stone Pit (f.n. Ashby Parva).

stæf OE, 'a staff, a stave, a rod'. *Flaxstaves* (f.n. Aylestone).

stede OE, 'a place, a site, a locality'. *Falstedes* (f.n. Cosby), *Greenstede* (f.n. North Kilworth), Lockstead (f.n. South Kilworth), *the wagonestede* (f.n. Ashby Magna).

steepyng ME, ppl.adj., 'that slopes precipitously, steep'. *Stepingakyr* (f.n. Westrill and Starmore).

steinn ON, 'stone'; often has adj. function 'stony'. ?Stemborough Mill. *Stainlandes* (f.n. Cosby), *steane* (f.n. Dunton Bassett).

stell OE (Angl), 'an enclosure'. *Donkkesteles* (f.n. Aylestone), *Shovel steale* (f.n. Ashby Parva).

stēor OE, 'a steer, a young bullock'. ?Steers Cl (f.n. Broughton Astley).

stēpel OE (Angl), 'a steeple, a tower'. *~ with too steples* (an affix of Wigston Magna).

stīg OE, **stígr** ON, 'a path, a narrow road, an upland path' (*v.* **sty-way**); almost impossible to distinguish from **stig** 'a sty, a pen', and as in some cases the el. developed late as *stile*, it thus may be confused also with names formed with **stigel**. In f.ns., the el. is best recognized when combined with names of townships, e.g. *Ashby Style* (Whetstone), *Glen Stile* (Aylestone), *Lairesty* (Ashby Parva), *Poultney stile* (North Kilworth). Note also *Grensty* (Blaby), *Hastye* (Broughton Astley), *Hechowsty* (Littlethorpe), *Hulstye* (Sutton in the Elms). ?*Hudwynsty* (Blaby), ?Kilworth Stile and ?Lankhorn Stile (Misterton) are problematical, while *grinste way* (Countesthorpe) and *Greenstie way* are perh. better thought of as a **sty-way**.

stig OE, 'a sty, a pen'. *Aylthmesty* (f.n. Ashby Magna), *Branhowstyes*, *le Dokestile* (f.ns. Cosby), ?*Hudwynsty* (f.n. Blaby), *le Styes* (f.n. Glen Parva, Wigston Magna), *Swinsties* (f.n. Ashby Magna).

stigel OE, 'a stile'. Big Stub Stile (f.n. Blaby), *Hallfeild stile* (f.n. Shawell), *Harestiles* (f.n. Ashby Parva), *Long lane stile* (f.n. Wigston Magna), ?Kilworth Stile, ?Lankhorn Stile (f.ns. Misterton), (*at*) *mill stile* (f.n. Frolesworth).

stinck ME, 'a foul smell'. *Stinckley* (f.n. Peatling Parva).

stoc OE, 'a religious place; a place where cattle stand for milking in outlying pastures; a cattle farm; a dairy farm (esp. an outlying one); a secondary settlement'. *Grenestokysmere*, ?*le Stokis* (f.ns. Cosby), *Lubstock* (f.n. Ayleston), *the litle Stock*, *the Stock* (f.ns. Broughton Astley), ?Stockshill (f.n. Dunton Bassett, Leire), *Stokfurlong'* (f.n. Littlethorpe).

stocc OE, **stokkr** ON, ' a tree-trunk, a stump, a stump, a stock, a log'. Stockwell Ho. *Stockhill* (f.n. Peatling Magna), *Stock Lands* (f.n. Aylestone), ?Stockshill (f.n. Dunton Bassett, Leire), *stockwell* (f.n. Dunton Bassett, Glen Parva, Knighton),?*le Stokis* (f.n. Cosby), Stoxwell (f.n. Ashby Parva).

stock eModE, 'livestock'. ?Stock Randles (f.n. Frolesworth).

stōd OE, 'a stud, a herd of horses'. *stodyhill* (f.n. Dunton Bassett).

stōd-fald OE, 'an enclosure for horses'. *Stotfold* (f.n. Swinford), *Stotfoldlow* (f.n. Bitteswell).

stolpi ON, **stolpe** ME, 'a stake, a stump, a post'. *stoophill*, *Stowpyng* (f.ns. Oadby).

stǫng ON, 'a pole, a stave'; also used in ME as a standard of measure, 'a pole'. ?Stonetree (f.n. Gilmorton).

storc OE, 'a stork'. Stork's Nest (f.n. South Kilworth).

stǫrr[2] ON, **star** ODan, 'sedge, bent-grass'. Starlands (f.n. Ashby Parva), Star Pits (f.n. Peatling Parva).

strēam OE, 'a stream'. *the Streme lane* (f.n. Gilmorton), *Whatle stream* (f.n. North Kilworth).

strēaw OE, 'straw'. Straw Cl (f.n. Blaby), Straw Mdw (f.n. Westrill and Starmore), Straw Rick Cl (f.n. Bitteswell).

strengr ON, 'a water-course'. *stringlandes* (f.n. Dunton Bassett).

strēt OE (Angl), 'a Roman road, a paved road, a street'. High St (Lutterworth), Main St (Ashby Magna, Ashby Parva, Kimcote, Willoughby Waterleys), *Bysselowstrett*, *Spowtewell Strete* (Wigston Magna), *the Common street* (Countesthorpe), *þe ealdan stræt* (Claybrooke Parva), *Hautestrete* (Aylestone), *the kinges high streete*, *the Towne Streete* (Bitteswell), *Queenes high way called common street* (Ashby Parva), *the streete* (Cotesbach), *the streete way* (Shawell); Street Cl (f.n. Ashby Parva, Claybrooke Magna), *Streetfield* (f.n. Bruntingthorpe, Catthorpe, Lutterworth), *Streete furlonge* (f.n. Shawell, Swinford), *streete leas*, Streetway Cl (f.ns. Claybrooke Parva), Street Seed Cl (f.n. Ashby Parva).

strica OE. 'a strip of land'. *le Strykfurlong* (f.n. Bitteswell).

***strīp** OE, a narrow tract of land'. Strip (f.n. Ashby Parva).

stubb OE, 'a stub, a tree-stump'. *Applebystub furlong* (f.n. Aylestone), *Big Stub Stile* (f.n. Blaby), *Elrenestubb'* (f.n. Knighton), *elrestobslade* (f.n. Kimcote), *Elrynstub* (f.n. Bitteswell), *Elstub* (f.n. North Kilworth), ?*Stubbiescroft close* (f.n. Knaptoft), Stubway (f.n. Leire).

stubbil ME, 'stubble'. Stubble Cl (f.n. Broughton Astley), Top Stubble (f.n. Shawell).

*stump OE, 'a tree-stump, the stump of something'. *Appleby Stumpe* (f.n. Aylestone), *the ould Mill stoumpe* (f.n. Oadby).

stykke ME, 'a stick, a twig', **stick** ModE, used also of 'a timber tree'. North Kilworth Sticks.

stylt ME, 'a post, a pile, a prop'. Stult Bridge.

*stynt OE, 'stint, limit'. *the Stint* (f.n. Leire).

*sty-way ME, 'a pathway, a narrow road, a footpath'. *Greenstie way, Styway* (f.ns. Blaby), *grinstie waye* (f.n. Countesthorpe), *Stye wayes* (f.n. Wigston Magna).

sulh OE, 'a plough, a ploughland (i.e. the amount of land which could be cultivated with one plough)'. Sowledge (f.n. Gilmorton).

sundor-land OE, 'land set apart for some special purpose, detached land'. *Sinderland* (f.n. Wigston Magna), *sinderlond* (f.n. South Kilworth), Sunderlands (f.n. Foston), *Synderlands* (f.n. Countesthorpe).

sūr OE, adj., 'sour, damp, coarse' (of land). *Sourdole* (f.n. Cosby).

sūð OE, adj., 'south, southern'. South Kilworth. *sotham* (f.n. Gilmorton), South Fd (f.n. Aylestone), *Sowfeild* (f.n. Whetstone), *Sowthfelde* (f.n. Oadby).

*swalg OE (Angl), 'a pit, a pool'. Swallowgore (f.n. Claybrooke Parva).

swan[1] OE, 'a swan'. *Swannes nest* (f.n. Blaby), Swans Nest (f.n. Arnesby, Leire).

swang emodE, 'a swamp'. *Swang furlong* (f.n. Whetstone).

swæð OE, 'a track', **swathe** ME, 'a strip of grassland'. *Sixswathes* (f.n. North Kilworth), Swathes Mdw (f.n. Broughton Astley).

swēte OE, adj., 'sweet, pure, pleasant'. Sweetham (f.n. Claybrooke Magna), *le Swetegres* (f.n. Cosby), ?*Swetynges* (f.n. Wigston Magna).

swīn OE, **svín** ON, 'a swine, a pig'. Swinford. The Swimmings (f.n. Swinford), *Swinie hill* (f.n. Whetstone), *Swinsties* (f.n. Ashby Magna), *Swynncoate* (f.n. Kimcote).

tægl OE, **taile** ME, 'a tail'; used topographically of 'a tail of land' or 'the bottom end of a pool or stream'. *Taylliholm* (f.n. Wigston Magna).

tǣsel OE, 'a teasel'. *Taselhill* (f.n. Wigston Magna).

temple ME, 'a temple'; alluding to properties of the Knights Templar. *Minstreton Temple* (f.n. Misterton).

tēn OE, numeral, 'ten'. Ten Lands, Ten Leys (f.ns. Lutterworth), ?*Tinwillowes* (f.n. Oadby).

tenement ME, 'a tenement, a dwelling'. *Becke tenement* (Wigston Magna), *the Tenement of the Beadhouse of Leicester, the Tenement of Thomas Winterton* (Kimcote).

tentour ME, 'a tenter, a frame for tenting cloth'. *tenteres* (f.n. North Kilworth), Tenter Piece (f.n. South Kilworth), Tenters (f.n. Lutterworth).

tēoða OE, 'a tithe, a tenth'. Tithe Barn Lodge. Tithe Mdw (f.n. Claybrooke Magna), *the tithe peece* (f.n. Ashby Parva, Aylestone, Catthorpe, Claybrooke Parva, Dunton Bassett, Wigston Magna), Top Tithe (f.n. Arnesby), Tythe Land (f.n. Cosby), *Tythe medo* (f.n. Kilby), the Tythe Yard (f.n. Lutterworth).

tēoðung OE, 'a tenth part, a tithing'. *Kitehill or tything piece* (f.n. Bruntingthorpe).

thing ME, 'property'. *Seyves thing* (f.n. Oadby).

terrace ModE, 'a raised level place for walking; a row of houses on a level above the general surface, a row of houses of a uniform style'. *Wickliffe terrace*

(Lutterworth).

thist(e)ly ME, adj., 'thistly, abounding with thistles'. *le thisteliholm* (f.n. Aylestone),Thistley Cl (f.n. Peatling Magna), Thistly Mdw (f.n. Blaby).

thistle-down eModE, 'the down which crowns the seeds of thistle and by means of which they are carried along by the wind'. Thistledown Baulk (f.n. South Kilworth).

three-corner ModE, adj., 'having three corners, triangular'. Three Corner Bit (f.n. Blaby), Three Corner Cl (f.n. Ashby Parva, Bruntingthorpe, Claybrooke Magna, Cotesbach, Peatling Magna), Three Corner Fd (f.n. Arnesby).

three-cornered ModE, adj., 'having three corners, triangular'. Three Cornered Cl (f.n. Claybrooke Magna, Cotesbach, Dunton Bassett, Shawell, Shearsby, Willoughby Waterleys), Three Cornered Debdale (f.n. Shawell), Three Cornered Piece (f.n. Blaby).

threten ME, numeral, 'thirteen'. *Threthen rodes* (f.n. Aylestone).

tilie ME, 'a husbandman'. ?Tilles Grave (f.n. Kimcote).

tinkere ME, 'a tinker'. Tinkers Hill (f.n. Dunton Bassett).

toft ODan, late OE, 'a curtilage, a messuage, a plot of land in which a dwelling stands'. Knaptoft. *Algerystoft*, *Reddeleiz tofth*, *Toftis* (f.ns. Wigston Magna), *Estoftes*, *scortestoft*, Willows Toft (f.ns. Kimcote), *halley tafts*, *Tafts* (f.ns. Whetstone), Little Toft (f.n. Claybrooke Magna), Marslin Tofts, Rye Tofts, *Toftes* (f.ns. Gilmorton), *Nedertoftes* (f.n. Kilby), *Newetoft*, *the toftes* (f.ns. Aylestone), *taftes* (f.n. Peatling Magna), Tafts Mdw (f.n. Leire), *Toftes* (f.n. Blaby, Cosby, Claybrooke Parva).

tōh OE, adj., 'tough, sticky'. *Towborrowe* (f.n. Broughton Astley).

toll-gate ModE, 'a toll-gate, a toll-bar, a turnpike'. Toll Gate Fm, Toll Gate Ho. Oadby Toll Gate (f.n. Oadby), Toll Gate (f.n. North Kilworth), Tollgate Cl (f.n. Bitteswell, South Kilworth).

tōm OE adj., 'empty, void of content'. ?Tomley Hall.

top ModE, adj., 'topmost, uppermost'. Top Cl, Top Fd (f.ns. Broughton Astley), etc.

topp OE, 'the top, the top of a bank or hill'. Hill Top Fm (Walcote, Walton). Nether Top (f.n. Glen Parva), Top Hill (f.n. Broughton Astley, Dunton Bassett, Frolesworth), Tunnel Top (f.n. Dunton Bassett).

*tōt-hyll OE, 'a look-out hill'. *Toote Hill* (f.n. Arnesby, Aylestone).

trade ME, 'a track'. *Gandertreyde* (f.n. Knighton).

trak ME, 'a track, a trail'. Top Track (f.n. Swinford).

trani ON, 'a crane' (the bird). *Tranemere* (f.n. Leire).

trenche ME, 'a cutting, a ditch'. Trench Cl (f.n. Bitteswell).

trēow OE, **tré** ON, 'a tree'. Ash Tree Cl (f.n. Cosby), Crooked Tree Cl (f.n Arnesby), Crook Tree Mear, *the Gospell tree* (f.ns. Shearsby), *crucked tree* (f.n. Kilby), Crow Trees (f.n. Ashby Parva), Oak Tree (f.n. Misterton), Oak Tree Cl (f.n. Dunton Bassett), Oak Tree Mdw (f.n. Willoughby Waterleys), ?Stonetree (f.n. Gilmorton).

trespas ME, 'an encroachment'. The Trespass (f.n. Willoughby Waterleys).

triangle ModE, 'a triangle', also used adj. as 'triangular'. Triangle Bit (f.n. Broughton Astley).

trog OE, 'a trough', also used topographically as 'a narrow valley'. ?Stonetree (f.n. Gilmorton).

*trun OE, adj., 'circular, round', usually describing a physical feature which turns in some sort. *Trunland* (f.n. Knighton), ?*The Turn* Fd (f.n. Cosby).

tū OE, numeral, 'two'. ~ *with too steples* (an affix of Wigston Magna), Two Acre Spinney. *Twobrokes* (f.n. Wigston Magna), (*on*) *Two furlongs* (f.n. Whetstone), *Twotherenhul* (f.n. Glen Parva).

tūn OE, 'a farmstead, a village, an estate', **tún** ON, 'a farmstead'. Aylestone, Broughton Astley, Dunton Bassett, Foston, Gilmorton, Knighton, Misterton, Sutton in the Elms, Walton, Wigston Magna; Town End Fm. Lost farmsteads are: *Alstertune* (Shawell), Cogington (Swinford), ?*Conston* (Frolesworth), *Dutu'* (Westrill and Starmore), ?*harpston* (Aylestone), Harton (Countesthorpe), *Hungerton* (Wigston Magna), ?*Nafferton* (Foston), ?*Nottestone* (Lutterworth), ?Weston (Broughton Astley), *Wethington* (Aylestone). Common in f.ns.: e.g., *Buueton* (Foston), Cogington Hollow (Swinford), *Harton Field* (Whetstone), *Hungertonhill* (Wigston Magna), ?*Nafferton close* (Foston), *Northentowne* (Aylestone), Top 'Arton (Willoughby Waterleys), ?Westons Willows (Broughton Astley); Town Cl (Ashby Parva, Aylestone), *the Towne furlong, the towne headland* (Catthorpe), Town Hay (Broughton Astley), *the Town Side* (Bruntingthorpe). Recurring are *Townhill* (Aylestone, Claybrooke Magna, Claybrooke Parva), *the Townes ende* (Ashby Parva, Aylestone, Broughton Astley, Claybrooke Parva, Dunton Bassett, Gilmorton, Sutton in the Elms) and *the towne street* (Ashby Magna, Ashby Parva, Bitteswell).

tunge OE, **tunga** ON, 'a tongue'; used topographically of 'a tongue of land'. *Schortgatetunge* (f.n. Bitteswell), *Tongue doles* (f.n. Bruntingthorpe), *tounge* (f.n. Ashby Parva).

tūnscipe OE, 'the site of a village'. Township (f.n. Bittesby).

turf OE, 'turf, greensward'. Turdills (f.n. Lutterworth), Turway (f.n. Kimcote).

turnepe eModE, 'a turnip'. Turnip Cl (f.n. Ashby Parva, Kimcote), Turnip Fd (f.n. Ashby Parva), Turnip Hill (f.n. Broughton Astley).

turnepike ME, ' a revolving pole bearing spikes and serving as a barrier', **turnpike** ModE, 'a road on which a toll is payable and along which movement is controlled by barriers'. Turnpike Cl (f.n. Bitteswell, Blaby, Cosby), Turnpike Mdw (f.n. Arnesby), Turnpike Road (f.n. Claybrooke Magna, Glen Parva).

twēgen OE, numeral, 'two'. *Tweyston'* (f.n. Cosby).

twelf OE, numeral, 'twelve'. *twelue acres* (f.n. Cotesbach), Twelve Acre Wood (f.n. Bitteswell) etc.

twēntig OE, numeral, 'twenty'. Twenty (f.n. Shawell).

twinn OE, adj., 'double, twofold'. Twin Glebe (f.n. Arnesby).

twisled OE, ppl.adj., 'forked'. *Tuyseldeweye* (f.n. Kimcote).

þæc OE, **þak** ON, 'thatch, material for thatching'. *Thacheholme* (f.n. Littlethorpe), Thacker (f.n. South Kilworth), *Thakeslade* (f.n. Cotesbach), *Thatchcroft* (f.n. Whetstone).

þe, the ME, def.art., 'the'. Early instances are *þe Dale, þe Ryme, þe Slade* (f.ns. Blaby), *þest rygeway, þe Wattri* (f.ns. Oadby).

*þefa OE, 'brushwood, bramble' or the like. *Theeves* (f.n. Kimcote), ?*Thefedayle* (f.n. Blaby), ?*Theuesgraue* (f.n. Knighton).

þēof OE, **þjófr** ON, 'a thief, a robber'. ?*Thefedayle* (f.n. Blaby), ?*Theuesgraue* (f.n. Knighton).

þicce¹ OE, 'a thicket, dense undergrowth'. *the Thick* (f.n. Bruntingthorpe), Thick Mdw (f.n. Countesthorpe), *Thykleyes* (f.n. Oadby).

þicce² OE, adj., 'thick, dense'. Tythorn Hill. Thythorne Cl (f.n. Willoughby Waterleys).

þistel OE, 'a thistle'. Thistle Hall. Shallow Thistles (f.n. Arnesby), *Thisle close* (f.n. Cotesbach), Thistle Fd (f.n. Bitteswell), Thistle Hill (f.n. Cosby).

þorn OE, 'a thorn', a thorn-tree', the hawthorn'; perh. in some f.ns., collectively 'a stand or thicket or a wood of thorn-trees'. Thornborough Fm, Thornborough Spinney, Tythorn Hill. Common in f.ns.: Cattern, *Crowethorne, le Smalthorn'*, Thorn Bush Cl (Bitteswell), *Copthorne* (Broughton Astley, Catthorpe), *Crothorne, Smale thorne* (Ashby Parva), *Crowethornhul* (Knighton), *Foston Thorne* (Blaby), *Hie Thorne* (Lutterworth), Langthorne, *Street thorne* (Shearsby), ?*Lankhorn Stile* (Misterton), *Maidethorne* (Cosby), Moult Thorne Leys (Gilmorton), *Odebie thornes, Spelthorn* (Oadby), *Peatlin thorne, Thorneborrow* (Claybrooke Parva), Small Thornes, *Widdowes Thornes* (North Kilworth), *Sowfield thorns* (Whetstone), Thone, *torningsway* (Dunton Bassett), *le Thornehill* (Knaptoft), *the Thornes* (Arnesby, Peatling Magna), *Three Thorns* (Kimcote), Thythorne Cl (Willoughby Waterleys).

þornig OE, adj., 'thorny, growing with thorns'. *Thorney Close* (f.n. Aylestone, Knaptoft), Thorny Fd (f.n. Broughton Astley, Oadby), *Thorney Furlong* (f.n. Misterton), *Thorny slade* (f.n. Broughton Astley).

þorp ON, 'a secondary settlement, a dependent outlying farmstead or hamlet'. Bruntingthorpe, Catthorpe, Countesthorpe, Littlethorpe, Primethorpe, Ullesthorpe. *Thorp medow, Underthorpe* (f.ns. Catthorpe).

þræll ON, 'a thrall, a serf'. *Thrallyn* (f.n. Aylestone).

þrēo OE, numeral, 'three'. (*on*) *Three forlongs* (f.n. Whetstone), Three Furlongs, *Three Thorns*, (f.ns. Kimcote), the 3 Rood Land (f.n. Dunton Bassett), *Threos* (f.n. Blaby).

þridda OE, adj., 'third'. *Thirden heades* (f.n. Leire).

þūma OE, 'a thumb'; perhaps used of a very small creature, such as a dwarf or hobgoblin. ?Tomley Hall.

þverr (þvert neut.) ON, adj., 'athwart, lying across'. *Thwertdole* (f.n. Ashby Parva), *Twerforlonghauedlandes* (f.n. Cosby).

þyrne OE, **þyrnir** ON, 'a thorn-bush'. *Abbethirne, Thurnedale* (f.ns. Kilby), *Bratherne hill* (f.n. Blaby), *Holoughtherne, Polwelthirne, Westingtherne* (f.ns. Cosby), *Prestesthirne* (f.n. Wigston Magna), *le Thernefeld* (f.n. Ashby Magna), *Thion hedge* (f.n. Broughton Astley), *Thurnborow* (f.n. Broughton Astley, Gilmorton, Lutterworth, Sutton in the Elms), *Thyon* (f.n. Sutton in the Elms), Thyon Mdws (f.n. Willoughby Waterleys), ?*Turnhades* (f.n. Leire), *Twothernhul* (f.n. Glen Parva), *Waterthirne* (f.n. Knighton).

***þyrning** OE, 'a place growing with thorns'. *turnyng waye* (f.n. Dunton Bassett).

þyrs OE, **þurs** ON, 'a demon, a giant'. Rush Pitts (f.n. Lutterworth), Thrush Slade (f.n. Ashby Parva), *Thurspitt* (f.n. Catthorpe).

uferra OE, comp.adj., 'higher, upper'. *Blakelondis ouerende* (f.n. Cosby), *Holbrocouerende* (f.n. Oadby), *Hungertonesikeouerende* (f.n. Wigston Magna), *Ouermlnehill, le ouermylneholme, Over meadow* (f.ns. Aylestone), *le Ouerwold* (f.n. Bitteswell), *Over blacklandes, Over Throwlesworthe waye* (f.ns. Ashby Parva), *the Overfeild* (f.n. Bruntingthorpe), *the Over Flat* (f.n. Lutterworth), *Over*

Locke (f.n. Cotesbach), *the Over meadowe* (f.n. Blaby), *Over Tomley* (f.n. Catthorpe).

under OE, prep., 'under, beneath, below'. Under Dam Cl, *Underhill*, Understone (f.ns. Leire), *under how* (f.n. Whetstone), *under Rie hill*, Underthorpe (f.ns. Catthorpe).

upper ME, adj., 'higher'. *Uper Longlands* (f.n. Gilmorton), Upper Mdw, Upper Row (f.ns. Blaby).

valeie ME, 'a valley'. Valley Fm, Valley Lane.

vangr ON, 'an in-field'. *all wronge* (f.n. North Kilworth), Ballong Corner, Hang Woong (f.ns. South Kilworth), *blindemans wong, broade wong, Godewynwong* (f.ns. Frolesworth), *Cobaldeswong, le Moriwong* (f.ns. Wigston Magna), *Cuttedwong* (f.n. Shawell), Dunton Wound (f.n. Lutterworth), *Erewerde Wongg, Neddrewong* (f.ns. Ashby Magna), *flaxlandeswong', Osbernwong', le Spitelwong'* (f.ns. Cosby), *le Geldiswong* (f.n. Knighton), *Heythingwong, Julianwong, Midulwong* (f.ns. Blaby), *Rayneswombe, Reddwombe* (f.ns. Ashby Parva), *Sitheswong, Wolleswong* (f.ns. Bitteswell), *Wolueswong'* (f.n. Catthorpe).

vápnatak ON, **wæpengetæc** late OE, **wapentac** ME, 'a wapentake', a sub-division of a county, corresponding to OE **hundred**. Guthlaxton Wapentake.

varði ON, 'a cairn, a heap of stones'. *Warhthou* (f.n. Ashby Magna).

verge ModE, 'the bounds or limits of a place; a planted strip at the side of a road'. *verges way* (f.n. Shearsby).

vestr ON, adj., 'west, westerly'. *Wester Holme* (f.n. Glen Parva), Westernholme (f.n. Whetstone).

vewe ME, 'a formal inspection or survey of ground', ModE, 'a prospect' and 'an expectation'. Views (f.n. Gilmorton).

vikerage ME, 'a vicarage'. The Vicarage (Arnesby, Ashby Magna, Bitteswell, Claybrooke Parva, Countesthorpe, Dunton Bassett, Kilby, Swinford, Whetstone), *the Vicaridge house* (Cosby, Peatling Magna).

vikere ME, 'a vicar'. *Vicar leyis* (f.n. Kilby), *the Vicars Cowe Close* (f.n. Claybrooke Parva), *the vicars hadland* (f.n. Oadby), *Vicars Meddowes* (f.n. Peatling Magna), *the Vicars peice, Vicars willowes* (f.ns. Arnesby).

village ME, 'a village'. Village Mdw (f.n. Bitteswell).

víkingr ON, **wīcing** or **wicing** OE, 'a viking'. ?Wigston Magna.

vrá ON, **wro** ME, 'a nook, a corner of land'. *Folewellewro* (f.n. Knighton), *long Roes* (f.n. Frolesworth), *Wowe* (f.n. Kimcote), *le Wroo* (f.n. Cosby).

*****wacu** OE, 'a watch, a wake'; poss. also in p.ns. 'a watching-place'. Wakeley Fm. *Wackefeld* (f.n. North Kilworth), Mill Wakefield, Wakelow (f.ns. South Kilworth), *Wakeley* (f.n. Ashby Parva), The Wakelins (f.n. Dunton Bassett), Waklin (f.n. Leire).

wād OE, 'woad'. Little Woad Ground (f.n. Westrill and Starmore), Wadders, *Wadgorslade* (f.ns. Cosby), Warden (f.n. Frolesworth).

waful ME, adj., 'poor, miserable'. *Woefull Lees* (f.n. Ashby Parva).

wagan eModE, 'a waggon, a cart'. *the wagonested* (f.n. Ashby Magna), *wagonewaye* (f.n. Dunton Bassett).

wald OE (Angl), 'woodland, high forest land', **wald, wold** ME, 'an elevated stretch of open country or moorland'; in later development in p.ns., may be confused with **ald** and **holt**. Bruntingthorpe Holt, Gilmorton Holt, Holt Fm, Holt Ho., Holt Lane, Walton Holt. *Brode old fielde*, ?*the old ditch, Smale old* (f.ns. Cotesbach), the Holt (f.n. Gilmorton, Misterton), Holt Cl, *Wollandes gutter* (f.ns. Ashby Parva), *the old brook*, *the Olde meadow*, *Wytewold'* (f.ns. Kimcote), Old Fd (f.n. Blaby, Broughton Astley, Shearsby), *the Olt field* (f.n. Bruntingthorpe), Oult Fd (f.n. Dunton Bassett), *Old Lands Leyes*, *Segould* (f.ns. North Kilworth), Old Wey Cl, the Oult Highway (f.ns. Dunton Bassett), *le Netherwold*, *le Ouerwold*, *Woldfelde* (f.ns. Bitteswell), *the owld*, *Smalewalt* (f.ns. Shawell), *Thorpp Woldfeld* (f.n. Countesthorpe), *Waldeforlong'* (f.n. Cosby), *Waud* (f.n. South Kilworth), *Wauda* (f.n. Westrill and Starmore), *le Wold'* (f.n. Catthorpe).

walh OE (Angl), 'a Briton, a serf'. Walcote, Walton.

walh-hnutu OE (Angl), 'a walnut-tree'. Walnut Cl (f.n. Broughton Astley).

walk ModE, 'a walking-place; a path; a range of pasture'. Church Walk, Holly Walk Spinney, Long Walk. The Walks (f.n. Ashby Magna).

wall OE (Angl), 'a wall'. *atte Halle Wal* (f.n. Oadby), the Wall Cl (f.n. Aylestone), ?*Wallslade* (f.n. Catthorpe).

wareine ME, 'a game preserve; a piece of ground for breeding rabbits, a warren'. Warren Fm. Cow Warren (f.n. Misterton), *Misterton Warren* (f.n. Cotesbach), Rabbit Warren (f.n. Cosby), the Warren (f.n. Lutterworth).

wāse OE, 'mud, ooze; a muddy place'. *Ouze acers* (f.n. Whetstone), *Wasedale* (f.n. North Kilworth).

wateryng eModE, vbl.sb., ppl.adj., 'a place where cattle and other farm animals (are taken to) drink'. (*at*) *hogges wateringe*, *the watring pitt* (f.ns. Aylestone).

(ge)wæd OE, 'a ford'. Little Ward (f.n. Lutterworth), *Schakulwade* (f.n. Blaby), ?Wadbourne Mdw (f.n. North Kilworth).

wægn, wægen OE, 'a waggon, a cart'. *le Waynford* (f.n. Aylestone).

wælisc OE (Angl), adj., 'British (not Anglo-Saxon); unfree'. *Walschemore* (f.n. Cosby), *welchmore* (f.n. Leire).

wæsce OE, 'a place for washing', of sheep, of wheels of carts etc. Names in Wash Brook are likely to contain this el., but may occasionally belong with ***wæsse**. ?Wash Brook. ?Wash Brook (f.n. Lutterworth), ?Washbrook Cl (f.n. Willoughby Waterleys), ?Washbrook Fd (f.n. Arnesby), the Wash Pit (f.n. Bruntingthorpe, Gilmorton, Peatling Parva), Washpit Cl (f.n. Arnesby, Foston), Wash Pit Mdw (f.n. Frolesworth, Misterton), Washpitt Leyes (f.n. Kimcote).

*wæsse OE, 'a wet place, a swamp, a marsh'. ?Wash Brook. ?Wash Brook (f.n. Lutterworth), ?Washbrook Cl (f.n. Willoughby Waterleys), ?Washbrook Fd (f.n. Arnesby), The Wassal (f.n. North Kilworth).

wæter OE, 'water, an expanse of water, a lake or pool, a stream or river' or, as first el., 'near to a stream or pool; wet, watery'. Willoughby Waterleys. *Brode water* (f.n. Kilby), *the Water close* (f.n. Aylestone), *Watergall Closes* (f.n. Ashby Parva), *Water furrowes* (f.n. with various spellings (note esp. *Water Thorees*) in Ashby Parva, Aylestone, Blaby, Claybrooke Parva, Cosby, Kilby, Kimcote, Knighton, Leire, North Kilworth), Water Laggs (f.n. Lutterworth), *the water lane end* (f.n. Shawell), *Waterthirne* (f.n. Knighton), Waterlees (f.n. Arnesby, Frolesworth).

wæterig OE, adj., 'watery'; also used as a sb. 'a watery place'. Watery (f.n. Leire), *watrie* (f.n. Dunton Bassett), *þe Wattri* (f.n. Oadby), *le Wattrie* (f.n. Wigston Magna); the Watery Cl (f.n. Frolesworth), *Watery furlong* (f.n. Catthorpe), Watery Pitt (f.n. Lutterworth), *watrey leyes* (f.n. Wigston Magna).

weard OE, 'watch, protection'. ?*Warhthou* (f.n. Ashby Magna).

wearg-trēow OE, **waritreo** ME, 'a gallows, a tree where felons were hanged'. ?*Wartres* (f.ns. Cosby).

weg OE, 'a way, a road'. ?Sanvey Lane, Woodby Lane, Woodway Lane, Woodway Rd. Freq., esp. with the name of a local township, e.g. *Asscebywey* (Bitteswell), *Blaby Way*, *Lotherworth way* (Blaby), *Peatlinge waye*, *Sadington way* (Arnesby), Starmer way (Kimcote); or signifying long-distance routes, e.g. *Chestreway* (Cosby), *London way* (Arnesby), *Stamford Way* (Aylestone), *Winchester Way* (Blaby). Early pers.ns. may be compounded, e.g. *Alfledeweye* (Whetstone), *Aylwordwaye*, *Edrichewey* (Bitteswell), or a local structure prefixed, e.g. *kirkeweye* (Kimcote), *Milnwey* (Blaby). Recurring are Greenway (Frolesworth, Gilmorton) and *Wodewey* (Blaby, Leire).

wella OE, **well(e)** (Angl), 'a well, a spring, a stream'. Bitteswell, Shawell; Cauldwell Fm, Cauldwell Lane, Cordals, Elwells Fm, Horsewell Lane. Freq. in f.ns.: with pers.ns. or surns., e.g. *Osberneswelle* (Ashby Magna), *pippines well*, *Ravens well* (Arnesby); with religious associations or superstitions, e.g. Bridewell (North Kilworth, South Kilworth), Holywell (Shawell, Wigston Magna), *Ladywell* (Whetstone), *Thursputwelle* (Catthorpe); with wild fauna, e.g. Buckwell (Misterton), Cromwell (Wigston Parva), Dowells (South Kilworth), *Mussel* (Arnesby). The commonest recurring name is *Caldwell* (with various spellings in Arnesby, Ashby Parva, Bruntingthorpe, Claybrooke Parva, Kimcote, Leire). *Blackwell* recurs (Ashby Magna, Broughton Astley, Knighton), as does Broadwell (Arnesby, Ashby Magna, Cotesbach, Gilmorton), *Fowlewells* (with various spellings in Aylestone, Catthorpe, Kimcote, Littlethorpe) and *stockwell* (Dunton Bassett, Glen Parva, Knighton).

west OE, **vestr** ON, adj., 'western, west'. *Wastrow* (f.n. Blaby), *Westbrookfeild* (f.n. Ashby Magna), *Weste Well* (f.n. Ashby Parva), *le Westing'* (f.n. Cosby), ?Westons Willows (f.n. Broughton Astley).

*wester OE, adj., 'west, western'. Westdale Fm, Westrill, Westrill Spinney. Westerhill (f.n. South Kilworth).

westerne OE, adj., 'west, western, westerly'.?Westons Willows (f.n. Broughton Astley).

westmest OE, superl.adj., 'most westerly', *v.* **westerne**. *wesmessoe* (f.n. North Kilworth).

weðer OE, 'a wether, a castrated ram'. *Wethercliuemere* (f.n. South Kilworth), Wethers Cl (f.n. Foston), Wethersdale (f.n. Leire).

weyour ME, 'a pond'. *the Wire hole* (f.n. Kimcote), *Wyarleese* (f.n. Misterton), *wyer arme* (f.n. Wigston Magna).

wharf ModE, 'a structure built along waterways and railways so that barges and trucks may load and unload'. Aylestone Wharf (f.n. Aylestone), Wharf Piece (f.n. Ullesthorpe), *Wharf road* (Wigston Magna).

whinny ME, adj., 'growing with whins and gorse-bushes'. Winney Doles (f.n. Willoughby Waterleys), ?Winneymeg (f.n. Cotesbach).

wīc OE, 'a farm, a dairy farm, a building or collection of buildings for a special purpose'. ?*dunninc wicon* (f.n. Ullesthorpe).

wice OE, 'a wych-elm'. *Witcham corner* (f.n. Aylestone), *witchgraue* (f.n. Wigston Magna).

*wīchām OE, 'an Anglo-Saxon settlement adjacent to a surviving Romano-British small town'. ?*dunninc wicon* (f.n. Ullesthorpe).

wīd OE, adj., 'wide, spacious'. *wide dickes* (f.n. Dunton Bassett).

widewe ME, 'a widow, a widower'. ?Widow Bushes (f.n. Swinford).

widu early OE, 'a wood'. ?Widow Bushes (f.n. Swinford).

wigga OE, 'a beetle; that which moves or wiggles'. ?Wigston Parva. ?*Wiggin Well* (f.n. Misterton).

*wiht OE, 'a bend; a curving recess, a bend in a river or valley'. White Hill (f.n. Lutterworth).

wilde OE, adj., 'wild, uncultivated, desolate'. Wildmore (f.n. Leire), *Wild Willows* (f.n. Oadby).

*wilig OE (Angl), 'a willow'. Willoughby Waterleys; Willow Brook Fm. Fairly freq. in f.ns.: *at the willowe* (Shearsby), *Mr Belgraves Willowes* (North Kilworth), *Cornerwylow* (Littlethorpe), *the parsonage willowes* (Frolesworth), Raven Willow Leys (Claybrooke Parva), *Sutton Willowes* (Sutton in the Elms), *Tinwillowes*, *Wild Willows* (Oadby), Top Willows (Willoughby Waterleys), *Vicars willows* (Arnesby), Westons Willows (Broughton Astley), Willowbeds (Gilmorton), Willow Cl (Cosby, Leire), *Willowes* (Kimcote, North Kilworth), *Willowes Close* (Aylestone), *Willow Lays* (Misterton), Willow Pits (Blaby), Willows Toft (Kimcote).

wind-mylne ME, 'a windmill'. The Windmill (Arnesby). *windemill laies* (f.n. Leire), *the Windmill* (Aylestone), Windmill Cl (f.n. Broughton Astley, Dunton Bassett), Windmill Fd (f.n. Bitteswell), Windmill Hill (f.n. Peatling Parva, Shawell), ?Windmill Pool (f.n. Lutterworth), *Wyndmill gate* (f.n. Wigston Magna), *wyndmill way* (f.n. Shawell).

winter[1] OE, 'winter'; in p.ns., used of streams which run or places which are used in winter. Winterfield Spinney. Winter Gutter (f.n. Catthorpe), *winterhill* (f.n. Peatling Parva).

wīðig OE, 'a withy, a willow'. Witherbed (f.n. Cosby), Withy Beds (f.n. Leire), *Wythebeck*, *Wythibed* (f.ns. Westrill and Starmore), *Wythy beddes* (f.n. Broughton Astley).

*wīðign OE, 'a willow, a willow copse'. *Wethington'* (f.n. Aylestone).

wodyard ME, 'an enclosure in which wood is chopped, sawn or stored'. Woodyard (f.n. Bitteswell).

wōh OE, adj., 'twisted in shape, crooked'. *Long oho* (f.n. Whetstone), *Woham* (f.n. North Kilworth), *le Wokehauedeland* (f.n. Cosby), Woulands (f.n. Bitteswell), *Wouelond* (f.n. Kimcote), Wow (f.n. South Kilworth).

workhouse ModE, 'a place of public employment for the poor'. *Union Workhouse* (Blaby, Lutterworth).

worð OE, 'an enclosure'. Frolesworth, Lutterworth, North Kilworth, South Kilworth, Stamore. *Maywordeshom* (f.n. Kimcote), *Wrthegraue* (f.n. Wigston Magna).

wrang OE, adj., **vrangr** ON, adj., 'crooked, twisted in shape'. *ranglandes* (f.n. Aylestone, Dunton Bassett), *Wranglandes* (f.n. with various spellings in Cosby, Glen Parva, Kilby, Kimcote, Knighton, Swinford, Wigston Magna), *Wrongedole* (f.n. Glen Parva), *le Wrongweye* (f.n. Cosby).

wraðu OE, 'a prop, a support'. ?*Long Rathes* (f.n. Countesthorpe), ?*Rath Hades* (f.n. Willoughby Waterleys).

wrenna OE, ' wren'. *Wrensloes* (f.n. Cosby).

wudu OE, 'a wood, a grove, woodland'; also 'wood, timber'. Wood Bridge, Woodby Lane, Wood End Fm, Woodmarket, Woodway Lane, Woodway Rd. *Brokeswode* (f.n. Aylestone), Hazlewood (f.n. Ashby Parva), *Sharwood* (f.n. Countesthorpe), *Wodewey* (f.n. Countesthorpe, Leire), Wooder Mdw (f.n. North Kilworth), *Wood Lane* (f.n. Misterton).

wulf OE, 'a wolf'. *Wolfil* (f.n. Wigston Magna), *Wolfoushull* (f.n. Bitteswell).

wyrm, **wurm** OE, 'a reptile, a snake'; also 'a dragon', **worm** ME, 'an earthworm, an insect'. ?*Wormedale* (f.n. Peatling Magna).

yerdland ME, 'a square measure of about 30 acres, a yardland'. *Cooks half yardland*, *Wales half yardland* (f.ns. Broughton Astley), Halfyard Lands (f.n. Shearsby), *Seeres half yardland* (f.n. Cosby).

yonge ME, adj., 'lately begun, lately formed'. Youngfield (f.n. South Kilworth).

INDEX OF THE PLACE-NAMES
OF GUTHLAXTON HUNDRED

This index includes all the major names and minor names in the Introduction and in the main body of the work but not in the section The Elements in Guthlaxton Hundred's Place-Names. Field-names in lists (a) and (b) are not indexed. The names of the townships are printed in capitals. Lost names are printed in italic.